The Age of Du Pont de Nemours
Politics, Law and Physiocracy in the Ancien Régime *to the American Republic*

OXFORD UNIVERSITY STUDIES IN THE ENLIGHTENMENT
– formerly *Studies on Voltaire and the Eighteenth Century* (*SVEC*),
is dedicated to eighteenth-century research.

General Editor
Gregory S. Brown, University of Nevada, Las Vegas

Associate Editors
Jenny Mander, University of Cambridge
Alexis Tadié, Sorbonne Université

Ex-officio
Nicholas Cronk, University of Oxford

Editorial Board
Katherine Brading, Duke University
Jean-Luc Chappey, Université de Paris Panthéon-Sorbonne
Andrew Curran, Wesleyan University
Schmuel Feiner, Bar-Ilan University
Amy Freund, Southern Methodist University
Emily Friedman, Auburn University
Aurélia Gaillard, Université Bordeaux – Montaigne
Charlotte Guichard, Centre national de la recherche scientifique
Catherine M. Jaffe, Texas State University
Bela Kapossy, Université de Lausanne
Minchul Kim, Sungkyunkwan University
Avi Lifschitz, University of Oxford
Anton Matytsin, University of Florida
Pierre Musitelli, Ecole normale superieure
Nathalie Ferrand, Ecole normale superieure
Christy Pichichero, George Mason University
Siofra Pierce, University College Dublin
Glenn Roe, Sorbonne Université
Kelsey Rubin-Detlev, University of Southern California
Neil Safier, Brown University
Ayana O. Smith, Indiana University
Karen Stolley, Emory University
Geoffrey Turnovsky, University of Washington
Thomas Wallnig, University of Vienna
Masano Yamashita, Colorado University

Consultative Editors
Elisabeth Décultot, University of Halle
Andrew Jainchill, Queen's University
Andrew Kahn, University of Oxford
Lawrence Klein, University of Cambridge
Christophe Martin, Sorbonne Université
Kate Quinsey, University of Windsor

THE AGE OF DU PONT DE NEMOURS
POLITICS, LAW AND PHYSIOCRACY IN THE ANCIEN RÉGIME *TO THE AMERICAN* REPUBLIC

Edited by

ANTHONY MERGEY

and

ARNAULT SKORNICKI

Published by Liverpool University Press on behalf of
© 2025 Voltaire Foundation, University of Oxford
ISBN: 978 1 83624 283 3
eISBN: 978 1 83624 285 7
ePUB: 978 1 83624 287 1

Oxford University Studies in the Enlightenment 2025:06
ISSN 2634-8047 (Print)
ISSN 2634-8055 (Online)

Institut d'Histoire du Droit Jean Gaudemet (UMR 7184)
de l'Université Paris-Panthéon-Assas.
Institut des Sciences sociales du Politique (UMR 7220)
de l'Université Paris Nanterre.

Voltaire Foundation
99 Banbury Road
Oxford OX2 6JX, UK
www.voltaire.ox.ac.uk

A catalogue record for this book is available from the British Library

The correct style for citing this book is
Anthony Mergey and Arnault Skornicki (eds), *The Age of Du Pont de Nemours: politics, law and physiocracy in the* Ancien Régime *to the American Republic*
Oxford University Studies in the Enlightenment
(Liverpool, Liverpool University Press, 2025)

Cover illustration: Pierre Samuel du Pont de Nemours (1739-1817), Joseph Decreux. 1795-1798. Courtesy of Hagley Museum and Library.

Printed and bound by CPI Group (UK) Ltd, Croydon CR0 4YY

The manufacturer's authorised representative in the EU for product safety is:
Easy Access System Europe, Mustamäe tee 50, 10621 Tallinn, Estonia
https://easproject.com (gpsr.requests@easproject.com)

Oxford University Studies in the Enlightenment

THE AGE OF DU PONT DE NEMOURS
POLITICS, LAW AND PHYSIOCRACY IN THE *ANCIEN RÉGIME* TO THE AMERICAN REPUBLIC

This book aims to retrace the life and work of Pierre-Samuel Du Pont de Nemours, a multifaceted man whose influence extended from the Parisian salons of the eighteenth century to the shores of the New World, by exploring the unique trajectory of his life, drawing on a wealth of documentation and contemporary accounts. This individual study not only does justice to a man whose work and ideas continue to inspire academics around the world, but also explores a part of Franco-American history that is often overlooked.

Du Pont de Nemours is a well-known figure who has been the subject of numerous studies. Therefore, his hectic and tumultuous life has been the subject of several biographies, and he is best known for his membership in the 'sect of Economists' founded by François Quesnay and the marquis de Mirabeau in 1757. While significant, these studies are limited in that the ideas he defended and the actions he took in the political, administrative and legal spheres still remain largely unknown. Consequently, this makes the originality of the present work twofold: it takes Du Pont de Nemours out of the realm of physiocratic studies to focus on his thought and action, and also lifts him from the rut of the history of economic thought to expand into the history of law and socio-history of political ideas.

In light of Du Pont de Nemours's career, the volume adopts a bilingual approach and features essays in both English and French, with the aim of enabling readers to grasp the scope of Du Pont de Nemours's legacy, understand the challenges he faced and appreciate the long-lasting contributions he made to modern society.

Contents | Table des matières

Foreword | Préface   ix

ANTHONY MERGEY *and* ARNAULT SKORNICKI, Introduction:
Pierre-Samuel Du Pont de Nemours – a journey through the
eighteenth century   1

I. Public action, private happiness | Action publique, bonheur privé

JULIA L. ABRAMSON, Family business at Du Pont de Nemours,
Père et Fils & Cie: Huguenot connections, credit and capital
in post-revolutionary France and America   21

II. A lawyer in action | Un juriste en action

JEAN-BAPTISTE MASMÉJAN, Du Pont de Nemours et la
question hospitalière: un éclairage des enjeux sanitaires à la
fin du dix-huitième siècle   61

SÉBASTIEN LE GAL, Du Pont de Nemours and the
maintenance of public order   79

THÉRENCE CARVALHO, Abolir la contrainte par corps: le
combat du jurisconsulte Du Pont de Nemours   99

III. A political thinker challenged by the Revolution and the Republic | Un penseur politique à l'épreuve de la Révolution et de la République

THIERRY DEMALS *and* ALEXANDRA HYARD, Politique
et économie politique chez Pierre-Samuel Du Pont: les
annotations au *Contrat social* de Jean-Jacques Rousseau   121

viii   *Contents | Table des matières*

CHRISTOPHE LE DIGOL, From one world to another: how
Du Pont de Nemours became a revolutionary   161

LIANA VARDI, A physiocratic mandate: Du Pont de Nemours
and *L'Historien*   177

ANNIE LÉCHENET, Du Pont de Nemours et la république des
'propriétaires du sol'   203

IV. War and peace between nations | Guerre et paix entre nations

ANTONELLA ALIMENTO, Commercial treaties and the
emergence of a political economy of peace: Du Pont de
Nemours, inspirer of the Eden Treaty and supporter of the
renewal of the *Pacte de famille* (1782-1790)   229

ALFRED STEINHAUER, Sur l'intérêt bien entendu des nations
éclairées: la correspondance entre Thomas Jefferson et Du
Pont de Nemours à propos de l'affaire de la Louisiane   253

SIMONA PISANELLI, Du Pont de Nemours: colonies, slavery
and economic growth   271

V. Du Pont's American dream | Le rêve américain de Du Pont

GABRIEL SABBAGH, Du Pont de Nemours, coauteur des *Lettres
d'Abraham Mansword* (1771-1772) et critique (1773-1789) de
De Lolme: le modèle politique anglais confronté avec une
Amérique rêvée   291

AYA TANAKA, Pontiana: Du Pont de Nemours's physiocratic
dream in America   311

MANUELA ALBERTONE, Des finances et des banques
américaines: autour des rapports entre Du Pont de Nemours
et Thomas Jefferson   327

—

ANTHONY MERGEY *and* ARNAULT SKORNICKI, Du Pont de
Nemours, between physiocratic loyalty and political versatility   347

Bibliography   379

Indices   417

Foreword | Préface

Pierre-Samuel Du Pont de Nemours is undoubtedly one of those historical figures whose complex and rich story resonates far beyond his own time. His intelligence and commitment as a philosopher, economist, administrator, politician and industrialist have left their mark on French and American history. This book aims to retrace the life and work of this multifaceted man, whose influence extended from the Parisian salons of the eighteenth century to the shores of the New World.

Born in 1739, Du Pont de Nemours was above all an enlightened man, trained by the Enlightenment. His early economic works, deeply influenced by the ideas of François Quesnay and the physiocrats, quickly placed him at the heart of the intellectual debates of his time. A prolific writer, he set about the arduous task of reconciling economic freedom with the common good, advocating unfettered agriculture and nascent industry.

But it was not only as a theoretician that Du Pont distinguished himself. A man of action, he was involved in the political affairs of his time. An influential adviser to several of Louis XVI's ministers, he played a crucial role in attempts to reform the *Ancien Régime*. His involvement in the Estates General of 1789 and his support for a constitutional monarchy demonstrated his desire to see France evolve towards a fairer and more balanced system, which led him to embrace the republican idea a few years later.

Far from being confined to France, Du Pont's career took on a transatlantic dimension after the French Revolution. Forced into exile, he emigrated to the United States, where he was reunited with his son, Eleuthère Irénée. Together, they founded the DuPont company, which would become one of the jewels in the crown of the American chemical industry. Through this industrial adventure, Du Pont de

Nemours reveals a new facet of his genius, combining innovation and entrepreneurship with an enlightened vision of progress.

This book sets out to explore this unique trajectory, drawing on a wealth of documentation and contemporary accounts. The aim is to do justice to a man whose work and ideas continue to inspire. By studying the life and thought of Pierre-Samuel Du Pont de Nemours, we are exploring a part of Franco-American history, a history woven of revolutions, innovations and resilience.

In light of Du Pont's career, we felt it appropriate to adopt a bilingual approach, using both English and French in the contributions that make up this book, which are the work of researchers from France and elsewhere, some of whom are also English speakers.

We would also like to extend our sincere thanks to those without whom this book, the fruit of a symposium held in Paris in December 2017, would never have seen the light of day. We are thinking of:

- The municipality of Nemours, represented by Valérie Lacroute, who is currently mayor, and Anne-Marie Marchand, her predecessor from 2017 to 2020.
- DuPont France, in the person of Martin Virot, who was CEO at the time of the conference.
- The Hagley Museum and Library, and particularly David Allen Cole, its former executive director, and Andrew Engel.
- The Mission de recherche Droit et Justice.
- The Institut d'histoire du droit Jean Gaudemet (UMR CNRS 7184) of Paris-Panthéon-Assas University.
- The Institut des sciences sociales du politique (UMR CNRS 7220) of the University Paris Nanterre.
- The Ecole doctorale d'histoire du droit, philosophie du droit et sociologie du droit (ED 8) of Paris-Panthéon-Assas University.
- Oxford University Studies in the Enlightenment, and particularly Gregory S. Brown, general editor.
- All the administrative staff, doctoral students and students who contributed to the smooth running of the conference.

We hope that this book will enable readers to grasp the scope of Du Pont de Nemours's legacy, understand the challenges he faced and appreciate the long-lasting contributions he made to modern society.

Anthony Mergey and Arnault Skornicki

Introduction: Pierre-Samuel Du Pont de Nemours – a journey through the eighteenth century

ANTHONY MERGEY

Paris-Panthéon-Assas University

ARNAULT SKORNICKI

University Paris Nanterre

i. From Du Pont to Du Pont de Nemours: the career of a multifaceted thinker and political player

The name Du Pont de Nemours has long been part of our collective imagination, probably more so in the United States than in France. What was originally a gunpowder factory, founded in 1802 by Eleuthère Irénée Du Pont de Nemours (1771-1834), has in just over two centuries become one of the largest industrial chemical groups, with headquarters in Wilmington, Delaware, in the north-east of the United States.[1] A pioneer in the plastics revolution, notably with the discovery of nylon, and in the development of other materials such as polymers, DuPont is now one of the agrochemical giants in a highly competitive sector, although in recent years the group, aware that it is evolving in a world that is increasingly informed regarding environmental issues, has gradually moved away from chemicals to position itself as a player in innovative specialty products to meet new challenges. The family firm's history, image, success, adventures and scandals have never left anyone indifferent, and this is still true today. Hollywood has recently taken up the not-always-golden legend

---

1. E. I. Du Pont de Nemours and Company, since its merger with Dow Chemical in September 2017, is now called DuPont de Nemours, better known as DuPont.

of the family business in two acclaimed films.[2] A recent portrait of the family and the industrial company also occupied the pages of the newspaper *Le Monde* for an entire week in the summer of 2020.[3]

At the origin of this entrepreneurial dynasty is Eleuthère Irénée Du Pont de Nemours. But, to repeat the question posed by the *Le Monde* journalist in the first part of his investigation: how did a French family name come to be attached to that of a multinational chemical company, DuPont? The answer lies in the story of Eleuthère Irénée's father, Pierre-Samuel Du Pont de Nemours (1739-1817), who, following the coup d'état of 18 fructidor An v (4 September 1797) led by the Directoire with the help of the Jacobins, fearing for his person, his family and his possessions, decided to embark on the *American Eagle* to emigrate across the Atlantic with some of his family, including Eleuthère Irénée, at the end of 1799.

Pierre-Samuel Du Pont de Nemours was born in Paris in 1739, the son of Samuel Dupont, a watchmaker from a Huguenot family in Rouen, and Anne Alexandrine de Montchanin, also a Protestant, from a noble but wealthless Burgundian family. He married Nicole Charlotte Le Dée de Rancourt in 1766 and had two sons, Victor-Marie and Eleuthère Irénée.[4] Widowed following the premature death of his wife in 1784, he married Françoise Robin,[5] widow of his friend Pierre Poivre, eleven years later. He died in 1817 in Wilmington, in what was soon to become the fiefdom of the Du Pont family. The man who created one of the richest families in the United States was no stranger to the limelight. An economist, publicist, philosopher, journalist, adviser, politician, administrator, diplomat and entrepreneur, Pierre-Samuel Du Pont de Nemours was one of a host of multifaceted figures who, from the end of the *Ancien Régime* to the Empire, lived through and participated in the major phases of France's turbulent history,

---

2. The misadventures of John Eleuthère Du Pont (1938-2010), convicted of murder, have been the subject of two films: a drama, *Foxcatcher*, by Bennett Miller (2014), and a documentary, *Team Foxcatcher*, by Jon Greenhalgh (2016). The story of the lawyer Robert Bilott, who denounced the polluting practices of the DuPont company in the early 2000s, was told in the feature film *Dark waters*, by Todd Haynes (2019).

3. Aureliano Tonet, 'Du Pont de Nemours, une saga franco-américaine', *Le Monde*, six-part series published from 18 to 24 August 2020.

4. They had another son, Paul François, born in 1769, who died the following year.

5. See Maurice Pérouse, 'Françoise Robin, la citoyenne Du Pont de Nemours', *La Revue des deux mondes* (1985), p.578-86.

Introduction

often taking on a significant role, albeit as a minor player. The ability to survive these turbulent and dangerous times, particularly the revolutionary period, while managing to keep one's head on one's shoulders, literally and figuratively, undoubtedly illustrates a certain endurance that some might describe as opportunism or, at the very least, that could cast slight doubt on the uprightness of the character, whose choices and decisions may have fluctuated according to his personal, political or business interests. Be that as it may, because it is always difficult to define and judge an individual's position in light of past historical circumstances, the fact remains that, in view of his life's journey(s) and thought(s), Pierre-Samuel Du Pont de Nemours, a tireless lover of new ideas with an overflowing imagination, stands out as one of the great minds of his time.

The colloquium held in Paris, on the premises of Paris-Panthéon-Assas University, on 14 and 15 December 2017, aimed, by bringing together researchers from different disciplinary fields, to shed light on and understand certain aspects of the thought and action of Pierre-Samuel Du Pont de Nemours. As far as we know, this was the first and remains the only symposium devoted entirely to him. The unprecedented nature of this scientific event is even more surprising given that Du Pont de Nemours is a well-known figure who has been the subject of numerous studies. Three things are clear.

The first is that Du Pont's hectic and tumultuous life has been the subject of several biographies, some of which tend towards hagiography in places. The main ones are *Du Pont de Nemours et l'école physiocratique* by Gustave Schelle, published in 1888; *Du Pont de Nemours, honnête homme* by Denise Aimé-Azam, published in 1933; *Du Pont de Nemours, soldat de la liberté* by Pierre Jolly, published in 1956; *Pierre Samuel Du Pont de Nemours* by Ambrose Saricks, published in 1965; and *Bourgeoisie et révolution: les Du Pont de Nemours (1788-1799)* by Marc Bouloiseau, published in 1972. A few comments are in order. Gustave Schelle's work, despite its somewhat reductive title, has the merit of being the first comprehensive study devoted to Du Pont's life, from his childhood to his death, and it is based on unpublished sources. But it remains somewhat superficial on certain aspects of the thought and actions of our character – whose life 'fut partagée entre son désir de trouver la vérité et son amour pour l'humanité et la justice'[6] – and has an unfortunate tendency to use excessive praise, a fault frequently found in the writings of nineteenth-century biographers. As Sébastien

6. Gustave Schelle, *Du Pont de Nemours et l'école physiocratique* (Paris, 1888), p.4.

Le Gal recalls in his contribution to this book, Du Pont's first biographer praised his honesty, his moderation and his condemnation of violence: 'Ses principes étaient ceux de la modération; son but, de perfectionner le gouvernement sans violence. Il s'opposa, autant qu'il le put, aux fureurs de l'anarchie.'[7] This image was repeated in the twentieth century by the art historian and writer Denise Aimé-Azam,[8] whose brief preface, written by Edouard Herriot, one of the leading French politicians of the interwar period, pays a rather pompous tribute to Du Pont de Nemours, in which he seems to celebrate himself. Moderation, uprightness, enlightenment, fine liberal views, loyalty to oneself and, above all, the merit of a 'Français d'origine moyenne' who had risen to the top through his talents and hard work are not unlike the career of the president of the Radical Party. However, Herriot did not stop on this narcissistic note, and, above all, praised Du Pont's role as a transmitter of the 'idéal républicain qu'il incarne', according to him, in North America.[9] Following Schelle's approach, Pierre Jolly traces the history of an individual and places it in a more global context, showing how he brings together the *Ancien Régime* with the nineteenth century and the Old and New Worlds.[10] However, despite its obvious contribution, this work sometimes tends to exaggerate the role played by Du Pont. Ambrose Saricks' study of Du Pont is very detailed, drawing on previously unpublished information from the vast amount of correspondence preserved by the Eleutherian Mills Historical Library, but remains focused on the political dimension.[11] Finally, Marc Bouloiseau's book is original in that it considers Pierre-Samuel and his two sons as the founders of a veritable family business, from the perspective of a social history of 'collective psychology', but it focuses on just ten years, from the eve of the Revolution to the coup d'état of 18 brumaire.[12]

---

7. Jules Monchanin, *Notice sur la vie de Du Pont de Nemours* (Paris, 1818), p.31.
8. Denise Aimé-Azam, *Du Pont de Nemours, honnête homme* (Paris, 1933).
9. Edouard Herriot, 'Préface', in Aimé-Azam, *Du Pont de Nemours, honnête homme*, p.i-ii.
10. Pierre Jolly particularly emphasises the fact that, while Eleuthère Irénée was the founder of the great American firm in technical and functional terms, his father is often presented as the one who was the 'moral' driving force behind the company in its early years. See Pierre Jolly, *Du Pont de Nemours, soldat de la liberté* (Paris, 1956), p.220.
11. Ambrose Saricks, *Pierre Samuel Du Pont de Nemours* (Lawrence, KS, 1965).
12. Marc Bouloiseau, *Bourgeoisie et révolution: les Du Pont de Nemours (1788-1799)* (Paris, 1972).

Introduction

Secondly, Du Pont is best known for his membership of the 'sect of Economists' founded by François Quesnay and the marquis de Mirabeau in 1757. He is rightly regarded as one of the main propagandists of the economic doctrine of the physiocrats, which helped lay the foundations of liberalism. For proof of this, it is sufficient to list the many and varied publications that deal mainly or incidentally with the thought and proposals of Du Pont, the physiocrat and economist, before, during and after the revolutionary period. These include the writings of Eugène Daire, Edouard Mossion, Georges Weulersse, Jules Conan, Catherine Larrère, James McLain, Pierre-Henri Goutte, Gérard Klotz, Philippe Steiner and, very recently, Gilles Jacoud. This is just a small sample of the substantial body of work on the political economy of the physiocrats, and thus of Du Pont de Nemours in part or in full.

The third and final observation, which is shorter but no less important, follows on from the first two: these biographical and economic studies show that other facets of Pierre-Samuel Du Pont de Nemours have yet to be explored and put into perspective. And it must be said that the ideas he defended and the actions he took in the political, administrative and legal spheres are still largely unknown. A few recent pioneering studies have paved the way, either by researchers who agreed to form the conference's scientific committee or chair sessions during the two-day event or even by the organisers themselves. We are thinking, for example, of the exchanges with America explored by Manuela Albertone;[13] the sensitive and sensualist literary Du Pont addressed by Liana Vardi;[14] Du Pont the historian and critic of England dealt with by Richard Whatmore;[15] Du Pont the cosmologist studied by Julien Vincent;[16] and Du Pont the publicist and constitutionalist studied by Anthony Mergey.[17] Now that the path has been mapped out, it seems desirable to explore it further.

---

13. Victor Riqueti de Mirabeau and Pierre-Samuel Du Pont de Nemours, *Dialogues physiocratiques sur l'Amérique*, ed. Manuela Albertone (Paris, 2015).
14. Liana Vardi, *The Physiocrats and the world of the Enlightenment* (Cambridge and New York, 2012).
15. Richard Whatmore, 'Dupont de Nemours et la politique révolutionnaire', *Revue française d'histoire des idées politiques* 20 (2004), p.335-51.
16. Julien Vincent, '"Un dogue de forte race": Dupont de Nemours, ou la physiocratie réincarnée (1793-1807)', *La Révolution française* 14 (2018), p.1-34.
17. Anthony Mergey, 'Le contrôle de l'activité législative de la nation en 1789: l'opinion de Dupont de Nemours', *Journal of interdisciplinary history of ideas* 3:5 (2014), p.1-33.

6   *Anthony Mergey and Arnault Skornicki*

Consequently, the originality of the present work is twofold. The first aim is to take Du Pont de Nemours out of the realm of physiocratic studies, or at least out of the strict framework of Quesnay's sect, to focus on Du Pont's thought and action after the break-up of the school. In short, it is a question of undertaking a long history of physiocracy beyond its origins, in the face of the upheavals of the time, and related as well to the genesis of French liberalism at the turn of the century. It should be remembered that, at the time of the conference, we were also commemorating the bicentenary of the death of Germaine de Staël, who died on 14 July 1817, some three weeks before Du Pont de Nemours, who died on 7 August.[18] The other aim is to get Du Pont de Nemours out of the rut of the history of economic thought. Not, of course, to exclude the latter from our collective work: most of the contributions in this volume deal with the close links between Du Pont's economic thought and his political reflections, and some of their authors are themselves economists and historians of economic thought. However, our ambition lies elsewhere: in the desire to restore the versatility and variety of the work and actions of Pierre-Samuel Du Pont de Nemours. From a methodological point of view, to renew the approach to works on our character, a dual perspective has been adopted: on the one hand, the history of law and, on the other, a socio-history of political ideas. Du Pont lends himself even more easily to these approaches because he is a 'thinker on the move', whose thinking is closely linked to his actions in the political, administrative and legal spheres.

In light of the above, a question arises: in what way does Du Pont de Nemours reveal the 'century'? By century, we do not mean the eighteenth chronological century, but that 'période-charnière' for modern political and economic language referred to by Reinhart Koselleck, which he places roughly between 1750 and 1850,[19] and comparable to Voltaire's use of the term in *Le Siècle de Louis XIV* to characterise the seventeenth century. Du Pont lived through and survived all the political regimes up to the beginning of the Restoration, and often participated in their creation and operation. The interest of his position as a privileged

18. In this respect, the links with what would later be known as the 'Coppet Group', led by Mme de Staël, deserve to be explored in greater depth. See Germaine de Staël-Holstein and Pierre-Samuel Du Pont de Nemours, *De Staël-Du Pont letters: correspondence of Madame de Staël and Pierre Samuel Du Pont de Nemours and other members of the Necker and Du Pont families*, ed. and translated by James F. Marshall (Madison, WI, 1968).

19. Reinhart Koselleck, *L'Expérience de l'histoire*, ed. Michael Werner, translated by Alexandre Escudier (Paris, 2011), p.8-9.

Introduction 7

witness and actor is redoubled by the considerable body of work he left behind: a polygraph and graphomaniac, author of numerous printed publications in various formats (books, memoirs, libels, speeches, etc.) in a host of genres and fields of knowledge (political economy, of course, but also constitutional law, criminal law, natural history, cosmology, theatre, etc.), not to mention countless administrative works. The imprint of the 'century' is evident not only in the changes to his surname (from Du Pont to Du Pont de Nemours), but also in the astonishing variety of his intellectual and socioprofessional activities. His versatility and polygraphy also raise the question of his intellectual and political identity. Du Pont emerges as an original specimen of this milieu of *scholarly expertise*, formed in the crucible of the reforming elites of the late monarchy, at the crossroads of the Republic of Letters and the political-administrative world, which flourished under the Revolution and the Empire.[20] Original, because he did not follow the *cursus honorum* of the *Ancien Régime* jurist and specialised early on in economic and financial issues, while enjoying a remarkable longevity that was, so to speak, both biological and political.

In short, this book aims to capture the whole trajectory of Pierre-Samuel Du Pont de Nemours, both diachronically and synchronically: at the different stages of his professional and intellectual career from the *Ancien Régime* to the beginning of the Restoration, and through the different facets of his public and private activities (administrator and legislator, economist and political thinker, businessman and head of family).

ii. The three circles of Du Pont de Nemours

Why focus on Du Pont, who is not generally counted among the leading intellectual and political figures in the canon of the Enlightenment and the Revolution? It is safe to say, however, that Pierre-Samuel was not a minor public figure or a third-rate author. During the last two decades of the *Ancien Régime*, his social rise took him to the very top of

---

20. It would be useful to compare him with a figure whose long and important career is fairly characteristic of these reformist circles and who has been studied in depth by Dominique Margairaz, *François de Neufchâteau: biographie intellectuelle* (Paris, 2005). On the notion of expertise under the *Ancien Régime*, see *Fields of expertise: a comparative history of expert procedures in Paris and London, 1600 to present*, ed. Christelle Rabier (Newcastle, 2007); *Parole d'experts: une histoire sociale du politique (Europe, XVIᵉ-XVIIIᵉ siècle)*, ed. Marion Brétéché and Héloïse Hermant (Rennes, 2021).

the ministerial ranks; during the Revolution, he was briefly president of the National Assembly; and, in America, he was in dialogue with Thomas Jefferson. His work as an economist, journalist, political thinker and philosopher also commands respect for its scope and, very often, for the quality of its content; it helped to stimulate public debate on several issues from the mid-1800s to the beginning of the Restoration. Du Pont's career unfolded in three circles, which, as they grew with the century, picked up their political and intellectual transformations along the way.

Family: between business, Protestantism and politics

Far from focusing on the private man, the study of this circle constantly brings us back to the public figure because a large part of his investment tends towards one objective: perpetuating the family as a dynasty. The Du Pont family, even before it became a major industrial firm and a multinational, was first and foremost a political enterprise that grew in stature over time; the intimate and patrimonial aspects are closely interwoven with the Parisian, American and Protestant social and professional circles. The fact is well-known, almost proverbial: the economist Pierre-Samuel had little business acumen, unlike his second son, Eleuthère Irénée. As Julia Abramson shows in the present volume, this never prevented him from finding investors in circles of trust.

However, the more Du Pont feels sidelined in politics, the more he invests himself in his grand project for an American colony, studied here by Aya Tanaka. His dream of America, tinged with utopianism, can in fact be read as a temptation and an attempt at a reasoned and disillusioned retreat. Relegated to the background under the Directoire, he seemed reduced to the position of commentator, making his journal *L'Historien* (1795-1797) his observatory of political life. This meagre spiritual power was confirmed by his appointment as a member of the Institut, 'a frivolous dignity like all the others'. It did not satisfy Du Pont, who noted with bitterness the decline of the doctrine of the Economists and his relative political decline. Unable to integrate the new post-Terreur ruling elites, he felt driven into exile,[21] unable to 'ni influer sur aucune autorité, ni exercer aucune

---

21. Jean-Luc Chappey, 'The new elites: questions about political, social, and cultural reconstruction after the Terror', in *The Oxford handbook of the French Revolution*, ed. David Andress (Oxford, 2015), p.556-72.

Introduction

autorité'.[22] But he also spoke to his lover, Mme Lavoisier, with a touch of ardour, about his grand project: a physiocratic colony of 'trois cents familles' destined to become the Athens of modern times[23] or a new Rome of which he would be the modern 'Numa' – no less.

Julia Abramson here looks back at the entrepreneurial history of Du Pont and his children. No fewer than four companies were founded in America: the first to buy and operate land in the United States; the second for his son Victor-Marie, dedicated to transatlantic trade, dissolved in 1802; the next, known as 'Du Pont de Nemours, Père et Fils & Cie', in Paris; and a fourth established by Eleuthère Irénée in Delaware, in which Du Pont's company also invested, which met with unexpected, spectacular and lasting success, since it is to this day one of the major companies of American and world capitalism. Although Pierre-Samuel was not the founder of this famous company, his imprint is twofold. On the one hand, it was his close ties with the chemist Lavoisier that set Eleuthère on the path to the gunpowder industry. On the other hand, his transatlantic connections formed a solid basis for alliances between the company and the American political elite, particularly in Delaware, which have endured to the present day.

Ironically, Du Pont *l'Economiste* never showed much business acumen. Not that he was a pure theoretician, because for a long time he practised economics as a statesman and not as an entrepreneur, holding positions at the Bureau de commerce before the Revolution and then at the Paris Chamber of Commerce in 1808. Be that as it may, he is living proof that a competent administrator in public affairs does not always make a shrewd entrepreneur in private affairs.[24] Julia Abramson explains this is due less to a lack of talent than to a lack of time and, subsequently, professionalism, with *business* being just

---

22. Letter to Mme Lavoisier, 22 fructidor An VII (8 September 1799), quoted in Bouloiseau, *Bourgeoisie et révolution*, p.235.
23. Letter to Mme Lavoisier, 2 brumaire An VII (23 October 1798), quoted in Bouloiseau, *Bourgeoisie et révolution*, p.234-35.
24. 'Les vertus publiques se composent des vertus privées. Celui-là ferait un mauvais administrateur politique ou d'Etat, qui n'aurait pas pu, ou pas su ou pas voulu être un bon administrateur particulier pour ses associés, ses amis et ses parents' (letter from Du Pont de Nemours to Mme de Staël, 19 pluviôse Year VIII [8 February 1800]), in Staël-Holstein and Du Pont de Nemours, *De Staël-Du Pont letters*, p.15).

10   *Anthony Mergey and Arnault Skornicki*

one of Du Pont's many occupations. However, Pierre-Samuel had put together a solid project and was able to convince a few investors within the Swiss bank: Bidermann, a naturalised Frenchman with Girondin sympathies who married Eleuthère's daughter, as well as Jacques Necker and his older brother, the scholar and banker Louis Necker de Germany (1730-1804). The strength of the interests and connections is obvious here; it outweighs the strength of the ideas and the political and intellectual disagreements with the minister and rival of Turgot. *Business* was seen as a personal affair, a family affair and a network affair.[25]

Du Pont was spared by Necker, who refrained from damaging his career and even entrusted him in 1778 with the task of finding the means to collect complete data to establish a reliable picture of the balance of trade.[26] On the eve of his departure for the United States in 1799, the former minister even sent him a letter of recommendation to his merchant friends in New York.[27] This was also the starting point of a friendship with his daughter, Mme de Staël. Necker and Germaine talked business and politics respectively.

State: from reformer to revolutionary

The breadth of Du Pont's administrative skills, often acquired on the job, is surprising, whether regarding finance, local administration, fiscal and constitutional issues, or social questions such as assistance to the poor and the sick, as Jean-Baptiste Masméjan shows here through the issues of hospital reform. Was Du Pont the inventor of ambulatory medicine? Or public–private partnerships? This wide range of expertise in the sciences of government was his main asset in standing the test of time and surviving regime changes. From a recognised but rather precarious position as a journalist and administrator, Du Pont rose through the ranks at the start of the Revolution

---

25. See Julia Abramson, 'Put your money where your friends are: finance and loyalty in a nineteenth-century Du Pont shareholder report', https://www.hagley.org/librarynews/put-your-money-where-your-friends-are-finance-and-loyalty-nineteenth-century-du-pont (last accessed 25 November 2024). On the question of trust in political economy, see Henry C. Clark, *Compass of society: commerce and absolutism in Old-Regime France* (Lanham, MD, 2007).
26. Letter from Du Pont de Nemours to Necker, 25 December 1778, in Staël-Holstein and Du Pont de Nemours, *De Staël-Du Pont letters*, p.3-5.
27. Letter from Necker to Du Pont de Nemours, 3 August 1799, in Staël-Holstein and Du Pont de Nemours, *De Staël-Du Pont letters*, p.12-13.

Introduction   11

to become an important figure in French political life, albeit not without a certain amount of upheaval.

As Christophe Le Digol's analysis reveals, Du Pont was both a man of two minds who took advantage of the Revolution to add a noble flavour to his surname and a coherent reformer who drew all the consequences from the great physiocratic motto, 'Liberté, propriété, sûreté',[28] whether in terms of his constant opposition to corporal punishment, as Thérence Carvalho shows, or in terms of his conception of public order, explored by Sébastien Le Gal. Du Pont was nevertheless aware of the relative precariousness of his position, always dependent on the good pleasure of the great, right up to the very end of the *Ancien Régime*. Despite a successful career and a well-established reputation, he was disgraced during a cabinet reshuffle.[29] However, like so many other deputies of the Third Estate, he was not inclined towards anti-nobility radicalism when the work of the Estates General began in May 1789;[30] it was not so much the bourgeois in him that made the Revolution, as the Revolution that made him a moderate revolutionary. Unfortunately, the Revolution did not have the desired effect on his wealth or his career.[31]

In the aftermath of Thermidor, Du Pont's constitutional proposal to the Thermidorian Convention, set out in *Du pouvoir législatif et du pouvoir exécutif convenables à la République française*, was close to

28. See Arnault Skornicki, 'Liberté, propriété, sûreté: retour sur une devise physiocratique', *Corpus* 66 (2014), p.16-36.
29. As early as the summer of 1788, he felt threatened by the new controller general of finances, Loménie de Brienne, of whom he was not a client; see letter to Dr Hutton, 24 June 1788, quoted in Bouloiseau, *Bourgeoisie et révolution*, p.43. Later, he emphasised to his son how lucky he was to inherit his father's connections: 'C'est un double et bien grand avantage que de commencer avec des amis puissans, tout acquis, qu'il est aisé de ne pas perdre, et que l'on peut s'attacher de plus en plus chaque jour' (letter to Eleuthère Irénée, Paris, 15 November 1789, quoted in Bouloiseau, *Bourgeoisie et révolution*, p.24).
30. Timothy Tackett, *Becoming a revolutionary: the deputies of the French National Assembly and the emergence of a revolutionary culture (1789-1790)* (Princeton, NJ, 1996); French translation: *Par la volonté du peuple: comment les députés de 1789 sont devenus révolutionnaires* (Paris, 1997).
31. Before the Revolution, his real-estate holdings included three houses (one in Bois-des-Fossés and two in Rouen) according to Saricks (*Pierre Samuel Du Pont de Nemours*, p.130). But his material situation remained precarious: 'La Providence qui s'intéressait à ma famille nous a ruinés quant à la fortune; m'a fait perdre le fruit de 28 années de travail et a détruit même ce que j'avais d'illusion', he explained to Eleuthère Irénée in a letter at the end of 1791, quoted in Bouloiseau, *Bourgeoisie et révolution*, p.25.

the Constitution finally adopted in 1795: on the one hand, to curb popular passions by a census suffrage favouring property owners; on the other, to share executive power to ward off any risk of Caesarism. Nonetheless, he remained determined to fight against the Robespierrist legacy, contributing directly to its black legend[32] and demonstrating uncompromising vigilance. Liana Vardi's study of the journal *L'Historien* reveals Du Pont's relative independence of mind, as he was far more critical of the new regime than might have been imagined. *L'Historien* is not really what its title suggests: it is a daily newspaper, an almanac of the present for historians of the future, of which Du Pont is the main worker and the soul, but which remains a collective work, dealing with constitutional as well as economic issues. Far from praising the 'bourgeois' republic of the Directoire, this journal was concerned that the deputies still had too many former Jacobin 'terrorists' in their ranks, that the division of powers and the Constitution were being repeatedly violated, and even that fundamental rights such as forced loans were being violated. While protesting his republicanism, Du Pont opposed the division of émigré property and frequented the Club de Clichy. It is therefore easy to understand why he was targeted by the repression that followed the coup d'état of 18 fructidor An v.

From then on, Du Pont's distrust of revolutionary upheavals was constant, even obsessive. All revolution carries with it a state of war against its enemies, who are likely to threaten freedom; it is indispensable only as a necessary evil and a shock remedy; it is subject to a condition of brevity, without which it can sweep away the three great principles of freedom of action, security of persons, and ownership of property. At a time when conflict with neighbouring kingdoms had just broken out, Du Pont publicly stated his definition of revolution:

> Une *révolution* est une secousse passagère pour arriver à un *gouvernement* et à l'établissement de la *liberté*. Tant que la révolution dure il n'y a point de liberté, car il y a guerre; et en toute guerre les battus et les vaincus ne sont pas *libres*.
>
> La liberté commence au moment où il se fait une convention pour vivre en paix, et où *une constitution* s'établit; car alors on commence à respecter les droits de tous et de chacun.

32. P.-S. Du Pont de Nemours, *Du pouvoir législatif et du pouvoir exécutif, convenables à la République française* (Paris, Chez Du Pont, 1795), p.3-4; P.-S. Du Pont de Nemours, *Avant-dernier chapitre de l'histoire des Jacobins: lettre de M. Du Pont aux citoyens constitutionnaires* (Paris, De l'imprimerie de l'auteur, 1796).

Introduction 13

> Plus on aime la *liberté*, plus on doit craindre de multiplier *les révolutions*, qui en suspendront au moins passagèrement l'exercice.[33]

In this passage, Du Pont does seem to admit the need for revolution in certain circumstances. But he underlines the tension between the ends it sets itself (the establishment or re-establishment of freedom) and the means it employs (the overthrow of the established order by illegal or even violent means): the latter, if they are perpetuated, risk swallowing up the former by postponing its accomplishment *sine die*.

The ordeal of the Montagnard Convention got the better of Du Pont's revolutionary scruples. Drawing a gloomy assessment of the period, he now anathematised the very principle of revolution but refused to join the counter-revolutionary camp, while at the same time proclaiming his love of constitutions.[34] It was as if he had dreamed of a constitution without revolution.

One phrase sums up his state of mind: 'quiconque veut jouir du fruit de son travail, quiconque veut avoir la sûreté de sa vie a l'esprit conservateur.'[35] *Conservative*: the word is out. No more than the *political reaction* coined by Benjamin Constant at the same time,[36] the adjective *conservateur*, which Chateaubriand turned into a noun with political credentials during the Restoration, can be burdened with retrospective meanings. While Du Pont certainly claimed to be a member of the 'parti des amis de l'ordre',[37] his conservatism appeared to be quite liberal.

---

33. P.-S. Du Pont de Nemours, 'De l'amour de la constitution et de celui de la liberté', in *Correspondance patriotique entre les citoyens qui ont été membres de l'Assemblée nationale constituante*, vol.2 (Paris, De l'imprimerie de Du Pont, 1791), p.70-79 (73).
34. 'Tu connais également ma haine et ma résistance contre toutes les révolutions dont les meilleures et les plus sages sont toujours un amas de calamités et de ruines' (letter to his eldest son Victor, 28 vendémiaire An IV [20 October 1795], in Bouloiseau, *Bourgeoisie et révolution*, p.114).
35. *L'Historien* 177 (27 floréal An IV [16 May 1796]), p.679-80, quoted by Liana Vardi in her contribution to this volume.
36. Benjamin Constant, *Des réactions politiques* (n.p., n.n., 1796). See the study by Jean Starobinski, *Action et réaction: vie et aventures d'un couple* (Paris, 1999).
37. In the words of his collaborator Louis-Philippe de Ségur (*L'Historien* 158, 8 floréal An IV [27 April 1796], quoted by Liana Vardi in her contribution to this volume).

International: from diplomacy to American exile

The day after Du Pont's death, the baron de Gérando said of him: 'On eût cru voir en lui le citoyen du Monde: la Pologne, l'Amérique, d'autres pays encore ont reçu l'influence de son zèle; et cependant y eut-il jamais aussi un meilleur Français?'[38] Beyond the emphasis typical of the laudatory genre, the phrase refers to the public image of the character as well as to the reality of his international mobility, sometimes chosen (Poland), sometimes forced (America). Beyond the case of Du Pont, the international and transatlantic dimensions of physiocracy have been well explored by scholars. The involvement of the Economists in colonial administration and their plans to redefine French imperial policy have been highlighted,[39] as has their deliberate strategy of internationalisation.[40] A recent thesis has drawn up a comprehensive comparative table of the circulation of their political, legal, and economic ideas in the Europe of the Enlightenment. Based on a wealth of often unpublished documentation, it shows Du Pont's commitment to the conversion of princely courts and administrations.[41] The thesis that the European ruling elites were massively acculturated to physiocracy will certainly not be accepted, as physiocracy by no means became the undisputed model of 'economic government', to use Quesnay's famous expression, in Europe. But neither can we ignore

---

38. Joseph-Marie de Gérando, *Notice sur M. Dupont de Nemours, lue à la séance générale de la Société d'encouragement pour l'industrie nationale, le 23 sept. 1818* (Paris, n.d.), p.4.

39. In particular Paul-Pierre Le Mercier de La Rivière (intendant of the Windward Islands between 1759 and 1764), but also the brother of the marquis de Mirabeau, Jean-Antoine (governor of Guadeloupe between 1753 and 1755). See André Labrouquère, *Les Idées coloniales des physiocrates (documents inédits)* (Paris, 1927); Louis-Philippe May, *Le Mercier de La Rivière (1719-1801): aux origines de la science économique* (Paris, 1975); Florence Gauthier, 'Le Mercier de La Rivière et les colonies d'Amérique', *Revue française d'histoire des idées politiques* 20:2 (2004), p.37-59; Loïc Charles and Paul Cheney, 'The colonial machine dismantled: knowledge and empire in the French Atlantic', *Past & present* 219:1 (2013), p.127-63; Pernille Røge, *Economistes and the reinvention of empire: France in the Americas and Africa, c.1750-1802* (Cambridge, 2019).

40. *La Diffusion internationale de la physiocratie (XVIII⁰-XIX⁰)*, ed. Bernard Delmas *et al.* (Grenoble, 1995).

41. Thérence Carvalho, *La Physiocratie dans l'Europe des Lumières: circulation et réception d'un modèle de réforme de l'ordre juridique et social* (Paris, 2020), p.322-32.

Introduction 15

the extent to which its ideas, themes and watchwords circulated and were sometimes translated into public policy.[42]

The contributions in this volume on these issues focus on two areas: on the one hand, Du Pont's strictly diplomatic activities, from the negotiations on the Eden-Rayneval trade treaty of 1786[43] to his role in the sale of Louisiana and his proposals on the Family Pact, which Alfred Steinhauer discusses in this volume, and, on the other, his intellectual relations with North America, which began well before his exile in 1799.[44] They reveal the breadth of his thinking in the fields of international relations, colonial policy and comparative politics.

If there was one subject on which Du Pont de Nemours remained firm in his principles, it was slavery. Simona Pisanelli's investigation clearly shows that Du Pont did not just contribute to the abolitionist argument; he theorised the transition from slavery to wage labour or, to put it in Marxist terms, from the slave mode of production in the French colonies to the capitalist mode of production. Slavery is contrary to man's natural rights, since it constitutes a violation of his primitive property: that of his own body, or 'personal property'. But Du Pont also tried to demonstrate its economic irrationality, arguing that free labour would be less costly than slave labour (which is far from proven). Du Pont's argument also ties in with a central thesis of physiocracy that Le Mercier de La Rivière developed repeatedly: far

---

42. On this point we differ from S. L. Kaplan and S. A. Reinert. The rich volume coordinated by them aims to deconstruct the thesis of the European success of physiocracy by highlighting the vigour of anti-physiocracy (a notion that is not well defined elsewhere), in a variety of high-quality contributions that rightly restore the importance of other currents in the political economy of the eighteenth century. In so doing, the volume partially proves what it sets out to refute: not, of course, the strict application of the physiocratic programme, which never really had any examples, but the centrality of physiocracy in European debates, and hence its international dissemination. See *The Economic turn: recasting political economy in Enlightenment Europe*, Steven L. Kaplan and Sophus A. Reinert (New York, 2019), especially p.11-15.

43. Orville T. Murphy, 'DuPont de Nemours and the Anglo-French commercial treaty of 1786', *The Economic history review* 19:3 (1966), p.569-80.

44. This is illustrated in particular by his correspondence with Benjamin Franklin between 1768 and 1789; see *The Papers of Benjamin Franklin*, https://franklin-papers.org/ (last accessed 25 November 2024). On the links forged between French elites and American revolutionaries in Paris, see Philipp Ziesche, *Cosmopolitan patriots: Americans in Paris in the age of Revolution* (Charlottesville, VA, 2010).

from being distinct or even conflicting, 'relativement au Corps social, *le juste et l'utile sont inséparables*.'[45] However, Du Pont, less farsighted and rigorous than Condorcet, hardly anticipated the cost of entering the 'free labour' market. Worse still, in response to the objection of the large planters that whites could not withstand the tropical climate, he sometimes locked himself into racial prejudice, even if it was for the good cause of abolition.

On other subjects, however, his practical experience and his wisdom as an administrator led him often to break with a doctrinaire attitude. In the service of Foreign Minister Vergennes, Du Pont had to put physiocratic conceptions of international relations to the test of realpolitik and invent a 'practical cosmopolitanism', to use the expression coined by Peter Sahlins and taken up by Antonella Alimento in her contribution. Du Pont played a role in the invention of diplomacy through trade in the eighteenth century.[46] He thus re-evaluates the role of 'negotiations', in other words, power relationships, and does not rely solely on the force of example and evidence. The main conclusion is that freedom cannot be unilateral and that it is conditional on reciprocity. Physiocracy could therefore not be reduced to a utopia or the musings of theorists in chambers, despite the accusations of certain contemporaries such as Rousseau and Galiani. At an advanced age, Du Pont declared before the Institut that rulers should 'ne [...] point songer à l'*Utopie*' and give time to improve things, even quoting Necker to back up his philosophical moderation.[47]

This need for gradual reform is confirmed by the example of free trade. As a good physiocrat, Du Pont was a resolute and unconditional supporter of free trade. As a government adviser, he recognised that the 1786 treaty with the United Kingdom, while failing to achieve free trade, was an excellent step in that direction. France had nothing to fear, he explained, and could reasonably hope to redress

---

45. Paul-Pierre Le Mercier de La Rivière, *L'Intérêt général de l'Etat, ou la Liberté du commerce des blés* (Amsterdam and Paris, Desaint, 1770), p.99 (original emphasis).

46. *The Politics of commercial treaties in the eighteenth century: balance of power, balance of trade*, ed. Antonella Alimento and Koen Stapelbroek (Cham, 2017); John Shovlin, *Trading with the enemy: Britain, France, and the 18th-century quest for a peaceful world order* (New Haven, CT, and London, 2021).

47. 'Discours du 20 vendémiaire An VIII [12 October 1799]', in Pierre-Samuel Du Pont de Nemours, *Quelques mémoires sur différens sujets, la plupart d'histoire naturelle, ou de physique générale et particulière*, 2nd edn (Paris, 1813), p.374-84 (383).

Introduction   17

the imbalance between the economies of the two countries thanks to
its demographic advantage, while finding in it a genuine guarantee
of peace between the two empires. Relying on Montesquieu and
Quesnay to support the thesis of gentle commerce, he added that,
because of such a partnership, 'no war can be lasting in Europe.'[48]
However, by demanding an independent committee empowered to
establish breaches of the treaty since 1786, he did not rule out
recourse to armed conflict to enforce it: 'A la différence de Quesnay et
de Turgot', notes Richard Whatmore, 'il en vint à considerer la guerre
comme le moyen le plus sûr et le plus efficace de restaurer l'ordre
naturel.'[49] Later, however, when Bonaparte consulted him about his
plan for an expedition to Egypt, Du Pont warned him, not without
premonition, of the dangers of imperialist hubris and the cloud of
wars it would bring.[50]

In her contribution, Manuela Albertone also demonstrates Du
Pont's ability to adapt in another field, that of banking and credit,
by studying an unpublished manuscript from 1812 intended for the
American government. At the end of his career, conscious of the
demonetisation of the physiocratic doctrine, Du Pont was forced
to reposition it in the face of the international success of Adam
Smith and his *Wealth of nations* (1776) and the emergence of new
generations of British (David Ricardo, Thomas Robert Malthus)
and French (Jean-Baptiste Say) economists. He himself participated
in the construction of a 'post-physiocratic political economy' by
paying lip service to the principle of a national bank, adapting the
physiocratic tax doctrine to the young American republic, and,
finally, approving certain protectionist measures aimed at fledgling
factories.

***

These three circles – family, government and international – are
not so much concentric as intertwined. They unfold the prolific and
polymorphous activity of a person who, in keeping with the times,

---

48. Pierre-Samuel Du Pont de Nemours, *Lettre à la Chambre du commerce de
    Normandie, sur le mémoire qu'elle a publié relativement au traité de commerce avec
    l'Angleterre* (Rouen and Paris, chez Moutard, 1788), p.74-75.
49. Whatmore, 'Dupont de Nemours et la politique révolutionnaire', p.344.
50. Letter dated 5 floréal Year VI (24 April 1798), in Bouloiseau, *Bourgeoisie et
    révolution*, p.135-36.

does not entirely compartmentalise private happiness and public action, entrepreneurial ambitions, and political projects. Far from being a pale reflection of the times, Du Pont's multifaceted work has the dimensions of the century, and perhaps of a world that he helped to shape. This book has no other ambition than to reveal some of his most remarkable works.

I

Public action, private happiness |
Action publique, bonheur privé

Family business at Du Pont de Nemours, Père et Fils & Cie   25

solicitations moved his investors to sponsor his business does not accurately express the nature of their interactions. As shown in the following pages, it is more accurate to state that his appeals did not fully discourage them from investing, despite manifest problems in the venture. As we discover, impetus for the early supporters' positive response reflected conceptions of investment and profit that related more to group cohesion and mutual aid among founder and capitalists than to hope of accumulation.

Any argument about Protestant culture and capitalist activity invites appraisal in light of the Weberian thesis.[6] *The Protestant ethic and the 'spirit' of capitalism* remains a reference for discussions of capitalism and Protestantism despite limitations for describing historical capitalist practices in Catholic France. In Weber's analysis, Protestantism and capitalism have an affinity. Wealth signifies that divine favour may be conferred upon its holder, and its loss might point to a fall from grace. This epistemology of the divine guides the individual in social behaviour.[7] By contrast, what emerges here is a social practice different from, and often at odds with, the Weberian epistemology. Du Pont emphatically underlined his family's Protestant cultural heritage, however, he critiqued Christianity as a revealed religion that fetishises the life of Jesus, and he had little interest in promoting Christian or Protestant dogma as such. At the same time, religion, broadly speaking, remained at the forefront of his public and intellectual activities. Like many of his contemporaries, Du Pont viewed civil religion favourably, as a vehicle for promoting a moral society. His publications that imagine an inclusive, 'natural' religion dwell upon universally available positive virtues, such as forgiveness and love of other humans. The relativist or cosmopolitan aspect of this attitude is traceable to favoured writers such as Montaigne, and

---

    Choudhury and Daniel J. Watkins, underline the centrality of religion and religious controversy in eighteenth-century society.

6.   Other points of reference include the renewal of interest in political economy and French economic history, as in *The Economic turn: recasting political economy in Enlightenment Europe*, ed. Steven L. Kaplan and Sophus A. Reinert (New York, 2019), and scholarship at the intersections of economics and religion, as in *Recent developments in economics and religion*, ed. Paul Oslington *et al.* (Northampton, 2018) and *The Oxford handbook of Christianity and economics*, ed. Paul Oslington (New York, 2014).

7.   Max Weber, *The Protestant ethic and the 'spirit' of capitalism and other writings* (1905), ed. and translated by Peter Baehr and Gordon C. Wells (New York, 2002).

26 *Julia L. Abramson*

Du Pont knew earlier statements about deistic, or 'natural', religious philosophy, including in the writing of Rousseau.[8] At the same time, his own proposals for dogma and practice suitable for the state and for families also responded to the violent rupture with tradition and reinvention of cult associated with revolutionary deism. For Du Pont, then, Protestantism was a defining feature of his personal history within his family network and extended kinship circles, and it was also a platform, although not the only one, for maintaining connections with others, including through acts of generosity, forgiveness and reciprocity. The next pages examine how Du Pont's personal and idiosyncratically Protestant ethos of capitalism informs the founding of Du Pont de Nemours, Père et Fils & Cie, and provides an explanatory tool for the founder's writings addressing the company's demise. Considering the topics of religion and business in tandem yields insight into Du Pont's biography and into an intriguing episode in the social history of business, while bringing into view the complex texture of the historical period.

'[D]ans les événemens qui nous arrivent, Dieu seul sait s'ils nous sont avantageux ou funestes'[9]

Issues of religion traversed the social and political upheaval of the 1790s and roiled milieus Du Pont frequented. Throughout 1790-1791 the Constituent Assembly engaged in epochal debates about religious freedom, individual rights and the state. At issue were the traditional status of the Catholic Church and of religion in French society. On 22 March 1790 Du Pont was among eleven *commissaires* elected to the new Comité d'aliénation des domaines nationaux, charged with supervising the sale of ecclesiastical and royal holdings, thereby raising money for the nation while paring down Church patrimony

---

8. Michel de Montaigne, 'Des cannibales', in *Les Essais* (1580), ed. Claude Pinganaud (Paris, 2002), p.156-64; Jean-Jacques Rousseau, 'Profession de foi du vicaire savoyard', *Emile, ou de l'éducation* (1762), in *Œuvres complètes de Jean-Jacques Rousseau*, ed. Bernard Gagnebin and Marcel Raymond, vol.4: *Emile. Education. Morale. Botanique* (Paris, 1969), book 4, p.565-635; and see C. J. Betts, *Early deism in France: from the so-called 'déistes' of Lyon (1564) to Voltaire's 'Lettres philosophiques' (1734)* (The Hague, 1984).

9. Pierre-Samuel Du Pont de Nemours, *Mémoires de Pierre Samuel Du Pont de Nemours adressés à ses enfans, le 4 septembre 1792*, HML, Winterthur Manuscripts, W2-4796, ch.4, p.4.

and power.[10] In January 1791 the Assembly attempted to subdue the Catholic clergy by demanding that they take the Ecclesiastical Oath transferring their allegiance from the pope and French monarchy to the new constitution.[11] As an alternative to Catholicism as the civil religion, some advocated substituting an atheistic Cult of Reason, however, the Assembly ratified Robespierre's deistic Cult of the Supreme Being in 1794. By this time, Du Pont had resigned from the revolutionary legislature and fallen out of favour. He became interested, however, in a deistic cult of *théophilanthropie* imagined as still another alternative.[12]

Like the statesman Jacques Necker and many other contemporaries, Du Pont believed a civil religion to be essential for social cohesion. Long accustomed to reflecting on theology, in his youth Du Pont studied 'la métaphysique' and considered a career as a pastor. By the 1790s, Du Pont tried his hand at creating a new theology: his *Philosophie de l'univers* develops a 'physique et [...] morale universelles'. In published form it was accompanied by a dialogic prose 'poème' titled *Oromasis* that describes the genesis of the universe and of life. Governed by 'natural' and 'universal' laws of attraction and reciprocity, these phenomena are at the same time characterised by mystery, or a divine aspect. Du Pont refers to this text as his 'philosophical testament', reflecting awareness that its authorship might be among his last acts. He states in its preface that he began

10. 'Séance du 22 mars 1790', in *Archives parlementaires de 1787 à 1860: recueil complet des débats législatifs & politiques des chambres françaises. Première série (1789 à 1799)*, ed. Jérôme Mavidal and Emile Laurent, 96 vols (Paris, 1867-1990), vol.12 (1881), p.299.

11. Albert Mathiez, *Rome et le clergé français sous la Constituante* (Paris, 1911); Michel Vovelle, *Religion et Révolution: la déchristianisation de l'An II* (Paris, 1976); Timothy Tackett, *Religion, revolution, and regional culture in eighteenth-century France: the Ecclesiastical Oath of 1791* (Princeton, NJ, 1986); Yann Fauchois, *Religion et France révolutionnaire* (Paris, 1989); Dale K. Van Kley, *The Religious origins of the French Revolution: from Calvin to the Civil Constitution 1560-1791* (New Haven, CT, 1996).

12. Albert Mathiez, *La Théophilanthropie et le culte décadaire: essai sur l'histoire de la Révolution 1796-1801* (Paris, 1903), p.109-14; Saricks, *Pierre Samuel Du Pont de Nemours*, p.261-62; Mona Ozouf, 'Déchristianisation', in *Dictionnaire critique de la Révolution française: événements*, ed. François Furet and Mona Ozouf (Paris, 1992), p.79-99, and 'Religion révolutionnaire', in *Dictionnaire critique de la Révolution française: institutions et créations*, ed. F. Furet and M. Ozouf (Paris, 1992), p.311-28; Liana Vardi, *The Physiocrats and the world of the Enlightenment* (Cambridge and New York, 2012), p.273-75.

28   *Julia L. Abramson*

the essay while in hiding and fearing for his life as the Revolution radicalised. The first version is dated 22 December 1792, Year I of the Republic, likely indicating the time he began the draft. In a manner typical for Du Pont as an author, he later returned repeatedly to the topic, publishing revised editions of the text through the 1790s.[13]

It is germane to Du Pont's situation that the lack of positive standing of Protestants remained a contentious topic through the 1790s and that debates about citizens' rights and the appropriate relationship of religion and state continued in the Constituent Assembly throughout Du Pont's tenure. Broad trends towards tolerance appeared in eighteenth-century society, yet they coexisted with intolerance and traditionalism, and tension emerging from ideological differences between these currents was characteristic. The 1685 ordinance signed by Louis XIV revoking the Edict of Nantes stood through 7 November 1787, when Louis XVI signed the Edict of Versailles reinstating limited civil legitimacy for Protestants.[14] The new statute did not grant equal positive rights to non-Catholics. Its first two articles extended elements of civil tolerance to 'ceux de nos sujets qui professent une autre religion que la religion catholique, apostolique et romaine'. Protestants and conceivably other minority sects – 'ceux qui professeront une religion différente de la religion catholique' – are still deviant relative to practitioners of the normative religion of the state. In August 1789, article 10 of the *Déclaration des droits de l'homme et du citoyen* addressed religious freedom in a new though still qualified statement. Meanwhile, incidents of anti-Catholic and anti-Protestant violence occurred through the country. At length, a law of 7 May 1791 reframed the issue: 'Nul ne doit être inquiété pour ses opinions, même religieuses, pourvu que leur manifestation ne trouble pas l'ordre public établi par la loi.'[15] The tolerance which had at times been practised despite the law was now universal in principle, within limits as needed to maintain 'public order'. But sects now stood on equal footing, and religion no longer founded the metaphysics for

13. Pierre-Samuel Du Pont de Nemours, *Philosophie de l'univers* (Paris, De l'imprimerie de Du Pont, [1793]); 2nd edn (Paris, De l'imprimerie de Du Pont, fructidor An IV [1796]). Du Pont, *Philosophie de l'univers* [1793], p.6 and 8-9.

14. Barbara de Negroni, *Intolérances: catholiques et protestants en France, 1560-1787* (Paris, 1996), p.212-14; Arno J. Mayer, *The Furies: violence and terror in the French and Russian revolutions* (Princeton, NJ, 2000), p.487-88.

15. Yann Fauchois, 'La difficulté d'être libre: les droits de l'homme, l'Eglise catholique et l'Assemblée constituante, 1789-1791', *Revue d'histoire moderne et contemporaine* 48:1 (2001), p.71-101 (73).

Family business at Du Pont de Nemours, Père et Fils & Cie   29

the state. Reconceptualised, it was now one among many 'opinions', or affections, of the individual.

Du Pont's public engagement with the politics of religion and his writings on religion from this period invite attention to the Protestant ancestry and Huguenot connections he evokes in describing his family, including their minoritarian status. Use of the phrase 'religion prétendue réformée' and abbreviation 'R.P.R.' to designate Protestantism can be traced back to the sixteenth century. The edict that Henri IV signed to grant limited civil liberties to reformers was the 'Edit de Nantes en faveur de ceux de la religion prétendue réformée' (1598).[16] To label the beliefs a 'so-called' reformed religion suggests peculiarity on the part of reformers and scepticism about the legitimacy of reform practices. The statute affirmed in this way the minoritarian status of Protestants in Catholic France, even as it extended measures of tolerance to them.[17] The phrase 'religion prétendue réformée' remained in use through the next two centuries. In 1792, while in hiding, Du Pont also wrote his personal and family memoir, or autobiographical testament, shortly before penning the 'philosophical testament' mentioned earlier. In his memoir, Du Pont used the phrase 'R.P.R.' ironically, as he described the very real Protestant faith and cultural identification of multiple generations of his extended family and others who played important roles in the family history, such as the chevalier de Jaucourt, the encyclopedist and critic of papal abuse of power whose prominent family were Protestant and who had taken in Du Pont's mother during her youth.[18] Du Pont's irony underlines the cruelty of the cultural erasure implied in the locution and defiantly refuses its attempts at suppression.

Protestant culture and deistic philosophy have been little considered in Du Pont's trajectory. The omission easily leads to the assumption or

16. Diane C. Margolf, 'Identity, law, and the Huguenots of early modern France', in *Memory and identity*, ed. B. Van Ruymbeke and R. J. Sparks, p.26-44 (29), and see Roland Mousnier, *L'Assassinat d'Henri IV, 14 mai 1610* (Paris, 1964); Daniel Ligou, *Le Protestantisme en France de 1598 à 1715* (Paris, 1968); and Mack P. Holt, *The French wars of religion, 1562-1629* (Cambridge, 1995).
17. Didier Poton and Patrick Cabanel, *Les Protestants français du XVIᵉ au XXᵉ siècle* (Paris, 1994); *Protestants d'Aunis, Saintonge et Angoumois*, ed. Pierre Boismorand *et al.* (Paris, 1998); Patrick Cabanel, *Juifs et protestants en France: les affinités électives (XVIᵉ-XXIᵉ siècle)* (Paris, 2004) and *Histoire des protestants en France (XVIᵉ-XXIᵉ siècle)* (Paris, 2012); *Protestants, protestantisme et pensée clandestine en France*, ed. Geneviève Artigas-Menant *et al.* (Paris, 2004); Daniel Benoît, *Les Frères Gibert: pasteurs du 'Désert' puis du 'Refuge'* (Paris, 2005); Carolyn Chappell Lougee, *Facing the Revocation: Huguenot families, faith, and the king's will* (New York, 2016).
18. Du Pont, *Mémoires*, ch.1, p.11; for the Jaucourt family: ch.2, 3, 6, 15.

conclusion that his life reflected a desacralising and anti-clerical era of Enlightenment to a disaffected modernity. Yet the vexed, minority status of Protestants in France came repeatedly to the fore in his lifetime, and not only during the revolutionary decade. In fact, as Du Pont attests in his memoir, Protestant culture shaped his sense of personal identity and family history. He portrayed himself as part of a group that shared elements of the Protestant cultural identity and history and who in this were distinct from the majority of the French. During the 1790s, Du Pont's Protestant culture and deistic philosophy provided coherence and perhaps comfort in the face of chaotic experience. Practically, Protestant connections and Protestant-friendly sympathisers were vital to his career. For the firm Du Pont de Nemours, Père et Fils & Cie, ties articulated through Protestant culture motivate its capitalisation despite the likelihood of failure since its inception.

Moral accounting: Du Pont, Bidermann and the Necker brothers

The *Compte rendu par Du Pont (de Nemours) aux actionnaires de la Compagnie*, or shareholder report, of 18 April 1808 is an accounting and company history to date, thirty-four manuscript pages in length. Du Pont's company was supposed to engage in maritime commerce such as provisioning French ships sailing the Atlantic, implying a broad scope for activity and profit. Instead, states Du Pont: 'rien de cela n'était des affaires lucratives.' The report lists obstacles such as new trade treaties (under Napoleon), tax laws governing resident aliens in America, prejudices of American judges against French people, betrayal by an American associate, volatility in the New World real-estate market. In short, *forces majeures* of all descriptions surprised him: 'les malheurs se sont enchaînés.' The remarks suggest he met with bad luck but also point to a lack of preparation on his part to establish the business:

> J'avais appris en Amérique ce que nul d'entre nous ne savait avant notre départ que les lois de la commandite n'y étaient pas respectées; que toutes les sociétés y étaient regardées comme pures et simples, que tous les associés y étaient solidaires et que chacun pouvait au choix des créanciers y être poursuivi pour la totalité de ses engagemens sociaux. [...] en France [...] les principes sont différents.[19]

---

19. Pierre-Samuel Du Pont de Nemours, *Compte rendu par Du Pont (de Nemours) aux actionnaires de la Compagnie* (18 April 1808), HML, L1-526.

Family business at Du Pont de Nemours, Père et Fils & Cie   31

Towards the end of the report, Du Pont announces plans to dissolve the company. Without cash to pay off investors, he will convert shares to holdings in the gunpowder company begun by his second son.[20] From the vantage of 1808, the future of Eleuthère Irénée's company was not assured, thus Du Pont's manoeuvre did not appear to benefit his shareholders. As his biographer observes, the move absolved Du Pont of his company's debts and foisted them onto his son.[21]

Beyond obstacles Du Pont names in the *Compte rendu*, further problems can be identified. The company's commercial activity was not Du Pont's sole obligation nor the work that most interested him. During 1808, he was serving as the elected vice president of the fifteen-member Chamber of Commerce of Paris while also editing Turgot's manuscripts and publications to create an edition of his mentor's collected works.[22] Despite Du Pont's noted industry, it is difficult to imagine how he could devote much attention to his firm. A letter he wrote to Victor-Marie described his busy weekly schedule: 'The next morning for the business of my own Company, correspondence, accounts, investments &c. in my office [...] This arrangement, you see, is very regular, but energetic.'[23] Du Pont likely devoted as little as one morning weekly to the company, possibly less, and the firm exhibited worrisome limitations. Intriguingly, letters from his investors show that they had found his business proposition problematic from the very beginning.

Among Du Pont's largest shareholders was Jacques Antoine Bidermann (1751-1817), the banker and *brasseur d'affaires* or big businessman, as contemporaries knew him, originally from Winterthur, Switzerland, who had come to Paris in 1789. Under the officially more tolerant regime, foreign-born and Protestant Bidermann was naturalised in France in 1790. His vast company Senn, Bidermann & Cie had installations throughout France, Switzerland and Belgium as well as in India. It manufactured *toiles peintes* in Alsace, imported merchandise from India and sold all of these goods. From his

20. Du Pont, *Compte rendu*.
21. Saricks, *Pierre Samuel Du Pont de Nemours*, p.331-32.
22. Anne-Robert-Jacques Turgot, *Œuvres de M. Turgot, ministre d'Etat, précédées et accompagnées de mémoires et de notes sur sa vie, son administration et ses ouvrages*, ed. Pierre-Samuel Du Pont de Nemours, 9 vols (Paris, 1808-1811).
23. P.-S. Du Pont de Nemours to Victor-Marie Du Pont (3 April 1803), in Saricks, *Pierre Samuel Du Pont de Nemours*, p.320 and p.421, n.52, who cites the translation of Bessie Gardner Du Pont in *Du Pont de Nemours, 1739-1817*, vol.2 (Newark, DE, 1933), p.85.

32 *Julia L. Abramson*

position in the Bureau de commerce, Du Pont had earlier dealt with Bidermann's firm, such as, in 1787, handling documents relating to patents and privileges for business and manufacturing activities in parts of France.[24] Initially a political moderate like Du Pont, Bidermann collaborated with him on the Girondiste review *La Chronique du mois, ou les Cahiers patriotiques*, contributing an article in early 1792 in favour of a liberal economy.[25] In March of the same year, he took up the task of administering the provisioning of Paris. Later in the year, radicalising 'patriotically' with the Revolution, Bidermann became one of three members of the Directoire des achats des subsistances générales de la République.[26] Bidermann was the largest single outright investor in Du Pont's company. He purchased thirteen shares at the standard price of 'deux mille dollars ou piastres fortes' apiece.[27]

Another Swiss Protestant shareholder, Louis Necker de Germany (1730-1804) was a wealthy mathematician, banker and trader, and the older brother of Du Pont's former patron Jacques Necker.[28] Necker

24. Letter from P.-S. Du Pont to Senn, Bidermann & Cie dated 'Paris 9.bre [novembre] 1787', HML, W2-326; to M. de La Boullaye, Paris (November 1787), HML, W2-327 and W2-328; and the enclosure 'Etablissement proposé par la maison Senn et Bidermann', HML, W2-329. See also Charles Poisson, *Les Fournisseurs aux armées sous la Révolution française: le Directoire des achats (1792-1793) – J. Bidermann, Cousin, Marx-Berr* (Paris, 1932), p.36-38, 40, 45-46; Jean Bouchary, 'Les manieurs d'argent sous la Révolution française: le banquier Edouard de Walckiers', *Annales historiques de la Révolution française* 86 (1938), p.133-55 (144); Herbert Lüthy, *La Banque protestante en France de la Révocation de l'Edit de Nantes à la Révolution*, vol.2: *De la banque aux finances (1730-1794)* (Paris, 1961), p.629, n.63, p.667-73, p.723, p.730; Louis Bergeron, *Banquiers, négociants et manufacturiers parisiens du Directoire à l'Empire* (Paris, 1978), ch.3, p.65-86. See also Richard Munthe Brace, 'General Dumouriez and the Girondins 1792-1793', *The American historical review* 56:3 (1951), p.493-509 (498-99), and Jacques Godechot, 'The business classes and the Revolution outside France', *The American historical review* 64:1 (1958), p.1-13 (9), who refer to Poisson.

25. Jacques Antoine Bidermann, 'Article VII. D'un commerce national', *La Chronique du mois, ou les Cahiers patriotiques* (Paris, Imprimerie du Cercle social, An III [January 1792]), bound in vol.1, p.83-88.

26. Entry for 21 June 1793, in *Archives parlementaires de 1787 à 1860*, ed. J. Mavidal and E. Laurent, vol.67 (1905), p.35-41; Poisson, *Les Fournisseurs*, p.51.

27. P.-S. Du Pont de Nemours to J. Necker (8 April 1801), in *De Staël-Du Pont letters: correspondence of Madame de Staël and Pierre Samuel Du Pont de Nemours and other members of the Necker and Du Pont families*, ed. and translated by James F. Marshall (Madison, WI, 1968), p.65.

28. See Lüthy, *De la banque aux finances*, p.235-37, 405-406, 505-507, 621-22, and Johannes Hermann, *Zur Geschichte der Familie Necker* (Berlin, 1886).

de Germany purchased one share, at $2000, after closely interrogating Du Pont and Victor-Marie about the company. Writing to Victor-Marie, Necker de Germany asked: '1. De quelle somme est son fond capital? 2. En combien d'actions est-il partagé? 3. Les sociétés en commandite sont elles permises en Amerique de façon que chaque associé commanditaire ne soit responsable que de sa mise en fond? [...] 12. devez vous monsieur etre longtems absent?' Later in the same letter, he continued: 'Quel terme et quelles facilités accordez vous le payement?'[29] The questions that Necker de Germany asked and his limited implication suggest that he did not find Du Pont's business proposal attractive. Why, then, did he, along with Bidermann, place money and trust with an associate having apparently limited business skills and inadequate time to nurture their investments?

The most widely recognisable (then as now) investor was Necker de Germany's younger brother Jacques Necker (1723-1804). A banker, Necker served several terms under as many titles as France's principal financial official. He was finance minister then director general of finances (1776-1781); director general of finances and minister of state (1788-1789); and finally prime minister of finances (1789-1790). After Du Pont had served the French state, including while his friend Jacques Turgot (1727-1781) was controller general (1774-1776), Necker recalled Du Pont to government service later in 1776.[30] Twenty years thereafter, Du Pont tried repeatedly to persuade Necker to buy shares in his company. Each time, Necker refused, and on 21 March 1801 he brusquely rejected an invitation to become a partner, writing to Du Pont: 'un associé de plus seroit inutile.'[31] That Necker refused to buy shares outright disappointed Du Pont, who thought the endorsement would bring the company success. Victor-Marie wrote as much to Necker: 'Il [P.-S. Du Pont] disait souvent, *Nôtre Etablissement aura les plus grands succès si Monsieur Necker en augure bien.*'[32] Other letters

---

29. *De Staël-Du Pont letters*, Necker de Germany to V.-M. Du Pont (5 March 1801), p.48; see also V.-M. Du Pont to Necker de Germany (21 March 1801), p.52-56; V.-M. Du Pont to Necker de Germany (18 August 1801), p.101-102.

30. H. Lüthy, *De la banque aux finances*, p.228-33, 239-42, 369-420, 458-60, 464-68, 496-97, 503-508, 519-21, 555-60, 565-72, 741-42, 771-72; Henri Grange, *Les Idées de Necker* (Paris, 1974); Jean Egret, *Necker, ministre de Louis XVI, 1776-1790* (Paris, 1975); Robert D. Harris, *Necker: reform statesman of the Ancien Régime* (Berkeley, CA, 1979) and *Necker and the Revolution of 1789* (Lanham, MD, 1986).

31. J. Necker to P.-S. Du Pont de Nemours (21 March 1801), in *De Staël-Du Pont letters*, p.60.

32. V.-M. Du Pont to J. Necker (8 April 1801), in *De Staël-Du Pont letters*, p.63.

from Necker consist mostly of questions, recalling those his brother asked. In these letters, Necker's writing style is laconic, contrasting starkly with the expansive verve of his published treatises. His letters about Du Pont's venture communicate scepticism kept in check by civility.

In view of Necker's wariness about the business proposal, it is striking that he did substantially assist Du Pont with his company. On 20 July 1801, Jacques Necker offered to the company, on a three-year term, $9833.40 worth of American stocks that 'ne sont pas en mon nom' and several months of accrued interest, while laying out conditions for eventual repayment. He had offered a similar sum as cash as early as April of the same year.[33] The offer made available five times more capital than what the majority of outright investors provided, as most purchased a single share each at $2000. The gesture was also discreet, as the loan terms avoid explicitly associating Necker's name with Du Pont's company. Necker's manoeuvre suggests generosity and circumspection. French grandees had made indirect and invisible investments at least since the mid-seventeenth century, as legal and economic historian Amalia D. Kessler has shown. For those forbidden, due to caste, to engage in commerce, the practices usefully maintained discretion.[34] Such practices provided precedents for the technical aspect of Necker's commitment to Du Pont. Their transaction took place in a changed, post-revolutionary social context, however, begging the question why Necker chose to assist Du Pont even as he avoided purchasing stock.

Insofar as business interactions are social exchanges that articulate connections among participants, to answer this question requires a change in perspective to focus on relationships and their contexts. Outside of the ostensibly 'rational' or objective matter of the original business proposal's economic feasibility, Du Pont's later shareholder report underlines that personal and social ties, first and foremost, bound investors and the non-shareholding benefactor to the founder. To review the list of their names is to see that relationships within

---

33. J. Necker to V.-M. Du Pont (20 July 1801), in *De Staël-Du Pont letters*, p.98-99, and see also J. Necker to V.-M. Du Pont (19 April 1801), p.76; V.-M. Du Pont to J. Necker (14 May 1801), p.84-87; V.-M. Du Pont to J. Necker (29 July 1801), p.100.

34. Amalia D. Kessler, 'Limited liability in context: lessons from the French origins of the American limited partnership', *The Journal of legal studies* 32:2 (2003), p.511-48 (516-24).

this group formed multiple 'layers of superimposed networks'[35] spanning business, friendship and marriage. Correspondingly, Du Pont activates the form of the *compte rendu* itself as a hybrid whose rhetoric simultaneously pursues multiple ends. In this he followed the famous precedent of one of his mentors and the indirect supporter in the business venture. Jacques Necker's *Compte rendu au roi* (1781) was a best-selling, widely read instance of a complex realisation of the genre. Known as the first public account of the French nation's finances, Necker's text is a multivalent document ultimately concerned with statecraft and governance.[36] Du Pont knew this document, as did a large swathe of French readers. Following its precedent, and in keeping with the many criss-crossing ties that bound founder and investors, numerical accounting is only one of several tasks that Du Pont's report performs.

The narrative that Du Pont crafted for his shareholders voices a dramatic, multilayered tale whose main plot revolves around the author's sense of credit and debt, figured as primordially social in nature. By relating his own story with the business story, Du Pont implicates his investors, also his designated readers, in the outcomes of both adventures. The report guides its audience towards ideals of reciprocity and mutual aid. By rhetorical means, Du Pont places moral pressure on his interlocutors, signalling them to respond according to his vision. In view of this moral accounting, the document can be understood as a 'genre of the credit economy'.[37] That is, Du Pont's elaboration of the shareholder account as a discursive form also naturalised among the population of its recipients capitalist practices that it explored.

The list of twelve shareholders in the 1808 report indicates that the community of founder and investors was bound by multiple strands of interwoven connections. The list of course includes the founder, but also Du Pont's second wife and her daughter. Bidermann, who had by

35. I borrow this phrase from Carolyn Chappell Lougee (appears as Carolyn Lougee Chapell), 'Family bonds across the Refuge', although her study does not address Du Pont. In *Memory and identity*, ed. B. Van Ruymbeke and R. J. Sparks, p.172-93 (183).

36. For the debate about Necker's text, begin with Harris, *Necker: reform statesman of the Ancien Régime*, p.217-35, and Joël Félix, 'The problem with Necker's *Compte rendu au roi* (1781)', in *The Crisis of the absolute monarchy: France from Old Regime to Revolution*, ed. Julian Swann and Joël Félix (Oxford, 2013), p.107-26.

37. Mary Poovey, *Genres of the credit economy: mediating value in eighteenth- and nineteenth-century Britain* (Chicago, IL, 2008).

36 *Julia L. Abramson*

now also served with Du Pont on the Parisian Chamber of Commerce and whose son would become an associate of Eleuthère Irénée and a family member through marriage to Eleuthère Irénée's daughter, and Bidermann's business partner, the Swiss Jean Johannot (1748-1829), both feature on the list. Like Bidermann, Johannot had established residency in Paris, and he knew Jacques Necker and Necker's daughter, the novelist, essayist and critic of Napoleon Mme de Staël. In 1801, Du Pont had written to Necker about Johannot's role within his company, taking care to point out connections: 'Les actionnaires plus faibles nomment des syndics pour les représenter. C'est actuellement le Citoyen Johannot bien connu de vous et de Madame votre fille.'[38] Mme de Staël, a friend and correspondent of Du Pont's since 1797, also appears on the 1808 list. Upon Necker's death in 1804, she had inherited Du Pont's debt to him, now converted into company shares after all.[39]

In describing the company's affairs for this group in the *Compte rendu*, Du Pont conflates its losses with those of his family and himself, eventually using a metaphor of martyrdom to bring his investors around to support his cause. He begins by explaining that the commingling of company and personal funds is due to accident. As he states, he was surprised to learn that in America, unlike in France, it was impossible to separate personal from corporate responsibility for loss in business.[40] This topic had been raised as a concern by Necker de Germany (cited above) and also by Jacques Necker prior to their investments. As if to avoid the sticky topic, Du Pont will invoke imperatives other than profit. Implicit references to honour and friendship indicate the response that the founder hoped for from investors, ties with whom he considered to be reciprocal. Facing losses and dissolution of the company, Du Pont notes that 'je

38. P.-S. Du Pont de Nemours to J. Necker (8 April 1801), in *De Staël-Du Pont letters*, p.65. On Johannot, see Lüthy, *De la banque aux finances*, p.669, 671.

39. For shareholders listed in the 1808 report, see Saricks, *Pierre Samuel Du Pont de Nemours*, p.424-25, n.104, who borrows from B. G. Du Pont, *Du Pont de Nemours*, p.104-106, and *Life of Eleuthère Irénée Du Pont from contemporary correspondence*, 11 vols (Newark, DE, 1923-1926), vol.8, p.303-306.

40. See Matthew H. Elbow, *French corporative theory, 1789-1948: a chapter in the history of ideas* (New York, 1953); Kessler, 'Limited liability in context'; Andrew Shankman, *Crucible of American democracy: the struggle to fuse egalitarianism & capitalism in Jeffersonian Pennsylvania* (Lawrence, KS, 2004); Andrew M. Schocket, *Founding corporate power in early national Philadelphia* (DeKalb, IL, 2007).

suis la principale victime' of the whole operation. He twice repeats a promise to 'sacrifice' personally as necessary, so that his shareholders can at least recover their capital. The alternative as he envisions it would be worse. To incur their disappointment, he continues, would be a mortal blow: '[I]l me serait mortellement pénible qu'ils crussent avoir à se plaindre de moi.' The language of ultimate sacrifice ('mortally painful'), which is hyperbolic in this case, echoes literary language in accounts of deaths for the Protestant cause, such as in the martyrology *Les Tragiques* that Huguenot soldier and writer Agrippa d'Aubigné authored during the wars of religion. With this metaphor Du Pont describes his own kind of martyrdom to the conjoined causes of business and the well-being of his associates. At the same time, he admits, as the narrative continues, that his shareholders 'ont une sorte de droit de ne juger que par les Evenemens'.[41] That is, they really have no obligation to credit his good intentions – to forgive his debts to them – since the company has not fared well. His language veers away from taking on responsibility for the shortfall. Instead, it suggests that any dishonour would come from the investors. Were they to lack forgiveness for the founding partner, the breach of trust could have, as he implies, fatal consequences for him. The report reframes the business problem as a moral responsibility which it then displaces onto the shareholders.[42]

Investment or 'éblouissement'? Du Pont and the long shadow of John Law

The audacious quality of Du Pont's business scheme contrasts notably with the fiscal caution he exercised in his public functions. Among family and friends, he was known, as his biographer states, to be uniquely persuasive, even when they perceived, as in this case, that his 'exuberance [...] was no adequate substitute for sound business sense'.[43] In letters, his sons and family intimates remarked with chagrin that Du Pont often influenced them against their own better judgement. Like the brilliant 'spokesmen for credit' that Marx would later deem essential motivators of capitalist production, Du Pont

---

41. Du Pont, *Compte rendu*.
42. For another instance of 'moral accounting', in Du Pont's argument against slavery: Caroline Oudin-Bastide and Philippe Steiner, *Calculation and morality: the costs of slavery and the value of emancipation in the French Antilles* (Oxford, 2019).
43. Saricks, *Pierre Samuel Du Pont de Nemours*, p.272.

38   *Julia L. Abramson*

possessed qualities of charisma and vision proper to the 'swindler and prophet'.[44] Yet, while he pushed to obtain credit, cash and forgiveness from investors, he remained cautious in other contexts, counselling against any possibility of speculation and financial sophistry in matters of state. An ambivalent figure that Marx named in this context was John Law, the Scot associated with the orchestration during the Regency of Philippe d'Orléans (1715-1723) of the 'System' designed to replace France's traditional royal financial institutions and to reduce the nation's debt.[45] After 1720, when the speculative bubble associated with Law's scheme burst, the debacle echoed through the eighteenth century and beyond,[46] to Du Pont's fascination. Du Pont's intervention in the 1769 crisis of the Compagnie des Indes, then under Necker's advisement, critiqued its monopoly as counter to liberty, and its activities as fraudulent insofar as they produced 'gains apparents', or illusory profits, in reality detrimental to the state. In a work ostensibly about commerce, but largely a critique of the Compagnie including several chapters on its history, Du Pont compared its disarray, due to excessive speculation, to its earlier condition under Law. At that time, 'l'esprit & l'art de la charlatanerie' characterised the System's operations, designed, as he wrote, to produce 'éblouissement', or dazzlement, that hoodwinked investors.[47] In 1790, when the Constituent Assembly addressed the national debt, Du Pont again revived the spectre of Law. In a lengthy speech, he invoked the 1720 events and exhorted his colleagues to address the debt directly, imploring them to avoid issuing paper *assignats* susceptible to inflation because, as he argued, lacking in immutable intrinsic value.[48]

44. Karl Marx, *Capital: a critique of political economy*, translated by David Fernbach, vol.3 (London, 1991), p.572-73.

45. Antoin E. Murphy, *John Law: economic theorist and policy maker* (Oxford, 1997); Arnaud Orain, *La Politique du merveilleux: une autre histoire du système de Law (1695-1795)* (Paris, 2018).

46. *The Great mirror of folly: finance, culture, and the crash of 1720*, ed. William N. Goetzmann *et al.* (New Haven, CT, 2013); Julia L. Abramson, 'Narrating "finances" after John Law: complicity, critique, and the bonds of obligation in Duclos and Mouhy', *Finance and society* 2:1 (2016), p.25-44.

47. P.-S. Du Pont, *Du commerce et de la compagnie des Indes*, 2nd edn (Paris, Delalain, 1769), p.3, 90-91, 156; for Law see especially ch.2-3, p.76-164. See also John Shovlin, *The Political economy of virtue: luxury, patriotism, and the origins of the French Revolution* (Ithaca, NY, 2006), p.124-25; Anoush Fraser Terjanian, *Commerce and its discontents in eighteenth-century French political thought* (Cambridge, 2013), p.147-62.

48. P.-S. Du Pont de Nemours to the Assemblée nationale constituante, 'Séance

Family business at Du Pont de Nemours, Père et Fils & Cie 39

By contrast, such caution was missing at the founding of Du Pont de Nemours, Père et Fils & Cie, while, within the networked group of investors, Du Pont was an enthusiast among fellow speculators. The overlapping networks among shareholders reflected connections that Du Pont cultivated throughout his career, including early associations with Quesnay and physiocracy, service to the French state under Turgot and Necker, engagement with the Revolution before its radical phase and his fall from grace, and ties of marriage and friendship. Investors for Du Pont's transatlantic venture included bankers, financiers and business people who engaged in demonstrably unsound speculation, for their friend's sake. What remains to be seen is exactly how the reciprocal connections informed not only their common interest in business but also their tolerance for risk.

Social politics and the Protestant experience

Beyond personal and family references in his autobiography, Du Pont took an active interest in French Protestants as a group. Upon immigration to the United States in 1799, he packed a personal library that included many works on Protestant history and related topics such as religious toleration and law in the Protestant state of Geneva. He brought a copy of the great *Dictionnaire historique et critique* (1697) by Pierre Bayle, a Huguenot who fled to Holland in 1681 due to religious persecution, then from Rotterdam published literary and philosophical works on tolerance and Calvinism and against superstition; the *Dictionnaire* would be seen as an essential prelude to the next century's enlightened currents. The oldest volume in Du Pont's library was Pierre Matthieu's *Histoire des derniers troubles de France* (Lyon, n.n., 1604) about the wars of religion and reigns of Henri III and Henri IV. Du Pont's library inventory cites Claude Carloman de Rulhière's treatise on Protestant history in France from the start of the reign of Louis XIV, *Eclaircissemens historiques sur les causes de la révocation de l'Edit de Nantes, et sur l'état des Protestants*

---

du 25 septembre 1790', in *Archives parlementaires de 1798 à 1860*, ed. J. Mavidal and E. Laurent, vol.19 (1884), p.224-37. See also Saricks, *Pierre Samuel Du Pont de Nemours*, p.191-94; Seymour Edwin Harris, *The Assignats* (Cambridge, 1930); Rebecca L. Spang, 'The ghost of Law: speculating on money, memory and Mississippi in the French Constituent Assembly', *Historical reflections / Réflexions historiques* 31:1 (2005), p.3-25 (17), and n.46-48 cites Alexandre Lameth, *Histoire de l'Assemblée constituante*, vol.2 (Paris, 1829), p.55-57, 65, 138, 631.

en France, depuis le commencement du règne de Louis XIV, jusqu'à nos jours: tirés de différentes archives du gouvernement (2 volumes, Geneva, François Dufart, 1788). He brought Gacon de Louancy's *Lettres de deux curés des Cévènes sur la validité des mariages des Protestans, et sur leur existance légale en France* (London, n.n., 1779) and volumes related to Françoise d'Aubigné, Mme de Maintenon, of Huguenot heritage and the granddaughter of Agrippa d'Aubigné, including several drawn from the *Lettres de Madame de Maintenon* (9 volumes, Amsterdam, Bruyn, 1755-1756) and *Mémoires pour servir à l'histoire de Madame de Maintenon, et à celle du siècle passé* (6 volumes, Maastricht, Dufour et Roux, 1778; original publication Amsterdam, Au dépens de l'auteur, 1755) authored or edited by the Protestant writer and outspoken defender of religious tolerance Laurent Angliviel de La Beaumelle.[49] These topics in Du Pont's shipped library highlight the breadth and specificity of his interests, and further underline how religious discourse – like 'finance', political economy and their discursive extensions – permeated the culture.

Pertinently for Du Pont's trajectory and outlook, religious elements had shaped the transition of France's financial administration from Turgot to Necker and unusual structure of Necker's nomination, affecting Du Pont. At issue, once again, was the status of Protestants in Catholic France, even as the transition reflected debates in political economy. Following the success of regional policies that he had enacted while serving as the *intendant* of Limoges, Turgot had been named controller general in 1774, only to be caught in the crosshairs of the *guerre des farines* of 1775.[50] Amid the controversy, publication of Necker's treatise *Sur la législation et le commerce des grains* (1775), arguing for a controlled grain market to moderate prices, contributed to his visibility. Necker cannily emphasised the plight of the majority, in pithy statements marked by oratorical flourish such as memorable chiasmus: 'Enfin, & c'est ici la considération la plus importante, il n'y a nulle égalité entre le désir de réaliser du bled contre l'argent

---

49. Packing list (1799), HML, W2-5129, and Evald Rink, 'A family heritage: the library of the immigrant Du Ponts' (n.d., unpublished, courtesy of the Hagley Library), p.46.

50. On the 'flour wars' begin with Louise A. Tilly, 'The food riot as a form of political conflict in France', *The Journal of interdisciplinary history* 2:1 (summer 1971), p.23-57; Vladimir S. Ljublinski, *La Guerre des farines: contribution à l'histoire de la lutte des classes en France, à la veille de la Révolution* (Grenoble, 1979); Steven L. Kaplan, *The Bakers of Paris and the bread question, 1700-1775* (Durham, NC, 1996).

& le besoin d'échanger son argent contre du bled.'[51] As Necker's published essay circulated, popular unrest grew in Paris over the prices of bread, wheat and flour. Yet, after Turgot was demoted (on 12 May 1776), Necker's ascent (leading to Du Pont's recall to service following Turgot's fall) was surprisingly slow. The minister Maurepas finally promoted Necker on 22 October, after a delay apparently due to considerations of social standing as affected by religion.[52] As a Protestant Swiss in Catholic France, Necker could not carry the usual title of controller general. Nonetheless, the understanding was that he would perform the office's work.[53] Necker was also excluded from sitting on councils, such as the Conseil d'Etat, to which his duties would normally have granted him access.[54] While Necker was known for wealth gained through banking and business, as director general of France's finances, he exercised in office the moderation his writings emphasise.[55]

Beyond Necker's ability to guide the political economy, due to his civil status, his promotion brought into view issues of religion, individual rights and state power in a manner unseen at Turgot's accession two years earlier. As the formal structure of Necker's appointment divorced his duties from their habitual title, the mathematician Condorcet sarcastically described the turn of events in a letter to his friend Turgot:

---

51. J. Necker, *Sur la législation et le commerce des grains*, 2 vols in 1 (Paris, Pissot, 1775), p.65.

52. Vicomte Othénien d'Haussonville [Gabriel Paul Othénien de Cléron, comte d'Haussonville], *Le Salon de Mme Necker: d'après les documents tirés des archives de Coppet*, vol.2 (Paris, 1882), p.106-108. See also Egret, *Necker*, p.44-45, p.45, n.151, p.52.

53. Egret, *Necker*, p.37-47.

54. Egret, *Necker*, p.56-58.

55. E.g. Jacques Necker, *Eloge de Jean-Baptiste Colbert, discours qui a remporté le prix de l'Académie française en 1773* ([Paris], J. B. Brunet, 1773). And see Egret, *Necker*, p.61; Gilbert Faccarello, 'Galiani, Necker and Turgot: a debate on economic reform and policy in eighteenth-century France', in *Studies in the history of French political economy from Bodin to Walras*, ed. Gilbert Faccarello (London, 1998), p.120-95 (145). Kaplan also sees in Necker's writings a 'down-to-earth epistemology': 'The grain question as the social question: Necker's antiphysiocracy', in *The Economic turn*, ed. S. L. Kaplan and S. A. Reinert, p.505-84 (515). Political scientist Aurelian Craiutu finds in Necker's later writings on political economy an ideology of moderation and the preference for bargaining, compromise and incremental advance: *A Virtue for courageous minds: moderation in French political thought (1748-1830)* (Princeton, NJ, 2012), p.114-57.

42 *Julia L. Abramson*

Cela est plus qu'incroyable. M. de Maurepas exerce notre foi, et le Gouvernement va devenir aussi mystérieux que la théologie. Ce mystère-ci est une véritable trinité. La finance sera gouvernée comme le monde. Le chef du Conseil [the ageing Maurepas] a tout à fait l'air du Père éternel dont la place doit être vacante depuis quelque temps dans la rue de Sèvres. M. Taboureau [the figurehead holding the controller title] représentera l'enfant Jésus ou l'agneau, dont il aura la mansuétude. Pour M. Necker, c'est assurément le Saint-Esprit, et il faut lire les actes des apôtres pour avoir idée du fracas qui accompagnera sa venue.[56]

Condorcet's comparison of the trio of principal state officers to the Holy Trinity draws attention to the bizarre aspect of the multiple appointments. The caricature of the principal financial officers as the Christian Eternal Father, Infant Jesus and Holy Spirit alludes to the power of Maurepas and Necker and mocks the customary and legal hierarchy that placed Catholic before Protestant. Condorcet's *bon mot* ironically points to moral bankruptcy in the state.

Condorcet's jibe underscores that France's pious doctrine of the single faith and state has conjured a hypocritical charade. Along with lawyer, liberal censor and minister of state Lamoignon de Malesherbes, Protestant pastor Rabaut Saint-Etienne and others, Turgot had in the 1770s campaigned to broaden religious tolerance, paving the way to the Edict of Versailles.[57] Necker's appointment to high office, like passage of the 1787 Edict, indicates tolerant tendencies at Versailles[58] and the state's readiness to defy its own doctrine for political expediency. Such is, for Condorcet, the sorry state of French finance and *le monde*, or the rest of society. It is a further irony that Necker was known for his personal sobriety and religiosity. Necker's intellectual biographer notes that he was 'un croyant sincère' who saw religion as a feature of human existence.[59] As a public figure, Necker,

---

56. Condorcet to Turgot, dated '22 oct 1776, à La Roche-Guyon'. Jean-Antoine-Nicolas de Caritat, marquis de Condorcet, and Anne-Robert-Jacques Turgot, baron de L'Aulne, *Correspondance inédite de Condorcet et de Turgot 1770-1779*, ed. Charles Henry (Paris, 1883), letter 240, p.291. Citing this source, Egret, *Necker*, p.50 and n.2, mistakenly attributes part of this quotation to Turgot.

57. Pierre Grosclaude, *Malesherbes témoin et interprète de son temps* (Paris, 1961), p.559-602; see also p.355-87, 411-41.

58. Haussonville, *Salon de Mme Necker*, p.106.

59. Grange, *Les Idées de Necker*, p.515.

Family business at Du Pont de Nemours, Père et Fils & Cie   43

like Du Pont, believed religion essential for civil society.[60] His long first term and two subsequent stints at the head of France's finances, in times of formidable turbulence, bear witness to the Swiss' capacity as an administrator and analyst of the times.

Protestantism and reciprocity in Du Pont's first network

In his 1792 autobiography, Du Pont heavily emphasises his people's Protestantism and Huguenot connections across the detailed picture of his historical family network. Like other documents in which he iteratively crafted and rehearsed material, the autobiography testifies to Du Pont's deliberate, persistant efforts in self-fashioning. His *Mémoires* read as a manifesto that articulates values as well as describes events. Its pages fortify memory of the author's past and seek to colour the future through the designated audience of first readers, Du Pont's children. Du Pont rhetorically constructs the narration about self and family history as a bridge. It must connect the uncertain present of his writing with a hoped-for future as well as with the past that it makes tangible. Two-way chronological telescoping – recalling from the past in order to energise the future – reflects what historian Natalie Zemon Davis has termed the 'planning tendency'. For Du Pont, writing during the early 1790s in fear for his life, retrospection and prolepsis aid in portraying his people as a coherent group capable of history and legacy. Drawing kith and kin into the narrative fold, his narration calls forth, in Davis' phrase, a 'sense of the relations between the living and the dead, that is, of the arrow of family fortunes in historical time'.[61]

The Terror's escalation as Du Pont – in hiding and under threat of the guillotine – wrote his *Mémoires* undoubtedly prompted him to a reckoning about his own life, expressed in an accounting metaphor from his economic writings about physiocracy that nonetheless emphasises the human aspect of his journey. During four months in seclusion, he recorded his history, addressed to his sons for their edification should

---

60. Jacques Necker, *De l'importance des opinions religieuses* (London and Paris, Panckoucke and Thou, 1788). See also Grange, *Les Idées de Necker*, p.517-614. For intersections of politics and religion, and notions of civil religion and theocracy: Ronald Beiner, *Civil religion: a dialogue in the history of political philosophy* (Cambridge, 2011).

61. Natalie Zemon Davis, 'Ghosts, kin, and progeny: some features of family life in early modern France', *Daedalus* 106 (spring 1997), p.87-114 (92). See also Lougee, 'Family bonds across the Refuge', p.176 and p.189, n.19.

44 *Julia L. Abramson*

he die. They will, he states, be the 'produit net' of his existence, should it be cut short. The preface opens on a note of existential aporia: 'Incertain, mes chers enfans, si j'aurai jamais le bonheur de vous revoir, et de quelle manière je sortirai de ma retraite actuelle [...] Si le dénouement arrivait avant la fin de l'histoire, vous suppléerez aux lacunes comme vous pourrez.'[62] Some pages later, he refers again to the danger of early death. Recalling an uncle who married at age sixty-nine and fathered two children, and his grandmother, still strong and active at eighty-four, he wrote that he was 'enchanté' at the vigour of his relatives which 'me donne une attitude heureuse pour mon âge avancé, s'il avance, et si je ne laisse pas ma tête à la fin de ce récit.'[63] With early, non-natural death looming urgently as a real possibility, Du Pont likely felt compelled to underline what he thought most important. At the same time, the heated debates on individual liberty and religious toleration that had taken place during his term in the Constituent Assembly were within recent memory. Although the debates had resulted in increased toleration for religious minorities, including Protestants, in the law of 7 May 1791, the statements were qualified and hard won, and clerical factions continued to lobby for Catholicism as the unique state religion.[64]

In these contexts, Du Pont's enumeration of his Protestant identity and heritage affirms their very existence, along with his own, hedging against annihilation. From the first sentence, the *Mémoires* emphasise shared Protestant identity: 'Notre Famille est protestante, et normande.'[65] The unusually placed comma in the manuscript weights the first adjective, adding to its prominence to further foreground the family religious tradition. Despite the long timeline of violent and coercive attempts to suppress Protestantism, the family have persisted. Du Pont's emphasis also resists secularising currents associated with Enlightenment thought and the Revolution. If Du Pont here highlights Protestantism as a defining feature of his family culture, subsequent pages reveal it as the organising principle for his thoughts throughout the narrative.

In the four opening chapters (of fifteen in total), Du Pont describes

---

62. Du Pont, *Mémoires*, [prefatory dedication], p.1.
63. Du Pont, *Mémoires*, ch.1, p.7.
64. A proposal for a separation of Church and state would only later be developed before the Revolutionary Convention, by Protestant Boissy d'Anglas (21 February 1795). See Fauchois, 'La difficulté d'être libre'.
65. Du Pont, *Mémoires*, ch.1, p.1.

his ancestry, drawing himself and, by extension, his two young sons as specific products of a long Protestant lineage and as nodes in an international web of interconnected Protestant families and individuals. He establishes links within the Huguenot 'Refuge' or diaspora that followed the Revocation of the Edict of Nantes, recording that paternal ancestors fled France to seek asylum in England, Switzerland, Holland and 'Carolina' in North America.[66] Their descendants, he writes, are now connected with the foreign nations, yet remain close to France. From his mother's family of 'très zélés Protestans', the Monchanins, there are descendants in France, but also Prussia, Switzerland, India, England.[67] The Monchanins, he repeats, were all 'Huguenots'.[68] He repeatedly mentions their convictions: 'Je vous ai dit qu'on était dans ma famille huguenots très zélés.'[69] He notes connections to Protestant financiers and bankers, through 'riches Financiers' on his mother's side.[70] On his father's side, he traces connections to the Cottin-Tassin clan of bankers and traders and possible paternal descendance from a *maître des comptes*.[71]

It is essential to underline that, in addressing his family's Protestant heritage, Du Pont does not weigh on religious creed. He states that he does not consider himself a Christian: 'en étudiant la métaphysique et la théologie, j'avais cessé d'être chrétien.' He indignantly deconstructs the universally damning notion of original sin, and critiques the fetish for the life of Jesus as the founding story for Christianity as a revealed religion. Referring to the conception of Christ as a redeemer, Du Pont finds horror and insanity, impiety and calumny, in imagining a deity appeased by a human sacrifice. Moreover, he writes, if the deity is both god and man ('absurd', 'inconceivable'), it is pointless that he should offer 'himself to himself' as a means of redemption. Most of the global population, Du Pont continues, is not Christian. From the perspective of Christianity, nine tenths of humanity are therefore damned, unjustly. This failure, he reasons, makes the

---

66. See also Henry Algernon DuPont, *The Early generations of the Du Pont and allied families*, 2 vols (New York, 1923), and John C. Hall, *Abraham DuPont: a Huguenot flees to Carolina, 1695: the DuPont-Buyck lineages* (Baltimore, MD, 2016).
67. Du Pont, *Mémoires*, ch.2, p.3.
68. Du Pont, *Mémoires*, ch.2, p.2.
69. Du Pont, *Mémoires*, ch.6, p.1.
70. Du Pont, *Mémoires*, ch.2, p.5.
71. Du Pont, *Mémoires*, ch.1, p.6. For the Cottin and Tassin families, see Lüthy, *De la banque aux finances*.

Christic sacrifice even less worthwhile and the more horrifying.[72] Clearly, Du Pont does not look to Christian scripture to provide the last word on any ultimate question. At the same time, issues of spirituality and religion preoccupy him enough that he borrows time and takes space to address them in the memoir.

In fact Du Pont focuses on connections among people who are Protestants, whether present or remembered, while applying reason to select scriptural references that reflect favoured values, in a manner typical for a deistic response to established Christian creed. For Du Pont, ideals of reciprocity, generosity and forgiveness are essential. Throughout the memoir, he emphasises the reciprocal nature of Protestant and family connections, for him social and cultural in nature, and underlines the receiving and giving of assistance: 'D'ailleurs, il est toujours bon de connaître les parens. on ne sait d'où l'on peut <u>recueillir</u> des successions, ni qui l'on peut avoir à secourir.'[73] He approves of assisting others, disapproves of those unwilling to do so. His exemplary mother, he proudly explains, advanced money to a female relative, helping the young woman to establish a shop and make her way in the world: 'Ma mère l'aida par des avances d'argent à monter à Rouen une boutique de Marchande de modes. Elle vint alors à Paris faire ses emplettes, et je la vis pour la première fois. Elle n'avait pas encore <u>vingt-six ans</u>.'[74] Along with several relatives, Du Pont contributed to the building and outfitting of a ship for the benefit of other family members. That this kind of shared contribution is described as 'très commun dans les pays maritimes'[75] does not discount the help as merely banal, but rather implies that to fail to help would be unusual. He admires his maternal godmother, Françoise de Monchanin, who embodied these ideals: 'C'était la bonté, la piété, l'économie, et la générosité mêmes. La plus pauvre de toute la famille, seule elle a toujours assisté tous les autres, seule elle a pu faire des dons considérables: avare pour elle, prodigue pour autrui. [...] c'était un des plus nobles cœurs que le Ciel eut formés.'[76] While expressing conflicted sentiments about his father, Du Pont praises pious women in his family for their exemplary character and support of others.

72. Du Pont, *Mémoires*, ch.6, p.5
73. Du Pont, *Mémoires*, ch.1, p.5.
74. Du Pont, *Mémoires*, ch.1, p.12.
75. Du Pont, *Mémoires*, ch.1, p.13.
76. Du Pont, *Mémoires*, ch.2, p.9.

Family business at Du Pont de Nemours, Père et Fils & Cie   47

In labelling his family culture as specifically Protestant, Du Pont emphasises generosity and aid as first principles that bolster the social group through reciprocal obligation. Giving, he establishes, is an investment that begets gifts or produces dividends. Among the family examples, he also invokes a biblical instance in a citation he attributes to his mother: 'C'est comme la cruche de la Veuve; plus elle verse, et plus Dieu permet qu'elle se remplisse.'[77] The reference is the Old Testament verse about the exiled prophet Elijah's encounter at Sarepta with the widow of Zarephath: 'Car ainsi parle le SEIGNEUR, le Dieu d'Israël: "Cruche de farine ne se videra / jarre d'huile ne désemplira / jusqu'au jour où le SEIGNEUR / donnera la pluie à la surface du sol."'[78] Du Pont's formulation emphasises the presence of the widow ('la Veuve') with her pitcher, and narrows the role of the deity while erasing the voice of the prophet. His syntax endows the first feminine subject pronoun ('*elle* verse') with ambiguity, although the first *elle* likely stands for the pitcher (miraculously dispensing) rather than the widow (generously pouring). The story highlights that, for Du Pont, gifts and gift-giving are totems of the network. Where his mother and also his godmother embody the fabled widow's self-abnegating generosity, Du Pont's admiration for his female relatives weighs on the principle of social investment, whereby connections produce benefits that can be redistributed as needed.

To be sure, the exchange of favours and help, whether monetary gifts or social introductions, was unique neither to Protestants nor to more or less Protestant networks. Rather, for early moderns, the exchange of favours and cultivation of networks were finely honed practices, essential to social life and getting along, that Du Pont encountered in many contexts. Neither the salons he frequented early in his career, nor spheres of government in which he worked, nor the city of Paris where he lived for decades were particularly 'Protestant'. Nor did Du Pont's social life involve uniquely Protestants, as his long, close relationship with Turgot demonstrates. Gift exchange and regard for reciprocity were part of the broadly shared social practices. Essential to the clientelism and patronage still at work among elites, such exchanges also wove together social groups and communities more generally.[79] As social forms, gift exchange

---

77. Du Pont, *Mémoires*, ch.6, p.3.
78. 1 Kings 17.14, *La Bible: traduction œcuménique de la Bible, comprenant l'Ancien et le Nouveau Testament* (Paris, 1993), p.420.
79. David Garrioch, *Neighborhood and community in Paris, 1740-1790* (Cambridge,

and the trading of favours undoubtedly held special fascination for Du Pont, who strived deliberately, as he explains in his autobiography, to elevate his status. In the changing political economy, debates about the role of reciprocity took place with increasing frequency and urgency through the century,[80] however, reciprocity still informed business exchanges, which often pursued credit flow over monetary profit. For this reason, states social and economic historian Pierre Gervais, 'whatever lesson the past held [...] was not contained in the numbers of an account, but in the intangibles which underpinned the relationship it represented.'[81]

Even as Du Pont participated in multiple networks, he chose in his autobiography to emphasise Huguenot ancestry as a defining feature in his story. Beginning with his first, family network, Huguenot connections set the precedent for Du Pont's later cultivation of reciprocal ties. As he sought to bequeath knowledge of the heritage to his children by codifying it in writing and to cultivate their social capacity by exposure to his principles, he praised as innate, positive features of Protestantism its encouragement of observation and reason and its accessibility to the individual:

> La supériorité marquée des peuples protestants sur les peuples catholiques, quant à la raison, à la moralité, à l'étendue et à la vigueur de l'esprit, tient à ce que les premiers demandent moins à la foi aveugle, plus à l'observation, au raisonnement; à ce que leurs offices religieux se font dans une langue familière aux auditeurs, et sont principalement tournés vers la morale; et surtout à la prière domestique faite en commun.[82]

1986); Sharon Kettering, *Patrons, brokers, and clients in seventeenth-century France* (New York, 1986); Timothy C. W. Blanning, *The Culture of power and the power of culture: Old Regime Europe, 1660-1789* (Oxford, 2002).

80. Shovlin, *The Political economy of virtue*; Geneviève Lafrance, *Qui perd gagne: imaginaire du don et Révolution française* (Montreal, 2008); Paul Cheney, *Revolutionary commerce: globalization and the French monarchy* (Cambridge, MA, 2010); Pierre Rosanvallon, *La Société des égaux* (Paris, 2011); Terjanian, *Commerce and its discontents*; Charles Walton, 'Capitalism's alter ego: the birth of reciprocity in eighteenth-century France', *Critical historical studies* (2018), p.1-43.

81. Pierre Gervais, 'Why profit and loss didn't matter: the historicized rationality of early modern merchant accounting', in *Merchants and profits in the age of commerce, 1680-1830*, ed. Pierre Gervais *et al.* (London, 2014), p.33-52 (52).

82. Pierre-Samuel Du Pont de Nemours, *Sur les institutions religieuses dans l'intérieur des familles, avec un essai de traduction nouvelle de l'Oraison dominicale* (Paris, October 1806; read before the Institut national 31 October 1806), p.5-6.

Yet the same features led him to question Protestantism as doctrine and instead to favour religions generally as social practices within a polity that could promote morality. Dogma, in his perspective, could not be persuasive: 'un homme pieux et de bon sens ne pouvait être ni Protestant, ni Catholique; [...] il fallait respecter la morale uniforme et divine dans toutes les religions, mépriser dans toutes le dogme [...] se soumettre à l'usage, à la foi, du Pays [...] Ma patrie religieuse en France était ma famille.'[83] The plea for tolerance combines with the admonition to respect the laws of the land. Any 'religious homeland' within France was his first network of family and their connections. He emphasises ties among people over dogma.

If Protestant cultural particularity helps the family cohere, it also could support further extensions to the network. Inasmuch as Du Pont found religion useful for promoting morality and cohesion among groups, he encouraged piety within his family as the social microcosm. Du Pont's autobiography figures Protestantism as a feature of personal culture that is also common to a group. It is not an orthodoxy about the supernatural, a required ritual or a recommendation for the nation. At the same time that he was elaborating these ideas in his autobiographical testament, on the public-facing side in his 'testament philosophique' Du Pont developed an even more inclusive vision through a new cosmology for the now-republican state.[84] This composition, too, underlines that religions must adapt to local circumstances. *Autres temps, autres mœurs.*

Du Pont's personal identification as Protestant enables connection and action across an international and transhistorical web of contacts. In the autobiography, his evocation of a Protestant family history retrospectively constructs an inheritance that advances his professional and public activities. In this way he rehearses a dynastic story that he reifies for the future. Yet the conception of reciprocity extends beyond family to include friends and associates such as his investors. Ties from within what has advisedly been called the 'réseau international de la banque protestante' emerged from filiations crossing the Protestant diaspora or 'internationale huguenote'.[85] This web did

---

83. Du Pont, *Mémoires*, ch.6, p.6.
84. In *Irénée Bonfils* and *Philosophie de l'univers*. See Saricks, *Pierre Samuel Du Pont de Nemours*, p.336 and p.425, n.114; Julien Vincent, '"Un dogue de forte race": Dupont de Nemours, ou la physiocratie réincarnée (1793-1807)', *La Révolution française* 14 (2018), p.1-34 (3); see also p.6-10, 13-15.
85. Herbert Lüthy, *La Banque protestante en France de la Révocation de l'Edit de Nantes*

not consist uniquely of individuals who identified as Protestant. Nor was a more or less Protestant network the only one for Du Pont and his investors. At the same time, Du Pont's autobiography, with its emphasis on Protestant networks, and his contemporaneous writings on religion, share with the later company accounting a preoccupation with binding social ties, inclusiveness and reciprocal obligation. As the business declined beyond any hope of rescue, and as he wrote the 1808 shareholder report, Du Pont turned again to the subject of religion in two new short publications about values, faith and society. In 1808 as in 1792 – during the venture's final days as during its prehistory and conception – Du Pont's intermingled trains of thought clarify aspects of the business venture.

In the shareholder report, the list of Protestant associates includes the founder, the principal shareholder Bidermann, Bidermann's partner Johannot, Necker de Germany, the important shadow supporter Jacques Necker, and Necker's daughter Mme de Staël. To be clear, Du Pont does not explicitly reference the common Protestant heritage in the *Compte rendu*. Yet the fact remains that shared experiences, including de facto Protestant status, drew founder and investors together across other divides. The shareholder report implicitly acknowledges economic disparities between Du Pont and his wealthier investors and his failure in the business. The *Mémoires*, for their part, had been coloured by the writer's vulnerability as a fugitive from the Revolution. In both the autobiography and the shareholder report, Du Pont develops themes of loyalty and self-abnegation to underline the mutuality of obligation within his networks. In this way he rhetorically negotiates his own positions, with their multiple weaknesses, shoring up defenses through the maintenance, despite all, of his ties to others.

à la Révolution, vol.1: *Dispersion et regroupement (1685-1730)* (Paris, 1959), p.11 and 32. Mark Greengrass notes the limits Lüthy places on his own memorable phrase in this work and critiques its misleading use in English-language works of history especially by Hugh Trevor-Roper; see 'Thinking with Calvinist networks: from the "Calvinist international" to the "Venice affair" (1608-1610)', in *Huguenot networks, 1560-1780*, ed. Vivienne M. Larminie (New York, 2018), p.9-27 (9-11).

'Préserves-nous de causer à personne le mal que nous ne voudrions pas éprouver'[86]

Rhetoric in the shareholder report, with its constant thread of autobiography, emphasises mutuality between founder and investors and shared circumstances despite different statuses. Just as the 1792 autobiography emphasised Protestant connections and reciprocity across the network, documents contemporary to the 1808 shareholder report and subsequent winding down of the business by 1811 underline the need for mutual obligation among members of any social group, pointing to an idiosyncratically Protestant ethos. As the firm moved towards its dissolution and Du Pont undertook to write its accounting, he published two essays about religion: *Sur les institutions religieuses dans l'intérieur des familles* (October 1806) and, anonymously, *Irénée bonfils, sur la religion de ses pères et de nos pères* (1808). Each work argues that an inclusive family religion and religious culture promote a harmonious and cohesive society.[87] The timing of their drafting and publication underlines the persistant salience of religious topics for Du Pont. In both texts, emphasis on values of reciprocity, generosity and inclusiveness mirrors the sensibility and strategy in the shareholder report, while further recalling passages in the earlier autobiography.

Following typically deist reasoning, *Irénée bonfils* sends up the idea that one religion is better than another, or that one should follow 'the religion of one's fathers' as a matter of course. The comedy turns on interpretations of the phrase 'ses pères' and concepts of family. Admonished to follow in the footsteps of 'ses pères', narrator 'Irénée bonfils', or Good Son Irénée, sets out to establish his paternal genealogy, the better to pinpoint that singular religion ('la religion') of his forefathers. Conveniently, he writes, '[m]a famille a depuis deux mille ans conservé, de génération en génération, des notes sur les principaux événemens qui l'ont intéressé, et particulièrement sur les opinions religieuses de ses membres.' The author identifies at least ten different religions in his 'family', including cults of the Druids, Romans, Catholics, Protestants, noting that each was 'la religion de ses pères'! But two millennia of family documents produce only confusion. Hyperbole combines with literalism to underline, through

---

86. Du Pont, *Sur les institutions religieuses*, p.13.
87. Pierre Samuel Du Pont de Nemours, *Irénée bonfils, sur la religion de ses pères et de nos pères* (Paris, 1808; insert to the *Journal des arts et des sciences*). See also Schelle, *Du Pont de Nemours et l'école physiocratique*, p.428.

52 *Julia L. Abramson*

ridicule, the futility of adhering without reflection to some notion of tradition. This point having been made, the narrator expounds a common-sense philosophy. Here, generous use of metaphor underlines a more naturalistic understanding of family. As he states, he knows for sure that all people are in some sense his 'cousins', and that the virtuous in this 'family' all seek to avoid the evils of vice, dereliction and crime. All those in this extended 'family' of the virtuous prize 'la fidélité à sa parole, l'exactitude à ses engagemens, l'équité, la charité, la générosité, la bienfaisance, le courage'. Du Pont's narrative ultimately targets fanaticism and exclusiveness as dangerous tendencies associated with narrow preference for specific dogma. Whatever the chosen creed, respecting reason, cherishing humanity and keeping one's word are the essential elements of actual religious spirit.[88]

From the perspective of values so clearly elaborated here and in the earlier autobiography, we can see that the shareholder report communicates about a situation where it is impossible for Du Pont to live out ideals he cherishes and recommends to others. He is not able to keep his word or live out the ideal of reciprocity towards the network of investor-shareholders consisting of co-religionists, business associates, friends and family. There is no money to pay out dividends or return the original capital investments to his shareholders. In this circumstance, dynamic, reciprocal engagement in the common project gives way to an unbalanced relationship. Having been a collaborator at the hopeful beginning of the venture, the founder is now a debtor to his investor-creditors. Du Pont's text *Sur les institutions religieuses* offers further insight into the implications of this situation and Du Pont's attitude in the shareholder report. As a complement to the conceptual visions for religion expressed in earlier texts, Du Pont here elaborates practices and prayers for families that will inculcate moral values and guide 'peoples' of a nation throughout the day. Du Pont's commentary on and revision of the prayer 'Notre Père', or 'Oraison dominicale' (Matthew 6.9-12), are telling. His commentary avoids demands placed on the deity and the imperative mode. Instead, he substitutes contemplation of divine goodness that can inspire the faithful to use human qualities of choice and will towards moral ends, including responsibility, generosity and forgiveness. These essential, sweetening elements are unfortunately minimised, as he writes, in the traditional 'Our Father', thus

88. Du Pont, *Irénée bonfils*, p.16.

Family business at Du Pont de Nemours, Père et Fils & Cie   53

j'ai cru devoir suppléer aussi, d'après d'autres discours de JESUS-CHRIST, à *l'omission* qu'ils [earlier translators and interpreters] y ont faite de sa grande maxime: *quod tibi fieri nos vis, alteri ne feceris [What you do not want done to you, do not do to others]*, qui est l'abrégé de la morale du Christianisme et de celle de toutes les Religions: car il n'y a pas deux morales.[89]

The Latin statement of the Golden Rule that Du Pont includes has numerous biblical semantic equivalents such as in Matthew 7.12 and 22.39 and Luke 6.31.[90] Linguistically it more closely follows Tobias 4.16: 'Quod ob alio oderis fieri tibi, vide ne tu aliquando alteri facias.' Its language is also nearly identical to the recommendation in the Rule of Benedict of Nursia about courtesies for welcoming guests from other monasteries: '*Quod tibi non vis fieri, alio ne feceris.*'[91] Reciprocity and implied equality among people are the most essential values, while hesitation to offend is recommended. Du Pont here announces that he will add these values into a new version of the Lord's Prayer. This rhetorical signposting incites curiosity in the reader to discover the new statement of the best-known biblical prayer.

In a revised and much lengthened new prayer, Du Pont's formulations of the Golden Rule rearrange elements of Tobias 4.15-16 and the usual 'Our Father' of Matthew 6.9-12 and – intriguingly considering his business predicament – also omit references common to both source verses that pertain to debt. In his French-language prayer, Du Pont places value on socially useful work ('utile à nous

---

89. Du Pont, *Sur les institutions religieuses*, p.11.
90. '12. Faites donc aux hommes tout ce que vous voulez qu'ils vous fassent: car c'est là la loi & les Prophètes. 12. Omnia ergo quaecumque vultis ut faciant vobis homines, et vos facite illis. Haec est enim lex & Prophetae', Matthew 7.12, in Le Maistre de Sacy, *La Sainte Bible*, t.3, p.759; '31. Traitez les hommes de la même maniere que vous voudriez vous-mêmes qu'ils vous traitassent. 31. Et prout vultis ut faciant vobis homines, vos facite illis similiter', Luke 6.31, in Le Maistre de Sacy, *La Sainte Bible*, t.3, p.876.
91. Tobias 4.16, in Le Maistre de Sacy, *La Sainte Bible*, t.1, p.768. 'Règle de St Benoît / Regula S. Benedicti', '61. Comment recevoir un moine étranger [...] 61.13: Pourtant l'abbé fera bien attention: il ne gardera jamais un moine d'un autre monastère connu, sans l'accord de son abbé ou sans une lettre de recommandation. 61.14. Car la Bible dit: "Ne fais pas aux autres le mal que tu ne veux pas pour toi" [Tobie 4, 15.]', 'Caput LXI De Monachis peregrinis, qualiter suscipiantur. [...] 61.13 Caveat autem abbas ne aliquando de alio noto monasterio monachum ad habitandum suscipiat sine consensu abbatis eius aut litteras commendaticias, 61.14 quia scriptum est: *Quod tibi non vis fieri, alio ne feceris.*'

et aux autres') and exhorts readers to avoid causing harm ('le mal') that they themselves do not want to experience. He also restates a positive version of the Golden Rule ('faire à autrui le bien que nous désirerions qui nous fût fait').[92] Remarkably, he excises from the traditional formulations in Tobias any reference to payment connected with work and further edits out the recommendation to pay promptly what is owed. The biblical verse states: 'Tobias 4.15/4.16 lorsqu'un homme aura travaillé pour vous, payez-lui aussitôt [...] que la récompense du mercenaire ne demeure jamais chez vous. 4.16. Prenez garde de ne faire jamais à un autre, ce que vous seriez fâché qu'on vous fît.'[93] This verse underlines the contractual and promissory nature of payment for work or service through sensitivity to shifts in ownership based on fulfillment of expectations. Once work is complete, the 'récompense' (reward or payment) now belongs to the 'mercenary' or contractor ('*du* mercenaire'). In this sense, the expected payment has become a debt or even a theft, until given to the rightful owner. The new, negative statement of the Golden Rule evokes a method to avoid this harm. The exhortation here to avoid debt matches in meaning Matthew 6.12 in the usual Lord's Prayer: '12. Et remettez-nous nos dettes, comme nous les remettons à *ceux* qui nous doivent. 12. Et dimitte nobis debita nostra, sicut nos dimittimus debitoribus nostris.'[94] In French versions of this verse, 'dettes' is sometimes cited as 'péchés' or 'offenses'.[95]

In his revision of the prayer, Du Pont retains the latter as a verb (*offenser*) while also inserting qualifications that are out of keeping with the succinct biblical 'Notre Père': 'Agrées le repentir que nous inspirent nos fautes; fais qu'il ne demeure pas stérile; accordes-nous l'occasion et les moyens de les réparer, *s'il en est tems encore*, ou de les compenser *autant que le peut notre faiblesse*; – et que ta miséricorde, en nous faisant pardonner à ceux qui nous ont offensé, *daigne nous pardonner*

---

92. Du Pont, *Sur les institutions religieuses*, p.13-14.
93. Tobias 4.16 (some: 4.15), in Le Maistre de Sacy, *La Sainte Bible*, t.1, p.768.
94. Matthew 6.12, in Le Maistre de Sacy, *La Sainte Bible*, t.3, p.756.
95. Dominique Ancelet-Netter, '*Dettes* et *débiteurs* dans les versions françaises de la cinquième demande du *Notre Père* du XIIᵉ au XXIᵉ siècle: une mise en perspective par l'analyse sémantique', *Transversalités* 109 (2009), p.103-23; Jean-Paul Petitimbert, 'Les traductions liturgiques du "Notre Père": un point de vue sémiotique sur les théologies qui les sous-tendent', *Actes sémiotiques* 119 (2016), https://www.unilim.fr/actes-semiotiques/5594 (last accessed 28 November 2024).

ensuite.'[96] Du Pont's throat-clearing additions gently insist on human failings and susceptibility to error, and they evoke the real possibility of failure to redress wrongs. Had he retained the language of Tobias ('remettez-nous nos dettes'), such negotiation might succinctly have been expressed in the double meaning of *remettre* as remit (or pay) but also remand (or defer). What Du Pont has chosen is explanation, interpretation, circumlocution. The strategy enables him to avoid using the word *dette*.

Conclusion: calculating the 'produit net'

This incident of the founding and capitalisation, and subsequent dismantling, of a family firm is situated at the intersection of social, business and financial history, the history of capitalism, Atlantic and French–American relations, revolutionary migrations and the history of French Protestantism. The instance features an intriguing mismatch between expert investors and a lesser-quality investment. In this gap, the founder Du Pont's ability to establish his business owed to a web of connections consisting of family, friends and business associates, and specifically to Protestant associates who worked in banking and finance. Participants explicitly framed the capitalist wager as a strategy for accumulation or investment understood in the 'rational' economic sense. At the same time, the value of reciprocity informed the venture from inception. Investment in the business was a social endeavour that supported the founder and further fortified multidirectional ties among members of the group consisting of founder and investors. In this sense, the investments made were in the man: Du Pont himself. The investments supported in principle social and economic viability among members of the group as a whole. For some, investment provided an opportunity to perform an act of charitable aid. For the largest – and, at the time, wealthiest – investors, participation in capitalist speculation was also a humanistic gesture of redistribution.

Jacques Necker was the most sceptical and discreet of the initial investors, and his commitment was among the most generous. For him, religious conviction likely played a role. Necker had developed pragmatic views, holding that 'opinions religieuses' among the populace were essential so that executives could run a state. Subsequent to his time in office, he elaborated these ideas in works

---

96. Du Pont, *Sur les institutions religieuses*, p.14 (emphasis added).

56 *Julia L. Abramson*

specifying roles for religion in the political economy and across the wealth spectrum. For Necker, the wealth of the individual determines the extent of moral obligation.[97] In considering Du Pont's solicitations, Necker likely balanced reticence before an obviously questionable business proposition with the sense of obligation to provide aid. His intervention followed, in this way, the approach he imagined for the idealised legislator and *homme d'Etat* in view of the citizenry that he described in his 1775 essay about the French political economy:

> [L]e Législateur doit chercher la vérité. Rempli d'un saint effroi, à l'aspect du bien qu'il peut faire & qu'il ose tenter, il doit s'élever par la pensée au-dessus des différens motifs qui remuent la Société; il doit [...] lier dans sa bienfaisance tous ces ordres de Citoyens [...]; il doit sur-tout être le protecteur de cette multitude d'hommes [...]; qu'il est si doux de défendre contre l'oppression & le malheur, sans éclat & sans récompense.[98]

Following this paradigm even outside an official role in service to the state, Necker's wealth brought with it the 'saintly' and 'dread', or imperative moral, obligation to assist those in need. In other writings, Necker had voiced a further preoccupation with social fragilities entrained by excessive economic inequality. For example, he singled out how France's inheritance laws further concentrate wealth in already propertied hands, leading potentially to social and political instability: 'La loi des propriétés produisit les inégalités de fortune [...] les richesses mobiliaires s'accumulent dans la Société, tant que les révolutions extraordinaires ne viennent pas les détruire; [...] les disproportions deviennent plus frappantes.'[99] For Necker, excessive wealth inequality posed a practical problem for governance and the maintenance of a peaceful and prosperous society, as well as, in principle, a moral dilemma.[100] Under laws such as the inheritance

---

97. Necker, *De l'importance des opinions religieuses* and *Cours de morale religieuse* (Geneva, An IX [1800]).
98. Necker, *Sur la législation*, p.7-8. For Calvinism as a basis for 'investment' made as a gesture of social reciprocity without hope of monetary return, see Johan J. Graafland, 'Weber revisited: critical perspectives from Calvinism on capitalism in economic crisis', in *Calvinism and the making of the European mind*, ed. Gijsbert van den Brink and Harro M. Höpfls (Boston, MA, 2014), p.177-98 (197-98).
99. Necker, *Eloge de Jean-Baptiste Colbert*, p.42-43.
100. Necker, *Sur la législation*, p.17; see also p.17-24, 65, and Kaplan, 'The grain question as the social question', p.512-19.

Family business at Du Pont de Nemours, Père et Fils & Cie   57

statutes, those who live day to day from their work are 'dans un état continuel d'oppression et de détresse' because unable, in effect, to get ahead.[101] Just as Necker had left office in France with the country in his debt due to unpaid personal loans he had made to the state, it is likely that monetary return from Du Pont was not foremost in the mind of the Swiss. As for Bidermann, he continued to lend support to Du Pont and his ventures, such as by financing publication of Du Pont's edition of Turgot's works between 1808 and 1811, precisely as his friend was dismantling the unsuccessful business, and even as his own firm moved towards bankruptcy.[102]

Du Pont's shareholder report implies that the worst consequence of financial loss is the threat of diminished social capital and personal credit and the possibility of social exclusion from a network. The incident underlines both the *social* and the *sociable* nature, along with the cultural embeddedness, of economic, financial and commercial activity. The founder of Du Pont de Nemours, Père et Fils & Cie emphasised Protestant heritage, deistic philosophy and indeed business ventures as platforms for cultivating social reciprocity. For this failed firm, 'dividends' produced in the immediate term of the company's investment were uniquely social in nature. In the long run, the networking in which Du Pont excelled helped lay groundwork for the eventual profitable outcomes and extraordinary longevity later achieved by Eleuthère Irénée's company. This 'produit net' or net result is apparent in retrospect, although it only started to become visible a full generation following the life of Pierre-Samuel Du Pont de Nemours.

---

101. Necker, *Sur la législation*, p.65; see also p.71-72, 86-88.
102. Turgot, *Œuvres de M. Turgot*. By 1805, Bidermann had significantly divested himself of his firm's holdings; by 1810, his firm had crumbled; Napoleon's ministry of the public treasury refused assistance to the firm, which by its last years was involved in speculation not considered to be 'véritable commerce' due to excessive risk-taking. Lüthy, *De la banque aux finances*, p.673 and n.123.

II

A lawyer in action | Un juriste en action

Du Pont de Nemours et la question hospitalière: un éclairage des enjeux sanitaires à la fin du dix-huitième siècle

JEAN-BAPTISTE MASMÉJAN

Nantes Université

L'œuvre littéraire de Pierre-Samuel Du Pont de Nemours est conséquente par la variété des thèmes abordés: l'économie, la politique, la physiologie, l'histoire naturelle, la physique générale ou encore le domaine sanitaire. La question hospitalière n'a pas échappé non plus à son érudition. Elle apparaît en effet comme l'un des axes d'un plan de réforme politique et administrative lorsqu'il compose le *Mémoire sur les municipalités* en 1775 sur les indications de Turgot[1] et, plus spécifiquement, dans les *Idées sur les secours à donner aux pauvres malades dans une grande ville*,[2] édité en 1786 à la demande de l'Académie des sciences.

Un événement tragique est à l'origine de son projet en matière hospitalière: le 30 mai 1772 se produit un incendie d'une grande ampleur qui ravage l'Hôtel-Dieu de Paris.[3] Deux commissions successives se sont réunies afin d'envisager non seulement des travaux mais aussi une amélioration de son fonctionnement originel.[4] De nombreux projets furent proposés dont celui, ambitieux, de l'architecte

---

1. Nous retrouvons ce mémoire dans l'ouvrage de Gustave Schelle, *Œuvres de Turgot et documents le concernant*, 5 vol. (Paris, 1913-1923), t.4, et dans le recueil publié à l'instigation de Pierre-Samuel Du Pont de Nemours, *Les Œuvres posthumes de M. Turgot, ou Mémoire sur les administrations provinciales* (Lausanne, s.n.,1787).
2. Pierre-Samuel Du Pont de Nemours, *Idées sur les secours à donner aux pauvres malades dans une grande ville* (Philadelphie, PA, et Paris, Chez Moutard, 1786).
3. Jean Cheymol et René-Jean César, 'Hôtel-Dieu: treize siècles d'histoire… panégyrique ou réquisitoire', communication présentée à la séance du 26 novembre 1977 de la Société française d'histoire de la médecine, https://numerabilis.u-paris.fr/ressources/pdf/sfhm/hsm/HSMx1977x011x004/HSMx1977x011x004x0263.pdf (date de dernière consultation le 28 novembre 2024), p.9-10.
4. Jean Imbert, *Le Droit hospitalier de l'Ancien Régime* (Paris, 1993), p.49.

Poyet qui prévoyait la création d'un nouveau bâtiment circulaire pour un montant de 18 millions de livres. Or, les fonds qu'il conviendrait d'engager pour mener à bien son objectif dépassent très largement les coûts estimés de l'incendie qui s'élèvent à 600 000 livres.[5] De cette proposition naît une controverse à laquelle prendra part Du Pont en rédigeant ses *Idées*.[6] Cette réponse parachève l'abandon du projet de Poyet. Le coût exorbitant que requerrait sa proposition ne pouvait trouver un écho favorable tant l'Etat manquait cruellement de moyens financiers. Une solution de *statu quo* fut préférée par Necker qui fit réaliser des travaux de réparation sans grande envergure.

La parution de l'œuvre de Du Pont témoigne que ses *Idées* étaient susceptibles de répondre à un besoin impérieux d'engager une réforme d'ampleur, tant l'administration des hôpitaux était décriée à cette époque.[7] Les dysfonctionnements logistiques, économiques et sanitaires conduisent à des effets désastreux, le plus perceptible étant la forte mortalité qui règne en leur sein.[8] Ce constat conduit le physiocrate à défendre la nécessité d'opérer une profonde transformation des hôpitaux sur le plan tant philosophique qu'institutionnel. Ses réflexions nourrissent celles de ses contemporains dans le dernier quart du dix-huitième siècle, ce qui débouchera sur une importante refonte du droit hospitalier.[9] Si, dans un premier temps, ce courant

5. J. Cheymol et R.-J. César, 'Hôtel-Dieu', p.9.
6. Cet ouvrage connaît un certain succès parmi ses contemporains, mais aussi de fortes réprobations. Claude-Philibert Coquéau, dans son *Essai sur l'établissement des hôpitaux dans les grandes villes*, critique la conception minimaliste de l'action étatique que défend Du Pont dans le domaine hospitalier. Voir C.-P. Coquéau, *Essai sur l'établissement des hôpitaux dans les grandes villes* (Paris, De l'imprimerie de Ph.-D. Pierres, 1787), p.14 et suiv. Par ailleurs, Camille Bloch rapporte que l'ouvrage de Du Pont fut repris par des contemporains dont le Dr Tenon, qui synthétise la partie concernant les hôpitaux dans son rapport destiné à la reconstruction de l'Hôtel-Dieu de Paris. Voir Camille Bloch, *L'Assistance et l'Etat à la veille de la Révolution* (Paris, 1907), p.39.
7. C'est notamment le cas pour l'Hôtel-Dieu de Paris: l'incendie qui l'a ravagé en 1772 suscite de nombreux projets de rénovation et de réformes quant à son organisation, parmi lesquels s'inscrivent les *Idées sur les secours à donner pour les pauvres malades dans une grande ville*. L'*Encyclopédie* fait la synthèse des différentes critiques concernant l'Hôtel-Dieu de Paris. Voir l'article 'Hôtel-Dieu', dans *Encyclopédie, ou Dictionnaire raisonné des sciences, des arts et des métiers*, éd. Denis Diderot et Jean D'Alembert, 17 vol. (Paris, Briasson, 1751-1772), t.8 (1766).
8. Denis Diderot, 'Hôpital', dans D. Diderot et J. D'Alembert, *Encyclopédie*, t.8.
9. Nous reviendrons ultérieurement sur ces mutations. Cependant il convient d'ores et déjà de préciser qu'elles ont eu un impact crucial au crépuscule du dix-huitième siècle quant à la 'médicalisation' de l'hôpital. Voir Albert Soboul,

réformateur considère qu'il revient à l'Etat d'assurer la direction des hôpitaux, l'échec de cette ambition sous la Convention conduit au développement progressif de structures privées à but lucratif venant compléter les institutions existantes. Or, par une approche philosophique tout à fait originale, Du Pont apparaît en France comme l'un des pionniers de cette approche institutionnelle dualiste en faisant la part belle aux établissements hospitaliers privés.

Les *Idées* explicitées par Du Pont de Nemours vont donc bien au-delà de la simple considération de l'Hôtel-Dieu: elles proposent une nouvelle conception de l'administration hospitalière, tranchant radicalement avec celle de son époque, entravée par les privilèges et par leurs différentes origines et dévolutions.[10] Il s'agit dès lors d'analyser, à l'aune des idées de notre auteur, les enjeux économiques, philosophiques et administratifs des structures hospitalières, et d'en connaître leur postérité. Autrement dit, il s'agit de voir dans quelle mesure Du Pont de Nemours se singularise par ses idées politiques en ce qui concerne la philosophie de la santé et l'administration hospitalière au regard de l'évolution de la législation sanitaire. Les réflexions de Du Pont de Nemours traduisent une remise en question de la philosophie de l'action sanitaire d'Ancien Régime (i), ce qui a pour effet d'entraîner un renversement pyramidal dans la gestion des soins des malades (ii).

---

article 'Hospices/Hôpitaux', dans *Dictionnaire historique de la Révolution française* (Paris, 2005).

10. Du Pont trace déjà les esquisses de ses idées en matière hospitalière dans sa correspondance avec le margrave de Bade dès 1773. En commentant l'ouvrage de Jean-François Marmontel, *La Voix des pauvres, épître au roi sur l'incendie de l'Hôtel-Dieu* (Paris, Valade, 1773), il critique la politique dispendieuse du pouvoir royal dans le domaine sanitaire: 'L'amour des bâtiments, des monuments, des grandes dépenses et des longues comptabilités est encore si fort chez la plupart des gens en crédit qu'il est impossible de se flatter qu'ils abandonnent une si belle occasion de se livrer à leur goût pour les arts, pour les vastes entreprises et tout ce qui en résulte.' Il aspire à terme à une transposition de la logique libérale dans le domaine de l'assistance, entraînant ainsi une intervention minimaliste de l'Etat par la diminution de la pauvreté qui en résulterait. Voir 'Lettre de Du Pont au margrave de Bade de 1773', dans *Carl Friedrichs von Baden brieflicher Verkehr mit Mirabeau und Du Pont*, éd. Carl Knies, 2 vol. (Heidelberg, 1892), t.2, p.34. Sur cette question, voir l'article de Thérence Carvalho, 'La correspondance littéraire et politique de Du Pont de Nemours: vecteur de diffusion du modèle physiocratique en Europe', dans *Entente culturelle: l'Europe des correspondances littéraires*, éd. Ulla Kölving (Ferney-Voltaire, 2021), p.165-84.

i. Une remise en cause de la philosophie de l'action sanitaire d'Ancien Régime

Le jusnaturalisme physiocratique comme fondement d'une nouvelle organisation hospitalière

Le parc hospitalier français, nonobstant une immixtion progressive du pouvoir royal en la matière,[11] n'est pas uniforme dans son fonctionnement tant sur le plan financier que sur ses dévolutions. Cette organisation disparate remonte au Haut Moyen Age et continue sous l'Ancien Régime.[12] Déjà critiquée par Montesquieu pour ses multiples lacunes fonctionnelles et pour son caractère inopérant,[13] l'administration hospitalière fait face à des difficultés budgétaires croissantes à la fin de l'Ancien Régime. En effet, la fin du dix-huitième siècle cristallise l'épuisement économique d'une partie des établissements, dont le système reposait essentiellement sur l'octroi continu de privilèges et leur domaine foncier pour perdurer: les hôpitaux étaient souvent contraints de demander une aide financière toujours plus grande auprès du pouvoir royal pour maintenir leur activité. C'est notamment le cas de l'Hôtel-Dieu de Paris qui a bénéficié au cours de sa longue histoire de privilèges en ce qui concerne les octrois, les revenus de loterie, le droit de commerce sur la viande ou encore les biens de mainmorte, auxquels s'ajoutent les subsides accordés par le pouvoir royal pour maintenir l'activité de l'institution.[14] Par ailleurs, lorsque les hospices étaient créés à l'instigation d'un fondateur, ceux-ci devaient suivre la destination qui leur avait été donnée, au risque d'avoir des fonctions obsolètes ou inutiles.

Dans la lignée de Turgot dans son article 'Fondation' paru dans l'*Encyclopédie*,[15] Du Pont de Nemours se montre critique dans

---

11. Françoise Hildesheimer et Christian Gut, *L'Assistance hospitalière* (Paris, 1992), p.39-43.
12. Voir Michel Mollat, *Les Pauvres au Moyen Age* (Bruxelles, 2006).
13. Montesquieu fustige le rôle des hôpitaux car ils maintiendraient les populations pauvres dans l'oisiveté. Ainsi, les institutions d'assistance ne doivent intervenir qu'*a posteriori* de cette aisance économique, afin de pallier les crises conjoncturelles. Voir Montesquieu, *De l'esprit des lois* (Paris, 1979), livre 23, chap.29, p.135. Sur cette question, voir aussi Catherine Larrère, 'Montesquieu et les pauvres', *Cahiers d'économie politique* 59:2 (2010), p.24-43.
14. J. Imbert, *Le Droit hospitalier*, p.37-41.
15. Cette libéralité dans la création de fondations sanitaires est dénoncée par Turgot dans l'article 'Fondation' de l'*Encyclopédie*. Celles-ci peuvent être selon

ses *Idées sur les secours à donner aux pauvres malades dans une grande ville* sur les méfaits qu'engendrent les libéralités dans la création d'une fondation. Il ne souhaite pas pour autant que l'Etat administre les hôpitaux. En effet, le gouvernement a selon lui pour rôle de 'tourner au bien public et rendre utile à la société, l'énergie de toutes les passions particulières'[16] ce qui écarterait les 'vanités frivoles' qui peuvent animer la création d'un établissement par un fondateur, pour reprendre les mots de Turgot.[17] Du Pont de Nemours souhaite en somme une sécularisation de l'initiative charitable sans pour autant remettre en question les institutions existantes, voyant dans les dames de charité et les religieux des auxiliaires indispensables pour le soin des malades.

Le cheminement intellectuel de Du Pont de Nemours sur la question hospitalière, en partant d'un postulat jusnaturaliste, le pousse à la considérer sur la base d'un interventionnisme étatique limité, tout en tenant compte de la dimension lucrative de ce domaine. En effet, l'esprit qui guide ses réflexions sur la bonne gouvernance hospitalière est précisé explicitement:

> La morale, la politique, l'administration même sont aussi des sciences, dont les principes, comme ceux des autres sciences, doivent être cherchés dans la nature; et qui, comme les autres sciences, présentent une foule de problèmes, dont il faut espérer que la plupart deviendront susceptibles d'être rigoureusement résolus par le calcul, et les autres de l'être avec un degré d'approximation suffisant pour éclairer, dans la pratique, les intentions d'un gouvernement paternel.[18]

En s'inscrivant dans cette perspective jusnaturaliste, Du Pont de Nemours rejoint la conception du droit naturel du maître de l'Ecole, François Quesnay, qui le définit comme le 'droit que l'homme a aux choses propres à sa jouissance'.[19] Ce droit existerait antérieurement à toute association civile et serait régi par des lois naturelles. Suivant le triptyque défendu par les physiocrates, ce droit naturel consiste dans la jouissance de la propriété, de la liberté et de la

---

lui pire que les maux qu'elles entendent atténuer. Voir *Turgot: textes choisis*, éd. Pierre Vigreux (Paris, 1947), p.171-72.

16. P.-S. Du Pont de Nemours, *Idées sur les secours*, p.37.

17. Anne-Robert Turgot, article 'Fondation' dans l'*Encyclopédie*, cité par P. Vigreux dans *Turgot: textes choisis*, p.173.

18. P.-S. Du Pont de Nemours, *Idées sur les secours*, p.6-7.

19. François Quesnay, *Physiocratie, ou Constitution naturelle du gouvernement le plus avantageux au genre humain*, 2 vol. (Leyde et Paris, Merlin, 1768), t.1, p.1.

sûreté. Malgré la sociabilité naturelle des hommes rendant possible leur jouissance, la constitution de la société politique vise à assurer pleinement leur protection.[20] Fidèle au docteur dont il a compilé les écrits dans l'anthologie *Physiocratie*, Du Pont estime que l'homme disposerait de ces droits pour assurer sa conservation[21] et solliciter le concours de ses semblables à cette fin.[22] Il déduit dans ses *Idées* que l'homme, lorsqu'il peine à assurer sa survie par lui-même, recourt à des cercles de solidarité croissants en fonction des besoins que celle-ci requiert.[23] L'homme, en entrant en société, cherche à protéger et assurer pleinement sa conservation.[24] L'institution d'une autorité souveraine, chargée d'assurer la protection du droit naturel, et son déploiement, ne l'engagerait toutefois que de manière subsidiaire sur le plan de l'assistance. Du Pont de Nemours précise que, lors du passage de l'état de nature à la 'grande société',[25] l'intervention de l'Etat doit être minimale du point de vue des lois et institutions en la matière.[26] Ici, notre auteur fait prévaloir la proximité sociale, inhérente à la sociabilité naturelle, comme premier mode de secours.

Cette hiérarchisation des dispensateurs de soins se retrouve dans le *Mémoire sur les municipalités*. Les administrations subalternes seraient préposées à la surveillance de la police des pauvres et de fait des hôpitaux au niveau des municipalités de village[27] et/ou paroisses

---

20. Sur cette question, voir Anthony Mergey, *L'Etat des physiocrates: autorité et décentralisation* (Aix-en-Provence, 2010).

21. Quesnay dit en effet que 'Tout homme est chargé de sa conservation sous peine de souffrance, et il souffre seul quand il manque à ce devoir envers lui-même, ce qui l'oblige à le remplir préalablement à tout autre.' F. Quesnay, *Physiocratie*, p.24.

22. Sur cette question, voir Romuald Dupuy, 'Liberté et rationalité chez Quesnay', *Revue de philosophie économique* 12 (2011-2012), p.117-42.

23. Cette assistance est en effet plus conséquente à mesure que les secours proviennent de cercles de solidarité proches. Du Pont assure ainsi que la famille est le meilleur dispensateur d'aide. Voir P.-S. Du Pont de Nemours, *Idées sur les secours*, p.11. Vient ensuite celle des voisins, du village, de la paroisse, de la municipalité, de la province et de l'Etat.

24. 'Le fondement de la société est la subsistance des hommes, & les richesses nécessaires à la force qui doit les défendre.' F. Quesnay, *Physiocratie*, p.35.

25. P.-S. Du Pont de Nemours, *Idées sur les secours*, p.10.

26. P.-S. Du Pont de Nemours, *Idées sur les secours*, p.7.

27. A.-R.-J. Turgot et P.-S. Du Pont de Nemours, *Mémoire sur les municipalités*, p.573-74. Sur cette question, voir Eric Gojosso, 'Le *Mémoire sur les municipalités* (1775) et la réforme administrative à la fin de l'Ancien Régime', *Cahiers poitevins d'histoire du droit* 1 (2007), p.127-38.

d'arrondissement,[28] tandis que la grande municipalité serait chargée du partage des impositions et de l'octroi des secours aux provinces ayant subi une calamité.[29]

En conséquence, Du Pont de Nemours propose dans ses *Idées* une réforme complète des institutions hospitalières, en souhaitant l'établissement de petits hospices.[30] Cette conception jusnaturaliste se couple à des perspectives sensualistes qui forgent la singularité de ses propositions.

L'avènement d'une nouvelle philosophie sanitaire: le sensualisme en opposition à la centralisation administrative

L'influence notable du droit naturel sur Du Pont de Nemours est corrélée à une certaine philosophie sensualiste,[31] selon laquelle 'Toute sensation est une perception qui ne saurait se trouver ailleurs que

28. A.-R.-J. Turgot et P.-S. Du Pont de Nemours, *Mémoire sur les municipalités*, p.604-605.
29. A.-R.-J. Turgot et P.-S. Du Pont de Nemours, *Mémoire sur les municipalités*, p.612-13. Voir aussi A. Mergey, *L'Etat des physiocrates*.
30. 'L'établissement des maisons de santé ouvertes aux malades pensionnaires, devant être un objet de profit pour les entrepreneurs, le nombre n'en saurait être déterminé. Quoiqu'il fût à désirer qu'il y en eût sur chaque paroisse, il n'est pas vraisemblable qu'il s'en établisse promptement un aussi grand nombre. Et ce sera dans les paroisses les plus grandes, et où il y aura le plus de gens riches, qu'elles auront naturellement le plus de succès. L'administration de charité de ces paroisses, aurait l'intérêt à les exciter; ce qui serait peut-être nécessaire pour les trois ou quatre premières. On ne peut guère espérer qu'il s'en forme jamais plus de vingt dans Paris. Le curé, et les autres ecclésiastiques chargés d'y porter les secours spirituels, y exerceraient naturellement un droit d'inspection; et il paraît qu'on ne devrait pas tolérer qu'aucun de ces espèces d'établissements, s'élevât à plus de cent lits. Il faudrait toujours craindre de retomber dans la négligence des soins de détail, à laquelle les grandes administrations sont condamnées par la nature, et surtout dans les inconvénients de l'accumulation du mauvais air, et du mélange toujours si dangereux, des miasmes qui s'exhalent de la plupart des malades. Vingt maisons de santé, à cent pensionnaires chacune, recueilleraient deux mille malades, uniquement entretenus par la charité privée, et qui, ne coûtant rien aux fonds de la charité publique, laisseraient à ceux-ci la supériorité qu'il est si important de leur conserver sur les besoins.' P.-S. Du Pont de Nemours, *Idées sur les secours*, p.48-49.
31. La terminologie est anachronique en l'espèce sous cette dénomination. Celle-ci est en effet utilisée pour la première fois par Joseph-Marie de Gérando dans son *Histoire comparée des systèmes de philosophie relativement aux principes des connaissances humaines* (Paris, 1804). Voir Sylvain Auroux, article 'Sensations', dans *Dictionnaire européen des Lumières*, éd. M. Delon (Paris, 1997).

dans un esprit, c'est-à-dire, dans une substance qui se sent elle-même, et qui ne peut agir ou pâtir sans s'en apercevoir immédiatement',[32] et par voie de conséquence ce que 'l'âme éprouve en soi, elle les [les sensations] rapporte à l'action de quelque cause extérieure, et d'ordinaire elles amènent avec elles l'idée de quelque objet'.[33] Dans cette conception, l'action humaine résulterait d'un empirisme en vertu duquel les sensations perçues par l'homme engendreraient ses actions. Autrement dit, pour reprendre l'adage d'Helvétius dans *De l'esprit* (1758), 'Penser, c'est sentir.'

Du Pont de Nemours fait sienne cette philosophie lorsque, par exemple, dans sa correspondance avec le margrave de Bade dans les années 1770, il propose à ce dernier un plan de fêtes civiques: 'Le plaisir est le ressort moteur du genre humain. C'est le feu principe par lequel l'univers est animé. Il s'agit de le faire trouver à Votre peuple dans de grandes et belles fêtes peu coûteuses, mais très nobles, très propres à l'émouvoir, à lui faire chérir tous les liens sociaux, à le conduire aux vertus patriotiques.'[34] Il rajoutera plus tard dans un *Mémoire lu à la classe des sciences physiques et mathématiques de l'Institut national* que 'l'homme est un être sensible qui [...] n'a été ni une machine, ni un inspiré qui serait une autre machine; il a été une créature formée pour le travail, pour l'instruction, pour la raison, pour la conscience, pour la vertu méritoire et récompensée'.[35]

Quesnay a certainement influencé Du Pont à ce sujet. Alors collaborateur pour l'*Encyclopédie*, le docteur développe dans le *verbo* 'Evidence' une philosophie pouvant s'inscrire dans le courant sensualiste, à l'instar de Locke et de Condillac, selon laquelle les sens sont à l'origine des connaissances humaines.[36] Ces dernières déterminent ensuite les actions selon qu'elles produisent de la peine ou du plaisir.[37] C'est ce

---

32. Article 'Sensations', dans *Encyclopédie*, t.15.
33. Article 'Sensations', dans *Encyclopédie*, t.15.
34. 'Lettre de Du Pont de Nemours au prince héréditaire, sans date' (1773), dans *Carl Friedrichs von Baden brieflicher Verkehr*, t.2, p.150. Sur cette question, voir Manuela Albertone, 'Du Pont de Nemours et l'instruction publique pendant la Révolution: de la science économique à la formation du citoyen', *Revue française d'histoire des idées politiques* 20:2 (2004), p.353-71 (356).
35. P.-S. Du Pont de Nemours, *Mémoire lu à la classe des sciences physiques et mathématiques de l'Institut national, dans les séances du 21 juillet, du 11 et du 18 août 1806* (Paris, 1806), p.17.
36. François Quesnay, article 'Evidence', dans *Encyclopédie*, t.6.
37. Gérard Klotz et autres, 'Introduction: la physiocratie vouée aux gémonies?', dans *Les Voies de la richesse? La Physiocratie en question (1760-1850)*, éd. Gérard Klotz et autres (Rennes, 2017), p.7-39 (10).

que Quesnay appelle la 'liberté animale'. Toutefois, sans perdre cette liberté commune aux animaux, l'homme dispose aussi d'une 'liberté d'intelligence', lui permettant d'appréhender le moral et l'immoral conformément à l'ordre naturel voulu par Dieu.[38]

Du Pont de Nemours fonde ses propositions à partir de cette ontologie sensualiste. Il propose à cet égard une dualité institutionnelle qui se juxtaposerait: la première se chargerait des pauvres qui n'ont pas les capacités financières nécessaires, grâce au concours des plus riches et, subsidiairement, par la province ou l'Etat; la seconde concernerait les plus aisés pour qui les soins seraient payants, ou qui financeraient des personnes dans ces hospices lucratifs, afin de leur épargner une 'peine morale'. Pour lui, l'absence de cercles de solidarité familiaux, amicaux et locaux réduit le pauvre malade à être secouru dans une structure d'assistance. Or, cette dépendance et cette solitude heurteraient la sensibilité du bénéficiaire, par la peine qu'il pourrait ressentir en étant une charge pour la société. Aussi propose-t-il de créer:

> [des] maisons de santé, où l'on payerait pension, [et où] rien non plus ne doit être meilleur que dans les hospices gratuits: si ce n'est que la pensée qu'on n'est point à charge à la société, et qu'on ne reçoit que les secours honorables de l'amitié, de la bienveillance ou de la protection.
>
> Ce qui rend l'assistance de la charité publique pénible à recevoir, c'est l'idée de dénuement absolu qu'elle suppose. Il est amer de ne tenir à rien, de n'avoir point de famille, ou de n'en avoir qu'une totalement impuissante; de ne pouvoir trouver ni ami, ni protecteur.
>
> Il y a au contraire une sorte de gloire à intéresser les gens puissants, qu'on regarde comme meilleurs juges des qualités personnelles.[39]

Le plaisir qu'entraîne l'enrichissement constitue l'un des moteurs de l'action humaine, et il s'inscrit aussi dans une perspective sensualiste. Notre auteur déclare en effet 'qu'il faut enchaîner aussi à leur service' (c'est-à-dire des malades) 'l'intérêt', 'l'amour du gain'. 'Aux hospices uniquement de charité, il est possible, et il serait utile d'en ajouter d'autres qui produiraient le même effet pour les malades, et qui seraient un objet d'entreprise et de profit.[40] Ces initiatives

---

38. F. Quesnay, article 'Evidence', dans *Encyclopédie*, t.6. Sur cette question, voir Philippe Steiner, 'L'économie politique du royaume agricole: François Quesnay', dans *Nouvelle histoire de la pensée économique: des scolastiques aux classiques*, éd. Alain Béraud et Gilbert Faccarello, t.1 (Paris, 1993), p.230-36.

39. P.-S. Du Pont de Nemours, *Idées sur les secours*, p.45.

40. P.-S. Du Pont de Nemours, *Idées sur les secours*, p.40-41. Notre auteur s'inscrit

privées ne pourraient que constituer une réussite en raison de cette conception sensualiste. Il conviendrait ainsi de privilégier autant que possible des soins payants, qui, quoiqu'identiques aux hospices gratuits,[41] présenteraient l'avantage d'épargner au bénéficiaire une sensation d'avilissement. C'est la raison pour laquelle Du Pont parle de 'peine morale':[42]

> [Cet établissement] aurait à traiter, soit chez eux, soit dans les hospices gratuits des paroisses; parce que les soins d'un hospice où l'on paierait pension, étant moins humiliants à recevoir que ceux des hospices qui donneraient un secours gratuit, un grand nombre de personnes se détermineraient à y envoyer les malades auxquels elles prendraient intérêt. Les maîtres riches n'oseraient faire placer ailleurs leurs domestiques. Les gens aisés seraient sollicités par leur propre cœur et par ceux qui les entourent, pour y soutenir les artisans qui les auraient servis, ou qui seraient connus dans leur maison.
>
> Cette impulsion, qui, en multipliant les charités privées, pourrait procurer une économie d'un tiers à la charité publique, serait une raison pour que la charité publique elle-même contribuât à encourager les établissements d'où une telle économie résulterait.[43]

Suivant ce paradigme, l'internement à l'hôpital, qui à l'époque était dévolu aux pauvres ne pouvant se soigner par eux-mêmes, donne une sensation d'humiliation, d'avilissement d'être soigné et d'être dépendant de la société. Ainsi, le concours de maisons de santé, lucratives et payantes, transforme le processus de création d'hospices. Jusqu'alors, celui-ci relevait de l'initiative d'un fondateur animé par les vertus de la charité chrétienne, tourné vers son salut. Du Pont propose ainsi une évolution institutionnelle profonde à partir du sensualisme.

Cette conception novatrice s'oppose ainsi à la tradition pluriséculaire française. Il reste désormais à saisir sa pensée dans le contexte de son époque.

---

pleinement dans la continuité du maître de l'Ecole, François Quesnay, qui indique que l'Homme est mû par son intérêt personnel. Sur ce point, voir Karl Polanyi, *La Grande Transformation* (Paris, 1983), p.173.

41. P.-S. Du Pont de Nemours, *Idées sur les secours*, p.44-45.
42. P.-S. Du Pont de Nemours, *Idées sur les secours*, p.47.
43. P.-S. Du Pont de Nemours, *Idées sur les secours*, p.42-43.

ii. L'apport de la pensée sanitaire de Du Pont: décentralisation et précurseur de l'hôpital moderne

La décentralisation administrative: moteur de l'efficience curative

Du Pont prône la subsidiarité dans l'assistance aux malades étant entendu que, selon lui, l'action provinciale ou étatique ne doit intervenir qu'en faveur des plus pauvres qui ne peuvent compter sur leur entourage. Il se montre inquiet à l'égard d'une trop grande étatisation et concentration hospitalière. En effet, la compassion pour le malade se dégrade à mesure que l'éloignement grandit. Aussi, les grands établissements, outre leur coût financier conséquent, nuiraient à la qualité des soins dispensés en raison de la dissolution du lien social attachant le soignant au pauvre.[44] Du Pont de Nemours souligne à cet égard la forte mortalité qui touche l'Hôtel-Dieu de Paris, qui est due, d'après lui, au trop grand nombre de patients pris en charge. Cela ternirait la qualité du suivi des soins et favoriserait la transmission des maladies au risque de déclencher des épidémies.[45] Cette subsidiarité est affirmée sans équivoque: 'La société ne doit à tout individu, même en infirmité, lorsqu'il a une famille ou des liaisons d'amitié, de domicile, d'habitude, de circonstances qui suppléent à une famille, qu'une addition aux secours qu'il peut tirer de cette famille, et jusqu'au temps où recouvrant la santé, il redeviendra dans le cas de se soutenir lui-même par son travail.'[46]

Du Pont privilégie les cercles rapprochés pour les secours à délivrer. En plus d'une meilleure prise en charge par rapport aux hôpitaux qui sont souvent débordés, la subsidiarité permettrait aussi de faire des économies substantielles en ne faisant pas supporter à la société le coût des soins.[47] Il ne suggère pas pour autant que la 'charité publique' s'estompe. Il s'agit davantage de propositions qui visent à minimiser au maximum l'allocation de fonds pour les pauvres malades.[48] Notre auteur part du postulat que les petites structures sont davantage propices aux concours de bienfaisants qu'une grande administration centralisée.[49] En considérant la question hospitalière

---

44. P.-S. Du Pont de Nemours, *Idées sur les secours*, p.12.
45. P.-S. Du Pont de Nemours, *Idées sur les secours*, p.17-18.
46. P.-S. Du Pont de Nemours, *Idées sur les secours*, p.16.
47. P.-S. Du Pont de Nemours, *Idées sur les secours*, p.20.
48. P.-S. Du Pont de Nemours, *Idées sur les secours*, p.19-20.
49. P.-S. Du Pont de Nemours, *Idées sur les secours*, p.33-34.

sous l'empire du jeu de l'économie, Du Pont opère une mutation tout à fait singulière du droit hospitalier. L'assistance relevant selon lui du droit naturel, l'Etat doit garantir le droit hospitalier et non l'entraver.[50] Par conséquent, l'Etat n'a pas de légitimité particulière à intervenir dans ce domaine. L'objectif est d'infléchir au maximum l'action étatique. Cette prise de position est ancienne et déjà explicitée dès 1771 dans les *Ephémérides du citoyen*.[51]

Ses *Idées* sont laconiques en ce qui concerne le rôle des différents degrés d'administration et leur champ de compétence. Elles ne sont pour autant pas antinomiques avec le *Mémoire sur les municipalités*. Dans ce dernier, il est proposé que les propriétaires, au sein de leur paroisse, pourraient créer une administration préposée aux secours des pauvres malades à domicile.[52] De plus, la municipalité de district et la province seraient chargées de la police des pauvres, et donc des hôpitaux, alors qu'il revient à la municipalité générale d'allouer des fonds en cas de carence de ces institutions décentralisées. Cette organisation sera reprise dans l'édit de 1787 relatif aux assemblées provinciales.[53] Le cadre paroissial semble être celui dans lequel les pauvres malades domiciliés doivent être assistés. Les fondations religieuses pouvant pourvoir à ce rôle seraient secondées par des dons de bienfaiteurs.

Cette réforme au crépuscule de l'Ancien Régime n'entrave pas la tendance selon laquelle la gestion des hôpitaux devient de plus en plus tributaire de l'Etat royal. Un édit de 1780 'concernant la vente

---

50. Voir John Locke, *Traité du gouvernement civil* (Paris, 1991).
51. Par extension, Du Pont souhaite une intervention *a minima* de l'Etat au sujet des invalides: '3° Par rapport aux infirmes qui ne sauraient travailler et auxquels on droit des secours purement gratuits, il en coûte beaucoup moins et il vaut mieux pour leur bonheur les leur donner au sein de leur famille ou du moins dans leur domicile habituel où ils ont toujours quelques amis, quelques meubles, quelques facilités qui contribuent à adoucir leur existence que de les rassembler dans des édifices publics sous une administration dispendieuse et pédantesque et de les contraindre à une vie monastique.' P.-S. Du Pont de Nemours, 'Commentaire de l'article "Hôpital" de l'*Encyclopédie économique*', *Ephémérides du citoyen* 11 (1771), partie 1, p.167. Sur cette question, voir aussi Gustave Schelle, *Du Pont de Nemours et l'école physiocratique* (Paris, 1888), p.117-18.
52. P.-S. Du Pont de Nemours, *Mémoire sur les administrations provinciales*, p.65-66.
53. Voir l'édit 'portant création d'assemblées provinciales et municipales', dans *Recueil général des anciennes lois françaises, depuis l'an 420 jusqu'à la Révolution de 1789*, éd. Anasthase-Jean-Léger Jourdan et autres, 29 vol. (Paris, 1821-1833), t.28, p.364-66.

des immeubles des hôpitaux du royaume et le remploi des deniers'[54] s'inscrit dans le *continuum* d'un interventionnisme législatif en la matière.[55] Par celui-ci, les établissements en difficulté financière ont la possibilité de vendre leurs biens en contrepartie desquels le pouvoir royal leur verse les intérêts du produit des ventes. Une fois les dettes épurées ou diminuées, ces hôpitaux deviennent alors tributaires de l'administration royale quant à l'allocation de leurs ressources, et sont *de facto* sous la tutelle de l'Etat. Cet édit ne présente cependant pas de caractère discrétionnaire, et Necker, qui en est à l'origine, n'entend pas pour autant réprimer la charité privée, qui conserve une place centrale dans le soin des malades.[56]

A contrario, Du Pont de Nemours s'inspire directement du système anglais dont il reconnaît la filiation au travers de ses *Idées*.[57] Les hôpitaux anglais procèdent souvent à des soins à domicile, ce qui correspond également aux aspirations du physiocrate de réduire les hôpitaux en petites structures pour des raisons d'hygiène et de qualité des soins, et de privilégier les soins à domicile.[58] Son projet rejoint d'une certaine manière le système anglais établi par les différentes *poors laws*, qui fait de la paroisse le cadre administratif dans lequel s'organisent les secours.[59] Il en fut de même pour le royaume de France, qui avait pris une trajectoire identique avec l'ordonnance de Moulins de février 1566.[60] L'orientation différa par la suite avec la

54. Voir l'édit 'concernant la vente des immeubles des hôpitaux du royaume et le remploi des deniers', dans A.-J.-L. Jourdan et autres, *Recueil général*, t.26, p.257-62.
55. Voir l'édit 'portant qu'il sera établi un hôpital en chaque ville et bourg du royaume pour les pauvres malades, mendians et orphelins', dans A.-J.-L. Jourdan et autres, *Recueil général*, t.18, p.18-20.
56. Louis Trénard, 'L'idéologie révolutionnaire et ses incidences', dans *La Protection sociale sous la Révolution française*, éd. J. Imbert (Paris, 1990), p.95-204 (113).
57. Il affirme en effet qu'il 'ne propose rien de nouveau. Ce plan qui a paru humain, raisonnable, dicté par les principes d'une saine philosophie & d'une véritable charité, est suivi en Angleterre'. P.-S. Du Pont de Nemours, *Idées sur les secours*, p.26-27.
58. P.-S. Du Pont de Nemours, *Idées sur les secours*, p.26-27.
59. Robert Castel, *Les Métamorphoses de la question sociale* (Paris, 1995), p.90. Voir aussi Pierre-Louis Lauget et Françoise Salaün, 'Aux origines de l'hôpital moderne, une évolution européenne', *Les Tribunes de la santé* 3 (2004), p.19-28 (22).
60. L'article 73 de l'ordonnance de Moulins dispose: 'Enjoignons aussi à tous nos officiers tenir la main à l'observance de nos édits et Ordonnances sur le fait des hôpitaux, sur peine d'en répondre en leur propre et privé nom, pour leur défaut et négligence et sous mêmes peines faire rendre compte aux Commissaires,

74   *Jean-Baptiste Masméjan*

création des hôpitaux généraux, qui, bien que partielle, car toujours tributaire des particularismes locaux, entraîne une immixtion directe de l'administration royale. La France, contrairement à l'Angleterre, n'a jamais uniformisé ni pérennisé le financement des secours au niveau paroissial par des prélèvements obligatoires.[61]

Ainsi, Du Pont marque son opposition avec le système mis en place par Necker en privilégiant une administration hospitalière animée par le local, à l'image du système anglais, même si, contrairement à celui-ci, la charité privée demeure le cadre privilégié de financement. La nuance, de taille, est là: alors que Du Pont part du principe que l'Etat doit avoir un rôle subsidiaire, Necker envisage au contraire le développement d'une administration centralisée des établissements de charité, amorçant ainsi une logique d'étatisation de l'assistance.

Il reste maintenant à déterminer quelle est la postérité de l'œuvre littéraire de Du Pont sur cette question.

Un précurseur de l'avènement de la médicalisation de l'hôpital

Les écrits de notre auteur rejoignent des critiques adressées aux hôpitaux généraux qui gagnent en virulence à la fin de l'Ancien Régime. Ces derniers sont accusés d'encourager l'oisiveté et d'être davantage un propagateur de maladies qu'un véritable lieu de soins.[62] A l'occasion d'un commentaire sur la condition sociale en Russie, Du Pont de Nemours s'émeut que les hôpitaux soient des lieux 'où se trouvent le despotisme; ce qui prouve encore combien la gangrène

---

    commis pour le régime des biens et revenu d'iceux, afin qu'ils soient dûment employés et nécessitez des pauvres, comme il est requis. Et outre, ordonnons que les pauvres de chacune ville, bourgs et villages seront nourris et entretenus par ceux de la ville bourg ou village dont ils seront natifs et habitants, sans qu'ils puissent vaguer et demander l'aumône ailleurs, qu'au lieu duquel ils sont. Et à ces fins seront les habitants tenus contribuer à la nourriture des dicts pauvres selon leurs facultés, à la diligence des Maires, Echevins, Consuls et Marguilliers des paroisses, lesquels pauvres seront tenus prendre bulletin et certification des susdits, en cas que pour guérison de leurs maladies, ils fussent contraints venir aux villes ou bourgades où y a Hôtels-Dieu et Maladreries pour ce destiner.' Voir A.-J.-L. Jourdan et autres, *Recueil général*, t.14, p.209.

61. Sur la question hospitalière en Angleterre, voir Jacques Carré, *Ville et santé en Grande-Bretagne, XVIIIᵉ-XXᵉ siècles* (Clermont-Ferrand, 1989), et *The Hospital in history*, éd. Lindsay Granshaw et Roy Porter (Londres, 1989).

62. Pour Du Pont, la concentration de malades dans les hôpitaux véhicule davantage de maladies qu'elle n'en guérit. Voir P.-S. Du Pont De Nemours, *Idées sur les secours*, p.25.

et l'esclavage sont d'effroyables maladies'.[63] Le souci qu'a Turgot de ne pas entraver inutilement la liberté des indigents l'amène à procéder à la fermeture des dépôts de mendicité. Ce nouveau genre d'établissements, créé à la suite d'un arrêt du Conseil du roi en 1767[64] afin de suppléer les carences des hôpitaux généraux, vise à s'assurer de l'enfermement des vagabonds conformément à une déclaration royale de 1764.[65] Plutôt que de chercher des mesures de réclusion, Turgot souhaite s'assurer des secours dispensés aux indigents. C'est la raison pour laquelle il diligente une grande enquête dans le but de connaître et rationaliser le fonctionnement des institutions charitables. S'adressant aux évêques le 18 novembre 1774, Turgot souhaite soutenir, voire suppléer, les établissements en difficulté: 'S. M. [...] a désiré connaître les fonds qui étaient destinés à la subsistance des pauvres afin de les consacrer entièrement à leur destination et de suppléer en cas de besoin à leur insuffisance.'[66]

Du Pont critique également l'inutilité de l'enfermement des pauvres. Il accuse les hôpitaux d'entraver la jouissance des droits des plus pauvres. Dans les *Ephémérides*, celui-ci souligne: 'Que lorsqu'on a le malheur d'avoir des pauvres, il faut du moins respecter en eux le plus qu'il est possible la dignité d'homme, avoir soin qu'ils ne doivent en quelque façon qu'à eux-mêmes les secours dont ils ont besoin, & de bien garder de donner en aumône ce qu'on peut offrir au travail.'[67] Le physiocrate fustige aussi les dépôts de mendicité, qu'il accuse de fausser la concurrence en créant un 'monopôle privilégié', lésant ainsi les entrepreneurs des villes et faussant le respect des lois naturelles dans l'ordre social.[68]

Ainsi, les aspirations de Du Pont et Turgot, par leur critique de l'enfermement des pauvres, amènent à repenser l'hôpital comme une structure proprement médicale. A rebours de la logique du 'grand renfermement' des mendiants qui prévalait depuis le dix-septième

---

63. P.-S. Du Pont de Nemours, 'Bienfaisance en Russie', *Ephémérides du citoyen* 11 (1771), partie 1, p.237.
64. François-Henri de Boug d'Orschwiller, *Recueil des états, lettres patentes, arrêts du Conseil d'Etat et du Conseil souverain d'Alsace*, t.2 (Colmar, Chez Jean-Henri Decker, 1775), p.768.
65. Sur la déclaration de 1764, voir José Cubéro, *Histoire du vagabondage* (Paris, 1998), p.140-47.
66. La Courneuve, Archives nationales, Fonds des hospices et secours, F15 3590.
67. P.-S. Du Pont de Nemours, 'Commentaire de l'article "Hôpital" de l'*Encyclopédie économique*', p.167.
68. Cité par J. Imbert, *Le Droit hospitalier*, p.195.

siècle,[69] tous deux considèrent que le pauvre est essentiellement une victime de l'ordre politique et social de la société d'Ancien Régime. En s'opposant à la réclusion des pauvres, ils entendent borner les structures hospitalières aux seuls invalides. Si l'historiographie tend à considérer que les cliniques sont nées durant la Révolution,[70] Du Pont est un précurseur dans leur conception. Le physiocrate n'est pas le seul à proposer cette médicalisation. Dans une autre perspective, Piarron de Chamousset propose un projet avant-gardiste d'assurance-maladie à travers l'établissement d'une *maison d'association*. De façon plus pragmatique que le physiocrate, il propose une structure hospitalière originale, financée par des sociétaires, grâce à laquelle chacun d'eux serait soutenu en cas de maladie.[71]

La large place donnée à l'initiative privée n'est pas suivie au début de la Révolution. Les constituants, profitant des moyens considérables d'action obtenus grâce à l'avènement de la souveraineté nationale, disposent d'une latitude que n'a jamais pu avoir le pouvoir royal sous l'Ancien Régime.[72] Ils vont plus loin que Necker en ce qui concerne les biens des hôpitaux en cherchant à les vendre et les placer sous l'administration de l'Etat. De fait, une approche locale de l'assistance, plus proche des *Idées* de Du Pont, est rejetée. Imprégnés de la critique que fait Adam Smith des *poor laws*, les révolutionnaires s'inquiètent des conséquences financières désastreuses qu'amènerait une taxation locale, ainsi que la fixation des pauvres dans les paroisses. Michel-Augustin Thouret, collaborateur du Comité de mendicité sous la Constituante, résume en ces termes cette réticence: 'Il faut lire dans Smith, sur les richesses des nations, le tableau de ces vexations intestines qui déshonorent l'administration anglaise, et surtout les incroyables efforts de la législation dans ce royaume pour

---

69. Sur la question du 'grand renfermement', voir Michel Foucault, *Histoire de la folie à l'âge classique* (Paris, 1975), p.67-110.
70. L. Granshaw, 'Introduction', dans *The Hospital in history*, éd. L. Granshaw et R. Porter, p.1-18 (3).
71. Claude Humbert Piarron de Chamousset, *Plan d'une maison d'association, dans laquelle au moyen d'une somme très-modique chaque associé s'assurera dans l'état de maladie toutes les sortes de secours qu'on peut désirer* (s.l., s.n., 1754). Sur Piarron de Chamousset (1717-1783), voir F. Martin-Ginouvier, *Un Philanthrope méconnu du XVIIIe siècle: Piarron de Chamousset* (Paris, 1905).
72. Voir notre contribution, J.-B. Masméjan, 'Le comité de mendicité mandaté par la nation: vers une harmonisation de la politique d'assistance des valides (1790-1791)', *Cahiers Jean-Moulin* 2 (2016), https://revues.univ-lyon3.fr/cjm/index.php?id=280#bodyftn33 (date de dernière consultation le 28 novembre 2024).

lever des obstacles que le principe a toujours rendus invincibles et qu'il multiplie, pour ainsi dire, chaque jour dans tous les points de l'Angleterre.'[73]

Bien que les constituants partagent la méfiance de Du Pont à l'égard des grandes structures hospitalières, et souhaitent privilégier les secours à domicile, ils ambitionnent aussi d'harmoniser l'allocation des ressources en fonction des besoins des hôpitaux en les plaçant sous la tutelle de l'Etat.[74] Aussi prévoient-ils de médicaliser ces établissements en répondant aux besoins d'hygiène et de les décharger de leur population nombreuse,[75] même si la charité privée demeure toujours possible.[76]

La Convention montagnarde, par le décret du 23 messidor An II (11 juillet 1794), concrétise l'ambition des constituants en procédant à une nationalisation des hôpitaux.[77] Ce décret va plus loin que l'édit de 1780, en procédant cette fois-ci à la vente des biens des hôpitaux, tandis qu'une dizaine d'années auparavant, il ne s'agissait que d'une simple possibilité offerte aux administrations hospitalières. Aussi, ce décret prévoit la réunion de l'actif et du passif des hôpitaux et maisons de secours. L'ambition étatiste n'aura été que de courte durée. Le Directoire s'inscrit en rupture du programme en matière d'assistance que l'on retrouvait depuis la Constituante. Une loi du 16 vendémiaire An V (5 octobre 1796) consacre la jouissance des biens dont disposent les hôpitaux civils, afin qu'ils puissent assurer leur bon fonctionnement. Cette loi, dans son article premier, laisse au soin des municipalités la surveillance des hôpitaux, les libérant pour grande partie de l'administration centrale.[78] La veille, Lebrun explique cette évolution en des termes très proches de ceux de Du Pont de Nemours. Il dit que 'dans l'ordre commun, le lien des familles garantit ces secours et la nature en assure la perpétuité [...] la société en masse ou le gouvernement général de la société sont à une trop grande distance [...] il est de l'intérêt public bien calculé d'exciter la bienfaisance individuelle'.[79]

---

73. *Procès-verbaux et rapports du comité de mendicité de la Constituante 1790-1791*, éd. Camille Bloch et Alexandre Tuetey (Paris, 1911), p.41.
74. L. Trénard, 'L'idéologie révolutionnaire', p.152-53.
75. L. Trénard, 'L'idéologie révolutionnaire', p.138.
76. L. Trénard, 'L'idéologie révolutionnaire', p.174-75.
77. Jean-Paul Bertaud, 'La crise sociale (septembre 1792-juillet 1796)', dans *La Protection sociale*, éd. J. Imbert, p.205-84 (241-43).
78. Adolphe de Wateville, *Législation charitable* (Paris, 1843), p.41.
79. Jean Imbert, 'Vers le redressement: le Directoire', dans *La Protection sociale*, éd. J. Imbert, p.419-22 (422).

En prônant la subsidiarité et la gestion des affaires au local, cette disposition se rapproche incontestablement des doléances consignées dans ses *Idées*. Les administrations hospitalières doivent en effet se spécialiser pour faire face aux difficultés économiques et donner la priorité à l'internement des malades.

L'hôpital, qui jusqu'alors rejoignait son étymologie signifiant 'lieu d'accueil', sans opérer de catégorisation particulière dans la prise en charge des pauvres valides ou malades, se spécialise désormais au profit de ces derniers.

***

Du Pont de Nemours peut apparaître comme l'un des précurseurs prônant la médicalisation des hôpitaux, à une époque où la terminologie institutionnelle est encore floue et où il n'y a pas véritablement de segmentation précise des différentes catégories de personnes internées. Ses *Idées*, par une utilisation originale des pensées philosophiques de son temps, reconsidèrent en profondeur la logique sanitaire en privilégiant l'action locale en faveur des malades sous l'empire du droit naturel et du sensualisme. Ses aspirations sont partagées par nombre de ses contemporains quant à la nécessité d'une spécialisation médicale. Malgré l'ambition des constituants et des conventionnels de procéder à la nationalisation des hôpitaux, les difficultés logistiques et financières ont amené à un revirement au profit d'une conception locale de l'assistance sous le Directoire.

En définitive, le projet de Du Pont contribue à légitimer le rôle de l'initiative privée et lucrative en matière hospitalière, le positionnant ainsi comme l'un des concepteurs de la clinique privée moderne. Il augure de cette façon le rôle prépondérant que joue l'hospitalisation privée commerciale en France.[80]

---

80. Voir Olivier Faure et Dominique Dessertine, *Les Cliniques privées: deux siècles de succès* (Paris, 2012).

Du Pont de Nemours and the maintenance of public order

Sébastien Le Gal

University Grenoble Alpes

At first sight, the maintenance of public order seems to be a secondary issue in the thinking of Du Pont de Nemours, whose name, for the revolutionary period, is associated above all with economic issues.[1] Admittedly, as a physiocrat, he was committed to *sûreté* (safety) and endorsed the triptych consecrated by Le Mercier de La Rivière, 'Liberté, sûreté, propriété'.[2] However, in his writings prior to the Revolution, the maintenance of law and order – an expression that refers *lato sensu* to questions of maintaining public order, security and safety – hardly comes into play. The events compelled the man to grasp the reality of safety. If the Revolution, in the year 1789, brought about political and social upheaval through violence,[3] then Du Pont de Nemours was its first opponent. An account, most certainly hagiographical, of Du Pont de Nemours in the Assembly highlights his profound conviction: 'Ses principes étaient ceux de la modération; son but, de perfectionner le gouvernement sans violence. Il s'opposa, autant qu'il le put, aux fureurs de l'anarchie.'[4] In fact, in examining

---

The author would like to thank Pascale Rodary, legal English teacher (University Grenoble Alpes), for her precious help and suggestions in the translation of this article.

1. The references to Dupont de Nemours in J. Godechot's classic work are remarkable, whether on issues relating to ecclesiastical property, the *caisse d'escompte* or *assignats*. See Jacques Godechot, *Institutions de la France sous la Révolution* (Paris, 1985).
2. Paul-Pierre Le Mercier de La Rivière, *L'Ordre naturel et essentiel des sociétés politiques* (1767), in *Physiocrates: Quesnay, Dupont de Nemours, Mercier de La Rivière, l'abbé Baudeau, Le Trosne, avec une introduction sur la doctrine des physiocrates, des commentaires et des notices historiques*, ed. Eugène Daire, 2 vols (Paris, 1846), vol.2, p.445-638 (615).
3. Georges Carrot, *Révolution et maintien de l'ordre* (Paris, 1995).
4. Jules Monchanin, *Notice sur la vie de Du Pont de Nemours* (Paris, 1818), p.31.

80   *Sébastien Le Gal*

Du Pont's speeches as a deputy at the National Assembly, one is struck by the conjunction between his interventions and the demonstrations of violent popular support for the Revolution. Such an observation led the administrator and polygraph Jacques Peuchet[5] to utter harsh words against the physiocrat: on 13 July 1789 the people of Paris were arming themselves and were organising a bourgeois guard. Du Pont was the first of the deputies to show his support for the initiative by enlisting. Peuchet concluded that Du Pont 'saisit cette occasion pour faire un de ces traits de patriotisme fanfaron dont il a donné tant d'exemples dans sa vie', before adding the following words, in themselves gratuitous and even more cruel: 'M. Du Pont eut toujours un sabre et un fusil près de son lit depuis ce moment.'[6]

He was undeniably a zealous defender of order. He registered from the very first day as a national guard and, along with his son Eleuthère Irénée, during the early years of the Revolution, he did as much as he could to oppose threats and breaches of order, whether it was taking sides in the Nancy affair in August 1790,[7] later, during the Champ-de-Mars massacre in July 1791, or, of course, on 10 August.[8] Du Pont de Nemours stood firm to stop the 'insurrection machine'.[9] He defended the king, on 10 August 1792, during an episode that is often narrated and in which his courage cannot be denied. However, Du Pont showed this courage also on the stage of the National

---

5. Ethel Groffier, *Un Encyclopédiste réformateur: Jacques Peuchet (1758-1830)* (Quebec, 2009).

6. Jacques Peuchet, *Mémoires tirés des archives de la police de Paris pour servir à l'histoire de la morale et de la police, depuis Louis XIV jusqu'à nos jours*, 6 vols (Paris, 1838), vol.4, p.104.

7. Du Pont de Nemours's outspokenness on this occasion made a lasting impression, even on Michelet, who recalled his 'eloquent fury', to justify the violence of the means used to ensure the return of peace to Nancy. He published open letters protesting against the honour shown to the freed Swiss on their way to Paris from Brest after their amnesty. See his *Lettres de M. Du Pont à M. Pétion*, in *Histoire parlementaire de la Révolution française*, ed. Philippe-Joseph-Benjamin Buchez and Pierre-Célestin Roux, vol.14 (Paris, 1835), p.81-91 (there are two that have been republished and distributed by the printing house he founded, as Eugène Daire reminds us); Jules Michelet, *Histoire de la Révolution française*, vol.1 (Paris, 1952), p.875; Daire, *Physiocrates*, vol.1, p.236.

8. On 10 August 1792, Dupont de Nemours, along with his son Eleuthère Irénée, defended the king. For this oft-reported episode, see Philippe Sagnac, *La Révolution du 10 août 1792: la chute de la royauté* (Paris, 1909), p.263.

9. Georges Duby, *Histoire de la France: dynasties et révolutions, de 1348 à 1852* (Paris, 1987), p.316.

Assembly, when he became the unfailing advocate of the maintenance of public order, despite his detractors. The latter expressed themselves in the Assembly – the left wing including Robespierre who gradually imposed himself – and outside the Assembly – Marat who willingly took Du Pont de Nemours as a target. At the opposite end of the political spectrum Du Pont was equally hated: the abbé Barruel made him one of the intellectual promoters of the Revolution and depicted him as a philosopher who was 'hypocrite et mielleux', and even, ultimately, a 'sophiste'.[10]

In spite of the critics, Du Pont consistently denounced the unrest and violence, from the first popular demonstrations in the summer of 1789. Throughout his term in office at the National Assembly,[11] he stressed the need to preserve public order and to make the Assembly the best defence against any popular outbursts. His words soon became counterproductive as people turned away from him. The impact of his words shrank, as did the influence of the physiocrats. In short, Peuchet expressed a widespread feeling.

However, these attacks related less to the heart of Du Pont de Nemours's thinking, his economic thought, than to his propensity to denounce violent revolutionary actions and to demand intransigent maintenance of public order and the repression of unrest, in order to preserve property and people. 'Sous prétexte de cette humanité, qui presse un philosophe à rappeler la paix',[12] Du Pont de Nemours is said to have condemned the popular adherence to the Revolution.

Is there a basis in the physiocrat's thinking for this constant attachment to the maintenance of law and order, or is it a reaction to events as they happen? To answer this question, it is first necessary to understand the maintenance of public order in its relation to the cardinal notion of safety, dear to the physiocrats (i). Secondly, it is necessary to confront these reflections with events that occurred while Du Pont de Nemours was a deputy. Throughout his speeches to the National Assembly, he highlights the antinomy between the maintenance of public order and Revolution (ii), before denouncing the anarchy and seditious unrest that threaten national cohesion (iii).

---

10. Augustin Barruel, *Mémoires pour servir à l'histoire du jacobinisme*, vol.2 (Augsburg, Les librairies associées, 1799), p.145.
11. See Richard Whatmore, 'Dupont de Nemours et la politique révolutionnaire', *Revue française d'histoire des idées politiques* 20 (2004), p.335-51.
12. Barruel, *Mémoires*, p.145.

i. Policing and maintenance of public order as a manifestation of public safety in physiocratic thought

Du Pont de Nemours approaches the question of the maintenance of public order as a constituent element of safety, which is a cardinal notion in the thinking of the physiocrats.

Safety, as one of the elements of the 'trinité politique'[13] according to the formula of Le Mercier de La Rivière, is conceived in a logical hierarchy. From property, which is first, comes freedom, and safety guarantees it. The first two go hand in hand, one manifesting the enjoyment of the other:

> La propriété n'est autre chose que le droit de jouir; or, il est évidemment impossible de concevoir le droit de jouir séparément de la liberté de jouir: impossible aussi que cette liberté puisse exister sans ce droit, car elle n'aurait plus d'objet, attendu qu'on n'a besoin d'elle que relativement au droit qu'on veut exercer. Ainsi, attaquer la propriété, c'est attaquer la liberté; ainsi, altérer la liberté, c'est altérer la propriété; ainsi, PROPRIETE, SÛRETE, LIBERTE, voilà ce que nous cherchons.[14]

For his part, Du Pont de Nemours expresses his adherence and attachment to this trinity: it forms, according to him, 'l'ordre social dans tout son entier'.[15] In this, there is nothing original under the pen of Du Pont, who hardly differs from his physiocratic friends. However, perhaps better than his predecessors, he clarifies the sequence of these notions, by ranking them differently. While Le Mercier de La Rivière considered a triptych with safety (*liberté, propriété, sûreté*) at its core, Du Pont asserts: 'Point de propriété sans liberté; point de liberté sans sûreté.'[16] Security is a necessity that guarantees, at the very end of the chain, that a person will actually enjoy the rights they are entitled to. This is why, from the state of nature, Du Pont introduces safety as a necessity: among the 'besoins naturels de l'homme',[17] it is the corollary

---

13. Paul-Pierre Le Mercier de La Rivière, *Les Vœux d'un Français, ou Considérations sur les principaux objets dont le roi et la nation vont s'occuper* (Paris, Mme Vallat La Chapelle, 1788), p.25.
14. Le Mercier de La Rivière, *L'Ordre naturel*, p.615.
15. Pierre-Samuel Du Pont de Nemours, *De l'origine et des progrès d'une science nouvelle* (1768), in *Physiocrates*, ed. E. Daire, vol.1, p.335-66 (346).
16. Du Pont de Nemours, *De l'origine*, p.347.
17. Pierre-Samuel Du Pont de Nemours, *Abrégé des principes de l'économie politique* (1772), in *Physiocrates*, ed. E. Daire, vol.1, p.367-85 (367).

of rest (second), after subsistence (first). He emphasises the fact that it must be effective: 'Sûreté, sans laquelle la propriété et la liberté ne seraient que de droit et non de fait, sans laquelle le produit net serait bientôt anéanti, sans laquelle la culture même ne pourrait subsister.'[18]

In approaching the political order, the physiocrats are led to rethink the concept of state,[19] or rather its missions, by drawing the consequences of this political trinity induced by their economic precepts. In the state of society, safety again becomes a determining element, because it legitimises the existence of the state as guarantor of rights. Indeed, being a necessary consequence of the enjoyment of property, the state constitutes, in the words of Du Pont de Nemours, '[l']autorité tutélaire et souveraine, pour procurer la sûreté essentiellement nécessaire à la propriété et à la liberté, et qui s'acquitte de cet important ministère, en promulguant et faisant exécuter les lois de l'ordre naturel, par lesquelles la propriété et la liberté sont établies'.[20] From this point on, three essential state missions emerge: authority, good administration[21] and education.[22] In short, the physiocrats' conception of the state gathers around the missions of the police state, since education itself is conceived as a political right, ensuring sound enjoyment of property.

By *authority*, we mean 'la protection & la garantie à chacun envers & contre tous de sa liberté & ses propriétés'.[23] For Du Pont, this first mission will consist in the guarantee against disorder and against attacks targeting persons and property. Du Pont defines this mission as a duty of the state: 'le devoir de cette autorité est de protéger toutes les propriétés de tous genres, et de veiller à l'exécution des lois de l'ordre naturel, comme aussi à l'entretien et à l'amélioration du

---

18. Du Pont de Nemours, *De l'origine*, p.363.
19. Anthony Mergey, *L'Etat des physiocrates: autorité et décentralisation* (Aix-en-Provence, 2010).
20. Du Pont de Nemours, *De l'origine*, p.363.
21. Mergey, *L'Etat des physiocrates*.
22. Manuela Albertone, 'Instruction et ordre naturel: le point de vue physiocratique', *Revue d'histoire moderne et contemporaine* 33:4 (1986), p.589-607; Manuela Albertone, 'Du Pont de Nemours et l'instruction publique pendant la Révolution: de la science économique à la formation du citoyen', *Revue française d'histoire des idées politiques* 20:2 (2004), p.353-71.
23. Nicolas Baudeau and Pierre-Samuel Du Pont de Nemours, *Avis au peuple sur son premier besoin, ou Second traité économique sur le commerce des blés*, in *Discussions et développements sur quelques-unes des notions de l'économie politique*, vol.5 (Yverdon, Fortunato Bartolomeo de Felice, 1769), p.3-110 (61).

84 *Sébastien Le Gal*

patrimoine public.'[24] In so doing, he offers a more precise analysis than his predecessors in the sect.

Du Pont's studies of safety also offer a useful counterpoint to Montesquieu's contribution. Indeed, the author of *L'Esprit des lois* confers on safety a subjective nature – it is 'l'opinion que l'on en a', he writes[25] – as with every principle of government that he discusses (honour for the monarchy, virtue for the republic, fear for despotism). Political liberty, defined in relation to safety, is the principle that he discovers in the English monarchy, which is of an original type. A free government, it would secure citizens within the laws as well as in the opinion that citizens have of their laws, which, effectively, would preserve them from all arbitrariness. It has been written that what distinguished Du Pont de Nemours from Montesquieu was the physiocrat's reobjectification of security.[26] Nevertheless, has the dynamic character of safety conferred by the subjectification of the notion disappeared in the thought of Du Pont de Nemours? Nothing is less certain, as the study of the place of safety in the books of grievances of the bailiwick of Nemours suggests.

We know that Du Pont played a large part in the writing of these books of grievances – monumental books in terms of volume and number of contributions.[27] At the end of a meticulous inventory of the situation of the kingdom, Du Pont de Nemours concludes without concession:

> Le Tiers-état du bailliage de Nemours a déchiré le voile qui couvrait les plus profondes de ses plaies et de celles de tous les citoyens de son ordre dans le royaume.
>
> Il a montré que l'ignorance et l'avidité s'étaient étroitement alliées pour exciter et pour entretenir un état de guerre entre le gouvernement et la nation, plus particulièrement encore entre le gouvernement et le peuple.[28]

---

24. Du Pont de Nemours, *Abrégé des principes*, p.378.
25. In *De l'esprit des lois*, Montesquieu addresses safety as opinion twice: on the one hand by defining political freedom in the famous chapter 6 of book 11 ('La liberté politique dans un citoyen est cette tranquillité d'esprit qui provient de l'opinion que chacun a de sa sûreté') and on the other hand by dealing, once again, with political freedom, in his relationship with the citizen ('Elle consiste dans la sûreté, ou dans l'opinion que l'on a de sa sûreté') in chapter 1, book 12.
26. André Vachet, *L'Idéologie libérale: l'individu et sa propriété* (Paris, 1970), p.381.
27. *Archives parlementaires de 1787 à 1860: recueil complet des débats législatifs & politiques des chambres françaises. Première série (1789 à 1799)*, ed. Jérôme Mavidal and Emile Laurent, 96 vols (Paris, 1867-1990), vol.4, p.112-215. Hereafter cited as *AP*.
28. *AP*, vol.4, p.161.

For Du Pont de Nemours, not only does the France of Louis XVI suffer from the absence of a community of interests between the people and their rulers, but it is also deprived of the necessary harmony, by the society of orders. The aristocracy – by its privileges – contravenes the natural design of society: fiscal privileges – irrational taxation – are contrary to the natural order.[29] Recalling the words of Du Pont de Nemours – 'l'ignorance qui a excité la résistance de quelques nobles et d'une partie du clergé' – taken from *Sur les travaux que l'Assemblée nationale constituante a légués à l'Assemblée nationale legislative*, M. Albertone emphasises that the ignorance of this minority is the reason for the impossibility of carrying out reforms in the kingdom.[30] Ignorance is therefore a considerable vector of deregulation of society, which justifies a thorough reflection on instruction.[31] The state of war is asserted; the belligerents are named.

It is easy to understand Du Pont de Nemours's enthusiasm at the announcement of the convening of the Estates General: it is an opportunity to establish a new order of things, founded in a rational way, by reforms carried out with understanding. In Du Pont's words: 'rallier le peuple à son Roi, réprimer les abus d'un pouvoir désordonné sur les impositions; [et surtout] perfectionner toutes les relations sociales, favoriser tous les travaux utiles, établir le règne de la justice entre toutes les différentes classes de citoyens'.[32]

Thus a good government will have certain characteristics: 'Les hommes n'ont essentiellement besoin, pour être heureux, que de la Liberté Des Actions qui ne renferment point de délit, de la Sûreté des Personnes, et de la Propriété Des Biens. [...] Tout gouvernement, toute constitution dans lesquels les citoyens ont la jouissance bien assurée de ces trois sources de bonheur, sont de bons gouvernements et des constitutions respectables.'[33] Here is once again the political trinity of the physiocrats, this time in ascending rather than descending order. It is a way of expressing a certain subjectification of the political trinity. We can postulate that, without being of equal weight, the objective dimension – previously discussed – and the subjective dimension are

29. On the aristocratic regime in physiocratic thought, see Mergey, *L'Etat des physiocrates*, p.90.
30. M. Albertone, 'Du Pont de Nemours et l'instruction', p.360.
31. M. Albertone, 'Du Pont de Nemours et l'instruction', p.360.
32. *AP*, vol.4, p.161.
33. P.-S. Du Pont de Nemours, 'De l'amour de la constitution et de celui de la liberté', https://www.institutcoppet.org/de-lamour-de-la-constitution-et-celui-de-la-liberte/ (last accessed 7 December 2024; original emphasis).

in fact closely interwoven in the thought of Du Pont de Nemours, so that they feed into each other. While the objective element is at the origin of the state and the state must protect the community against the actions of a few, making the state a product of human weaknesses[34] – the result 'des éléments désordonnés et passionnels de l'homme'[35] – these same weaknesses are counterbalanced by man's nature. Indeed, in everyone, instinctive self-preservation creates resistance, which leads people to seek security for themselves and their possessions. In this way, Du Pont reinjects subjectivity into the meaning of safety. If subjectivity was residual in his earlier writings – as Du Pont de Nemours himself hardly emphasised it – it now explains many of the developments in the Nemours books of grievances. For him, safety naturally participates in the consolidation of society.

Du Pont de Nemours himself offers a key to understanding his investment in public life. In the past, Du Pont had assisted Turgot with this assertion in mind; there is no doubt that this idea was also a powerful driving force in the adventure of the Estates General: considering that society was not founded on solid foundations, Du Pont felt it necessary to help strengthen them; for him, the convening of the Estates General was clearly a historic opportunity.

In the Nemours books of grievances, the diagnosis made is one of the most serious: firstly, because the foundations of society are no longer only fragile but *neglected*, and, secondly, because the citizens' desire for safety is explicitly expressed.

Thereafter, Du Pont remained committed to these principles, as evidenced by his recurrent statements during the Revolution concerning strict law and order. Thus, the enrolment of P.-S. Du Pont and his son in the registers of the National Guard, from mid-July 1789, testifies to his attachment to public tranquillity. Very early on, he was concerned about events, as soon as they provoked a popular reaction, and, from the dispatch box, he was quick to denounce violence, in particular the summary execution of the governor of Launay and of the provost of merchants, Jacques de Flesselles, during the capture of the Bastille. For Du Pont, 14 July 1789 was less a sign of popular support for the political achievements of the National Assembly than an illustration of disturbances that had to be stifled before they threatened property and the entire social order.

34. Marie-Claire Laval-Reviglio, 'Les conceptions politiques des physiocrates', *Revue française de science politique* 37:2 (1987), p.181-213 (184).
35. Vachet, *L'Idéologie libérale*, p.385.

ii. Maintenance of public order and Revolution

Is revolution, by itself, a satisfactory instrument for the regeneration of institutions? It is not certain – far from it – that revolutionary action has the favour of Du Pont de Nemours. His speeches in the National Assembly demonstrate this.

ii. Maintenance of public order and Revolution

During the summer of 1789, the first divisions within the National Assembly began to emerge around the maintenance of public order and the response to popular reaction.[36] Du Pont de Nemours took an active part in determining the terms of the debate, at the risk of losing the moral ascendency acquired during the spread of physiocratic ideas.

On 20 July 1789, as the Great Fear was spreading, Lally-Tollendal expressed his worries at the dispatch box about the troubles that were multiplying: the Assembly had to respond to them and '[s']opposer aux torrents de sang qui sont prêts à couler',[37] without stifling popular support for the Revolution. Difficult balance! Du Pont de Nemours immediately took the floor to support him in his denunciation of the disturbances and attacks on property; he was joined by a few other influential deputies, notably Mounier. The very first heated exchanges between Du Pont de Nemours and Robespierre took place on the floor of the Assembly; others followed.

On 4 August 1789, Target presented to the National Assembly his *Rapport sur le projet d'arrêté [sic] relatif à la sûreté du royaume.* The necessity of this project had been defended by Du Pont a few days earlier.[38] Target and Du Pont had very little control over what followed. The facts are well known: the vicomte de Noailles spoke, then the duc d'Aiguillon, before, one after another, the deputies abandoned their privileges. The intervention of Du Pont de Nemours on the night of 4 August is not generally recorded (it is not mentioned by Michelet, Quinet, Thiers or Guizot): he imposed himself between Noailles and d'Aiguillon to demand the adoption of the initial *arrêté* (it is technically a *décret*, but the legal terms are not yet clearly fixed). He did so in terms characteristic of his thinking: 'Un désordre universel s'est emparé de l'Etat, à raison de l'inaction de tous les agents du

---

36. Jean-Clément Martin, *Violence et Révolution: essai sur la naissance d'un mythe national* (Paris, 2006).
37. Gérard de Lally-Tollendal, *AP*, vol.8, p.252.
38. Pierre-Samuel Du Pont de Nemours, *AP*, vol.8, p.253.

pouvoir; aucune société politique ne peut exister un seul moment sans lois et sans tribunaux, pour garantir la liberté, la sûreté des personnes, et la conservation des propriétés.'[39] For him, questioning social guarantees by overthrowing institutions leads to anarchy, and complete breakdown leads to chaos. Thus, he stands back from the flow of events and historic political decisions taken by the National Assembly. Nevertheless, at this date, despite receiving a slap in the face, Du Pont remains confident about the course of events. He is still convinced that the nation, through the adoption of the *Declaration of rights*, which he had called for[40] and regarding which the books of grievances of the bailiwick of Nemours give a precise account of his wishes,[41] can follow the path of reform that will lead to happiness. However, the course of events would change this optimism, and force him to deepen his reflection on the maintenance of public order.

Remarkably, Du Pont is still trying to find an answer within the context of his deep convictions as a physiocrat, and, consequently, within the ideas defended prior to the Revolution. As proof, let us recall one of his definitions of safety:[42] it is the means of ensuring that property and liberty are both de jure and de facto. But what is violence? Exactly the opposite! Violence is the denial of all liberty and property, and it is the responsibility of the public authorities to guarantee them. In this game, Du Pont de Nemours barely scratched the surface of the specificity of the *mesure de police*, by its very nature irreducible to a legal statement, since it manifests its need for effectiveness through constant rebalancing.[43]

In short, the public authorities must 'mettre obstacle au tumulte, au pillage, au meurtre, à l'incendie; car aucune de ces choses ne peut être à l'avantage de la société'.[44] Thus, Du Pont reminds us, once again, of the purpose of society – to preserve law and order, and

---

39. Pierre-Samuel Du Pont de Nemours, *AP*, vol.8, p.344.
40. Pierre-Samuel Du Pont de Nemours, *Examen du gouvernement d'Angleterre, comparé aux constitutions des Etats-Unis* (London and Paris, Chez Froullé, 1789), p.180-81.
41. Draft bill of rights contained in the books of grievances of the bailiwick of Nemours, *AP*, vol.4, p.161-62.
42. Pierre-Samuel Du Pont de Nemours, *De l'origine*, p.363.
43. Paolo Napoli, *Naissance de la police moderne: pouvoir, normes, société* (Paris, 2003); Paolo Napoli, 'Mesure de police: une approche historico-conceptuelle à l'âge moderne', *Tracés* 11 (2011), p.151-73.
44. Pierre-Samuel Du Pont de Nemours, *AP*, vol.11, p.668.

protect victims of assault – and the legality of the means that the constitution confers upon it.

In his eyes, this justifies the special status of the police force: it is the repositary of *majesté nationale* and, as such, its agents must benefit from special protection. Du Pont de Nemours logically comes to raise the question of recourse to military authority in the event of sedition. He describes soldiers as 'guerriers légaux de la nation': they can therefore be mobilised to maintain internal peace, at the request of the civil authorities. This is an opportunity for Du Pont de Nemours to recall the virtues of martial law,[45] of which he is one of the most ardent defenders.

To enlighten the debate, it is interesting to compare the words of Du Pont with those of Jacques de Guibert, the military philosopher who was very successful on the eve of the Revolution, before being widely scorned because of a misunderstood reform of the army carried out in 1788.[46] Guibert's reflections on the maintenance of public order were heard by the constituents – Rabaut Saint-Etienne,[47] Sieyès[48] but also, therefore, Du Pont de Nemours. This familiarity with Guibert's writings may also have been deepened through contact with Jean-Xavier Bureaux de Pusy,[49] an officer from the Ecole de Mézières, an engineer, a fine connoisseur of the subject and an

45. On martial law, see particulary Florence Gauthier, *Triomphe et mort du droit naturel en Révolution, 1789-1795-1802* (Paris, 1992), p.56-66 and 102-103, reprinted in 2014, p.75-85 and 127-28; Michel Pertué, 'La loi martiale', in *Mélanges Henri Jacquot* (Orléans, 2006), p.459-70.

46. Sébastien Le Gal, 'La réforme de la constitution militaire durant la pré-révolution (Guibert et le Conseil de la Guerre)', *Cahiers poitevins d'histoire du droit* 8-9 (2017), p.109-27.

47. Jean-Paul Rabaut Saint-Etienne, *Rapport de M. Rabaud sur l'organisation de la force publique*, in *AP*, vol.20, p.592-97. See also *Histoire des polices en France: des guerres de religion à nos jours*, ed. Vincent Milliot (Paris, 2020), p.224.

48. Vincent Denis and Bernard Gainot, 'De l'art du maintien de l'ordre chez Sieyès, 1791', in *Les Mémoires policiers, 1750-1850: écritures et pratiques policières du siècle des Lumières au Second Empire*, ed. Vincent Milliot (Rennes, 2006), p.219-33.

49. J.-X. Bureaux de Pusy was the son-in-law of Françoise Robin, who was to marry Du Pont de Nemours in September 1795. Pusy would also go to America and benefit from concessions in Delaware, as Du Pont de Nemours did. Struck off the list of emigrants, he returned to France and was appointed prefect by Bonaparte, first in the department of Allier, then the Rhône, and finally Genoa, where he died in office.

influential speaker on questions of military reform,[50] although, on the basis of current knowledge, this hypothesis is unverifiable.

Let us recall Guibert's contribution. In *De la force publique*,[51] a work written at the end of 1789 or the beginning of 1790 and published posthumously, Guibert offers an innovative reflection on the maintenance of public order, articulated with reference to new political law. In this short work, the author sets out a certain number of decisive principles: on the one hand, the distinction between the external force, the army, responsible for defending the integrity of the national territory, and the internal, civil force, ensuring the safety of citizens; on the other hand, the mobilisation of more substantial resources devoted to the public force, when it is a question of repressing 'troubles majeurs relatifs à la police et à l'ordre public'.[52] Guibert subtly distinguishes between, on the one hand, 'crises majeures', which constitute a 'danger de la liberté publique' and threaten the constitution itself, such as civil war or federalist secession, and, on the other hand, 'crises de subversion',[53] such as sedition. In the first case, it seems that the constitution can be suspended, if necessary, with the legislative power assuming the powers of public salvation; in the second case, Guibert justifies giving 'la puissance exécutive une plus grande autorité et de lui confier la direction et l'emploi de toute la force publique'.[54] Thus, 'dans cet état de trouble',[55] the executive power must be given the possibility of using armed force, as far as necessary. How can the justification for such a use of force be translated into law? Prior to any repressive action, by 'la proclamation de la tranquillité publique trouble'.[56] Otherwise, any use of coercion by the police, particularly through martial law, would be despotic.

On all these points, Du Pont de Nemours implicitly converged with Guibert, as illustrated by the debates of February 1790 on the seditious gatherings. Several questions then arose concerning the right of municipalities to request the presence of the National Guard and the army, recognised on 10 August 1789. As early as 22 February, Du Pont set out the relationship between public safety and the freedom of

---

50. Sébastien Le Gal, 'Origines de l'état de siège en France (Ancien Régime – Révolution)', doctoral dissertation, University Lyon 3, 2011.
51. Jacques de Guibert, *De la force publique* (1790), ed. Jean-Pierre Bois (Paris, 2005).
52. Guibert, *De la force publique*, p.55.
53. Guibert, *De la force publique*, p.55.
54. Guibert, *De la force publique*, p.55.
55. Guibert, *De la force publique*, p.55.
56. Guibert, *De la force publique*, p.55.

the people in terms of balance. His statement was as follows: 'la sûreté publique [sera établie] sans porter atteinte à la liberté du peuple.' The question then arises: that of establishing 'comment on empêchera que des scélérats, égarant son zèle [celui du peuple], ne le portent à des actions dont il serait le premier à gémir ou à rougir'.[57] The determination of this report is, obviously, still relevant today.

How are disorders of such magnitude possible? Guibert saw in these disorders a clear failure on the part of the public authorities, especially as they 'n'arrivent presque jamais sans des commotions préliminaires'.[58] Thus, for Guibert, the authorities must foresee and contain, so that sedition reveals the mere incompetence of public authorities. For his part, Du Pont de Nemours does not say anything different. In his speech of 22 February 1790, he deconstructed the mechanics of these gatherings, which originated in the activities of 'anarchists'. These gatherings demanded a severe response from the government, commensurate with the threat, by tracking down the individuals involved. In case of failure, if actions lead to violence, repression is imposed, followed by punishment, presented as the duty to ensure 'la garantie et les indemnités à fournir par les villes, paroisses et communautés où se seront commis des dommages, à ceux qui les auront essuyés'.[59] The sanction can thus be individual or collective – it is nothing other than the declared state of unrest, when a municipality rebels against the authority of the state or when the payment of taxes fails (both of which are examples envisaged by Guibert in his work).

With his vigorous discourse on policing, Du Pont de Nemours is the faithful theoretician of the police state, in line with physiocratic thinking. As the revolutionary troubles continued, he concluded that a state of internal war had developed, which forced him to consider the political priorities of the moment in a different way: they no longer presupposed ambitious economic and social reforms, conceived on the eve of the Revolution, but required the scrupulous application of the decrees of the Assembly for the preservation of public order through the use of public force. As Du Pont asserted: 'il y a guerre, il n'y a plus d'ordre public, ni de société.'[60] This justifies the multiple decrees of the Assembly 'contre les insurrections, contre les pétitions à main armée',[61]

57. P.-S. Du Pont de Nemours, *AP*, vol.11, p.667.
58. Guibert, *De la force publique*, p.55.
59. P.-S. Du Pont de Nemours, *AP*, vol.11, p.669.
60. P.-S. Du Pont de Nemours, *AP*, vol.11, p.668.
61. P.-S. Du Pont de Nemours, *AP*, vol.11, p.668.

including, in the end, the decree consecrating martial law in France.[62] Du Pont finds that his fears materialise when increasing numbers of municipalities openly oppose the application of the decrees of the National Assembly: Arles and soon Lons-le-Saunier, later Orléans and Mende, justify declaring a state of rebellion in order to give a legal basis to vigorous collective repression.[63]

Du Pont de Nemours, for once, is followed by significant speakers. Charles de Lameth supports him: 'La responsabilité des communes est un des plus sûrs moyens de rétablir la tranquillité publique.'[64] After him, Adrien Duport sums up word for word the provision proposed by Du Pont de Nemours: 'Lorsque, par un attroupement, il aura été causé quelque dommage dans une ville, paroisse ou communauté, il sera réparé par une imposition mise sur tous les habitants, au marc la livre de toutes leurs impositions directes: sauf le recours desdites communautés sur les biens de ceux qui auraient fomenté les désordres dont les dommages seraient résultés.'[65] However, this was a bitter victory for the physiocrat, because the diagnosis of the events was bleak. The year 1790 is definitely the moment when Du Pont de Nemours realised that events had brought the Revolution closer to the dreaded state of anarchy, even though he himself had warned very early on about the seditious drift of popular movements supporting the Revolution.

iii. Maintenance of public order, sedition and national cohesion

For Du Pont de Nemours, 14 July 1789 was the first alarm that soon heralded large-scale unrest and acts of collective violence, which, because of their repetition, called for an adapted response from the legislature. According to him, the troublemakers did not defend the achievements of the Revolution – at least, the political revolution of the first months – but rather carried the seeds of anarchy. Before his eyes, order gave way. Two episodes allowed Du Pont de Nemours to recall his unwavering commitment to public order: the debates on the constitutional treatment of sedition in February 1790, and the affair of the Châteauvieux Swiss Regiment in April 1792.

Firstly, with regard to the constitutional treatment of sedition,

---

62. P.-S. Du Pont de Nemours, 3 August 1790, *AP*, vol.17, p.579.
63. Le Gal, 'Origines de l'état de siège', p.303-14.
64. Charles de Lameth, *AP*, vol.11, p.682.
65. Adrien Duport, *AP*, vol.11, p.669.

Du Pont de Nemours offers a synthetic analysis of this danger to political freedom. This danger can be apprehended by studying the maintenance of law and order. The speech of 22 February 1790, which dealt with the constitutional treatment of sedition, led us not only to consider the engineering of the maintenance of public order, as we have seen, but also to recall that sedition was the last step of a process that the public authorities had not been able to contain. In this, there was a convergence of views between Du Pont de Nemours and Guibert. Nevertheless, in the face of events, it is necessary to go further and denounce the troublemakers.

Soon enough, Du Pont targets the Jacobin threat and describes the club as a new aristocracy: 'c'est parce que nous sommes décidés à ne vouloir jamais de la ci-devant noblesse des races et des fiefs, que nous ne voulons pas davantage de la nouvelle noblesse des sociétés usurpatrices.'[66] In the eyes of the physiocrat, members of the Jacobin Club are engaged in undermining the principles of the Revolution under the guise of spreading them. They are the most dangerous ferment of deadly anarchy. Du Pont sketches a weapon, all the more dangerous as it is solid, between the violent speeches uttered in the clubs, corruption, the payment of money to corrupt individuals to engage in violent actions, and the dissemination of untruths in libels and pamphlets. Du Pont details the workings of a plot that he describes as a veritable political counter-model. He denounces the protagonists in the following terms:

> Ils violent vos lois, en excitant à les violer. Ils ne sont pas les amis de la Constitution [...] ce sont des despotes qui, s'étant créés par séduction et par argent une armée indisciplinée, mais redoutable, veulent conserver leur empire, et, au risque de perdre notre constitution, notre liberté, notre commune patrie, veulent prolonger entre leurs mains le pouvoir de faire trembler tous les hommes de bien qui résisteront à leurs complots.[67]

However, the current denunciation should not be misleading: not only is it underpinned by mature reflection on the modalities of maintaining public order, detailed in the speech of February 1790, it is also fuelled by the author's involvement in the debate that divided the National Assembly on the subject of freedom of the press. Eventually, the physiocrat's conviction, forged over a long period of time, that the

---

66. Du Pont de Nemours, *Lettres de M. Du Pont à M. Pétion*, p.90.
67. P.-S. Du Pont de Nemours, *AP*, vol.17, p.579.

94 *Sébastien Le Gal*

instinct that lies dormant in each person makes them seek security is reinforced.

From then on, internal enemies are perceived as a small number of individuals who manoeuvre against the state and speculate on the blindness and lack of education of the masses. We can understand the violence of the exchanges between Du Pont and Robespierre in February 1790, the latter refining for the occasion a speech that was widely disseminated for the first time.[68] Both took up the arguments exchanged in the autumn of 1789, when martial law was under discussion: repression in the name of public order, defended by the one, was answered by the rights of the weakest and the revolutionary ideal of the other.

Then there's the matter of the Châteauvieux Swiss Regiment. Let us briefly review the events. French society was splintering in a poisonous climate. Opposition between the former nobility and the common people fuelled persistent and recurring tensions. In the army, they led to conflict and hostility. The Nancy affair in August 1790, with its dramatic results, aroused emotions and contrasting positions. The exasperated Swiss regiments stationed in the garrison rebelled against their officers. La Fayette sent General Bouillé to quell the soldiers, but the national guards and soldiers opened fire on each other, resulting, it was long said, in several hundred deaths and, according to recent historiography, 110.[69] The death of Lieutenant Desilles, who interfered in the name of national unity, was symbolic. Sedition was put down, and the soldiers were judged by an inflexible military justice system. Twenty-two of them were hanged, one *roué vif* (the last known example in France) and forty-one sent to prison. In the spring of 1792, the Legislative passed a law granting amnesty to the latter, who made a triumphant return trip from Brest to Paris, appearing before the Assembly to thank the deputies for this act of clemency.[70] Opinion was divided on whether to defend or denounce the amnesty. Not surprisingly, Du Pont de Nemours was among the latter. In his *Lettres à Pétion* (who was then mayor of Paris), Du Pont

---

68. Hervé Leuwers, *Robespierre* (Paris, 2014), p.140.
69. Jean-Clément Martin, *Nouvelle histoire de la Révolution française* (Paris, 2012), p.248.
70. Stanislas de Chabalier, 'Réparer l'injustice d'un châtiment par l'oubli: l'amnistie de soldats du régiment suisse de Châteauvieux (31 décembre 1791)', *Criminocorpus* 16 (2020), https://journals.openedition.org/criminocorpus/7842 (last accessed 29 November 2024).

vigorously denounced the mayor's shady dealings. He reminds us how necessary peace is for the proper application of the constitution, and puts forward the wish for stability and public order felt by the 'silent majority', to use an anachronistic expression, but one that relates quite well to this 'majorité sage, vertueuse, honnête [...] courageuse',[71] in a word, bourgeois and conservative, to which he assimilates himself. On this occasion, Du Pont de Nemours explicitly revives the physiocratic rhetoric of safety and the objectification of the notion. The good citizens wanted to denounce the lax policies of the deputies and the support of the Paris municipality (which organised a *fête de la liberté* to mark the return of the amnestied); they wanted 'l'égalité, la liberté, la propriété, la sûreté, la paix intérieure, le travail, l'abondance, et le respect pour les loix'.[72] The majority, who are attached to public order, represent public opinion, whose advocate Du Pont de Nemours is. They are opposed to the minority, which the authorities unthinkingly support, a 'minorité insensée, turbulente, coupable, révoltée contre la constitution'.[73] It is a war that shakes the nation to its core 'entre les défenseurs de la constitution et les usurpateurs de toutes les autorités publiques'.[74] Safety, the first duty of the constitution, is ignored in this war. Public opinion must be made aware of the arguments of both parties, the better to denounce the demagoguery of the agitating minority. By publishing and widely distributing these letters, Du Pont de Nemours also reintroduces the necessary relationship between maintaining public order and freedom of expression.

Indeed, the study of policing in the thinking of Du Pont de Nemours highlights the link between public tranquillity and freedom of expression. This close link is obvious for Du Pont de Nemours; it is no less so for other deputies, but has not always been emphasised. Reading the debates of 1790 brings these issues back into focus.

Article 11 of the *Declaration of human rights* states the principle in the most categorical terms: 'La libre communication des pensées et des opinions est un des droits les plus précieux de l'Homme.' As in most of the provisions of the *Declaration*, this right is limited by the law, which determines the abuses that its exercise may generate. Thus, in reaction to the preventive system of the Old Regime, the Assembly

---

71. Pierre-Samuel Du Pont de Nemours, *Seconde lettre de Monsieur Du Pont à Pétion* (Paris, n.n., 1792), 27 April 1792, p.1-2.
72. Du Pont de Nemours, *Seconde lettre*, p.1-2.
73. Du Pont de Nemours, *Seconde lettre*, p.1-2.
74. Du Pont de Nemours, *Seconde lettre*, p.1-2.

proclaims freedom as a principle, and control *a posteriori*. However, the reality check is painful, and the Assembly is confronted with a use of freedom of the press that quickly proves to be problematic, as much because of the flow of publications as because of the vigour of their expression. Criticism of the Assembly is sometimes vehement, which generates a difficult relationship with this freedom. Certainly, freedom of expression, and therefore of the press, is considered the first social guarantee in the political community. There is consensus on the principle. However, the battle is raging to determine the criminal threshold, which means identifying an abusive use.[75] The National Assembly debates on several occasions, without being able to deliberate, so delicate is it to express the general will in this matter. The deputies are faced with the difficult implementation of a freedom conceived up to now in the most absolute terms, in the wake of its defenders, during the course of the century.[76] Since then, this absoluteness has been considered the corollary of political freedom, so much so that 'l'arbre de la liberté politique ne croît que par l'influence salutaire de la liberté d'imprimer', according to Barère,[77] in response to one of the drafts of the decree under discussion. In sum, any project to limit the freedom of the press runs the risk of being considered 'une inquisition littéraire et politique, mille fois plus absurde que la censure royale et la tyrannie de l'ancienne police, sous lesquelles la raison, le génie et la liberté ont si longtemps gémi en France'.[78] At the same time, however, the virulence of certain journalists, first and foremost Marat, prompted the deputies to take up the question of the abuse of the right of freedom of expression. As early as the autumn of 1789, Malouet, the first, moved to note the distortion of parliamentary debates by libellists, invited the Assembly to debate. The question bounced back, until Sieyès, in an in-depth report of the Constitutional Committee on the question of the press on 20 January1790,[79] denounced writings inciting resistance against

---

75. This question is all the more difficult when the protagonists themselves embrace a political career while being journalists. See for example Johan Menichetti, 'Pierre-Louis Roederer (1754-1835): science sociale et législation', doctoral dissertation, University Paris-Est, 2020, p.364-87.
76. Bertrand Binoche, *Ecrasez l'infâme* (Paris, 2018).
77. Bertrand Barère quoted by Alma Söderhjelm, 'Le régime de la presse française pendant la Révolution française', doctoral dissertation, University of Helsingfors, 1900, vol.1, p.113.
78. Jacques Pierre Brissot, *Le Patriote français* (13 January 1790), cited by Söderhjelm, 'Le régime', vol.1, p.117.
79. Joseph-Emmanuel Sieyès, *Projet de loi contre les délits qui peuvent se commettre*

the law and the use of violence. Sieyès also called for the prosecution and punishment of the authors of these writings, for sedition. The draft was met with strong hostility.[80] In the summer of the same year, the debate began again. Du Pont de Nemours's speech is part of this new episode. It began on 31 July with Malouet's denunciation of Marat's writings fantasising about the counter-revolutionary plots woven around the king and the queen, and of Camille Desmoulins concerning the Feast of the Federation on 14 July 1790;[81] it continued with the heated adoption of a decree ordering the king's prosecutor at the Châtelet of Paris to prosecute the authors of the writings for the crime of *lèse-nation*.[82] This muddled context should not overshadow the contribution of Du Pont de Nemours's speech, both to the freedom of the press and to the problem of maintaining public order. In support of Malouet, the physiocrat denounced 'l'art horrible des *séditions*', practised by scoundrels driven by the desire to undermine social order by subverting good citizens (speculation on paper money being a preferred instrument). He concludes by mirroring the lawful right of petition and the dissemination of inflammatory, criminal writings: 'Nulle pétition ne doit être faite par forme d'insurrection ni à main armée; car alors elle est sédition, rébellion, révolte; et si vous les tolériez, ce serait alors que vous ne pourriez maintenir votre constitution, et que vous auriez une contre-révolution tous les quinze jours.'[83] The ensuing exchanges were lost in considerable confusion until the Assembly adopted a decree defended by Du Pont de Nemours (after having been refused the floor for the first time), referring the matter back to the Constitution Committee and the Committee of Criminal Jurisprudence to draw up a report on the subject... which never occurred.

---

    par la voie de l'impression, in *Histoire parlementaire de la Révolution française*, ed. Philippe-Joseph-Benjamin Buchez and Pierre-Célestin Roux, vol.4 (Paris, 1834), p.280-88.

80. For a review, see Söderhjelm, 'Le régime', vol.1, p.123-28.

81. Pierre-Victor Malouet, *AP*, vol.17, p.456.

82. Charles Walton, *La Liberté d'expression en Révolution* (Rennes, 2014), p.139-40; on the crime of *lèse-nation*, see Jean-Christophe Gaven, *Le Crime de lèse-nation: histoire d'une invention juridique et politique (1789-1791)* (Paris, 2016).

83. P.-S. Du Pont de Nemours, 3 August 1790, in *Réimpression de l'ancien Moniteur*, vol.5 (Paris, 1860), p.303.

98 — Sébastien Le Gal

***

In conclusion, let us take a leap of a few years, to the time of the Thermidorian Convention, when the new constitution to be given to France, that of the Directoire, is being debated. Du Pont de Nemours invites himself into the discussions, by publishing his *Observations sur la constitution proposée par la commission des Onze*. Recent events have proved him right: revolutionary violence has become an instrument of government. What should be the purpose of the constitution? Du Pont de Nemours's reply was:

> une République bien constituée, quelle que puisse être l'étendue de son territoire, serait le gouvernement le plus paisible et le plus moral; celui où chaque homme ayant le plus de liberté, pourrait le moins troubler la liberté et la propriété d'autrui; celui, par conséquent, sous lequel il vaudrait le mieux vivre, et sous lequel l'agriculture, les manufactures, le commerce, les sciences, les arts feraient les plus grands et les plus rapides progrès.[84]

Clearly, his convictions in terms of maintaining public order are intact, and they find justification in the course of the Revolution; too faint to be heard in 1790, is Du Pont de Nemours more audible in Year III, when the 'reign of law' becomes the keyword of the new political order?[85] The Thermidorians claimed to be attached to public order and tranquillity – the report of Sieyès on the law of the great police force, of the 1st germinal Year III (21 March 1795), then, a few months later, the creation of the Ministère de la Police générale, testify to this attachment to public order and tranquillity. However, the maintenance of the constitution at the cost of force and the invalidation of elections did not offer the guarantees expected by Du Pont de Nemours. His criticism of the Directoire focused on financial issues, and the regime's excessive collusion with the former Montagnards. Resigned, fructidorised,[86] he fled revolutionary France, the day after 18 fructidor, to seek a safe haven in America.

---

84. Pierre-Samuel Du Pont de Nemours, *Observations sur la constitution proposée par la commission des Onze* (Paris, Chez Du Pont imprimeur-libraire, 1795), p.49.
85. Milliot, *Histoire des polices*, p.251.
86. According to Eugène Daire, Du Pont de Nemours owed it to Joseph Chénier to have been struck off the deportation lists; see Daire, *Physiocrates*, vol.1, p.328.

Abolir la contrainte par corps: le combat du jurisconsulte Du Pont de Nemours

THÉRENCE CARVALHO

Nantes Université

'Du Pont de Nemours, jurisconsulte.' Ce rapprochement inattendu semble relever de l'oxymore et n'est pas sans susciter l'étonnement. En effet, si le physiocrate est connu pour ses qualités et ses compétences en matière d'économie politique, de journalisme, de droit public, d'administration ou encore de diplomatie, son intérêt pour certaines questions relatives au droit privé n'est presque jamais évoqué. Pourtant, à plusieurs moments de son existence, Du Pont n'hésite pas à revêtir les habits du jurisconsulte, spécialement au sujet de la contrainte par corps.

De formation à la fois littéraire et scientifique, ce fils d'horloger n'a jamais poursuivi des études de droit,[1] et ce, contrairement à certains de ses coreligionnaires en physiocratie comme le parlementaire Paul-Pierre Le Mercier de La Rivière[2] ou l'avocat du roi Guillaume-François Le Trosne.[3] Sa culture juridique, néanmoins honorable,

---

1.   Sur la vie et la formation de Du Pont, voir Ambrose Saricks, *Pierre Samuel Du Pont de Nemours* (Lawrence, KS, 1965); Pierre Jolly, *Du Pont de Nemours, soldat de la liberté* (Paris, 1956); Gustave Schelle, *Dupont de Nemours et l'école physiocratique* (Paris, 1888). Enfin, *L'Enfance et la jeunesse de Du Pont de Nemours racontées par lui-même* (Paris, 1906) constitue toujours une source digne d'intérêt.

2.   Pour des travaux sur la carrière et l'œuvre de Le Mercier de La Rivière, voir Bernard Herencia, 'Physiocratie et gouvernementalité: l'œuvre de Lemercier de la Rivière', thèse de doctorat, 2 vol., Paris Ouest Nanterre La Défense, 2011; Louis-Philippe May, *Le Mercier de La Rivière (1719-1801): aux origines de la science économique* (Paris, 1975).

3.   Le Trosne poursuit des études de droit à l'Université d'Orléans et devient le disciple du célèbre professeur Robert-Joseph Pothier. Pour une analyse renouvelée de la vie et l'œuvre de Le Trosne, nous nous permettons de renvoyer à notre présentation du recueil intitulé *Les Lois naturelles de l'ordre social* (Genève, 2019) qui réunit trois de ses textes majeurs: *De l'ordre social, De l'intérêt social* et ses *Vues sur la justice criminelle*. Voir également la thèse datée de Jérôme Mille,

relève donc de l'autodidaxie. Lecteur à la curiosité insatiable, il se tient régulièrement informé des actualités législatives en France et en Europe. A ce titre, les *Ephémérides du citoyen*, périodique du mouvement physiocratique qu'il dirige de mai 1768 à mars 1772, recensent attentivement les grandes réformes juridiques opérées à travers le continent au sein de la rubrique des 'Opérations louables faites depuis peu par les divers gouvernements de l'Europe'. De même, c'est parce qu'il affiche sans cesse ses convictions libérales dans la polémique sur la réforme du droit du commerce des grains que son journal est interdit en 1772 par le nouveau pouvoir en place incarné par le contrôleur général Terray et le chancelier Maupeou.

Plus largement, Du Pont s'est toujours opposé aux interprétations qui tendent à réduire la physiocratie à un courant strictement économique. Les physiocrates proposent en effet un projet global et universel dont l'objectif est d'aligner l'ordre juridique, social et économique sur les lois de l'ordre naturel. Consubstantielle au droit et au politique, leur pensée économique constitue une branche essentielle mais en aucun cas unique du mouvement. 'Vous avez trop rétréci la carrière de l'économie politique en ne la traitant que comme la *science des richesses*. Elle est la *science du droit naturel* appliqué, comme il doit l'être, aux sociétés civilisées. Elle est la *science des constitutions*' et 'celle de la *justice éclairée* dans toutes les relations sociales intérieures et extérieures', rappelle d'ailleurs Du Pont à Jean-Baptiste Say en 1815.[4] Reliant la loi naturelle à toutes les structures sociales, les physiocrates témoignent donc d'une approche juridique de l'économie. Ainsi, même leurs théories proprement économiques conduisent à un modèle de réforme de l'ordre juridique et social.[5]

Un Physiocrate oublié: G.-F. Le Trosne – étude économique, fiscale et politique (Paris, 1905); et l'ouvrage récent dirigé par Anthony Mergey et autres, *Guillaume-François Le Trosne: itinéraire d'une figure intellectuelle orléanaise au siècle des Lumières* (Le Kremlin-Bicêtre, 2023).

4. Cité par Eugène Daire, *Physiocrates: Quesnay, Dupont de Nemours, Mercier de La Rivière, l'abbé Baudeau, Le Trosne, avec une introduction sur la doctrine des physiocrates, des commentaires et des notices historiques* (Paris, 1846), p.397. Sauf indication contraire, les citations reproduisent l'emploi de l'italique des sources citées. Sur les désaccords entre Say et Du Pont de Nemours, voir Gilles Jacoud, 'Jean-Baptiste Say et la critique de la physiocratie: l'opposition à Pierre Samuel Dupont de Nemours', dans *Les Voies de la richesse? La Physiocratie en question (1760-1850)*, éd. Gérard Klotz et autres (Rennes, 2017), p.245-62.

5. Sur ce sujet, nous nous permettons de renvoyer à notre ouvrage: Thérence Carvalho, *La Physiocratie dans l'Europe des Lumières: circulation et réception d'un modèle de réforme de l'ordre juridique et social* (Paris, 2020).

Abolir la contrainte par corps 101

Les plus importantes observations juridiques de Du Pont se cristallisent autour d'un mécanisme singulier du droit des contrats: la contrainte par corps. Contrairement à l'esclavage ou à l'emprisonnement pour dettes, qui est avant tout conçu comme une peine, la contrainte par corps est d'abord un moyen comminatoire, c'est-à-dire une menace temporaire destinée à exercer une pression sur le débiteur de mauvaise foi. Dans l'ancien droit français, la contrainte par corps ne peut généralement s'appliquer que si le contrat le stipule expressément. L'ordonnance de Moulins de 1566 institue cependant le principe de la contrainte par corps judiciaire et durcit considérablement le système. Tout débiteur peut désormais être emprisonné quatre mois seulement après le prononcé de la décision par le juge.[6] Si le créancier parvient à prouver sa dette, la condamnation au paiement entraîne *ipso jure* la contrainte par corps. Cette extrême rigueur est atténuée par l'ordonnance de 1667 par laquelle Louis XIV interdit la contrainte par corps conventionnelle et abroge l'ensemble des règles précédentes.[7] Dorénavant, les débiteurs ne sont emprisonnés que dans des cas limitativement prévus par la loi[8] et à la condition que le juge approuve souverainement la mesure. A la fin de l'Ancien Régime, la contrainte par corps est donc devenue une voie d'exécution strictement encadrée par la loi.[9]

A deux moments très différents de sa vie, Du Pont s'illustre

6. 'Ordonnance sur la réforme de la justice, Moulins, février 1566', dans *Recueil général des anciennes lois françaises, depuis l'an 420 jusqu'à la Révolution de 1789*, éd. Anasthase-Jean-Léger Jourdan et autres, 29 vol. (Paris, 1821-1833), t.14, p.201, art.48.
7. *Ordonnance de Louis XIV, roy de France et de Navarre, donnée à Saint-Germain-en-Laye au mois d'avril 1667* (Paris, chez les associés choisis par ordre de Sa Majesté pour l'impression de ses nouvelles ordonnances, 1667), p.198, tit.34, art.1.
8. La contrainte par corps est alors essentiellement maintenue pour les dépens et restitutions de fruits de dommages-intérêts au-dessus de 200 livres (*Ordonnance de Louis XIV*, p.198, tit.34, art.2), contre les tuteurs et curateurs (p.199, tit.34, art.3), pour les deniers royaux (p.199-200, tit.34, art.5) et, plus généralement, pour les dettes entre marchands, pour lettres de change et faits de commerce (p.199, tit.34, art.4). L'ordonnance tolère néanmoins de multiples exceptions et conserve ainsi les anciens privilèges des foires, ports, étapes, marchés et villes d'arrêt (p.199-200, tit.34, art.5).
9. Sur l'histoire de la contrainte par corps, voir Nazlie Aïnouddine Sidi, 'L'évolution de la contrainte par corps du XVIᵉ au XXᵉ siècle', thèse de doctorat, Université de Poitiers, 2020; Marie-Hélène Renaut, 'La contrainte par corps: une voie d'exécution civile à coloris pénal', *Revue de science criminelle et de droit pénal comparé* 4 (2002), p.791-808; Jean-Philippe Lévy et André Castaldo, *Histoire du droit civil* (Paris, 2010), p.1013-23; Jean Bart, *Histoire du droit privé* (Paris, 2009),

comme un farouche adversaire de la contrainte par corps. Dans les deux cas, ses réflexions sont guidées par l'actualité législative et les grands principes libéraux qui l'animent. Dès 1773, dans le cadre de sa correspondance littéraire et politique qu'il entretient avec plusieurs souverains européens, le physiocrate critique sévèrement un nouvel édit promulgué par Louis XV sur le régime de la contrainte par corps. Sa réprobation prend toutefois un caractère confidentiel en demeurant limitée à un cercle de lecteurs prestigieux certes, mais extrêmement restreint (i). Deux décennies plus tard, par le décret du 9 mars 1793, la Convention décide, en s'épargnant tout véritable débat, d'abolir la contrainte par corps. Cette suppression est cependant rapidement remise en cause par le Directoire qui affiche son souhait de revenir en la matière aux dispositions antérieurement en vigueur. Du Pont choisit de combattre résolument le projet. Cette fois-ci, il n'est plus le modeste correspondant littéraire qui se confie à quelques princes étrangers mais l'honorable député du Loiret au Conseil des Anciens qui entend s'exprimer publiquement devant la nation. Son argumentation juridique a mûri et ses discours passionnés s'attaquent au principe même de l'exécution sur la personne (ii).

i. Abolir la contrainte par corps: un combat officieux sous l'Ancien Régime

Après l'interdiction des *Ephémérides du citoyen* en 1772, Du Pont décide d'utiliser sa plume et de faire jouer son réseau européen pour proposer une correspondance littéraire et politique aux princes enthousiasmés par les idées de l'école physiocratique. Le roi Gustave III de Suède, le margrave Charles-Frédéric de Bade, le comte polonais Joachim Litawor Chreptowicz et le duc de Courlande Pierre de Biron souscrivent alors un abonnement.[10] A l'aide de ce canal, Du

---

p.375-77 et 446; Jules Levieil de La Marsonnière, *Histoire de la contrainte par corps* (Paris, 1843).

10. A propos de la correspondance littéraire du physiocrate, nous nous permettons de renvoyer à notre article 'La correspondance littéraire et politique de Du Pont de Nemours: vecteur de diffusion du modèle physiocratique en Europe', dans *Entente culturelle: l'Europe des correspondances littéraires*, éd. Ulla Kölving (Ferney-Voltaire, 2021), p.165-84. Voir également les articles pionniers de Jochen Schlobach, 'Une correspondance littéraire de Du Pont de Nemours adressée à Stockholm et à Karlsruhe', dans *Nouvelles, gazettes, mémoires secrets*, éd. Birgitta Berglund-Nilsson (Karlstad, 1998), p.101-11, et 'Physiocratie, critique sociale et éducation princière: à propos d'un texte inconnu de Du Pont de

Abolir la contrainte par corps 103

Pont fait circuler en Europe un modèle politique et juridique propice à la refonte de la société et de la législation d'Ancien Régime. Dans une lettre du 15 janvier 1773 destinée à la cour de Bade, Du Pont formule pour la première fois son opinion sur 'un point important de législation civile' en critiquant sévèrement 'une nouvelle loi sur l'emprisonnement pour dettes'.[11] Il s'agit en réalité d'un édit royal portant règlement sur les contraintes par corps pour dettes civiles 'dans la ville, faubourgs et banlieue de Paris'. Ce texte, préparé par le secrétaire d'Etat de la Maison du roi, Phélypeaux de Saint-Florentin, et supervisé par le chancelier et garde des sceaux Maupeou, est adopté par Louis XV en novembre 1772 et enregistré par le Parlement de Paris le 2 janvier 1773.[12] Sans modifier la substance du droit de la contrainte par corps, l'objectif affirmé par cet édit est 'de prescrire des formes et d'établir des règles, à la faveur desquelles le créancier pourra désormais exercer avec plus d'effet ses droits contre son débiteur, sans que le débiteur soit exposé à la surprise et à la violence, et sans que le bon ordre et la tranquillité publique soient intervertis'.[13]

'L'emprisonnement pour dettes de commerce, qu'on appelle *contrainte par corps*, est établi en France comme dans presque toute l'Europe',[14] regrette l'ancien journaliste dès le début de sa lettre. En retenant les deux expressions comme synonymes, Du Pont perçoit davantage le mécanisme comme une peine que comme une voie d'exécution. Cette confusion du vocable, loin d'être inédite, est partagée par nombre de ses contemporains. Le physiocrate reproche surtout à la nouvelle législation d'autoriser les officiers-gardes du commerce à arrêter les débiteurs au sein même de leurs maisons et à toute heure de la nuit, s'ils sont accompagnés par un commissaire de

---

Nemours', dans *Chemins ouverts: mélanges offerts à Claude Sicard* (Toulouse, 1998), p.77-84.

11. 'Lettre de Du Pont à Charles-Louis de Bade, Paris, 15 janvier 1773. D'une nouvelle loi sur l'emprisonnement pour dettes et des principes relatifs à cette partie du droit civil', dans *Carl Friedrichs von Baden brieflicher Verkehr mit Mirabeau und Du Pont*, éd. Carl Knies, 2 vol. (Heidelberg, 1892), t.2, p.25.

12. *Edit du roi, portant création de dix officiers-gardes du commerce, et règlement pour les contraintes par corps pour dettes civiles dans la ville, faubourgs et banlieue de Paris, donné à Fontainebleau au mois de novembre 1772, registré en Parlement le 2 janvier 1773* (Paris, P.-G. Simon, 1773).

13. *Edit du roi*, p.2.

14. 'Lettre de Du Pont à Charles-Louis de Bade, Paris, 15 janvier 1773', p.25.

police.[15] Dans son argumentation, il se livre à une vigoureuse critique du droit romain:

> Cette disposition semble bien dure. La loi des XII tables qui, selon quelques commentateurs, permettait aux créanciers de couper leurs débiteurs par morceaux, est la seule que nous connaissions qui ait été plus dure encore. [...] Le débiteur insolvable était vendu pour l'esclavage et ses créanciers en partageaient le prix, ce qu'on appelait le couper par morceaux. Cette atrocité légale a duré longtemps.[16]

En réalité, ce passage de la loi des Douze Tables, rédigée en 451 et 450 avant J.-C., est nettement plus complexe. Dans ses *Nuits attiques*, Aulu-Gelle, grammairien romain du deuxième siècle de notre ère, indique de manière particulièrement sibylline que les créanciers d'un débiteur mis à mort peuvent '*partes secanto*',[17] expression qui peut être littéralement traduite par 'qu'ils coupent les parts'. Cette formule énigmatique a fait l'objet de multiples interprétations. Pour la plupart des historiens, le cadavre est découpé en autant de morceaux que de créanciers afin que chacun ait sa part. Aulu-Gelle insiste d'ailleurs sur l'inhumanité du châtiment et convient qu'on ne doit jamais y recourir.[18] D'autres proposent une lecture de la règle qui exclut toute acception sanglante: les créanciers se partagent simplement les biens du débiteur exécuté. Enfin, d'aucuns y ont vu une sorte de malédiction par laquelle le débiteur insolvable était voué aux dieux infernaux.[19] Quoi qu'il en soit, l'expression '*partes secanto*' laisse présumer de la division, matérielle ou imaginaire, de quelque chose – un corps, des biens, une âme – en plusieurs parties. Du Pont nous livre en somme

---

15. Il s'agit en fait de l'article 6 de l'édit: 'Les arrêts, jugements et sentences, portant contrainte par corps pour dettes civiles, pourront être mis à exécution dans l'intérieur des maisons, tous les jours et à toute heure; à l'exception toutefois des fêtes et dimanches [...]; Voulons néanmoins que lesdites contraintes ne puissent être mises à exécution pendant la nuit, sans l'assistance d'un commissaire, dont les frais de transport et vacation seront payés par la partie poursuivante, sauf à les répéter' (*Edit du roi*, p.4).
16. 'Lettre de Du Pont à Charles-Louis de Bade, Paris, 15 janvier 1773', p.26-30.
17. *Fontes iuris Romani anteiustiniani*, éd. Salvatore Riccobono, t.1 (Florence, 1941), p.33: '*Tertiis nundinis partis secanto. Si plus minusve secuerunt, se fraude esto.*' La formule peut se traduire par: 'Au troisième jour du marché, qu'ils coupent les parts. Si l'on a coupé plus ou moins, que cela soit sans inconvénient.'
18. Aulu-Gelle, *Les Nuits attiques*, t.3 (Paris, 1846), p.325: 'Quoi de plus atroce? quoi de plus barbare? Mais n'est-il pas évident qu'on a entouré la peine de cet appareil de cruauté, précisément pour n'avoir jamais à y recourir.'
19. Voir J.-P. Lévy et A. Castaldo, *Histoire du droit civil*, p.1011.

Le physiocrate poursuit en essayant de retracer à grands traits les origines historiques de la contrainte par corps:

> [Ce fut] chez des peuples où tous les droits de l'homme étaient méconnus, chez des peuples où l'esclavage était établi par une force cruelle et maintenu par d'odieuses lois, qu'à la suite de cet énorme désordre moral et politique, l'emprisonnement pour dette prit autrefois naissance. [...] On sait à quel point les patriciens des premiers temps de la République romaine opprimaient le peuple. [...] L'Europe s'est échappée aux lances et aux francisques des peuples du Nord que pour retomber sous les chaînes de plomb de la législation romaine: chaînes moins nobles et plus pesantes que celles du fer.[20]

Archaïque et contraire aux droits fondamentaux de l'homme, le droit romain est envisagé sur ce point comme un modèle juridique pernicieux qu'il convient absolument d'écarter. Aujourd'hui, 'les progrès des lumières ne permettant plus de donner aux créanciers la personne de leurs débiteurs, on a cru n'en devoir pas moins l'ôter à ceux-ci et on l'a mise en prison. Rien n'est plus conforme à l'esprit des lois romaines, ni plus contraire à l'humanité et à la raison éclairée',[21] conclut catégoriquement l'auteur. Partant, Du Pont s'inscrit, à l'instar de Voltaire,[22] Diderot,[23] Linguet[24] ou des révolutionnaires,[25] dans

---

20. 'Lettre de Du Pont à Charles-Louis de Bade, Paris, 15 janvier 1773', p.29-30.
21. 'Lettre de Du Pont à Charles-Louis de Bade, Paris, 15 janvier 1773', p.30.
22. Voir François Quastana, 'Du bon usage du droit romain: Voltaire et la réforme des législations civile et pénale', dans *Les Représentations du droit romain en Europe du Moyen Age aux Lumières* (Aix-en-Provence, 2007), p.203-31.
23. En 1776, Diderot écrit en ce sens: 'Notre Faculté de droit est misérable. On n'y lit pas un mot du droit français; pas plus du droit des gens que s'il n'y en avait point; rien de notre code ni civil ni criminel; rien de notre procédure, rien de nos lois, rien de nos coutumes, rien des constitutions de l'Etat [...] De quoi s'occupe-t-on donc? On s'occupe du droit romain dans toutes ses branches, droit qui n'a presque aucun rapport avec le nôtre; en sorte que celui qui vient d'être décoré du bonnet de docteur en droit est aussi empêché, si quelqu'un lui corrompt sa fille, lui enlève sa femme ou lui conteste son champ, que le dernier des citoyens'; 'Plan d'une université pour le gouvernement de Russie', dans *Œuvres complètes*, t.3 (Paris, 1875), p.409-551 (437). Sur la réception du droit romain par les encyclopédistes, voir Witold Wolodkiewicz, *Le Droit romain et l'Encyclopédie* (Naples, 1986).
24. Voir Stéphane Baudens, 'Linguet, critique du droit romain: un jurisconsulte iconoclaste au Palais', dans *Les Représentations du droit romain*, p.233-51.
25. Voir Xavier Martin, 'Images négatives de la Rome antique et du droit romain

la longue tradition des contempteurs du *jus romanum* que compte le dix-huitième siècle.[26]

Concrètement, cette loi sur la contrainte par corps est profondément inefficace car elle 'réduit le débiteur à l'état le plus triste, sans aucun profit et même avec perte pour le créancier, auquel elle enlève ordinairement jusqu'à l'espoir d'être payé jamais'.[27] En effet, comment le débiteur pourrait-il acquitter ses dettes dans l'oisiveté d'une prison? 'L'esclavage de cet homme est en pure perte, et pour lui-même, et pour ses créanciers, et pour la société entière',[28] assure le correspondant littéraire qui confond alors sans vergogne la contrainte par corps et l'esclavage pour dettes, c'est-à-dire la réduction en servitude du débiteur n'honorant pas ses obligations. Par conséquent, cette loi est 'non seulement une loi à ne pas faire, mais la plus éloignée des lois à faire pour assurer autant qu'il soit possible le payement des dettes'.[29]

En bon physiocrate, Du Pont avance aussi des arguments jusnaturalistes. L'édit royal est d'abord contraire au principe supérieur et naturel de la justice. 'Sœur de la bienfaisance', la justice 'ne punit que les coupables' et 'secourt les infortunés: et c'est à cela même qu'elle trouve du profit'.[30] Comment accepter dans ces conditions qu'une loi puisse enfermer un individu qui ne parvient pas, en toute bonne foi, à acquitter ses dettes? En ce sens, il rappelle dogmatiquement que, 'selon l'ordre naturel, *l'emprisonnement ne doit pas être prononcé contre le débiteur non frauduleux.*'[31] La contrainte par corps se révèle de la sorte entièrement contraire au droit naturel et précisément au triptyque 'liberté, propriété, sûreté' auquel tout législateur doit se plier pour

---

(1789-1814)', dans *Droit romain, jus civile, et droit français*, éd. Jacques Krynen (Toulouse, 1999), p.49-66.

26. Nous pouvons classiquement faire remonter cette tradition aux *Recherches de la France* (1560) d'Etienne Pasquier et à l'*Antitribonien* (1603) de François Hotman. Notons que l'opinion des physiocrates sur le droit romain est loin d'être unanime. Contrairement à Du Pont, Le Trosne estime que 'la source la plus pure où l'on puisse puiser' le droit civil et pénal 'est la collection qui nous reste des lois romaines. Si l'on en ôte ce qui s'y trouve de particulier aux mœurs de ce peuple, à sa forme de procéder, le surplus est tiré des vraies notions du juste et de l'injuste appliquées aux différentes actions que les hommes peuvent avoir et exercer'; *De l'ordre social*, dans *Les Lois naturelles de l'ordre social*, éd. T. Carvalho, p.187, n.81.

27. 'Lettre de Du Pont à Charles-Louis de Bade, Paris, 15 janvier 1773', p.30.

28. 'Lettre de Du Pont à Charles-Louis de Bade, Paris, 15 janvier 1773', p.30.

29. 'Lettre de Du Pont à Charles-Louis de Bade, Paris, 15 janvier 1773', p.28.

30. 'Lettre de Du Pont à Charles-Louis de Bade, Paris, 15 janvier 1773', p.31.

31. 'Lettre de Du Pont à Charles-Louis de Bade, Paris, 15 janvier 1773', p.28.

ne pas tomber dans l'arbitraire. Du Pont relie d'ailleurs intrinsè-
quement ces trois préceptes: 'Point de propriété, sans liberté; point
de liberté, sans sûreté.'[32] Dès lors, 'aucun prix ne saurait balancer
la liberté personnelle. Dans tout contrat, où l'un des stipulants
abandonnerait pour une somme déterminée sa propre personne que
la nature a rendu pour lui-même au-dessus de toute appréciation, il
y aurait toujours démence d'une part, séduction, abus de pouvoir et
tyrannie de l'autre; et par conséquent le contrat serait nul',[33] tranche le
disciple de Quesnay. Vingt ans plus tard, ce même raisonnement sera
précisément réutilisé par les conventionnels pour justifier l'abolition
de la contrainte par corps. Ainsi, lors de la séance du 9 mars 1793,
Danton énonce avec emphase à la tribune: 'Je demande que la
Convention nationale déclare que tout citoyen français, emprisonné
pour dettes, sera mis en liberté, parce qu'un tel emprisonnement
est contraire à la saine morale, aux droits de l'homme, aux vrais
principes de la liberté.'[34]

A la recherche d'un argument d'autorité, Du Pont s'appuie
également sur l'opinion de 'l'illustre et bon Marquis de Beccaria' qui
a 'très bien senti cette vérité' et 'a osé le dire dans les dernières éditions
de son excellent ouvrage'.[35] Effectivement, dans son fameux livre
Des délits et des peines (*Dei delitti e delle pene*) publié en 1764, Beccaria
distingue 'la faillite frauduleuse de la faillite innocente'.[36] La première
doit être punie avec la même rigueur que le faux-monnayage 'car
falsifier un morceau de métal gravé, qui est un gage des obligations
des citoyens, n'est pas un plus grand délit que falsifier ces obligations
mêmes'.[37] En revanche, la seconde, provoquée par la malchance ou la
malveillance d'autrui, ne saurait conduire le débiteur en prison et le
priver 'du seul et misérable bien qui lui reste, à savoir la liberté nue'.[38]
Du Pont reproche néanmoins à Beccaria de ne pas avoir justifié sa

---

32. Pierre-Samuel Du Pont de Nemours, *De l'origine et des progrès d'une science
nouvelle* (Londres et Paris, Desaint, 1768), p.28. Sur ces trois éminents principes
de la doctrine, voir A. Skornicki, 'Liberté, propriété, sûreté: retour sur une
devise physiocratique', *Corpus* 66 (2014), p.16-36.

33. 'Lettre de Du Pont à Charles-Louis de Bade, Paris, 15 janvier 1773', p.29.

34. Georges Jacques Danton, *Discours civiques de Danton*, éd. Hector Fleischmann
(Paris, 1920), p.56.

35. 'Lettre de Du Pont à Charles-Louis de Bade, Paris, 15 janvier 1773', p.28.

36. Cesare Beccaria, *Des délits et des peines*, éd. Philippe Audegean (Paris, 2009),
p.265.

37. C. Beccaria, *Des délits*, p.265.

38. C. Beccaria, *Des délits*, p.265.

position[39] et espère certainement que son travail permettra de combler cette lacune.

Enfin, le penseur tente d'anticiper la critique en réfléchissant à l'hypothèse d'un obligé de mauvaise foi, qui est justement la principale cible visée par le mécanisme de la contrainte par corps. Si un débiteur abuse de la clémence du droit 'pour se livrer à l'oisiveté ou pour dissiper ses gains en folles dépenses' sans jamais acquitter ses dettes, 'alors seulement il deviendra coupable'[40] et pourra être soumis à une peine, possiblement afflictive, mais qui ne doit jamais lui ôter sa liberté. La liberté est en effet l'unique moyen permettant au débiteur de travailler et de mettre un terme à son insolvabilité. Un endetté qui abuserait de cette liberté pourrait alors légitimement se trouver soumis à une inspection ou à une curatelle. Mais, par principe, 'aucune peine ne doit précéder le délit.'[41] Il faut donc attendre 'que sa conduite injuste et déraisonnable' ait démontré qu'il faille 'le regarder et le traiter comme une espèce de mineur'.[42]

En 1773, l'opinion de Du Pont en faveur de l'abolition de la contrainte par corps n'est reçue que par quelques prestigieux destinataires européens. Le texte n'est pas publié et demeurera à l'état de manuscrit jusqu'à la fin du dix-neuvième siècle. Pour sa part, l'édit royal continuera de s'appliquer jusque durant les premières années de la Révolution française, l'Assemblée nationale constituante sauvegardant implicitement le principe de la contrainte par corps au sein de son décret des 13-17 juin 1791 relatif pourtant à l'organisation du corps législatif.[43] Par la loi du 25 août 1792, la Législative supprime la contrainte par corps mais exclusivement pour le non-paiement des frais de nourrice. Les grands principes libéraux avancés pour justifier la mesure contrastent alors fortement avec sa portée extrêmement limitée.[44] Il faut finalement attendre le décret du 9 mars 1793 pour

---

39. 'Lettre de Du Pont à Charles-Louis de Bade, Paris, 15 janvier 1773', p.28: 'Il n'en a pas dit la raison.'
40. 'Lettre de Du Pont à Charles-Louis de Bade, Paris, 15 janvier 1773', p.31.
41. 'Lettre de Du Pont à Charles-Louis de Bade, Paris, 15 janvier 1773', p.31.
42. 'Lettre de Du Pont à Charles-Louis de Bade, Paris, 15 janvier 1773', p.31.
43. Art.54: 'En matière civile, toute contrainte légale pourra être exécutée sur les biens d'un représentant ou contre sa personne, tant que la contrainte par corps aura lieu, comme contre les autres citoyens'; *Recueil général des lois, décrets, ordonnances, etc., depuis le mois de juin 1789 jusqu'au mois d'août 1830*, 16 vol. (Paris, 1834-1837), t.2, p.210.
44. *Loi portant que la contrainte par corps ne pourra être exercée pour dettes de mois de nourrice, donnée à Paris, le 25 août 1792, l'An 4ᵉ de la liberté* (Paris, Imprimerie

Abolir la contrainte par corps

que la Convention nationale abolisse officiellement la contrainte par corps et libère les prisonniers pour dettes.[45] Le comité de législation est chargé de rendre un rapport sur les exceptions à apporter à cette extinction soudaine, notamment pour le fisc qui récupérera d'ailleurs l'usage de cette voie d'exécution à peine quelques jours plus tard.[46] Abrogée sans véritable discussion, la contrainte par corps va ressusciter sous le Directoire, au grand dam de Du Pont.

ii. Prévenir le rétablissement de la contrainte par corps: un combat officiel sous le Directoire

Après Thermidor, le souhait de revenir à l'ordre ancien se manifeste dans de multiples domaines, et de nombreuses voix affirment la nécessité d'offrir une meilleure garantie au commerce. Le 12 ventôse An V (2 mars 1797), une résolution du Conseil des Cinq-Cents propose l'abrogation du décret du 9 mars 1793 et le rétablissement de la contrainte par corps. Lorsque la résolution arrive au Conseil des Anciens, Du Pont, alors député du Loiret depuis octobre 1795, s'y oppose vigoureusement en évoquant les heures sombres de la Révolution: 'Je suis animé par l'indignation qu'inspire à tout ami de la liberté, le projet d'entraîner les conseils dans une marche rétrograde. [...] Je ne sais comment, après que nous avons été cinq cent mille en prison, il se trouve des hommes qui sont encore ragoûtés de la prison, et qui la proposent pour leurs concitoyens.'[47] Du Pont rattache ainsi la restauration de la contrainte par corps à la Terreur, ou du

---

nationale, 1792): 'L'Assemblée nationale considérant que chez un peuple libre, il ne doit exister de loi qui autorise la contrainte par corps, que lorsque les motifs les plus pressants le réclament; [...] L'Assemblée nationale, après avoir décrété l'urgence, décrète que la contrainte par corps ne pourra être exercée, à compter de ce jour, pour dettes de mois de nourrice.'

45. *Décret de la Convention nationale du 9 mars 1793, l'An second de la République française, qui donne l'élargissement des prisonniers détenus pour dettes, et qui abolit la contrainte par corps* (Paris, Imprimerie de Praut, 1793): 'La Convention nationale décrète que les prisonniers détenus pour dettes seront élargis, que la contrainte par corps est abolie; et charge son comité de législation de lui faire incessamment un rapport sur les exceptions.'

46. La loi du 30 mars 1793 rétablit la contrainte par corps pour les comptables des deniers de la République, les fournisseurs qui ont reçu des avances du Trésor public et les autres débiteurs directs de l'Etat.

47. 'Séance du Conseil des Anciens, du 18 ventôse An V', dans *La Législation civile, commerciale et criminelle de la France, par M. le baron Locré*, t.15 (Paris, 1828), p.463-70 (465-66).

moins à l'arbitraire qui la guidait, alors qu'il s'agit d'un héritage de l'Ancien Régime que la Convention n'avait pas rétabli. Ce 18 ventôse An v (8 mars 1797), Du Pont n'est toutefois, de son propre aveu, pas suffisamment préparé pour 'traiter avec la profondeur qu'elle mérite une question qui touche à la liberté'.[48]

C'est finalement six jours plus tard, lors de l'importante séance du 24 ventôse An v (14 mars 1797), que l'orateur expose méthodiquement ses arguments:

> Ne laissons plus revenir parmi nous les mœurs de l'esclavage, et gardons-nous de croire qu'ils puissent être favorables à aucune profession. [...] La peine spéciale que l'on propose contre les commerçants ne leur est pas appliquée une fois sur vingt pour leur propre faute, mais presque toujours pour de tristes évènements qui ne dépendaient pas d'eux, et dont ils sont les premiers à plaindre.[49]

Lecteur appliqué de Beccaria, Du Pont considère qu'il faut absolument distinguer l'escroquerie ou la banqueroute frauduleuse, qui constituent de véritables délits, de la faillite involontaire, dans laquelle le failli est sans reproche, et qui relève de la simple infortune. Les deux ne peuvent être sanctionnées par la même peine.[50] Fidèle aux grandes notions du droit pénal moderne, il poursuit: 'Songez, législateurs, que ce n'est point la grande sévérité des peines qui prévient et réprime les délits: c'est leur justice, et surtout leur *inévitabilité*, qui ne peut accompagner que les peines modérées, et dont l'équitable proportion avec les fautes se fait sentir d'elle-même.'[51] Par conséquent, Du Pont refuse de considérer la contrainte par corps comme une voie d'exécution. Il préfère sciemment se placer sur le terrain délictuel afin de mettre en évidence l'injustice de la mesure.

Revenir à l'ordre juridique ancien constitue une totale aberration. Jamais l'emprisonnement ne contribuera au paiement des dettes du débiteur insolvable.[52] Pis, en l'empêchant de travailler, la contrainte

---

48. 'Séance du Conseil des Anciens, du 18 ventôse An v', p.465.

49. P.-S. Du Pont de Nemours, *Opinion sur la contrainte par corps: s*éance du 24 ventôse An v [*14 mars 1797*] (Paris, Imprimerie nationale, germinal An v), p.4-5.

50. P.-S. Du Pont de Nemours, *Opinion sur la contrainte par corps*, p.5.

51. P.-S. Du Pont de Nemours, *Opinion sur la contrainte par corps*, p.10.

52. P.-S. Du Pont de Nemours, *Opinion sur la contrainte par corps*, p.11: 'La prison ne fait donc point payer le négociant lorsqu'il ne le peut. Elle ne saurait rien ajouter à ses efforts, il les a tous épuisés avant de faillir. Elle le déshonore et le torture en pure perte.'

Abolir la contrainte par corps 111

par corps 'lui ôte l'unique ressource qu'il pût avoir pour se tirer d'embarras et pour payer son créancier. Elle tue la poule qui aurait pondu des œufs d'or'.[53] Du Pont interroge alors les membres de la Chambre haute: 'Ne voyez-vous pas que le moyen est absurde; que la peine est absolument contraire à son objet; qu'elle s'oppose à votre désir qui est d'assurer autant qu'il soit possible le paiement de la dette?'[54] De plus, si la contrainte par corps ne peut pas faire payer celui qui n'en a pas le moyen, 'elle ne peut pas davantage faire payer celui qui, en ayant le moyen, n'en a pas la volonté.'[55] En effet, ce dernier maîtrise les échéances et, 'quand l'époque fatale approche, il sait fort bien augmenter ses dettes et disparaître, laissant à ses créanciers la vaine ressource de poursuivre un nom dont l'honneur est perdu, et qu'il changera lui-même en pays étranger.'[56] Quelle que soit la situation, la contrainte par corps se révèle ainsi foncièrement inefficace.

Tout comme dans sa lettre de 1773, Du Pont s'appuie sur un épisode de l'histoire juridique romaine en évoquant brièvement le nom de 'Lucius Papirius'.[57] Ce créancier patricien est demeuré tristement célèbre pour sa cruelle maltraitance du jeune Caïus Publius, qui travaillait à son service comme esclave pour acquitter les dettes de son père. Violenté et blessé sous les coups de son maître, il parvint à s'échapper et se plaignit dans tout Rome de la cruauté du créancier. Cet événement indigna profondément le peuple et le Sénat, dont la réaction législative fut immédiate. Sans abolir la contrainte par corps, la loi *Poetelia Papiria* de 326 avant J.-C. améliora considérablement la situation des débiteurs en adoucissant la loi des Douze Tables. Ils étaient désormais libérés à condition qu'ils prêtent serment d'abandonner leurs biens au créancier. De plus, la loi interdit de placer *in futurum* le corps du débiteur en servitude, ce qui transforma le régime des dettes.[58] A la tribune, Du Pont présente la contrainte par corps comme 'plus cruelle et plus absurde' que l'esclavage pour dettes: 'L'esclavage des Romains appropriait le travail du débiteur au profit du créancier. Du moins, puisqu'il y avait travail, tout n'était pas perdu pour celui qui en recueillait le fruit, ni pour la société: tout travail

53. P.-S. Du Pont de Nemours, *Opinion sur la contrainte par corps*, p.11.
54. P.-S. Du Pont de Nemours, *Opinion sur la contrainte par corps*, p.12.
55. P.-S. Du Pont de Nemours, *Opinion sur la contrainte par corps*, p.12.
56. P.-S. Du Pont de Nemours, *Opinion sur la contrainte par corps*, p.12.
57. P.-S. Du Pont de Nemours, *Opinion sur la contrainte par corps*, p.17.
58. Sur cette importante réforme, voir André Magdelain, 'La loi *Poetelia papiria* et la loi *Iulia de pecuniis mutuis*', dans *Jus imperium auctoritas: études de droit romain* (Rome, 1990), p.707-11.

112 *Thérence Carvalho*

est utile.'[59] Cette fois, le droit romain n'est donc pas entièrement condamné. Son évolution doit inspirer clémence et humanité aux législateurs de la République thermidorienne.

L'argumentation du député se fonde aussi largement sur des illustrations de droit comparé. Il évoque tour à tour le cas de l'Angleterre,[60] de la Hollande,[61] de Venise,[62] du Portugal[63] et de l'Espagne[64] afin de prouver que la résolution des Cinq-Cents conduirait à une législation 'plus rigoureuse que chez toutes les autres nations'.[65] Dans ces grands pays européens, connus pour leur vitalité en matière commerciale, le débiteur parvient le plus souvent à éviter la prison. Il ne peut être arrêté au sein de son domicile ou en pleine nuit. Or, abroger le décret du 9 mars 1793 reviendrait à rétablir l'édit royal de 1773, tant vilipendé par Du Pont dans sa correspondance littéraire et politique: 'L'ancien gouvernement qui respectait peu les domiciles, avait, depuis quelques années, établi l'usage barbare d'arrêter le débiteur chez lui, même pendant la nuit, par *des officiers du commerce*. C'était la plus odieuse violation de la liberté civile; et dans l'Europe entière, [...] cette atrocité n'avait lieu qu'en France.'[66] Le retour à l'ordre ancien conduirait dès lors la grande Nation à posséder la législation la plus cruelle et la plus sévère de tous ses voisins européens. Les Conseils, qui d'après la formule de Boissy d'Anglas sont censés incarner 'l'imagination' et 'la raison' de la République,[67] feraient donc mieux de s'inspirer des droits des Etats qui ne connaissent pas la contrainte par corps, à l'instar du Portugal qui jouit pour autant d'un commerce florissant.[68]

---

59. P.-S. Du Pont de Nemours, *Opinion sur la contrainte par corps*, p.17.
60. P.-S. Du Pont de Nemours, *Opinion sur la contrainte par corps*, p.19-20.
61. P.-S. Du Pont de Nemours, *Opinion sur la contrainte par corps*, p.19.
62. P.-S. Du Pont de Nemours, *Opinion sur la contrainte par corps*, p.20.
63. P.-S. Du Pont de Nemours, *Opinion sur la contrainte par corps*, p.21.
64. P.-S. Du Pont de Nemours, *Opinion sur la contrainte par corps*, p.22.
65. P.-S. Du Pont de Nemours, *Opinion sur la contrainte par corps*, p.29.
66. P.-S. Du Pont de Nemours, *Opinion sur la contrainte par corps*, p.20.
67. *Projet de constitution pour la République française, et discours préliminaire prononcé par Boissy d'Anglas, au nom de la Commission des Onze, dans la séance du 5 messidor An III* (Paris, Imprimerie de la République, messidor An III), p.41-42: 'Le Conseil des Cinq-Cents étant composé de membres plus jeunes, proposera les décrets qu'il croira utiles; il sera la pensée, et, pour ainsi dire, l'imagination de la République; le Conseil des Anciens en sera la raison: il n'aura d'autre emploi que d'examiner avec sagesse quelles seront les lois à admettre ou les lois à rejeter, sans pouvoir en proposer jamais.'
68. P.-S. Du Pont de Nemours, *Opinion sur la contrainte par corps*, p.21: 'On ignore

Abolir la contrainte par corps   113

A la Chambre haute, Du Pont doit répondre à de remarquables contradicteurs tels que Jean-Denis Lanjuinais, François Denis Tronchet et surtout Jean-Etienne-Marie Portalis. Ces trois éminents jurisconsultes prennent fermement position pour le rétablissement de la législation antérieure. D'après Lanjuinais, 'la contrainte par corps s'est introduite avec le commerce même. Dès le treizième siècle, il existait des villes qu'on appelait d'*arrêt*: l'usage a été ensuite transformé en statuts.'[69] Outre cet argument historique, le professeur de droit rennais jette le discrédit sur les circonstances de son abolition en 1793: 'C'est *Danton* qui l'a fait supprimer, après un discours de quelques minutes, appuyé par des tribunes armées; et à quelle séance fut porté ce décret qui ruina le commerce? dans la séance où l'on établit le tribunal révolutionnaire.'[70] Pour Tronchet, la liberté politique et civile 'ne consiste pas dans le droit de n'être jamais incarcéré'.[71] La contrainte par corps est aujourd'hui devenue une nécessité car de nombreux 'débiteurs de mauvaise foi parviennent à cacher leur fortune. La crainte de la contrainte la leur fera employer à satisfaire leurs créanciers'.[72] L'ancien avocat au Parlement de Paris défend ainsi la traditionnelle idée d'un paiement obtenu au moyen d'une forte pression psychologique exercée sur le débiteur pour le contraindre à exécuter volontairement sa propre dette. Il précise néanmoins: 'Qu'on se rassure; peu de créanciers sont disposés à retenir dans une prison inutilement, et à leurs frais, un débiteur qui par son travail pourrait arriver à les payer.'[73]

Pareillement, Portalis affirme que la contrainte par corps 'ne blesse en rien la liberté' puisqu'elle ne constitue qu'un simple 'moyen de

---

qu'en *Portugal* la contrainte par corps n'a pas lieu; que les Portugais ne sont pas une nation plus morale que les Français, tant s'en faut; que les Anglais chez qui la contrainte par corps est cependant plus rigoureuse que partout ailleurs, confient néanmoins, tous les ans, pour *cent vingt millions* de marchandises aux Portugais.'

69. 'Séance du Conseil des Anciens, du 18 ventôse An v', p.468-69. Sur Lanjuinais, voir l'article de Yann-Arzel Durelle-Marc, 'Jean-Denis Lanjuinais, juriste et parlementaire (1753-1827): une biographie politique', *Parlement[s]: revue d'histoire politique* 11:1 (2009), p.8-24.

70. 'Séance du Conseil des Anciens, du 18 ventôse An v', p.469.

71. 'Séance du Conseil des Anciens, du 18 ventôse An v', p.467. Concernant la vie et les idées de Tronchet, voir Philippe Tessier, *François Denis Tronchet, ou la Révolution par le droit* (Paris, 2016).

72. 'Séance du Conseil des Anciens, du 18 ventôse An v', p.468.

73. 'Séance du Conseil des Anciens, du 18 ventôse An v', p.468.

coaction pour forcer un débiteur de remplir ses engagements'.[74] Lors de la séance du 24 ventôse An V, le futur corédacteur du Code civil défend ardemment cette sage mesure éprouvée par l'expérience des temps anciens. Selon lui, 'il importe de lier le passé au présent et à l'avenir', et ce n'est pas parce qu'"une telle institution existait autrefois' qu'"il faut la proscrire'.[75] Il interpelle alors les Anciens: 'Le peuple français vous demande des lois sévères contre la mauvaise foi; profitons de cette heureuse disposition.'[76] Du Pont reproche à 'l'admirable discours de *Portalis*' l'idée selon laquelle '*l'exactitude dans le paiement des effets de commerce est d'une si haute utilité, que les lois ne doivent pas craindre de lui sacrifier même les sentiments de la compassion, même la liberté des citoyens*.'[77] Tandis que l'illustre jurisconsulte provençal avance qu'il faut une garantie plus forte pour les engagements de commerce, Du Pont s'appuie sur l'état du droit existant pour lui rétorquer: 'Eh bien! La chose existe dans nos lois, sans contrainte par corps. [...] La *garantie*, c'est le droit de saisir et de prendre, et de vendre tous les biens meubles et immeubles de celui qui n'a pas payé son billet, un seul de ses billets, au jour promis.'[78] Il n'y a que cette solide voie d'exécution qui soit véritablement utile, la contrainte par corps n'apportera, à l'inverse, que souffrance, humiliation et défaut de paiement.

Se dérobant dans des divagations chimériques, l'ancien physiocrate invoque des règles juridiques supérieures et immanentes: 'Il n'y a que Dieu et la nature qui sachent doser, soit les récompenses, soit les peines. Etudions leurs lois irréfragables, et ne les violons pas: faisons-en la base des nôtres.'[79] Lorsqu'il revient à des considérations plus tangibles, Du Pont conteste le manque de précisions concernant l'applicabilité de la loi: 'On prétend que ce n'est qu'*un principe* qu'on veut vous faire adopter aujourd'hui. Non point, mes collègues, ce

---

74. 'Séance du Conseil des Anciens, du 23 ventôse An V', dans *La Législation civile*, p.484-94 (491). Sur Portalis et ses positions, voir Jean-Luc A. Chartier, *Portalis, père du Code civil* (Paris, 2004); Joël-Benoît d'Onorio, *Portalis: l'esprit des siècles* (Paris, 2005); Marceau Long et Jean-Claude Monier, *Portalis: l'esprit de justice* (Paris, 1997).

75. Jean-Etienne-Marie Portalis, *Opinion sur la contrainte par corps: s*éance du 24 ventôse An V [*14 mars 1797*] (Paris, Imprimerie nationale, germinal An V), p.7.

76. J.-E.-M. Portalis, *Opinion sur la contrainte par corps*, p.22. Du Pont (*Opinion sur la contrainte par corps*, p.11) lui répond de la manière suivante: 'Faites des lois, *faites-les dures*, disait Portalis, *parce que vous êtes libres* (ce qui pour un orateur de son mérite, est un beau contre-sens, encore que *Montesquieu* soit derrière).'

77. P.-S. Du Pont de Nemours, *Opinion sur la contrainte par corps*, p.2.

78. P.-S. Du Pont de Nemours, *Opinion sur la contrainte par corps*, p.8-9.

79. P.-S. Du Pont de Nemours, *Opinion sur la contrainte par corps*, p.11.

Abolir la contrainte par corps

n'est pas seulement *un principe*; ce sont une multitude de lois positives dans l'énoncé vague d'une loi.'[80] En effet, la simple abrogation du décret de mars 1793 remettra 'en activité cinquante lois différentes'.[81] 'Comment de grands jurisconsultes, tels que ceux auxquels je réponds, ne voient-ils pas le danger de décréter législativement *des principes?*'[82]

L'orateur souligne, en outre, une dangereuse absence de cohérence dans la hiérarchie normative. A agir de la sorte,

> on regarderait comme fondamentales les lois décrétées en principe; comme réglementaires, les lois d'exécution. On ferait des lois *en principe*, une classe intermédiaire entre les lois constitutionnelles et les autres lois. Que le Conseil des Anciens ne mette pas le pied sur cette glu de prétendus principes. Tous les principes de nos lois sont et doivent être uniquement dans la déclaration des droits et des devoirs, et dans la constitution.[83]

Or, 'la déclaration des droits et des devoirs, et la constitution, sont rationnellement et textuellement contraires à la contrainte par corps.'[84] Effectivement, l'article 15 de la déclaration de 1795 dispose clairement: 'Tout homme peut engager son temps et ses services; mais il ne peut se vendre ni être vendu; sa personne n'est pas une propriété aliénable.'[85] De même, l'article 352 de la constitution du 5 fructidor An III affirme que la loi ne reconnaît 'aucun engagement contraire aux droits naturels de l'homme'.[86] Du Pont soulève ainsi, à juste titre, un réel problème d'inconstitutionnalité de la résolution. Sans exercer expressément un contrôle de constitutionnalité des lois, le Conseil des Anciens dispose d'un droit de veto absolu et doit, d'après l'article 88 de la constitution, refuser d'approuver 'les résolutions du Conseil des Cinq-Cents qui n'ont point été prises dans les formes prescrites par

---

80. P.-S. Du Pont de Nemours, *Opinion sur la contrainte par corps*, p.28.
81. P.-S. Du Pont de Nemours, *Opinion sur la contrainte par corps*, p.28.
82. P.-S. Du Pont de Nemours, *Opinion sur la contrainte par corps*, p.28-29. L'orateur considère ainsi que 'dans un seul article de loi, on vous fait prononcer et remettre en activité cinquante lois différentes' (p.28).
83. P.-S. Du Pont de Nemours, *Opinion sur la contrainte par corps*, p.29.
84. P.-S. Du Pont de Nemours, *Opinion sur la contrainte par corps*, p.29.
85. 'Déclaration des droits et des devoirs de l'homme et du citoyen', dans Jacques Godechot et Hervé Faupin, *Les Constitutions de la France depuis 1789* (Paris, 2006), p.102.
86. 'Constitution du 5 fructidor An III', dans J. Godechot et H. Faupin, *Les Constitutions de la France*, p.139.

la constitution'.[87] Le député exerce au fond pleinement sa mission en invoquant tous les arguments juridiques possibles afin d'empêcher l'adoption de la mesure.

En dépit des efforts de Du Pont, le Conseil des Anciens approuve en urgence et à une faible majorité la résolution, qui devient la loi du 24 ventôse An V. Le décret du 9 mars 1793 est abrogé, et le principe du rétablissement de la contrainte par corps est posé. Comme le craignait l'ancien physiocrate, la mise en application de cette législation évasive se révèle particulièrement laborieuse. Un an plus tard, une réorganisation complète du système s'impose. Ce sera la loi du 15 germinal An VI (4 avril 1798), qui encadre précisément le régime de la contrainte par corps en matière civile et commerciale. Conformément à l'ancien droit, elle ne peut être prononcée que dans les cas formellement prévus par la loi.[88] Toute stipulation dans un contrat en dehors de ces cas répute la clause non écrite.[89] La contrainte par corps doit également être ordonnée par le juge, qui, contrairement cette fois à l'ancien droit, perd toute liberté de choix. Enfin, la détention ne peut pas excéder cinq années.[90] Les principales dispositions seront reprises, avec quelques modifications, par les codificateurs napoléoniens aux articles 2059 à 2070 du Code civil. Arrêté neuf mois avant l'adoption de la loi, lors du coup d'Etat du 18 fructidor An V (4 septembre 1797), Du Pont, désormais suspecté de royalisme, ne sera finalement pas parvenu à faire entendre sa voix pour s'opposer à la réintroduction pleine et entière de cette singulière voie d'exécution.

***

Que ce soit sous l'Ancien Régime ou sous le Directoire, Du Pont nous offre, au sujet de la contrainte par corps, le visage d'un véritable jurisconsulte qui n'hésite pas à porter directement la contradiction à des grandes figures de la science juridique, telles que Lanjuinais, Tronchet ou Portalis. Après avoir échappé *in extremis* à la déportation, l'ancien député ne se juge plus en sûreté en France et part pour les Etats-Unis en septembre 1799. Il ne reviendra en France qu'en 1802

---

87. 'Constitution du 5 fructidor An III', p.112.
88. 'Loi du 15 germinal An VI', dans J. Godechot et H. Faupin, *Les Constitutions de la France*, p.501, tit.1, art.1.
89. 'Loi du 15 germinal An VI', p.501, tit.1, art.2.
90. 'Loi du 15 germinal An VI', p.508, tit.3, art.18, 6°.

sous le Consulat. Il faudra finalement attendre près de soixante-dix ans pour que ses conceptions libérales et humanistes triomphent enfin dans le droit civil français puisqu'il revient à la loi du 22 juillet 1867 d'abolir définitivement la contrainte par corps en matière civile et commerciale. Désireux de faciliter la croissance entrepreneuriale et le recours au crédit, le gouvernement de Napoléon III s'inscrit alors dans une logique d'assouplissement de la législation commerciale et même de dépénalisation du droit des entreprises en difficulté.[91] Le long combat mené par Du Pont apparaît dès lors comme précurseur. Animé par une fine compréhension des mutations économiques à l'œuvre, il se fonde sur la liberté individuelle, chère aux philosophes économistes du dix-huitième siècle, pour jeter les fondements qui permettront au capitalisme libéral du dix-neuvième siècle de prendre son essor.

---

91. Voir Nadine Levratto, 'Abolition de la contrainte par corps et évolution du capitalisme au XIX⁰ siècle', *Economie et institutions* 10-11 (2007), p.221-49.

III

A political thinker challenged by
the Revolution and the Republic |
Un penseur politique à l'épreuve de la
Révolution et de la République

Politique et économie politique chez Pierre-Samuel Du Pont: les annotations au *Contrat social* de Jean-Jacques Rousseau

THIERRY DEMALS

Université de Lille

ALEXANDRA HYARD

Université de Lille

Pierre-Samuel Du Pont (1739-1817) fut un économiste, au sens du dix-huitième siècle et au sens actuel, qui occupa différentes fonctions politiques sous l'Ancien Régime, la Révolution française et l'Empire napoléonien. Ce serviteur de l'Etat fut également un grand lecteur d'ouvrages de philosophie politique comme l'indique le catalogue de sa bibliothèque conservé à l'Eleutherian Mills Historical Library (Hagley Museum and Library), dépositaire des archives de la famille

---

Univ. Lille, CNRS, UMR 8019 – CLERSÉ – Centre lillois d'études et de recherches sociologiques et économiques, F-59000 Lille, France. Les auteurs remercient chaleureusement le Hagley Museum and Library (Wilmington, Delaware, USA) pour avoir financé cette recherche par l'octroi d'une bourse et facilité l'accès aux manuscrits de Pierre-Samuel Du Pont (DPDN Papers). Les auteurs tiennent à remercier Lucas Clawson pour sa précieuse aide matérielle. Une première version de cet article a été présentée au Research Seminar du Hagley Museum and Library, organisé par le responsable du Center for History of Business, Technology and Society, Roger Horowitz, le 15 mai 2018. Les auteurs remercient également l'ensemble des participants du séminaire ainsi que Anthony Mergey, Arnault Skornicki et le rapporteur anonyme pour leurs remarques suggestives. Ils demeurent néanmoins seuls responsables des éventuelles erreurs contenues dans cet article.

Du Pont.[1] Cette bibliothèque possède une pièce rare: un exemplaire du *Contrat social* (1762) de Jean-Jacques Rousseau (1712-1778) ayant appartenu à Du Pont et annoté de sa main. Ce sont les annotations laissées sur cet exemplaire qui fourniront la trame de cet article. Celles-ci portent sur le livre 1 du *Contrat social*, intitulé 'Où l'on recherche comment l'homme passe de l'état de nature à l'état civil, & quelles sont les conditions essencielles du pacte' et plus sommairement sur le livre 4 d'*Emile*.

Ces annotations firent l'objet d'un commentaire de la part de Jean A. Perkins dans son article intitulé 'Rousseau jugé par Du Pont de Nemours' au cours des années 1970.[2] Perkins y développait plusieurs idées: premièrement, elle présentait Rousseau comme 'l'un des mentors' (p.173) du jeune Du Pont; deuxièmement, elle insistait sur la proximité des annotations de Du Pont avec les grands écrits physiocratiques, y compris son propre ouvrage, *De l'origine et des progrès d'une science nouvelle*, paru en 1767 et considéré comme un résumé de l'ouvrage de Paul-Pierre Le Mercier de La Rivière (1719-1801), *L'Ordre naturel et essentiel des sociétés politiques* (1767); troisièmement, elle proposait de dater ces annotations en deux temps sur la base d'une analyse graphologique. Selon elle, les notes en marge des chapitres 1 à 4, d'une écriture très petite et resserrée, correspondaient aux années 1760-1770; celles en marge des chapitres 5 à 9, d'une écriture beaucoup plus large, étaient caractéristiques des années 1790.

Dans cette contribution, nous ne chercherons pas à discuter ce troisième point hors de notre compétence. Nous nous concentrerons sur les deux premiers: celui de savoir si l'on peut considérer Rousseau comme 'l'un des mentors' de Du Pont, et celui de savoir si les notes de Du Pont sont l'œuvre d'un physiocrate attitré.[3] Pour cela, nous procéderons en trois temps: d'abord le repérage des références à Rousseau dans les écrits de Du Pont consacrés au droit naturel; ensuite, la reproduction des annotations; troisièmement, l'examen de ces annotations.

---

1. *Liste des ouvrages de M. Du Pont*, Hagley Museum and Library (dorénavant HML), Longwood Manuscripts, L1-467, et *Liste des livres*, HML, Winterthur Manuscripts, W2-5131.
2. Voir Jean A. Perkins, 'Rousseau jugé par Du Pont de Nemours', *Annales de la Société Jean-Jacques Rousseau* 39 (1972-1977), p.171-96.
3. Dans son ouvrage *L'Economiste, la cour et la patrie: l'économie politique dans la France des Lumières* (Paris, 2011), p.194, Arnault Skornicki estime que 'Du Pont de Nemours reconsidère la physiocratie à l'aune de son opposition à Rousseau.'

i. Du Pont, Rousseau et le droit naturel

Ce que l'on connaît généralement de la relation entre les 'Economistes' et Rousseau réside en grande partie dans la correspondance entre le marquis de Mirabeau (1715-1789) et le Genevois tenue entre octobre 1766 et novembre 1767 (en particulier les lettres du 28 et du 30 juillet 1767), qui se clôt par un rejet du second de la doctrine politique des premiers, et une incompréhension manifeste de part et d'autre.[4]

Avant sa rencontre avec le marquis, Rousseau ne semble pas être un lecteur averti de la littérature physiocratique. On lui connaît une courte note manuscrite réduite à trois paragraphes tirés du premier chapitre de *Théorie de l'impôt* paru en 1760.[5] Il dit avoir emporté dans sa malle des écrits du marquis qu'il ne précise pas et deux traités de botanique (lettre du 31 janvier 1767). Rousseau étant devenu client du marquis, celui-ci l'abreuve d'ouvrages physiocratiques, bien entendu *Philosophie rurale* (1763), mais aussi *L'Ordre naturel et essentiel des sociétés politiques* de Le Mercier de La Rivière, les six premiers tomes des *Ephémérides du citoyen* et une brochure de l'abbé Nicolas Baudeau (1730-1792), *Exposition de la loi naturelle* (1767), repris dans les *Ephémérides* de 1767 (t.3, p.88-106), 'Du faste public et privé. Vrais principes du droit naturel'. Il lit quelques chapitres de ces ouvrages, les survole et n'en termine jamais la lecture. De son côté, Mirabeau lui fait part qu'il l'a beaucoup lu, qu'il lit actuellement *Julie, ou la Nouvelle Héloïse* (1761), mais il lâche cette phrase ambiguë: 'Je ne parle pas de vos ouvrages de politique, dont je ne serai pas bon juge' (lettre du 27 octobre 1766). Dans sa lettre du 26 juillet 1767, Rousseau lui adresse d'âpres critiques concernant la notion d'évidence, base sur laquelle les Economistes assoient la notion d'ordre naturel; le caractère abstrait, théorique, applicable universellement sans tenir compte des circonstances et des exceptions, de leur système, et donc la supposition d'un ordre connaissable par la raison à mesure de son perfectionnement et de la neutralisation des passions; la référence à une forme de

---

4. Voir J.-J. Rousseau, *Correspondance générale de J.-J. Rousseau, collationnée sur les originaux, annotés et commentés par T. Dufour*, t.16 et 17 (Paris, respectivement 1931 et 1932).

5. Rousseau résume les pages 1 à 10 de l'ouvrage de Mirabeau. Il paraphrase notamment ce passage: 'Tout le secret donc de la finance est que le peuple paye le plus qu'il est possible, & qu'il pense payer le moins.' Voir Gérard Namer, 'Mirabeau et Rousseau: réflexions sur un texte inédit'; Jean Fabre, 'Mirabeau, interlocuteur et protecteur de Rousseau', dans *Les Mirabeau et leur temps* (Paris, 1968), respectivement p.67-70 et p.71-90.

despotisme, légal et de surcroît héréditaire, qui serait compatible avec la liberté des individus; enfin le 'principe de population' qui est 'impossible à concilier avec l'origine des nations', c'est-à-dire l'idée que le rapport de la population aux subsistances (la 'population multiplicative') qui pousse les hommes à cultiver les mène vers les sociétés politiques.[6]

A n'en pas douter ces critiques de Rousseau sont tirées de sa lecture cursive de l'ouvrage de Le Mercier de La Rivière. C'est en effet cet ouvrage, plus que tout autre écrit physiocratique sur le droit naturel et l'origine des sociétés politiques, qui, dès sa parution, est considéré comme la bible politique de la physiocratie. C'est cet ouvrage que les commentateurs ultérieurs enquêtant sur la relation entre Rousseau et la physiocratie ont comparé au *Contrat social*.[7]

Du Pont annote les neufs chapitres du livre 1 du *Contrat social*, laissant sans commentaires les livres 2, 3 et 4. Ces chapitres traitent du premier état de l'humanité, appelé par 'état primitif' ou 'état de nature', ainsi que du pacte social, acte fondateur du second état de l'humanité, l'état civil ou politique. Ses annotations, postérieures à avril 1762, date de parution de l'ouvrage, sont nourries de la lecture et de la relecture du *Discours sur l'origine et les fondements de l'inégalité parmi les hommes* (1755), comme il l'explique dans son autobiographie écrite en 1792,[8] qui porte sur ces mêmes thèmes du premier état et du pacte fondateur. Les livres laissés sans notes concernent davantage le second état politique (souveraineté, gouvernement, volonté générale, formes de gouvernement, etc.).

On ne sait pas quand ces notes ont été rédigées, si elles l'ont été avant ou après sa conversion à la physiocratie en 1763. Avant cette date, on connaît peu, voire pas, d'écrits imprimés de Du Pont. Son biographe Ambrose Saricks, sur la foi de son autobiographie, mentionne deux plans pour la prise de Gibraltar antérieurs à février 1763, date du traité de Paris qui met fin au conflit avec la Grande-Bretagne, et un mémoire adressé au ministre Choiseul (1719-1785) dont on n'a pas trouvé de trace.[9]

6. Voir Céline Spector, *Rousseau et la critique de l'économie politique* (Bordeaux, 2017).
7. Voir par exemple Reinhard Bach, 'Rousseau et les physiocrates: une cohabitation contradictoire', *Etudes Jean-Jacques Rousseau* 11 (2000), p.9-82.
8. P.-S. Du Pont, *Mémoires de Pierre Samuel Du Pont de Nemours adressés à ses enfans, le 4 septembre 1792*, HML, Winterthur Manuscripts, W2-4796.
9. P.-S. Du Pont, *Mémoires*, chap.11, p.12-17. Ambrose Saricks, *Pierre Samuel Du Pont de Nemours* (Lawrence, KS, 1965), p.18.

Du Pont publie anonymement un premier ouvrage en juillet 1763, *Réflexions sur l'écrit intitulé: Richesse de l'Etat.*[10] L'écrit en question, paru en mai de la même année sous la plume de l'auteur Roussel de La Tour (1710?-1788?), conseiller au Parlement de Paris, proposait un impôt direct unique (la capitation) remplaçant les impôts existants et l'établissement de nouvelles classes de contribuables soumis à un impôt progressif sur la fortune. Guère polémiques, les *Réflexions* objectent simplement que Roussel de La Tour surestime le nombre des contribuables. On ne trouve dans cet ouvrage aucune référence à la *Théorie de l'impôt* de Mirabeau parue en 1760, pas plus que l'idée d'un impôt territorial assis sur le produit net de l'agriculture. Le vocabulaire physiocratique est absent. On note toutefois les expressions 'petite culture' et 'grande culture', mais Du Pont ne les tire pas de Quesnay ou de Mirabeau puisqu'il avoue n'avoir lu à cette date aucun de leurs écrits. Dans ses *Mémoires* (chap.12, f.34), il précise en effet qu'il lit 'd'après le conseil que me donnèrent les lettres de Mirabeau, les articles *Fermiers* et *Grains* de l'*Encyclopédie*', c'est-à-dire au second semestre 1763. Quant à *L'Ami des hommes* (1756) et la *Théorie de l'impôt*, c'est l'intendant de Soissons Charles-Blaise Méliand (1703-1768) qui les lui donne à lire et le met en contact avec Mirabeau.

Le second ouvrage de Du Pont, *Réponse demandée par Monsieur le marquis de M****, paraît en août 1763. Dans ses *Mémoires*, Du Pont précise qu'à cette époque il n'avait jamais lu d'ouvrage de Mirabeau: 'J'ignorais qu'il y eut un autre Mirabeau que le traducteur de l'Arioste.[11] Le bon intendant [Méliand] qui s'affectionnait à moi, me donna sur le champ *L'ami des hommes* et la *Théorie de l'impôt*! Je les dévorai, ne pouvant contenir le plaisir que je ressentais de me trouver dans la bonne route.'[12] Du Pont lit *L'Ami des hommes* et prend contact avec Mirabeau: 'Je me trouvais si heureux d'avoir quelques idées communes. Je lui demandai de vouloir bien continuer d'aider à mon instruction. Il m'avait appris que *la subsistance est la mesure de la population*: c'est la seule vérité qui lui soit entièrement propre.' Voici comment il présente quelques décennies plus tard cet ouvrage:

10. [P.-S. Du Pont], *Réflexions sur l'écrit intitulé: Richesse de l'Etat* (Londres, s.n., 1763).
11. Il s'agit probablement de Jean-Baptiste de Mirabaud (1675-1760), formé chez les Oratoriens, élu à l'Académie française en 1726 et secrétaire perpétuel de 1742 à 1755. Voir *Roland furieux, poème héroïque de l'Arioste, traduction nouvelle par M**** (La Haye, P. Gosse, 1741).
12. P.-S. Du Pont, *Mémoires*, chap.12, f.32.

Je lui [Mirabeau] fis promptement passer une seconde brochure qui se sentait des lumières nouvelles que j'avais puisées dans ses écrits. C'était une *Réplique* à un soi-disant *Marquis de M.* qui m'avait fait l'honneur de critiquer ma première production en tâchant d'établir que les Commerçants et les Artisans sont contribuables, et que les impôts dont on charge le commerce sont les meilleurs: système des *Colbertistes*, qui ne peut pas soutenir l'examen, et que je combattis avec une supériorité décidée quoique je fusse encore bien novice dans la carrière.[13]

L'écrit est composé de deux parties. La première partie est une continuation de la discussion sur l'imposition directe et sur le nombre de contribuables réels. La seconde partie roule sur le commerce extérieur et les droits de douane, probablement sous l'influence de Mirabeau. Cette seconde partie, plus générale et fouillée, contient une critique des droits de sortie et d'entrée considérés comme nuisibles aux intérêts de la nation. Du Pont dresse une critique en trois points de ce qu'il appelle les 'Colbertistes' dans ses *Mémoires*: la 'Confusion de l'intérêt du Commerce des Nationaux avec celui du commerce de la Nation';[14] la 'Persuasion que l'on peut vendre toujours, & n'acheter jamais';[15] et 'l'idée de richesse attachée à l'argent qui n'en est que le signe représentatif'.[16]

La seconde partie, qui ne traite pas d'impôt direct mais de droits de douane, est beaucoup plus générale. La question soulevée est celle de la liberté du commerce extérieur, qui amène une critique des principes de la science du commerce indiqués ci-dessus. Cette seconde partie contient davantage de thèmes physiocratiques (la primauté de l'agriculture 'mère du commerce', les voituriers classe dépendante de l'agriculture, la liberté de commerce), mais pas encore le vocabulaire physiocratique. Aucun nom d'auteur, aucun titre n'est cité.

Au cours de l'année 1764, Du Pont publie deux ouvrages, *De l'exportation et de l'importation des grains* et *Lettre sur la différence qui se trouve entre la grande et la petite culture*, qui contiennent manifestement à la fois les éléments de la doctrine et le vocabulaire: 'Reprises', 'avances annuelles', 'richesses d'exploitation', 'intérêts des premiers

---

13. P.-S. Du Pont, *Mémoires*, chap.12, f.32. Sauf indication contraire, les citations reproduisent l'emploi de l'italique des sources citées.
14. P.-S. Du Pont, *Réponse demandée par Monsieur le marquis de M*** à celle qu'il a faite aux Réflexions sur l'écrit intitulé: Richesse de l'Etat* (Londres, s.n., 1763), p.14-15.
15. P.-S. Du Pont, *Réponse*, p.15.
16. P.-S. Du Pont, *Réponse*, p.15.

fonds', 'produit net', 'classe productive', 'classe stérile', 'propriétaires du revenu ou produit net', 'prix commun du marché général', 'prix commun fondamental'. Sont mentionnés le *Tableau économique*, les articles 'Fermiers' et 'Grains', *L'Ami des hommes, Philosophie rurale*. De même note-t-on des références aux agronomes Henri Louis Duhamel Du Monceau (1700-1782) et Henri Patullo (?-1784).

En novembre 1767, Du Pont édite une compilation d'articles récents de Quesnay sous le titre de *Physiocratie, ou Constitution naturelle du gouvernement le plus avantageux au genre humain* qu'il préface d'un long 'Discours de l'éditeur'.[17] Ce 'Discours' est concomitant d'un certain nombre de travaux visant à préciser la philosophie qui sous-tend les écrits des Economistes et à les arrimer à une philosophie du droit naturel. Il reproduit notamment en tête de sommaire l'article 'Droit naturel' de Quesnay paru une première fois sous le titre 'Observations sur le droit naturel des hommes réunis en société' dans le *Journal de l'agriculture, du commerce et des finances* de septembre 1765. Quesnay livre également 'Despotisme de la Chine' dans les *Ephémérides du citoyen* de mars-juin 1767. Paraît aussi *L'Ordre naturel* de Le Mercier de La Rivière, qui circule sous forme manuscrite dès le premier semestre 1767 et qui est publié un peu plus tard la même année.[18]

Dans ce 'Discours', Du Pont fait sienne la formule de Quesnay – 'le droit que l'homme a aux choses propres à sa jouissance'[19] – et examine un certain nombre de notions, telles que 'l'homme isolé', 'l'état sauvage' ou 'l'association primitive', en vue de soutenir l'idée que, quel que soit l'état de développement atteint par l'humanité, le principe de conservation justifie le travail, l'accumulation et la mise en sûreté des biens, et implique des règles de justice et de bienfaisance précisant le droit, la liberté de chacun et leur limite. Une référence à Rousseau apparaît:

> C'est parce qu'on a, *de droit naturel*, la *propriété* de sa personne, qu'on a le *droit* de réclamer contre tout autre ce qu'on a acquis par le travail, par *l'emploi de sa personne*; de même, (pour me servir de l'expression

---

17. P.-S. Du Pont, 'Discours de l'éditeur', dans *Physiocratie, ou Constitution naturelle du gouvernement le plus avantageux au genre humain*, 2 vol. (Leyde et Paris, Chez Merlin, 1767-1768), t.1, p.i-cxx.

18. Bernard Herencia, 'Présentation', dans Paul Pierre Lemercier de La Rivière, *L'Ordre naturel et essentiel des sociétés politiques* (Genève, 2017), p.9-38 (15).

19. P.-S. Du Pont, 'Discours de l'éditeur', p.iii.

128 *Thierry Demals and Alexandra Hyard*

énergique de J. J. Rousseau) qu'on a *le droit de retirer son bras de la main d'un homme qui voudrait le retenir malgré nous.*[20]

Du Pont cite également cette phrase dans ses notes au *Contrat social.*[21] Il la lit dans un sens lockéen en la reliant à la propriété de ce qui a été acquis par le travail, c'est-à-dire la 'propriété mobiliaire', et soutient que cette propriété était reconnue par les 'hommes sauvages'.[22] L'association primitive & naturelle' se soumet aux mêmes principes que les sociétés ultérieures, à cette différence près qu'elle ne nécessite pas la création d'une autorité tutélaire trop coûteuse pour le peu de biens à protéger. C'est un état où les individus sont propriétaires de leur personne et des richesses mobilières acquises par le travail de

20. P.-S. Du Pont, 'Discours de l'éditeur', p.xxix-xxx.
21. La phrase est tirée d'*Emile, ou De l'éducation*, t.1, selon la copie de Paris (Jean Néaulme, 1762), partie 1, p.108. Rousseau prend l'exemple du jardinier Robert qui enseigne à un enfant (Emile) la culture afin de lui expliquer l'origine de la propriété. Le jardinier montre à l'enfant les différents travaux de la terre (labourer, ensemencer, arroser, etc.). Le jardinier laboure la terre pour l'enfant, 'il [l'enfant] en prend possession en y plantant des fèves; et sûrement cette possession est plus sacrée et plus respectable que celle que prenoit Nunès Balbao de l'Amérique méridionale au nom du roi d'Espagne, en plantant son étendard sur les côtes de la mer du Sud.' Les fèves lèvent et le jardinier dit à l'enfant: 'Cela vous appartient; et lui expliquant alors le terme d'*appartenir*, je lui fais sentir qu'il a mis là son temps, son travail, sa peine, sa personne enfin; qu'il y a dans cette terre quelque chose de lui-même qu'il peut réclamer contre qui que ce soit, comme il pourroit retirer son bras de la main d'un autre homme qui voudroit le retenir malgré lui.' Chez Rousseau, comme chez Du Pont, la phrase est une justification de la propriété par le travail et de la propriété mobilière. Du Pont reprend cette phrase dans plusieurs écrits (*De la vie pastorale*, manuscrit de 1787 ou *prima*, HML, W2-4732, f.1; *Philosophie de l'univers*, 1793, 3ᵉ éd., Paris, Chez Goujon fils, 1798, p.103). Il reprend aussi plusieurs fois l'exemple de Nunès Balbao (voir *Du contrat social, ou Principes du droit politique*, Amsterdam, Chez Marc Michel Rey, 1762, livre 1, chap.9, p.43).
22. Voir le texte original de Locke: 'Though the Earth, and all inferior Creatures be common to all Men, yet every Man has a *Property* in his own *Person*. This no Body has any right to but himself. The *Labour* of his Body and the *Work* of his Hands, we may say, are properly his. Whatsoever then he removes out of the State that Nature hath provided, and left in it, he hath mixed his *Labour* with, and joyned to it something that is his own and thereby makes it his *Property*. It being by him removed from the common state Nature placed it in, it hath by his *Labour* something annexed to it, that excludes the common right of other Men. For this *Labour* being the unquestionable Property of the Labourer, no man but he can have a right to what that is once joyned to'; John Locke, *Two treatises of government* (1690), éd. P. Laslett (Cambridge, 1960), chap.5, 'Of property', §27, p.305-306.

Politique et économie politique chez Pierre-Samuel Du Pont 129

leur personne.[23] Quand viendra l'étape des défrichements et de la culture, une autorité tutélaire sera nécessaire pour protéger la récente propriété foncière. 'Cet état est heureux; il est certainement préférable à celui des hommes qui vivent dans une société mal constituée, & dont les *Loix positives* contrarient les *Loix de l'ordre naturel*. Mais par sa nature, il n'est pas durable, & même il est loin encore du meilleur état possible de l'humanité.'[24]

Dans ce même 'Discours de l'éditeur', Du Pont se penche sur le phénomène de la guerre. Cet état est une suite de l'inégalité croissante des richesses, de la multiplication des hommes dont l'un des effets est de les rendre moins unis et de les pousser à la cupidité négative lorsqu'ils ne sont pas éclairés. Dès lors les sociétés s'écartent de l'ordre naturel (telle est l'histoire des sociétés): 'Voilà l'état de guerre; ce n'est pas, comme le pensèrent *Hobbes* & ses sectateurs, celui des hommes vivans dans la simplicité naturelle; c'est celui des hommes en société désordonnée; c'est celui où la *propriété* incertaine est sans cesse exposée à des violations clandestines, exercées sous les auspices d'une législation arbitraire.'[25] Du Pont esquisse alors une sorte d'histoire ternaire: (i) l'état d'association primitive ('anciennes peuplades de Chasseurs & de Pâtres') plus heureux que (ii) les 'sociétés imparfaites & semi-policées', et (iii) les sociétés politiques qui suivent l'ordre naturel.[26]

De l'origine et des progrès d'une science nouvelle, datée de 1768 mais paraissant en décembre 1767, est une commande de Diderot désireux de publier chez l'éditeur Desaint une version condensée du célèbre ouvrage de Le Mercier de La Rivière.[27] On y retrouve la plupart des éléments doctrinaux contenus dans le 'Discours de l'éditeur', notamment l'assertion selon laquelle 'il y a une société naturelle, antérieure à toute convention entre les hommes, fondée sur leur

23. P.-S. Du Pont, 'Discours de l'éditeur', p.xxxvii.
24. P.-S. Du Pont, 'Discours de l'éditeur', p.xxxv.
25. P.-S. Du Pont, 'Discours de l'éditeur', p.lxxiii.
26. P.-S. Du Pont, 'Discours de l'éditeur', p.lxxiv.
27. Lettre de Du Pont à Le Mercier de La Rivière (novembre 1767), HML, W2-11, f.11: 'Vous verrez par la brochure dont je vous envoye le manuscrit que Desaint m'avait demandé, que Diderot m'avait commandé et que vous m'aviez prié de faire, vous verrez, dis-je, que je me conduis autant que je peux conséquemment à mes principes. J'ai idée que cette brochure qui ne répond à personne fera bien autant d'effet que plusieurs des réponses du cher abbé Baudeau. Diderot pense de même. Il m'a beaucoup excité à la faire imprimer le plus tôt possible, on y travaille. Je vous enverrai des exemplaires avec ceux de la Physiocratie qui ne sont pas encore entièrement achevés mais dont vous recevrez toujours le Discours préliminaire avec cette lettre.'

130   *Thierry Demals and Alexandra Hyard*

constitution, sur leurs besoins physiques, sur leur intérêt évidemment commun'.[28] Du Pont évoque un 'état primitif' où les hommes ont déjà 'des *droits* et des *devoirs* réciproques':

> Les *droits* de chaque homme, antérieurs aux conventions, sont la *liberté* de pourvoir à sa subsistance & à son bien-être, la *propriété* de sa personne, & celle des choses acquises par le travail de sa personne. Ses *devoirs* sont le travail pour subvenir à ses besoins, & le respect pour la liberté, pour la propriété personnelle, & pour la propriété mobiliaire d'autrui.[29]

Avec cette différence toutefois que Du Pont s'intéresse moins à la société naturelle de l'état primitif qu'au stade agricole et plus généralement à la société politique. Le physiocrate ne fait aucune mention de Rousseau.

En 1770 Du Pont recense l'ouvrage *Essais sur les principes de finances*, publié anonymement l'année précédente,[30] qui lui permet de revenir à la philosophie politique et de critiquer deux conclusions de l'auteur: d'une part que le gouvernement des sociétés politiques serait une forme de gouvernement paternel, d'autre part que le despotisme serait une suite de la conquête territoriale par des chefs militaires. Deux erreurs manifestes, puisque, d'une part, l'auteur confond le gouvernement paternel caractéristique des associations primitives, telles que la famille, et le gouvernement des sociétés politiques apparues avec l'agriculture. D'autre part, l'auteur saisit mal l'essence du despotisme: ce gouvernement n'est pas lié à la conquête de territoires par des chefs de guerre qui soumettent la population de ces territoires conquis. Les chefs militaires ne se transforment pas en despotes arbitraires (privant le peuple de lois), mais, se fondant dans la société conquise, ils se transforment en propriétaires. Ce qu'ils ont établi, c'est un gouvernement féodal. En revanche, un gouvernement féodal déliquescent peut générer le despotisme, qui est le produit d'un dérèglement des sociétés politiques. Là encore, aucune référence à Rousseau.

---

28. P.-S. Du Pont, *De l'origine et des progrès d'une science nouvelle* (Londres et Paris, Desaint, 1768), p.17.
29. P.-S. Du Pont, *De l'origine*, p.17-18.
30. L'auteur de cet ouvrage, Jean-Baptiste-Bertrand Durban (1732-1808), est directeur de la Régie de 1759 à 1775 et sera premier commis du contrôleur général Calonne de 1784 à 1787. Il est également auteur d'un *Eloge de Colbert* (1773) et d'un *Traité de l'impôt* (An VI [1797]).

Néanmoins ce texte est instructif pour sa distinction entre gouvernement paternel et gouvernement de la nation, distinction qui rejoint celle de Rousseau dans l'article 'Economie' entre le 'chef de famille' et le 'chef de l'Etat', encore appelé 'premier magistrat' ou 'législateur'.[31] Le premier fait la loi, le second l'exécute. Cette distinction est suivie d'une seconde dans le *Contrat social* entre gouvernement et souveraineté. Du Pont a bien senti cette distinction,[32] quoiqu'il l'entende différemment. Pour Rousseau, en théorie le premier magistrat ou le législateur n'est pas souverain: il 'rédige' les lois proposées au consentement du peuple. Le peuple est souverain en tant qu'il s'identifie à la volonté générale.[33] Du Pont distingue le législateur qui énonce, rédige, déclare les lois, et le 'légisfacteur' qui fait les lois (avec ce codicille: 'Ce n'est point aux hommes à faire les lois').[34] Le législateur souverain, c'est Dieu ou la nature ordonnée:

> Comment les reconnaître [les lois de la république]? Par l'examen, par la réflexion, par la raison. Il n'y a point d'autre autorité législative. Cette autorité si nécessaire et si bienfaisante n'appartient pas aux mortels: Dieu se l'est réservée. Il l'a placée dans la nature des choses, et n'a donné à l'homme pour discerner celle-ci, que la raison. Aussi dans aucune langue, on n'a employé le mot Légis-FACTEUR, ni aucun mot qui eût le même sens; car ce n'est point aux hommes à faire les loix. On a nommé ceux qui sont chargés de les énoncer, de les rédiger, de les déclarer, Légis-LATEURS, parce que leur fonction est de rechercher dans les rapports entre les hommes, leurs besoins, leurs droits, leurs devoirs, leurs travaux, quelles sont les loix que la sagesse universelle a prescrites au bon sens et de les porter, de les élever aux yeux de tous, resplendissantes de leur propre lumière.[35]

31. J.-J. Rousseau, *Discours sur l'économie politique* (1755) (article 'Economie ou œconomie (morale & politique)' de l'*Encyclopédie* de Diderot et D'Alembert), dans *Œuvres politiques* (Paris, 1989), p.119-52 (121).

32. Voir aussi Anne-Robert-Jacques Turgot, dans *Œuvres de Turgot et documents le concernant*, éd. Gustave Schelle, 5 vol. (Paris, 1913-1923), t.2 (1914), p.660: 'ce livre [le *Contrat social*] se réduit à la distinction précise du souverain et du gouvernement; mais cette distinction présente une vérité bien lumineuse, et qui me paraît fixer à jamais les idées sur l'inaliénabilité de la souveraineté du peuple dans quelque gouvernement que ce soit.'

33. Voir Blaise Bachofen, *La condition de la liberté: Rousseau, critique des raisons politiques* (Paris, 2002), p.254-55.

34. [P.-S. Du Pont], *Du pouvoir législatif et du pouvoir exécutif, convenables à la République française* (Paris, Chez Du Pont, 1795), p.127.

35. [P.-S. Du Pont], *Du pouvoir*, p.127-28.

132 *Thierry Demals and Alexandra Hyard*

C'est une reprise de Le Mercier de La Rivière: 'Il est sensible que dans la main des hommes, le pouvoir législatif n'est point le pouvoir de faire des loix nouvelles; qu'il se réduit à publier celles qui sont déjà faites par Dieu même, & à sceller le sceau de l'autorité coërcitive dont le Souverain est le dépositaire unique.'[36] Mais ici le pouvoir législatif réside dans le souverain, monarque héréditaire, en tant qu'il est dépositaire de l'évidence, et 'il faut regarder cette évidence *comme étant la divinité elle-même*.'[37]

Dans un manuscrit non daté (1771?), intitulé *Elémens de philosophie économique*, Du Pont revient sur les premières sociétés afin de donner sens à la distinction entre sociétés chasseresses et sociétés pastorales. Il dresse un portrait positif des secondes, plus paisibles et en marche vers l'étape agricole. L'agriculture suppose en effet 'des préliminaires indispensables qui ne produisent rien par eux-mêmes et qui ne font que préparer la terre à être cultivée'.[38] Les sociétés de chasseurs ne peuvent s'engager dans de tels préliminaires et de telles dépenses: '[L'agriculture] n'a pu être l'occupation des premiers hommes [...] elle n'a pû naître que chés les Peuples Pâtres, à qui les bestiaux assuraient déjà une nourriture abondante, et donnaient par là le loisir de se fabriquer les instruments nécessaires, de se livrer à des travaux longtemps infructueux, celui d'attendre les récoltes tardives.'[39] Mais quelle que soit la société, chasseresse, pastorale ou agricole, le respect de la propriété est un droit fondamental. Récuser ce droit, c'est entrer dans la violence et le remplacer par le droit du plus fort. Ce qui sous-entend que sans le respect de ce droit les sociétés primitives seraient en état de guerre, ce qui n'est pas exactement la conclusion de Rousseau, à savoir que par essence les sociétés naturelles ne connaissent pas la guerre. Et Du Pont de qualifier de 'prétendus raisonneurs', ceux 'qui ont voulu réduire tous les droits naturels des hommes entr'eux à ceux de la force ou du pouvoir physique'.[40]

En 1773, dans sa correspondance avec le margrave de Bade (1728-1811), Du Pont fait une recension en plusieurs épisodes de l'ouvrage de François-Jean de Chastellux (1734-1788), *De la félicité publique, ou Considérations sur le sort des hommes dans les différentes époques*

---

36. [Paul-Pierre Le Mercier de La Rivière], *L'Ordre naturel et essentiel des sociétés politiques*, 2 vol. (Londres et Paris, Nourse, Desaint, 1767), t.2, p.472.
37. [P.-P. Le Mercier de La Rivière], *L'Ordre naturel*, t.2, p.471.
38. P.-S. Du Pont, *Elémens de philosophie économique*, HML, W2-4579, f.11.
39. P.-S. Du Pont, *Elémens*, chap.5, f.22.
40. P.-S. Du Pont, *Elémens*, f.56-57.

de l'histoire, paru l'année précédente.[41] Il revient sur quelques-unes de ses idées: tout d'abord celle selon laquelle les sociétés présentes qu'il appelle politiques, quoique plus développées, n'ont pas pour autant rompu avec l'état primitif – elles en portent la trace. Les sociétés présentes – qu'il appelle 'grandes sociétés politiques' et 'empires' – ne sont que la suite de cet état primitif, la conséquence de la 'multiplication des familles' et du 'perfectionnement naturel des lumières'.[42] Ensuite, l'idée selon laquelle l'état de l'homme isolé (qui aurait abandonné femme et enfant, perpétuant son espèce par des 'rencontres fortuites'), est un 'état qui n'a jamais existé, attendu que, bien loin d'être naturel, il aurait été contre la nature'.[43] C'est une fiction qui ne caractérise pas l'état primitif. Enfin, l'idée selon laquelle les sociétés primitives ne sont pas des états en guerre virtuelle ou perpétuelle. Ces sociétés qui ne disposent pas de grandes richesses sont paisibles dès lors qu'elles s'appuient sur une structure de droits et de devoirs. Elles ne connaissent pas le brigandage, lequel ne peut apparaître que s'il y a des richesses à prendre chez les voisins, ce qui ne peut se produire que si les sociétés ont une capacité à multiplier leurs richesses, c'est-à-dire si elles sont agricoles. Du Pont emploie ici le mot 'brigandage'. Ce mot, employé par Mirabeau et Quesnay, semble plutôt rare chez lui.[44] Du Pont réitère une nouvelle fois contre Chastellux quelques-uns de ses thèmes favoris: dans l'état primitif, les guerres ne peuvent apparaître avant l'établissement de l'agriculture, et les sociétés suivent une marche naturelle qui les conduit à satisfaire d'abord les besoins plutôt que les plaisirs; 'le despotisme n'a jamais été un gouvernement primitif'[45] – c'est une corruption des sociétés politiques établies sur l'agriculture.

Dans un manuscrit de 1787 (ou *prima*), Du Pont présente les sociétés pastorales comme le 'troisième état naturel de l'homme'.[46]

41. *Carl Friedrichs von Baden Brieflicher Verkehr mit Mirabeau und Du Pont*, éd. Carl Knies, 2 vol. (Heidelberg, 1892), t.2.

42. P.-S. Du Pont, recension de la *Félicité publique*, dans *Carl Friedrichs von Baden Brieflicher Verkehr*, t.2, p.47.

43. P.-S. Du Pont, recension de la *Félicité publique*, dans *Carl Friedrichs von Baden Brieflicher Verkehr*, t.2, p.48.

44. Dans le *Traité de la monarchie* (1757-1759), éd. G. Longhitano (Paris, 1999), p.14, 25, Mirabeau décrit les sociétés de brigands comme des rejets des premières sociétés paternelles ou patriarcales n'ayant pour objet que 'l'invasion et l'attaque', 'la rapine', la 'lésion d'autrui'. Voir aussi F. Quesnay, 'Le droit naturel' (1767-1768), dans *Physiocratie*, t.1, p.1-38 (26).

45. P.-S. Du Pont, recension de la *Félicité publique*, dans *Carl Friedrichs von Baden Brieflicher Verkehr*, t.2, p.63.

46. P.-S. Du Pont, *De la vie pastorale: troisième état naturel de l'homme. Changement*

Ce sont des sociétés de chasseurs qui ont évolué vers des mœurs plus douces et plus paisibles. Ce sont des familles qui se sont rendu compte qu'il était plus avantageux et moins aléatoire d'élever les bêtes plutôt que de les chasser (accroissement des moyens de subsistance) à condition toutefois de protéger la propriété de chaque pâtre. Cette définition est l'occasion pour Du Pont de mentionner Rousseau: 'Il devient juste alors que chacun respecte le troupeau de son voisin, car le lui enlever, serait encore dérober les tems, les fatigues, la *partie de sa personne*, (j'emploierai toujours en ce cas l'expression de *Jean Jacques*) consumés au travail de la garde et de l'éducation des bestiaux.'[47] Du Pont tente donc ici de rapprocher les sociétés pastorales des sociétés agricoles. Les deux sociétés ont à peu près les mêmes traits si ce n'est qu'elles ne sont pas arrivées au même stade de l'appropriation: pour l'une le bétail (propriété mobilière), pour l'autre la terre (propriété mobilière et foncière). Ces sociétés sont paisibles si elles se dotent d'une structure de droits et de devoirs comme l'avait fait la société familiale primitive. La paix suppose le respect de la propriété. Ces sociétés ont un ennemi commun: leurs richesses étant plus abondantes, elles doivent se protéger des sociétés plus pauvres que sont les sociétés chasseresses. Il faut alors des chefs militaires qui assurent la garde des troupeaux sans usurper la propriété de chacun des membres. Ce souci de la défense pousse les petites sociétés pastorales à se transformer en 'une confédération de petites républiques'.[48] Cette idée est présente dans les notes au *Contrat social*.

En 1792, Du Pont écrit son autobiographie qui s'arrête à sa rencontre avec Quesnay et Turgot et qui contient trois références à Rousseau. La première occurrence déjà citée indique qu'à la fin des années 1750 ou au début des années 1760, la pauvreté de Du Pont

---

qu'elle introduit dans la forme de la Société. Elle n'en apporte aucun dans les droits de ses membres, chap.8, f.1. Il s'agit d'un chapitre manuscrit (HML, W2-4732) destiné à un ouvrage, *Observations sur les principes et le bien des républiques confédérées*, qui ne paraîtra pas. La date nous est connue grâce à une lettre de Franklin à Du Pont datée du 9 juin 1788 dans laquelle celui-ci dit avoir reçu ce chapitre (*The Writings of Benjamin Franklin*, t.9, New York, 1906, p.658-60). La lettre de Franklin éclaire le titre de l'ouvrage. Inspiré par l'exemple américain, Du Pont projette d'écrire un ouvrage sur l'origine et les progrès de l'idée de confédération, idée que l'on trouve dans les notes au *Contrat social*. Franklin lui répond non pas sur les sociétés pastorales, mais sur la confédération américaine en train de naître.

47. P.-S. Du Pont, *Vie pastorale*, f.1.
48. P.-S. Du Pont, *Vie pastorale*, f.2.

Politique et économie politique chez Pierre-Samuel Du Pont 135

l'oblige à se séparer de ses livres: 'Il ne me resta que le Discours sur l'inégalité des conditions, l'esprit des loix et les commentaires de César [...]. J'y ai joint dans la suite la lettre à d'Alembert sur les spectacles, le contrat social, et Emile: jusqu'à vingt-deux ans je n'ai pas eu d'autre bibliothèque.'[49] La deuxième occurrence un peu plus tardive est à replacer dans le contexte du conflit entre Corses et Génois. Du Pont imagine un plan de constitution pour la Corse:[50]

> Les succès militaires ne peuvent être durables qu'autant qu'ils sont soutenus par une bonne constitution civile et politique, et par de bonnes loix. J'avais dans la tête le Contrat social, Montesquieu, et plusieurs de mes propres idées qui se sont fondues depuis dans la doctrine des économistes. Je devais proposer des institutions si sages, si parfaitement liées l'une à l'autre, que, surtout venant des plus habiles et des plus braves de l'armée, elles devaient avoir le suffrage universel. Nous fondions ainsi une république dont l'agriculture aurait été la base, et la liberté du commerce le soutien; où les citoyens auraient eus [*sic*] la plus grande étendue de droits politiques, dont le Roi n'aurait été que le premier Magistrat, et nous étions contens de cette autorité bornée jointe au droit magnanime des bienfaits.[51]

La troisième occurrence apparaît au chapitre 13, dans lequel Du Pont narre sa rencontre avec Quesnay et l'influence que celui-ci a exercée sur lui:[52]

---

49. P.-S. Du Pont, *Mémoires*, chap.10, f.97. La *Lettre à D'Alembert* est publiée en 1758, le *Contrat social* et *Emile* en 1762.

50. Du Pont semble placer son propos dans un contexte de guerre contre les Génois puis contre les Français. En 1768 la Corse passe sous administration française. Du Pont sous-entend dans cet extrait qu'il réfléchit à un plan de gouvernement pour cette île et indique les sources de sa réflexion, c'est-à-dire ses lectures antérieures à sa conversion auxquelles il surajoute ses propres idées qui lui ont fait rejoindre la physiocratie. Aussi mentionne-t-il conjointement le 'suffrage universel', la 'plus grande étendue des droits politiques', la primauté de l'agriculture et la 'liberté du commerce'. Deux lettres de Turgot à Du Pont du 13 mars et 12 avril 1771 (dans *Œuvres de Turgot et documents le concernant*, t.3, p.476-78, 480-83) indiquent que Turgot a reçu de Du Pont un plan de constitution pour la Corse qui diverge de celui de Rousseau. Le *Plan de gouvernement* de Rousseau rédigé en 1765 est resté à l'état de manuscrit. Turgot et Du Pont, semble-t-il, en avaient quelques renseignements. On ne sait que peu de choses sur le plan de Du Pont. Turgot ne soulève que des questions juridiques, telle la peine de mort dont Du Pont souhaite l'abolition.

51. P.-S. Du Pont, *Mémoires*, chap.10, f.2-3.

52. Cet extrait n'est pas daté, mais il semble postérieur à l'extrait précédent, donc postérieur à 1764-1765.

136   *Thierry Demals and Alexandra Hyard*

En effet quelle que puisse être la distribution du pouvoir exécutif et la puissance tribunitienne qui sont l'objet de nos constitutions; et de quelque manière dont les Peuples soient représentés, ils seront riches, nombreux, heureux, puissans, et de bonnes mœurs si l'agriculture est florissante, si le travail est en honneur, si le commerce prospère, si l'on jouit de la liberté des pensées et des actions, de la sûreté des Personnes, et de la propriété des biens. Et au contraire si la liberté, la sûreté, la propriété ne sont pas suffisamment garanties, si le travail, l'agriculture, et le commerce dépérissent le Pays deviendra inhabitable, quelles que soient l'étendue des droits politiques et les formes établies pour en faire usage. Ce n'est donc pas la *science du Contrat social* dont les bases étaient dans Jean-Jacques Rousseau, c'est celle de l'*Economie Politique* que Mr. Quesnay a cultivée, ou pour mieux dire créée.[53]

On saisit dans cet extrait toute la différence qui le sépare des deux extraits précédents. *Exit* la philosophie politique de Rousseau. La question constitutionnelle devient secondaire relativement à la question économique: 'quelque manière dont les Peuples soient représentés', 'quelles que soient l'étendue des droits politiques et les formes établies pour en faire usage', écrit-il. Les mots 'république', 'suffrage universel' disparaissent. Cependant, si l'économie politique physiocratique est clairement affirmée, la politique physiocratique l'est un peu moins (les notions de despotisme légal et d'autorité tutélaire unique ne sont pas mentionnées), ce qui est peut-être un effet de recomposition du passé.

En 1793, Du Pont entreprend la rédaction de *Philosophie de l'univers*, ouvrage qui lui permet de croiser à nouveau Rousseau. Le texte contient trois occurrences. La première est la reformulation d'une critique qu'il a déjà adressée à Rousseau et qui se trouve également dans les notes au *Contrat social*, à savoir que l'homme isolé est une invention:

Jamais l'homme n'a erré solitaire dans les bois, abandonnant la femelle qui venait de le rendre heureux, comme l'ont prétendu l'insensé *Hobbes*, et cet éloquent menteur *Jean-Jacques*, qui, cependant, aimait la vérité. L'homme, après avoir joui, n'êtait pas si dénué du besoin de jouir encore. Quand l'amour n'est point corrompu, chaque faveur qu'il obtient lui en fait désirer une nouvelle. L'intelligence humaine a toujours compris l'utilité de l'assistance dans le travail; et l'affection, si naturellement redoublée par le plaisir, l'a toujours plus vivement portée à cette assistance mutuelle. Elle a toujours établi

---

53. P.-S. Du Pont, *Mémoires*, chap.13, f.41.

Politique et économie politique chez Pierre-Samuel Du Pont

entre l'homme et sa compagne un commerce de pensées, de soins, d'attentions et de services, une volupté de l'âme, qui les a ramenés avec plus de délices à la volupté des sens.[54]

La première association, c'est le couple; viennent ensuite la famille et le peuple. La deuxième occurrence est d'un moindre intérêt: 'Voudriez-vous être *Jean-Jacques*, avec son éloquence, ses idées originales et fortes, ses passions énergiques; et sa susceptibilité, son orgueil indomptable, son ingratitude raisonnée, ses torts envers Madame de *Warens*, et la honte persévérante d'avoir mis ses cinq enfans à l'hôpital, ou seulement sa calomnie contre une pauvre servante pour le petit ruban rose broché d'argent?'[55] La troisième occurrence est la rengaine tirée d'*Emile*. La morale naturelle de l'homme consiste à ne pas faire à un autre ce qu'on ne voudrait pas qu'il nous fasse:

> Chacun se voit assiégé de besoins, et veut la liberté de travailler pour y satisfaire. Chacun sait donc qu'il ne doit pas troubler le travail des autres qui ont des besoins semblables.
>
> Chacun veut jouir de ce que son travail lui a procuré. Il sent que le lui enlever, ce serait, comme dit *Rousseau*, le priver de la partie de sa personne qu'il a employée, usée, dans le travail; et qu'il a droit d'en défendre le produit, ainsi qu'il aurait droit de retirer son bras des mains d'un homme qui voudrait le retenir malgré lui. Chacun sait donc qu'il doit respecter pareillement la propriété des autres sur le fruit de leur travail.
>
> Rien là-dedans ne dépend des conventions, ni des sociétés politiques. C'est la *Morale naturelle* de l'homme dans l'état le plus sauvage. Dans cet état primitif, celui qui n'a point chassé, ou qui a chassé sans succès, n'a aucun droit de s'emparer du gibier de celui qui a chassé heureusement. Il ne peut, s'il en a besoin d'une partie, que la lui demander comme un bienfait, ou lui proposer un marché, un échange, soit en choses à son usage, soit en services présens ou futurs. Si, au lieu de recourir à cette voie amiable [...] il voulait prendre le gibier de force, il y aurait GUERRE: et cette guerre serait *juste* de la part du Propriétaire, *injuste* de la part du Ravisseur.[56]

L'homme est un être sensible et intelligent: il a 'des sensations, des sentimens, des raisonnemens, des passions, de la liberté, de la volonté,

---

54. P.-S. Du Pont, *Philosophie de l'univers*, p.59-60.
55. P.-S. Du Pont, *Philosophie de l'univers*, p.71-72.
56. P.-S. Du Pont, *Philosophie de l'univers*, p.103-104.

et du pouvoir actif'.[57] A la différence d'une machine, il doit subir les conséquences, bonnes ou mauvaises, de ses actions. Il en est de même des nations:

> Quand les Nations sont ignorantes sur leurs vrais intérêts, ou agitées par des passions, soit haineuses, soit dissipatrices; quand leurs Loix sont vicieuses ou impuissantes, leur Administration faible ou corrompue, les capitaux se consument, l'Agriculture dépérit, le Commerce languit, le Travail est découragé, une pauvreté générale attaque les Citoyens, les disettes locales se multiplient; et les gens de bien pâtissent de tous ces maux comme les méchans.[58]

ii. Les annotations de Du Pont au *Contrat social* et à *Emile*[59]

Textes de Rousseau	Annotations de Du Pont
Du Contract social,[60] Livre I	
Chapitre II: Des premières Sociétés	
|5| La plus ancienne de toutes les sociétés et la seule naturelle est celle de la famille. Encore les enfans ne restent-ils liés au pere qu'aussi longtems qu'ils ont besoin de lui pour se conserver. Sitôt que ce besoin cesse, *le lien naturel se dissout.* Les enfans, exempts de l'obéïssance qu'ils devoient au pere, le père exempt des soins qu'il devoit aux enfans, *rentrent tous également dans l'indépendance.* S'ils continuent de rester unis ce n'est plus *naturellement* c'est *volontairement*, et la famille elle-même ne se maintient que par convention.	C'est beaucoup trop dire. Il reste entre les enfans et le Pere un lien naturel fondé sur ce que les enfans n'ayant point demandé la vie le Pere est obligé de contribuer toujours et autant qu'il peut à la leur rendre plus douce; et encore sur ce que celui-ci ayant rempli ce devoir par une multitude de secours gratuits et d'instructions profitables, les enfans qui eussent péri sans ces services essentiels que le père leur a rendus lui en doivent une vive et perpétuelle reconnaissance qui les oblige à le respecter profondément, et à l'assister à leur tour de tout leur pouvoir, à rendre à la vieillesse ce qu'il a prêté à leur enfance. Si ce lien est *volontaire* il n'en est pas moins *naturel*, et c'est parce qu'il est *naturel* qu'il devient *volontaire*: c'est parce que la nature de l'homme différente de celle du Tigre le rend propre à connaître la justice, à éprouver la gratitude, et à la conduire d'après leurs règles et leur impulsion.

---

57. P.-S. Du Pont, *Philosophie de l'univers*, p.116.
58. P.-S. Du Pont, *Philosophie de l'univers*, p.117-18.
59. Les textes de Rousseau et les annotations de Du Pont sont reproduits à l'identique. Seuls les s allongés 'ſ' ont été remplacés par des 's'. Les chiffres entre les barres renvoient à la pagination des éditions originales de 1762. Les phrases soulignées par Du Pont apparaissent en italique, sauf mention contraire.
60. J.-J. Rousseau, *Du contrat social*, HML, N* JC179. R864c.

|6| La famille est donc si l'on veut le premier modèle des sociétés politiques; le chef est l'image du pere, le peuple est l'image des enfans, et tous étant nés égaux et libres *n'aliénent leur liberté* que pour leur utilité.	Personne n'aliène la liberté, c'est-à-dire le droit de travailler et d'acquérir et de jouir sans nuire à autrui. Mais chacun respecte la liberté des autres et tous se plaisent à se prêter des secours réciproques, et il en doit être de même en toute société. Si une seule liberté était aliénée il n'y aurait plus de société par rapport à celle-là. Elle serait un état de guerre qui est l'opposé de l'état de sociétés celui-ci consiste dans la garantie réciproque de toutes les libertés et l'obligation des secours mutuels.

Chapitre III: Du droit du plus fort

|12| Convenons donc que force ne fait pas droit et *qu'on n'est obligé d'obéir qu'aux puissances légitimes*. Ainsi ma question primitive revient toujours.	On n'est obligé d'obéir qu'à la raison et à la justice. Les Puissances légitimes sont celles qui sont établies pour faire respecter la justice et la raison par les foux et par les méchans. Si elles quittaient cette fonction sacrée pour le plaisir féroce de faire respecter leurs volontés arbitraires, elles ne seraient plus des Puissances *légitimes*; mais elles pourraient être encore des puissances, alors ce serait à la prudence seul à calculer jusqu'à quel point il peut être sage de leur obéïr. La convention qui a établi une Puissance ne peut donc la rendre légitime qu'autant que celle-ci se conforme aux vues de raison, de justice et d'utilité publique qui l'ont fait établir. Hors de là on rentre dans l'état de guerre, plus ou moins atroce, plus ou moins cachée, plus ou moins funeste.

Chapitre IV: De l'esclavage

|13| Si un particulier, dit Grotius, *peut aliéner sa liberté et se rendre esclave d'un maître*, pourquoi tout un peuple ne pourroit-il pas aliéner la sienne et se rendre sujet d'un roi?	Un homme peut engager ses services à tems limité. Il est valet et non esclave. Il garde une portion de liberté et le droit de rentrer dans l'autre sa convention remplie. Un homme ne peut pas aliéner toute sa liberté celle des sentimens du cœur, celle de se marier, ni même le travail entier de la vie, parce qu'il y aurait besoin dans un tel marché que nulle compensation ne peut égaler le sacrifice de la liberté entière ou de la vie entière d'un homme; que celui qui consentirait à en prendre l'engagement ferait le marché d'un homme privé de sens; et que tout marché d'un homme en démence est nul en loi, et non obligatoire. Un homme peut encore moins vendre ou engager la liberté de ses enfans à laquelle ils ont un droit direct et qui n'est point à lui. Voyez plus bas page 15 où cela est très bien développé.

|18| [L]a guerre privée ou d'homme à homme ne peut exister, ni dans l'état de nature où il n'y a point de propriété constante, ni dans l'état social où tout est sous l'autorité des loix.

La guerre privée ou d'homme à homme peut exister et existe souvent dans l'état primitif que Rousseau appelle ici l'état de nature et precisement parce que dans cet état il y a des propriétés constantes. Celle de la personne et celle des objets choses acquises par le travail, comme les armes la proie prise à la chasse, les fruits cueillis, la cabane etc. mais cette guerre qui peut emporter jusqu'au droit de tuer l'assaillant redoutable, n'emporte nullement celui de le tuer que pour sa pressante conservation et l'ennemi réduit à l'impuissance n'est plus qu'un malheureux qui demande de la pitié et même des secours.

Les combats particuliers, les duels, les rencontres sont des actes qui ne constituent point un état; et à l'égard des guerres privées, autorisées par les établissemens de Louis IX roi de France et suspendues par la paix de Dieu, ce sont des abis du gouvernement féodal, système absurde s'il en fut jamais, contraire aux principes du droit naturel, et à toute bonne politie.

La guerre n'est donc point une relation d'homme à homme, mais une relation d'Etat à Etat, dans laquelle les particuliers ne sont ennemis qu'accidentellement.

|22| Ces mots *esclavage*, &, *droit*, sont contradictoires; ils s'excluent mutuellement.[61]

Il est impossible de mieux dire.

Chapitre V: Qu'il faut toujours remonter à une première convention

---

|24| Un peuple, dit Grotius, peut se donner à un roi. Selon Grotius un peuple est donc un peuple avant de se donner un roi. Ce don même est un acte civil, il suppose une délibération publique. Avant donc que d'examiner l'acte par lequel un peuple élit un roi, il seroit bon d'examiner l'acte par lequel un peuple est un peuple. Car cet acte étant nécessairement antérieur à l'autre est le vrai fondement de la société.

Les hommes ne se sont jamais donnés *à un Roi*. Ils se sont quelquefois donnés *un Roi* c'est-à-dire qu'ils ont nommé un premier Magistrat pour diriger l'emploi des forces de la confédération sociale au maintien des droits et de la liberté de tous et de chacun des individus dont elle est composée. Et l'autorité des Rois n'a et ne peut avoir d'autre titre légitime.

|25| La loi de la pluralité des suffrages est elle-même un établissement de convention, et suppose au moins une fois l'unanimité.

La loi de la pluralité des suffrages n'est pas dans son origine un établissement de convention. Elle est l'expression d'un fait physique, qui est que le pouvoir de se faire obéir appartient au plus grand nombre et que ce plus grand nombre une fois d'accord, il faut ou que le plus petit cède à sa volonté ou qu'il s'établisse un état de guerre entre le plus grand nombre et le plus petit nombre. Alors ceux-ci ne sont plus en sociétés dont la plus faible seulement a le choix ou de s'accomoder avec le premier à la manière des traités de Paix, ou de courir les risques d'une guerre inégale.

---

61. Les mots sont mis en italique par Rousseau.

Chapitre VI: Du pacte Social

|26| Je suppose les hommes parvenus à ce point où les obstacles qui nuisent à leur conservation dans l'état de nature, l'emportent par leur résistance sur les forces que chaque individu peut employer pour se maintenir dans cet état. Alors cet état primitif ne peut plus subsister, et le genre humain périroit s'il ne changeoit sa manière d'être.

Rousseau n'a jamais eu d'idée bien nette de l'état de nature. On voit par son Discours sur l'inégalité des conditions qu'il a supposé dans cet état l'homme isolé et courant les bois à la manière des singes. Mais ceci n'est point l'état de nature de l'homme. L'homme nait et vit naturellement en famille parce qu'étant susceptible des plaisirs de l'amour en tout tems le male et la femelle n'ont aucune raison de s'éloigner l'un de l'autre quand ils se sont joints et sont au contraire portés par leur attrait très vif et très naturel à prolonger cette liaison et à s'assister réciproquement de tout leur pouvoir. De sorte que le premier enfant naissant sans que le Pere et la Mere aient eu la moindre envie de se séparer, et cet enfant dans les besoins et les grâces établissent entre eux un nouvel attrait de secours réciproques et de nouveaux motifs d'union restant dans cet état de faiblesse intéressante jusqu'à la naissance d'un second enfant et par delà les liens de la famille se trouvent formés dès la première génération et cette famille est une société naissante qui dès que le grand Père est mort devient par les branches diverses une société de familles confédérées. Personne dans cette confédération naturelle n'a songé à aliéner ni à restraindre aucun de ses droits mais au contraire à en étendre l'usage par les secours des confédérés.

|28| Ces clauses bien entendues se réduisent toutes à une seule, savoir *l'aliénation totale de chaque associé avec tous ses droits à toute la communauté.*

Nul associé ne s'aliène avec tous ses droits à toute la communauté nul associé n'entend perdre la moindre partie de ses droits. Tous les associés au contraire sont convenus de réunir toutes leurs forces pour conserver en leur entier les droits de tous et de chacun. Mais Rousseau comme la plupart des publicistes a cru que dans l'état primitif tout homme avait droit à tout et il n'avait pas songé que ce droit vague à tout était même dans l'état sauvage restreint pour chaque homme à ce qu'il peut acquérir par son travail: et que jamais il ne s'est atendu à s'emparer par force du produit du travail d'autrui. Que toute tentative d'usurpation de ce genre dans l'état sauvage produirait une guerre qui serait injuste de la part de l'usurpateur et si visiblement injuste que par la seule exposition du fait tout tiers sauvage survenant se mettrait contre lui.

|29| [C]omme il n'y a pas un associé sur lequel on n'acquiere le même droit qu'on lui cède sur soi, *on gagne l'équivalent de tout ce qu'on perd*, et plus de force pour conserver ce qu'on a.

On ne perd rien à s'unir on s'assure sa conservation et de ce qu'on a et de ce qu'on peut acquérir, et un plus grand nombre de moyens plus efficaces pour faire des acquisitions.

|29| Si donc on écarte du pacte social ce qui n'est pas de son essence, on trouvera qu'il se réduit aux termes suivans. *Chacun de nous met en commun sa personne & toute sa puissance sous la suprême direction de la volonté générale; & nous recevons en corps chaque membre comme partie indivisible du tout.*

Ce n'est pas là le véritable énoncé. Le voici: *chacun de nous emploiera sa persnne et toute sa puissance pour garantir à chacun de nous la sureté de sa personne, la liberté d'acquérir, et la conservation de ce qu'il aura acquis.*

|30| Cette personne publique qui se forme ainsi par l'union de toutes les autres prenoit autrefois le nom de *Cité*, & prend maintenant celui de *République* ou de *corps politique*, lequel est appelé par ses membres *Etat* quand il est passif, *Souverain* quand il est actif, *Puissance* en le comparant à ses semblables. A l'égard des associés ils prennent collectivement le nom de *peuple*, & s'appellent en particulier *Citoyens* comme participans à l'autorité souveraine, et *Sujets* comme soumis aux loix de l'Etat.[62]

C'est dans cette nomenclature excellente dans la notion précise et juste que Rousseau donne du *Souverain* et dans la distinction d'avec le *Gouvernement* que consiste le principal mérite de ce livre. Ce mérite est très grand et c'est une partie de la science de l'économie politique qui appartient à Jean Jacques et n'appartient qu'à lui. Mais aussi c'est la seule dont il ait eu des idées nettes ou vraies.

---

62. Les mots sont mis en italique par Rousseau.

Politique et économie politique chez Pierre-Samuel Du Pont   143

Chapitre VII: Du Souverain

|36| [Q]uiconque refusera d'obéir à la volonté générale y sera contraint par tout le corps: ce qui ne signifie autre chose sinon *qu'on le forcera d'être libre.*

Forcer d'être libre est une expression qui a plus d'éclat que de clarté et de vérité. Etre libre c'est jouir de tous ses droits de propriété et de tous les moyens naturels d'acquérir et de travailler sans nuire à autrui. On ne peut forcer un homme d'être libre, on le laisse tel; on lui garantit l'usage de sa liberté. Cette liberté n'a de limites naturelles et justes que les libertés et les propriétés des autres hommes sur lesquelles il ne lui est pas permis d'empiéter. On forcera donc l'homme porté à l'usurpation de laisser les autres libres, c'est-à-dire de respecter leurs droits et leur propriété. On l'y forcera quoi qu'il soit citoyen comme on y forcerait tout étranger qui tenterait les mêmes violations des droits d'autrui. Le citoyen qui attaque la liberté ou la propriété d'un autre citoyen, cesse en cela d'être membre de l'Etat. Il est poursuivi non par une loi particulière et relative à la qualité de citoyen qu'il avait revêtue, mais par la loi générale en vertu de laquelle tous les citoyens se sont promis garantie réciproque pour toutes leurs libertés et toutes leurs propriétés. Qui que ce soit qui y porte atteinte devient ennemi de l'Etat Le Citoyen qui refuserait aux autres la contribution ou l'assistance convenue pour la Sureté des propriétés et des libertés tandis que les autres ont garanti les siennes, est dans le cas d'un homme qui ne voudrait pas payer; il pourrait être contraint car alors il a rompu le pacte social autant qu'il était en lui et s'est mis en guerre avec ses amis et confédérés. La Société ne force que ses ennemis. Ses citoyens sont libres. Mais malheur à eux s'ils veulent changer cet état honorable utile et doux contre celui d'ennemis de la Patrie.

Chapitre VIII: De l'état civil

|37| *Quoiqu'il se prive dans cet état de plusieurs avantages qu'il tient de la nature, il en regagne de si grands.*

Il ne se prive d'aucun des avantages qu'il tenait de la nature. La nature ne lui avait jamais donné d'autre droit que celui de jouir des biens acquis par son travail. Elle lui avait toujours interdit toute usurpation de ceux acquis par le travail d'autrui. Il reste en Société dans le même état et soumis à la même loi. Sa situation est seulement améliorée en ce que les moyens d'acquérir sont augmentés et ses acquisitions garanties par une plus grande somme de forces. La société qui réprime les voleurs n'est pas plus juste que le sauvage qui défend sa proie mais elle est plus puissante.

|38| Ce que l'homme perd par le contract social, c'est sa liberté naturelle & *un droit illimité à tout ce qui le tente & tout ce qu'il peut atteindre**

*on ne peut trop répéter que dans l'état naturel et sauvage l'homme n'avait pas *un droit illimité à tout ce qui le tentait et qu'il pouvait atteindre.* Il faut reconnaitre que ce droit était limité par la justice et par la raison dès que la chose dont le sauvage pouvait être tenté avait déjà été acquise par un autre. Le vol est proscrit par une loi de la nature antérieure à toute convention. Le droit illimité du sauvage ne s'étendait donc qu'aux choses qui n'étaient encore à personne. Celui de l'homme en société est précisément le même. Il n'est pas vrai que la propriété ne puisse être fondée que sur une convention sociale. Elle peut seulement et doit être reconnue et garantie par ces conventions. Mais le gibier pris à la chasse est une propriété dont la possession et le travail sont le titre très suffisant; et les troupeaux élevés par les soins du Pâtre et la récolte du champ défriché et cultivé par les mains du laboureur sont dans le même cas.

|38| [I]l faut bien distinguer *la liberté naturelle qui n'a pour bornes que les forces de l'individu*, de la liberté civile qui est limitée par la volonté générale.

Ce serait un principe atroce et démenti par l'expérience universelle que celui qui mettrait en maxime que *la liberté naturelle n'a pour bornes que les forces de l'individu.* Elle a comme la liberté civile qui n'est que la même liberté *la justice pour bornes.* Et ce serait calomnier l'homme sauvage que de dire qu'il ne peut pas reconnaitre la justice. Les animaux même les plus féroces en ont quelque idée.

Chapitre IX: Du domaine réel

|40| Car l'État à l'égard de ses membres est maitre de tous leurs biens par le contract social, qui dans l'État sert de base à tous les droits.

L'État n'a droit aux biens d'aucun de ses membres par le contrat social que relativement aux étrangers et alors il est aux droits des citoyens qu'il garantit. Mais il n'a pas lui même le droit de violer la propriété de ces citoyens, car c'est pour la protéger qu'il a été institué et s'il y portait atteint [sic] il violerait le contrat. C'est ce que font les gouvernemens arbitraires.

|41| *Le droit de premier occupant, quoique plus réel que celui du plus fort*, ne devient un vrai droit qu'après l'établissement de celui de propriété.

Le droit du premier occupant pour les choses qu'on peut réellement occuper dans l'état de nature, comme la proie, les fruits, la cabane et son petit enclos et les armes et les outils et les vétemens tels quels est si réel et si respectable que le plus fort ne peut violer ce droit sans injustice, sans guerre, sans s'exposer à des représailles que la justice révoltée des peuples sauvages rend très cruelles. Dès qu'il y a vie et travail il y a droit de propriété.

|41| [M]ais l'acte positif qui le rend propriétaire de quelque bien l'exclud de tout le reste.*

*L'acte positif qui rend un homme propriétaire d'un bien ne l'exclut point du droit de s'emparer des autres biens dont aucun autre homme n'est encore propriétaire.
Il lui laisse en entier celui d'acquérir de ces autres hommes par échange service ou convention.

|41| En général, pour autoriser sur un terrain quelconque le droit de premier occupant, il faut les conditions suivantes. Premièrement que ce terrain ne soit encore habité par personne; secondement qu'on n'en occupe que la quantité dont on a besoin pour subsister. En troisième lieu qu'on en prenne possession, non par une vaine cérémonie, mais par le travail et la culture, seul signe de propriété qui au défaut de titres juridiques doive être respecté d'autrui.

La première et la troisième condition sont justes et naturelles. La seconde est superflue comme comprise dans la troisième. Rousseau convient ici lui-même que la culture est un titre de propriété qui doit être respecté par autrui. [Ça a été] le moyen naturel d'acquérir la propriété des terres aussi voyons nous que les bois et les pâtures et les près qui ne demandent que peu ou point de culture sont longtems restés en communautés et l'on en trouve encore dans cet état. Mais les champs qu'il faut labourer, les vignes et les jardins qu'il faut créer ont toujours un maitre.

|43| Quand Nuñez Balbao prenoit sur le rivage possession de la mer du sud et de toute l'Amérique méridionale au nom de la couronne de Castille, étoit-ce assez pour en déposséder tous les habitans et en exclurre tous les Princes du monde?

Ces prises de Possession des voyageurs n'ont jamais rien signifié que lorsque de véritables colons les ont suivies.

|44| Ceux d'aujourd'hui s'appellent plus habilement Rois de France, d'Espagne, d'Angleterre etc. En tenant ainsi le terrain, ils sont bien sûrs d'en tenir les habitans.	Il n'y a pas longtems que nos Rois s'appellaient encore Rois des Francs *Francorum Rex* tandis que les Rois d'Angleterre s'entitraient *Rex franciae* parce que ceux-ci prétendaient un droit d'hérédité sur le sol tandis que les autres régnaient sur la nation, par ses lois et par son suffrage. Les Rois qui ont porté le titre de leur nation étaient originairement des chefs de Peuples chasseurs ou dont l'association remonte a un tems antérieur à la culture du territoire et qui la plus part ont conquis avec cette nation le territoire d'un peuple cultivateur.
|44| Ce qu'il y a de singulier dans cette aliénation, c'est que, loin qu'en acceptant les biens des particuliers la communauté les en dépouille, elle ne fait que leur en assurer la légitime possession, *changer l'usurpation en un véritable droit, et la jouissance en propriété.**	*il n'aurait pas fallu dire sur la vague précédente changer *l'usurpation* en *droit* et la *jouissance* en *propriété* car le premier qui cultive un champ ne l'usurpe sur personne et la culture lui donne un véritable droit.
|45| De quelque manière que se fasse cette acquisition, *le droit que chaque particulier a sur son propre fond est toujours subordonné au droit que la communauté a sur tous*, sans quoi il n'y auroit ni solidité dans le lien social, ni force réelle dans l'exercice de la Souveraineté.	La communauté n'a aucun droit sur les fonds ni sur les possessions d'aucun particulier que celui de les garder et protéger. Pour exercer cette protection elle a quelquefois le droit d'exposer même la vie des particuliers en les convoquant pour la guerre; mais elle n'a pas celui d'en faire mourir un seul, ni de lui infliger la moindre peine arbitrairement. Elle peut de même prendre un héritage pour le service public de la guerre ou des chemins. Mais elle ne le peut que pour des choses de simple décoration et elle ne le doit jamais sans une indemnité suffisante. Dans le cas de la défense de l'Etat la communauté peut s'emparer provisoirement d'un héritage et le détruire ou dégrader. Elle doit alors indemnité large au Propriétaire où le salut public n'est pas intéressé elle doit traiter de gré à gré et ne prendre possession qu'après avoir satisfait le maitre du sol. Mais les mœurs doivent noter d'une sorte d'infamie l'homme qui vis-à-vis de la communauté voudrait abuser de son droit et mettre un prix par trop excessif à la portion de son bien dont le public a besoin.

Emile,[63] Livre IV

---

63. J.-J. Rousseau, *Emile, ou De l'éducation*, 2 vol. (Amsterdam et Paris, Jean Néaulme, 1765), t.2, HML, N LB 511a.

|177| Une ignorance absolue sur certaines matieres est peut-être ce qui conviendroit le mieux aux enfans: mais qu'ils apprennent de bonne heure ce qu'il est impossible de leur cacher toujours. Il faut, ou que leur curiosité ne s'éveille en aucune manière, ou qu'elle soit satisfaite avant l'âge où elle n'est plus sans danger. Votre conduite avec vôtre élève dépend beaucoup en ceci de sa situation particulière, des sociétés qui l'environnent, des circonstances où l'on prévoit qu'il pourra se trouver, etc. Il importe ici de ne rien donner au hazard, et si vous n'étes pas sur de lui faire ignorer jusqu'à seize ans la différence des sexes ayez soin qu'il l'apprenne avant dix.*

*la grande difficulté quant à l'ignorance des sexes se trouve lorsque l'on a [à] élever ensemble des enfans de sexe différent. La familiarité des petits jeux, le hazard, un instant de solitude, peut être leur procurer des lumières funestes à leur repos, leur santé, à leurs mœurs. La fraternité ne garantit point des impressions et de l'impulsion de la nature dans l'âge ou les sens commencent à se développer.

|297, n.21| Mais si on lui cherche querelle à lui-même, comment se conduira-t-il? Je réponds qu'il n'aura jamais de querelle, qu'il ne s'y prêtera jamais assez pour en avoir. Mais enfin poursuivra-t-on, qui est-ce qui est à l'abri d'un soufflet ou d'un démenti de la part d'un brutal, d'un ivrogne ou d'un brave coquin, qui, pour avoir le plaisir de tuer son homme, commence par le deshonorer? C'est autre chose; il ne faut point que l'honneur des citoyens ni leur vie soit à la merci d'un brutal, d'un ivrogne ou d'un brave coquin, et l'on ne peut pas plus se préserver d'un pareil accident que de la chûte d'une tuile. Un soufflet ou un démenti reçu et enduré ont des effets civils que nulle sagesse ne peut prévenir et dont nul tribunal ne peut venger l'offensé. L'insuffisance des loix lui rend donc en cela son indépendance; il est alors seul magistrat, seul juge entre l'offenseur et lui; il est seul interprète et ministre de la loi naturelle, il se doit justice et peut seul se la rendre, et il n'y a sur la terre nul gouvernement assez insensé pour le punir de se l'être faite en pareil cas. Je ne dis pas qu'il doive s'aller battre, c'est une extravagance; je dis qu'il se doit justice et qu'il en est le seul dispensateur. Sans tant de vains édits contre les duels, si j'étois souverain je réponds qu'il n'y auroit jamais ni soufflet, ni démenti donné dans mes Etats, et cela par un moyen fort simple dont les Tribunaux ne se mêleroient point. Quoi qu'il en soit Emile sait en pareil cas la justice qu'il se doit à lui-même, et l'exemple qu'il doit à la sureté des gens d'honneur. Il ne dépend pas de l'homme le plus ferme d'empêcher qu'on ne l'insulte, mais il dépend de lui d'empêcher qu'on ne se vante long-tems de l'avoir insulté.*

*J'ai vu des gens qui travaillaient pour chercher le sens de cette note et le véritable conseil de J J Rousseau. Jeune lecteur ne t y trompes pas: *tu te dois justice sans doute et un exemple à la sureté des honnestes gens.* Cela ne signifie point pour que tu doives te battre une fois pour éviter d'y revenir par la suite. Un homme honnête et sensible ne doit jamais se battre que quand il s'agit de sauver sa vie ou celle d'un autre homme attaqué et en danger. Mais il doit toujours faire rougir celui qui l'insulte. Le moyen est simple. C'est de montrer dans toute sa conduite tant de sagesse, tant de cette noble et tranquille audace qui accompagne la vertu et qui pour elle et pour la vérité ne craint de déplaire à personne, que chacun saisi de respect sente que la raison et non la faiblesse a empêché l'offensé d'exposer sa vie et celle d'autrui le moyen (nous ne pouvons trop répéter) de ne se point battre et de n'être pas déshonoré, c'est d'avoir pour champions l'estime et la considération publique et de les opposer à l'insolence des étourdis. Ce moyen vaut bien l'art de l'escrime, et tant pis pour ceux qui trop avilis pour être capable de l'employer, sont forcés d'avoir recours à leur épée! Il faut que les hommes soient braves, sans doute, j'espère que mon fils ne sera pas poltron, qu'il saura affronter le danger le plus terrible quand il s'agira d'en préserver sa mère, sa sœur, sa femme ou ses enfans, qu'il ne redoutera point le crédit ni l'autorité des hommes puissans quand il faudra protéger l'innocent infortuné, qu'il ne craindra pas la persécution et les revers. Si son devoir l'appelle à servir l'humanité par des exemples ou des travaux importans, qu'il méprisera le fer de l'ennemi s'il est destiné à déffendre sa patrie, mais que jamais entrainé par un faux point d'honneur il ne s'exposera volontairement à voir palpiter à ses pieds, baigné de sang et rendant les derniers soupirs, son semblable égorgé par ses mains.

148   *Thierry Demals and Alexandra Hyard*

iii. Les notes de Du Pont

Les annotations des neufs chapitres du livre 1 du *Contrat social* sont ici regroupées en quatre thèmes.

La famille et les premières sociétés

Du Pont annote un passage du chapitre 2 où Rousseau qualifie la famille de 'société naturelle', mais aussi de 'premier modèle des sociétés politiques', arguant qu'elle est issue d'un 'lien naturel' et ne peut se proroger que par un acte volontaire des membres qui la constituent et se maintenir que par convention. Dans le *Discours sur l'inégalité* Rousseau imagine en effet un 'pur état de nature' dans lequel l'individu est dépourvu de tout sentiment familial ou filial: 'Telle fut la condition de l'homme naissant; telle fut la vie d'un animal borné d'abord aux pures sensations, & profitant à peine des dons que lui offroit la Nature', écrivait-il.[64]

Le premier sentiment naturel est celui de la conservation. Avec le temps et l'expérience, se forme une 'idée assez grossière des engagements mutuels et de l'avantage de les remplir'. Rousseau qualifie de 'première révolution',[65] la sortie de cet état animal et l'établissement de familles, révolution qui induit une sorte de propriété, celle des outils, des armes et de l'habitation commune où logent 'les maris & les femmes, les pères & les enfans': 'L'habitude de vivre ensemble fit naître les plus doux sentiments qui soient connus des hommes, l'amour conjugal, & l'amour paternel. Chaque famille devint une petite société d'autant mieux unie que l'attachement réciproque & la liberté en étoient les seuls liens.'[66] La conséquence de cette révolution, c'est l'abandon de la 'vie simple & solitaire',[67] l'accroissement du confort, le désir de posséder les nouvelles commodités, la comparaison avec autrui, la jalousie, l'envie et l'inégalité.

Dans le 'Discours de l'éditeur', Du Pont emploie les expressions de 'société naturelle', et d''association primitive et naturelle' pour désigner la famille. Mais il ne fait aucun doute pour lui que la famille reste une association fondamentalement naturelle, même lorsqu'elle

---

64. J.-J. Rousseau, *Discours sur l'origine & les fondements de l'inégalité parmi les hommes* (Amsterdam, Chez Marc Michel Rey, 1755), p.123, 104.
65. J.-J. Rousseau, *Discours sur l'inégalité*, p.113.
66. J.-J. Rousseau, *Discours sur l'inégalité*, p.114.
67. J.-J. Rousseau, *Discours sur l'inégalité*, p.115.

Politique et économie politique chez Pierre-Samuel Du Pont 149

devient volontaire.[68] Le fait qu'elle soit volontaire ne supprime pas le lien naturel originel. Les mêmes expressions sont donc prises dans un sens différent: Rousseau pense la discontinuité et la rupture, la nature finissant par se dissoudre dans la politique; Du Pont pense la continuité, la politique ne devant pas supprimer la nature, mais au contraire l'imiter, la reproduire, la prolonger.

Du Pont pointe aussi cette conséquence que Rousseau tire de sa définition de la famille comme premier modèle des sociétés politiques, à savoir que les enfants ont aliéné leur liberté et se sont soumis à leur père 'pour leur utilité'. Il soutient au contraire que personne dans la famille n'a aliéné sa liberté définie ici comme le 'droit de travailler et d'acquérir et de jouir sans nuire à autrui'. La société familiale s'ordonne, comme toutes les sociétés naturelles ou politiques bien réglées, sur la base du respect de la liberté de chacun et de la réciprocité. Sans ce respect de la liberté de chacun, la famille ne serait plus une société naturelle, mais deviendrait selon Du Pont un 'état de guerre', un état où l'on aliène sa liberté, où les libertés ne sont pas garanties, c'est-à-dire l'antithèse d'une société.

A plusieurs endroits de son commentaire, Du Pont emploie les expressions de 'confédération naturelle', de 'sociétés de familles confédérées', correspondant à l'étape décrite par Rousseau qui suit l'établissement des familles, celle de leur regroupement, de leur sédentarisation et du remplacement du droit naturel par le droit civil. Pour Du Pont, la confédération de familles est une suite naturelle de la 'multiplication des familles': 'Personne, annote-t-il, n'a songé à aliéner ni à restreindre aucun de ses droits, mais au contraire à en étendre l'usage par les secours des confédérés.'[69]

Dans ses différents écrits, Du Pont recourt à des expressions similaires: 'société de familles', 'familles confédérées', 'associations ou simples confédérations de familles sans administrateurs réguliers'.[70] Il va même jusqu'à présenter la société pastorale comme une 'confédération de petites républiques'[71] et écrit un peu plus tard que 'tout ménage est devenu une famille et toute famille un peuple.'[72] Le

---

68. P.-S. Du Pont, 'Discours de l'éditeur', p.xvi, xxxiii.
69. P.-S. Du Pont, recension de *Félicité publique*, dans *Carl Friedrichs von Baden Brieflicher Verkehr*, t.2, p.47.
70. P.-S. Du Pont, recension des *Essais sur les principes des finances, Ephémérides du citoyen* 3 (1770), p.158-95 (166-67 et 173-74).
71. P.-S. Du Pont, *Vie pastorale*, f.2.
72. P.-S. Du Pont, *Philosophie de l'univers*, p.60.

mot 'confédération' lui semble propre.[73] Le Mercier de La Rivière emploie l'expression 'confédération générale' concernant les nations et leurs relations, non les familles.[74] Dans sa recension des *Essais sur les principes des finances*, il explicite cette notion: 'Une nation est une société de familles qui ont chacune séparément leurs propriétés & leurs intérêts particuliers, & leur sureté à défendre les unes contre les autres, & contre les ennemis du dehors. C'est pour assurer ainsi leurs propriétés, leur liberté, leurs droits évidemment reconnus par tous, que ces familles se sont confédérées.'[75]

L'état de nature et l'état primitif

Pour Rousseau l'état de nature ou la condition de l'homme naturel est une construction théorique visant à expliquer la dénaturation de l'homme et l'avènement de l'état civil. Rousseau conçoit cet état comme une fiction: c'est 'un état qui n'existe plus, qui peut-être n'a point existé, qui probablement n'existera jamais, mais dont il est nécessaire d'avoir des notions justes pour bien juger de cet état présent', écrit-il.[76]

L'état de nature n'est pas une expression des plus courantes chez Du Pont. Il emploie dans ses notes l'expression 'état naturel et sauvage', mais dans ses propres ouvrages il lui préfère celles d''état

---

73. L'expression 'familles confédérées' se trouve chez Pierre Jurieu, *Histoire critique des dogmes et des cultes* (Amsterdam, s.n., 1704), p.121, et plus nettement chez Pierre Bayle, *Œuvres*, t.3 (La Haye, s.n., 1727), partie 1, §cxviii, p.352, dans un passage distinguant des familles indépendantes et sans gouvernement et des familles confédérées sous certaines lois. Jean-Jacques Burlamaqui (*Principes du droit naturel*, Genève, s.n., 1748, partie 1, chap.4, p.59) est peut-être le plus proche de la définition proposée par Du Pont lorsqu'il écrit: 'l'état de FAMILLE. Cette société est la plus naturelle & la plus ancienne de toutes, & elle sert de fondement à la *société nationale*: car un peuple ou une *nation* n'est qu'un composé de plusieurs familles.' Pour Burlamaqui, il existe une 'simple société de nature' (*Principes*, p.62) distincte de la société civile: 'Originairement le genre humain n'étoit distingué qu'en familles & non en peuples. Ces familles vivoient sous le gouvernement paternel de celui qui en étoit le chef, comme le père ou l'ayeul. Mais en suite étant venues à s'accroître & à s'unir pour leur défense commune, elles composèrent un corps de nation, gouverné par la volonté de celui, ou de ceux à qui on remettoit l'autorité. De là vient ce qu'on appelle le gouvernement civil & la distinction de souverain & de sujets' (*Principes*, p.62).
74. [P.-P. Le Mercier de La Rivière], *L'Ordre naturel*, t.2, p.231.
75. P.-S. Du Pont, recension des *Essais sur les principes des finances*, p.166-67.
76. J.-J. Rousseau, *Discours sur l'inégalité*, p.lxix-lxx.

Politique et économie politique chez Pierre-Samuel Du Pont

primitif'[77] ou d'"état primitif et sauvage',[78] avec cette gradation parfois soulignée d'"état le plus sauvage'.[79] La plus grande fréquence des épithètes 'primitif' et 'sauvage' peut s'expliquer par le fait qu'il n'y a pas lieu selon lui de considérer qu'il existe un état qui serait naturel uniquement et un autre qui ne le serait plus et serait uniquement politique. Les sociétés politiques (si elles ne sont pas déréglées) sont des émanations du droit naturel, des prolongements ultérieurs des sociétés naturelles, non une rupture d'avec le droit naturel. L'emploi des épithètes 'primitif' et 'sauvage' est en outre possiblement lié aux lectures de Du Pont, notamment les récits de voyages.[80] Ces récits démontrent que l'état primitif décrit par Rousseau n'a que peu de rapport avec ce que l'on peut connaître du passé lointain.

Notons que dans l'article 'Droit naturel' Quesnay distingue deux états de nature hypothétiques successifs: 'l'état de l'homme isolé' ou 'état de pure nature' et 'l'état de multitude' où les hommes communiquent entre eux. L'état de pure nature ou de 'pure indépendance' est un état dans lequel les hommes satisfont à leurs besoins par le travail plutôt que par l'"usurpation sur le droit de possession d'autrui' ou la 'guerre' dont les résultats sont moins assurés.[81] Cet état de solitude disparaît progressivement avec l'apparition de l'association familiale, établissement qui suivant l'ordre naturel est dirigé par un chef, membre le plus fort de cette association. L'état de multitude qui advient alors conduit à l'établissement de conventions, d'une autorité souveraine et de lois positives destinées à protéger l'usage par les hommes de leur droit naturel. Car cet état qui ne connaît encore ni pâturage ni agriculture est moins paisible que l'état isolé: 'il faut les [les hommes réunis] envisager comme des peuplades de Sauvages dans des déserts, qui y vivroient des productions naturelles du territoire,

---

77. P.-S. Du Pont, *De l'origine*, p.17; recension de la *Félicité publique*, dans *Carl Friedrichs von Baden Brieflicher Verkehr*, t.2, p.47; *Philosophie de l'univers*, p.103.
78. P.-S. Du Pont, *Philosophie de l'univers*, p.56-57.
79. P.-S. Du Pont, *Philosophie de l'univers*, p.103.
80. Dans le 'Discours de l'éditeur', p.xxxi-xxxii, Du Pont mentionne les *Mémoires sur l'état de l'Amérique septentrionale* sur les sauvages de Louisiane. Il prend aussi l'exemple des Ostiakes sans donner de référence. L'anecdote qu'il raconte ressemble à celle racontée par Louis Moreri, *Le Grand Dictionnaire historique*, t.8 (Paris, Les libraires associés, 1759), p.141. Voir aussi Jacques-Philibert Rousselot de Surgy, article 'De la Sibérie', dans *Mélanges intéressans & curieux*, t.3 (Paris, Lacombe, 1766), p.15-204.
81. F. Quesnay, 'Le droit naturel', p.11.

ou qui s'exposeroient par nécessité aux dangers du brigandage, s'ils pouvoient faire des excursions chez des Nations où il y auroit des richesses à piller.'[82]

Dans son célèbre ouvrage, Le Mercier de La Rivière consacre peu de pages aux premières étapes des sociétés humaines précédant l'apparition de la culture et de la propriété, attendu que pour lui l'homme est 'social' par nature. L''ordre primitif de la nature' ou encore la 'société primitive' sont composés d'hommes 'vivant naturellement en société', ayant entre eux des droits et devoirs réciproques, ce qu'il exprime ainsi: 'Dans le premier état où le genre humain se présente à nous, je veux dire, dans la société naturelle, universelle & tacite'.[83]

Pour Du Pont, la description de l'homme primitif proposée par Rousseau est doublement fautive. Tout d'abord, écrit-il en note, 'Rousseau n'a jamais eu d'idée bien nette de l'état de nature. On voit par son Discours sur l'inégalité des conditions qu'il a supposé dans cet état l'homme isolé et courant les bois à la manière des singes.' Dans le *Discours sur l'inégalité*, Rousseau s'appuyait sur une hypothèse imaginaire, une fiction, selon Du Pont, celle d'un homme sans relation avec autrui, sans liens familiaux, voulant les droits sans les devoirs. Il dessinait un homme

> errant dans les forêts sans industrie, sans parole, sans domicile, sans guerre & sans liaisons, sans nul besoin de ses semblables, comme sans nul désir de leur nuire, peut-être même sans jamais en reconnoître aucun individuellement, l'homme sauvage sujet à peu de passions, & se suffisant à lui-même, n'avoit que les sentimens & les lumières propres à cet état, qu'il ne sentoit que ses vrais besoins, ne regardoit que ce qu'il croyoit avoir intérêt de voir, & que son intelligence ne faisoit pas plus de progrès que sa vanité.[84]

La seconde supposition fautive du raisonnement rousseauiste est d'attribuer à l'homme primitif un droit illimité sur tout, comme le fait Hobbes. Ainsi pointe-t-il cette phrase de Rousseau: 'Ce que l'homme perd par le contract social, c'est sa liberté naturelle & un droit illimité à tout ce qui le tente & tout ce qu'il peut atteindre.' Sa réponse est qu'il est erroné de supposer que l'homme primitif disposait d'un tel droit et était dépourvu de toute idée de justice naturelle. Le droit illimité sur les choses et les terres qui conduit à prendre ce qui est à

---

82. F. Quesnay, 'Le droit naturel', p.26.
83. [P.-P. Le Mercier de La Rivière], *L'Ordre naturel*, t.1, p.22, 31.
84. J.-J. Rousseau, *Discours sur l'inégalité*, p.91.

autrui est assimilé à un vol. Le droit du sauvage a une limite fixée par la loi naturelle qui est de ne s'étendre qu'aux choses et aux terres qui ne sont à personne. Il n'y a donc pas lieu de distinguer sur une telle base la liberté naturelle et la liberté civile et de soutenir que l'une n'a de limite que les 'forces de l'individu' et n'est applicable qu'à l'état primitif et que l'autre ne dépendant que de la volonté générale échapperait au droit naturel. Toutes deux sont bornées par la justice. Ce raisonnement est également tenu dans le 'Discours de l'éditeur' et dans d'autres écrits.[85] Un propos similaire est exprimé par Quesnay: 'Quelques Philosophes absorbés dans l'idée abstraite du droit naturel des hommes, qui laisse à tous un droit à tout, ont borné le droit naturel à l'état de pure indépendance des hommes les uns envers les autres, & à l'état de guerre entr'eux pour s'emparer les uns & les autres de leur droit illimité.'[86]

Dans ces annotations Du Pont relève également cette phrase de Rousseau affirmant qu'il n'y a pas de 'guerre privée ou d'homme à homme' dans un état de nature sans 'propriété constante', ni même dans un 'état social' gouverné par des lois. Dans le premier état où 'l'inégalité est à peine sensible',[87] l'absence de propriété annihile sensiblement toute forme de rivalité. Rousseau cite à l'appui cette phrase de Locke: 'Il ne sauroit y avoir d'injure où il n'y a point de propriété.'[88] Dans l'état social, ce sont les lois positives protégeant la propriété qui empêchent la rivalité. En revanche cet état ne supprime pas les guerres d'Etat à Etat. Du Pont répond que la guerre privée ou d'homme à homme peut exister dans un état primitif pour la raison précisément qu'il y a des propriétés constantes, au moins la propriété de la personne, celle des choses acquises par le travail de chasse ou de cueillette, celle encore des instruments de travail et du logis. En dépouillant l'état primitif de ces propriétés constantes, Rousseau n'a pas perçu qu'il pouvait y avoir guerre entre les hommes, avec toutefois cette limite que le droit naturel de conservation interdit de tuer le rival. Pour autant il ne rejoint pas Hobbes et sa vision d'un état de guerre caractérisant la 'simplicité naturelle'.[89] Dans d'autres écrits, il

---

85. P.-S. Du Pont, 'Discours de l'éditeur', p.vi, xv; recension de la *Félicité publique*, dans *Carl Friedrichs von Baden Brieflicher Verkehr*, t.2, p.48; *Philosophie de l'univers*, p.59.
86. F. Quesnay, 'Le droit naturel', p.8.
87. J.-J. Rousseau, *Discours sur l'inégalité*, p.98.
88. Cette phrase est tirée de l'*Essai philosophique concernant l'entendement humain*, traduit par P. Coste (Amsterdam, s.n., 1742), livre 4, chap.3, §18, p.454.
89. P.-S. Du Pont, 'Discours de l'éditeur', p.lxxiii.

soutient au contraire qu'il n'y a pas de guerre avant l'état agricole,[90] voire avant l'état pastoral, pour la raison qu'il y a peu de richesses à convoiter. Autre manière de dire que l'état agricole ne produit ses effets bénéfiques que sous 'un gouvernement paisible' et la protection d'une autorité tutélaire.

Propriété

Cette question est délicate chez Rousseau.[91] Dans l'état de nature rousseauiste se trouvent entremêlées deux explications, voire deux justifications de l'appropriation privative: le droit du premier occupant qui peut être considéré comme une forme d'usurpation, et le droit issu du travail qui 'n'a rien d'évident'[92] et qui est contestable lorsqu'il s'agit de s'approprier plus que la consommation nécessaire à sa conservation.[93] Cette question est illustrée par deux exemples bien connus (que Du Pont ne commente pas), le poseur de clôture du *Discours sur l'inégalité* et le planteur de fèves du livre 2 d'*Emile*. Le point important chez Rousseau est de distinguer entre propriété et possession (c'est-à-dire un usage non associé à un droit de propriété privatif). Cette distinction permet d'asseoir l'idée que la propriété sur les choses et sur la terre n'est pas naturelle, qu'elle est une dégradation, une dénaturation de l'état de nature, puisque cet état est caractérisé par la communauté des biens (choses et terres).

Dans le *Discours sur l'inégalité*, l'individu qui, dans l'état de nature, s'approprie le terrain qu'il vient d'enclore est qualifié d'imposteur par Rousseau pour n'avoir pas respecté un commandement: 'Les

---

90. P.-S. Du Pont, recension de *Félicité publique*, dans *Carl Friedrichs von Baden Brieflicher Verkehr*, t.2, p.54.

91. On se reportera à Robert Derathé, *Jean-Jacques Rousseau et la science politique de son temps* (Paris, 1950); B. Bachofen, *La condition de la liberté*; Mikhaïl Xifaras, 'La destination politique de la propriété chez Jean-Jacques Rousseau', *Les Etudes philosophiques* 66 (2003), p.331-70; Rudy Le Mentheour, 'Au berceau de l'appropriation: Rousseau, Locke et l'enfance du propriétaire', *Annales Jean-Jacques Rousseau* 50 (2012), p.161-82; C. Spector, *Rousseau et la critique de l'économie politique*.

92. Céline Spector, 'L'inaliénabilité de la liberté', dans *Rousseau et Locke: dialogues critiques*, éd. Céline Spector et Johanna Lenne-Cormuez, Oxford University Studies in the Enlightenment (Liverpool, Liverpool University Press / Voltaire Foundation, 2022), p.181-207.

93. J.-J. Rousseau, *Discours sur l'inégalité*, p.143-44: 'Ignorez-vous [...] qu'il vous falloit un consentement exprès et unanime du genre humain pour vous approprier une substance commune de tout ce qui alloit au-delà de la vôtre.'

Politique et économie politique chez Pierre-Samuel Du Pont 155

fruits sont à tous, [...] la terre n'est à personne.'[94] Ce commandement rappelle une vieille distinction entre le domaine de Dieu et le domaine des hommes.[95] Le domaine de Dieu, ce sont des terres et des choses laissées à l'usage commun de tous les hommes sans pour autant leur conférer de titre de propriété; le domaine des hommes relève non pas du droit naturel, mais du droit positif. Ainsi, dans l'état de nature la cueillette des fruits de la nature ou la chasse au gibier ont pour fin une possession justifiée par le droit de conservation, une possession acquise par la force, non une appropriation privative exclusive, à la différence de l'acte d'enclore une terre qui apparaît comme une appropriation illégitime de biens communs. Dans ce premier état de nature où la terre n'appartient à personne, les hommes ne sont que des occupants sans titre d'un domaine qui appartient à Dieu, dont ils peuvent jouir des fruits sous l'hypothèse d'une abondance de biens (choses, terres). Le processus d'appropriation privative se déroule par deux révolutions – l'appropriation du logis, des armes et des outils, et l'appropriation de la terre pour la cultiver – signes de la fin irréversible de l'état de nature. Dans le *Contrat social*, l'état de nature est décrit comme un état de liberté et de conservation, sans guerre et sans 'propriétés constantes'. Dès lors que les propriétés deviennent constantes, l'état de nature se dégrade et fait insensiblement place à un état de guerre.

La propriété par le travail qui s'origine dans le second traité de gouvernement civil de Locke dérive de la propriété de la personne.[96] C'est la règle qui doit régir toute appropriation privative. Un point cependant sépare Locke et Rousseau, c'est que le premier ne distingue pas propriété et possession. Ces deux notions étant confondues, toute cueillette des fruits de la nature, toute terre cultivée pour ses fruits s'apparentent à des appropriations privatives légitimes – à la condition qu'elles soient limitées à la conservation de l'individu, qu'elles ne se transforment pas en un droit à tout, et qu'elles soient proportionnées au travail dépensé préalablement. Cette limitation ne doit pas être comprise comme une condamnation de l'échange et de l'accumulation des produits de la terre.[97] Les annotations de Du Pont reprennent la

---

94. J.-J. Rousseau, *Discours sur l'inégalité*, p.102.
95. C'est la reprise d'une vieille question qui traverse la patristique et la scolastique et qui est débattue par exemple par Thomas d'Aquin, *Summa theologiae* (1266-1274), traduit par Ceslas Spicq (Paris, 1934), II^a II^{ae}, q.66, art.1 et 2.
96. J. Locke, *Two treatises of government*, §27.
97. J. Locke, *Two treatises of government*, §46, p.318: '*the exceeding of the bounds of his just Property* not lying in the largeness of his Possession, but the perishing of any thing uselesly in it.'

position de Locke: le cueilleur a un droit de propriété par son travail, de même le chasseur et le cultivateur. Comme chez Locke, il n'y a pas de discontinuité ou de rupture qui ferait apparaître l'état civil.

Dans le *Contrat social*, Rousseau fournit une justification du droit du premier occupant sous certaines conditions, notamment l'exclusion de la conquête coloniale qui est une appropriation non légitime de terres. L'idée générale est que l'homme a droit à tout ce qui lui est nécessaire, et que dans l'état civil une loi positive peut lui donner la propriété à l'exclusion des autres, mais, une fois sa part déterminée, 'il doit s'y borner et n'a plus aucun droit à la communauté'.[98] Rousseau énumère subséquemment les conditions de possibilité du droit d'occupation (c'est-à-dire des conditions légitimes du droit d'appropriation): (i) le terrain doit être non habité; (ii) il ne doit être occupé que pour satisfaire les besoins nécessaires; (iii) seuls 'le travail et la culture' justifient son appropriation. Il ajoute, suggérant une sorte de droit éminent de la communauté, que quelle que soit la forme de l'appropriation légitime 'le droit du particulier sur son propre fonds est toujours subordonné au droit que la communauté a sur tous.'[99]

Du Pont interprète ce passage de Rousseau de la façon suivante: le droit du premier occupant est un droit sur les produits de la nature, le gibier chassé, le logis, les armes, les outils et une portion de terre, bref sur des produits du travail. Ce droit est donc déjà un droit de propriété: 'Dès qu'il y a vie et travail il y a droit de propriété', annote-t-il. Ensuite, la propriété sur les choses et sur la terre n'est pas un droit exclusif tant qu'il existe des biens qui ne sont la propriété de personne, donc vacants, ou qu'on peut les obtenir par 'échange, service ou convention'. Enfin, des trois conditions énoncées par Rousseau, Du Pont rejette logiquement la seconde qui limite l'occupation à la satisfaction du nécessaire.[100]

Du Pont rejette le droit éminent de la communauté (ou de l'Etat dans l'état civil) au motif que la communauté n'a aucun droit sur les propriétés des particuliers (sauf lors de circonstances exceptionnelles

---

98. J.-J. Rousseau, *Du contrat social*, chap.9.

99. J.-J. Rousseau, *Du contrat social*, chap.9.

100. Le droit du premier occupant est une expression assez rare dans les écrits physiocratiques. Il ne semble pas qu'on la trouve chez Quesnay et Mirabeau. En revanche on peut la lire chez Guillaume-François Le Trosne, *Recueil de plusieurs morceaux économiques* (Amsterdam et Paris, Desaint, 1768), p.18, et Nicolas Baudeau, *Explication du Tableau économique à Madame de **** (1767; Paris, Delalain, 1776), p.23. Les expressions 'premier occupant' ou 'premier défricheur' sont associées à la justification des avances foncières.

Politique et économie politique chez Pierre-Samuel Du Pont 157

telles que la guerre). Il termine ce passage en distinguant deux types de royaumes: ceux dont les rois gouvernent sur une nation ou un peuple et ceux gouvernant sur un territoire par hérédité. Les premiers sont généralement issus des sociétés chasseresses antérieures à la culture des terres.

La première convention, le pacte social et la pluralité des suffrages

Dans le chapitre 5 du *Contrat social*, Rousseau attribue à Grotius l'assertion selon laquelle 'un peuple [...] peut se donner à un roi'[101] et lui objecte qu'avant de poser l'existence de cet acte de soumission il faut poser que le peuple préexiste au roi et qu'il a nécessairement dû se constituer en tant que peuple avant de délibérer et de se donner à un roi ou d'élire un roi, la délibération étant la preuve que le peuple est une entité et non une masse informe d'individus isolés. Ce qu'il faut examiner en premier lieu, c'est donc 'l'acte par lequel un peuple est un peuple' et 'le vrai fondement de la société', c'est-à-dire l'acte fondateur.

Dans sa réponse, Du Pont emploie non pas le mot 'peuple', mais celui d'hommes ou d'individus formant une 'confédération sociale'. Il note en marge de ce passage que 'les hommes ne se sont jamais donnés *à un Roi*', mais qu'ils 'se sont quelquefois donnés *un Roi*, c'est-à-dire qu'ils ont nommé un premier Magistrat'. Il dénie l'idée de première convention,[102] et s'en tient à la convention civile qui nomme un roi ou un premier magistrat pour défendre la liberté des individus. Ni lui ni Rousseau ne mentionnent à cet endroit la propriété et sa sécurité comme justification du souverain, mais seulement le 'maintien des droits et de la liberté de tous et de chacun des individus'.

Rousseau fait ensuite une distinction entre la 'loi de la pluralité des suffrages'[103] et 'l'unanimité': la pluralité est un établissement de

---

101. Hugo Grotius, *Le Droit de la guerre et de la paix*, traduit par Jean Barbeyrac, 2 vol. (Basle, Chez E. Thourneisen, 1746), t.1, livre 1, chap.3, §8, p.121. Rousseau conteste également cette autre assertion de Grotius soutenant que, si un individu peut aliéner sa liberté et se soumettre à un maître, 'pourquoi tout un peuple ne pourroit-il pas aliéner la sienne et se rendre sujet d'un roi', assertion que lui-même et Du Pont rejettent.

102. Dans *L'Etat des physiocrates: autorité et décentralisation* (Aix-en-Provence, 2010), p.38-66, Anthony Mergey remarque que, si le pacte social, sous ses deux aspects (association et soumission), se trouve dans les textes physiocratiques, cette notion perd beaucoup de son importance dans le raisonnement physiocratique qui confère à l'homme une sociabilité naturelle.

103. Rousseau emploie trois fois l'expression 'pluralité des suffrages' dans le *Contrat*

convention qui suppose au moins une fois 'l'unanimité', c'est-à-dire lors de l'acte fondateur. Il faut un accord unanime du peuple pour admettre une convention qui stipule que le petit nombre doit 'se soumettre au choix du grand'.[104]

Du Pont répond que la loi de pluralité des suffrages n'est pas une convention, mais 'l'expression d'un fait physique', c'est-à-dire le fait que le plus grand nombre l'emporte sur le plus petit. De sorte que, soit le plus petit nombre accepte la volonté du plus grand nombre, soit il la refuse et entre dans un 'état de guerre'. Si le petit nombre refuse, tout se passe comme s'il constituait une société différente qui se mettrait en guerre contre la société du plus grand nombre. Comme dans les relations internationales, le conflit se résoudrait soit par l'acceptation d'un traité de paix, soit par l'acceptation des 'risques d'une guerre inégale'.

Du Pont n'oppose ici aucune objection de fond à la pluralité des suffrages qu'il réduit à un fait physique et ne lui oppose pas l'évidence comme guide de la décision publique, ce qui le différencie par exemple de Le Mercier de La Rivière. Chez ce dernier, la loi de pluralité des suffrages correspond à une situation où l'opinion est ignorante et divisée,[105] à la différence de l'évidence qui, quand on l'a reconnue, met tout le monde d'accord (c'est-à-dire l'unanimité): 'Toute nation qui croit que l'autorité doit être acquise à la pluralité des suffrages, & qui donne à cette pluralité le pouvoir de tenir la place de l'évidence, n'a certainement pas une connaissance évidente de l'ordre qui constitue son meilleur état possible.'[106] Du Pont ne

---

social outre le chap.6: livre 1, chap.5, 'Qu'il faut toujours remonter à une première convention', p.25; livre 4, chap.2, 'Des suffrages', p.239; livre 4, chap.4, 'Des comices romains', p.274.

104. *Du contrat social*, livre 1, chap.5, p.25.

105. Voir aussi Nicolas Baudeau, 'Les doutes éclaircis ou réponse aux objections de M. l'abbé de Mably', *Ephémérides du citoyen* 7 (1768), p.208-10. L'abbé critique la pluralité des suffrages lorsqu'elle concerne la 'législation positive' ou 'l'adminis-tration': 'c'est livrer, écrit-il, l'ordre social à la multitude des intérêts particuliers exclusifs' (p.209). Le *Dictionnaire de l'Académie françoise dédié au roy*, t.1.2 (Paris, Coignard, 1718), précise que l'expression est employée dans les ouvrages de droit romain ou canon, les traités de guerre et de paix, les traités ecclésiastiques. Voir aussi [Hilaire Dumas], *Histoire des cinq propositions de Jansenius* (Liège, s.n., 1700), p.123: 'Le droit commun & naturel de toutes sortes d'assemblées est de conclure à la pluralité des suffrages, à moins qu'il n'y ait quelque Statut qui en ordonne autrement: l'Eglise mesme dans les Conciles Généraux ou Provinciaux en use de la sorte.' De même le *Journal des sçavans* (1703), p.565.

106. [P.-P. Le Mercier de La Rivière], *L'Ordre naturel*, t.1, p.136.

semble pas employer l'expression 'pluralité des suffrages' dans *De l'origine* ou dans le 'Discours de l'éditeur'. En revanche, l'expression apparaît dans le *Mémoire sur les municipalités* en 1775,[107] lorsqu'il réfléchit à la procédure de vote dans le système d'assemblées territoriales qu'il échafaude avec Turgot. Il y précise (i) que le vote et le nombre de suffrages sont liés non pas à l'individu (selon la règle: un homme, un vote), mais au montant de produit net ou de revenu qu'un propriétaire retire de sa terre; (ii) que cette disposition permet d'avoir des assemblées peu nombreuses et moins tumultueuses et des délibérations avoisinant l'unanimité; (iii) que la pluralité est une notion imprécise qui se décline suivant l'importance de la question à débattre (pluralité simple, grande pluralité, ou très grande pluralité); (iv) que dans certains cas le vote par tête est préférable (par exemple, pour empêcher que les citoyens riches et grands propriétaires n'abusent de leur avantage). Dans ce projet d'assemblées, les objets de la délibération porteraient uniquement sur l'impôt, les biens publics (routes, corvées) et la police des pauvres.

***

Le présent article a cherché à éclaircir deux questions: la première était celle de l'influence de Rousseau sur la pensée politique de Du Pont, la seconde était d'évaluer le caractère physiocratique de ses annotations au *Contrat social* et à *Emile*.

Quant à la première question, il nous semble difficile d'affirmer que Rousseau est l'un des mentors de Du Pont dans les années 1760. Les références au Genevois sont peu nombreuses dans les premiers écrits comme dans les derniers. En outre, les annotations font apparaître un point de divergence majeur au milieu d'un accord large sur la théorie du droit naturel. En effet, Du Pont ne conçoit pas de rupture franche entre l'état naturel (ou primitif) et l'état civil et, consécutivement, de distinction nette entre des sociétés familiales primitives qui – suivant l'assertion de Rousseau – seraient gouvernées selon la nature, et des sociétés politiques, plus tardives, qui seraient gouvernées par des conventions. Cette distinction n'est pas opératoire pour Du Pont. Il y a au contraire une continuité: les sociétés politiques (si elles sont bien réglées) ne se sont pas séparées de la nature, comme Rousseau le prétend. Et surtout, il n'y a pas un état d'indépendance de l'individu

---

107. [P.-S. Du Pont et A.-R.-J. Turgot], *Mémoire sur les municipalités*, dans *Œuvres de Turgot et documents le concernant*, t.4, p.568-621.

qui aurait été perdu avec l'avènement des sociétés politiques, une liberté naturelle qui aurait été troquée contre un gain d'utilité, comme le pense Rousseau. Une telle proposition peut se lire chez Quesnay, dans 'Droit naturel': 'Ainsi les hommes qui se mettent sous la dépendance, ou plutôt sous la protection des lois positives et d'une autorité tutélaire, étendent beaucoup leur faculté d'être propriétaires, et par conséquent étendent beaucoup l'usage de leur droit naturel, au lieu de le restreindre.'[108]

Quant à la seconde question, la réponse est plus mitigée. Du Pont est incontestablement physiocrate à la fin de l'année 1763, mais il faut noter l'absence dans ses notes de deux notions importantes, constitutives de la philosophie physiocratique – la notion d'évidence qui permet de connaître l'ordre naturel et la notion de despotisme légal qui est le gouvernement le plus avantageux qui suit les lois de l'ordre naturel –, alors qu'elles sont présentes à des degrés divers dans ses écrits imprimés, ce qui rend incertaine la datation des annotations.

---

108. F. Quesnay, 'Le droit naturel', p.28.

From one world to another: how Du Pont de Nemours became a revolutionary

Christophe Le Digol

University Paris Nanterre

> Un des caractères qui ont distingué le plus grand nombre des membres de l'Assemblée nationale constituante, a été l'entière abnégation de tout intérêt personnel, même de celui dont la séduction est la plus entraînante pour les cœurs sensibles et les âmes élevées, l'intérêt si puissant de la gloire dont on sent qu'on est digne.
>
> – Du Pont[1]

Someone who regularly attends political gatherings might greet the words of Pierre-Samuel Du Pont de Nemours with a smile, for an observer who frequents politicians is not inclined to spontaneously grant them the virtue of self-abnegation. Everyone deplores the fact that altruism is probably not their strongest quality. Politics is usually described as a world where calculation and strategy reign almost supreme. Everyone fights fiercely to win the slightest advantage and seeks in every possible way to increase their own political credit. This is how power works, whether it be political or not. Only professional politicians describe their activities in terms of altruism, disinterest and self-sacrifice. The Constituent Assembly had barely broken up when Du Pont de Nemours wrote the words quoted above.[2] They resonate

---

1. *Correspondance patriotique entre les citoyens qui ont été membres de l'Assemblée nationale constituante*, vol.1 (Paris, De l'imprimerie de Du Pont, 1791), 9 October 1791, p.10. All translations are my own unless otherwise indicated.
2. A few years later, in 1794, Du Pont sent a letter to the *Décade philosophique* in which he expressed a similar point of view: 'C'est Dupont qui a fait voir qu'outre l'obligation de ne pas nuire, le droit naturel entraînait le devoir de servir ses semblables'; 'Economie rurale', *La Décade philosophique, littéraire et politique* 26 (20 nivôse An III), p.69-84 (76).

like an epitaph praising the collective action of a heterogeneous and even motley group which, against all odds, had forbidden itself to run for the Legislative Assembly that was to succeed it. Despite their differences, the members of the Constituent Assembly were apparently driven by a desire for the common good, a desire to serve the general interest to which they had even sacrificed their personal interest.

Written in October 1791, these words were undoubtedly the finest tribute that could be paid to the work accomplished by the Constituent Assembly, the fate of whose members was for a time shared by the author. This epitaph denied there was any personal interest in the reasons which governed their actions, not even the interest of the 'glory' to which they could have legitimately laid claim. Implicitly, it implied that, in accordance with their noblest acts (the *Declaration of the rights of man and of the citizen*, the waiver of their own privileges, and their refusal to be re-eligible for the future assembly, for example), it was the general interest that guided their action and perhaps even justified it. The historical enigma of the Constituent Assembly's reasons for acting has since remained one of the main interpretative issues of the French Revolution: the question *why?* After all, their individual destinies were very closely intertwined, to the point of identity, with the fate of a nation which they – perhaps more than others – had helped to bring about politically.[3] But is it even possible to treat as a homogeneous group a set of deputies who, undoubtedly having heterogeneous stories and reasons for acting, found themselves gripped by political logic and interdependencies which led them, against their own wills, towards political horizons that they had neither foreseen nor anticipated? Assigning a single reason to the collective actions of those who, subsequently, became revolutionaries was an element in the power play in which, as we see with Du Pont, the revolutionaries themselves were already involved, immediately embroiled as they were in the struggles over the legitimate interpretation of their action. These struggles continued even after the dissolution of the Constituent Assembly. And they have continued to be waged up until the present day, even if, now that time

---

3. On this point, see the writings of Emmanuel Sieyès, who theorised the question of the political existence of the nation, in particular in *Qu'est-ce que le Tiers Etat?*, first published in Paris in 1789; English translation (abbreviated) available online as *What is the Third Estate?*, https://pages.uoregon.edu/dluebke/301ModernEurope/Sieyes3dEstate.pdf (last accessed 4 December 2024).

How Du Pont de Nemours became a revolutionary   163

has done its work, they have gradually become more or less limited to the historiographical dimension.[4]

Moving from the members of the Constituent Assembly to Du Pont de Nemours himself, we can reasonably agree that he did not exclude himself from 'the greatest number of the members of the national Constituent Assembly'. The personality trait he generously attributed to his colleagues was also recognised in him by his contemporaries. The public homage paid to him on his death in 1817 was unanimous in saying as much: a member of his maternal family, the Montchanins, underlined the nobility of his soul[5] and Joseph-Marie de Gérando, who was one of his friends, insisted on the qualities of his heart.[6] But, without calling into question the judgement of his contemporaries,[7] or even that of the authors who have written his biography, one can wonder whether it is possible to establish his human qualities as a motive for his revolutionary commitment. Can concern for others and the common good, or a taste for freedom and equality, sociologically explain his commitment to a new regime where everything needed to be done afresh, as the same regime had by now undone everything? If his contemporaries were able to reasonably think and write as much, the researcher, for his or her part, must absolutely try to understand the properly social conditions underlying the propensity to disinterestedness in that *homme double*, Pierre-Samuel

4. As Timothy Tackett shows in *Becoming a revolutionary: the deputies of the French National Assembly and the emergence of a revolutionary culture (1789-1790)* (Princeton, NJ, 1996).
5. 'Son âme était noble, élevée, généreuse.' Jules Monchanin, *Notice sur la vie de Du Pont de Nemours* (Paris, 1818), p.1.
6. 'C'est dans le cœur de M. Dupont de Nemours qu'il faut chercher le principe et la source de tout ce qu'il a été, de tout ce qu'il a fait. Son cœur bien connu nous donne le secret de sa vie et de ses ouvrages. Deux sentiments qui se confondent l'un dans l'autre, quand ils sont sincères, et qui se confondaient réellement en lui, l'amour du bien, l'amour de la vérité, l'animaient et avaient chez lui le caractère d'une passion exaltée, passion qui sembla s'accroître encore avec le tems, loin d'éprouver ce relâchement que l'âge, les mécomptes rendent trop communs chez les autres hommes: ces deux sentimens s'épanchaient avec une candeur et une bonne foi singulières qui régnaient dans tous ses rapports avec les autres, parce qu'elles régnaient dans toutes ses méditations intérieures.' Joseph-Marie de Gérando, *Notice sur M. Du Pont de Nemours, lue à la séance générale de la Société d'encouragement pour l'industrie nationale, le 23 septembre 1818*, extract from the *Moniteur* of 16 October 1818, p.2.
7. For example Pierre Jolly, *Du Pont de Nemours, soldat de la liberté* (Paris, 1956), p.2-5.

164   *Christophe Le Digol*

Du Pont de Nemours. The historian Christophe Charle defines 'les hommes doubles' as mediators who 'appartiennent conjointement à deux niveaux culturels d'habitude séparés et servent de passeurs entre eux'.[8] In the case of Du Pont, being a double man was associated with a kind of socialisation that was unusual for the time.

The logic of the double man

Dupont or Du Pont? Some biographers have felt it necessary to comment on a graphic curiosity which in their view is basically rather trivial: the two spellings are used by Pierre-Samuel himself and by his family. Any serious biographer has a duty to dispel any doubt as to the identity of their subject: logically, the two spellings could correspond to two different individuals. The first virtue of precision is therefore to attest to the existence of a *single* individual, despite the variant spellings. From Denise Aimé who, in 1933, felt obliged to explain her use of the two spellings depending on the circumstances[9] to the historian Marc Bouloiseau who also justified his choice of spelling in his very first note,[10] the play on names is somewhat problematic as this practice was so different from the current use of patronymics[11] –

8.   On the notion of the 'homme double', see Christophe Charle, 'Le temps des hommes doubles', *Revue d'histoire moderne et contemporaine* 39:1 (1992), p.73-85 (73).

9.   'Ni les écrivains, ni les journalistes du XVIIIe siècle, ni les économistes, ni les historiens actuels ne se sont mis d'accord sur le nom de Dupont, la plupart l'écrivent ainsi, d'autres, moins nombreux, Du Pont. Pierre-Samuel lui-même a constamment usé et même souvent à des dates très rapprochées, des deux formes, sa signature liant les deux mots, permettant de lire de l'une ou de l'autre façon. Les registres de Rouen écrivent tous Du Pont, ceux de Wilmington également et la famille s'est toujours appelée ainsi depuis. L'auteur a pris le parti d'écrire Dupont quand il s'agit de son héros et que le nom est seul et Du Pont dès que les mots "de Nemours" s'y adjoignent'; Denise Aimé-Azam, *Du Pont de Nemours, honnête homme* (Paris, 1933), p.2, n.1.

10. 'On sait que le nom des Du Pont est écrit tantôt en un mot, tantôt en deux par les intéressés eux-mêmes. Nous adoptons la seconde forme qui est plus souvent usitée. D'abord le père, Pierre Samuel, député du bailliage de Nemours aux Etats généraux de 1789, ajouta entre parenthèses ce complément qui le distinguait de son collègue Dupont (de Bigorre); puis les parenthèses disparurent'; Marc Bouloiseau, *Bourgeoisie et révolution: les Du Pont de Nemours (1788-1799)* (Paris, 1972), p.11, note 1.

11. Other biographers, writing in the nineteenth century, such as Eugène Daire and Léonce de Lavergne, preferred to use the spelling 'Dupont de Nemours'. See *Physiocrates. Quesnay, Dupont de Nemours, Mercier de La Rivière, l'abbé Baudeau,*

especially as this game continued at the start of the French Revolution when Pierre-Samuel, then deputy of the bailiwick of Nemours, added 'de Nemours' to his name to distinguish himself from his colleague Dupont, deputy of Bigorre, who also sat in the Constituent Assembly.[12] On this occasion, the name used was also adopted for political reasons: arising from a practical, specific concern for distinction, it now and forever identifies Dupont or Du Pont with the place Nemours, as he claimed to be its representative. Thus, a practical logic of distinction became a perennial identity, transmissible and transmitted to his descendants.

These two spellings were perhaps not unrelated to the social aspirations that Pierre-Samuel fostered from an early age. Tossed between two social worlds, that of the bourgeoisie and that of the nobility, he espoused the values of the Protestant bourgeoisie to which his paternal family belonged: rigour, thoroughness, the importance of hard work and a job well done. His father, who held a position as watchmaker to the king and with whom – on his own admission – Pierre-Samuel's relations were strained, had a very prosaic relationship to the social order. Becoming a watchmaker seems to have been the only social horizon he envisioned for his son, and he would spare no efforts to orient him in that direction. As soon as he could, he withdrew his son from the Viard boarding house where he had initially agreed to place him, under pressure from his wife. When the latter died, he apprenticed his son to learn the profession of watchmaker. The prospect was far from alluring to Pierre-Samuel, who was full of the stories his mother had always told him and inspired by the high level of literacy she had taught him to enjoy. Of noble but poor origin, Anne Alexandrine de Montchanin had nevertheless received a very good education, influenced by the Enlightenment. When her mother died, her education was taken over by Mme d'Epenilles. Her father was then the manager of the estates of her husband, the marquis de

---

Le Trosne, avec une introduction sur la doctrine des physiocrates, des commentaires et des notices historiques, ed. Eugène Daire, 2 vols (Paris, 1846), p.309-34; Léonce de Lavergne, *Les Economistes français du dix-huitième siècle* (Paris, 1870), p.381-435. More recently, Edna Hindie Lemay uses the spelling 'Dupont, Pierre-Samuel' in her *Dictionnaire des constituants, 1789-1791,* 2 vols (Paris, 1991), vol.1, p.314-17.

12. This addition was immediately emphasised by another of his biographers, Gustave Schelle, in *Du Pont de Nemours et l'école physiocratique* (Paris, 1888), p.7. On family-name legislation in the eighteenth century and during the French Revolution, see Anne Lefebvre-Teillard, 'Le nom et la loi', *Mots: les langages du politique* 63 (2000), p.9-18.

166   *Christophe Le Digol*

Jaucourt. In Paris, she received an aristocratic education far above her condition and never fully recovered from being excluded from this world and sent back to her family at the age of sixteen. In the unfinished memoirs that Pierre-Samuel wrote in 1792, intended for his children, long pages are devoted to describing this painful episode:

> Un des plus grands malheurs qui puisse arriver à une jeune fille est d'être élevée dans une famille plus riche et plus illustre que la sienne, comme enfant de la maison; d'y contracter les besoins de l'opulence et de l'amour-propre, et d'être ensuite renvoyée, comme cela ne manque presque jamais, au destin qui devait résulter pour elle du véritable état de ses parents. J'en ai vu plusieurs exemples très fâcheux. Les gens riches, dans ce cas-là, croient avoir été bienfaisants: ils se sont seulement procuré pendant quelques années une poupée qui leur a fait plaisir. Mais ils lui ont donné une âme, et l'âme de la poupée est déchirée en cent façons lorsqu'elle a perdu sa petite bonne. J'invite ceux qui voudront élever de jolis enfants pauvres dans leur maison à y songer. Ont-ils l'envie et le pouvoir de les rendre riches? ils font bien. Veulent-ils les renvoyer à leur pauvreté, ou même à un état médiocre? ils leur préparent des moments dont l'amertume ne peut être exprimée.
>
> C'est précisément ce qu'éprouva ma mère: elle partit de l'hôtel de Jaucourt fondant en larmes, étouffant de soupirs et de sanglots. Elle avait environ seize ans et son frère Alexandre la prit chez lui.[13]

By 'chance', there was a man staying at her brother's house when she was taken in; this was the man she was later to marry. The biographical break of her sixteenth birthday was followed by a fall in social status for which her lifestyle until that age had not prepared her: belonging to the penniless nobility, she married a bourgeois whose relationship to the world was very different from her own. However, she tried to give her son the best possible education: contrary to custom, and after two unhappy episodes, her husband allowed her to keep her son at her side. Noting that her son was good at mathematics, she introduced him to D'Alembert, who recommended a mathematics teacher to her.[14] From this education, Pierre-Samuel acquired a certain taste for knowledge and an immoderate inclination for the aristocratic world of which his mother had given him a glimpse. Coincidentally, Pierre-Samuel was also sixteen when his mother died in 1755. It is hard not

13. *L'Enfance et la jeunesse de Du Pont de Nemours racontées par lui-même* (Paris, 1906), p.54-55.
14. *L'Enfance*, p.94.

How Du Pont de Nemours became a revolutionary

to notice that mother and son both suffered from a traumatic event at the same age. And, while these two events were not of the same nature, they nevertheless had similar effects on the way mother and son related to the aristocracy. One effect was that Pierre-Samuel was ambitious to be part of the world from which his mother had been excluded and which had fascinated him so much – a desire, in a way, for social revenge:

Through the stories and education his mother gave him, Pierre-Samuel symbolically got one foot into this world to which he did not belong, but to which he aspired and which he identified with his beloved mother. The figure of the father and that of his mother each represented a social horizon for the young Du Pont, but with unequal chances of success: the figure of the father embodied the assurance of a career traced out before him, one that would bring no surprises but was also without glamour; the figure of the mother represented the promise of a career to be conquered in an aristocratic world whose splendour did not belong to him by birth.

> Elle me faisait lire Corneille et appuyer sur ces vers:
> Je ne dois qu'à moi seul toute ma renommée
>> A l'exemple des dieux, j'ai fait beaucoup de rien.
>> Ma valeur est ma race, et mon bras est mon père.
>> Et puis elle me parlait de sa race.
>> Elle ne trempait pas mon corps dans le Styx, il n'en avait point encore la force: elle élevait mon âme aux nues et l'arrosait d'ambroisie. Vous en trouverez quelque chose dans mon portrait que vous avez, qui a été fait à l'âge de cinq ans, ressemblant quoique très médiocre; les yeux n'en sont pas enfantins, mais penseurs fiers et tendres.
>> Je ne puis me dissimuler aujourd'hui que ma mère, en cultivant chez moi les passions glorieuses, me donnait des défauts. Elle avait tous les préjugés de la noblesse comme elle en avait les manières et l'apparente grandeur. Elle semait sur son fils le dernier grain de ses espérances et de ses chimères de roman, elle le rendait propre à toute espèce d'entreprise, mais aussi à toute espèce de ridicule et de vanité.[15]

When his wife died, his father had to struggle against these aspirations; he felt they were romantic musings that he ought not to encourage. The father figure thus embodied a social order of which the young Du Pont was constantly being reminded through the demand that he should be satisfied with his own destiny. In reality,

15. *L'Enfance*, p.65-66.

these were 'calls to order', worded with all the authority given to them by eighteenth-century society. Apprenticeship to the profession of watchmaker, and the transmission of paternal responsibility, defined a social future that was already mapped out. In this logic, education must be focused primarily on general knowledge, but above all on useful skills. If Du Pont senior had granted his wife permission for their son to enter the boarding house run by M. Viard, it was on the imperative condition that he would not learn versification, a practice considered as worldly as it was futile. However, a general education was undoubtedly seen as necessary if one was to make a good impression on clients belonging to the upper aristocracy. The marquis d'Argenson, for example, was one of Du Pont senior's clients. One can understand the exasperation of a father confronted with the whims of a son who refused to accept his most likely future in order to follow the chimeras of a path he was not meant to take.

In contrast, the mother figure expressed the romanticism of a lost paradise, glimpsed from the stories she loved to tell her son, but this was a paradise to which her rank and fortune did not allow her natural access.[16] We are surely obliged to interpret the conduct of Anne Alexandrine de Montchanin as the transfer of her social aspirations to her son, who was very early on given the task of conquering a place in a world which had slipped away from her after she had tasted its sweetest sap during her stay with an aristo-cratic family imbued by Enlightenment values. Attending the salon of Mme d'Urfé for a short time, an enthusiast for esotericism, gave young Pierre-Samuel a glimpse of the splendour of a world that was initially beyond his grasp. During this episode, described at length in his unfinished memoirs, he refused to play the game expected of a man on the make at court, focusing instead on the truth while he was still very young. His desire to belong to this world was strong – but not, it seems, at any cost. Perhaps this should be seen as an effect of his liking for mathematics and for rational explanations of the world around him.

16. In a letter sent to Thomas Jefferson on 21 April 1800, Du Pont de Nemours spoke of his social background: 'Je suis obligé d'être un habile Négociant et un bon Directeur de compagnie, puisque Dieu m'a fait pauvre, et que, n'étant plus homme public, je ne puis espérer d'être encore utile au genre humain, et parvenir à de grands et honorables travaux qu'avec les capitaux d'autrui, par conséquent à condition de les faire prospérer.' *The Correspondence of Jefferson and Du Pont de Nemours, with an introduction on Jefferson and the physiocrats*, ed. Gilbert Chinard (New York, 1971), p.12.

How Du Pont de Nemours became a revolutionary   169

This tension between the paternal figure and the maternal figure, between a destiny that the social world naturally tended to impose on him and the (to put it mildly) unlikely path to which his upbringing inclined him, is a key to reading and interpreting the social strategies that Pierre-Samuel Du Pont de Nemours adopted upon the death of his mother. The two spellings of his surname – at least, this is the hypothesis that we are putting forward – reflect the tension between the paternal figure and the maternal figure, between a bourgeoisie characterised by work and rigour on the one hand, and the Enlightenment nobility, imbued with the desire to improve the human condition and the functioning of the social world, on the other. Each fork in the road his career followed expressed this social tension, one that limited his field of social possibilities, whether (in retrospect) they were to be deemed daring or conservative. Du Pont de Nemours clearly belonged to the very particular category of the double man, an intermediary between two social universes which, if they clashed ever more violently at the end of the eighteenth century, coexisted to a certain extent in the person of Pierre-Samuel.

Services and servitudes

If they are to grasp Pierre-Samuel's revolutionary commitment, sociologists and historians need to question the social strategies he developed and implemented very early on. A whole world separated the romantic young man from the deputy vigorously engaged in the work of the Assembly. The trials and errors, the blunders and the failures of his youth were a reflection of structural inequality when it came to social opportunities for gaining access to jobs in the administration of state monopolies. Du Pont was deprived of the economic capital which would have enabled him to buy a position related to his aspirations, and he was also a Huguenot; the desires of his imagination inclined him to apply for a place as a military engineer, or even to become a doctor like Quesnay, Louis XV's doctor, who enjoyed the influence at court that the favour of Mme de Pompadour had procured for him.[17] Without the ascendency that a high birth could have conferred on him, without assets or sufficient income, he was forced to opt for the only social strategy offering him some

---

17. The amount of time it takes to acquire medical knowledge as compared with the social profitability of this position undoubtedly soon discouraged him from taking this path, as his memoirs suggest.

170   *Christophe Le Digol*

hope, however modest: to obtain the favour of a powerful figure who
would offer him a position in the administration of the kingdom. (It
is worth remembering that the kingdom was a space with limited
autonomy, and subordinate to the intrigues of the court.) The marquis
d'Argenson, whose brother was then minister of War, was the first in a
long line of powerful figures whom Du Pont solicited for their favours.

> Mon caractère alors prit une grandeur au-dessus des vanités qui
> avaient ébloui ma jeunesse et de tout intérêt particulier. Je songeai
> moins à la fortune et à la gloire, dont l'espérance m'avait d'abord
> déterminé au travail, qu'à la félicité, à la prospérité auxquelles je
> pouvais élever ma patrie. Je ne vis plus, dans les ministres, des
> protecteurs qui m'étaient nécessaires, mais des instruments dont
> j'avais besoin, pour faire régner les vérités utiles dont la beauté et la
> simplicité touchaient également ma tête et mon cœur.
>   Tel est le sentiment qui depuis cette époque a dirigé ma vie
> entière. On a cru que j'avais servi beaucoup de ministres. Cela
> n'est pas vrai. M. Turgot seul excepté, parce qu'il était digne de
> commander à moi et au monde, je me suis servi de beaucoup de
> ministres et je les ai fait servir malgré leurs préjugés, malgré leurs
> erreurs, malgré leurs défauts, malgré leurs vices, et, ce qui est plus
> fort, malgré leurs préventions contre moi et contre ma doctrine,
> à une multitude d'opérations paternelles et à promulguer des lois
> sages et salutaires, qu'avait dictées cette doctrine conservatrice de
> la propriété, fondatrice de la liberté. J'ai cherché le pouvoir dans les
> mains qui l'avaient, et je l'ai dirigé à faire le bien. Ce que j'y pouvais
> trouver d'avantages personnels, n'a plus été qu'en arrière ligne dans
> ma pensée.[18]

Forced to act as a pawn in the game of curial logic, he called on
two types of 'protectors': obtaining their favour required qualities
often contrasted with one another. The first type was the court
aristocrat, who naturally appreciated the qualities attached to the
courtier, notably his art of social conversation, and his ability to
seduce his interlocutors or to turn away from them with ease when
his 'protector' fell out of favour.[19] The second type corresponded to
the learned man well established at court, such as D'Alembert or

---

18. *L'Enfance*, p.186-87.
19. On this aspect, the anecdote that Du Pont tells about the disgrace suffered by
    Dr Quesnay on the death of Mme de Pompadour clearly shows the game that
    courtiers played. *L'Enfance*, p.257.

Dr Quesnay.[20] The social game in which he then indulged was quite different: knowledge, rigour and a capacity for work regulated the level of relations and exchanges. The first type required the qualities proper to the courtier and a type of behaviour with which Du Pont complied only reluctantly, when he had no choice; the second encouraged a relationship primarily based on work and intelligence, and then on knowledge and merit. To gain the favour of the former, he needed first to acquire knowledge from the latter. Between these two types of protectors, Du Pont sometimes had to choose, as this anecdote about M. de Choiseul shows:

> Je regardais comme un des premiers devoirs de ma reconnaissance envers les 'gracieusetés' de M. de Choiseul, de lui rendre compte de ma liaison avec M. Quesnay, de l'amitié qu'il avait prise pour moi, et des leçons qu'il voulait bien me donner. J'ignorais que M. de Choiseul s'était brouillé depuis peu de temps avec Mme de Pompadour, qu'il redoutait les conseils que Quesnay pouvait lui donner, et qu'il haïssait fortement le docteur. [...] frappé de la froideur qui succédait à ses manières caressantes, je lui demandai la cause de ce changement et en quoi j'avais eu le malheur de lui déplaire. Il m'emmena dans un arrière cabinet et me dit: 'Je ne suis point changé; vous ne me déplaisez pas. Vous avez dû remarquer que je vous veux du bien depuis le premier jour que je vous ai vu. Je vous l'ai montré en mille occasions. Mais c'est vous qui changez de carrière. Je vais vous parler comme à un homme que j'estime, et que je crois incapable d'abuser de ce que je lui dis. Les amis de M. Quesnay ne sont pas les miens: choisissez.' J'avais pour M. de Choiseul de l'inclination et même de la reconnaissance, quoiqu'il n'eût jamais rien fait pour moi que de m'ouvrir sa porte et de me parler obligeamment. Mais entre un sage, un grand homme, un philosophe éclairé qui m'honorait d'une affection sincère et daignait m'instruire chaque jour comme son enfant, et un ministre aimable et puissant qui ne pouvait me bien connaître, ni m'accorder qu'un intérêt superficiel, la différence, la distance me parurent si énormes que je n'hésitai pas un instant.[21]

This tension between his taste for knowledge and the need to seduce protectors so as to apply that knowledge and make a living out of it conditioned the aspirations and social trajectory of Du Pont de

---

20. On the contribution of Quesnay to physiocracy, see Arnault Skornicki, *L'Economiste, la cour et la patrie: l'économie politique dans la France des Lumières* (Paris, 2011), p.183-220.
21. *L'Enfance*, p.238-39. See Skornicki, *L'Economiste*, p.231-33.

172   *Christophe Le Digol*

Nemours. The role he played in the administration of the kingdom, like the position he occupied within it, would always be conditional on the grace or disgrace of the ministers likely to employ him. During a career that might be deemed – correctly, it seems – as particularly fortunate given his slender chances of success at the death of his mother, he was appointed inspector general of manufactures by his friend Turgot, then controller general of finances; he was then an economic expert under Vergennes before becoming commissioner general of commerce under Calonne. His positions in the administration of the kingdom meant that he was ennobled in December 1783.[22] A few years earlier, in 1772, the king of Sweden had made him a knight of the Royal Order of Vasa. These honours not only consecrated his gradual integration into the administrative hierarchy of the kingdom, but above all demonstrated the fulfilment of the dreams and aspirations that his mother had transmitted to him.

Judging Du Pont's social success does not consist just in meticulously recording the objective positions that he successively occupied in the royal administration. If we focus merely on the list of his administrative functions, it can be difficult to identify and interpret the reasons for his revolutionary commitment. On the eve of the Revolution, he was one of the two secretary-clerks of the Assembly of Notables, in the 1787 Assembly and subsequently in that of 1788.[23] However, he complained bitterly that he was not being remunerated at the level of the services he had performed for the Assemblies of Notables: the archbishop of Sens, Etienne-Charles de Loménie de Brienne, '[lui] fait payer [son] attachement à Mr. De Vergennes, la part [qu'il a] eue aux projets utiles de Mr. Calonne, et l'amitié de Mr. Fourqueux'.[24] The honour of being secretary-clerk of the first

---

22. 'Terres et titres coûtaient donc fort cher. Presque toute la noblesse du mérite, d'origine récente, qui n'avait pas trouvé au berceau une fortune assise, déplorait cette précarité. Hauts fonctionnaires, astreints par leur rang à entretenir une façade sociale qui reposait sur le produit de leur emploi, dépendaient de la bonne volonté ou de l'amitié des ministres. Plus que quiconque ils ressentaient l'arbitraire d'une telle sujétion. Qu'ils aient cessé de plaire et ils se retrouvaient sans crédit, sans argent, mortifiés dans leur chair et leur orgueil. Leurs déceptions étaient d'autant plus vives que leur splendeur passée avait été plus grande. Pour rembourser leurs dettes ils en contractaient de nouvelles, toujours plus accablantes'; Bouloiseau, *Bourgeoisie et révolution*, p.40.
23. On this period, see Ambrose Saricks, *Pierre Samuel Du Pont de Nemours* (Lawrence, KS, 1965), p.99-144.
24. Letter of 24 June 1788 to Dr Hutton, in Bouloiseau, *Bourgeoisie et révolution*, p.43.

Assembly of Notables should have satisfied him. Du Pont nevertheless wished to keep his position as secretary-clerk in the second Assembly of Notables, and he succeeded. But when Necker came to power, replacing Loménie de Brienne, this resulted, to his anger, in a reduction of the means allocated to him to fulfil his administrative functions as inspector general of commerce. He then had to part with several employees – in his professional duties as well as in his domestic service – whom he no longer had the means to maintain.[25]

In his strategies for acquiring and maintaining his administrative posts, Du Pont was thus confronted with a peculiarity of the administration of the *Ancien Régime*: the blurred distinction between public means and private resources. This raised the issue of the adequacy of the means for the post to which he was appointed; these means depended on the favour of the appointing authority. In fact, his social success did not necessarily translate into suitable financial comfort: the property he acquired and the variable remuneration he received for his administrative responsibilities were not sufficient to protect him from need. Thus he retained the 'éthos social de la bourgeoisie professionnelle', which did not suit his recent status as a noble: he tirelessly counted and checked money that was spent, asking his children to contribute to the family's efforts.[26] Everything suggests that even his social success, quite exceptional given his origins, still did not free him from the forms of social domination on which he had depended since his adolescence.

The difficulties that Du Pont encountered during his administrative 'career' prompted him to question social logic based on the primacy of birth or patrimonial domination, as well as to oppose the system of favours that organised access to certain state positions, the length for which they could be held and the material resources arbitrarily allocated to their holders. The allocation of resources was indexed not necessarily to the needs of the administrative organisation but to the credit the holder enjoyed with the minister. Under the *Ancien Régime*, Du Pont therefore faced a fundamental contradiction between his fascination with the aristocratic universe to which he had always wished to belong, and his opposition to the principles and functioning of a royal administration heavily dependent on court

25. For more information on Du Pont's economic situation, see Bouloiseau, *Bourgeoisie et révolution*, p.37-40.
26. Bouloiseau, *Bourgeoisie et révolution*, p.19; on this historical point, see Norbert Elias, *La Société de cour* (Paris, 1985), p.47-48.

174 *Christophe Le Digol*

logic. The eminently social constraints to which he was subjected led him to draw lessons from the lack of recognition of his own merits. In fact, he tended to develop a vision of the world based on knowledge and competence as a principle of allocation of positions dependent on the organisation of state monopolies. Social merit as a system of access and distribution of 'administrators' to positions dependent on the functioning of the state became a political objective which, from his point of view, did not necessarily justify a general questioning of the monarchy.[27]

***

The memory of Pierre-Samuel Du Pont de Nemours had, it seems, almost completely faded when Gustave Schelle published his intellectual biography in 1888, showing his influence on the formation of the physiocratic school in the eighteenth century.[28] What justified saving Du Pont de Nemours from the oblivion to which history had consigned him was linked in no way to his political role in the advent of a new world, but to his contribution to the renewal of the framework of an economic philosophy that sought to describe the economy in its real movement. As a political economist, he contrived to act politically according to a certain ethic of 'scientific' truth to which he was attached. In this sense, his political action was driven by the desire to reform a state and a society for the satisfaction of the general interest, and to promote their proper functioning so as to allow the most deserving to act without being hampered by logic which favoured individuals without merit. It was probably in this sense that, as early as October 1791, he decided that the work of the Constituent Assembly must be governed by the general interest, as each member

27. Perhaps we should ponder the effects of his apprenticeship as a watchmaker on his vision of how the social world works. The results achieved by a watchmaker stem from his knowledge, thoroughness and skill. In the same way, the social world appeared to Du Pont as a regulated universe whose mechanisms should provide individuals with the position that their merits justify. In the world of the *Ancien Régime* in which Du Pont moved, knowledge was in no way a principle that structured action and its results. The favour which dispensed grace and disgrace was a very capricious principle which rarely rewarded the efforts made and the results obtained.

28. 'Du Pont de Nemours, dont le nom est aujourd'hui presque oublié, a été, dans sa jeunesse, l'un des principaux vulgarisateurs des théories de Quesnay'; Schelle, *Du Pont de Nemours et l'école physiocratique*, p.1.

How Du Pont de Nemours became a revolutionary 175

of the Assembly had contributed, as much as their means and ideas permitted, to the realisation of the Constitution of 1791.

If his revolutionary commitment was not unconnected to the practical necessities of stabilising or even improving his economic and social situation for himself and his children, as his correspondence clearly reveals, we must not forget how much he had at heart the affairs of the kingdom of France. This family necessity was accompanied by the promotion of a rational vision of the functioning of the economy and of the state.[29] As a double man, it is hardly surprising to find him hired within the Société des Trente (Society of the Thirty) to influence the elections to the Estates General. This society brought together great court aristocrats, great gentlemen of the robe, and thinkers belonging to the Third Estate.[30] At the end of this campaign, he was elected deputy to the Estates General. He was to be one of the deputies most involved in the work of the Assembly, playing a part in numerous committees and even becoming chairman of the agriculture and trade committee. He also wrote numerous pieces, notably contributing to the struggle for the redefinition of the administrative organisation of the kingdom.[31] However, thanks to the 'radicalisation' of political

29. On Du Pont's revolutionary commitment, see Richard Whatmore, 'Dupont de Nemours et la politique révolutionnaire', *Revue française d'histoire des idées politiques* 20 (2004), p.335-51.

30. On the Société des Trente, see Jean Egret, *La Pré-Révolution française (1787-1788)* (Paris, 1962), p.326-31.

31. Among these published interventions, one shall mention *De la manière la plus favorable d'effectuer les emprunts qui seront nécessaires, tant afin de pourvoir aux besoins du moment, que pour opérer le remboursement des dettes de l'Etat dont les intérêts sont trop onéreux, par un député du bailliage de Nemours à l'Assemblée nationale* (Paris, Chez Baudouin, 1789); *Discours prononcé à l'Assemblée nationale, par M. Du Pont, sur les banques en général, sur la caisse d'escompte en particulier, et sur le projet du premier ministre des finances relativement à cette dernière* (Paris, Chez Baudouin, 1789); *Discours prononcé à l'Assemblée nationale par M. Du Pont sur l'état & les ressources des finances* (Versailles, Chez Baudouin, 1789); *Observations sur les principes qui doivent déterminer le nombre des districts et celui des tribunaux dans les départemens, par M. Du Pont* (Paris, Imprimerie nationale, 1790); *Opinion de M. Du Pont, député de Nemours, sur le projet de créer pour dix-neuf cent millions d'assignats-monnaie, sans intérêt, exposée à l'Assemblée nationale, le 25 septembre 1790* (Paris, Chez Baudouin, 1790); *Principes constitutionnels relativement au renvoi et à la nomination des ministres: discours prononcé à la Société des amis de la liberté et de la constitution de 1789, dans leur séance du 20 octobre 1790, par M. Du Pont, député de Nemours à l'Assemblée nationale* (Paris, Imprimerie nationale, 1790); *Rapport fait, au nom du Comité de l'imposition, par M. Du Pont, député de Nemours, sur les impositions indirectes en général et sur les droits à raison de la consommation des vins,*

positions, his moderate interventions would gradually cause him to lose his political influence. The French Revolution, in which he nevertheless actively participated, did not allow him to obtain any more stable positions; relinquishing his privileges and the pensions he enjoyed worsened his economic situation, and he was forced to ask for the support of the pensions committee.[32] His dual status under the *Ancien Régime* certainly enabled him to contribute resources and knowledge from which the Constituent Assembly would be able to take advantage, but nevertheless prevented him from drawing the consequences of the political logic that he had nevertheless helped to create.

He went into hiding in Cormeilles-en-Parisis, where he pretended to be an old doctor; here, between 3 September and 3 November 1792, Du Pont de Nemours wrote his *Mémoires* for his children.[33] He had narrowly escaped Paris after taking up arms to defend the king at the Tuileries. In financial difficulty, he had endeavoured to become a printer while he was still a member of the Constituent Assembly. With the financial support of his friend Lavoisier, he bought printing presses and, in this way, continued to participate in the political turmoil in Paris. The growing influence of the Jacobins made him fear that the work of the Constituent Assembly, his work, was under threat. And this was true – in more ways than one.

---

    et des boissons en particulier (Paris, Imprimerie nationale, 1790); *De quelques amélio-rations dans la perception de l'impôt et de l'usage utile, qu'on peut faire des employés réformés, par M. Du Pont, député de Nemours* (Paris, Imprimerie nationale, 1791).

32. Bouloiseau, *Bourgeoisie et révolution*, p.58.

33. We should at this point reflect on this first part of the life of Du Pont de Nemours, knowledge of which comes almost exclusively from his unfinished memoirs. We must not forget that the sequence of the episodes that compose them stems solely from the author's memory. Intended for his children, the memoirs appear as a self-presentation whose function was to transmit, in addition to information on Du Pont's family and life, a family morality congruent with the meaning of the history in which its author had played a part since 1789.

A physiocratic mandate: Du Pont de Nemours and *L'Historien*

LIANA VARDI

University at Buffalo, SUNY

How does one come out of the Terror and ensure a stable government and the safety of French citizens? By supporting the Constitution and the rule of law. As a member of the Conseil des Anciens in the newly established Directory, Pierre-Samuel Du Pont de Nemours parsed each vote for the readers of his daily newspaper, *L'Historien,* so as to render comprehensible his concerns and guide them to support his positions. These initially revolved around fear of a resurgence of revolutionary violence either from surviving Jacobins or from the ultraroyalists. Du Pont's position was coupled with a distrust of the Directorate that favoured the radicals, convinced that the real threat came from the right. Du Pont's position cohered with the upcoming elections, as he and his collaborators sought to ensconce a liberal centre. His brand was rooted in physiocracy, supporting the interests of landowners and the protection of property. Aurelian Craiutu would deem *L'Historien*'s editorial board candidates for his theory about the emergence of moderation as an ideological stance in this period, although, as the author admits, moderation was elusive during the Directory, and centrism, ill-defined.[1] How far Du Pont and his friends strived for the *juste milieu,* in whatever way they phrased it, is what this article seeks to elucidate.

I am grateful for the Henry Belin Du Pont Research Grant, Hagley Library and Archives, Wilmington, Delaware, March 2019, June 2019 that allowed me to complete the research for this article.

1. Aurelian Craiutu, *A Virtue for courageous minds: moderation in French political thought (1748-1830)* (Princeton, NJ, 2012), ch.6, *passim.*

178   *Liana Vardi*

The 1795 Constitution

In 1795, the Convention's wartime government having overstepped its bounds, and the Constitution of 1793 never implemented and now viewed as too radical, the Assembly set itself to devise a new constitution, better suited to the post-Thermidorian realignment of forces.[2] A committee of eleven was struck; input solicited. Du Pont offered his own model in response to the deviations that had culminated in the Terror, so that a new government might be established on a healthy and sustainable basis.[3] One is aware from the start that it is the physiocrat speaking. Government mismanagement and corruption

---

2. The literature on the Terror, Thermidor and the Directory is growing by leaps and bounds. At the time of writing, I was able to peruse newer and older studies, among others: Bronislaw Baczko, *Comment sortir de la Terreur* (Paris, 1989); Bronislaw Baczko, *Politiques de la Révolution française* (Paris, 2008); Marc Belissa and Yannick Bosc, *Le Directoire: la République sans la démocratie* (Paris, 2018); Michel Biard and Marisa Linton, *Terreur! La Révolution française face à ses démons* (Malakoff, 2020); *Les Noblesses françaises dans l'Europe de la Révolution*, ed. Philippe Bourdin (Rennes, 2010); Howard Brown, *Ending the French Revolution* (Charlottesville, VA, 2006); *Taking liberties: problems of a new order from the French Revolution to Napoleon*, ed. Howard Brown and Judith Miller (Manchester, 2002); *Le Directoire: forger la République 1795-1799*, ed. Loris Chavanette (Paris, 2020); Loris Chavanette, *Quatre-vingt-quinze: la Terreur en procès* (Paris, 2017); Malcolm Crook, *Elections in the French Revolution* (Cambridge, 1996); Marcel Gauchet, *Robespierre: l'homme qui nous divise le plus* (Paris, 2018); Hugh Gough, *The Newspaper press in the French Revolution* (London, 1988); Patrice Gueniffey, *Le Nombre et la raison: la Révolution française et les élections* (Paris, 1993); Patrice Gueniffey, *La Politique de la Terreur* (Paris, 2000); Auguste Kuciski, *Les Députés au corps législatif, Conseil des Cinq-Cents, Conseil des Anciens, de l'An IV à l'An VII* (1905; Delhi, 2019); Georges Lefebvre, *La France sous le Directoire (1795-1799)*, ed. Jean-René Suratteau (Paris, 1984); Evelyne Lever, *Paris sous la Terreur* (Paris, 2019); Martin Lyons, *France under the Directory* (Cambridge, 1975); Sergio Luzzatto, *L'Automne de la Révolution: luttes et cultures politiques dans la France thermidorienne* (Paris, 2001); Jean-Clément Martin, *Les Echos de la Terreur: vérités d'un mensonge d'Etat 1794-2001* (Paris, 2018); Jean-Clément Martin, *La Terreur: vérités et légendes* (Paris, 2017); Jeremy D. Popkin, *La Presse de la Révolution: journaux et journalistes (1789-1799)* (Paris, 2011); Jeremy D. Popkin, *The Right-wing press in France, 1792-1800* (Chapel Hill, NC, 1980); Pierre Serna, *La République des girouettes, 1789-1815 et au-delà: une anomalie politique, la France de l'extrême centre* (Seyssel, 2005); *Républiques sœurs: le Directoire et la Révolution atlantique*, ed. Pierre Serna (Rennes, 2009); Michel Troper, *Terminer la Révolution: la Constitution de 1795* (Paris, 2006); Denis Woronoff, *La République bourgeoise: de thermidor à brumaire 1794-1799* (Paris, 1972).
3. Pierre-Samuel Du Pont de Nemours, *Du pouvoir législatif et du pouvoir exécutif, convenables à la République française* (Paris, Chez Du Pont, An III [1795]).

A physiocratic mandate: Du Pont de Nemours and L'Historien 179

had created economic havoc, especially in the countryside. But it is when he comes to define the Nation that his programme displays its ideological bent.

What is a Nation, he asks, and who belongs to it? A Nation is an assembly of property-owners. Should they decide, independently, to sell their land to people from other countries, the Nation would cease to exist. It is therefore by the will of property-owners that a Nation exists. Those who do not own property are foreigners (étrangers), to be valued and respected, who can of course become full citizens by buying land. Those who only possess moveable wealth can buy land as well. Property, however tiny, offers its owners full citizenship. Those who cannot afford it by any stretch of the imagination, while members of society, should be treated with kindness and consideration. Moreover, the non-propertied, for example renters, can by special dispensation be granted the rights of the propertied. They can also be given administrative positions and, of course, serve in the army and the National Guard, as long as the local administrator vouches for their good behaviour. Nowhere are taxpayers mentioned, because, presumably, only landowners would be liable in this physiocratic vision.

So who gets to vote? Du Pont much approves the Constituent Assembly's reliance on the parish-level, tiered elections, adopted for the Estates General, and laments the silencing of rural voices through the creation of districts that combine and eliminate voting by individual communes. It is a heinous system, invented by city-dwellers. Graduated elections should be restored in order for villages to be represented at primary assemblies. There they would elect deputies to the district-level assemblies and so on.

What kind of system would they be voting for? First and foremost, a republican one, with a single representative assembly, divided into two branches. One, composed of two thirds of deputies, would propose legislation; the other third would discuss it. Elections for both would be held simultaneously. The members of the second chamber or 'Senate' would be chosen from among elected deputies and all deputies would serve for four years, staggered through annual elections. People would therefore go to the polls every year, but electoral assemblies would dissolve at the end of each electoral period. None of this nonsense of sections sitting indefinitely as had been the case since August 1792. Moreover, as the Revolution had revealed, entirely new legislatures had wanted to enact further revolutions. As a result, the Revolution had spun out of control. What was wanted now was stability and respect for established laws, not constant innovation.

180   *Liana Vardi*

The guiding principles for the National Assembly would be ensconced in a 'Declaration of rights and duties', stressing liberty, equality, fraternity and security. It had been a grave error to leave out duties from the initial document of 26 August 1789 (never mind that of 1793). All must use their reason to reach decisions, both as representatives of the localities that had elected them and as men of conscience who could consider the issue at hand impartially. Purity of purpose plays an important role here to prevent the sort of partisan voting that had darkened the days of the Convention.

Like the Convention itself, Du Pont assumed that the new Legislature would keep some of its old members, so that elections would only be partial. Continuity was crucial, as previous regimes had shown by ignoring this fact. Experience, which for Du Pont was tied to a familiarity with fundamental principles and how to apply them, was a way to guarantee stability. Before this, however, the Assembly must be cleansed. About a hundred deputies with blood on their hands were to be purged immediately, while fellow travellers of the Jacobins would be eliminated later.[4]

The discussion of the executive branch comes in last. It was to be composed of ministers elected by the Legislature in order to administer the laws. Du Pont saw the need for only six ministries but added a 'prime minister' who also presided the Senate. He granted each ministry power in their own domain, although they had to report all their activities to the Legislature as well as their plans for the coming year. His proposed constitution, Du Pont assured his readers, would prevent the emergence of a dictatorial authority, the reign of a single man, a king, being utterly superfluous. Once all understood where their self-interest lay, they would understand the orientation and raison d'être of the laws.

This proposal is remarkably similar to the version adopted by the Convention, even if its rationale differed from Du Pont's. The major difference was the creation of an executive of five directors (elected by the Council of the Elders) independent of the Legislature.

Du Pont was among the newly elected deputies to the higher Chamber (the Elders), that which he had equated with a Senate in his

---

4. When, to the contrary, 500 (or two thirds) of the *conventionnels* were to stay in the new assembly, including those recently amnestied, and only one new third elected, Du Pont was among those who vigorously protested; this marked much of the subsequent conflicts between the right and the left of the councils. Much hope was then placed on subsequent elections to replace the radicals.

own proposal, composed, indeed, of somewhat older men than those who sat in the Council of Five Hundred.

L'Historien

Du Pont published a daily paper named *L'Historien*, issued from October 1795 until suppressed on 5 September 1797. In this paper, Du Pont and his steadfast collaborator,[5] Jean Charles Bienaymé, would summarise the day's events at the Assembly, one following the Conseil des Cinq-Cents and the other the Conseil des Anciens. There was some editorial commentary, but the day's deliberations were presented straightforwardly.

In their 'Prospectus', the editors stated:

> L'époque où le gouvernement constitutionnel a été établi, doit être décisive pour la France et pour l'Europe. C'est d'elle que *L'Historien* doit partir; c'est en marquant les pas qui se feront désormais vers le bonheur du genre humain, c'est en indiquant les fautes et les méprises qui pourraient égarer sur la route, que peut-être aura-t-il l'avantage d'aider à quelque bien, de diminuer quelque mal: seule ambition des citoyens qui concourront à sa rédaction. La vérité sera leur loi, l'utilité leur but; et dans la crainte de le manquer, ils prendront, autant qu'il dépendra d'eux, le soin si nécessaire d'éviter l'ennui.[6]

But *L'Historien* will also report foreign items of news and assess them in relation to policy (*politique*), agriculture, manufactures, commerce, subsistance and population. *L'Historien* will engage with all of these as they are part of the newspaper's project, which dares to take this name in order to collect odd (*curieux*) and faithful materials for

---

5. There were various others over time, until it fell back to Du Pont and Bienaymé. On 5 floréal An IV (24 April 1796), *L'Historien* announced that Bienaymé would be in charge of the Conseil des Anciens, and Sauvo of the Cinq-Cents (issue 155). Starting with the lengthy reports on the Babeuf conspiracy (vol.5), Du Pont writes the political and cultural notices and Bienaymé reports on the councils. As a result, we find fewer reports from the councils. Sometimes (and increasingly so in the following year), the Conseil des Anciens appears more frequently than the Cinq-Cents and sometimes the opposite. What is more, reports on the armies take up more and more space. Noticeably, from volume 9, more is said about peace negotiations. It is also when F. D. Budan joins the team to report on internal and foreign news, although he would not last long. As additional daily features, the newspaper lists the plays performed on that day and stock-market fluctuations.
6. Hagley Library, no.B2019.D85, f.1-40.

182 *Liana Vardi*

historians of the future. The paper would come out daily, sometimes in greater and sometimes lesser length depending on the selection made by the *Journal des débats et des décrets* about what matters, but 'il formera toujours, en trois mois, deux volumes, au moins de 45 feuilles chacun.'

This would change in spring 1797 when Du Pont, glowing from the success of the recent elections, announced a new era for the journal:

> Les premiers auteurs de cet ouvrage périodique, la plupart membres des deux conseils dès l'année dernière, et réunis par le désir de résister de toutes les manières à toute tyrannie, de concourir à la complète destruction des habitudes révolutionnaires, au retour de la morale et de la justice, de la consolidation du gouvernement constitutionnel, au rétablissement de la paix intérieure, aux succès de l'agriculture, à la renaissance des manufactures, du commerce et des arts, se flattent de trouver un puissant renfort dans leurs collègues du nouveau tiers au corps législatif. Et ils le leur demandent.[7]

There is little present foreign danger, he adds, and this renders internal problems more evident. 'La dépravation, la corruption, le pillage, le gaspillage et l'incapacité détruisent presque à chaque moment les puissantes ressources que présentent à nos finances la nature des choses et l'activité de la nation.' Intrigue has not disappeared, so this is no time to abandon the pen. This will only be possible once honesty and enlightenment in all public affairs will have unmasked crime and ignorance. There is still one year of struggle left and then, hopefully, it will be over. But they will reduce the format, producing monthly volumes with less bulky issues. The end of the war reducing the need to report political news, this would be replaced by more philosophy and literature.[8]

The first issue appeared on 1st prairial Year IV (22 November 1795), but a preliminary discourse of 200 pages was inserted later into the first volume, recapitulating activities since 5 brumaire, the day the new Constitution came into effect.[9] To break down the

---

7. Vol.13, issue 547, 2 prairial An v, 21 May 1797, p.3-4.
8. Strewn among the issues one finds reviews of Benjamin Constant, Mme de Staël, André Morellet, Jacques Necker, Beccaria, Vauvenargues, Helvétius, and a selection of economic texts assembled by Roederer.
9. Vol.2, issue 64, 24 January 1796, p.345-47. Two months after the start of publication, in response to a letter, Du Pont explains why they privilege politics over entertainment. They mean, by recapitulating the day's debates at the two councils, to inform their readers promptly, even more so than the *Moniteur* or

A physiocratic mandate: Du Pont de Nemours and L'Historien   183

material gathered in seventeen volumes, I am focusing here on what especially concerned Du Pont: constitutional rigour, the economy, the revival of factionalism, the fate of the émigrés, and how to maintain harmony in a body filled still with deputies implicated in the Terror. The deep engagement with the elections of the Year v will follow and worries about a potential coup against the Legislature.[10] Over time, the newspaper reported less on discussions in the councils as letters from collaborators and readers took up more and more space, bolstering and sometimes challenging its positions. *L'Historien* would then respond. Most letter-writers were anonymous (a position that Du Pont would endorse when the Directory ordered that all articles be signed, taking the responsibility for the content personally) and, as Jeremy Popkin has noted in his study of the right-wing press, their identities are impossible to reconstruct.[11] It might well be that JBS is actually Jean-Baptiste Say, and the old man who was listened to in his youth, Forbonnais.[12] The most frustrating is 'P.N.', who seems to merge with the editors by 1797. Ambrose Saricks lists Morellet, Forbonnais, Peuchet, Jollivet and Lanjuinais as collaborators, but their names do not appear.[13] One of Du Pont's fellow deputies and a personal friend, Félix Faulcon, a frequent contributor, was happy to sign his letters.

Républicain français, of crucial debates and decisions. Deputies hand them copies of their speeches, and, when they do not, *L'Historien* is there to remind them what they have argued. 'Mais quand on n'a que des notes fugitives, il faut *un jour* pour entrer dans l'esprit d'un orateur, pour se pénétrer de son ame, pour retrouver, d'après les phrases qu'il a incontestablement dites, celles qui leur ont servi de liaison naturelle.' They will not change their focus, but they will rather try to improve and expand it. They appreciate greatly the opinions stated by their collaborators in the rubric 'nouvelles politiques'. They read many foreign gazettes and use them in their discussion of foreign affairs (p.348, original emphasis).

10. The interested reader will also find in *L'Historien* discussions of Saint-Domingue, religion, and particular attention paid to the war in Italy and the bulletins issued by Napoleon. An example of its stance on religion is offered in issue 559 of 14 prairial An v, 2 June 1797, p.197: 'Le gouvernement n'a pas le droit d'obliger le protestant ou le juif de payer les prêtres du catholique, pas plus que de contraindre le catholique à entretenir le mollah du musulman, ou les uns de salarier les médecins des autres.'

11. See Popkin, *The Right-wing press*, p.xvi-xvii.

12. Issue 44, 4 January 1796, p.49-51. See the BnF entry about Véron de Forbonnais: https://data.bnf.fr/ark:/12148/cb12141360c (last accessed 21 December 2024).

13. Ambrose Saricks, *Pierre Samuel Du Pont de Nemours* (Lawrence, KS, 1965), p.242.

184 *Liana Vardi*

Du Pont was up to his old tricks, having learned nothing from his conflict with Turgot over his 'revisions' of *Réflexions sur la formation et la distribution des richesses* that the future controller general had submitted in 1766 to Du Pont's journal *Ephémérides du citoyen*. JBS complained on 21 November 1796 that his article had been altered to an attack on the minister of Justice, accusing him of tyranny.[14] Had he written this, he would be guilty of lying. He firmly disavowed the opinions that were attributed to him. Du Pont admitted to adding a few words and ideas. His other friends knew that he sometimes stressed and sometimes softened their arguments. What is more, he monitored ministers more than other men, but, in attacking them, reluctantly, he was engaging in a defensive war. From this we may conclude that it is possible to treat the contributions of outsiders to *L'Historien* as reflecting Du Pont's opinions, unless he expressly stated otherwise.

Constitutionalism

Abiding by the Constitution has been viewed by historians as a sign of conservatism, nay, of reaction, or at least a will to disrupt. 'Formalism', as Du Pont explained, was the only way to make the system work,[15] although even he recognised that it could be unduly cumbersome. Thus, he complained that discussions, especially regarding demands by the Directory (already 'illegal' given the strict division of powers), took so long at the Council of Five Hundred that, by the time they reached the Elders, emergency was invoked and ritually agreed upon, despite Du Pont's and others' protests. There was heated debate on the Directory's request to name judges in districts where none had been elected. This was a direct intervention in the supposedly autonomous judicial system. The Directory continually asked for funds, but the councils hesitated before granting the ministries monies to pursue the war. Yet, even Du Pont conceded, urgent requests were legitimate when the needs of internal and external security were at stake.[16] Du Pont expressed his constitutionalist credo early, and it is worth reproducing:

> Les Français ne doivent plus avoir qu'une *politique intérieure*; c'est de vivre en paix, de rendre à leur constitution une sorte de culte, et

14. Issue 366, 1 frimaire An IV, 21 November 1796, p.247.
15. Issue 366, 1 frimaire An IV, 21 November 1796, p.78.
16. See issue 5, 29 November 1795, p.77.

A physiocratic mandate: Du Pont de Nemours and L'Historien 185

de consolider leur gouvernement. La chose est très facile; la fatigue universelle y conduirait aussi. Toutes les constitutions [...] méritent des égards et de la soumission car elles sont toutes des moyens de faire respecter les droits des hommes, d'obliger à l'accomplissement de leurs devoirs, d'encourager le travail, de conserver les propriétés, de protéger les familles, d'augmenter les subsistances, les jouissances, les plaisirs doux et honnêtes. Toutes les constitutions doivent être appuyées de tout le pouvoir de bons citoyens; car on ne peut les renverser que par des révolutions.[17]

Fear of a Jacobin revival is central to Du Pont's concerns to the point of paranoia. There is to be no change in the system. The government *applies* the laws; it's not there to innovate. Anything that smacks of the Convention is to be mistrusted: demands by the Directorate that might lead to seizure of power by the 'terrorists' or the creation of clubs that would foment factionalism.[18] This overzealous oversight by Du Pont and his *confrères* generated the states of emergency that he so decried.[19] Without them, the executive was stuck, unable to fulfil its administrative functions.[20] One has to pinch oneself to remember that the regime was meant to perdure, so aware are we of its collapse.

P.N. states that 'L'emprunt forcé a été une mesure tyrannique.' The tyranny of the Directorate was a constant rant, so convinced were the self-proclaimed constitutionalists that they meant to weaken the Legislature, and their outrage would focus on the treatment of émigrés and former 'terrorists', and the nature of communications between the directors and the councils.[21]

17. Issue 1, 1 prairial An IV, 22 November 1795, p.11-12 (original emphasis). On Du Pont's constitutionalism, initially based on the *Declaration of the rights of man and of the citizen* and then on the 1791 Constitution, as well as on the king's veto, see Anthony Mergey, 'Le contrôle de l'activité législative de la nation en 1789: l'opinion de Dupont de Nemours', *Journal of interdisciplinary history of ideas* 3:5 (2014), p.1-33.

18. Issue 4, 4 frimaire An IV, 25 November 1795, p.53, and issue 13, 10 frimaire An IV, 1 December 1795, p.203.

19. Bailey Stone, *Rethinking revolutionary change in Europe* (Lanham, MD, 2020), p.169-72. In his self-justification, La Révellière-Lépeaux blames the hostility and counter-revolutionary nature of the two councils and the duplicity of Carnot for the fructidor coup but also the Constitution for not granting a power of veto to the executive. *Mémoires de La Révellière-Lépeaux, publiés par son fils*, 3 vols (Paris, 1895), vol.2, p.59-65.

20. See Howard Brown, *War, Revolution, and the bureaucratic state* (Oxford, 1995).

21. See for example, issue 36, 27 December 1795, p.570, comment by Logicien: 'Observations sur le décret du 3 brumaire, qui exclut de la législature et des

186 *Liana Vardi*

What was a sign of royalism? The Cinq-Cents struggled with its definitions of reaction. Those who opposed the decree of 9 floréal that ordered the division of the property of émigrés, penalising, for example, parents of an absconded future heir, were accused of being the fomenters of the 13 vendémiaire reactionary uprising and, hence, of being pro-royalist.[22] The laws of 3 and 4 brumaire,[23] passed in the last days of the Convention, declared respectively that returned émigrés and refractory priests were forbidden from running for office and that, by contrast, a general amnesty for 'revolutionary acts' was accorded imprisoned *conventionnels*, so that they might be eligible. His own deletion from a list of émigrés in Rouen taking its jolly good time, Du Pont argues at the Conseil des Anciens that the time has come to move along proposals to hasten the procedure.[24]

Could the Terror return? No, deems a letter-writer, because experience will have taught people that serving on arbitrary commissions only leads to the guillotine. Yet *L'Historien* responds with the following: '*La terreur, nous dit-on, ne reviendra pas; car elle est déjà revenue avec les commissaires et les administrateurs nommés par le pouvoir exécutif.* Nous aurions à publier une multitude de ces lettres bien appuyées de faits: nous leur répondons à toutes: *elle ne durera pas; car elle est contraire aux intérêts autant qu'aux devoirs du gouvernement.*'[25]

---

    fonctions administratives et judiciaires les parens et alliés d'émigrés. Ce décret est une atteinte portée à la constitution dans le moment où elle vient d'être acceptée par le peuple.' At the meeting of the Cinq-Cents on 4 nivôse, the proposed exclusion of Jean-Jacques Aymé gives rise to heated debate (p.574-83).

22. In issue 63 of 3 pluviôse An IV, 23 January 1796, p.300, Du Pont shares the version of the oath of 21 January that he would have preferred: 'Je jure la haine, ou ce qui est plus efficace et plus noble que la haine, je jure une résistance intrépide à la royauté et à toute espèce de tyrannie, quels que soient le nombre et la puissance des tyrans. Je jure zèle, fidélité, amour, à l'humanité, à l'égalité, à la république, à la sûreté, à la justice, à la constitution.' Du Pont sustains André Morellet's plea on behalf of the families of émigrés threatened by the law of 9 floréal. He publishes and sells Morellet's work (issue 56, 16 January 1796, p.238-40). Despite Du Pont's objection, the reinvigoration of the law of 9 floréal is declared urgent and is voted on 14 January (issue 56, 16 January 1796, p.245-46).

23. On Du Pont's stance on the law of 3 brumaire, see 'Opinion de Du Pont (de Nemours) sur la résolution relative à la loi du 3 brumaire', session of 27 brumaire An V (Paris, Imprimerie nationale, frimaire An V).

24. Issue 73, session of 13 pluviôse An IV, 3 February 1796, p.500. See Marc Bouloiseau, *Bourgeoisie et révolution: les Du Pont de Nemours (1788-1799)* (Paris, 1972), p.112-13.

25. Issue 85, 25 pluviôse An IV, 14 February 1796, p.670.

By now, Du Pont is bolder in his attacks, and through him one can gauge the increasing appeal to republican conservatives among their readers, that is, those afraid of the radicals still in their midst. We encounter more appeals to moderation, meaning a middle ground between the excesses of the far right and those of the far left. As one correspondent puts it:

> J'avoue que les constitutionnels, qui tiennent principalement à la constitution comme l'unique moyen de protéger les personnes et les propriétés, ont à cet égard quelque affinité avec les aristocrates qui ont été surtout révoltés par les attaques faites à leur bien et à leur vie. Ils me paraissent, entre eux et dans le même rapport où vous êtes, citoyens modérés, amis de la révolution, mais que vous ne voulez ni pillarde, ni sanglante, avec les jacobins, qui ne cherchent qu'à bouleverser, tuer, et prendre. [...] Je conclus qu'il faut se rapprocher des constitutionnels et de se joindre à un centre commun, qui est celui du gouvernment.[26]

Du Pont views himself as the regime's conscience, reminding the Directory and the deputies to follow procedures and to respect the constitution. At the Conseil des Anciens on 6 June, he once more insists on its primacy: 'Lorsque nous nous trouvons entre deux loix constitutionnelles et des loix réglementaires, dont les dispositions sont inconciliables, notre choix ne peut pas être et n'est jamais douteux. Nous regardons la loi constitutionnelle comme règle; la loi réglementaire qui pourrait y déroger, comme une erreur, que la bonne intention qui l'a dictée ne canonise pas, et nous suivons la constitution.'[27]

On the economy

While most of the discussion in *L'Historien* is circumstantial, responding to immediate events, Du Pont offered the continuity of his Enlightenment beliefs and his peculiar branch of political economy. He intervened in all fiscal debates, not least as a member of the committee with oversight of the treasury. He contributed his views about the devaluation of the *assignat*, then of the *mandat*, on the *biens*

26. Issue 118, 28 ventôse, 28 March 1796, letter from correspondent L'Indépendant about his concept of moderation.
27. Issue 198, 8 prairial An IV, 27 May 1796, p.283.

nationaux, banking, lotteries, indirect taxes, with a consistent physio-cratic outlook.[28]

His philosophy might be summarised as he presented it to the Institut:

> Le citoyen Du Pont de Nemours remarquant le lien qui existe entre les différentes sciences [...] a établi que la plupart des questions d'économie politique, et surtout celles qui tiennent aux causes et aux effets du prix des productions et des marchandises, pouvaient donner lieu à l'emploi de la plus haute géométrie, qui seule les décidera avec une entière exactitude, et sans laquelle on n'arrive, par le raisonnement ordinaire qu'à un résultat moral et vague. Il a offert en exemple l'effet de la liberté donnée au commerce, ou de la suppression d'une taxe sur une denrée ou une marchandise: effet qui ne peut être bien exprimé, que par deux courbes correspondantes, serpentines et assymptotes. Il a invité les savans de la classe des sciences physiques et mathématiques, à tourner leurs recherches vers ces *courbes politiques*, qui sont peut-être innombrables.[29]

His physiocratic principles guided his responses to economic questions. Du Pont objected to additional taxes in December 1795 because landowners and farmers could not afford them. Costs had gone up by one fifth because the labour force had been conscripted, raising wages for the remainder, and horses had been requisitioned. At the same time the war, the seizure of noble properties and other disruptions had reduced produce by one fifth. Payment of rents in *assignats* had further reduced agricultural profits. The rich should not pay for the poor: this would generate resentment.[30] Du Pont would continue to plead on behalf of landed interests throughout his

---

28. Issue 11, 11 frimaire An IV, 2 December 1795, p.174. One might note that Du Pont de Nemours, Père et Fils & Cie were official printers of *assignats* at that time. Yet he wrote to Félix Faulcon on 12 May 1795: 'Mes prophécies sur les assignats ne se sont que trop réalisées. A présent je suis en réquisition à Paris, pour travailler à la régénération des Finances. L'entreprise serait aisée, si la convention n'en parlait pas trop, ou en parlait avec plus de lumières', in 'Lettres de Du Pont de Nemours à Félix Faulcon', ed. Gilbert Chinard, *French American review* 1:3 (1948), p.174-83.

29. Issue 227, 15 messidor An IV, 3 July 1796, p.16-17 (original emphasis).

30. *L'Historien*, vol.1, 9 December 1795, p.281-85. He adds that no one will be able to pay half of the forced contribution in kind, since they have used up their reserve in the last round of taxation. Payments by those poorer three quarters of the population will be in *assignats* and coin, removing both from circulation. Issue 23, p.366-67.

A physiocratic mandate: Du Pont de Nemours and L'Historien   189

mandate. His objections to special levies *because* he makes them on behalf of the propertied, even when supported by statistics, become controversial for that reason for the left wing in the councils.

Du Pont gets his own back in his denunciation of *babouvisme*:

> C'est ici la guerre de la propriété contre le pillage de la subsistance contre une famine qui deviendrait sans remède, de la liberté contre la tyrannie la plus hideuse, de la vertu contre le crime. Ces intérêts sont assez grands pour étouffer tout autre sentiment, pour rallier quiconque n'est pas en démence, quiconque veut jouir du fruit de son travail, quiconque veut avoir la sûreté de sa vie a l'esprit conservateur. Français, donnons-nous mutuellement cet exemple et cet appui; n'ayons d'ennemis que les méchans.[31]

He is simultaneously engaged in a struggle with the official press, *L'Ami des loix* and *La Sentinelle*. Du Pont denounced the subsidies they received from the Directory, possibly out of peevishness that he did not benefit from the same handout.[32] Louvet of *La Sentinelle* attacked Du Pont who retorted, '[il] m'accuse de conspirer avec la noblesse – qui n'existe plus – de conspirer avec la Suisse, qui n'existe pas; de prêcher la paix, que seuls les directeurs et les conseils ont le droit de juger.' Robert Lindet, meanwhile, sent *L'Historien* a letter where he tried to account for his role in the establishment of the revolutionary tribunal. Du Pont has no interest in giving Lindet a platform.[33] Finally, Du Pont loses patience:

> Après avoir longtems opposé le mépris de la calomnie, la patience échappe. Provoqué depuis trois mois, dans L'Ami des Loix, par Dom Poultier; par Dubois de Crancé, par leur associé Robert Lindet que ses crimes passés et présens ne peuvent déterminer au silence; dans La Sentinelle par Louvet, qui se montra un moment digne de mieux faire; dans le Journal de Paris par Sergent, osant menacer d'un procès criminel en réparation; L'Historien, qui le conjure aujourd'hui pour la première fois; dans le Journal des Patriotes de 89, par Naulin, reste du tribunal révolutionnaire; enfin par l'aristocrate Meimieu,

---

31. Issue 177, 27 floréal An IV, 16 May 1796, p.679-80.
32. Issue 148, 28 germinal An IV, 17 April 1796, p.197. 'On avait annoncé la suppression de la solde des journaux *stipendiés*. [...] L'*Ami des loix* a dit que c'était *malgré lui qu'on le payait*. La *Sentinelle* n'a rien dit sur ce point: mais les distributions continuent; et c'est encore une des dépenses auxquelles on applique le produit des rigueurs de l'emprunt forcé' (original emphasis).
33. Issue 154, 4 floréal An IV, 23 April 1796, p.271-72. He then threatens to take *L'Historien* to court for claiming that he received 6 million worth of subsidies.

qui rédige les articles de l'Abbréviateur signés Benoit Le Franc, quoi qu'il ne soit ni benoit, ni franc, ni abréviateur, je veux en finir avec ces messieurs. Je veux [...] Mais, que puis-je faire de plus cruel pour eux? ne les ai-je pas tous nommés? [...] Que puis-je dire de plus fort en ma faveur? ne viens-je pas de donner le catalogue complet de mes détracteurs et de mes ennemis?[34]

Then, in February 1797, Dubois-Crancé accused the great majority of journalists of serving the royalists, nonetheless distinguishing between the

royalistes d'opinion soupirant après la tranquillité, après la paix, regrettant un règne où ils avaient l'une et l'autre, amis de la république si elle assure leur repos; et les royalistes actifs qui méditent le renversement de la république, et veulent que les privilèges se rétablissent, dussent périr tous les français, tous les propriétaires échappés à la tyrannie execrable de Robespierre.[35]

Starved for funds, the state resorts to tariffs to raise revenue and Du Pont, while admitting their necessity until peace revived commercial treaties, nonetheless made plain his disapproval:

Il y aurait beaucoup d'autres choses à considérer relativement aux douanes: elles sont un reste des préjugés de la barbarie. L'avantage prétendu d'avoir par elles, un état des importations et des exportations, est totalement illusoire; il ne peut jamais valoir à la curiosité ce qu'il coûte au commerce. En quelques sens que les douanes frappent le commerce, c'est toujours à son détriment.[36]

---

34. Issue 208, 28 prairial An IV, 16 June 1796, p.436-37.
35. Vol.11, issue 446, 21 pluviôse An V, 9 February 1797, p.91-92. He names the newspapers called *Le Précurseur*, *Le Messager du soir*, *Les Actes des Apôtres* and *L'Eclair*. He reminds us that the name of Jardin, editor of the *Courier républicain* and the author of the *Journal des élections*, is compromised by documents that have been seized, related to the Babeuf conspiracy.
36. Issue 29, 20 December 1795, p.469, speech of 25 frimaire and of 26 frimaire An IV, issue 30, p.484-86. See also 'Opinion de Du Pont de Nemours sur la résolution du premier messidor, relative à l'urgence des paiements et aux négociations à faire par la trésorerie' (Paris, Imprimerie nationale, messidor An V [1797]), Newberry Library, IL, case FRC 18066. He concludes: 'Les négociations à la trésorerie; les anticipations au corps législatif; l'urgence au Directoire.'

A physiocratic mandate: Du Pont de Nemours and L'Historien 191

He actually suggests the opposite: a one fifth reduction in tariffs.[37] He is especially appalled by the attacks on privacy that searches would entail were monopolies and inspectors reinstated. Once again, his physiocratic principles are invoked, through long explanations, and his vocal opposition made him stand out. Bienaymé sums up the discussion:

> Dans son opinion, que nous donnerons textuellement, il a combattu l'adoption de la résolution: il a établi que le système des économistes sur la contribution foncière et sur les impôts indirects; et pour faire sentir que l'on voulait revenir au privilège exclusif de la vente de tabac, il a déclaré qu'on avait remis à la commission un mémoire d'une compagnie qui offrait de faire à la nation un fonds de douze millions, à condition qu'il lui serait permis d'introduire les tabacs en exemption du droit proposé et de les fabriquer dans une manufacture particulière.[38]

Du Pont was trying time and again to educate his colleagues, instead of bowing to economic necessity:

> Il serait plus simple à cet égard et plus prudent d'étudier les principes des hommes dont les cheveux ont blanchi dans l'application à la science de l'économie politique, que de chercher à les tourner en ridicule. Cette science dit que tout ce qui viole la liberté des personnes et des domiciles est mauvais, que tout ce qui s'éloigne de la morale est funeste. [...] L'avidité fiscale accompagne presque toujours l'ineptie politique.[39]

On the particulars of tobacco, he argued that fraud would be more advantageous to the clerks and guards who would turn a blind eye to contraband. Similarly, he points out all the hidden costs of raising tolls on canals.[40] In both cases he is particularly anxious that the old tax-farming system not be reintroduced, demonstrating that the revenues would go into the hands of financiers instead of the state. He counsels turning to foreign investment instead, which would flow in as long as there was a profit to be made, and the republic guaranteed

---

37. Allowing Du Pont to reiterate his argument that collecting duties in coins would bring in far more (issue 30, p.484-86).
38. Issue 370, 5 frimaire, 25 November 1796, p.313.
39. Issue 370, 5 frimaire, 25 November 1796, p.313.
40. Issue 411, 16 nivôse, 5 January 1797, p.244-52, and issue 467, 12 ventôse, 2 March 1797, p.418-32.

the security of the investments. The state would benefit from the increased value of properties along the new canals.

He repeats the same criticism regarding tolls on roads, which would do nothing to improve them. He admonishes the Council of the Elders: 'Non, mes collègues, elle n'est pas une question de voierie; elle est purement une question de finance et d'imposition.'[41] Tolls were incompatible with liberty, and the revenues would be a fraction of what it would cost the government to enforce them. Moreover, there would be no guarantee that the taxes would go towards new roads or their upkeep.

What is more, he thundered, taxation had reached its maximum. A nation might be viewed as a sponge, but it cannot disgorge more water than it has:

> Qui donc ose dire que ce ne soit pas assez? qui ose être friand d'une addition des maux? Et que regrette-t-on? les commis aux aides? aux entrées, aux gabelles? la violation des domiciles? l'arrestation des voyageurs? le droit de faire retourner nos poches, et de mettre la main sous ou sur la jupe de nos femmes et de nos filles? Eh bien! [...] On les regrettera en vain. Notre constitution ne permet pas qu'on les rétablisse. Nous avons au moins gagné la liberté personnelle, et le droit d'être maîtres dans notre maison.[42]

In fine, Du Pont believed that more savings were in order, and was particularly preoccupied by the state of the treasury. Recall that he sits on the Committee that oversees its expenditures. He stresses that there are many problems with the organisation of the treasury that demand a prompt reform, because, even if it were properly organised, the treasury in the past four years experienced the chaos that resulted from paper money, 'de ses dégradations successives, des rehaussemens illusoires que lui ont procuré quelques actes de despotisme, quelques moments d'une plus grande terreur, et la fureur des réquisitions, et la démence du maximum, et l'ignorance arbitraire, insolente, cupide, qu'ont déployé à la fois pres de 50,000 ordonnateurs disséminés sur toute la France'.[43]

When it comes to subsidies to manufactures, Du Pont wants priority given to those that would then be able to function independently.[44]

---

41. Issue 467, 12 ventôse, 2 March 1797, p.418-32.
42. Issue 569, 24 prairial, 12 June 1797, p.346-47.
43. Issue 562, 17 prairial, 5 June 1797, p.242.
44. Issue 557, 12 prairial, 31 May 1797, p.170.

A physiocratic mandate: Du Pont de Nemours and L'Historien

More surprising is that, besides concern for the pocketbooks of landowners, Du Pont has nothing to say, nor reports about, the misery of the citizenry in these years. Instead, we get a denunciation of the Maximum as one of the greatest evils that has befallen mankind. If *révolution bourgeoise* there is, it lies here.

The centre

The Legislature lurches forwards, facing impediments in its way, especially once the directors become frustrated by the constitutional limits placed on them and the slow pace of the Legislature's two councils, endlessly wrangling about procedures. The directors attempt to set the legislative agenda time and again, despite being forbidden to do so. Their hands are tied while they must address rebellions in the countryside, the renewal of the Vendée; conspiracies which were dreaded and one that had already materialised in 1796 with Babeuf and Buonarotti. Du Pont's anti-Jacobinism remains palpable, and, unlike some of his fellow constitutionalists, he does not distinguish between Montagnards and milder Jacobins:

> L'auteur a raison de regarder comme des insensés très coupables ceux qui voudraient ramener ou l'ancien gouvernement, ou quoique ce soit qui eut avec lui quelque ressemblance.
>
> On les contiendra par les seules forces de la raison et de la constitution perpétuellement réclamées.
>
> Il paraît trop oublier les jacobins, insensés furieux qui voudraient ramener le gouvernement révolutionnaire et les proscriptions de Marat ou de Babœuf. Ceux-là ne bavardent point; ils frappent. Ils se tiennent actuellement prêts à frapper, et on ne les contiendra que par la force physique.[45]

So, while the Directory sees the threat emanating from the right, Du Pont minimises that risk, as one can see from his response to the closing of the Club de Clichy, along with those of Noailles and Salm.[46] As far as Du Pont is concerned, there is a difference between clubs that correspond and have branches throughout France and meetings

---

45. Issue 588, 13 messidor, 1 July 1797, p.182.
46. Issue 583, 8 messidor, 26 June. On Clichy, see Popkin, *The Right-wing press*, p.84-88; Augustin Challamel, *Les Clubs contre-révolutionnaires* (Paris, 1895), p.490-506; and David Mindock, 'The role of the Clichy Club in the French Revolution from October 26, 1795 to September 4, 1795', MA dissertation, University of Wisconsin, 1969.

194 *Liana Vardi*

of like-minded deputies that are not otherwise allowed constitutionally to meet together, at the Club de Clichy. He is one of its estimated 300 members.[47] But he is not wedded to its existence:

> Il serait surtout notre espoir dans la réunion des hommes qui ont quelques vertus et quelques talens, réunion qui doit s'opérer, non pas à Clichy, non pas à l'hôtel de Salm, mais chacun à son poste, indiquant à toutes les atrocités, le but où il faut tendre, et le chemin, non pas le plus court, mais le plus sûr pour y arriver.

and a contributor to add, seemingly addressing right-wing extremists:

> De grands exemples devraient pourtant leur ouvrir les yeux; ils voyent Cochon, ils voyent Thibaudeau, qui pourraient, s'ils le voulaient, se croire plus compromis qu'eux, marcher courageusement dans la carrière de l'ordre et de la justice, mépriser les fantômes de vendémiaire créés par ceux qui les ont combattus; ils les voyent, soutenus par l'opinion publique, exercer énergiquement leurs fonctions, aux applaudissemens des honnêtes gens et au désespoir des factieux.[48]

L'Historien had already reported on the shenanigans of the Noailles circle:

> On dit qu'il y a un comité intérieur secret de membres qui se sont choisis eux-mêmes, et que l'existence de ce comité n'est pas même soupçonnée par ceux que fait mouvoir cette ame invisible. On dit aussi que le comité a prévenu les membres obéissans qu'il fallait par tous les moyens empêcher une discussion régulière et soutenue dans le conseil des anciens, sur la grande question des séquestres et du partage des biens des pères et mères, ayeux et ayeules, bisayeux et bisayeules des émigrés. Les rôles distribués; on parlera peu; on criera beaucoup, on frappera le plancher du talon et de la canne, on toussera, on se mouchera pendant les discours de quelques orateurs; on dira pour les autres, *appuyé*; on tachera de faire naître quelque incident, quelque querelle particulière qui détourne l'attention, qui anime une partie du conseil, qui afflige l'autre.[49]

---

47. Issue 589, 14 messidor, 2 July 1797, p.196.
48. Issue 470, 15 ventôse, 5 March 1797, Ségur again.
49. Issue 146, 26 germinal, 15 April 1796, p.165-66, letter to the editor signed Anticipation. On moderates, see Serna, *La République des girouettes*, p.267-74.

A physiocratic mandate: Du Pont de Nemours and L'Historien

As Jourdan des Bouches-du-Rhône put it: 'Il n'y a de société à Clichy que parce qu'il y a dix-huit mois nous avons trouvé formé le club de Noailles.'[50]

There is no scholarly consensus on the political line taken by the Club de Clichy, because it could not agree on a single ideological stance. There were royalists mainly of the constitutional monarchist persuasion, republican constitutionalists, moderate centrists, some that would have liked to see an eventual revision of the Constitution, and those who stuck to the *juste milieu*.[51] Throughout *L'Historien* we similarly find Du Pont and his supporters trying to work out where moderation lay and what it possibly meant. They positioned themselves as centrists, but of what order, and who exactly formed the opposition was sometimes unclear. There was no doubt about the Jacobins, whom they detested and associated with chaos and terrorism. They also dissociated themselves from the die-hard royalists who wanted a return to the Old Regime, but the centre did not hold.[52]

The nuances, as in this letter from Ségur addressed to *L'Historien*, were very clear to observers of the government, but the lines are murkier to us:

> Les partis qui peuvent influer sur nos destinées, et qui doivent fixer l'attention du gouvernement, sont les trois suivans: Le parti des jacobins qui s'arrogent avec hypocrisie le titre de patriotes. Le parti des amis de l'ordre, qui s'appelle parti des honnêtes gens, et qui tenant au gouvernement tel qu'il soit, pour que le gouvernement protège les personnes et les propriétés, n'aurait peut-être pas fait la république, mais est aujourd'hui le plus solidement républicain. Enfin un troisième parti intermédiaire qui, troublé par le souvenir de ses

50. Issue 612, 12 thermidor An v, 25 July 1797, p.95.
51. See 'Nécessité du juste milieu', issue 501, 16 germinal, 5 April 1797, p.242-46.
52. See W. R. Fryer, *Republic or Restoration in France? 1794-7, the politics of French royalism, with particular reference to the activities of A. B. J. d'André* (Manchester, 1965), p.234-36. On the troubled centre: issue 570, 25 prairial, 13 June 1797, p.363-64. 'Depuis qu'une multitude innombrable d'hommes ont été métamorphosés en girouettes accident qui a toujours été plus commun en France qu'en tout autre pays, il y aurait une véritable inhumanité à persécuter les girouettes qui ont de tout tems été répandues dans toutes les classes de la société. Il est vrai qu'elles occupent ordinairement une place élevée, mais qui n'a rien de féodal. Elles sont dociles par essence et n'ont jamais été du parti de l'opposition. Elles obéissent aux loix de la nature et les indiquent sans violence à l'homme en société. Elles suivent avec plaisir le vent de la faveur; et pour peu que le gouvernement saisisse celui de l'opinion publique, il les fera marcher avec un souffle.'

égaremens passés, par ses torts successifs envers les deux autres, et par la chaleur inquiète de son imagination et de son ambition, veut entraîner le gouvernement à combattre, à ménager les deux autres partis qu'il appelle royaliste et anarchiste, et à se placer ainsi dans une position précaire, insoutenable, bordée de précipices.

Le parti des honnêtes gens est formé d'hommes bien élevés, de propriétaires, de négocians, de cultivateurs, de jeunes gens instruits et de cette immensité respectable de citoyens qui ont horreur du crime et de l'injustice. Les uns aiment la république; les autres qui n'aiment pas cette forme de gouvernement, comme trop orageuse, sont prêts à changer d'opinion s'ils voient dans cet état de chose le respect des propriétaires et des personnes, le règne des loix et la tranquilité. Ils sont las d'orages, et s'ils s'agitent, c'est par la crainte de voir renaître les malheurs passés, ils craignent [...] presque également le triomphe des émigrés et celle des jacobins.[53]

Yet another correspondent, Cassandre, attempts to define the centre.[54] He too isolates three ideological trends or parties in the country. Faced with the radicalism of two of them, there is no option for those who believe in 'la raison, la morale, la bonne foi et la constitution', detested and threatened as they are by the other two, but to form a third party. This party is that of sensible men, like the editors of *L'Historien*, for whom the Constitution is a harbour. It is the party of *honnêtes gens*, who, unfortunately, are too often dupes. The second consists of the prejudiced, enthusiasts who want the return of the Old Regime and Louis XVIII; they are *frondeurs*. The remaining party is that of the ambitious, who want a ruler who is not a Bourbon who will safeguard their power, wealth and impunity. Whether it be a party of the left (already envisaging military rule) or not, it is striking that the advocates of a middling position repeatedly place themselves within moderate conservatism, clearly differentiated from ultraroyalism. The left treated anyone who did not share their ideas as a royalist, much to the distress of moderate republicans. *L'Historien* situates moderation more clearly as the constitutionalist road that refuses a perpetual revolution or a counter-revolution.

Thus P.N. responds:

---

53. Issue 158, 8 floréal An IV, 27 April 1796, letter from P. L. Ségur.
54. Like La Fenêtre, Cassandre appears to be Faulcon, as he reveals in his memoirs where he employs the same language. Issue 588, 14 messidor, 1 July 1797, p.181-82.

A physiocratic mandate: Du Pont de Nemours and L'Historien

197

Vincet amor patria. Celui des trois partis qui l'emportera, mon cher
Cassandre, est le parti [...] qui se tient fidèlement attaché à la constitution; celui à qui les révolutions, les prolongations de révolution, les
contre-révolutions font également horreur. C'est qu'il est le seul qui
soit pour la paix, la liberté, pour la propriété, pour la sûreté de tous
les citoyens.

The elections of the second set of deputies (one-third replacement
of existing legislators) is much on everyone's mind, and *L'Historien*
attempts to reach the famous *honnêtes gens*:

Peuple Français, séant aujourd'hui en ton trône impérial, sois-y
grand, sage et modéré: c'est ce qu'il faut toujours recommander aux
souverains.

Tes représentans ont demandé à tes électeurs une déclaration
très simple en elle-même, et qui était dans le cœur de tous les bons
citoyens; car c'est celle de s'opposer à de nouveaux crimes, à de
nouveaux malheurs, à de nouveaux combats, à de nouveaux pillages,
à tout changement qui ne pourrait résulter que d'une nouvelle
révolution, ou d'une contre-révolution également dangereuse. [...]

Que cela te serve seulement d'instruction pour choisir des
représentans qui te connaissent parfaitement et qui te soient
parfaitement connus; qui te rendent l'estime que tu leur auras
prouvée en leur déléguant tes pouvoirs. [...]

Songe que tes ennemis voudraient le désordre pour annuler tes
élections, peut-être pour déployer la force, pour *vendémiairiser*.[55]

The wording is significant. The short-lived royalist uprising is treated
as the left's invention. But, at the same time, indifference, isolation
and disunion were to be feared more than at any other time in the
Revolution, one contributor had already admonished in January.[56]
Du Pont's colleague at the Cinq-Cents, Félix Faulcon, warned against
criticising the government, saying that now was the time to rally
around the Constitution.[57]

---

55. Issue 487, 2 germinal, 22 March 1797, Du Pont de Nemours, 'Au peuple',
    p.17-18.
56. Issue 409, 14 nivôse, 3 January 1797, 'Avis aux honnêtes gens'.
57. Letter to *L'Historien*, 'Sur l'aveuglement de l'esprit de parti', issue 452, 27
    pluviôse An v, 15 February 1797, p.179-83. Faulcon had shared his concern that
    the elections of a single deputy from various parts of the country would reduce
    the new third to perhaps thirty out of 250. He urged therefore journalists to
    convince electors to vote for local candidates. Issue 420, 25 nivôse, 14 January
    1797, p.385-86.

198 *Liana Vardi*

Du Pont shared his preferences among potential candidates, moderates who had once supported a constitutional monarchy: Desmeuniers, Morellet, Boissy d'Anglas, Quatremère de Quincy for the Five Hundred and Emmery for the Elders. He added Gorguerrau, Jolivet, Demousseaux and Sécard. He also stated his discontent when Desmeuniers, Gorguerrau, Morellet and Sécard were removed from the electoral list, following the bad advice of Merlin de Douai, and to the glee of the Jacobins. He wished that some departing deputies might run again such as Boissy, Lanjuinais, Durand-Maillane, Fermont, Olivier-Gérente, Johannot and Pelet de La Lozière.[58] In other words, these elections should give pride of place to known moderates.

Du Pont and the Clichyens were successful in the nomination of a new director to replace the one rotating off. Based on what the press was reporting, Barthélémy, ambassador to Switzerland, was at the top of the Clichy Club's list while the Club de Noailles favoured Merlin de Douai, minister of Justice. As the 'right' had secured more seats in the Legislature with the Year V elections, Barthélémy easily secured the post.[59]

L'Historien reported on the manoeuvres by Merlin.[60] Following a decision from the minister, reported by the executive, Du Pont commented: 'Il résulte de cet arrêté un moyen très simple d'exclure des assemblées primaires, tous les individus que le gouvernement, ou l'administration centrale du département jugerait à propos d'en écarter. A la veille même du premier germinal, il suffira de les inscrire sur une liste d'émigrés, comme on vient de le pratiquer à l'égard de Félix Lepelletier.' A celebratory note was struck in the wake of the conservative electoral victory (especially evident in the Cinq-Cents):

> Les membres des deux nouveaux tiers s'embrassent avec une effusion dans laquelle on reconnaît d'une part le plaisir de recevoir un secours honorable et longtems attendu, de l'autre celui de trouver un point d'appui dont la solidité est éprouvée comme la vertu qui en est la base. [...]
>
> On avait semé des craintes sur l'effet de quelques restes des préjugés de l'ancien régime. Mais tous les membres des deux conseils

58. See issues 472, 17 ventôse An v, 7 March 1797, p.497-98; 497, 12 germinal An v, 1 April 1797; 504, 19 germinal An v, 8 April 1797; 508, 23 germinal An v, 12 April 1797.
59. See issues 551, 6 prairial An v, 25 May 1797; 553, 8 prarial An v, 27 May 1797. Barthélémy would be deported after the fructidor coup.
60. Issue 477, 22 ventôse An v, 12 March 1797, p.581-82.

A physiocratic mandate: Du Pont de Nemours and L'Historien   199

sont des magistrats du régime nouveau. Ils sont les sénateurs de la république. C'est d'elle et de sa constitution qu'ils tiennent leur pouvoir. [...]

Mille biens sont à faire, mille maux à réparer, et l'on n'y peut parvenir que par la raison, la justice, la bonté, l'application à discerner ce qui est utile.[61]

As they set about dismantling the legislation on the émigrés and their properties that they had so contested, they frightened the left:

Le conseil [des Cinq-Cents] ferme la discussion, et adopte la rédaction suivante:

La loi du 3 brumaire est abrogée; la loi du 14 frimaire est également abrogée, à l'exception de l'article qui confirme la loi du 20 vendémiaire. Les fonctionnaires publics suspendus reprendront leurs places [...]. Cela est un droit, disent une foule des membres. Les loix des 21 floréal et 18 fructidor sont abrogées.[62]

This was not the end of the reversals: 'Sur la proposition de Thibaudeau, le conseil arrête que la commission lui présentera des articles additionnels qui tendront au rapport des loix particulières qui ont suspendu divers représentans du peuple de l'exercice de leurs fonctions, en exécution de la loi du 3 brumaire.' This did not go down

---

61. Issue 548, 3 prairial An v, 22 May 1797, 'Aspect des deux conseils' by P.N. and Medius, p.17-19, p.26-31. On the elections of the Year v, see Jean-René Suratteau, 'Les élections de l'An v aux Conseils du Directoire', *Annales historiques de la Révolution française* 301:154 (1958), p.21-63; Gueniffey, *Le Nombre et la raison*, p.475-510; Albert Mathiez, 'Les élections de l'An v', *Annales historiques de la Révolution française* 6:35 (1929), p.425-46. Melvin Edelstein, *The French Revolution and the birth of electoral democracy* (Farnham, 2014), ch.12, *passim*. Bernard Gainot, 'Le contentieux électoral sous le Directoire: monisme et pluralisme dans la culture politique de la France révolutionnaire', *Revue historique* 642:2 (2007), p.325-53.

62. Issue 538, 22 floréal An v, 11 May 1797, p.124. Félix Faulcon had also initially been enthusiastic about the new third, but was soon disenchanted as they fomented more factionalism. Faulcon now isolated five tendencies in the councils: 'La montagne royaliste, les royalistes modérés [that he associates with the Club de Clichy], les constitutionnels sages, les constitutionnels exagérés et la montagne anarchiste'; *Mélanges législatifs, historiques et politiques pendant la durée de la Constitution de l'An III* (Paris, 1801), p.288-90. Who joined whom in debates was therefore crucial. He notes that the moderate royalists drifted towards the radical royalists, while his ultraconstitutionalists allied themselves with the Mountain.

200 *Liana Vardi*

easily. Trouble was brewing on several fronts, however much Du Pont wished it just to peter out. Already on the evening of 19 May,

> ils ont formé des rassemblemens dans les faubourgs Saint-Antoine et Saint-Marceau, et dans plusieurs autres cantons de la ville, de petites troupes d'hommes, les uns ivres, les autres feignant de l'être, et mêlés avec quelques restes des furies de guillotine, et quelques autres femmes de mauvaise vie. Le ministre de la police a été instruit que plusieurs représentans du peuple devaient être assassinés à domicile, et les membres du directoire dans leur palais.[63]

Du Pont called for calm and unity from his position as president of the Council of the Elders for the month of Thermidor.

Jourdan des Bouches-du-Rhône stated at the Five Hundred:

> On ne cesse de calomnier le conseil des Cinq Cents, on dénature nos intentions pour les accuser. Des sociétés populaires se propagent, les anarchistes lèvent la tête; c'est Paris qui est le rendez-vous des conspirateurs, le foyer de la sédition, des scélérats connus y paraissent [...] (oui, oui dit un membre des émigrés).[64]

> Si l'on ne se bat pas à Paris, ce n'est pas la faute des pamphlétaires et des afficheurs. On vient de placarder sur tous les murs une comparaison entre l'armée d'Italie et le club de Clichy. Les rapprochemens tendent à prouver que l'influence du club de Clichy empêche la paix, fait mourir de faim les rentiers, les pensionnaires et les employés, fait baisser les inscriptions, etc. tandisque l'armée d'Italie a négocié les préliminaires de la paix, envoyé de l'argent et relevé le crédit public. On y remarque surtout cette expression: Le conseil des cinq cents s'il s'écarte de la constitution, ne forme que 500 hommes – L'armée d'Italie, si la constitution est violée, offre 200,000 bayonnettes.[65]

Worse is envisaged, but Du Pont remains sanguine a few weeks before the 18 fructidor coup: 'On sait que les barrières doivent être fermées; on sait que 100 ou 130 représentans du peuple doivent être arrêtés ou consignés dans leurs maisons; on sait que l'on doit faire des visites domiciliaires. Si ce numéro paraît, la moitié du péril sera passée; si le suivant est publié, il n'y aura presque plus à craindre.'[66]

Yet troops were massing around Paris, 21,000 total. Du Pont

---

63. Issue 545, 30 prairial An v, 19 May 1797.
64. Issue 605, 30 messidor An v, 18 July 1797.
65. Issue 615, 10 thermidor An v, 28 July 1797, p.139.
66. Issue 629, 24 thermidor An v, 11 August 1797.

A physiocratic mandate: Du Pont de Nemours and L'Historien 201

concludes that ministers of War and of the Police Petiet and Cochon were dismissed so they might not present any opposition. It was rumoured that General Bonaparte celebrated 14 July with toasts to the Directory and the Conseil des Anciens, but refused to do so for the Five Hundred.[67] As far as *L'Historien* was concerned, the army had been misinformed on the attacks on the Constitution and needed to be enlightened on this.[68] Besides the popular movements in Paris and the arrival of troops in the capital, the Conseil des Cinq-Cents was involved in a power struggle with the directors. Among their grievances was that ministers they liked had been dismissed, while they retained Merlin de Douai who was their main target as well as that of 'public opinion'. Du Pont recognised that the Five Hundred had gone too far:

> En terminant il a fait remarquer que l'on n'avait peut-être pas assez pris garde que la nature même de ces deux autorités qui étaient aujourd'hui dans la lutte dont on craignait le résultat nécessitait entre eux une sorte de surveillance jalouse. Mais il a invoqué la sagesse du conseil des Anciens, placé par la constitution comme le modérateur de celui des Cinq Cents, et l'a invité à s'interposer entre ces deux rivaux, et à prévenir ainsi les déchiremens que produirait nécessairement le choc que les factions toujours actives voudraient déterminer.[69]

On 3 September, Du Pont addressed the Anciens at length on debts to lenders and the time allowed for repayment.[70] The next day, 18 fructidor, under the orders of General Augereau, soldiers cleared both houses, resulting in the arrest and exclusion of 177 deputies. Carnot and Barthélémy were purged from the Directory, leaving a triumvirate of Barras, La Révellière-Lépeaux and Reubell in charge.

Du Pont's presses were smashed, and he and his son Irénée were taken to La Force prison, accused of conspiring against the internal and external security of the Republic by preaching for the return of the monarchy and the dissolution of the republican government.[71] After an appeal to La Révellière, they were immediately released on order of La Révellière, Barras and Reubell. No charges were brought

---

67. Issue 616, 11 thermidor An v, 29 July 1797, p.145-46.
68. Issue 621, 16 thermidor An v, 3 August 1797.
69. Issue 640, 5 fructidor An v, 22 August 1797.
70. Issue 652, 17 fructidor An v, 3 September 1797, 247.
71. Paris, Archives nationales de France, AFIII/463, dossiers 2804-2806. Wilmington, DE, Hagley Museum and Library, microfilm, Archives nationales reel 7, accession 700 Du Pont de Nemours.

against them, but Du Pont was asked to resign from the Council of the Elders, which he did on 27 fructidor.[72]

***

Du Pont had seemingly two goals as deputy: to keep Jacobinism at bay, sticking firmly to a constitutionalist position (and we can only go on what we read in his newspaper, correspondence, except on family matters, having been lost or destroyed), and to introduce physiocratic principles into the economy. The question remains about his political allegiances, what brand of moderation he embraced, and whether his constitutionalism flirted with the royalists. Opinions differed at the time and still do among historians. It was easier several decades ago still to view him as a royalist counter-revolutionary 'at heart' than it is today, when the dossier on political allegiances during the Directory has been reopened.

Barras in his memoirs dubs him the leader of the new *tiers* elected in 1795, while referring to him as 'notre ami'.[73] For Thibaudeau, a typical centrist, Du Pont was a royalist, even if a mild one, not necessarily hostile to the Republic.[74] Georges Lefebvre counts *L'Historien* among the moderate newspapers, while at the same time calling Du Pont a constitutional monarchist. For Jeremy Popkin, Marc Belissa and Yannick Bosc, Du Pont was a moderate.[75]

As we have seen, it was difficult to pinpoint political positioning during the regime, given the responses to ever-changing circumstances. Marc Bouloiseau therefore views Du Pont as a maverick, pursuing his own reasoning, irritating both sides of the chamber.[76] Saricks denies that he was an active royalist, viewing him instead as a committed republican during the Directory.[77] I conclude that Du Pont's stance was that of a constitutional centrist, a position that can be viewed as conservative, but not reactionary, and which in the nineteenth century would emerge as political and economic liberalism. For Du Pont these went together, as he had argued time and again as a member of the Council of the Elders and editor of *L'Historien*.

72. AF III/463, dossier 2806, including letters of 21 and 27 fructidor An v, 7 and 13 September 1797.
73. *Mémoires de Barras* (Paris, 2010), p.232.
74. A. C. Thibaudeau, *Mémoires sur la Convention et sur le Directoire*, vol.2: *Directoire* (Paris, 1824), p.12.
75. Lefebvre, *La France sous le Directoire*, p.79, 221, 315; Popkin, *The Right-wing press*, p.117; Belissa and Bosc, *Le Directoire*, p.144.
76. Bouloiseau, *Bourgeoisie et révolution*, p.113-15.
77. Saricks, *Pierre Samuel Du Pont de Nemours*, p.251.

Du Pont de Nemours et la république des 'propriétaires du sol'

ANNIE LÉCHENET
Université Claude Bernard Lyon 1

i. Introduction: un échange entre Du Pont de Nemours et Jefferson

En 1815, Pierre-Samuel Du Pont de Nemours signale à Thomas Jefferson que 'les trois républiques unies de la nouvelle Grenade, de Carthagène et de Caracas [lui] ont fait demander [ses] idées sur la constitution à laquelle elles voudraient s'arrêter ne regardant leur état actuel que comme révolutionnaire et provisoire', et qu'il lui envoie le projet qu'il a réalisé de cette constitution.[1]

Il est frappant de remarquer que, dans les troubles de leur indépendance, c'est à Du Pont de Nemours, qui a été membre du Comité de Constitution à l'Assemblée constituante française en 1791, que ces républiques s'adressent, et que c'est à Jefferson, son ami et correspondant américain de longue date, que Du Pont envoie son projet lorsqu'il s'agit de leur espoir commun de diffusion de la république. A cette époque[2] il se sent en effet très proche des

---

1. Pierre-Samuel Du Pont de Nemours, *Lettre à Jefferson* (7 décembre 1815), dans *The Correspondence of Jefferson and Du Pont de Nemours, with an introduction on Jefferson and the physiocrats*, éd. Gilbert Chinard (1931; New York, 1971), p.227. Cette demande semble avoir été faite à Du Pont de Nemours par Manuel Palacio-Fajardo, indépendantiste vénézuélien lors de son séjour à Paris en 1814. Ambrose Saricks, *Pierre Samuel Du Pont de Nemours* (Lawrence, KS, 1965), p.346.
2. Il est vrai que Du Pont de Nemours a soutenu la lutte des républiques américaines dès leurs combats pour leur indépendance. Mais, ayant prôné d'abord le 'despotisme légal', puis, en 1789, une monarchie constitutionnelle, Du Pont de Nemours n'a *explicitement* soutenu la république qu'à partir de 1792. Réfutant le reproche de versatilité politique qui lui a été adressé, Anthony Mergey et Arnault Skornicki montrent sa constante recherche d'une 'politique rationnelle qui consacrerait la propriété, la liberté, la sûreté, l'égalité,

Américains du Nord dans leur défense commune de la réalisation de la république au point de l'histoire humaine où il leur a été donné de vivre. Une de ses dernières lettres met en garde James Monroe à l'égard de la coalition 'des Rois et des Pairs en Europe' contre 'la République américaine, dernier espoir du monde'.[3] Ou encore, voici comment il parlait en 1811 de la République américaine: 'une république qui respecte la liberté de la presse, qui est aujourd'hui la dernière des Républiques qui aient existé, la dernière espérance de celles qui sont à naître, et qu'elle propagera comme une mère Abeille.'[4]

Pour lui la république est la forme normale, c'est-à-dire correspondant à 'la nature, la morale, l'équité', et en réalité universelle, de l'organisation et de la vie politiques: 'Si l'on excepte les nations entièrement abusées on trouvera partout des sentiments républicains. Et même sous un certain aspect tous les Etats sont déjà des Républiques, ou très prêts à le devenir.'[5] Ce qu'il entend par 'république', qu'il nomme aussi parfois 'gouvernement représentatif',[6] est, classiquement, une forme de gouvernement exercée par 'le véritable souverain' (mais nous verrons plus précisément ce qu'il entend par 'véritable souverain') par le biais d'une représentation non héréditaire, donc élective, limitant les pouvoirs du gouvernement, notamment par la séparation de ses branches, ainsi que par 'les mœurs, un louable esprit

---

l'obéissance à la loi et le respect de la constitution' (voir ci-dessous, p.347-77), ce qu'il a finalement espéré trouver dans la république.

3. P.-S. Du Pont, *Lettre à James Monroe* (26 février 1817), dans G. Chinard, *The Correspondence*, p.276.

4. P.-S. Du Pont, *Lettre à Jefferson* (12 décembre 1811), dans G. Chinard, *The Correspondence*, p.172.

5. P.-S. Du Pont, *Lettre à Jefferson* (12 décembre 1811), dans G. Chinard, *The Correspondence*, p.176.

6. De même James Madison, principal concepteur de la Constitution américaine, écrit: 'Une république, par quoi j'entends un gouvernement dans lequel l'idée de représentation est mise en place' (Alexander Hamilton et autres, *Le Fédéraliste*, éd. et traduit par Anne Amiel, Paris, 2012, p.136), s'opposant par là à toute la tradition des républiques antiques, notamment grecques, qui pour lui correspondent plutôt à la notion de 'pure démocratie, par quoi [il] entend une société comprenant un petit nombre de citoyens qui s'assemblent pour administrer le gouvernement en personne' (*Le Fédéraliste*, p.135). '[A] pure democracy, by which I mean a society, consisting of a small number of citizens, who assemble and administrate the government in person [...] A republic, by which I mean a government in which the scheme of representation takes place', dans J. Madison, *Writings*, éd. Jack N. Rakove (New York, 1999), p.164.

Du Pont de Nemours et la république des 'propriétaires du sol'   205

public',[7] esprit du peuple lui-même fait de 'respect pour les droits, d'amour de la patrie, de zèle pour la liberté, et de dévouement le plus héroïque pour la Patrie'.[8]

Cependant cette conception assez répandue à cette époque recouvre des sens précis et variés chez les différents penseurs et acteurs, et c'est le cas pour Du Pont de Nemours, qui a commencé à penser et à agir sous la monarchie française – il a dès cette époque aidé les républiques américaines, comme il le rappelle à Madison en 1815: 'Quand les Etats-Unis se formèrent, j'étais déjà dans les places influentes, et je tâchai avec quelque succès de leur rendre les services qui pouvaient dépendre de moi'[9] – et dont la pensée maintenant républicaine sera toujours construite sur 'les rapports naturels' énoncés par les théories des 'Economistes' ou 'physiocrates'.

Or l'une des pierres angulaires de sa conception du 'gouvernement représentatif' est son affirmation d'un droit de vote très précisément restreint aux propriétaires de terre. On trouvait déjà cette position chez certains protagonistes de la Révolution anglaise de 1649, tel le modéré Ireton, et, dans les premiers temps des républiques américaines, chez certains partisans du *statu quo ante*, tel Edmund Pendleton, président de la Convention de Virginie en 1776. Mais, dès avant l'Indépendance, le débat avait lieu dans les colonies anglaises d'Amérique entre partisans d'un droit de suffrage réservé aux propriétaires de terre et ceux d'un droit de suffrage simplement censitaire, attaché aux diverses formes de propriété,[10] voire, chez certains, d'un droit de suffrage universel – des chefs de famille. Dès la Constitution de 1787, c'est le suffrage censitaire que propose Madison, tout comme la quasi-totalité des acteurs de la Révolution française. La position de Du Pont de Nemours semble étonnante de la part d'un républicain épris de liberté en ce début de dix-neuvième siècle, et c'est sur cette question que portera l'essentiel de la réponse de Jefferson, ainsi que l'argumentation en retour de la part de Du Pont.

---

7. P.-S. Du Pont, *Mémoire sur l'agriculture et les manufactures aux Etats-Unis*, envoyé au Président Madison, 18 janvier 1816, dans G. Chinard, *The Correspondence*, p.245.
8. P.-S. Du Pont, *Lettre à Jefferson* (25 mai 1808). dans G. Chinard, *The Correspondence*, p.125.
9. P.-S. Du Pont, *Lettre à Madison* (25 juillet 1815), dans G. Chinard, *The Correspondence*, p.225.
10. Derek Heater, *A Brief history of citizenship* (Edimbourg, 2004); Chilton Williamson, *American suffrage from property to democracy, 1760-1860* (Princeton, NJ, 1968).

206 Annie Léchenet

Il est proposé dans cette étude d'examiner principalement cette conception, et les raisons sur lesquelles la fonde Du Pont de Nemours: s'agit-il de raisons purement politiques au sens constitutionnel, de principes moraux, en termes notamment de droits naturels, ou de raisons fondées sur 'la science de l'Economie politique [qui] ne doit pas être ignorée, ni négligée aux Etats-Unis'?[11]

Pour ce faire, la source principale étudiée sera le débat entre Jefferson et Du Pont de Nemours, notamment au sujet du projet de Constitution fait par Du Pont pour 'les trois républiques unies de la nouvelle Grenade, de Carthagène et de Caracas',[12] parce que les différences de position entre ces deux républicains permettent non seulement de comprendre certains aspects de la pensée de Jefferson – ce qui est l'objectif le plus fréquemment recherché parce qu'on estime que Jefferson est agrarien et qu'il y aurait un 'possible attrait de sa part pour les théories physiocratiques'[13] – mais aussi de saisir le raisonnement politique de Du Pont de Nemours. C'est en effet dans les derniers temps de sa correspondance avec Jefferson que Du Pont, devenant de plus en plus désireux de convaincre un Jefferson de plus en plus réservé,[14] a, d'une certaine manière, récapitulé avec force les différents aspects de sa pensée et le lien entre eux.

11. P.-S. Du Pont, *Lettre à Jefferson* (12 décembre 1811), dans G. Chinard, *The Correspondence*, p.172.

12. Lettres de Jefferson à Du Pont (24 avril 1816), dans G. Chinard, *The Correspondence*, p.256-60, et réponse de Du Pont à Jefferson (12 mai 1816), p.260-68.

13. Lucia Bergamasco, 'Thomas Jefferson et Du Pont de Nemours: un dialogue décalé', dans *Entre deux eaux: les secondes Lumières et leurs ambiguïtés (1789-1815)*, éd. Anouchka Vasak (Paris, 2012), p.203-36. Mais ce dialogue 'décalé' montre particulièrement bien à celles et ceux qui l'étudient (Bergamasco, Chinard) que Jefferson n'adhère pas aux idées de Du Pont de Nemours, parce qu'il n'est ni physiocrate, ni même agrarien (Annie Léchenet, 'Indépendance et citoyenneté dans la république selon Jefferson', thèse de doctorat, Université de Nancy, 1990). Manuela Albertone analyse précisément les points de convergence et de divergence entre les pensées des deux hommes politiques dans *National identity and the agrarian republic: the transatlantic commerce of ideas between America and France (1750-1830)* (Farnham, 2014) et dans l'article du présent ouvrage.

14. *Correspondence between Thomas Jefferson and Pierre Samuel Du Pont de Nemours, 1798-1817*, ed. Dumas Malone (New York, 1930).

ii. Le droit de vote n'appartient qu'aux propriétaires de terre

C'est principalement par la réponse de Jefferson que nous connaissons le projet de Du Pont pour les républiques d'Amérique du Sud, projet dont le texte se trouve maintenant dans une collection privée.[15] La structure générale du mécanisme représentatif conçu par Du Pont[16] consiste en un échelonnement de nombreux degrés de vote, les électeurs choisissant leurs conseillers communaux, lesquels élisent à leur tour ceux du canton, lesquels élisent ceux des districts, puis à leur tour ceux des cercles, puis à leur tour enfin les membres de l'Assemblée nationale – ce que Jefferson raillera un peu en disant: 'Vos trois ou quatre raffinages ont il est vrai une apparence séduisante. Nous pouvons penser à première vue que le dernier extrait en serait la pure substance d'alcool, trois ou quatre fois rectifiée' – et d'ajouter: 'mais en proportion qu'ils sont de plus en plus sublimés, ils sont aussi de plus en plus éloignés du contrôle de la société.' Il conclut de manière assez rédhibitoire: 'Votre processus produit donc une structure de gouvernement de laquelle le principe fondamental de la nôtre est exclu.'[17] Le principe de Jefferson en particulier est que 'l'action des citoyens en personne dans les affaires qui sont à leur portée et dans leur compétence, et dans toutes les autres par des représentants, choisis

---

15. G. Chinard, *The Correspondence*, p.lxv. Sur la découverte en 2015 de ce manuscrit, voir les notes 9 et 10 de la contribution de Gabriel Sabbagh, dans le présent ouvrage.

16. Cette structure reproduit celle conçue, alors sur un plan purement administratif, dans le *Mémoire sur les assemblées provinciales ou sur les différents degrés de municipalités*, que Du Pont avait rédigé en 1775 à la demande de Turgot et à partir des idées de celui-ci, dit-il dans son édition posthume des *Œuvres* de Turgot: définition des 'territoires dont l'administration pourrait être confiée aux différents degrés de municipalités', instruction du peuple et même 'répartition des impôts' sur les seuls 'propriétaires de terre'. Mais Pierre Rosanvallon analyse cependant que dans ce texte, pour Turgot/Du Pont, 'c'est encore autant le territoire que l'individu qui est représenté.' Pierre Rosanvallon, *Le Sacre du citoyen* (Paris, 1992), p.63.

17. 'Your three or four alembications have indeed a seducing appearance. We should conceive prima facie, that the last extract would be the pure alcohol of the substance, three or four times rectified; but in proportion as they are more and more sublimated, they are also farther and farther removed from the control of society [...] Your process produces, therefore, a structure of government from which the fundamental principles of ours is excluded'; T. Jefferson, *Lettre à Du Pont de Nemours* (24 avril 1816), dans G. Chinard, *The Correspondence*, p.257. Toutes les traductions des textes de Jefferson dans cet article sont réalisées par mes soins.

immédiatement et révocables par eux-mêmes, constitue l'essence d'une république.'[18] La raison pour laquelle Jefferson désapprouve les nombreux degrés de représentation conçus par Du Pont et 'l'éloignement du contrôle de la société' qu'ils produisent, est une raison de préservation des libertés et de la liberté, car des représentants hors de contrôle seront 'inévitablement saisis d'un esprit de corps ou de parti'.[19]

Quant à la proposition de Du Pont de réserver le droit de vote aux seuls propriétaires de terre, Jefferson la critique brièvement dans cette lettre, disant seulement: 'Vous avez d'abord tenu pour zéros tous les individus qui n'ont pas de terre, qui constituent le plus grand nombre dans toute société qui existe depuis longtemps.'[20] Par ailleurs, et dès l'élaboration de la Constitution républicaine de la Virginie en 1776, Jefferson était partisan du suffrage universel des chefs de famille, ce qui mesure l'écart entre les pensées des deux correspondants.

Du Pont de Nemours argumente dans de nombreux passages, et notamment dans sa réponse du 12 mai 1816, en faveur du vote réservé aux propriétaires de terre, et donne des raisons de différents ordres – ce dont nous allons tenter de comprendre la logique, car ces différents 'niveaux' de raisons semblent en quelque sorte emboîtés, du plus superficiel au plus profond.

iii. Raisons politiques

Contre les 'élections populaires'

Du Pont donne d'abord des raisons qui sont d'ordre constitutionnel, ou politique à proprement parler: dans sa réponse (qui laisse percer quelque contrariété) aux objections de Jefferson à son projet sud-américain, il estime que les Etats-Unis, ayant 'conservé [de l'Angleterre] ses mauvaises lois civiles et tous ses mauvais usages', mettent en

---

18. 'I believe [...] that action by the citizens in person in affairs within their reach and competence, and in all others by representatives, chosen immediately and removable by themselves, constitutes the essence of a republic'; T. Jefferson, *Lettre à Du Pont* (24 avril 1816), dans G. Chinard, *The Correspondence*, p.258.
19. 'Whenever, therefore, an esprit de corps, of party, gets possession of them, which experience shows to be inevitable, there are no means of breaking it up'; T. Jefferson, *Lettre à Du Pont* (24 avril 1816), dans G. Chinard, *The Correspondence*, p.258.
20. 'You first set as zeros all individuals not having lands, which are the greater number in every society of long standing'; T. Jefferson, *Lettre à Du Pont* (24 avril 1816), dans G. Chinard, *The Correspondence*, p.257.

œuvre la loi des 'Elections absolument populaires', dont il garde une expérience de violences et de déraison, car elles sont aux mains d'"électeurs de cabaret'. Pour lui de telles élections sont sous l'influence des 'taverniers'. C'est que, de manière générale, il se méfie du pouvoir politique du peuple, ayant eu l'expérience de 'tous les maux causés par les ouvriers et journaliers métamorphosés en Politiques, défigurés en membres du souverain dont [il] a été le triste témoin en France'.[21]

Cette 'horreur' et ce 'dégoût' exprimés explicitement par Du Pont de Nemours ne se justifient pas seulement par l'expérience de la violence et de l'inaptitude des ouvriers à être 'politiques', car plus fondamentalement il estime que leur absence de qualification recouvre une dépendance à l'égard des corrupteurs et des tyrans: 'Cette classe d'ouvriers des grandes fabriques où le travail est autant divisé qu'il puisse l'être ne contribue aucune félicité, ni aucune puissance: elle est une tare pour les Nations. Elle n'oppose et ne peut opposer aucune résistance aux Conquérans. C'est principalement pour elle et par elle que les Tyrans font la loi.'[22]

Cette argumentation condense sans doute plusieurs des arguments classiques en faveur du suffrage censitaire entendu dans son sens le plus général: incapacité intellectuelle à distinguer 'le véritable intérêt du pays', comme chez Madison,[23] mais aussi incapacité en quelque sorte morale, risque de corruption, liée à une dépendance analogue à celle des domestiques pour Sieyès et l'ensemble des penseurs de cette époque.[24] Ces deux premières incapacités débouchent sur une véritable incapacité politique: celle de 'ne contribuer aucune félicité, ni aucune puissance' pour une nation, d'être plutôt pour elle une 'tare'. Or il ne s'agit plus ici des domestiques de l'époque précédente, mais bien sans doute des ouvriers salariés, soumis à la division du travail dans 'les grandes fabriques', et l'Economiste qu'est Du Pont

---

21. P.-S. Du Pont, *Lettre à Jefferson* (12 mai 1816), dans G. Chinard, *The Correspondence*, p.261 et 265.

22. P.-S. Du Pont, *Lettre à Jefferson* (17 mai 1812), dans G. Chinard, *The Correspondence*, p.199.

23. Annie Léchenet, *Jefferson-Madison, un débat sur la République* (Paris, 2002), p.72-81.

24. Ainsi Sieyès demande-t-il d'exclure les domestiques du droit de vote en les définissant comme 'ceux qu'une dépendance servile tient attachés, non à un travail quelconque, mais aux volontés arbitraires d'un maître' (*Observations sur le rapport du Comité de Constitution, concernant la nouvelle organisation de la France*, Versailles, 2 octobre 1789, p.22, cité par P. Rosanvallon, *Le Sacre du citoyen*, p.155).

210 *Annie Léchenet*

indique ici à quel point il fonde ses raisonnements politiques sur les fonctions économiques que remplissent les membres d'une société. Peut-être la division du travail expose-t-elle ceux qui la subissent à une triple fragilité intellectuelle, morale et donc politique, qui peut faire d'eux l'instrument passif des tyrans.[25]

Et ce que vise Du Pont, c'est aussi une sorte d'archaïsme du peuple, comme lorsque celui-ci demandait le maintien du pacte de subsistance entre lui et le roi, contre la liberté du commerce des grains.[26] Il ne s'agit donc ici pas tant d'un jugement moral sur le peuple que d'un jugement politique, d'un jugement sur une inaptitude politique dont les constitutions républicaines doivent être préservées.

'Montrer la loi'

Mais la politique a un sens bien particulier pour Du Pont de Nemours, comme pour tous les physiocrates: par exemple si Du Pont a accepté de rédiger un projet de constitution pour les républiques d'Amérique du Sud, c'est pour contribuer à les faire 'sortir du cahos [*sic*] actuel de l'Amérique espagnole' et ce non pas tant par des constitutions que 'par des gouvernemens'.[27] Pour lui, la question importante n'est pas celle de l'Etat, et de sa constitution, républicaine ou non, mais celle du gouvernement, comme 'organe de la société' éditeur des lois, comme l'analyse Catherine Larrère.[28] Et les lois, pour être bonnes, émanent de la nature, nature des choses et nature de la 'société civilisée'. Ainsi, selon Du Pont de Nemours, si l'on dit (à juste titre) 'législation', et

25. Je remercie Arnault Skornicki pour cet échange au cours duquel il a analysé la spécificité de l'argument de la division du travail par rapport au risque de corruption en considérant que les manœuvres, isolés, seraient plus faciles à séduire, à acheter, y compris par de vaines promesses comme le pacte de subsistance.

26. Catherine Larrère, *L'Invention de l'économie au XVIIIe siècle: du droit naturel à la physiocratie* (Paris, 1992), p.221-68.

27. P.-S. Du Pont, *Lettre à Jefferson* (26 mai 1815), dans G. Chinard, *The Correspondence*, p.218. Cet engagement de Du Pont fait écho à celui de Le Mercier de La Rivière, qui, se désolant en 1772 de l'état déplorable de la Pologne ('Nobles Polonois, je ferai peu de commentaires sur ces deux institutions, l'esclavage de vos paysans et l'espèce de proscription prononcée contre la bourgeoisie; il vous est facile d'en juger par les effets qu'elles ont produits'), rédige un texte de proposition de réformes constitutionnelles, *L'Intérêt commun des Polonais*; voir Le Mercier de La Rivière, *Pour la Pologne, la Suède, l'Espagne et autres textes: œuvres d'expertise (1772-1790)*, éd. Bernard Herencia (Genève, 2016).

28. C. Larrère, *L'Invention de l'économie*, p.232.

non pas 'légisfaction', c'est parce que les hommes ne *font* pas les lois, 'ils les portent au milieu de la société', parce qu''ils les reconnaissent comme conformes à la raison suprême'.[29] En 1811, il tient des propos similaires à Jefferson:

> C'est que l'on a senti, au moins confusément, qu'il s'agissait de bien comprendre le principe de la *loi*, qui doit toujours être dans la nature, dans la morale, dans l'équité; et que la Loi étant ainsi conçue, il n'est plus question que de la montrer, de la démontrer, de la porter, de la présenter brillante de son pur éclat, appuyée de l'assentiment général et de la force sociale, à l'obéissance des citoyens.[30]

Le problème est donc pour Du Pont de Nemours que le peuple ne pouvant pas (re)connaître les principes de la nature, il faut premièrement 'ne pas admettre [les dernières classes du peuple] dans les Assemblées électorales', car on risquerait d'en venir à la structure politique de la 'démocratie pure': 'Les Préjugés populaires influeront sur les loix, et donneront au Gouvernement une teinte de cette *démocratie pure* que vous avez reconnue n'être que l'ébauche d'une société civilisée, et ne pouvoir, ni ne devoir subsister chez une nation qu'une profonde étude des droits, des devoirs, et de l'intérêt commun aura élevée au plus haut degré de la science morale.'[31]

Il faut instruire le peuple

'L'instruction se place en effet au cœur de la théorie physiocratique, car des lois immuables de l'ordre naturel découlait la nécessité d'une conscience universelle des fondements de la science économique et de son acceptation', analyse Manuela Albertone.[32] Mais, pour les garçons du peuple, cette instruction semble viser un objectif plus moral que cognitif: s'il faut, tout en excluant le peuple des assemblées électorales,

---

29. P.-S. Du Pont de Nemours, *Maximes du Docteur Quesnay*, dans *Physiocrates: Quesnay, Dupont de Nemours, Mercier de La Rivière, l'abbé Baudeau, Le Trosne, avec une introduction sur la doctrine des physiocrates, des commentaires et des notices historiques*, éd. Eugène Daire, 2 vol. (Paris, 1846), t.1, p.389-93 (390).
30. P.-S. Du Pont, *Lettre à Jefferson* (12 décembre 1811), dans G. Chinard, *The Correspondence*, p.177.
31. P.-S. Du Pont, *Lettre à Jefferson* (12 janvier 1812), dans G. Chinard, *The Correspondence*, p.194.
32. Manuela Albertone, 'Du Pont de Nemours et l'instruction publique pendant la Révolution: de la science économique à la formation du citoyen', *Revue française d'histoire des idées politiques* 20:2 (2004), p.353-71 (354).

l'instruire, c'est pour lui procurer un accès à la connaissance de la 'société civilisée' en ce que celle-ci comporte dans sa nature même un ensemble de 'droits et de devoirs' c'est-à-dire une moralité conforme à 'l'intérêt commun' que Du Pont nomme aussi 'amour de la patrie', ou 'patriotisme', 'but prioritaire de l'instruction primaire' selon Manuela Albertone.[33] Cette instruction des enfants du peuple nécessite un réseau de 'petites écoles', dont Du Pont ne cesse de recommander à Jefferson l'institution en Amérique, sous forme d'écoles primaires pour tous les garçons, pourvues de 'petits livres classiques' rédigés à cette intention. 'Si ce degré de lumière était général, il deviendrait presque indifférent quelles que fussent les constitutions',[34] dit-il dans la même lettre à Jefferson, indiquant bien par là le but politique de cette instruction, qui est d''assurer [...] la stabilité politique et sociale':[35] 'Toute l'instruction véritablement et journalièrement usuelle, toutes les sciences pratiques, toute l'activité laborieuse, tout le bon-sens, toutes les idées justes, toute la morale, toute la vertu, tout le courage, toute la prospérité, tout le bonheur d'une nation, et surtout d'une République, doivent partir des écoles primaires, des petites écoles.'[36]

iv. Raisons morales: la mise en œuvre des droits naturels pour l'ordre et le bonheur général

Nous n'avons jusqu'ici présenté que des raisons en quelque sorte négatives, celles qui amènent Du Pont de Nemours à exclure les dernières classes du peuple du droit de vote, raisons par lesquelles il commence par répondre aux objections de Jefferson sur un plan politique. Il enchaîne dans cette même lettre du 12 mai 1816[37] avec des raisons positives pour donner le droit de vote aux propriétaires de terre et à eux seuls, raisons qui reprennent celles énoncées dans le grand nombre de lettres de conseils et même de mémoires divers envoyés à Jefferson entre 1800 et 1816. Ainsi, après avoir dénoncé 'la Tyrannie d'en haut [et] celle d'en bas',[38] il déclare décrire comment

33. M. Albertone, 'Du Pont de Nemours et l'instruction', p.365.
34. P.-S. Du Pont, *Lettre à Jefferson* (14 avril 1812), dans G. Chinard, *The Correspondence*, p.195.
35. M. Albertone, 'Du Pont de Nemours et l'instruction', p.369.
36. P.-S. Du Pont, *Lettre à Jefferson* (21 avril 1800), dans G. Chinard, *The Correspondence*, p.12.
37. G. Chinard, *The Correspondence*, p.260-68.
38. Celle de 'la monarchie et de la noblesse, et celle de la roture'.

il est 'sorti de là', et affirme que c'est 'en consultant la justice, et pour conseiller, non pour maître, l'Intérêt public'.[39] S'ensuit donc un énoncé conjoint de 'la justice' et du 'droit naturel', dont va découler la 'société civilisée', qui n'est elle-même que comme le prolongement, ou plutôt, selon Catherine Larrère, 'l'application',[40] du droit naturel.

Les droits naturels au fondement des droits politiques

Dans les textes adressés aux Américains Jefferson et Madison, Du Pont de Nemours fonde très clairement le droit politique des seuls propriétaires de terre: 'Il y a dans la propriété foncière un intérêt permanent et une habitude de travaux utiles qui deviennent un gage de raison',[41] écrit-il en 1811. Pendleton en 1776 et Ireton en 1649 employaient les mêmes termes, notamment ceux d'"intérêt permanent'. Mais ces raisons en quelque sorte psychologiques sont elles-mêmes fondées sur une raison plus fondamentale, de l'ordre du droit naturel prolongé en loi de la société civilisée.[42] Ainsi un niveau plus profond des raisons pour lesquelles Du Pont de Nemours souhaite restreindre le droit de vote aux seuls propriétaires de terre est sa conception du caractère naturel – et fondamental – du droit de propriété.

'Tout homme reçoit de la nature le droit de vivre'[43] dit Du Pont de Nemours, ce qui signifie aussi, très clairement formulé avant lui par Le Mercier de La Rivière, que 'le droit de pourvoir à sa conservation renferme le droit d'acquérir, par ses recherches et par ses travaux, les choses utiles à son existence.'[44]

39. G. Chinard, *The Correspondence*, p.262.
40. C. Larrère, *L'Invention de l'économie*, p.194.
41. P.-S. Du Pont, *Lettre à Jefferson* (12 décembre 1811), dans G. Chinard, *The Correspondence*, p.176.
42. Pour une analyse exhaustive et approfondie de la conception physiocratique du droit naturel de propriété et de son rôle de fondement d'un 'rapport entre droit naturel, liberté et propriété', dont sont tirées des 'conséquences politiques et institutionnelles', nous ne pouvons dire mieux qu'Arnault Skornicki, dans 'Liberté, propriété, sûreté: retour sur une devise physiocratique', *Corpus* 66 (2014), p.16-36. Les affirmations de Du Pont de Nemours présentées ici sont donc à situer dans le cadre de ces analyses: 'Avec Locke, et contre Rousseau, [les physiocrates] tiennent la propriété privée pour naturelle et antérieure à l'état civil'(p.19).
43. P.-S. Du Pont de Nemours, *Abrégé des principes de l'économie politique*, dans E. Daire, *Physiocrates*, t.1, p.367-85 (382).
44. P.-S. Du Pont de Nemours, *De l'origine et des progrès d'une science nouvelle*, dans E. Daire, *Physiocrates*, t.1, p.335-66 (342).

214 Annie Léchenet

De ce droit naturel de propriété, et même de ce 'fait de nature' qu'est la propriété,[45] découle d'abord une hiérarchie naturelle, dont le respect indique ce que l'on propose d'appeler les raisons morales de la position de Du Pont au sujet du droit de vote:

> La justice m'a dit que chacun devait être maître sur son champ et dans sa maison, ceux qui n'ont ni champ ni maison, qui ne mangent que par *salaire*, et ne logent que par contrat, ne sont et ne doivent être dans aucune société complètement les égaux de ceux dont ils ont sollicité le toit et le pain, qui les hébergent et qui les nourrissent, de ceux à qui Dieu, le travail, les capitaux qu'il a procurés, la nature et l'équité, ont confié l'importante magistrature de produire les récoltes, de les conserver pour l'intérêt de tous, de les distribuer par de libres conventions.[46]

Du côté des propriétaires du sol, découle de leur droit naturel de propriété un droit que nous pourrions appeler de 'gestion': 'La justice m'a dit que chacun devait être maître sur son champ et dans sa maison [...]. Personne ne peut avoir que par délégation aucun droit sur ce dont il n'est pas propriétaire.'[47]

C'est pourquoi, après avoir expliqué pourquoi ceux qui ne sont pas propriétaires de terre (c'est-à-dire pas seulement les plus basses classes) ne peuvent être dotés du droit de vote – nous y reviendrons –, Du Pont de Nemours énonce sa doctrine fondamentale: 'Les propriétaires du sol tiennent nécessairement au Pays, ils en sont les co-souverains, car il est à eux.' Et en conséquence voici leurs possibilités de comportement, selon leurs droits: 'Ils peuvent l'exploiter à leur fantaisie. Ils

---

45. Selon les analyses de Rafe Blaufarb, 'pour les physiocrates, la propriété n'était pas une construction juridique ou historique, mais "l'essence de l'ordre naturel et essentiel de la société [...] une branche de l'ordre physique" [Le Mercier de La Rivière, *L'Ordre naturel et essentiel des sociétés politiques*, Londres, Jean Nourse, 1767].' Et Rafe Blaufarb fait remarquer que, s'il s'appuie sur les formulations de Le Mercier de La Rivière, elles 'auraient aussi bien pu se baser sur celles de Pierre-Samuel Du Pont de Nemours, qui recourt à des arguments similaires et presque au même langage dans *De l'origine et des progrès d'une science nouvelle* en 1767'; Rafe Blaufarb, *L'Invention de la propriété privée: une autre histoire de la Révolution*, traduit par Christophe Jaquet (Ceyzérieu, 2019), p.36-37.
46. P.-S. Du Pont, *Lettre à Jefferson* (12 mai 1816), dans G. Chinard, *The Correspondence*, p.262. Souligné par Du Pont.
47. P.-S. Du Pont, *Lettre à Jefferson* (12 mai 1816), dans G. Chinard, *The Correspondence*, p.262.

Du Pont de Nemours et la république des 'propriétaires du sol' 215

peuvent le vendre; et ne sauraient abdiquer leur part de la *souveraineté* qu'en vendant leur héritage.'[48]

En revanche tous les autres membres de la société, étant 'les membres d'une République universelle et sans magistratures, répandus dans tous les autres Etats', ont certes droit aux libertés humaines: 'la liberté, l'exemption des contributions, la sûreté de leurs personnes et de leurs biens'[49] d'une part, et aussi 'le droit naturel d'exprimer sa pensée sur toute chose'.[50] Mais ces droits humains n'impliquent pas le droit de vote, car c'est la propriété foncière que régit, ou plutôt régule, le gouvernement de la société: 'Le droit naturel d'exprimer sa pensée [...] n'importe aucunement celui de *délibérer*, de *voter*, de *prononcer* sur les affaires d'autrui [...]: car la société n'est faite que pour conserver à chacun ce qu'il a, sans porter atteinte à la liberté, ni à la propriété de qui que ce soit.'[51]

Ou, en d'autres termes: 'L'homme qui ne possède que sa personne et des biens mobiliers ne peut avoir droit qu'à la liberté de sa personne, à la propriété de ses biens, à la faculté d'en disposer comme il l'entend.'[52] Comme les autres physiocrates, Du Pont de Nemours va donc, pour protéger le statut et les intérêts de toute propriété privée, plus loin que les partisans du pur suffrage censitaire, ceux qui fondent le droit de vote par exemple sur le paiement d'un cens.[53] Du Pont n'accorde le droit de vote qu'aux seuls propriétaires *de terre*,[54] et ne laisse aux autres membres de la société, y compris les propriétaires de 'biens mobiliers',[55] que les libertés personnelles.

48. P.-S. Du Pont, *Lettre à Jefferson* (12 mai 1816), dans G. Chinard, *The Correspondence*, p.263. Souligné par Du Pont.

49. P.-S. Du Pont, *Lettre à Jefferson* (12 décembre 1811), dans G. Chinard, *The Correspondence*, p.174.

50. P.-S. Du Pont, *Lettre à Jefferson* (12 mai 1816), dans G. Chinard, *The Correspondence*, p.262.

51. P.-S. Du Pont, *Lettre à Jefferson* (12 mai 1816), dans G. Chinard, *The Correspondence*, p.262. Souligné par Du Pont.

52. P.-S. Du Pont, *Lettre à Jefferson* (12 mai 1816), dans G. Chinard, *The Correspondence*, p.263.

53. Le suffrage censitaire a en général pour justification la crainte de la subversion de toute propriété privée, qui pourrait survenir si on accordait le droit de vote à des non-propriétaires. Voir par exemple le raisonnement d'un Madison, opposant, dans un raisonnement plus étrange qu'il ne paraît au premier abord, les 'droits des personnes' et les 'droits de la propriété' (A. Léchenet, *Jefferson-Madison*, p.39-48).

54. De terre productive, il va sans dire.

55. Qui, pour les physiocrates, ne sont pas réellement producteurs de richesse.

Le droit de propriété chez Du Pont et chez Jefferson

Pour mieux comprendre, on peut mesurer ici la distance de la pensée de Du Pont de Nemours avec celle de son interlocuteur Jefferson. Celui-ci, bien seul en son temps,[56] est partisan dès 1776 du suffrage universel des chefs de famille:

> J'étais partisan d'étendre le droit de vote – en un mot d'être citoyen – à tous ceux qui ont l'intention de vivre en permanence dans ce pays. Que l'on prenne les conditions que l'on veut comme preuves de cette intention, que ce soit le fait d'y résider depuis un certain temps, ou d'y avoir sa famille, ou d'y avoir de la propriété, l'une quelconque ou toutes ensemble. Tout homme qui a l'intention de vivre dans un pays doit souhaiter le bien de ce pays, et a un droit naturel à concourir à sa préservation.[57]

Cette position de Jefferson est cohérente avec sa conception des droits fondamentaux. Pour Jefferson le droit fondamental n'est pas celui de propriété, qui n'est qu'un droit 'municipal', c'est-à-dire réglé différemment par différentes sociétés, à l'échelon de la municipalité ou de la nation, et donc en outre variable dans l'histoire humaine – et de manière plus ou moins conforme au droit naturel.[58] Ainsi,

56. Un des rares penseurs de cette époque, Destutt de Tracy, très proche de Jefferson par la pensée, est lui aussi partisan du suffrage universel: 'Tous les citoyens doivent être également appelés dans les assemblées dont il s'agit, et y voter de la même manière', écrit-il dans son *Commentaire et revue de L'Esprit des lois de Montesquieu* (Caen, 1992, p.153). Par ailleurs, 'la restriction du droit de suffrage par le cens est brièvement abandonnée par la Constitution de 1793 mais rétablie dès la Constitution de l'an III'; Philippe Blacher, 'L'étendue du suffrage universel sous la IIe République', *Revue française d'histoire des idées politiques* 38:2 (2013), p.257-68.

57. 'I was for extending the right of suffrage (or in other words the rights of a citizen) to all who had a permanent intention of living in the country. Take what circumstances you please as evidence of this, either the having resided a certain time, or having a family, or having property, any or all of them. Whoever intends to live in a country must wish to have this country well, & has a natural right of assisting in the preservation of it'; T. Jefferson, *Lettre à Edmund Randolph* (26 août 1776), dans *Thomas Jefferson: writings*, éd. Merrill Peterson (New York, 1984), p.756.

58. Pour l'étude du rapport de Jefferson à la propriété, on peut consulter Joyautpaul Chauduri: 'Possession, ownership and access: a Jeffersonian view of property', *Political inquiry* 1 (1973), p.78-95; Stanley N. Katz, 'Thomas Jefferson and the right to property in revolutionary America', *Journal of law and economics* 19 (1976), p.467-88; Jean M. Yarbrough, *American virtues: Thomas Jefferson on the*

comme pour Locke,[59] le droit naturel pour Jefferson n'est pas le droit de propriété, mais le droit d'usufruit de la terre: 'La terre [*the earth*] est donnée comme une réserve commune aux hommes pour qu'ils la travaillent et en vivent.' En conséquence, le gouvernement et les lois peuvent être justes ou injustes, c'est-à-dire conformes ou non au droit naturel, de 'travailler et de vivre', ou encore de 'poursuivre le bonheur', comme il sera inscrit dans la Déclaration d'Indépendance américaine: 'Si, pour encourager l'industrie, nous permettons qu'elle [la terre] soit l'objet d'une appropriation, nous devons prendre garde qu'un emploi soit fourni à ceux qui sont exclus de l'appropriation. Si nous ne le faisons pas, le droit fondamental de travailler la terre revient à celui qui n'a pas d'emploi.'[60] Ainsi, lorsqu'en 1789 Du Pont de Nemours travaille avec Lafayette à un projet de 'Déclaration des droits' pour la France, qu'ils soumettent pour avis à Jefferson, celui-ci leur suggère de supprimer le droit de propriété du rang des droits naturels et de le remplacer par le droit à la poursuite du bonheur.[61]

---

   character of a free people (Lawrence, KS, 1998); Jean M. Yarbrough, 'Jefferson and property rights', dans *Liberty, property, and the foundations of the American Constitution*, éd. Ellen Frankel Paul et Howard Dickman (Albany, NY, 1989), p.65-84; Maurizio Valsania, 'Thomas Jefferson and private property: myths and reality', *Ricognizioni: rivista di lingue, letterature e culture moderne* 7 (2020), p.123-36.

59. Dans *A Discourse on property: John Locke and his adversaries* (Cambridge, 1978), James Tully analyse que la propriété est pour Locke un droit naturel et formel, lié à la subsistance, et pouvant se réaliser différemment dans les diverses formes que peut prendre la société. Un certain nombre de lecteurs discutent actuellement des 'complexités et ambiguïtés troublantes' au sujet du droit de propriété chez les penseurs du dix-septième siècle, dont Locke, et chez les hommes d'Etat du dix-huitième, contre la 'perception commune du caractère sacré de la propriété'; Michael Kammen, 'The rights of property, and the property in rights: the problematic nature of "property" in the political thought of the founders and the early republic', dans *Liberty, property*, éd. E. F. Paul et H. Dickman, p.1-22.

60. 'The earth is given as a common stock for man to labor and live on. If for the encouragement of industry we allow it to be appropriated, we must take care that other employment be provided to those excluded from the appropriation. If we do not, the fundamental right to labor the earth returns to the unemployed'; T. Jefferson, *Lettre à Madison* (28 octobre 1785), dans M. Peterson, *Thomas Jefferson*, p.840-43.

61. *Lafayette's draft of a Declaration of Rights* (juin 1789), annoté de la main de Jefferson. *The Papers of Thomas Jefferson*, t.15, éd. Julian P. Boyd (Princeton, NJ, 1950), p.230-33. Ce texte est également disponible sur le site *Founders online*, sous le titre mentionné ci-dessus. Sur le sens du droit à la poursuite du bonheur, on peut consulter Annie Léchenet, 'Le républicanisme américain: Jefferson et la

218 *Annie Léchenet*

Et c'est de la 'Déclaration des droits' de ... 1793 dont Jefferson sera proche.

v. Raisons d'économie politique

Or cette différence dans la conception des droits, notamment du droit de propriété comme naturel ou comme municipal, a des conséquences non seulement sur le droit de vote, mais sur tout le sens de l'institution politique – et ce sera le troisième 'niveau' auquel nous proposons d'analyser la conception de Du Pont de Nemours.

Jefferson: les 'petits propriétaires de terre'

Si la propriété est un droit municipal, et que le droit fondamental est celui de l'usufruit de la terre, Jefferson n'hésite alors pas à concevoir une intervention de l'Etat pour modifier la propriété, de sorte à la rendre conforme au droit naturel. Il écrit par exemple, dès 1785:

> Je suis conscient qu'une répartition égale de la propriété est impraticable. Mais les conséquences de cette énorme inégalité, productrice de tant de misères pour la masse de l'humanité, sont telles [il est alors en France, et horrifié, comme les physiocrates,[62] par la propriété féodale des terres] que les législateurs ne peuvent inventer trop de plans pour subdiviser la propriété, en prenant seulement garde que leurs subdivisions aillent de pair avec les affections naturelles de

---

poursuite du bonheur', dans *Histoire raisonnée de la philosophie morale et politique: le bonheur et l'utile*, éd. Alain Caillé et autres (Paris, 2001), p.499-503.

62. Comme l'a montré Arnault Skornicki, écrivant: 'Les Economistes font donc jouer la propriété comme droit naturel contre la propriété féodale', dans 'Liberté, propriété, sûreté', p.32-33. Rafe Blaufarb place précisément les physiocrates comme les premiers et les plus fermes défenseurs de la propriété dans son sens moderne, la 'propriété pleine et indivisible', par opposition au système féodal d'allocation des terres sous le régime de la tenure (R. Blaufarb, *L'Invention de la propriété privée*, p.63-70). En Amérique anglaise du Nord, la plupart des terres sont, dès la colonisation, détenues sous la forme de la tenure *allodiale*, c'est-à-dire libre de tout engagement de type féodal, et c'est en France que Jefferson découvre l'étendue de ce que sont pour lui les méfaits de la féodalité (voir A. Léchenet, 'Indépendance et citoyenneté', notamment le chap.3.3-1). Sur l'opposition à la féodalité et la conception 'moderne' de la propriété libre et entière, Jefferson est en plein accord avec les physiocrates. On verra ci-dessous un motif précis de leur commune opposition à la féodalité à propos des terres laissées incultes pour la chasse.

Du Pont de Nemours et la république des 'propriétaires du sol'   219

l'esprit humain [il pense à l'abolition du droit d'aînesse et à la division égale entre tous les enfants].[63]

Et cette législation sur la propriété est pour lui profondément reliée aux conditions sociales du maintien de la république dans sa vertu, sa capacité de résistance à la corruption, à la dégénérescence:

> Il est encore trop tôt pour dire que dans notre pays tout homme qui ne peut trouver d'emploi, mais qui peut trouver de la terre non cultivée, aura la liberté de la cultiver, moyennant le paiement d'un loyer modéré. Mais il n'est pas trop tôt pour pourvoir par tous les moyens possibles à ce qu'aussi peu d'hommes que possible soient sans une part de terre. Les petits propriétaires de terre sont la partie la plus précieuse d'un Etat.[64]

Il ne s'agit donc pas seulement de la mise en œuvre du droit naturel d'usufruit de la terre, ou de la poursuite du bonheur, mais aussi du maintien de la république, seule forme qui réalise le second des droits naturels fondamentaux pour Jefferson, le droit à l'auto-gouvernement. C'est pour cela que Jefferson est partisan du suffrage de 'quiconque

---

63. 'I am conscious that an equal division of property is impracticable, but the consequences of this enormous inequality producing so much misery to the bulk of mankind, legislators cannot invent too many devices for subdividing property, only taking care to let their subdivisions go hand in hand with the natural affections of the human mind'; T. Jefferson, *Lettre à Madison* (28 octobre 1785), dans M. Peterson, *Thomas Jefferson*, p.841.

64. 'It is too soon yet in our country to say that every man who cannot find employment, but who can find uncultivated land, shall be at liberty to cultivate it, paying a moderate rent. But it is not too soon to provide by every possible means that as few as possible shall be without a little portion of land. The small landholders are the most precious part of a state'; T. Jefferson, *Lettre à Madison* (28 octobre 1785), dans M. Peterson, *Thomas Jefferson*, p.842. Cette proposition peut sembler inspirée de Harrington, qui fait dépendre le maintien de la république de l'existence d'une classe de petits propriétaires agriculteurs et pour cela institue une loi agraire de partage permanent des terres et la colonisation de nouvelles contrées. Certes Jefferson discute ici de l'attribution des terres 'vierges' de l'Ouest en évitant leur achat par 'des grandes compagnies à capitaux', qui les revendraient ensuite de manière spéculative, et son raisonnement semble assez proche, par sa structure, de celui de Harrington. Cependant pour Jefferson d'autres bases économiques que la terre – comme le commerce, et aussi l'industrie, qui pour lui doit rester de taille modeste, voire familiale... – peuvent servir de support à l'indépendance économique, qui devient dès lors morale et sociale, puis politique.

220 *Annie Léchenet*

désire vivre dans ce pays'. Car seuls des citoyens économiquement indépendants peuvent voter de manière indépendante.[65]

Du Pont de Nemours: n'imposer que la propriété foncière

Revenons à Du Pont, qui est le principal auteur et acteur dont nous voulons ici comprendre la pensée. Lui aussi pense une articulation entre les lois et la structure de la société, mais elle va en quelque sorte dans l'autre sens,[66] de la société et de ses 'vérités arithmétiques et morales'[67] vers le gouvernement, et en particulier vers son 'système de finances': il s'agit de faire en sorte que la société se développe selon son ordre juste, qui est lui-même le prolongement de la nature et du droit naturel.

L'essentiel est donc pour lui le système de contribution à l'Etat, ce qu'il nomme 'commencer par le commencement, par une bonne constitution de commerce',[68] qu'il développait d'abord dans son *Petit traité sur les finances des Etats-Unis*.[69]

Pour Du Pont de Nemours, il ne faut imposer que la propriété de la terre. Il le dit dès 1811 à Jefferson, lui recommandant de construire un 'nouveau système de finances',[70] notamment en critiquant 'l'erreur' née de 'l'envie de faire contribuer tout le monde, particulièrement les Ouvriers, les commerçans, les capitalistes'. Pour lui ce sont au contraire

65. Ainsi pour Jefferson le droit de suffrage ne dépendant pas de la propriété, *a fortiori* pas de la propriété foncière, mais du rapport moral à l'Etat que constitue l'indépendance économique, de tout type qu'elle soit, il est inconditionnel.

66. Pour Jefferson, l'Etat peut en partie influencer les formes de la société, en favorisant la propriété d'une taille réduite aux possibilités de travail d'une famille. Pour le physiocrate qu'est Du Pont, 'la propriété n'est pas instituée pour participer à l'Etat, mais c'est l'Etat qui est institué pour la propriété' analyse Arnault Skornicki dans *L'Economiste, la cour et la patrie: l'économie politique dans la France des Lumières* (Paris, 2011), p.240.

67. P.-S. Du Pont, *Lettre à Jefferson* (14 avril 1812), dans G. Chinard, *The Correspondence*, p.194.

68. P.-S. Du Pont, *Lettre à Jefferson* (26 mai 1815), dans G. Chinard, *The Correspondence*, p.218.

69. Ce traité, que l'on croyait perdu, vient d'être retrouvé par Manuela Albertone, qui l'étudie dans sa contribution insérée dans cet ouvrage. N'ayant pu en prendre connaissance jusqu'à présent, je me base sur des lettres à Jefferson, qui en reprennent la substance: les lettres du 12 décembre 1811 (dans G. Chinard, *The Correspondence*, p.172-77), la longue lettre du 25 janvier 1812 (p.179-93), la lettre du 14 avril 1812 (p.193-96) et celle du 17 mai 1812 (p.196-200).

70. P.-S. Du Pont, *Lettre à Jefferson* (12 décembre 1811), dans G. Chinard, *The Correspondence*, p.173.

Du Pont de Nemours et la république des 'propriétaires du sol'   221

les seuls propriétaires de terres agricoles qui doivent contribuer. Bien plus: 'La concession faite par les propriétaires à l'état politique d'une partie quelconque du revenu de territoire [...], loin de leur faire aucun tort et de leur causer aucun mal, est au contraire pour eux un très grand bien, le plus grand bien qu'ils puissent désirer.' Il existe à ce choix des raisons économiques, car l'absence d'imposition des autres travaux (qui sont pour les physiocrates des travaux qui donnent non de la production, mais seulement de la richesse, c'est-à-dire dérivée de la production), 'laisse à toutes les espèces de travaux la plus grande liberté dont ils puissent jouir et la plus vive concurrence qui puisse les animer', évite le paiement d'intérêts sur les produits de la terre, et donc pousse à 'cultiver les terres [même les terres médiocres] le mieux et au meilleur marché qu'il soit possible et en rend pour leurs Propriétaires le revenu le plus haut possible'[71] – ce qui est économiquement fondamental pour les physiocrates, dont l'un des grands combats porte contre le maintien en jachère des terres, notamment par les nobles en vue de leurs chasses.[72]

Mais il existe aussi, puisque ce sont des 'vérités arithmétiques et morales qui conduisent à bannir des Finances tout arbitraire', des raisons plus morales, énoncées en termes de droits – et de là, toujours sans solution de continuité, des raisons politiques, que nous rappelons ici, énoncées cette fois par Du Pont au sujet de l'imposition.

Les raisons morales se présentent donc en termes de droits, et ces droits sont différents pour les différentes classes de la société:

---

71. P.-S. Du Pont, *Lettre à Jefferson* (25 janvier 1812), dans G. Chinard, *The Correspondence*, p.181.
72. Cette nécessité de cultiver le plus de terres possible, par opposition au maintien de terres incultes par la noblesse pour la chasse, est fondamentale pour les physiocrates, comme l'a montré A. Skornicki. On trouve cette même indignation contre les terres laissées incultes pour la chasse chez Jefferson, qui les constate lors d'un séjour à Fontainebleau: 'Je me demandai quelle pouvait être la raison pour laquelle sont condamnés à mendier tant d'hommes qui ont la volonté de travailler, dans un pays où il y a une proportion très considérable de terres non cultivées? Ces terres sont laissées en repos seulement pour le plaisir de la chasse' ('I asked myself what could be the reason so many should be permitted to beg who are willing to work, in a country where there is a very considerable proportion of uncultivated lands? These lands are undisturbed only for the sake of game'; T. Jefferson, *Lettre à James Madison*, 28 octobre 1785, dans M. Peterson, *Thomas Jefferson*, p.841).

222 *Annie Léchenet*

> Les droits des hommes qui ne possèdent que leurs Personnes et des
> effets mobiliers,[73] doivent être religieusement respectés en tout pays,
> par toutes les nations, par tous les Gouvernemens. [...] Il entre dans
> les droits de ces membres de la classe des *salariés* d'aller chercher leur
> salaire où il leur plaît, de le gagner comme il leur plaît, de faire pour
> lui les conventions qui leur plaisent.[74]

Ainsi Du Pont ajoute-il immédiatement: 'Ils ne sont réellement
membres ni sujets d'aucune nation qu'autant qu'il convient à leur
intérêt et à leur bienveillance.'

Il y aurait ainsi trois sortes de conséquences politiques très graves à
leur faire payer des impôts. Imposer les non-propriétaires, c'est d'abord
leur donner un pouvoir indu et destructeur de l'ordre naturel: 'Vous ne
prétendriez pas que [l'homme qui ne possède que sa personne et des
biens mobiliers], parce qu'il a besoin de manger, eût le droit d'obliger les
propriétaires de terre à cultiver, pour le nourrir, car alors les Propriétaires
ne seraient plus les *propriétaires*, ils seraient devenus des *esclaves de la Glèbe*.'[75]

D'autre part ils se croiraient membres du souverain, ce qui est un
'défaut d'idées justes sur ce que sont les sociétés politiques, les propriétaires du sol, et les hommes industrieux non-propriétaires et sur ce que
la société doit à chacun d'eux',[76] ce qui a une troisième conséquence
politique fondamentale:

> Quand on s'écarte de ces bases de la société civilisée et constituée;
> quand on croit ou quand on laisse croire que ceux qui n'ont que
> leurs bras ou des biens purement mobiliers, sont autant *citoyens* que
> les propriétaires du territoire et ont droit, ou d'en demander part
> sans l'acquérir, ou de délibérer sur les lois de ces propriétés qu'ils
> ne possèdent pas, on fomente les orages, on prépare les révolutions,
> on ouvre la voie aux Pisistrates, aux Marius, aux Césars, qui se font
> plus *démocrates* que ne le veulent la nature, la justice et la raison, pour
> devenir *Tyrans*, violer tous les droits, substituer aux loix leurs volontés
> arbitraires, offenser la morale, avilir l'humanité.[77]

---

73. Rappelons que ces droits sont les libertés personnelles, dont la liberté d'avoir des
  propriétés et d'en user.

74. P.-S. Du Pont, *Lettre à Jefferson* (12 mai 1816), dans G. Chinard, *The Correspondence*,
  p.263.

75. P.-S. Du Pont, *Lettre à Jefferson* (12 mai 1816), dans G. Chinard, *The Correspondence*,
  p.263 (c'est Du Pont qui souligne).

76. P.-S. Du Pont, *Lettre à Jefferson* (12 décembre 1811), dans G. Chinard, *The
  Correspondence*, p.174.

77. P.-S. Du Pont, *Lettre à Jefferson* (12 décembre 1811), dans G. Chinard, *The
  Correspondence*, p.174-75 (c'est Du Pont qui souligne).

Il ne faut pas lire ici pure défiance à l'égard de la dépendance et de l'incapacité des salariés, mais au contraire une confiance dans le bon sens d'une classe qui se croirait opprimée d'être imposée, car Du Pont de Nemours poursuit immédiatement ainsi: 'Dans une république qui veut être paisible, durable, exempte de troubles, il faut donc faire en sorte qu'il n'y ait pas une classe qui soit ou qui puisse se croire opprimée, et veuille des protecteurs pour opprimer à son tour: car il s'en trouve, et c'est un rôle très recherché.'

Un tel sentiment serait justifié: 'Quand le travail ou le Commerce sont gênés, tous les Travailleurs, tous les Négocians ont droit de réclamer, et de prouver que l'on attente contre l'intérêt public à leur liberté naturelle.'[78]

Il s'agit donc bien ici d'économie politique, dans le sens le plus fort du terme, puisqu'il s'agit de fonder la politique sur l'économie, elle-même fondée en nature et en morale, centralement par des thèses sur l'imposition, qui vont ensuite s'appliquer au droit de vote: ceux qui produisent les richesses, et donc paient les impôts, sont ceux qui prennent part au gouvernement, donc font les lois… et l'imposition.

vi. Conclusion: Du Pont et Jefferson, deux sens différents de la république et de l'agriculture

Pour conclure, nous voyons que la souveraineté n'appartient pour Du Pont de Nemours qu'aux propriétaires de terre, pour des raisons tant politiques et négatives, en termes d'exclusion des 'dernières classes du peuple', que morales et positives, fondées sur le droit naturel de propriété, et surtout pour des raisons d'économie politique: 'Les droits de cité et de souveraineté, celui de siéger et de délibérer dans les Assemblées politiques, celui d'élire, celui de promulguer ou de faire exécuter les loix, appartiennent exclusivement aux Propriétaires de terres, parce qu'il n'y a qu'eux qui soient membres d'une République particulière, ayant un territoire, et le devoir de l'administrer.'[79]

Ou, plus clairement encore, selon les termes déjà cités: 'Les propriétaires du sol tiennent nécessairement au Pays, ils en sont les co-souverains, car il est à eux. Ils peuvent l'exploiter à leur fantaisie. Ils peuvent le vendre; et ne sauraient abdiquer leur part de la *souveraineté*

---

78. P.-S. Du Pont, *Lettre à Jefferson* (12 décembre 1811), dans G. Chinard, *The Correspondence*, p.175.

79. P.-S. Du Pont, *Lettre à Jefferson* (12 décembre 1811), dans G. Chinard, *The Correspondence*, p.174.

qu'en vendant leur héritage.'[80] Le terme de 'co-souverains' semble renvoyer à celui de 'copropriétaires' et à la logique de celui-ci, puisque le droit d'exercer leur 'souveraineté', qui est elle-même une 'part', est ici assimilé à un droit de gestion, et même d'"exploiter à leur fantaisie'. Ce terme de 'copropriétaire' du royaume avait d'ailleurs déjà été employé par Le Mercier de La Rivière,[81] et cette idée clairement exprimée par Du Pont de Nemours dès 1794 dans une proposition de gouvernement pour la France: il faut, disait-il 'déclarer le droit de *souveraineté*, que possèdent collectivement sur le pays les propriétaires qui, en vendant chacun leur héritage, pourraient aliéner la totalité du territoire.'[82]

Proposons une remarque pour apporter un élément à la comparaison entre Du Pont de Nemours, plutôt libéral et physiocrate, et Jefferson, plutôt républicain, et bientôt 'Républicain-Démocrate', du nom du parti qu'il fonda en 1791 avec Madison. Pour Du Pont de Nemours comme pour Jefferson, l'agriculture est la base du rapport moral des citoyens à la république, c'est pourquoi sans doute Du Pont souhaitait convaincre Jefferson d'appliquer ses idées, en matière d'instruction du peuple et de finances publiques. Mais c'est tant le sens de la république que celui du rapport des citoyens qui est différent chez les deux correspondants.

Du Pont fonde la valeur économique sur la terre, travaillée par les bras et les capitaux de l'agriculteur: 'Conserver, additionner, *transformer*, acquérir des richesses, sont des choses à la portée de l'intelligence et du travail de l'homme. En *produire* n'appartient qu'à Dieu. Dieu seul, en organisant la Nature, l'a rendue productrice.'[83]

Or Jefferson dit aussi cela à maintes reprises, mais tout d'abord il pense que l'agriculteur doit garder sa propriété le plus possible à l'échelle familiale, être un *husbandman*, un 'mesnager' pour parler comme Olivier de Serres. Et Jefferson n'en déduit pas un système

---

80. P.-S. Du Pont, *Lettre à Jefferson* (12 mai 1816), dans G. Chinard, *The Correspondence*, p.263.

81. P.-P. Le Mercier de La Rivière, *L'Ordre naturel et essentiel des sociétés politiques* (1767), dans E. Daire, *Physiocrates*, t.2, p.445-638. Notons cependant que, pour Le Mercier de La Rivière, il s'agit du souverain comme 'copropriétaire du produit des terres de sa domination' (p.627).

82. Pierre-Samuel Du Pont de Nemours, *Du pouvoir législatif et du pouvoir exécutif, convenables à la République française* (Paris, Chez Du Pont, 1795), ch.14, p.116. Souligné par Du Pont.

83. P.-S. Du Pont, *Lettre à Jefferson* (25 janvier 1812), dans G. Chinard, *The Correspondence*, p.186. Souligné par Du Pont.

politique censitaire fondé sur la propriété terrienne – sans doute parce que pour lui la valeur de la production agricole est qu'elle fournit à la république bien plus que de la valeur économique: elle est une base morale et sociale, celle de l'indépendance, que nous proposons d'entendre comme le paradigme d'une condition sociale qui permet de participer vertueusement à la république, puisque celle-ci doit reposer sur une société qui tend à la démocratie. En effet, l'important pour Jefferson est cette indépendance économique obtenue par ce qu'il nomme 'l'honnête industrie', qui peut s'exercer dans d'autres types d'activités économiques que strictement l'agriculture, pourvu qu'elle reste à taille familiale et permette un juste échange économique, moral et de là politique entre concitoyens. Jefferson part de l'agriculture comme base productive dans la société, mais aussi il fait d'elle le modèle de la condition économique et sociale des citoyens d'une république, puisque la démocratie économique et sociale construite par des citoyens indépendants lui apparaît de plus en plus comme la condition de la survie de la république.

Loin de ce sens paradigmatique de l'agriculture, Du Pont de Nemours entend l'agriculture dans un sens réel et fait d'elle la base réelle d'une république juste. Si Du Pont de Nemours place la moralité de l'agriculteur dans son efficacité économique productive, et réserve à celui-ci le droit de vote et de citoyenneté, c'est parce que seuls les intérêts de l'agriculteur propriétaire de terre, permanents et attachés, peuvent donner lieu à une saine gestion de la grande copropriété qu'est la république – sans doute une république que nous appellerions de nos jours une république 'libérale'.

IV

War and peace between nations |
Guerre et paix entre nations

Commercial treaties and the emergence of a political economy of peace: Du Pont de Nemours, inspirer of the Eden Treaty and supporter of the renewal of the *Pacte de famille* (1782-1790)

Antonella Alimento

University of Pisa

Despite having passed into history as a free-trade agreement, the Eden Treaty (1786) did not in fact liberalise trade between France and Great Britain in a generalised manner. A result of intense negotiation, the treaty, which took its name from the English negotiator William Eden, significantly reduced import duties on certain French agricultural products, such as wine, brandies and vinegar, in exchange for the reciprocal admission of hardware, subject to the payment of duties ranging from 10 to 15 per cent of the value of the goods. Both nations reserved the right to retain preferential agreements previously signed with other partners, in Great Britain's case with Portugal through the Methuen Treaty (1703), and in France's with Spain by virtue of the third Family Compact (1763) and the explanatory convention of 1768. Furthermore, Great Britain continued to apply its navigation acts, the legislation that prevented foreign ships from docking in English ports in the event that they shipped goods not produced by the country whose flag the ship was flying.

The man who negotiated the tariffs and which English goods would be excluded in France from the new regime of relative freedom[1]

---

1. England's woollen cloth, and cloth made from cotton mixed with silk, as well as the goods imported by the English East India Company were not included in the agreement in the absence of reciprocal treatment: the British government had in fact opposed the entry of French silks. The criterion followed when drawing up the tariffs was the contraband premium, due to which the rates varied from 10 per cent to 12 per cent to 15 per cent depending on the type of

230 *Antonella Alimento*

was not Du Pont, who had officially joined the French administration thanks to Turgot who had appointed him *inspecteur général du commerce* in 1775. Instead, the negotiations were conducted by Gérard de Rayneval, who, on behalf of the minister of Foreign Affairs, Charles de Vergennes, in September 1784 presented to a reluctant George Crauford, the English negotiator who in 1785 was substituted by William Eden, the guidelines that the French would be following:

> Que les sujets des deux nations contractantes jouiront respectivement dans les deux royaumes des avantages qui y sont accordés aux nations les plus favorisées, tant pour la navigation que pour le commerce, toutefois que cela ne dérogera pas aux traités subsistants, et principalement à celui d'Utrecht de 1713; à moins qu'il n'y est quelque chose que nous croyons devoir changer ou expliquer pour le bien général.[2]

In effect, the Franco-British commercial treaty, as Marie Donaghay has persuasively demonstrated, did not originate from purely physiocratic convictions, and, if any 'doctrine guided the French in the exchange of hardware for wine, brandy and vinegar, it was "most favoured nation". The duty on hardware was the same as that on the goods of most favoured nations before the general prohibition in 1785 – a prohibition the French planned to lift.'[3]

While the goals and inspiring principles of the Eden Treaty had little in common with the economic objectives and political presumptions pursued by physiocracy, the operation carried out by Du Pont cannot be described solely as a rhetorical exercise of

---

products and goods in question. There are many studies of the Eden Treaty, and I recommend Pascal Dupuy, 'French representations of the 1786 Franco-British commercial treaty', in *The Politics of commercial treaties in the eighteenth century: balance of power, balance of trade*, ed. Antonella Alimento and Koen Stapelbroek (Cham, 2017), p.371-99.

2. Quoted in John Holland Rose, 'The Franco-British commercial treaty of 1786', *The English historical review* 23:92 (1908), p.709-24 (712). Despite the fact that the Utrecht commercial treaty (1713) had officially been ratified by the British Parliament, its most important parts, articles 8 and 9, had not. See Antonella Alimento, 'Commercial treaties and the harmonisation of national interests: the Anglo-French case (1667-1713)', in *War, trade and neutrality: Europe and the Mediterranean in the seventeenth and eighteenth centuries*, ed. Antonella Alimento (Milan, 2011), p.107-28.

3. Marie Donaghay, 'The exchange of products of the soil and industrial goods in the Anglo-French commercial treaty of 1786', *The Journal of European economic history* 19:2 (1990), p.377-401 (399).

Commercial treaties and the emergence of a political economy of peace   231

a skilled propagandist. According to Donaghay's interpretation, in the *Lettre* à la Chambre du commerce de Normandie[4] that Du Pont published anonymously in 1788 to respond to the criticisms levelled at the treaty in France, he used the argument for commercial freedom because it 'would appeal to the influential Shelburne, whose free-trade proclivities were well known to the Foreign Ministry, and his "pupil" William Petty', and because it would not offend the susceptibilities of the English nation.[5]

In reality Du Pont, who in 1779 had become *inspecteur général des manufactures* 'pour faire plaisir à M. de Vergennes',[6] very soon took on the role of 'adviser on economic affairs'[7] in the powerful Foreign Ministry which, after the death of Maurepas in 1781, had de facto control of the French government's decision-making with regard to trade. Contrary to what is commonly believed, 'trade diplomacy' was not born in the nineteenth century with advisors of the calibre of Richard Cobden and Michel Chevalier, who thanks to their intellectual prestige and the networks to which they belonged managed to successfully conclude the negotiations that, in 1861, ended with the signing of the Franco-British commercial treaty that reopened trade relations between the two countries after the failure of the Eden Treaty, and the return of the system of prohibitions enacted by the Convention in 1793.[8]

The part played by Du Pont before and during the negotiations that led to the Eden Treaty (ratified on 26 December 1786) demonstrates beyond any shadow of doubt that, in the course of the eighteenth century, commercial agreements were losing their mainly political nature: after being used for so long to subordinate the economies of countries rich in gold and silver but in need of political protection, commercial treaties had effectively become the foremost

---

4. *Lettre à la Chambre du commerce de Normandie, sur le mémoire qu'elle a publié relativement au traité de commerce avec l'Angleterre* (Rouen and Paris, chez Moutard, 1788). This was written on 12 February – see p.244-47.
5. Donaghay, 'The exchange of products', p.401.
6. Gustave Schelle, *Du Pont de Nemours et l'école physiocratique* (Paris, 1888), p.203.
7. Orville T. Murphy, 'DuPont de Nemours and the Anglo-French commercial treaty of 1786', *The Economic history review* 19:3 (1966), p.569-80 (571 and 580).
8. See David Todd, *L'Identité économique de la France: libre-échange et protectionnisme, 1814-1851* (Paris, 2008), p.19-41, and Geoffrey Allen Pigman, *Trade diplomacy transformed: why trade matters for global prosperity* (London, 2016), p.42-50.

232 *Antonella Alimento*

instrument of 'international trade as diplomacy', as Geoffrey Pigman has pointed out.[9]

The correspondence he exchanged with Vergennes, along with the six *Mémoires*[10] that he wrote in 1786, in the midst of the negotiation, clearly demonstrates that Du Pont knowingly resorted to the instrument of the commercial treaty in order to neutralise the potential causes of conflict between the two historic enemies and, in that way, to secure peace in Europe.[11]

Du Pont made a decisive contribution to the creation of 'trade diplomacy' by making maximum use of the economic training he had acquired while editor of the *Ephémérides*, the work he performed

9.   Pigman, *Trade diplomacy transformed*, p.1-26.

10. The six *Mémoires* are kept in the Archives du ministère des Affaires étrangères, La Courneuve, henceforth AAE, Mémoires et documents (MD) Angleterre 65. On 23 January 1786, Du Pont sent Vergennes the first two, the *Réflexions sur le bien que peuvent se faire réciproquement la France et l'Angleterre*, f.3-8, and the *Observations sur les motifs particuliers qui peuvent déterminer le traité de commerce*, f.9-21 (published with Edouard Boyetet's *Observations* in *Recueil de divers mémoires, relatifs au traité de commerce avec l'Angleterre faits avant, pendant et après cette négociation*, vol.1, Versailles, Baudouin, 1789, p.109-37), along with an accompanying letter, in AAE, Correspondance politique (CP) Angleterre 555, f.63r-63v. A copy of the *Troisième mémoire sur le Traité de commerce entre la France et l'Angleterre: observations sur la note concernant la base du traité de commerce, communiquées par Monsieur le comte de Vergennes à Monseigneur le contrôleur général*, f.23-175v, can be found in London, National Archives, Public Record Office, Privy Council, I, box 123; see Charles Walton, 'The fall from Eden: the free-trade origins of the French Revolution', in *The French Revolution in global perspective*, ed. Suzanne Desan *et al.* (Ithaca, NY, 2013), p.44-56 and 193-97 (194). The fourth, entitled *Remarques sur les observations faites au comité du 9 août 1786, relativement à la lettre confidentielle de M. Eden*, f.199-223, was sent to Vergennes on 15 August 1786, with an accompanying letter, available in Paris, AAE, CP Angleterre 557, f.170-83. The fifth, *Observations sur les avantages que trouvera la France dans la diminution des droits actuellement imposés à l'entrée des marchandises françaises en Angleterre*, is at f.199-223. The sixth, *Mémoire sur les opérations qui sont à faire dans l'intérieur du royaume pour que la concurrence ouverte par le traité de commerce, entre les manufactures anglaises et les françaises, ne soit pas nuisible à ces dernières*, f.226-34v, was published by Du Pont as an annex to the *Lettre à la Chambre du commerce de Normandie* with the title *Sixième mémoire sur le traité de commerce avec l'Angleterre, remis aux deux ministres le 30 septembre 1786*, p.94-102.

11. On the role of commercial treaties as means with which to neutralise trade conflict, see Alimento and Stapelbroek, *The Politics of commercial treaties*, and Antonella Alimento, 'Il controverso cammino verso la reciprocità: pratica diplomatica e riflessione economica nella Francia d'Ancien Régime', *Società e storia* 165 (2019), p.549-65.

As secretary to Turgot, and above all the experience that, from March 1785, he gained as *inspecteur général du commerce* in charge of the 'collection & du dépôt des tarifs & des loix commerciales des nations etrangeres' under the control of the three ministries – Foreign Affairs, Navy and Finances – interested in those matters,[12] as well as his membership of the Comité d'administration de l'agriculture, an advisory body headed by Gravier de Vergennes, the foreign minister's grandson.[13]

As Murphy has persuasively argued, 'the germ of the Anglo-French commercial treaty lies in the Dupont-Vergennes correspondence at the beginning of 1782.'[14] In essence, Du Pont suggested to Vergennes that peace could be consolidated by neutralising the economic rivalry between France and Great Britain by the signing of a commercial treaty. For, by establishing profitable business relationships, the two countries would be mutually obligated to respect the peace. In his role as advisor, on 25 November 1782 Du Pont wrote to Vergennes encouraging him to exploit '[le] besoin de s'accommoder' that both countries had in order to obtain, in the course of the peace negotiations,

> des conditions réciproques et respectivement avantageuses [...]. Il y a trois questions dont la préface me semble être: nous faisons une paix sincère et dans le dessein de nous obliger réciproquement au lieu de nous nuire à l'avenir. Vous êtes une nation commerçante. Ne souhaitez-vous rien pour votre commerce? Que souhaitez-vous? Que feriez-vous en retour pour le nôtre? Car si vous ne voulez rien faire, vous ne devez rien demander. Ces trois questions peuvent être la conclusion de toute négociation lorsqu'on sera d'accord sur les points politiques et si V. E. ne les fait pas, les Anglais sont trop peu éclairés sur leurs véritables intérêts, trop vains et trop ulcérés pour les faire.[15]

---

12. See Loïc Charles and Guillaume Daudin, 'La collecte du chiffre au XVIIIe siècle: le Bureau de la balance du commerce et la production des données sur le commerce extérieur de la France', *Revue d'histoire moderne & contemporaine* 58:1 (2011), p.128-55.

13. Du Pont kept the position from 16 June 1785 to September 1787. It is important to underline that in 1779 Du Pont had been appointed by Necker to produce a report on the balance of trade of the first bureau for the balance of trade, led by Bruyard. See Charles and Daudin, 'La collecte du chiffre', p.134.

14. Murphy, 'DuPont de Nemours', p.573.

15. Letter from Du Pont to Vergennes, 25 November 1782, in Paris, AAE, CP Angleterre, 539, published in Schelle, *Du Pont de Nemours et l'école physiocratique*, p.236.

234 *Antonella Alimento*

This letter of 25 November 1782 is important for two reasons. On the one hand, it demonstrates beyond reasonable doubt that the idea of the clause that Vergennes had inserted in the 1783 peace treaty, thereby breaking English resistance, fundamentally belonged to Du Pont. The clause in fact stipulated that, 'aussitôt après l'échange des ratifications, les deux hautes parties contractantes nommeront des commissaires pour travailler à de nouveaux arrangements de commerce entre les deux nations sur le fondement de la réciprocité et de la convenance mutuelles; lesquels arrangements devront être terminés et conclus dans l'espace de deux ans à compter du 1er janvier 1784.'[16]

At the same time, the letter also allows us to appreciate the originality of the thought processes of an administrator who, while remaining loyal to physiocratic pacifism, had the ability to interpret Quesnay's teaching in reformist terms. As I will argue in the first part of this essay, from 1782 Du Pont adopted the logic of the negotiation and the 'bons marchés', of the 'équivalent' and of the 'compensation des faveurs', of the 'arrangement' and the 'profit réciproque', expressions that recur frequently in his letters, as well as in his published and unpublished works of these years. Despite accusations of abstractness levelled at him from various quarters, in particular by his colleague and 'adversary' Boytet,[17] starting from 1782 Du Pont accepted the logic of the 'bon marché' because he maintained that only reciprocal concessions could make it possible to gradually arrive at the abolition of all obstacles to commercial freedom and thus to universal peace.

In the two sections of this essay, I will reconstruct the original reformist interpretation of the physiocratic doctrine on customs duties and more broadly of interstate relations envisioned by Du Pont. The analysis of the contribution he made to the signing of the Eden Treaty and the reaffirmation, after appropriate changes, of the Family

16. Schelle, *Du Pont de Nemours et l'école physiocratique*, p.34; John Ehrman, *The British government and commercial negotiations with Europe 1783-1793* (Cambridge, 1962), p.4, has underlined the fact that the definitive peace treaties of 1783 and 1784 called for all the belligerents to appoint commissioners to establish new trade agreements with Great Britain (article 9 of the treaty with Spain of 3 September 1783; article 7 of the treaty with Portugal, 20 May 1784, but applying only to Africa).

17. On the different mentalities and points of view, see Marie Donaghay, 'Calonne and the Anglo-French commercial treaty of 1786', *Journal of modern history* 50:3 (1978), p.1157-84.

Commercial treaties and the emergence of a political economy of peace

Compact makes it possible to follow the evolution of a thought that, in response to the challenges posed by the new, emerging powers of Russia and Prussia, and more so by English expansionism, subjected to critical scrutiny the free-trade strategy formulated by the physiocratic movement from the early 1760s, while at the same time retaining the aspiration of peace.

Between the 'jealousy of trade' and the 'nec plus ultra' of free trade: Du Pont's reformist choice and the Eden Treaty

As we know, the physiocratic movement believed that negotiations on tariffs and duties and the signing of trade treaties were the highest expression of *fausse politique*, or, in other words, of the policy that subordinated decision-making on trade issues to the dogma of the *balance du commerce*.[18] According to Le Trosne, the physiocrat who addressed the issue of the relationship between taxation and international relations most directly, the ruling classes of the European states would be best advised to abandon negotiations on tariffs and customs matters once and for all, given that, rather than guaranteeing peace, they only fed the hostility of nations:

> La combinaison des tarifs a paru un des objets les plus difficiles du gouvernement: & il l'est d'autant plus en effet qu'il est dénué de toute base, & qu'il n'a d'autre regle que la maniere très arbitraire d'envisager dans tel ou tel point le prétendu intérêt qu'on suppose etre celui de la nation. Cette politique est cependant généralement admise: elle entre dans tous nos traités: elle décide de la paix & de la guerre; elle concourt à perpétuer les haines nationales; elle établit la distinction singuliere des nations plus ou moins favorisées.[19]

The much desired equilibrium would not be achieved through the 'balance du commerce', because, Le Trosne held, this search implied 'un équilibre d'appauvrissement', whereas only by adopting a system

---

18. See Thierry Demals and Alexandra Hyard, 'Forbonnais, the two balances and the Economistes', *The European journal of the history of economic thought* 22:3 (2015), p.445-72.
19. Guillaume-François Le Trosne, *De l'ordre social, ouvrage suivi d'un traité élémentaire sur la valeur, l'argent, la circulation, l'industrie & le commerce intérieur & extérieur* (Paris, Chez les freres Debure, 1777), p.652; see also Guillaume-François Le Trosne, *Les Lois naturelles de l'ordre social*, ed. Thérence Carvalho (Geneva, 2019).

of free exchange was it possible to create the conditions for real economic development.

Furthermore, Le Trosne also thought that the country which first 's'inquiétera peu des sublimes & inintelligibles spéculations de la balance du commerce, qu'on dit avoir servi de base à des tarifs combinés il y a plus d'un siècle sur les intérêts du commerce, qu'on dit en même temps être sujets à des variations continuelles', would force 'les nations voisines [...] de recourir aussi à la liberté pour rétablir l'équilibre' since its example would have demonstrated the advantages of this choice:

> Malgré la liberté entiere de l'importation, son industrie n'auroit plus à craindre la concurrence dans aucune partie importante, & les autres nations ne pourroient soutenir la sienne. En vain s'obstinant à maintenir leur régime prohibitif, voudroient-elles repousser ses ouvrages par de nouveaux impôts, la contrebande encouragée par les circonstances sauroit vaincre les obstacles, & pénétrer malgré les tarifs: elle multiplieroit les importations en raison du bénéfice qu'elle trouveroit d'une part dans l'abaissement du prix de ses achats chez la nation libre, & de l'autre dans la cherté des droits d'entrée chez les autres. Les nations voisines seroient donc forcées de recourir aussi à la liberté pour rétablir l'équilibre.[20]

In *De l'ordre social*, Le Trosne explicitly argued that the removal of customs barriers that hindered the movement of goods and the emergence of competition 'ne se fera jamais par une convention générale; il n'y a que l'exemple qui puisse l'amener par degrés'.[21]

However, if conventions were of no use, the violation of the 'loi de la reciprocité du commerce & de la liberté des échanges' did not license acts of reprisal:

> Mais l'acte d'hostilité que commet une nation envers une autre en l'excluant de chez elle par des prohibitions & des impôts, en violant la loi de la réciprocité du commerce & de la liberté des échanges, n'autorise point les représailles [...] parce que loin de diminuer le mal, elles ne font que l'agraver, l'étendre & le rendre universel; parce que cette maniere de se venger & de repousser les prohibitions par des prohibitions, les impôts par des impôts, est aussi ruineuse &

---

20. Le Trosne, *De l'ordre social*, p.682.
21. Le Trosne, *De l'ordre social*, p.412.

Commercial treaties and the emergence of a political economy of peace   237

aussi funeste à la nation qui l'emploie, qu'à celle qui a été assez peu réfléchie pour en donner l'exemple.[22]

Instead of responding with acts of reprisal, the country subjected to discriminatory measures had to continue to 'maintenir la franchise & la liberté, ou de les rétablir, si l'on s'est laissé entraîner par l'exemple, & de prouver aux autres par les heureux effets qu'on retirera de cette modération, combien est solide & abondante la récompense attachée à l'observation inviolable de la justice'.

What it is essential to underline here is that, in Le Trosne's vision, respect for the 'loi de la réciprocité du commerce & de la liberté des échanges' would create the conditions for universal and lasting peace: 'La véritable manière de répondre à ces hostilités seroit de le faire par un manifeste de paix universelle & de liberté générale.' The nation that was the first to adopt a general system of freedom would have escaped the logic of war:

> la liberté entiere ne seroit-elle pas le meilleur moyen de parvenir à cet heureux état de paix perpétuelle? d'abord pour la nation qui l'établiroit la premiere, qui dès-lors n'auroit plus à craindre la jalousie de ses voisins; & qui, si elle pouvoit être attaquée, verroit par une confédération fondée sur l'intérêt commun, tous les autres peuples s'armer pour sa défense; & ensuite pour toute l'Europe, lorsque l'exemple des avantages rapides de la liberté auroit fait sentir aux autres nations la nécessité de l'établir.[23]

While he shared the conviction that there was an inseparable link between free trade and universal peace, during the American War of Independence Du Pont distanced himself from the policy of universal liberalisation proposed by Le Trosne. With time, Du Pont came to revalue the usefulness of negotiation and the search for agreements based on the 'devoir de la réciprocité', a strategy that Le Trosne, in *De l'ordre social*, had decisively rejected on the basis that any country truly aware of its 'véritables intérêts' 'ne forcera aucune nation à s'acquitter envers lui du devoir de la réciprocité: il attendra que l'exemple des avantages de la liberté détermine ses voisins à l'imiter'.[24]

22. Le Trosne, *De l'ordre social*, p.415.
23. Le Trosne, *De l'ordre social*, p.417, where he distinguishes his project, based on the respect of 'l'ordre', from that of 'Le bon abbé de Saint Pierre [qui] avait imaginé un projet de paix perpétuelle pour la république européenne'.
24. Le Trosne, *De l'ordre social*, p.427. It should be underlined that Le Trosne

238   *Antonella Alimento*

The turning point came during 1782, the year in which Vergennes assigned Du Pont to study how to transform Bayonne into a free port and the compensations to be given to the Ferme,[25] as well as the year in which he published the *Mémoires sur la vie et les ouvrages de M. Turgot*.[26] In this text, a genuine homage to his *maître*, Du Pont took inspiration from the tax initiatives taken by Turgot to put forward a proposal in line with what he had suggested to Vergennes in the aforementioned letter of 25 November. After having expressed his appreciation for the reform of *traites* that Turgot would have completed had he remained in office, Du Pont urged the French government to use the peace negotiations as an opportunity to sign a treaty 'qui assure à l'Amérique son indépendance, à toutes les Nations la liberté des mers & du commerce, & qui engage l'Angleterre à favoriser le nôtre, à la condition pour nous de rendre les mêmes faveurs ou d'équivalentes au sien'.[27]

The 'trade diplomacy' proposed by Du Pont therefore associated the freedom of navigation and trade between all nations with the concession of favours and equivalents that France had to grant to Great Britain 'pour obtenir de notre côté d'autres conditions avantageuses'.[28] Having abandoned the policy of unilateral action and adopted that of the 'devoir de la réciprocité', Du Pont focused his work on studying the mechanisms of compensation to be activated to reach a reciprocal

---

partially modified his proposal, so that in *De l'administration provinciale, et de la réforme de l'impôt* (Basel, n.n., 1779), book 1, ch.6, p.35, he exhorted the French government to 'forcer l'Angleterre à ouvrir avec nous un commerce absolument libre, à lever toutes ses barrieres & ses impôts d'entrée tant en Europe que dans les Colonies, en lui offrant en même tems d'en user de meme. Imposer une telle condition de paix, n'est pas dicter des loix dures à son adversaire; c'est profiter de son avantage pour faire cesser un état d'hostilité entretenu par la jalousie exclusive & par la cupidité aveugle; pour éteindre une haine nationale dont les motifs sont si mal vus, & les effets si funestes; pour établir une communication également utile aux deux Nations, fondée sur une réciprocité que la justice prescrit aux hommes & aux sociétés, qu'elles n'ont jamais pu violer sans méconnoitre leur véritables intérêts, & qui une fois admise, deviendroit le gage & le lien d'une paix solide'.

25. Work from which emerged the edict of 14 May 1784 that transformed Bayonne, along with Dunkirk, Lorient and Marseille, into a free port for trade with the USA.

26. *Mémoires sur la vie et les ouvrages de M. Turgot, ministre d'Etat* (Philadelphia, PA, n.n., 1782), 2 parts in 1 vol.

27. *Mémoires sur la vie*, p.171.

28. Letter from Du Pont to Vergennes, 23 November 1782, in Schelle, *Du Pont de Nemours et l'école physiocratique*, p.234.

Commercial treaties and the emergence of a political economy of peace   239

and generalised reduction of duties and above all to overcome the system of prohibitions that fuelled the increased smuggling which syphoned resources from the coffers of both countries.

The gradual dismantling of the customs system between France and Great Britain would lead to the 'nec plus ultra' that Du Pont wrote about in his letter of 25 November to Vergennes: 'Jusqu'à l'abolition réciproque de tous droits sur les marchandises des deux pays, qui serait le nec plus ultra, il y a une longue carrière. Il sera doux à votre cœur de l'avoir entr'ouverte.'[29]

Pending the complete liberalisation of trade between the two nations, from 1782 onwards Du Pont advised Vergennes to adopt a comprehensive strategy of reciprocal favours, which ranged from permission to sail freely between the islands 'du Vent et sous le Vent, peut-être aussi de Cayenne', as compensation for Britain's loss of trade with North America, and the admission 'des quincailleries et merceries anglaises en France, à la charge de supprimer le droit presque prohibitif qu'ils lèvent sur l'entrée de nos vins'.[30]

It is important to underline that Du Pont was using the strategy of compensation and reciprocity not only to harmonise the economic interests between France and Great Britain but also to reform the national economy; to emulate the English economic success, the different productive sectors of France had to change and submit themselves to the logic of reciprocity. All the arguments developed by Du Pont in favour of the signing of the commercial treaty with Great Britain reflected this approach and implied this interconnection.[31]

This original way of thinking about international relations in conjunction with the reform of domestic productive sectors is present in all six of the *mémoires* written by Du Pont in 1786 as well as in the 1788 *Lettre*. It emerges particularly clearly in the *Remarques sur les observations faites au comité du 9 août 1786*, of 15 August 1786, in

29. Letter from Du Pont to Vergennes, 25 November 1782, in Schelle, *Du Pont de Nemours et l'école physiocratique*, p.236.
30. Letter from Du Pont to Vergennes, 23 November 1782, in Schelle, *Du Pont de Nemours et l'école physiocratique*, p.233.
31. In the same letter of 23 November 1782, p.233-34, Du Pont declared himself certain that 'Les murmures de nos négocians nationaux seraient le seul obstacle, mais ces murmures seraient sans fondement dans le moment où vous leur assurez, en compensation, une part immense au commerce de l'Amérique Septentrionale et vraisemblablement la renaissance du commerce de la morue par un nouveau partage de Terre-Neuve ou par la restitution de Louisbourg et de l'Ile royale en tout ou en partie.'

which he examined 'les dispositions de réciprocité les plus propres pour determiner' the English government to lower its duties on French wines, whose sale was, in his opinion, 'l'affaire capitale'.[32] Among the goods that could guarantee reciprocal treatment ('objet naturel de reciprocité') Du Pont identified the 'toiles de coton et les mousselines de l'Inde' which Great Britain owned exclusively, just as France did its wine. He argued for the benefit of allowing the entry of English muslin on payment of a duty of 12 per cent of value, based on the principle that the national interest required the acquisition of this commodity through 'commerce réciproque' rather than a 'commerce qui n'a point de réciprocité' even if carried out directly by the French East India Company. Since it did not involve the sale of domestic products and manufactured goods, trade carried out by the French company was not to be favoured: 'on ne croit pas que l'interet de la Compagnie des Indes puisse à cet égard balancer l'intérêt National.'[33]

By contrast, the admission of English cotton fabrics necessarily implied the abolition of the privilege of exclusivity granted to those who, in France, introduced 'machines ingénieuses' and its transformation into an 'indemnité très moderée' to be offered in compensation for 'concessionnaires privilégiés'.[34] The admission also implied the dismantling of the system '[des] marques et des plombs' and 'l'entière liberté de la fabrication des draps qui les fait prosperer'.

On the basis of these considerations, Du Pont went so far as to state that, if, thanks to the treaty, the French administration was to give greater freedom to manufacturing production, 'on croit que ce ne serait pas un bien d'une médiocre conséquence que ce traité aurait fait à la Nation.'[35]

Given these positions, it comes as no surprise to see that Du Pont sided with those, such as Bouvard de Fourquereux, who endorsed the 'single duty' project originally conceived by Colbert and strongly desired by Turgot. Adopted only in 1790 due to the stubborn opposition of the Ferme, the reform provided for the abolition of internal *traites* and their displacement to the borders, a measure which, in the intention of the reformists and of Du Pont himself, had to be taken ahead of the application of the Franco-British treaty since only by

---

32. *Remarques sur les observations faites au comité du 9 août 1786*, 'Table des matiéres contenues dans ce mémoire', AAE, MD Angleterre 65, f.25-33 (31).
33. *Remarques sur les observations faites au comité du 9 août 1786*, f.185 and 49v.
34. *Remarques sur les observations faites au comité du 9 août 1786*, f.192v-93.
35. *Remarques sur les observations faites au comité du 9 août 1786*, f.194v.

Commercial treaties and the emergence of a political economy of peace 241

exempting French goods from internal duties could they compete on equal terms with British ones.[36]

Du Pont's adoption of this reformist strategy explains the closeness with Vergennes, who used commercial treaties to increase the competitiveness of the French economy and simultaneously to neutralise the clash with Great Britain and curb Russian expansion. As Jeff Horn noted, apart from the agreement with Great Britain, between 1778 and 1787 Vergennes signed no fewer than five such treaties: with the United States (1778), Portugal (1783), Holland (8 November 1785), Spain (24 December 1786) and Russia (11 January 1787).[37] Du Pont certainly had a hand in the elaboration of the 'Convention préliminaire du commerce' that the French government concluded with Sweden in 1784;[38] the existence of a *mémoire* probably datable to 1784 and partially written in Du Pont's hand[39] leads us to believe that Vergennes made the most of Du Pont's expertise to add flesh to his overall diplomatic strategy, which Peter Sahlins has so eloquently described as 'practical cosmopolitanism'.[40]

36. On Mahy de Cormeré, director of the Bureau pour la refonte des traites and author of the reform, and on the committee created on 14 October 1786 by Calonne to examine it, which included Boytet, Gérard de Rayneval and Du Pont, see John F. Bosher, *The Single duty project* (London, 1964), p.75-81.
37. See Jeff Horn, *The Path not taken: French industrialization in the age of revolution, 1750-1830* (Cambridge, MA, 2006), p.66, which is based on O. T. Murphy, *Charles Gravier, comte de Vergennes: French diplomacy in the age of revolution, 1719-1787* (Albany, NY, 1982), p.432-58 (434). On the importance of the Franco-Dutch treaty of alliance, Koen Stapelbroek, 'Reinventing the Dutch Republic: Franco-Dutch commercial treaties from Ryswick to Vienna', in *The Politics of commercial treaties*, ed. A. Alimento and K. Stapelbroek, p.195-215.
38. By virtue of this convention, France granted Sweden the renewal of the 1741 convention and offered Gustav III the island of Saint-Barthélemy in exchange for an entrepot in Gothenburg, where French products brought on French vessels, including colonial ones, were received without paying duties; see Ale Pålss, *Our side of the water: political culture in the Swedish colony of St Barthélemy, 1800-1825* (Stockholm, 2016), p.49-67.
39. The *mémoire*, entitled *Sur les traités de commerce actuellement à faire et sur les faveurs et la forme qui peuvent être données à différentes branches de notre commerce relativement à ces traités*, 144 pages long, a draft partly in the hand of Du Pont and organised in ten chapters, with a table of contents, is listed in Hagley Museum and Library, Wilmington, DE, Winterthur Manuscripts, papers of Du Pont de Nemours, series B: 'Writings, memoirs and political papers, 1763-1817', n.54.
40. Peter Sahlins, *Unnaturally French: foreign citizens in the Old Regime and after* (Ithaca, NY, and London, 2004), p.147.

242   *Antonella Alimento*

Treaties and geopolitics: Du Pont, the Family Compact and the critique of free trade

The strategy 'des faveurs réciproques' adopted from 1782 by Du Pont was predicated on the assumption that only by eliminating the commercial rivalry between the two great imperial powers would it be possible to guarantee peace in Europe. In the *Mémoire abrégé sur la position actuelle de l'Europe, le changement que la paix y peut apporter et les combinaisons de commerce auxquelles elle peut donner lieu* (1783), Du Pont made his position clear when he openly stated that the two nations also had a common geopolitical interest to defend: 'L'Angleterre et la France elles-mêmes, si elles jugent bien leur position et leurs intérêts futurs, peuvent trouver des avantages immenses à se faire des faveurs réciproques, qui de part et d'autre accroitraient leur population et leur richesse, qui tariraient entre elles la source et l'occasion des guerres, qui établiraient un lien dont elles peuvent avoir le plus grand besoin.'[41]

In this work Du Pont evidently alludes to the possible changes in the European balance of power that the alliance between Austria, Prussia and Russia would have brought to the total detriment of France and Great Britain. Referring to the 'projets ambitieux' of the ruling house of Austria and the prospect of an expansion of its empire, and referring also to Prussian opportunism, Du Pont outlined the contents of a political alliance aimed at safeguarding the existing balance on the continent: 'dans le cas d'une confédération de ces deux puissances avec la Russie, il arriverait que la Suède, le Dannemarc, la Pologne, la Turquie, les Princes d'Allemagne seraient en danger. La nécessité d'une alliance entre la France, l'Espagne, l'Angleterre, la Hollande, les petites puissances du Nord et la Turquie, serait alors indispensable.'[42]

Du Pont returned to this geopolitical vision, with more detail, in the *mémoire* entitled *Réflexions sur le bien que peuvent se faire réciproquement la France et l'Angleterre* (1786),[43] a manuscript in which he repeated that the two nations did not actually have conflicting

41. *Mémoire abrégé sur la position actuelle de l'Europe, le changement que la paix y peut apporter et les combinaisons de commerce auxquelles elle peut donner lieu*, in AAE, MD France 587, f.76-77.
42. *Mémoire abrégé sur la position actuelle de l'Europe*, f.76-77. See Jeremy J. Whiteman, *Reform, Revolution, and French global policy, 1787-1791* (Aldershot, 2003), p.26.
43. *Réflexions sur le bien que peuvent se faire réciproquement la France et l'Angleterre*, AAE, MD Angleterre 65, f.3-8.

commercial interests: Great Britain could not compete with France in the production of wines, and France could not compete with England in tin-mining and the wool industry. Hardware, fashion and cotton were the only sectors in which they might clash but, in his view, the process of emulation that the entry of these goods would trigger would have beneficial effects on the economies of both countries.

In this text, a valuable synthesis of his thinking of those years, Du Pont explicitly associated the maintenance of the hegemonic position of France and Great Britain to the signing of the commercial treaty: by overcoming their commercial rivalry, the two countries could have made their presence felt from the North Pole to the South Pole since no nation would have dared fire a single cannon shot without their permission. Prussia and Austria, Du Pont stressed, waged war only thanks to the subsidies that France and England gave them.

Thus the message issued by Du Pont in this work was apparent: by putting an end to their commercial rivalry, France and Great Britain could guarantee peace, the indispensable condition for the economic success of all nations:

> toutes les Puissances ont également interet à maintenir la Paix, parceque la Guerre, même la plus heureuse, épuise les Capitaux, rallentir [*sic*] les travaux de l'agriculture et du commerce, nécessite des emprunts qui absorbent les revenus publics et qui obligent de multiplier les impôts: de sorte que les Conquêtes même ne valent jamais ce qu'elles ont couté, et laissent les Nations qui les ont faites, moins puissantes et par conséquent moins imposantes qu'elles ne l'étaient auparavant.[44]

This 1786 work is important not only because it develops the argument of the beneficial effect of competition in increasing the spirit of emulation and the productive potential of national manufacturing, but also because it reflected the growing fears that the activism of Russia, Prussia and the house of Austria aroused in French diplomatic circles. The Treaty of Teschen of 1779, which ended the War of the Bavarian Succession, and the creation of the Fuirstendbund by Prussia were undermining France's role as guarantor of the 1648 settlement in Germany, which 'represented a substantial blow to France's continental prestige', as Gary Savage has rightly highlighted.[45]

The stabilising role that Du Pont had attributed to the commercial

44. *Réflexions sur le bien*, f.4.
45. Gary Savage, 'Favier's heirs: the French Revolution and the *secret du roi*',

244 *Antonella Alimento*

treaty did not, therefore, seem able to staunch this gradual loss of French stature and influence, in part because Great Britain did not respect the 'devoir de la réciprocité' which, in Du Pont's view, by ensuring the harmonious development of the two economies, drove the two partners to respect the peace.

Du Pont's change of attitude towards the British government is, in my opinion, the most interesting aspect of the *Lettre à la Chambre du commerce de Normandie*, which he wrote in February 1788 and published anonymously in order to rebut the accusation by the Chambre that the treaty was the cause of the crisis in the French manufacturing sector.

In this work, which he sent to Stanislaw II, the king of Poland, on 24 June 1788,[46] Du Pont defended the commercial treaty with arguments that he had already used in his correspondence with Vergennes and in the printed and manuscript works he wrote between 1782 and 1786: that in negotiations sovereign states needed to achieve reciprocal advantages. 'Il serait impossible de faire consentir une Puissance étrangère & indépendante à un marché où elle ne trouverait pas un avantage réciproque.' Even the positive role played by competition and emulation in the development of French manufacturing is strongly reaffirmed: 'le meilleur moyen d'élever au même degré l'industrie des deux Nations, & de rendre leur législation également parfaite, c'est d'établir entre elles une communication qui mette sans cesse des modèles & des objets d'émulation sous les yeux de celle qui est dans l'infériorité.' The argument that there would be increased tax revenue thanks to a substantial curbing of smuggling, a conspicuous feature of the 1786 *mémoires*, was given considerable space also in the *Lettre*, as was the need to protect the less developed sectors of the French economy with low taxation designed to render smuggling pointless: 'Plusieurs branches de notre industrie, que la concurrence ne stimulait point, sont restées dans une infériorité qui nécessite de conserver sur les marchandises Anglaises des droits d'entrée proportionnés à ce que couterait la contrebande.'[47]

With regard to this, it must be emphasised that many of Du Pont's considerations on excise policies, emulation and combating smuggling

---

Historical journal 41:1 (1998), p.225-58; see also Derek McKay and Hamish M. Scott, *The Rise of the great powers, 1648-1815* (London, 1983), p.229-34.

46. See Winterthur Manuscripts, papers of Du Pont de Nemours, series B: 'Writings, memoirs and political papers, 1763-1817', p.783.

47. *Lettre à la Chambre du commerce de Normandie*, p.73, 81 and 85 respectively.

Commercial treaties and the emergence of a political economy of peace 245

are broadly echoed in the arguments propounded by Daniel Trudaine in the 1750s and adopted by the intendant of commerce, Vincent de Gournay. The fact that both had seen the possibility of reforming trade with Great Britain by means of a policy of the *équivalent* explains the fact that the manuscript version of the *Lettre* available to us bears the motto 'Laissez faire et laissez passer. M. de Gournay, Intendant du commerce',[48] attributed to Gournay by Turgot in the *Eloge de Gournay*, which Du Pont had published in his *Mémoires sur la vie et les ouvrages de M. Turgot*, the second edition of which was published, significantly, in 1788.

But absent from the earlier writings is the strong attack which Du Pont made in the *Lettre* on British exclusivism. While he restated that universal peace depended on the Franco-British treaty – 'Le repos du Monde, & le nôtre sur-tout, tiennent donc presque uniquement à ce Traité' – in the *Lettre* he accentuated his criticism of a government which, despite having signed the treaty, showed that it wanted to keep its own fiscal and commercial regime unaltered. Writing to Vergennes of 1782, Du Pont said that the British had been 'trop peu éclairées sur leurs véritables intérêts'; in the fifth *mémoire* of 1786 he described the nation as 'à demi-barbare'; in the *Lettre* he accused the British government of behaving in a disloyal manner: 'leurs Douanes se sont entièrement écartées de l'esprit & de la lettre du Traité.'[49]

It is within this criticism that two decisive positions taken by Du Pont should be placed: one relates to the nature of commercial treaties and the other to power relationships between 'nations commerçantes' and 'royaumes agricoles'. Compared to the writings so far analysed, in the *Lettre* Du Pont placed free trade squarely at the centre of his thinking: while commercial treaties were an expression of the sovereign's will, commercial freedom was inscribed in the law of nations:

> L'esprit d'un Traité de Commerce est d'admettre tout ce qui n'a pas été nommément excepté. La liberté des échanges était de droit naturel entre les Nations, elle était l'usage de la propriété de leurs Citoyens, avant qu'on eût fait ni Traités ni Loix. Il ne faut point d'ordre spécial pour permettre ce qui est essentiellement conforme à la raison, à la liberté, aux droits de propriété, à la justice; c'est

48. Manuscript of the *Lettre à la Chambre du commerce de Normandie*, AAE, MD Angleterre 74, f.140. The motto was substituted in the published edition by 'Otez-lui ses liens, & laissez-le aller. Evangile selon S. Jean, C. XI, v. 44.'
49. *Lettre à la Chambre du commerce de Normandie*, p.87.

pour y porter atteinte, que l'expression de la volonté des Souverains devient indispensablement nécessaire; car en ce cas, on ne peut pas la présumer.[50]

Precisely because treaties were the expression of the sovereign will, Du Pont came to contemplate the possibility of war in the event that the spirit of the treaty was openly violated by one of the contracting parties: 'Elles ne peuvent manquer à leurs engagemens, sans s'exposer à s'entendre dire, par des Puissances indépendantes: LA BONNE FOI ou LA HONTE, & vraisemblablement LA GUERRE, & avec elle LA RUINE, & peut-être LA DESTRUCTION.'[51]

In this 1788 work, Du Pont seemed therefore not to fear a possible outbreak of war, and in this regard it is important to note that, to respond to the challenge launched by the partner, Du Pont turned to the typically physiocratic argument of the superiority of agricultural nations over manufacturing ones:

L'expérience de tous les tems a fait voir que successivement les Nations s'enlèvent les unes aux autres les Manufactures. L'Espagne actuellement nous débauche nos Ouvriers en soie, sur tout ceux qui soutenaient la Fabrique de bas [...] Mais on n'enlève point les Cultivateurs, ni la nature du sol, ni son heureuse exposition, ni les denrées privilégiées qu'il produit exclusivement. C'est donc sur les produits de la culture qu'il faut fonder d'une manière solide la prospérité & le Commerce d'un grand Empire.[52]

The invasion of Holland by Prussia in support of the stadtholder and against the patriots supported by France, and above all Great Britain's entry in August of 1788 into the Triple Alliance, which marked the end of the system of alliances built by Vergennes, certainly contributed to reinforcing in Du Pont the conviction that the British government was not only untrustworthy but also hostile. Significantly, in the *Lettre* Du Pont had condemned the fact that, in contravention of the terms of the treaty, the British government refused to recognise the role of consuls as 'Agens pour veiller l'une chez l'autre à leurs intéréts commerciaux, & à qui leurs Négocians puissent s'adresser, quand ils se trouvent exposés à des vexations contraires à l'esprit ou à la lettre du Traité, & à l'intention de leurs Souverains'. To remedy this

---

50. *Lettre à la Chambre du commerce de Normandie*, p.275.
51. *Lettre à la Chambre du commerce de Normandie*, p.268, n.8.
52. *Lettre à la Chambre du commerce de Normandie*, p.80-81.

blatant violation, Du Pont had requested that the British Parliament change the law that prevented 'que des Consuls étrangers jouissent chez eux de priviléges égaux à ceux que notre usage & celui de toutes les Nations assureraient aux leurs chez nous' or that 'une autre dénomination pour les personnes à qui seront confiées les fonctions dont le Traité avait dit que l'on chargerait des Consuls' be found.[53]

Further evidence of Du Pont's diminishing faith in the British government was his request for the creation of a mixed commission composed of 'hommes éclairés des deux Nations' in order to 'examiner les erreurs contraires aux principes qui ont servi de base au Traité & que l'on a pris de part & d'autre l'engagement de redresser de bonne foi'.[54]

The sense of reproach clearly evident in the *Lettre* turned into open hostility with the start of the Nootka Sound crisis in 1790: Du Pont, by this time a member of the National Assembly and a supporter of a moderate, commercial monarchy, shared Barnave's belief that Great Britain conspired against the Revolution. Armed with this certitude, he took to the field to prevent revolutionary France from abandoning the alliance with Spain, which to his mind was central to defending the commercial interests of France and its reputation in the system of states.

As is known, the Spanish government requested French support against Great Britain, and the 'patriots' took their cue from this request to raise three interlinked questions: that of control over diplomacy, that of the universal right to peace and that of who had the power to declare war. This set of problems, debated between 16 and 22 May 1790, was presented by Volnay, who proposed that a declaration of the law of nations be issued to repudiate the war. The proposal, which did not receive the unanimous consent of the 'patriots', was attacked by the 'right', who interpreted the 22 May 1790 decree – in which the French nation solemnly declared 'de renoncer à entreprendre aucune guerre dans la vue de faire des conquetes, et qu'elle n'emploiera jamais ses armes contre la liberté d'aucun peuple' – as a mere expedient to repudiate the Spanish alliance. In order to block this eventuality, between June and August 1790 the 'right' launched a violent anti-British campaign, and the stands taken by Du

53. *Lettre à la Chambre du commerce de Normandie*, p.276.
54. *Lettre à la Chambre du commerce de Normandie*, p.278.

248   *Antonella Alimento*

Pont in favour of the 22 May 1790 decree and against the rejection of the Family Compact should be seen as part of this.[55]

Du Pont in fact proposed that the constitutional question (the right to declare war) should be disassociated from the executive act (arming the fleet in support of the Spanish request and in compliance with the Family Compact), and on 19 May presented a draft decree in which he invited the Assembly to maintain 'en toutes leurs dispositions défensives les traités qui ont été conclus en son nom; mais ils seront successivement soumis à l'examen des Représentans de la Nation, pour aviser aux changemens, modifications, ou améliorations qui pourraient etre nécessaires dans les autres dispositions de ces traités.'[56]

What is important to underscore here is that, by taking this position, Du Pont effectively aligned himself with the mediation proposed by Mirabeau between 20 and 22 May (on the two competing powers) which led to the 22 May 1790 decree, and with the argumentation strategy set out by the *ministériels* in defence of the Family Compact. Tellingly, the *Journal de la Societé de 1789*, their mouthpiece, in June 1790 printed one of Du Pont's fierce attacks on Great Britain. In the 'Considération sur la position politique de la France, de l'Angleterre et de l'Espagne', he actually accused the 'puissance rivale' of wanting to take over Spanish commerce by forcing it to sign 'un traité de commerce très-avantageux pour la Grande Bretagne, et très-nuisible au commerce de la France et à celui de l'Espagne elle-même'.[57] Du Pont, who in the *Observation sur les motifs particuliers qui peuvent determiner le traité de commerce* (1786) had argued that due to its conceitedness Great Britain could not 'imaginer qu'une Nation continentale, qui n'est point représentée en Parlement, puisse jamais égaler leur industrie',[58] in this work of June 1790 expressed his certainty that Great Britain was using the crisis to 'nous enlever nos colonies de l'Amérique et de l'Inde, détruire notre marine et notre commerce, ruiner nos ports, nous réduire à n'être qu'une puissance continentale'. He therefore exhorted the Assembly not to call into question the

---

55. On these debates, see Marc Belissa, *Fraternité universelle et intérêt national (1713-1795): les cosmopolitiques du droit des gens* (Paris, 1998), p.199-200.

56. *Le Pacte de famille* can be read in the *Journal de la Société de 1789* (July 1790) on p.15-36. See also the *Opinion de M. Dupont sur l'exercice du droit de la guerre et de la paix, exposée à l'Assemblée nationale* (Paris, Imprimerie nationale, 19 May 1790).

57. 'Considération sur la position politique de la France, de l'Angleterre et de l'Espagne', *Journal de la Société de 1789* 4 (26 June 1790), p.5-29 (6).

58. *Observation sur les motifs particuliers qui peuvent déterminer le traité de commerce*, AAE, MD Angleterre 65, f.9-21 (20).

Family Compact because doing so would have diverted trade with Spain, which in his opinion was 'le plus avantageux de tous ceux que fait la France', into British hands.[59]

Du Pont further reaffirmed the strategic value of the alliance with Spain in *Le Pacte de famille* (1790), a text in which he revealingly used the expression 'équilibre de puissance' to argue that only by remaining united could the two nations avoid the start of war.[60] In the same text he reiterated the vital importance of the Spanish economy for the French economy: 'Notre commerce avec l'Espagne soutient nos Manufactures, & occupe un nombre considérable de nos matelots. Nous montrerions une indifférence coupable sur le sort de notre Peuple, si nous permettions qu'une Puissance Etrangère vint à main armée lui prescrire de nouvelles loix.'[61]

Undoubtedly in the course of 1790 Du Pont made the themes dear to the 'right' and the *ministériels* his own. Despite this, however, it is possible to underscore the presence of a firm line of continuity between the vision he expressed as the advocate of the Anglo-French commercial treaty (1782) and his support for the maintenance of the Family Compact (1790). Indeed, during the period in question Du Pont continued to believe in the strategy of negotiation based on the granting of reciprocal favours.

His ferocious attack on British expansionism, his defence of the French colonial empire against those who claimed 'qu'il ne nous est pas utile d'avoir des possessions lointaines; que nos colonies, de toute espèce, ne sont qu'un fardeau dispendieux',[62] and his support for the system of 'équilibre de puissance', which led him to wish for 'une guerre nationale',[63] were combined with a request strongly consistent with the strategy he had adopted in 1782, when he advised Vergennes to stabilise the European political system through the signing of a commercial treaty with Great Britain.

---

59. 'Considération sur la position politique', p.10.
60. Pierre-Samuel Du Pont de Nemours, *Le Pacte de famille et les conventions subséquentes, entre la France et l'Espagne* (Paris, Imprimerie nationale, 1790), p.147.
61. Du Pont de Nemours, *Le Pacte de famille et les conventions subséquentes*, p.141-42.
62. 'Considération sur la position politique', p.11: 'Quant aux écrivains et aux orateurs françois qui raisonnent ainsi, et qui se font applaudir pour raisonner ainsi, oseroient-ils avancer que nous n'avons pas besoin de Bordeaux, de Marseille, de Nantes, de Rouen, du Havre-de-Grace, de Saint-Malo, de l'Orient, de la Rochelle, de Bayonne, de Dunkerque! Perdons nos Colonies, et la plupart de ces ports seront détruits.'
63. 'Considération sur la position politique', p.25.

250   *Antonella Alimento*

It is noteworthy that in 1790 Du Pont used the same rhetorical expedient that he had employed in his letter to Vergennes to force Great Britain to negotiate. As in 1782, he called on Great Britain to abandon aggressive attitudes by making a choice predicated on reciprocity: if it did indeed want peace, Great Britain had to accept a 'désarmement réciproque'.[64]

Ever faithful to the reformist choice taken in 1782 and to the need to establish mutually binding economic relations, in *Le Pacte de famille*, Du Pont openly countered those who, on the basis of 'des principes généraux très philosophiques & très sages', claimed 'que la liberté & l'égalité sont l'âme du commerce'.[65] He defended the preferential treatment given by France to Spain by dint of the Family Compact with the observation that, as long as the nations did not create the conditions 'pour établir une complette fraternité entr'elles toutes',[66] it was necessary to ensure favourable treatment, as long as this was reciprocal. The fact that Great Britain, despite the 1786 commercial treaty, had decided not to repeal its navigation act demonstrated the need for France to remain loyal to the Family Compact, and to fight for the establishment of the principle of 'parfaite reciprocité':

> Nous aurions grand tort de donner au Commerce Anglais, en France, les mêmes privilèges dont y jouissent le Commerce Français & le Commerce Espagnol, tant que les Anglais réserveront chez eux, par leur acte de navigation, des priviléges particuliers au Commerce Britannique. Les Anglois nous traitant beaucoup moins favorablement que ne le font les Espagnols, il serait injuste de ne pas traiter les Espagnols en France plus favorablement que les Anglais. La parfaite réciprocité vis-à-vis de chaque Nation, est la seule loi qu'elles puissent invoquer & peut être le seul moyen de ramener à une meilleure conduite celles qui ont des principes peu favorables à la liberté des communications respectives.[67]

It is no surprise, then, to find that in *Le Pacte de famille* Du Pont went back to underlining the reformist potential of commercial agreements. Commenting on article 19 of the pact, he wrote that 'Les

---

64. 'Considération sur la position politique', p.20; only in the face of a refusal would French military support for Spain become essential because France could not allow itself to 'détruire les voisins dont la puissance et les engagemens garantissent l'Intégrité de ses possessions', p.30.
65. Du Pont de Nemours, *Le Pacte de famille et les conventions subséquentes*, p.59.
66. Du Pont de Nemours, *Le Pacte de famille et les conventions subséquentes*, p.59.
67. Du Pont de Nemours, *Le Pacte de famille et les conventions subséquentes*, p.59.

Commercial treaties and the emergence of a political economy of peace 251

alliances commerciales sont avantageuses en raison de ce qu'elles se rapprochent de la liberté.'[68]

The Du Pont of 1790 thus remained broadly loyal to the reformist approach he had set out in 1782. What should be highlighted is that, as a member of the National Assembly,[69] he stressed the pacifist nature of his proposal.[70] The only article that to his mind was incompatible with the values 'd'équité, de fraternité & d'intérêt bien entendu' adopted by revolutionary France was article 21, which denied access to the alliance to other powers:

> Rien n'est plus étrange que cet article. Le traité fait pour établir la paix & pour conserver à chacun ses possessions, toute puissance qui voudra s'unir dans les mêmes vues de conservation & de protection réciproque, & qui pourrait faire entrer dans la confédération des forces proportionnées, aux risques que sa position peut y apporter, doit pouvoir être admise à y accéder de l'avis des puissances déjà confédérées, qui ne peuvent ni ne doivent s'interdire d'avance cette liberté de recevoir dans leur confédération les Puissances dont le concours peut ensuite leur paroître utile à la sureté commune.
>
> La seule stipulation raisonnable est 'qu'il faudra l'aveu de toutes les nations confédérées, pour en admettre une nouvelle dans leur confédération'.[71]

Having changed, in his opinion, from an alliance between sovereigns to an alliance between nations, and thus a 'pacte national' and an instrument of balance with purely defensive purposes, the alliance with Spain ought to be expanded: 'Car plus il y a de confédérés pour se défendre, & plus il y a d'espoir d'en imposer à ceux qui voudraient attaquer.'[72]

---

68. Du Pont de Nemours, *Le Pacte de famille et les conventions subséquentes*, p.45. See Walton, 'The fall from Eden', p.44-56.

69. See Edna Hindie Lemay, *Dictionnaire des constituants, 1789-1791*, 2 vols (Paris, 1991), vol.1, p.415.

70. See Linda Frey and Marsha Frey, *The Culture of French revolutionary diplomacy: in the face of Europe* (London, 2018), p.29, on the rejection of war by Du Pont because 'each is ruined himself in the hope of ravaging others'.

71. Du Pont de Nemours, *Le Pacte de famille et les conventions subséquentes*, p.140, 47-49.

72. Du Pont de Nemours, *Le Pacte de famille et les conventions subséquentes*, p.45.

***

Du Pont's arguments in defence of the Family Compact unequivocally testify to his loyalty to the concept of 'international trade as diplomacy', and at the same time allow us to reflect on a broader issue, namely that of the level of continuity between the *Ancien Régime* and the revolutionary era, starting from the significant changes that emerged in the political and economic culture from the second half of the eighteenth century. At this time, Du Pont, bringing a decidedly reformist and pragmatic quality to Quesnay's teaching, prompted Vergennes to propose to Great Britain the stipulation of a commercial treaty aimed at neutralising the economic rivalry between the two countries and thus ensuring a lasting peace in Europe.

Sur l'intérêt bien entendu des nations éclairées: la correspondance entre Thomas Jefferson et Du Pont de Nemours à propos de l'affaire de la Louisiane

ALFRED STEINHAUER

Democritus University of Thrace

L'activité diplomatique de Pierre-Samuel Du Pont de Nemours reste bien moins étudiée que son activité en tant qu'économiste, membre du groupe des physiocrates. C'est celle-ci, en effet, et non la première, qui est mise en valeur dans la littérature sur le groupe.[1] Il est vrai que le rôle diplomatique qu'a joué Du Pont reste mineur par rapport à ses activités d'économiste, de publiciste et d'administrateur.

Mais ceci est regrettable, parce que Du Pont a bel et bien agi en tant que diplomate. L'apport de Du Pont – associé au ministre des Affaires étrangères pendant le ministère de Vergennes – a été important, comme le souligne notre collègue Mme Alimento dans le volume présent, au traité commercial avec l'Angleterre de 1786. Cependant ici on va s'intéresser à une autre intervention diplomatique de Du Pont de Nemours: son implication dans la vente de la Louisiane par la France aux Etats-Unis, ratifiée en 1803.

Cet article analyse la structure argumentative de sept lettres, échangées en 1802 et 1803, développée entre deux interlocuteurs: Thomas Jefferson, troisième président des Etats-Unis d'Amérique et un des Pères Fondateurs (*Founding Fathers*) de la jeune république, et Du Pont de Nemours, alors ancien dignitaire français exilé aux Etats-Unis. A première vue, l'écart de statut politique entre ces deux acteurs apparaît incommensurable. Non seulement Du Pont est, à

---

1. Mentionnons ici seulement les deux dernières synthèses parues sur le groupe physiocratique: Arnault Skornicki, *L'Economiste, la cour et la patrie: l'économie politique dans la France des Lumières* (Paris, 2011); Liana Vardi, *The Physiocrats and the world of the Enlightenment* (Cambridge et New York, 2012).

l'époque de la rédaction de ces lettres, un particulier, mais en sus il est un individu au statut précaire, un simple émigré. Toutefois, il est aussi un citoyen de la République des lettres, membre de ses réseaux, et finalement un ami personnel de Jefferson, qui le connaît et l'estime depuis longtemps. Ainsi, le ton usité dans ces lettres est celui de l'égalité respectueuse, qui autorise le maintien d'un air cordial, malgré la nature extrêmement sensible du sujet de la contestation. Car le dernier implique la question du devenir politique d'un territoire immense, détenu par la France et revendiqué par les Etats-Unis, devenir qui laisse dans ce même échange planer le spectre d'une guerre entre deux puissances *a priori* amies. Toutefois, il semble que Du Pont réussit même à convaincre son interlocuteur puissant du bien-fondé de son raisonnement, et on voit finalement le président des Etats-Unis s'incliner vers la solution préconisée par Du Pont, ouvrant la voie au traité de la cession de la Louisiane, qui sera finalement signé à Paris, le 30 avril 1803.

Là apparaît l'importance de cet échange discursif, dont la dimension performative – les effets pratiques si l'on veut – affecte les modalités historiques de la formation de l'Etat américain, tel que nous le connaissons. On ne saura jamais assez mesurer les répercussions d'une solution alternative, dont une conséquence éventuelle aurait pu être une guerre entre les Etats-Unis et l'Empire napoléonien.

Dans cet article, nous essaierons d'abord de saisir les stratégies discursives employées dans ce dialogue, avant de nous tourner vers sa base normative. C'est seulement ainsi que nous pourrons estimer la pertinence pratique de ce cadre, permettant aux interlocuteurs de s'exprimer avec franchise et sur un pied d'égalité. Nous allons donc analyser les artifices argumentatifs qu'emploie Du Pont de Nemours afin, d'une part, d'écarter la perspective de la guerre entre les deux Etats et, d'autre part, de présenter au président américain l'achat de la Louisiane comme la seule solution morale et rationnelle susceptible d'arranger le différend entre les deux nations. Nous exposerons comment Du Pont, employant une série de dispositifs rhétoriques bien connus, amène le président américain à une entente fondée sur une double base normative d'inspiration jusnaturaliste, à la fois morale, politique et économique.

C'est alors là que nous conclurons en soulignant l'importance capitale de la base normative qu'offre le droit naturel dans l'entente entre les deux acteurs. Nous pourrons ainsi apprécier le fait que le droit naturel n'est pas uniquement une structure théorique, mais aussi – et peut-être surtout – une matrice normative dans laquelle peut s'initier et se conclure un débat en forme juridique entre deux parties concernées raisonnables. L'égalité entre les parties et la norme de la *recta ratio* permettent alors la coordination des discours et la parité des arguments. Dans ce sens, nous montrerons que, même si l'on admet la différence que Hannah Arendt essaie d'établir dans *Sur la révolution* entre le fondement normatif de la Révolution française et celui de la Révolution américaine,[2] on ne saurait invalider cette méthode de raisonnement juridique, politique et économique universel. De cet échange discursif donc, nous étayerons l'argument selon lequel le droit naturel constitue un fondement d'une importance capitale pour la construction des cadres de la décision rationnelle et de l'entente politique au début de l'ère moderne. En effet, dans son domaine propre, éthico-juridique, si le droit naturel permet l'établissement de dualismes potentiellement conflictuels dans l'ordre de l'intérêt politique (naturel/civilisé, particulier/Etat, public/privé, national/ international), il offre simultanément un mécanisme permettant leur considération paritaire dans l'ordre de l'intérêt privé (du point de vue du particulier, propriétaire ou détenteur d'un office temporaire). Le même mécanisme est en œuvre dans la philosophie, où le droit naturel ne cesse d'être au dix-huitième siècle une nébuleuse conceptuelle, dans laquelle cependant s'élaborent les cadres d'un individualisme cohérent.[3] Si l'on examine la loi naturelle alors comme un dispositif,[4] on pourrait peut-être tirer quelques enseignements sur les modes de la rationalisation de la gouvernementalité pendant et après les Lumières.

---

2. Hannah Arendt, *Essai sur la révolution* (Paris, 1967), p.181-82.
3. Simone Goyard-Fabre, *Les Embarras philosophiques du droit naturel* (Paris, 2002), p.117.
4. Suivant Michel Foucault, Giorgio Agamben définit le dispositif de la manière suivante: 'Le terme dispositif nomme ce par quoi se réalise une pure activité de gouvernement sans le moindre fondement dans l'être. C'est pourquoi les dispositifs doivent toujours impliquer un processus de subjectivation. Ils doivent produire leur sujet'; Giorgio Agamben, *Qu'est-ce qu'un dispositif?* (Paris, 2007), p.26-27. Or, ce n'est pas manifestement le cas ici, car 'l'être' est bel et bien présent. Cependant, il s'agit de l'être ontologiquement minimal du droit naturel, l'animal intelligent et libre (porteur des attributs de la rationalité et de la volonté), dont le premier devoir est sa propre conservation (Grotius, Hobbes, Pufendorf, Locke, Quesnay), et à partir duquel s'échafaude le processus de subjectivation mentionné par Agamben.

i. Le désaccord entre Jefferson et Du Pont de Nemours sur la proposition à formuler à Napoléon

Le 25 avril 1802, Thomas Jefferson envoie à Pierre-Samuel Du Pont de Nemours, qui avait décidé de revenir en France, une lettre dans laquelle il lui assigne une fonction d'émissaire officieux à Paris. Outre le fait qu'il lui confie des lettres pour ses amis parisiens, il l'invite à transmettre aussi des instructions à deux représentants des Etats-Unis à Paris, le chargé d'affaires William Short et l'ambassadeur, le chancelier Livingston. En fait, dans cette lettre Jefferson expose immédiatement et clairement ses motivations à Du Pont afin de le convaincre de l'importance de sa mission, en l'incitant à lire les parties non chiffrées de sa lettre à Livingston. Par des mots très clairs, le président somme la France de céder la Louisiane aux Etats-Unis, en laissant planer le spectre d'une guerre: 'Je veux que vous maitrisez le sujet, parce que vous pourrez être capable d'exprimer au gouvernement de la France les conséquences inévitables de leur occupation de la Louisiane, [...] et que cette mesure coutera à la France, et peut-être dans un avenir pas si lointain une guerre.'[5]

En effet, la situation que décrit Jefferson résulte de l'évolution du statut juridique du territoire de la Louisiane. Ce territoire, qui est une colonie française depuis 1682, était passé sous contrôle espagnol en 1762 à la suite de la guerre – désastreuse pour la France – de Sept Ans. La jeune république américaine, soucieuse de ses intérêts commerciaux pour lesquels le débouché du Mississippi était vital, mais aussi pour maintenir le contact avec les nouvelles colonies du Tennessee et du Kentucky, avait négocié avec l'Espagne un accord de libre-échange, le traité de San Lorenzo, ratifié en 1795. Or, ce dernier fut remis en question avec la rétrocession de la Louisiane à la France par un traité secret de 1801, le traité de San Idelfonso. Concrètement, la souveraineté de la Louisiane était cédée à la France mais l'administration espagnole était maintenue.[6]

---

5. 'I wish you to be possessed by the subject, because you may be able to impress on the government of France the inevitable consequences of their taking possession of Louisiana; [...] and that this measure will cost France, and perhaps not very long hence, a war'; dans *The Correspondence of Jefferson and Du Pont de Nemours, with an introduction on Jefferson and the physiocrats*, éd. Gilbert Chinard (Baltimore, MD, 1931), p.46-47. Toutes les traductions dans cet article sont réalisées par mes soins.
6. Peter J. Kastor, *The Nation's crucible: the Louisiana purchase and the creation of America* (New Haven, CT, et Londres, 2004), p.36-37.

Il semble alors que depuis 1801 Jefferson avait commencé à organiser une offensive diplomatique afin d'obtenir le contrôle plus ou moins effectif du Mississippi et de la Nouvelle-Orléans, dans laquelle il avait enrôlé non seulement Pierre-Samuel, mais aussi, avant lui, son fils aîné, Victor Du Pont.[7] La question du 'réalisme' ou de l'"idéalisme' de Jefferson a été âprement discutée dans la bibliographie.[8] Mais sa lettre du 25 avril est formulée dans un langage nettement 'réaliste': considérant la présence de la France en Louisiane comme 'occupation', il la menace directement de guerre. Et dans sa lettre du 30 avril, Du Pont répond avec une apostrophe d'une simplicité étonnante: 'Celui de dire: *cédez-nous ce pays, sans quoi nous le prendrons* n'est pas du tout persuasif. *Nous le défendrons* est la première réponse qui se présente à tout homme.'[9] Le recours à la guerre entre alors comme sujet principal de la discussion, préparant le terrain à un recours à des artifices rhétoriques, dans lesquels celle-là sera réfutée méthodiquement, avec la mise en place d'un auditoire fictif.[10]

Ce rejet catégorique, formulé de la bouche de quelqu'un qui, en s'apprêtant à quitter les Etats-Unis en laissant derrière lui, comme il l'admet dans sa lettre précédente adressée à Jefferson en date du 26 avril, 'mes deux fils, leurs femmes, mes petits-enfants. Toute ma fortune et toutes les espérances de repos de mes vieux jours',[11] semble une attitude pour le moins imprudente. Mais cette divergence n'a pas lieu entre un émigré et un président: elle met en dialogue d'abord deux hommes des Lumières, deux amis de longue date et deux membres d'un même univers discursif.

ii. L'amitié entre Thomas Jefferson et Pierre-Samuel Du Pont de Nemours

La rencontre entre les deux hommes remonte à octobre 1787, quand Jefferson, alors ambassadeur des Etats-Unis en France, décrit Du Pont dans une lettre adressée à Robert Livingston comme un homme

---

7. Charles A. Cerami, *Jefferson's great gamble: the remarkable story of Jefferson, Napoleon and the men behind the Louisiana purchase* (Naperville, IL, 2003), p.137.

8. Leonard J. Sadosky, 'Jefferson and international relations', dans *A Companion to Thomas Jefferson*, éd. Francis D. Cogliano (Malden, MA, 2012), p.99-217 (200-201).

9. G. Chinard, *The Correspondence*, p.52.

10. Voir Chaïm Perelman, *L'Empire rhétorique, rhétorique et argumentation* (Paris, 2002), chap.2.

11. G. Chinard, *The Correspondence*, p.45.

258 *Alfred Steinhauer*

hautement savant et valeureux, occupant une position très distinguée dans le département du commerce.[12] Or, en 1787, Jefferson était déjà à Paris depuis trois ans, période durant laquelle il eut de nombreux contacts parisiens. Quand il arrive, en août 1784, c'est en tant que successeur présomptif de Benjamin Franklin, qui était en poste depuis 1777.[13] C'est probablement Franklin, qui restera à Paris jusqu'en 1785, qui l'introduit auprès des deux plus éminents salons parisiens de la fin de l'Ancien Régime: le salon d'Auteuil de Mme Helvétius, le lieu principal du 'couchant des Lumières', selon l'expression de Sergio Moravia, où se rencontrèrent plusieurs générations des Lumières, et celui de Mme Condorcet, installé à l'Hôtel des Monnaies.[14] Or, Du Pont connaissait Condorcet depuis 1770: tous les deux fréquentaient le salon de Julie de Lespinasse, leur relation s'étant affermie grâce à leur collaboration au sein du ministère Turgot de 1774 à 1776.[15] Il est d'ailleurs fort possible que ce soit chez elle que se rencontrèrent Jefferson et Du Pont.

A la suite de cette rencontre, on constate que, rapidement, des écrits de Du Pont figurent parmi les ouvrages que Jefferson envoyait régulièrement aux Etats-Unis.[16] Il est certain aussi qu'il est influencé par la

12. 'A person of great wealth and knowledge, and holding a very distinguished office in the department of commerce'; lettre à Robert R. Livingston, dans Robert F. Haggard, 'The politics of friendship: DuPont, Jefferson, Madison and the physiocratic dream for the New World', *Proceedings of the American Philosophical Society* 153:4 (2009), p.419-40 (422). La position à laquelle se réfère Jefferson n'est pas précisée, mais, selon Georges Weulersse, à la chute de Calonne en 1787, Du Pont tenait les charges suivantes: inspecteur de commerce, garde du dépôt des lois étrangères sur le commerce et les douanes, commissaire général du commerce extérieur et intérieur. Georges Weulersse, *La Physiocratie à l'aube de la Révolution (1781-1792)* (Paris, 1985), p.36.
13. Thomas Jefferson, *Autobiography of Thomas Jefferson 1743-1970* (New York et Londres, 1914), p.97.
14. Ian McLean, 'The Paris years of Thomas Jefferson', dans *A Companion to Thomas Jefferson*, éd. F. D. Cogliano, p.110-27 (119); Sergio Moravia, *Il tramonto dell'illuminismo: filosofia e politica nella società francese (1770-1810)* (Rome et Bari, 1986).
15. Elisabeth Badinter et Robert Badinter, *Condorcet (1743-1794): un intellectuel en politique* (Paris, 1988), p.59 et 118.
16. En 1788, Jefferson envoie en Amérique une copie de la *Lettre à la Chambre de commerce de Normandie*, qui est une défense du traité commercial entre la France et l'Angleterre de 1786 (R. F. Haggard, 'The politics of friendship', p.423). Le recensement des publications de Du Pont que Jefferson a envoyées en Amérique serait probablement d'un grand intérêt pour l'histoire des idées, mais nous n'avons pas tenté de l'entreprendre.

La correspondance entre Jefferson et Du Pont à propos de la Louisiane   259

pensée physiocratique, dont Du Pont a été l'un des derniers membres influents encore actifs dans les années 1780-1790.[17] De son côté, Du Pont posait dès la fin des années 1760 sur l'Amérique un regard favorable; ainsi, en 1769, le dixième volume des *Ephémérides du citoyen* commence par un article de Benjamin Franklin. Pendant la Révolution française, les deux hommes se rapprochent davantage, dans la mesure où Jefferson favorise le parti des Américanistes, proche des Economistes physiocratisants.[18]

Ainsi, en 1800, Jefferson, devenu depuis président des Etats-Unis, insiste sur cette 'longue expérience de fidélité et amitié personnelle'[19] qui l'attache à Du Pont, le considérant comme 'un des plus grands hommes de son temps' et comme 'l'homme le plus habile en France'.[20] Quant à Du Pont, il considère Jefferson comme une personne hautement intelligente, talentueuse et 'un des grands gouverneurs des nations'.[21]

Le fait que les deux auteurs ne discutent jamais en détail du fondement de leurs convictions communes n'est pas preuve de désaccord: bien au contraire, il pointe vers l'existence d'une base normative commune. Celle-ci soutient une méthode de rationalisation, qui se déploie, comme nous allons le montrer dans la précieuse lettre de Du Pont du 30 avril, afin de présenter une solution 'économique' au différend. C'est sur ce socle normatif que nos deux interlocuteurs semblent trouver un terrain d'entente sur cette question politique aride. Il est notamment intéressant ici de suivre de près l'argumentation développée par Du Pont, si on la considère comme un artifice rhétorique destiné à un seul auditeur, le président américain.[22]

17. Manuela Albertone, 'Thomas Jefferson and French economic thought: a mutual exchange of ideas', dans *Rethinking the Atlantic world: Europe and America in the age of democratic revolutions*, éd. Manuela Albertone et Antonino De Francesco (New York, 2009), p.123-46 (130).
18. Joyce Appleby, 'What is still American in the political philosophy of Thomas Jefferson?', dans *The Enlightenment: critical concepts in historical studies*, t.5: *Revolutions*, éd. Ryan Patrick Hanley et Darrin McMahon (Londres et New York, 2010), p.287-309.
19. 'My long experience of your personal faith and friendship' (lettre du 1er février 1803, G. Chinard, *The Correspondence*, p.66).
20. 'One of the very great men of the age [...] the ablest man in France' (lettres à James Madison, 4 avril 1800, et à Thomas Mann Randolph, 17 janvier 1799, citées par R. F. Haggard, 'The politics of friendship', p.423).
21. Lettre à Mme de Staël, 8 avril 1801, citée par R. F. Haggard, 'The politics of friendship', p.423.
22. Chaïm Perelman et Lucie Olbrechts-Tyteca, *Traité de l'argumentation* (Bruxelles, 2008), §8.

iii. La structure argumentative de la lettre de Du Pont du 30 avril 1802

Dans la riche lettre du 30 avril 1802, Du Pont reconnaît l'importance du sujet dont il fait 'le but principal de [s]on voyage', puisqu'une guerre entre les deux nations le mettrait face à un dilemme: se priver du 'doux asile de l'Amérique' ou procéder à 'une abdication entière de [s]a patrie natale'.[23] Cependant, il use d'un exercice de rhétorique en réfutant méthodiquement la demande de Jefferson dans sa formulation initiale. En mettant en scène un auditoire imaginaire français, en employant donc le procédé de l'hypotypose, il essaie d'obtenir l'adhésion du président pour une solution pacifique, esquissée au gré des arguments présentés. Avec cette invention rhétorique, il commence par lui présenter une illustration du 'bon sens' des Français, tout en s'esquivant derrière la pluralité assumée de l'auditoire fictif: 'permettez-moi-même de vous opposer quelquefois le langage de ceux avec lesquels j'aurai à traiter.'[24] C'est ainsi que Du Pont commence avec le point de vue militaire. Assumant, dans un argument fondé sur la structure du réel, la position de Bonaparte, l'argument souligne que lui, en tant que militaire, sera irrité des demandes belliqueuses de Jefferson. Du Pont complète par une amplification due au favoritisme de son environnement. Même si Napoléon voudrait accepter la demande des Américains, il aurait du mal à le faire, puisqu'il est encerclé de ministres qui 'ne peuvent conserver leur place qu'en encensant perpétuellement l'orgueil militaire'.[25] Donc le premier argument de Du Pont vise précisément à montrer l'inefficacité de la menace de la guerre: 'Voici comme on lui parlera pour soutenir par des raisons politiques l'*irritation* qu'aura excitée la menace, plus ou moins enveloppée de protestations, de le déposséder malgré lui.'[26] Aussi, dans une première étape est étayée l'antithèse entre la suggestion initiale de Jefferson et la position présumée de Bonaparte, une figuration qui aboutit immanquablement à l'éventualité d'une guerre entre deux pays censés être amis.

Ensuite, dans la prosopopée imitant la scène qui se déroulerait en France à la réception de l'ultimatum, Du Pont avance un second argument, cette fois-ci de nature géopolitique, élargissant le sujet.

---

23. G. Chinard, *The Correspondence*, p.48.
24. G. Chinard, *The Correspondence*, p.49.
25. G. Chinard, *The Correspondence*, p.49.
26. G. Chinard, *The Correspondence*, p.49 (souligné par Du Pont).

La correspondance entre Jefferson et Du Pont à propos de la Louisiane   261

Dans un discours censé reproduire le raisonnement d'un conseiller fictif de Napoléon, il accuse les Etats-Unis, et Jefferson même, d'être possédés 'd'une ambition de conquête'.[27] Par cette tournure, il montre que le signe de guerre émis par Jefferson serait interprété comme un indice politique d'agressivité généralisée. Sous le masque de la personne fictive, Du Pont complète l'artifice rhétorique, passant des conséquences possibles aux conséquences certaines, assumant alors que l'ambition américaine de conquérir le Mexique ne faisait plus guère de doute. L'amplification est effectuée et, par cet artifice, l'attitude des Etats-Unis est considérée comme universellement 'agressive'.

C'est à ce moment précis qu'entre en scène un troisième personnage: il s'agit du moraliste, qui s'adresse maintenant à Jefferson non en tant que Français à un Américain, mais en tant que 'Philosophe ami de l'humanité'.[28] Assumant l'hypothèse énoncée comme valide, il peut entraîner l'adhésion de Jefferson à une solution pacifique, en illustrant les conséquences inévitables d'une invasion du Mexique par les Etats-Unis pour l'économie politique et morale de ces derniers.

Ces trois arguments forment ainsi une argumentation rhétorique empruntant la topique de la 'pente savonneuse' (*slippery slope*), avec cette idée que la conquête de la Louisiane conduirait fatalement à des suites funestes, surtout pour les Etats-Unis eux-mêmes, ce qui enclencherait une cascade d'effets nocifs synonymes d'un impérialisme débridé. Et on retrouve ici aussi les traces d'un discours, bien étudié par J. G. A. Pocock, celui de la dialectique de l'expansion et de la corruption des Etats, une tradition remontant à Polybe et reprise par Machiavel, très répandue dans l'Amérique prérévolutionnaire, et avec laquelle Du Pont semble familier.[29]

Dans ce contexte, Jefferson est amené par Du Pont au rôle de l'auditoire universel. Il est positionné dans le but de juger, en philosophe moral et politique, les dangers du bellicisme. En peignant les conséquences néfastes, Du Pont insiste sur leurs aspects économiques et civilisationnels: 'Le Mexique, animé par une révolution, et porté à la hauteur de votre civilisation par vos citoyens qui s'y domicilieraient, qui pour lui quitteraient votre territoire et cesseraient de l'améliorer, serait ce qu'on pourrait imaginer de plus funeste à votre paix, à votre

---

27. G. Chinard, *The Correspondence*, p.49.
28. G. Chinard, *The Correspondence*, p.50.
29. J. G. A. Pocock, *The Machiavellian moment: Florentine political thought and the Atlantic republican tradition* (Princeton, NJ, 1975), p.524.

liberté, à votre prospérité.'[30] Ainsi, la guerre contre la France est rejetée non pas pour des motifs qui intéresseraient celle-ci, mais pour le bien des Etats-Unis qui seraient immanquablement marqués par le bellicisme. Or, ce dernier, du point de vue de la philosophie, est nocif et il faudrait bien le 'déraciner de votre nation, en lui montrant dans quelle suite de malheurs l'entraînerait cette tentation fatale'.[31]

Ayant établi l'hyperbole de la certitude d'une guerre avec le Mexique et ses conséquences pour les Etats-Unis, dans le quatrième volet de son argumentation, Du Pont assume la figure du patriote, bien connue de Jefferson.[32] Il évoque alors le sentiment anti-anglais de Jefferson dans une diatribe de politique internationale, qui analyse d'une part les rapports de forces, surtout maritimes, et d'autre part la situation légale internationale, entre l'Angleterre, la France et les Etats-Unis. Suivant cette perspective, seule l'Angleterre profiterait selon lui d'un conflit entre les Etats-Unis et la France: 'On dira que ces sentiments si pacifiques à l'égard des Anglais, si hostiles et déjà s'exprimant en menace à l'égard des Français [...] montrent en faveur de l'Angleterre une partialité dont la nation et le gouvernement français doivent être choqués et aussi inquiets que vous le paraissez vous-mêmes.'[33] Ces réflexions ne sont pas que 'pragmatistes', car on pourrait supposer qu'elles fonctionnent aussi comme une sorte d'incitation, rappelant à Jefferson son passé diplomatique, et le rôle joué par la France pendant la Révolution américaine: 'Il n'y a que la France qui désire que vous soyez une puissance maritime. Il n'y a que les Anglais qui le craignent.'[34] La guerre est encore écartée comme solution, tandis que Du Pont passe, à travers la discussion du statut légal et de l'importance économique de la Louisiane, insensiblement de la discussion sur une guerre à la discussion sur un éventuel traité.

C'est à ce point qu'intervient une dernière figure, celle de l'honnête homme, pour démontrer la faiblesse de la proposition de Jefferson au niveau du droit. Après le rejet de l'ultimatum américain, la France serait forcée à considérer des mesures à plus long terme, minant les relations entre les deux pays et 'tous les malheurs que nous voulons empêcher auraient lieu'.[35] Après avoir réfuté l'option de la guerre,

---

30. G. Chinard, *The Correspondence*, p.50.
31. G. Chinard, *The Correspondence*, p.51.
32. Voir Th. Jefferson, *Autobiography*, p.138.
33. G. Chinard, *The Correspondence*, p.51.
34. G. Chinard, *The Correspondence*, p.52.
35. G. Chinard, *The Correspondence*, p.52.

La correspondance entre Jefferson et Du Pont à propos de la Louisiane 263

Du Pont articule une série de solutions pour résoudre la crise de la Louisiane. La dernière est exprimée solennellement dans une adresse personnelle à Jefferson en tant que président des Etats-Unis, personnification de l'intérêt national de son pays:

> Hélas! Monsieur Le Président, la liberté des contrats, le goût naturel de tous les peuples, de tous les individus pour les richesses, et la pauvreté avec laquelle toutes les grandes puissances sont sans cesse attaquées, à laquelle il n'y a que les puissances de second ordre qui échappent, ne vous laissent qu'un moyen quand vous n'avez point d'échange de même nature à offrir. C'est l'acquisition, et c'est le paiement en argent.[36]

La multiplication des points de vue et l'échange des rôles entre les différents personnages indiquent la difficulté du problème. Le déploiement de tout l'arsenal rhétorique, la prosopopée, l'évocation de Jefferson d'abord diplomate, ensuite homme d'Etat et finalement président sont des échelons d'un discours persuasif bien rodé qui amène au point final, la cession de la Louisiane pour une somme d'argent. Or, cette solution est présentée non seulement comme morale (provenant de la solidarité historique des deux pays) mais aussi comme juste (à l'égard du droit) et – surtout – économique. Intervient alors le renversement de la rationalité de l'agir typique de l'époque classique, entre passion (ici de conquête) et intérêt.[37] L'argument s'achève alors avec un calcul de dépenses qui a l'avantage d'indiquer aussi bien le profitable que le moral. Une base d'entente semble alors se profiler. Laissant pour le moment le récit historique en suspens, il convient désormais d'aborder la question des fondements normatifs de cette rhétorique.

iv. Les fondements normatifs de l'entente entre Jefferson et Du Pont

Nous avons vu dans cette lettre l'effort entrepris par Du Pont afin d'exorciser le spectre de la guerre. Il faut bien croire, d'un côté, que le déploiement de cet artifice rhétorique n'y est pas pour rien, et qu'une menace de guerre planait vraiment autour de ces délibérations. De l'autre, il est peu probable qu'une recherche historique serait capable

---

36. G. Chinard, *The Correspondence*, p.53.
37. Voir Albert Hirschman, *The Passions and the interests: political arguments for capitalism before its triumph* (Cambridge, MA, 2013).

d'établir à quel point les suggestions de Du Pont furent décisives pour la décision finale de Jefferson. Cependant, il est permis de spéculer que les arguments de Du Pont ont atteint, à un certain point au moins, leur objectif.

Le fait que Du Pont emploie tout son arsenal rhétorique, avec lequel Jefferson est familier, montre le sérieux de l'affaire. Car, d'un côté, les deux interlocuteurs s'entendent forcément étant donné qu'ils appartiennent aux mêmes réseaux sociaux des Lumières et partagent leurs valeurs.[38] Mais, de l'autre, ces mêmes valeurs, en se concrétisant et en se particularisant, entrent dans la délibération comme contestables.[39] Comment trancher entre volontés souveraines? Comment savoir lequel des deux droits prévaut, celui de la France ou celui des Etats-Unis sur un même objet, ici fort considérable, la Louisiane, vu son histoire, son étendue et sa position stratégique? Toute l'argumentation déployée consiste alors à détacher la question du niveau de la décision souveraine de l'entrée en guerre, pour l'attacher à une logique de type utilitariste du calcul des coûts et des bénéfices d'un traité conclu pacifiquement.

Pour opérer ce changement et persuader Jefferson, nous avons vu Du Pont mettre en scène une suite de personnes fictives: le général, le conseiller d'Etat, le philosophe, le patriote et enfin l'honnête homme. Or, ce dispositif fait partie de la culture commune qui unit nos deux protagonistes. Il suit, dans ses lignes générales, la division quadripartite des devoirs, ou offices, ou rôles sociaux de la tradition cicéronienne, décrite principalement dans *De officiis* (1, 30-32). On sait que Jefferson appréciait l'héritage cicéronien.[40] Or, au dix-huitième siècle, la tradition cicéronienne fait partie de la science politique du droit naturel, dans la mesure où elle est reprise dans la théorie des entités morales de Pufendorf dans le *De jure naturae et gentium* (1, 1).[41] Ce dernier ouvrage se trouve, en traduction française, dans une liste

---

38. Wladimir Berelowitch et Michel Porret, 'Introduction', dans *Réseaux de l'esprit en Europe des Lumières au XIXᵉ siècle*, éd. Wladimir Berelowitch et Michel Porret (Genève, 2009), p.11-28 (13-14).

39. Voir C. Perelman, *L'Empire rhétorique*, p.47.

40. Voir Paul A. Rahe, 'Cicero and the classical republican legacy in America', dans *Thomas Jefferson, the classical world and early America*, éd. Peter S. Onuf et Nicholas B. Cole (Charlottesville, VA, et Londres, 2011), p.248-64 (249).

41. Les entités morales signalent chez Pufendorf les traits moraux, naturels (d'origine divine), aussi bien que d'institution humaine, que nous assignons aux personnes et aux choses et qui façonnent nos attitudes envers elles (obéissance, respect, etc.). Ce sont des schémas d'évaluation subjective mais qui participent à

que Jefferson prépare pour l'éducation de son neveu en 1785.[42] De son côté, Du Pont adhère à une version jusnaturaliste, comme tous les physiocrates, inspirée surtout de Locke.[43] On en trouve une belle formulation en 1767, dans une petite somme intitulée *Vrais principes du droit naturel*, qui clôt le commentaire d'un ouvrage de l'écrivain Hubner sur l'histoire du droit naturel: 'La Loi naturelle termine, en un seul mot, toutes ces vaines discussions, en prononçant que c'est toujours non seulement une *injustice*; mais encore une *absurdité pernicieuse* pour les Nations en corps, tout de même que pour les Hommes en particulier, de chercher son avantage dans le préjudice d'autrui.'[44]

Il faut bien noter la fonction attribuée aux verdicts du droit naturel, qui coïncident souvent avec la fameuse 'évidence' des physiocrates. Celle-ci est censée, chez eux, achever toute discussion entre intérêts divergents, par l'admission unanime de la vérité.[45] Mais la théorie, ou plutôt la constellation des théorèmes associés au droit naturel, fonctionne aussi comme un mode de réflexion autorisant des représentations des affaires politiques et sociales sous un angle universaliste.[46] Il permet alors de comparer les arguments de différentes prétentions particularistes dans une perspective plus générale, fondée sur des règles pratiques de validité universelle. Ce même raisonnement est saillant chez Jefferson dans son texte le plus fameux, la *Déclaration d'indépendance* des Etats-Unis de 1776.[47] Or, pour Hannah Arendt, l'influence du droit naturel sur la *Déclaration d'indépendance* américaine

---

      un ordre normatif objectif (comme un titre, une charge, etc.). Voir Heiki Haara, *Pufendorf's theory of sociability: passions, habits and social order* (Cham, 2018), p.24.

42. Dans sa lettre à Walker Maury, du 19 août 1785, *The Papers of Thomas Jefferson*, t.8, éd. Julian P. Boyd (Princeton, NJ, 1953), p.411.

43. Catherine Larrère, *L'Invention de l'économie au XVIIIᵉ siècle: du droit naturel à la physiocratie* (Paris, 1992), p.195-204.

44. *Ephémérides du citoyen* 3 (1767), p.179 (l'emploi de l'italique est celui de la source).

45. 'L'accomplissement de la loi naturelle repose donc objectivement sur la nécessité physique de l'Ordre établi par le Créateur et subjectivement sur l'évidence qui contrait l'intérêt au nom de l'intérêt sensible [...] Voilà la réalité et le sens de la morale dans le système physiocratique: elle est l'instrument de la réalisation physique de l'ordre qui jaillit de la loi naturelle. Ordre désirable à l'homme éclairé parce qu'il réalise le plus grand bonheur de celui qui s'y soumet.' André Vachet, *L'Idéologie libérale: l'individu et sa propriété* (Paris, 1970), p.279.

46. Daniel Chernillo, *The Natural law foundations of modern social theory: a quest for universality* (Cambridge, 2013), p.5.

47. Philippe Raynaud, *Trois révolutions de la liberté: Angleterre, Amérique, France* (Paris, 2009), p.148.

266 *Alfred Steinhauer*

est limitée,[48] car elle considère que Jefferson 'ne savait pas de façon très précise de quelle sorte de bonheur il parlait quand il faisait de cette "quête du bonheur" un des droits inaliénables de l'homme'.[49] Or, comme le montre Annie Léchenet, ce bonheur se lie étroitement avec une idée jusnaturaliste d'indépendance socio-économique qui fonde sa morale républicaine.[50] Si Arendt s'insurge contre le droit naturel, c'est qu'elle le considère comme un socle normatif ayant trahi ses promesses, et non pas comme un type de rationalisation politique.

Et l'unité de ces principes, qui fonde la multiplicité des discours jusnaturalistes, est une unité non pas de contenu mais de méthode. La particularité du droit naturel moderne est toute méthodique, comme le soulignent tant Michel Villey que Mario Scattola.[51]

---

48. Il convient ici de citer Arendt *in extenso*: 'Quand Jefferson et les hommes de la Révolution Américaine – à l'exception peut-être de John Adams – émettaient leurs généralités, la vérité de leur expérience se manifestait rarement. Certains, il est vrai, vitupéraient "les absurdités de Platon", mais cela n'empêchait pas que leur pensée fût prédéterminée par "l'esprit brumeux" du philosophe Grec plutôt que par leurs propres expériences chaque fois qu'ils essayaient de s'exprimer dans un langage conceptuel. [...] Ainsi la grandeur de la Déclaration de l'Indépendance ne doit rien à sa conception d'une loi naturelle' (H. Arendt, *Essai sur la révolution*, p.186-87).

49. H. Arendt, *Essai sur la révolution*, p.184.

50. Annie Léchenet, 'Le républicanisme américain: Jefferson (1743-1826) et la poursuite du bonheur', dans *Histoire raisonnée de la philosophie morale et politique*, t.2: *Des Lumières à nos jours*, éd. Alain Callé et autres (Paris, 2007), p.133-38 (138). On pourrait objecter que pour Jefferson la propriété des terres reste une institution civile (p.134), tandis que pour les physiocrates elle est une institution découlant du droit naturel. Il faut bien mettre en relief ici deux choses: d'abord ce point, longuement débattu déjà en France entre Du Pont et Turgot, n'a pas suffi à faire éclater le cadre jusnaturaliste, articulé autour de l'individu égal aux autres dans son droit de la conservation de soi (Grotius, *De iure praedae commentarius*, chap.2; Hobbes, *De cive*, chap.2.1; Pufendorf, *De officio hominis et civis*, chap.3.2; Spinoza, *Tractatus theologico-politicus*, chap.16; Locke, *Second treatise*, chap.2, §6). Ensuite, l'institution de la propriété, en Amérique post-coloniale, dans la mesure où elle inclut la possession d'esclaves, ne saurait être discutée dans ce cadre.

51. Michel Villey, *La Formation de la pensée juridique moderne: cours d'histoire de la philosophie du droit* (Paris, 1975), p.573-74. 'This methodological and epistemological complex was the real foundation of modern natural law, and aside from some general speculative hypotheses, like the state of nature, it was common to all currents of modern natural law'; Mario Scattola, '*Scientia iuris* and *ius naturae*: the jurisprudence of the Holy Roman Empire in the seventeenth and eighteenth centuries', dans *A History of the philosophy of law in the civil law world, 1600-1900*, éd. Damiano Canale et autres (Dodrecht, 2009), p.1-41 (22).

En insistant plutôt sur la forme de rationalité propre au droit naturel, on peut en souligner un second aspect, à savoir la liaison qu'elle établit entre le politique et l'économique, qui, dans notre cas, permet de balancer les types d'action à considérer: guerre ou paix. Ce trait est notamment présent dans la conception physiocratique du droit naturel dont Du Pont fut l'un des promoteurs: il forme le socle d'une science sociale totale, ambition chère à la physiocratie.[52] Ainsi, ce discours permet également, à un troisième niveau, de lier les discussions d'ordre politique à une morale du calcul des intérêts, unissant le normatif et le pragmatique. De cette manière, Du Pont présente l'enfreinte du droit des traités entre les Etats-Unis, l'Espagne et la France que serait la conquête de la Louisiane comme une faute aussi bien morale qu'économique.

C'est ainsi qu'on arrive au troisième élément-clé émanant de la tradition rationaliste liée au droit naturel, un cadre de négociations interindividuelles entre Etats, préfigurant le droit international. L'Etat est conçu comme un individu politique, et ses droits sont les mêmes que ceux de l'individu dans l'état de nature, des droits dont l'extension est virtuellement illimitée, ou plutôt limitée par ceux des autres puissances.[53] La proposition de Du Pont suggère ainsi une transaction entre les Etats-Unis et la France, sur le modèle d'un marchandage entre individus: 'La France vous demandera le plus qu'elle pourra, vous offrirez le moins que vous pourrez.'[54] Et, dans la lettre du 12 mai 1802, il présente le prix de l'acquisition comme une aubaine: 'Vous pourrez payer vos dettes en moins de quinze ans. Quand, pour acquérir Nouvelle Orléans et la Floride, et pour le faire sans guerre, vous devrez reculer cette époque de trois ou quatre années, vous aurez fait un excellent marché, même pécuniairement.'[55]

Entrant dans la logique de Du Pont, même s'il laisse encore planer le spectre d'un éventuel conflit, Jefferson invoque aussi la pauvreté financière des Etats-Unis: 'Nous sommes un peuple agricole, pauvres en argent, et déjà fortement endettés.'[56] En outre, il insiste sur

---

52. A. Skornicki, *L'Economiste*, p.238.
53. Mario Scattola, 'Before and after natural law: models of natural law in ancient and modern times', dans *Early modern natural law theories: contexts and strategies in the early Enlightenment*, éd. Timothy J. Hochstrasser et Peter Schröder (Dordrecht, 2003), p.1-30 (23), et M. Villey, *La Formation de la pensée juridique moderne*.
54. G. Chinard, *The Correspondence*, p.53.
55. G. Chinard, *The Correspondence*, p.55.
56. 'We are an agricultural people, poor in money, and owing great debts' (lettre du 1er février 1803, G. Chinard, *The Correspondence*, p.67).

l'honnêteté de ses démarches et souligne la candeur de ses propos: 'Vous voyez, mon cher ami, avec quelle franchise je communique avec vous sur ce sujet, que je ne vous cache rien, et que j'essaie de tourner notre amitié privée vers le bien de nos pays respectifs. Et quelle fin plus noble peut avoir une amitié personnelle que de maintenir la paix entre deux nations.'[57]

Quelques mois après, le traité de la cession étant signé, Jefferson, dans la dernière lettre concernant le sujet, tient à remercier Du Pont de ses services:

> De ma part et de la part de mon pays, je vous remercie pour les aides que vous lui avez données, et je vous félicite d'avoir vécu pour nous donner ces aides dans une transaction pleine des remerciements des millions d'hommes pas encore nés, et qui vont marquer la face d'une partie du globe si étendue que maintenant composent les Etats-Unis de l'Amérique.[58]

En effet, la conclusion heureuse de cette affaire double presque l'étendue des Etats-Unis, qui recouvrent désormais une partie considérable du continent nord-américain.

***

En guise de conclusion, quelques remarques doivent être formulées. On peut d'abord regretter que la correspondance de Du Pont ne soit pas davantage mise en valeur. Par ses nombreuses activités politiques, administratives, journalistiques et privées, il reste un acteur et un témoin de première importance de l'histoire de l'âge des révolutions. Naviguant entre les postes de journaliste, de prosélyte de Quesnay, de conseiller de princes, comme le margrave de Bade,[59] et

---

57. 'You see, my good friend, with what frankness I communicate with you on this subject; that I hide nothing from you, and I am endeavoring to turn our private friendship to the good of our respective countries. And can private friendship ever answer a nobler end than by keeping two nations at peace' (G. Chinard, *The Correspondence*, p.68).

58. 'For myself and my country, I thank you for the aids you have given in it; and I congratulate you on having lived to give those aids in a transaction replete with blessings to unborn millions of men, and which will mark the face of a portion on the globe so extensive as that which now composes the United States of America' (lettre du 1er novembre 1803, G. Chinard, *The Correspondence*, p.80).

59. Thérence Carvalho, *La Physiocratie dans l'Europe des Lumières: circulation et réception d'un modèle de réforme de l'ordre juridique et social* (Paris, 2020).

de ministres comme Vergennes, ardent propagateur du libre-échange, de la rationalisation de l'administration et de la taxation, de la liberté des Américains, Pierre-Samuel Du Pont de Nemours a développé une volumineuse correspondance dont la publication complète serait d'un intérêt considérable pour l'histoire des Lumières françaises et transatlantiques.

Ensuite, en ce qui concerne l'histoire des idées, non seulement la sociabilité des Lumières contient-elle des idées et un consensus théorique, mais elle produit aussi des effets pratiques, comme le confirme la recherche récente. La sociabilité est en effet un terrain dans lequel s'organise la diffusion des idées,[60] s'articule le fonctionnement d'espaces stratégiques sociaux[61] ou enfin, comme nous espérons l'avoir montré, s'effectue la discussion des grandes questions de haute politique éclairée. C'est le lieu où les valeurs propres aux Lumières sont précisées et débattues, en se matérialisant, ou pas, dans les faits.[62] En établissant des conditions de confiance non seulement nationales mais aussi transnationales, les Lumières seraient alors cruciales pour la formation d'un système international de droit public.

Finalement, et ce dernier point mérite davantage de considération, nous ne pouvons qu'estimer la contribution du droit naturel en tant que fondement d'une logique évaluative opératoire unissant les sphères du public et du privé, du local et de l'universel, mais aussi séparant les nouvelles entités politiques victorieuses qui émergent sur les ruines des sociétés traditionnelles. Ces entités, l'individu et l'Etat, apparaissent sur une base, multiforme dans ses aspects mais unie sur les principes et la méthode, qui est en grande partie empruntée à la philosophie du droit naturel moderne, laquelle véhicule les valeurs capitales de la tradition juridique occidentale, comme l'a décrit Richard Berman.[63] Il faut également suivre le chemin emprunté par les traditions de la civilité républicaine, comme l'a démontré J. G. A. Pocock. On voit alors, au-delà du jeu politique auquel s'adonnent nos deux interlocuteurs, se profiler un socle normatif complexe, axé sur des valeurs

---

60. A. Skornicki, *L'Economiste*, p.285.
61. Antoine Lilti, 'Sociabilité mondaine et réseaux intellectuels: les salons au XVIIIe siècle', dans *Réseaux de l'esprit*, éd. W. Berelowitch et M. Porret, p.89-104 (96).
62. *Républiques sœurs: le Directoire et la Révolution atlantique*, éd. Pierre Serna (Rennes, 2009); Manuela Albertone, *National identity and the agrarian republic: the transatlantic commerce of ideas between America and France (1750-1830)* (Farnham, 2014); M. Albertone et A. De Francesco, *Rethinking the Atlantic world*.
63. Harold J. Berman, *Law and revolution: the formation of the western legal tradition* (Cambridge, MA, et Londres, 1983), p.12.

mais aussi sur des stratégies d'évaluation du risque géopolitique, qui permet la résolution pacifique de leur différend souverainiste.

Pour terminer, à la suite de la discussion qui a suivi la communication de cet article, Mme Albertone a évoqué l'existence d'un texte de Du Pont sur la *Déclaration de Virginie* commenté par le marquis de Mirabeau. Il semble que la liaison des penseurs physiocrates avec l'Amérique et spécialement avec les idées de Jefferson s'inscrive dans la longue durée, mais cela nécessiterait une autre enquête avec un horizon différent. Quant à Mme Alimento, elle a fait remarquer qu'il faudrait plutôt distinguer les niveaux normatif et pragmatique dans la proposition de Du Pont. Nous montrons, dans la version finale, comment la liaison de ces deux est établie. En effet, nous pensons que ce qui importe, c'est la portée universaliste du discours jusnaturaliste qui est crucial pour l'élaboration d'une base de politique raisonnée. On ne devrait certainement pas surestimer l'impact de ce discours sur le cours des événements; mais on ne devrait pas non plus oublier que sa multivalence, la souplesse que cette rationalité autorise, en permettant de passer du militaire à l'économique et du moral au politique dans un cadre discursif et axiologique cohérent, fondé sur la liberté et l'égalité statutaire entre les personnes, a permis un vrai progrès politique qui est loin d'avoir épuisé sa dynamique. Ceci d'autant plus qu'apparaissent les risques d'un monde fragmenté entre des logiques et des valeurs mutuellement incompatibles.

Du Pont de Nemours: colonies, slavery and economic growth

SIMONA PISANELLI

University of Salento

In the second half of the eighteenth century, the issue of slavery was so complex that different opinions about it were to be expected. From a general and long-term point of view, the Enlightenment authors considered it necessary to abolish slavery to build a fairer and more progressive social order. However, while agreeing with its abolition, the same authors tended to argue – sometimes even bitterly – about the policies to adopt, given their forecasts on the short-term effects of the abolition of slavery.

Diderot, Rousseau, Voltaire and, above all, Montesquieu[1] – who officially launched the debate – are only some of the thinkers who insisted on the importance of man's emancipation and on the use of free labour in order to modernise the working of the economy. Among them, Du Pont de Nemours had an important place. He explicitly 'defendit les gens de couleur',[2] speaking about colonialism and trying to demonstrate that slavery was not economically profitable. Du Pont's conviction was so strong that he could not avoid arguing with Turgot, who did not share his ideas on the matter.

This article aims to deal with the following issues:

1. Denis Diderot, 'Supplément au *Voyage* de Bougainville', in *Opuscules philosophiques et littéraires* (Paris, De l'imprimerie de Chevet, 1796), p.187-270. Jean-Jacques Rousseau, *Du contrat social, ou Principes du droit politique* (Amsterdam, Chez Marc Michel Rey, 1762). Voltaire, *L'A, B, C: dix-sept dialogues traduits de l'anglais de Monsieur Huet*, ed. Roland Mortier and Christophe Paillard, in *Œuvres complètes de Voltaire*, vol.65A (Oxford, 2011), p.169-348; Voltaire, *L'Homme aux quarante écus*, ed. Brenda M. Bloesch, in *Œuvres complètes de Voltaire*, vol.66 (Oxford, 1999), p.211-409. Charles-Louis de Secondat de Montesquieu, *De l'esprit des lois*, vol.1 (Geneva, Barillot & fils, 1748).
2. A. Boullée, 'Dupont de Nemours', in *Annuaire de la Société Montyon et Franklin pour l'an 1835*, no.3: *Bulletin des hommes utiles* (Paris, 1835), p.147-50 (149).

271

272   *Simona Pisanelli*

- how Du Pont fitted into the context of the debate on slavery;
- why Du Pont considered wage labour more productive than slave labour;
- why, although Turgot was one of the men Du Pont most valued (both for his scientific analyses and for his human qualities), the two came to a disagreement on slavery.

i. Du Pont and the debate on slavery

As the literature shows, almost all the authors involved in the debate about slavery considered its economic aspects, although they placed different degrees of importance on them. For this reason, before dealing with Du Pont's analyses of the economic consequences of the employment of slaves in sugar plantations,[3] it seems useful to sum up the cultural environment in which the debate in favour of or against abolition developed.

For introductory purposes, it is useful to mention Montesquieu's reflections on slavery as an essential reference point, especially from a legislative perspective. His interest in colonial issues (and slavery) lasted until his later years, and he always thought that, 'avant d'être en mesure de simplement *penser* l'abolition de la traite et de l'esclavage, quitte à la refuser ou la différer, il fallait s'être pleinement convaincu de leur caractère illégitime.'[4]

In book 15 of his *Esprit des lois*, expressly devoted to slavery, Montesquieu never discusses in detail the economic aspects of the issue. However, in chapter 5 of the same book, 'De l'esclavage des nègres',[5] he brings together 'les fausses doctrines économiques et

---

3. As is well-known, France and Great Britain used the capital invested in the West Indies to experiment with the plantation economy. A single entity, owning the land and slaves, ran an economic unit characterised by monoculture. Of the different crops, sugar cane was the one that most characterised the European colonies in the Caribbean, so much so that historians have spoken of a true 'sugar revolution'; Philip D. Curtin, *The Rise and fall of the plantation complex: essays in Atlantic history* (Cambridge, 1999), p.73-85; Russell R. Menard, *Sweet negotiations: sugar, slavery, and plantation agriculture in early Barbados* (Charlottesville, VA, 2006), p.123-36; Patrizia Delpiano, *La schiavitù in età moderna* (Bari, 2009), p.26; Maxine Berg and Pat Hudson, *Slavery, capitalism and the industrial revolution* (Cambridge, 2023), p.27-29.
4. On Montesquieu's pioneering role in the fight against slavery, see Jean Ehrard, *Lumières et esclavage: l'esclavage colonial et l'opinion publique en France au XVIIIᵉ siècle* (Brussels, 2008), p.141, 151.
5. Montesquieu, *De l'esprit*, p.389-90.

les préjugés de l'orgueil européen pour [...] montrer la sottise et la cruauté' of slavery.[6] He sarcastically demolished the most common preconceived notions used to justify the employment of slaves in the American colonies. For instance, he rejected the idea that the price of sugar would be higher, due to the employment of free workers rather than slaves: the latter received in exchange only enough to eat and dress themselves.

Montesquieu supported the abolitionist line, but his well-known realism pushed him to propose a strategy of gradually freeing the slaves. According to him, the legislative activity of republican nations and democratic countries should pay special attention to the consequences, especially in the short term, of the liberation of a large number of slaves. Too many freed slaves could indeed constitute a 'multitude de nouveaux pauvres',[7] becoming a burden for society. As he admitted, a philosopher can only propose *ex ante* and in the abstract 'les règlements qu'une bonne république doit faire là-dessus', but it is clear that everything depends on the specific situations of each country. Thus, he proposed progressive emancipation, in order to guarantee the maintenance of the social balance: 'l'Etat peut affranchir toutes les années, un certain nombre d'esclaves qui par leur âge, leur santé, leur industrie peuvent se procurer les moyens de vivre', to avoid the risk of becoming the new poor. But, in order to 'guerir le mal dans sa racine', preventing new forms of slavery from being surreptitiously established, it was necessary for more and more free workers to replace the freed slaves in the kinds of work previously carried out by the latter.[8] As a result, Montesquieu highlighted the social effects of generally accepted economic prejudices and made realistic proposals for a progressive solution to the problem of slavery.

In the same years when Montesquieu was discussing the illegitimacy of slavery, physiocracy put forward its proposals in terms of economic reforms, 'celebrating agriculture as the sole source of riches, free international trade over monopoly trade, and free labour over slave labour'.[9] All physiocrats agreed on the importance of free work: only

6. Russell Parsons Jameson, *Montesquieu et l'esclavage: étude sur les origines de l'opinion antiesclavagiste en France au XVIIIe siècle* (Paris, 1911), p.292. See also Ehrard, *Lumières et esclavage*, p.151.

7. Montesquieu, *Pensées et fragments inédits de Montesquieu*, ed. G. Gounouilhou, vol.1 (Bordeaux, 1899), p.148.

8. Montesquieu, *De l'esprit*, p.392-94.

9. Pernille Røge, *Economistes and the reinvention of empire: France in the Americas and Africa, c.1750-1802* (Cambridge, 2019), p.4.

the employment of free labourers in agriculture ensures a *produit net*, since wage work stimulates the creativity of labourers. By promoting technical progress, wage work guarantees an increase in productivity and, as a consequence, in national wealth. Nevertheless, not all physiocrats linked the indispensability of free labour to the abolition of slavery, and some of them had an ambiguous approach to the issue.

On the one hand, the physiocratic leader Quesnay never directly dealt with the issue of slavery, though it was evident that it violated the 'abstract idea of the natural right of all to everything'[10] that he placed at the basis of the equivalence between 'natural laws' and 'human laws'.[11] Driven by his prudent attitude, Quesnay simply remained silent on the matter.[12] Other supporters of free labour were forced to find ways to preserve – or rather reorganise – slave labour in the colonies because of their political responsibilities. Among these, it is worth mentioning Le Mercier de La Rivière and Pierre Poivre, intendants of Martinique and Ile-de-France respectively.[13]

On the other hand, Du Pont was one of the period's most coherent authors in fighting slavery. From an ethical point of view, his position was not particularly different from that of other Enlightenment thinkers (who considered slavery responsible for general moral degradation and a deep distortion of social relations). As far as the economic effects of slavery are concerned, Du Pont's analysis was detailed and profound, since he put the relationship between slavery and the economy at the centre of his thinking, emphasising the role of free labour. His aim was to demonstrate to both individuals and governments of European countries that using slaves on colonial plantations was not at all as profitable as most of them believed.[14] To pursue this goal, he used the 'science de l'Economie politique [qui]

10. François Quesnay, 'Le droit naturel', in *Œuvres économiques complètes et autres textes*, ed. Christine Théré *et al.*, 2 vols (Paris, 2005), vol.1, p.111-23.

11. Simona Pisanelli, 'Political power vs "natural laws": physiocracy and slavery', *History of economic thought and policy* 6:1 (2017), p.67-85 (69-73).

12. Alain Clément, 'Du bon et du mauvais usage des colonies: politique coloniale et pensée économique française au XVIIIᵉ siècle', *Cahiers d'économie politique / Papers in political economy* 56:1 (2009), p.101-27.

13. On Le Mercier de La Rivière, see Florence Gauthier, 'Le Mercier de La Rivière et les colonies d'Amérique', *Revue française d'histoire des idées politiques* 20:2 (2004), p.37-59. On the different ways in which the two intendants managed slavery in the colonies, see Pisanelli, 'Political power vs "natural laws"', p.73-83.

14. Also Mirabeau insisted on proving that free labour is more productive than servile labour; Pierre Le Masne, 'La colonisation et l'esclavage vus par les physiocrates', *L'Economie politique* 71:3 (2016), p.101-12.

démontre chaque jour ces principes à ceux qui la cultivent; et c'est parce qu'elle les démontre rigoureusement, qu'elle est une Science; et c'est parce que ces principes mènent directement au bonheur de tous les hommes, et sont conformes à la dignité de notre espèce, qu'elle est une Science respectable'.[15]

This science, if properly interpreted, suggested that the entrepreneur – who wants to achieve significant results – should invest in wage labour[16] according to completely different criteria from those underlying the institution of slavery. From the pages of the *Ephémérides du citoyen*, Du Pont led a real information campaign on the damage that slavery was causing to the economy and social organisation of the country, also making some proposals to overcome it.[17] The next section will focus on Du Pont's commentaries on Saint-Lambert's short novel *Ziméo*[18] and Jean-François Butini' *Lettres africaines*.[19] Although neither Saint-Lambert nor Butini visited the West Indies and thus had direct experience of slave life,[20] their works offered the editor of the *Ephémérides* an opportunity to develop a

15. Pierre-Samuel Du Pont de Nemours, 'Ziméo, ou de l'esclavage des nègres par Jean-François de Saint-Lambert', in *Ephémérides du citoyen, ou Bibliothèque raisonnée des sciences morales et politiques* 6 (1771), part 2, p.178-246 (218-19).

16. It should also be noted that Du Pont suggested a policy of 'forts salaires': 'Veux-tu t'enrichir? Respecte les droits de tes subalternes, excite-les au travail par de forts salaires, ne sois pas seulement juste envers eux, sois bienfaisant, sois noble, et ne crains point de perdre ce que tu confieras à leur activité, qui te le rendra toujours avec usure' (Du Pont, 'Ziméo', p.220-21).

17. From the pages of the *Ephémérides*, the abbé Baudeau also argued with supporters of slavery.

18. Saint-Lambert (1716-1803) belonged to the first generation of ideologues who made an important contribution to the planning of political and social reforms. See François Picavet, *Les Idéologues: essai sur l'histoire des idées et des théories scientifiques, philosophiques, religieuses, etc. en France depuis 1789* (Paris, 1891), p.144-57; Sergio Moravia, *Il tramonto dell'illuminismo: filosofia e politica nella società francese (1770-1810)* (1968; Rome and Bari, 1986), p.47-48. Saint-Lambert's main work is the *Poème des saisons*, an example of 'didactic poetry' used in the second half of the eighteenth century to address important questions in the history of ideas (Moravia, *Il tramonto dell'illuminismo*, p.62). This is also the aim of his novel *Ziméo*.

19. Jean-François Butini (1747-1805), a lawyer, was a member of the Assemblée nationale in 1793 and of the Comité and Conseil législatif in 1794-1795. In addition to the *Lettres africaines* (1771), he published the *Traité du luxe* (1774) and a *Projet de code civil* (1796).

20. *Fictions coloniales du XVIIIe siècle: Ziméo, Lettres africaines, Adonis, ou le Bon Nègre, anecdote coloniale*, ed. Youmna Charara (Paris, 2005), p.8.

276 *Simona Pisanelli*

more complete and complex argument about the economic aspects of slavery.[21]

ii. Servile work and free work: from inefficiency to the spread of scientific progress in the economy

In his *Ziméo*, Saint-Lambert suggested moral motivations in favour of the abolition of slavery. Such motivations were shared by Du Pont, who agreed with the main message of the novel: African peoples were more backward than European peoples only with reference to their scientific and technological capabilities, not in relation to attitudes of the mind. In fact, Africans lacked two important instruments: (a) the compass, which, 'en facilitant les voyages, nous fait partager les lumières de tous les lieux'; (b) the press, which 'nous a rendu propre l'esprit de tous les âges'.[22] However, Europeans themselves discovered both of them rather late and only by chance. Therefore, it would be enough to gift them to Africans and to all those people who still did not know them, and all of humanity would benefit.

These reflections, very close to those of Montesquieu, confirmed the general attention that Enlightenment thinkers favourable to abolition paid to the moral aspects of the issue. Nevertheless, as mentioned earlier, Du Pont improved his reflections, shifting the focus to the economic problem: 'Mr. de Saint-Lambert est un poète sublime' but 'nous sommes des calculateurs, non pas froids, mais sévères.' In addition, 'les gens que nous avons à persuader ne sont pas moins sensibles au calcul de leur intérêt qu'au tableau de leurs devoirs.'[23]

Du Pont aimed to demonstrate to the slave-owners that the use of force would not guarantee the maximum level of productivity of the slaves.[24] On the contrary, they would have achieved nothing or 'peu de chose', which 'lui coûterait cent fois plus qu'il ne vaut'.[25] Each citizen, convinced that he was pursuing his own interests, ended up causing problems both to himself and to his society, because of his ignorance of the fundamental principles of political economy:

---

21. Caroline Oudin-Bastide and Philippe Steiner, *Calcul et morale: coûts de l'esclavage et valeur de l'émancipation (XVIIIᵉ-XIXᵉ siècle)* (Paris, 2015), p.38-39, 45-46.
22. Jean-François de Saint-Lambert, *Ziméo*, in Du Pont, 'Ziméo', p.211.
23. Du Pont, 'Ziméo', p.216-17.
24. Oudin-Bastide and Steiner, *Calcul et morale*, p.42-43.
25. Du Pont, 'Ziméo', p.221.

Du Pont de Nemours: colonies, slavery and economic growth   277

> Les particuliers qui ont des esclaves comme les gouvernements qui les tolèrent [...] croient que c'est une grande économie; que le travail des esclaves auxquels on ne paie ni gages, ni salaires, est à bien plus bas prix que ne pourrait être celui d'hommes libres [...] enfin, que si l'on employait ceux-ci à la culture de nos colonies, le sucre serait trop cher.[26]

According to Du Pont, the investment in slaves is a bad investment:

> Car si l'on tient compte des frais d'achat des nègres, de la nécessité d'amortir rapidement cette dépense de premier établissement, en raison de la faible durée de la vie des esclaves, de la mauvaise qualité de leur travail, des frais que leur surveillance exige,[27] on trouve un taux de salaires tellement élevé qu'on est à peu près sûr d'avoir toujours des ouvriers libres pour le même prix sans faire violence à personne.[28]

This gross miscalculation could have been avoided if greed had not blinded the owners of the plantations and, what is worse, the governments, that uncritically accepted their views.

According to Du Pont's meticulous calculations,[29] published in his commentary on Saint-Lambert's *Ziméo*, the cost of employing each slave amounted to 420 *livres*.[30] Du Pont asked why the same work could not be done by poor Europeans (20 to 25 million of them), who would have been willing to work in the American plantations, improving their miserable condition. Du Pont, who was aware of the slaver-owners' view, rhetorically anticipated the answer that they would use to justify the continuation of slavery: 'On nous dira que les blancs ne pourraient pas travailler sous le climat brûlant des Antilles.'[31]

The question had already been a subject of discussion since 1748, the year of the publication of *De l'esprit des lois*. Montesquieu had suggested that the legislator should intervene in order to correct 'the

26. Du Pont, 'Ziméo', p.217.
27. Du Pont explained more explicitly what he meant when he talked about 'frais de surveillance' of slaves: he was referring to the need 'd'avoir sur un petit nombre de nègres, un autre nègre oisif, pour lutter à coups de fouet contre la paresse inhérente à tout esclave, et qui est son premier moyen de se venger du maître qui l'opprime' (Du Pont, 'Ziméo', p.225).
28. Du Pont quoted in Gustave Schelle, *Du Pont de Nemours et l'école physiocratique* (Paris, 1888), p.106.
29. Oudin-Bastide and Steiner, *Calcul et morale*, p.40-41.
30. See the table in Du Pont, 'Ziméo', p.233-35.
31. Du Pont, 'Ziméo', p.236.

278 *Simona Pisanelli*

influence of physical environmental factors in the event that they lead to excesses. [...] When an excessive subordination of man to the natural influence of the environment upsets the balance, it is necessary to react starting from moral factors.'[32]

Du Pont's response to the hypothesis that only men of colour can survive by working in prohibitive climatic conditions is much more sarcastic. He reminds us that the origin of the colonies of the West Indies is due to the 'blancs de toutes les nations de l'Europe: *flibustiers* [...]; *boucaniers* [...], *planteurs* de tabac'. The white man not only did not suffer from the climatic conditions of the Antilles, but he also benefited from 'la vie la plus laborieuse et la plus dure'.[33]

Du Pont's reasoning appears very similar to the one Condorcet developed in his *Réflexions sur l'esclavage des nègres* (published in 1781 and reprinted in 1788). According to the latter, white and black human beings are similar in everything. Therefore, both of them are able to provide the same kind of work under the same conditions. In addition, Condorcet completed his discourse, dealing with the paradoxical position of people who stated that, due to the torrid climate of the American colonies, only black slaves would be able to work profitably on the plantations. Even in this case, Condorcet commented, it was not clear why blacks should work as slaves and not as wage workers.

Comparing the way Condorcet and Du Pont elaborated their

32. Sergio Cotta, 'Introduzione', in Montesquieu, *Lo spirito delle leggi*, vol.1 (Turin, 2005), p.7-30 (26) (my translation). See also Raymond Aron, *Le tappe del pensiero sociologico* (Milan, 1972). However, it was not enough simply to enact a new law to abolish slavery. To introduce such a far-reaching change without indicating the exact means necessary for a new social order would have been a serious mistake. In 1836, Charles Dain still noted that the process of economic and social reform required the contribution of science: the politician could ask the philosopher for his support in order to identify the most appropriate ways to free slaves. Like Montesquieu, Dain criticised the principle of absolute correspondence between 'loi naturelle' and 'loi positive': 'Croyez-vous à une Providence gouvernant le monde, ou n'y croyez-vous pas? Croyez-vous comme l'a écrit Buffon, à un système de lois établies par le Créateur pour la conservation des choses et le développement des êtres? Ou, encore mieux, croyez-vous que ces lois sont nécessaires, non pas établies, mais éternelles et incréées?' See Charles Dain, 'De l'abolition de l'esclavage, suivi d'un article de M. Fourier' (1836), in *Abolitionnistes de l'esclavage et réformateurs des colonies, 1820-1851: analyse et documents*, ed. Nelly Schmidt (Paris, 2000), p.633-44 (639-40). It was necessary to get rid of the institutions of the Old World to create new ones, adapted to the New World under construction.

33. Du Pont, 'Ziméo', p.237 (original emphasis).

abolitionist reflections, one might have the impression that – at least in one case – Du Pont's reasoning was less rigorous than Condorcet's. Du Pont seemed to hesitate momentarily in the building of his theory and to end up reacting to a prejudice with another prejudice, emphasising the physical and intellectual superiority of the European white man:[34]

> Il faut convenir d'une chose: l'homme blanc d'Europe, quand il est exercé par le travail du corps, est une des espèces les plus vivaces et le plus robustes que le Ciel ait placées sur la terre. *Il l'emporte à cet égard sur le nègre, sur l'asiatique Indien, et sur les naturels d'Amérique, même dans leur propre climat.* C'est donc un préjugé de croire qu'il ne pourroit soutenir en liberté le même travail que ceux-ci supportent dans les fers.[35]

But, despite this logical 'weakness', Du Pont continued his campaign, radically condemning slavery. According to him, Europeans committed a real crime by killing the natives and uprooting Africans from their continent, putting them to work on sugar-cane plantations in a country (America) which had physical characteristics that were unsuitable for this kind of crop. Instead, it would have been more useful to establish a peaceful relationship with the Africans, teaching them the techniques of processing sugar cane.[36] Then, both of them would have benefited from international trade.[37] On an ideal plane, assuming that Africans had freely determined to produce sugar and to maintain trade relations with Europeans, Du Pont's reasoning would have been legitimate and correct and, therefore, worthwhile. Nevertheless, on the practical level, Du Pont seemed to neglect a significant aspect in his economic analysis. In fact, while it is true that he suggested the employment of European agricultural workers in the colonies and made proposals in other domains to promote a higher rate of employability, it is also true that he did not establish a

---

34. See David Allen Harvey, 'Slavery on the balance sheet: Pierre-Samuel Dupont de Nemours and the physiocratic case for free labor', *Journal of the Western Society for French History* 42 (2014), http://hdl.handle.net/2027/spo.0642292.0042.008 (last accessed 10 December 2024).
35. Du Pont, 'Ziméo', p.237 (emphasis added).
36. Oudin-Bastide and Steiner, *Calcul et morale*, p.44.
37. Gilles Jacoud, 'L'esclavage colonial: une comparaison des approches de Say, Sismondi et des saint-simoniens', *Œconomia: history, methodology, philosophy* 6:3 (2016), p.363-402 (380).

280

Simona Pisanelli

rigorous programme to facilitate the re-employment of former slaves as free workers.[38]

Reviewing the *Lettres africaines* by Jean-François Butini (1771), Du Pont seemed to admit that his previous theoretical vision was not completely satisfactory, and he agreed with Butini, who considered that 'rendre la liberté aux nègres qui sont actuellement dans nos Colonies' and employing them as free labour 'seroit avantageux pour leurs maîtres actuels'.[39] Du Pont published Butini's entire letter, in which the author explained the advantages deriving from the use of freed slaves in the colonies. For the purpose of this article, it is enough to refer only to the sections that highlight the importance of education and technological progress in the work of former slaves in agriculture (and in handicrafts):

> Qu'on accorde une liberté absolue aux nègres, qu'on métamorphose les esclaves en artistes, en ouvriers, en manoeuvres, en domestiques, et je soutiens qu'on procurera le profit des maîtres, de l'Etat considéré sous le double rapport de Métropole et de Colonie, enfin celui des esclaves. [...] En usant de violence, [les maîtres] rencontrent à chaque pas [...] la résistance éternelle de la liberté. Imaginez à présent que les nègres sont libres, et voyez ces hommes qui rompoient un joug pésant [...], guidés sur-tout par l'espoir du gain, étaler les résultats de leur industrie. Aujourd'hui ils n'ont que des mains, *alors ils auront de l'intelligence et des yeux*. Aujourd'hui la plupart des terrains situés dans l'intérieur de l'Isle, sont condamnés à une stérilité éternelle [...]; *alors la plupart des terrains seront cultivés, parce que les charmes de la liberté et la certitude de trouver du travail, retiennent les manœuvres autour de leurs foyers*.[40]

Du Pont could only share Butini's prediction, since before him he had also stated that, through the daily improvement of methods, the freed slaves would be able to double their productivity:[41] the

---

38. Morever, the risk was to condemn the freed slaves to a partial enjoyment of their freedom, since they still lacked not only material, but also intellectual means typical of free men. As far as this aspect is concerned, see Condorcet's proposals of worthwhile solutions (progressive abolition of slavery, compensation for former slaves, education, etc.).

39. Pierre-Samuel Du Pont de Nemours, 'Lettres africaines, ou histoire de Phédima et d'Abensar par Mr. Butini', *Ephémérides du citoyen, ou Bibliothèque raisonnée des sciences morales et politiques* 8 (1771), part 2, p.68-118 (80).

40. Du Pont, 'Lettres africaines', p.87-88 (emphasis added).

41. Du Pont, 'Ziméo', p.239.

Du Pont de Nemours: colonies, slavery and economic growth   281

'esclave est inepte' only when 'il n'a aucun intérêt de perfectionner son intelligence.' In such a situation, the conflict between owners and slaves will continue because, through laziness, the slave reappropriates a tiny part of himself 'que le maître a volée en gros'. From this point of view, the slave will be 'dans un véritable état de guerre toujours subsistante' against his owner.[42]

The issue of slaves' 'laziness' was recurrent in the debate of the period. For instance, Condorcet rejected the idea of people of colour being lazy by character,[43] willing to work only if forced to do so in slavery:

> Il n'y a de peuples vraiment paresseux dans les nations civilisées, que ceux qui sont gouvernés de manière qu'il n'y aurait rien à gagner pour eux en travaillant davantage. Ce n'est ni au climat, ni au terrain, ni à la constitution physique, ni à l'esprit national qu'il faut attribuer la paresse de certains peuples; c'est aux mauvaises lois qui les gouvernent.[44]

A similar view can also be found in authors of the Scottish Enlightenment. According to Adam Smith, unlike wage workers, slaves rarely use their ingenuity to reduce their workload, and this happens for a very simple reason: 'Should a slave propose any improvement of this kind, his master would be very apt to consider the proposal as the suggestion of laziness, and of a desire to save his own labor at the master's expense. The poor slave, instead of reward

---

42. Du Pont, 'Ziméo', p.238. Pierre Poivre suggested a new 'humanitarian' policy as a possible way to improve the relationships between slaves and masters. If owners treated slaves better, the latter would see the former as protectors. Remaining faithful to them, the slaves would not hesitate to defend the owners' land as if it was their own property from any possible attempts at conquest, in times of both peace and war; Pierre Poivre, 'Discours aux habitants de l'Isle de France' (1767), in *Œuvres complettes de P. Poivre, intendant des isles de France et de Bourbon, correspondant de l'Académie des sciences, etc., précédées de sa vie, et accompagnées de notes* (Paris, Fuchs, 1797), p.199-232.

43. Condorcet had already rejected this hypothesis in his notes on Pascal's *Pensées*: 'On dit que les nègres sont paresseux: veut-on qu'ils trouvent du plaisir à travailler pour leurs tyrans? Ils sont bas, fourbes, traîtres, sans mœurs: eh bien, ils ont tous les vices des esclaves, et c'est la servitude qui les leur a donnés. Rendez-les libres, et plus près que vous de la nature, ils vaudront beaucoup mieux que vous.' Jean-Antoine-Nicolas de Caritat, marquis de Condorcet, *Eloge par Condorcet et pensées de Pascal* (Paris, 1832), p.104.

44. Jean-Antoine-Nicolas de Caritat, marquis de Condorcet, *Réflexions sur l'esclavage des nègres* (Paris, 2009), p.76. See also Montesquieu, *De l'esprit*.

282 *Simona Pisanelli*

would probably meet with much abuse, perhaps with some punishment.[45] Increasing productivity in the presence of slave labour is impossible, especially without an 'enlightened' administrator heading the productive process. In his *Notice sur la vie de P. Poivre* (1786), Du Pont took as an example the experience of Pierre Poivre, who was a successful 'Intendant des Isles de France et de Bourbon' (1767-1772). He was known for having imported a variety of rice requiring little irrigation from Cochinchina (a region of current Vietnam). Du Pont regretted that, 'après le départ de Poivre, la culture de ce grain si important ayant été *abandonnée aux esclaves nègres, qui l'arrosèrent comme l'autre riz*; l'espèce du riz sec, qui aurait pu, de cette colonie, passer en Europe, et qui devrait enrichir aujourd'hui nos provinces méridionales, fut détruite à l'Isle de France.' The negative consequences of the lack of labour specialisation also had an impact on the European economy: 'parmi les maux humains sans nombre que *l'esclavage et la stupidité qui en est la suite*, ont causés au genre humain, il faut encore compter celui-là.'[46] Slaves could not be blamed for such a failure, as they had not received the proper education and training in order to apply the most appropriate cultivation methods for particular crops.

In short, although 'l'arithmétique politique' seemed to be able to 'prouver que [...] des ouvriers libres ne coûteroient pas plus, seroient plus heureux, n'exposeroient point aux mêmes dangers, et feroient le double d'ouvrage',[47] many intellectuals had still not accepted these economic motivations and did not consider the abolition of slavery a priority.[48] Among them, curiously, Turgot – one of the greatest

---

45. Adam Smith, *An Inquiry into the nature and causes of the wealth of nations*, ed. R. H. Campbell and A. S. Skinner, 2 vols (Oxford, 1979), vol.2, p.545-1080 (684). See also Stefano Fiori, *Ordine, mano invisibile, mercato: una rilettura di Adam Smith* (Turin, 2001), p.188, and Akihito Matsumoto, 'Priestley and Smith against slavery', *The Kyoto economic review* 80:1 (2011), p.119-31 (126-27).
46. Pierre-Samuel Du Pont de Nemours, *Notice sur la vie de M. Poivre, chevalier de l'Ordre du roi, ancien intendant des Iles de France et de Bourbon* (Philadelphia, PA, and Paris, Chez Moutard, 1786), p.18-19 (emphasis added).
47. Du Pont, 'Ziméo', p.245-46.
48. The expression *arithmétique politique* was introduced by William Petty in England in the second half of the seventeenth century, but it spread throughout Europe, especially in France, in the eighteenth century. Here, contaminated by the encounter with the calculation of probabilities (and German descriptive statistics), *arithmétique politique* became a method of analysis for several Enlightenment thinkers. See Pierre Crépel, 'Arithmétique politique et population dans les métamorphoses de l'*Encyclopédie*', in *Arithmétique politique dans la France du XVIIIᵉ siècle*, ed. Thierry Martin (Paris, 2003), p.47-70 (47).

theorists of the *perfectionnement indéfini de l'homme* – continued to consider the persistence of slavery in the economy useful. The next section will focus on the reasons for the disagreement between Turgot and Du Pont, despite their lasting friendship and cooperation.

iii. The controversy between Du Pont and Turgot

It is well-known that Du Pont worked with Turgot for a long time. In 1769-1770, as editor of the *Ephémérides*, Du Pont published the latter's *Réflexions sur la formation et la distribution des richesses*. It was a schematic summing-up of the basics of political economy – 'une espèce de catéchisme économique'[49] – that Turgot had written in 1766, on the occasion of two Chinese students' visit to France. In it, Turgot explained how a country increases and distributes its wealth,[50] through one hundred fundamental proposals (commented on by Du Pont).

The passages of particular interest to us are those from paragraph 19 to paragraph 27, where Turgot analysed five different methods by which landowners could make their land profitable: (1) with wage workers, (2) with slaves, (3) transferring the product in exchange for rent, (4) partial colonisation (also called *métayage*), (5) rental (the latter method, although the most advantageous, only seemed possible in countries that were already rich, where farmers were able to anticipate agricultural investments).

In the original version of the *Réflexions*, Turgot devoted only paragraph 21 to the method of exploiting slaves. According to Gustave Schelle, who edited Turgot's complete works (1913-1923), the reference to the original version is very important, because of the sometimes significant modifications that Du Pont introduced in the following edition for the *Ephémérides*. Du Pont added two paragraphs on slavery, provoking a harsh reaction from Turgot, as their exchange of letters proves.

In order to highlight the different visions of Turgot and Du Pont on slavery, it seems useful to proceed by first indicating what Turgot

49. Léonce de Lavergne, *Les Economistes français du dix-huitième siècle* (Paris, 1870), p.238.
50. Condorcet – who was his faithful collaborator and biographer – defined this short but extremely valuable work by Turgot as 'le germe du traité sur la richesse des nations du célèbre Smith'; see Jean-Antoine-Nicolas de Caritat, marquis de Condorcet, 'Vie de M. Turgot' (1786), in *Œuvres de Condorcet*, ed. Arthur O'Connor and François Arago, vol.8.5 (Paris, 1847), p.5-233 (45).

284   *Simona Pisanelli*

wrote about the use of slaves in agriculture and then to report the additions made by Du Pont. Finally, it would be interesting to recall the complaints of Turgot, who firmly demanded that his friend restore the original version of the text or, if not, state explicitly that the author did not agree with the changes that the editor had introduced.

According to Turgot, the practice of employing slaves in agriculture dates back to the early days of society, when it was virtually impossible to find men willing to work the land in the service of others. Some more ferocious individuals used violence to force others to work, reducing them to slavery. Although self-proclaimed masters had deprived slaves of the opportunity to exercise their 'droits de l'humanité', they could not avoid providing them with at least what they needed to survive: it was not a matter of money to spend as they wished, but 'cette espèce de salaire est bornée au plus étroit nécessaire et à leur subsistance. Cette abominable coutume de l'esclavage a été autrefois universelle',[51] and it was still prevalent at the time of Turgot.

Nevertheless, Turgot was convinced that this custom was destined to stop with the disappearance of small nations, constantly at war among themselves. Indeed, wars produced slaves more than any other historical event. According to Turgot, after the birth of great nations like England, France and Spain, there was a radical change concerning the slavery issue. In fact, whatever wars they may wage, whatever prisoners they may capture, the quantity of slaves would never reach the same levels as in the past. In any case, the number of new slaves would be insufficient to satisfy the needs of the economy. In short, the slaves would be 'une bien faible ressource pour la culture de chacune des trois nations'.[52]

This is the content of paragraph 21 of Turgot's *Réflexions*, without taking into account the additions of Du Pont. The latter modified the text with his own considerations, but without warning the reader of the *Ephémérides* that they were not Turgot's reflections.

With reference to the origins of society, Du Pont did not describe uncritically the mechanism of recruiting men to cultivate the land

---

51. Anne-Robert-Jacques Turgot, *Circulaire aux officiers de police des villes (1727-1781)* (Paris, 1914), p.546-47. Here, the edition consulted is that of Estang because it provides a double version of the text: Turgot's original Réflexions and the modified one published by Du Pont, first in the *Ephémérides*, then in his edition of the *Œuvres de Turgot*. Estang took care to indicate in regular font the sentences by Turgot and in *italics* those by Du Pont.
52. Turgot, *Circulaire*, p.547.

Du Pont de Nemours: colonies, slavery and economic growth 285

instead of the owners, but talked about that age as 'temps d'ignorance et de férocité', in which the strongest men mercilessly massacred the defeated. The same was happening in that period with the 'sauvages d'Amérique': 'l'introduction de la culture adoucit un peu les mœurs' even if it did not completely correct them. Thus, the conquerors of the eighteenth century, instead of massacring prisoners, understood that it was more profitable to make them 'travailler la terre comme esclaves'.[53]

These modifications by Du Pont do not seem to significantly change Turgot's thinking. However, the publisher took the liberty of adding entire sentences to the original text, starting with the title of paragraph 23 of the *Réflexions*: 'Combien la culture exécutée par les esclaves est peu profitable et chère pour le maître et pour l'humanité'. Turgot had never expressed himself in terms of the benefit or damage of slavery from an economic point of view. All these reflections, like the following, are attributable to Du Pont:

> Les esclaves n'ont aucun motif pour s'acquitter des travaux auxquels on les contraint avec l'intelligence et les soins qui pourraient en assurer le succès; d'où suit que ces travaux produisent très peu. Les maîtres avides ne savent autre chose, pour suppléer à ce défaut de production qui résulte nécessairement de la culture par esclaves, que de forcer ceux-ci à des travaux encore plus rudes, plus continus et plus violents.[54]

The relentless exploitation of slaves, without guaranteeing them adequate treatment and sufficient means of subsistence, meant that they were destined to live a very short life. This forced the masters to buy new slaves continually. Turgot was aware of this aspect, but refrained from adding that owners 'payent un capital considérable pour se procurer ces mauvais ouvriers'.[55]

The words of Du Pont were much more eloquent than those of Turgot who – in a letter dated 2 February 1770 – reproached him for them: 'Vous m'avez encore beaucoup changé le morceau de l'esclavage. Ce que vous avez dit sur son origine ne s'éloigne pas de mes idées, excepté que je n'aurais pas dit qu'on ne se bat que par faiblesse, mais surtout je n'aurai pas substitué à un sommaire

53. Du Pont in Turgot, *Circulaire*, p.545-46.
54. Du Pont in Turgot, *Circulaire*, p.545.
55. Du Pont in Turgot, *Circulaire*, p.545.

286   *Simona Pisanelli*

marginal un morceau d'éloquence.'[56] Turgot demanded that Du Pont restore everything back to the original version. Otherwise, he would be forced to write a letter to the *Mercure*,[57] in order to clarify that the editor was solely responsible for all additions concerning the economic disadvantages of slavery.[58]

Only a few days later, on 6 February 1770, Turgot returned to the issue to dissociate himself even more clearly from the words of his friend and collaborator, stressing the fact that, beyond the undeniable injustices implicit in the institution of slavery, there are groups of citizens who economically benefit from it:[59]

> Franklin a aussi montré que le travail des noirs est plus cher qu'il ne paraît au premier coup d'œil, à cause des remplacements, mais je n'en pense pas moins que dans nos Iles, il y a un avantage à avoir des esclaves, non pour la colonie, mais pour le possesseur qui veut avoir des denrées d'une grande valeur vénale pour faire une prompte fortune par le commerce. Je crois avoir donné, dans mon ouvrage même, les raisons qui rendent le travail des esclaves utile dans un pays où l'on veut que la richesse et le commerce précèdent la population.[60]

In a further letter, dated 20 February 1770, Turgot reinforced his idea, radically opposed to that of Du Pont. Slavery is an abominable, barbaric, unjust custom at all stages of society, 'même dans [son] enfance'. But, according to Turgot, from a practical point of view, 'l'injustice est souvent utile à celui qui la commet et celle de l'esclavage l'est tout comme une autre.'[61]

56. Anne-Robert-Jacques Turgot, *Œuvres de Turgot et documents le concernant*, ed. Gustave Schelle, 5 vols (Paris, 1913-1923), vol.3, p.374.
57. Turgot probably refers to the *Mercure de France*, originally born as a periodical of worldly entertainment (1672) and, in the second half of the eighteenth century, transformed into a means of expression for more moderate philosophers. See Andrea Tagliapietra, *Che cos'è l'illuminismo? I testi e la genealogia del concetto* (Milan, 2000), p.376.
58. On the controversy between Turgot and Du Pont, see also David Brion Davis, *Il problema della schiavitù nella cultura occidentale* (Turin, 1971), p.483-85, and Gianluigi Goggi, 'Diderot–Raynal, l'esclavage et les Lumières écossaises', *Lumières* 3 (2004), p.52-94 (68-69).
59. Clément, 'Du bon et du mauvais usage des colonies', p.118-19.
60. Turgot, *Œuvres de Turgot et documents le concernant*, vol.3, p.375.
61. Turgot, *Œuvres de Turgot et documents le concernant*, vol.3, p.378. See also Michel Herland, 'Penser l'esclavage: de la morale à l'économie', in *L'Economie de l'esclavage colonial*, ed. Fred Célimène and André Legris (Paris, 2012), p.53-76 (68-69).

As correctly pointed out in an important work about the costs of slavery, 'Du Pont fut sans doute désagréablement surpris de voir son calcul d'emblée rejeté par l'un de ses plus proches amis.'[62] Nevertheless, this disagreement between Du Pont and Turgot, linked by a close relationship of friendship and collaboration, reveals an important aspect of the cultural environment of the time. The agreement between the Enlightenment thinkers on the general theme of human emancipation did not prevent the taking of different positions on a scientific and practical level on the issue of slavery.

In any case, the quarrel with Turgot did not weaken Du Pont's analytical effort to hasten the abolition of slavery, as demonstrated by writings published and commented on in subsequent issues of the *Ephémérides*.

***

As we have seen, the debate on slavery during the Enlightenment developed on two levels: the first focused on the juridical and ethical aspects of the phenomenon, whereas the second concentrated on the economic aspects.

As is well-known, the analysis of the legal and ethical distortions produced by slavery was emphasised by Montesquieu, who pointed out that the legislator had the task of creating patterns of institutions consistent with the realisation of the essence of human nature and conducive to the progressive development of humanity. From this point of view, it was evident that slavery was a phenomenon which had negative effects at every level of economic and social organisation. In fact, such effects concerned both slaves and owners: in the long term, both would be involved in the same process of human and ethical degradation. This plan of the argument was widely shared by most Enlightenment thinkers and if, to return to Du Pont, we look at the *Ephémérides*, this is fully evident. Nevertheless, Du Pont – and with him other thinkers (like Condorcet, A. Smith, etc.) – was convinced that the emphasis on legal and moral aspects was not enough to push the owners to give up slaves. According to him, it was also necessary to demonstrate that slavery was economically disadvantageous. Therefore, Du Pont set about demonstrating that the use of slaves in agriculture represented an obsolete kind of work organisation which hindered the introduction of innovative processes and, consequently,

---

62. Oudin-Bastide and Steiner, *Calcul et morale*, p.51.

the growth of the economy. He pointed out that the conditions of material deprivation in which slaves were forced to live led to a permanent conflict that prevented all forms of social progress. By contrast, it was precisely such a conflict that had negative economic impacts, especially with regard to the introduction and spread of technical progress. While owners, by profiting from the increasing use of slaves, did not promote investment in the improvement of economic processes, the slaves tended to avoid unnecessary efforts to increase their labour productivity, as the effects of new production practices would increase their workload. As a consequence, the existence of an insoluble conflict between owners and slaves coincided with the perpetuation of an economically inefficient and disadvantageous production system for the owners themselves.

In addition, the institution of slavery was inconsistent with the aspirations of emancipation expressed by Enlightenment societies. In the light of the social evolution, institutional modernisation and spread of technical progress of the age, slavery could no longer be tolerated. As Du Pont continually emphasised, it was to be condemned by both individuals and governments.[63] All this appeared to be absolutely evident, if analysed from the point of view of the 'science de l'économie' which had the 'vocation à transformer les gouvernements et les sociétés'.[64] Only the abolition of slavery could allow the reorganisation of society in accordance with 'reason' and with the sense of humanity that must guide individual and collective choices.

63. Du Pont, 'Ziméo', p.217.
64. Manuela Albertone, 'Deux générations autour de l'Amérique', in Victor Riqueti de Mirabeau and Pierre-Samuel Du Pont de Nemours, *Dialogues physiocratiques sur l'Amérique*, ed. M. Albertone (Paris, 2015), p.7-51 (8).

V

Du Pont's American dream |
Le rêve américain de Du Pont

Du Pont de Nemours, coauteur des *Lettres d'Abraham Mansword* (1771-1772) et critique (1773-1789) de de Lolme: le modèle politique anglais confronté avec une Amérique rêvée

GABRIEL SABBAGH

Université Paris Diderot

A la mémoire d'Arnold Heertje (1934-2020)
qui m'apprit beaucoup et ne sera pas oublié.

En 1772, Du Pont de Nemours, qui éditait les *Ephémérides*, publia dans ce journal, qui était l'organe des physiocrates, les *Lettres d'Abraham Mansword, citoyen de Philadelphie, à ses compatriotes de l'Amérique septentrionale, traduites du Pennsylvany's chronicle*. Le *Pennsylvania chronicle and universal advertiser* n'était pas un journal fictif. L'introduction de Du Pont donnait des détails véridiques sur ce journal, sans doute fournis par Benjamin Franklin, mais Abraham Mansword n'avait jamais existé, pas plus que les *Lettres* en anglais. Au nombre de deux, datées des 12 avril et 15 mai 1771, elles furent publiées pour la première fois dans la première partie de l'année 1772.[1]

Il y a eu plusieurs interprétations de ces *Lettres*, qui divergeaient

---

L'aide d'Arnold Heertje, qui a mis à ma disposition l'exemplaire de la Fondation Heertje des *Ephémérides*, fut précieuse. Cet article est dédié à sa mémoire. Je remercie Manuela Albertone, Loïc Charles, Bernard Herencia, Pierre Le Masne, Christine Théré, Liana Vardi et Richard Whatmore pour des échanges utiles ainsi que Herre de Vries, de l'atelier Restauratie Nijhoff Asser, dont les techniques photographiques ont révélé des fragments d'épreuves corrigées par Du Pont, confirmant l'attribution présentée dans la suite de ce texte.

1.　Voir *Ephémérides* 11 (1771), p.74-112, et *Ephémérides* 12 (1771), p.6-45. Ces tomes auxquels on renverra librement dans la suite reçurent l'approbation du censeur les 14 février et 25 avril 1772. Le journal paraissait souvent en retard et divers tirages existent. Pour une étude du journal, on se reportera à Bernard Herencia, *Les 'Ephémérides du citoyen' et les 'Nouvelles Ephémérides économiques', 1765-1788* (Ferney-Voltaire, 2014). Cet ouvrage sera dorénavant désigné par Herencia (2014).

sur leur auteur supposé, et qui seront mentionnées à la fin de cette étude. Je propose ici en examinant d'autres textes de Du Pont une explication nouvelle du mystère de ces *Lettres*: elles esquissent dès 1771 un projet de Constitution pour une république confédérale américaine qui n'est évidemment pas encore née, tout en annonçant, notamment dans les conditions d'entrée dans les 'Etats provinciaux', le mémoire sur les assemblées municipales de Du Pont et Turgot, rédigé plus tard.[2]

Notre explication est que ces *Lettres* furent d'abord une critique du modèle anglais et furent provoquées par la publication à Amsterdam chez Van Harrevelt[3] en 1771 du livre de de Lolme, *Constitution de l'Angleterre*.

Franklin contribua sans doute de manière décisive à stimuler Du Pont: l'essentiel des *Lettres* est bien un projet physiocratique[4] d'une loi fondamentale pour une république américaine, irrigué par les contacts entre Du Pont et Franklin; le 15 juin 1772[5] Franklin écrivait à Du Pont: 'Abraham Mansword's Advice to his Countrymen is very good. I hope they will have more of it.' Dans une des dernières lettres conservées de Franklin à Du Pont, du 9 juin 1788, il est question d'un

---

2. Voir *Œuvres de Turgot et documents le concernant*, éd. Gustave Schelle, 5 vol. (Paris, 1913-1923), t.4, p.568-628, et, pour une anticipation négligée, développée par Mirabeau, *Supplément à la théorie de l'impôt* (La Haye, P.-F. Gosse, 1776), dorénavant cité comme Mirabeau (1776). Sur l'ouvrage publié sous l'anonymat par Butré en 1775, *Principes sur l'impôt, ou la Liberté et l'immunité des hommes et de leurs travaux* (Londres, Chez les libraires associés), p.132-48, voir Gabriel Sabbagh, 'An unrecorded physiocratic précis by Charles Richard de Butré and the experiment of Karl Friedrich of Baden-Durlach in Dietlingen', *The European journal of the history of economic thought* 24:1 (2017), p.1-24. Pour les assemblées représentatives, on renvoie à Anthony Mergey, *L'Etat des physiocrates: autorité et décentralisation* (Aix-en-Provence, 2010), et pour le mémoire de Du Pont et Turgot à Eric Gojosso, 'Le *Mémoire sur les municipalités* (1775) et la réforme administrative à la fin de l'Ancien Régime', *Cahiers poitevins d'histoire du droit* 1 (2007), p.127-38. A noter que les citations données dans le présent texte respectent l'orthographe de leurs auteurs.

3. Il ne s'agit pas d'une fausse adresse: Du Pont se trompa en écrivant en 1773 dans sa *Lettre à Scheffer* (voir plus loin) que le livre avait été imprimé à Londres, peut-être parce que l'auteur y résidait alors.

4. Il nuance la doctrine des Economistes sur un point intéressant, à la p.36 de la seconde *Lettre*, en assimilant aux propriétaires fonciers 'ceux qui sont pensionnés par l'état'; voir la note 15 du présent texte.

5. La première lettre connue de leur correspondance date de mai 1768: Du Pont envoie à Franklin le recueil *Physiocratie*. La correspondance de Franklin est numérisée: franklinpapers.org (date de dernière consultation le 10 décembre 2024).

écrit, apparemment perdu, de Du Pont, *Ouvrage sur les principes et le bien des républiques en général.* C'est manifestement le projet envoyé à Franklin en décembre 1787.[6] Du Pont sera toujours intéressé par ces questions, et un de ses derniers écrits, daté mars 1815, sera un manuscrit de 140 pages adressé aux 'Républiques Equinoxiales, et à celles qui leur seront naturellement confédérées', inspiré par le mouvement de libération des colonies espagnoles d'Amérique du Sud.[7] Une copie de ce texte, dédicacée par Du Pont au savant et homme politique sud-américain Manuel Palacios Fajardo, fut découverte récemment et sommairement décrite,[8] même si le monde savant semble l'avoir ignoré. Les renseignements obtenus alors confirment qu'il s'agissait là encore d'un projet constitutionnel pour une confédération éventuelle des colonies espagnoles. Je reviendrai rapidement plus tard sur ce texte.

Le plan de l'exposé privilégie la juxtaposition de quelques textes. Notre point de départ consiste à prouver qu'en 1773 Du Pont écrivit une lettre au comte Scheffer destinée à Gustave III de Suède,[9] qui était une critique explicite du livre de de Lolme. Cette *Lettre à Scheffer*[10]

---

6. Voir Ambrose Saricks, *Pierre Samuel Du Pont de Nemours* (Lawrence, KS, 1965), p.132, qui indique qu'il s'agissait de républiques confédérées.

7. La correspondance entre Du Pont et Jefferson était jusqu'à présent une des rares sources d'information sur ce texte, que l'on croyait perdu.

8. Voir Freeman's, *Catalogue de vente* (22 octobre 2015), n° 210. Le manuscrit avait appartenu à un membre de la famille Du Pont et n'était probablement jamais parvenu à son destinataire. Je remercie la librairie William Reese, l'acquéreur en 2015, pour m'avoir renseigné sur ce manuscrit qui est maintenant dans une collection privée.

9. Les Archives royales de Stockholm (je remercie Lena Animmer) et la bibliothèque de l'université d'Uppsala (je remercie Kia Hedell) possèdent les lettres de Du Pont envoyées à Gustave III (par l'entremise de son conseiller le comte Scheffer); j'ai pu obtenir une copie du manuscrit, non daté, de cette lettre, écrit de la main de Du Pont, conservé dans la collection de S. Rosenhane le jeune, H 260, à la bibliothèque de l'université d'Uppsala. Le texte présente des différences stylistiques intéressantes, mais négligeables pour cette étude, avec les versions imprimées de cette lettre. La plus connue est celle publiée presque à l'identique, à partir des archives de Bade, par Carl Knies, *Carl Friedrichs von Baden brieflicher Verkehr mit Mirabeau und Du Pont*, 2 vol. (Heidelberg, 1892), t.2, p.214-31: Du Pont était pensionné par le margrave de Bade et Gustave III et leur envoyait très souvent les mêmes lettres. Cet ouvrage de Knies sera dorénavant désigné par Knies (1892).

10. J'abrège ainsi le titre (courant, il n'y a pas de page de titre séparée) de la brochure qui est: *Lettre à M. le comte Charles de Scheffer.*

294 *Gabriel Sabbagh*

parut en 1788, datée du 20 août 1773, sous deux formes différentes[11] et servit d'ossature (certaines pages sont intégralement reprises) à des notes ajoutées par Du Pont à la traduction française d'un livre de Stevens (même s'il fut attribué à Livingston), *Examen du gouvernement d'Angleterre*, publié en 1789.[12]

La section i présentera brièvement les *Lettres d'Abraham Mansword* et le livre de de Lolme, et établira que ce livre fut rigoureusement interdit en 1771 par la censure et autorisé seulement en 1785, ce qui permit de le diffuser dès lors en France et d'en débattre librement. On montrera comment la *Lettre à Scheffer* critique (dès 1773) le livre de de Lolme en reprenant des motifs de la seconde des *Lettres d'Abraham Mansword*, ce qui fournit un indice pour l'attribution de cette seconde *Lettre* à Du Pont.

La section ii signalera des écrits significatifs de Du Pont portant sur des thèmes des *Lettres*, notamment sur la religion de Du Pont, qui est le déisme, sur l'impact des spectacles, des cérémonies et des beaux-arts, et d'autres dans lesquels il évoque l'Angleterre et adopte sur son histoire, parfois avant l'apparition du livre de de Lolme, des vues opposées à certaines de celles de ce livre. Notre résultat principal, que les *Lettres* furent d'abord une réponse à de Lolme à qui on opposa, sur l'instigation probable de Franklin, un hypothétique modèle américain, découle de la confrontation de ces textes. Une conjecture secondaire formulée dans la section ii est que le livre de de Lolme provoqua également une bonne partie de la discussion juridique et philosophique entre Condorcet et Turgot comparant en 1771 les systèmes juridiques anglais et français.

11. Elle fut publiée (anonymement) dans un journal fondé par Honoré-Gabriel de Mirabeau, *Analyse des papiers anglois* 34-36 (1788), p.241-48, 265-72, 283-96 et séparément. On renverra à ces numéros quand on citera la *Lettre à Scheffer*. Le seul exemplaire connu de moi de la brochure séparée, sans doute celui de Du Pont, est à la Hagley Library que je remercie pour son aide; Gustave Schelle, *Du Pont de Nemours et l'école physiocratique* (Paris, 1888), p.276 et 411, qui ignora le rapport précis avec le livre de Stevens et le journal de Mirabeau, signala la brochure, alors que la publication dans le journal est analysée par François Quastana, *La Pensée politique de Mirabeau (1771-1789), 'républicanisme classique' et régénération de la monarchie* (Paris, 2007), p.512, qui a ignoré le nom de son auteur. Le livre de Schelle sera dorénavant désigné par Schelle (1888).

12. *Examen du gouvernement d'Angleterre, comparé aux constitutions des Etats-Unis* (Londres et Paris, Chez Froullé, 1789). Une conséquence de ce travail est que l'on peut maintenant attribuer avec une totale certitude à Du Pont au moins deux notes de cet ouvrage, les II, 69-120, et XVI, 154-71, puisqu'elles reprennent littéralement plusieurs passages de la *Lettre à Scheffer*.

La section iii tentera d'identifier l'auteur ou les auteurs des *Lettres*. J'expliquerai pourquoi certains passages doivent être attribués à Du Pont, notamment dans la seconde *Lettre*, pourquoi les attributions antérieures de ces *Lettres* ne sont pas satisfaisantes et ce qu'apporte l'exemplaire de la Fondation Heertje.

i. Les *Lettres d'Abraham Mansword* et le livre de de Lolme

Les Lettres d'Abraham Mansword

La première *Lettre* débute par un préambule déiste invoquant 'Mes frères en Dieu' et mettant sur le même plan le Christ et saint Paul (p.78). La censure supprima là une phrase sur 'la loi des chrétiens (prêchant l'amour du prochain) [qui] n'est que la nature sanctifiée par la révélation'. Les pages sur la bienfaisance (p.77), la réunion des forces et l'intérêt commun (p.80) sont semblables à des considérations du 'Discours préliminaire' (œuvre de Du Pont) du recueil *Physiocratie*.[13] Vient ensuite un développement sur le droit de propriété, la liberté et la justice, qui débouche sur une défense des colonies contre le 'système mercantile' de la métropole et prédit une 'révolution' (p.91), et sur une vision d'une 'confédération' (p.95) avec une esquisse de ses 'loix constitutives'. L'instruction est indispensable: 'Il nous faudra [...] des Ecoles publiques & gratuites' (p.98). Cette dernière phrase aurait pu être écrite par de nombreux physiocrates, mais on pense d'abord à Le Mercier de La Rivière.[14]

La seconde *Lettre* critique sévèrement le parlement anglais, la 'vénalité' et la 'corruption' de ses membres et le fait que les 'Députés n'y portent point le vœu commun de leur District & [...] n'ont aucun compte à rendre à leurs commettants' (p.14). L'auteur recommande au contraire que les 'Etats provinciaux s'assemblent [...] pour qu'il leur soit rendu compte de ce qui s'est passé dans les Etats Généraux', puis décrit l'assemblée des Etats généraux qui doit se faire de manière solennelle car 'les vérités les plus utiles ne pénètrent [...] que par l'entremise de nos sens: il faut donc que ces vérités [...] présentent un

13. Voir P.-S. Du Pont dans F. Quesnay, *Physiocratie, ou Constitution naturelle du gouvernement le plus avantageux au genre humain*, 2 vol. (Leyde et Paris, Merlin, 1768), p.x (réunion des forces) et xxxiv-xxxvi (bienfaisance et intérêt commun).
14. P.-P. Le Mercier de La Rivière, *De l'instruction publique, ou Considérations morales et politiques sur la nécessité, la nature et la source de cette intruction* (Stockholm et Paris, Didot l'aîné, 1775), p.20: 'il ne suffit pas d'établir un grand nombre d'écoles publiques & gratuites.'

296 *Gabriel Sabbagh*

grand spectacle' (p.14-16). Une dizaine de pages (p.23-31) décrivent la cérémonie et évoquent 'les Beaux Arts' et les 'danses & repos champêtres' qui montrent 'qu'une société d'hommes justes [...] ne peut être qu'une société d'hommes heureux' (p.30). A la page 19 un passage remarquable permet au 'Chef' de 'jurer ou promettre' d'observer les lois fondamentales et mentionne 'ceux de nos Freres qui ne croient pas qu'il leur soit permis de rien jurer': l'auteur du texte est opposé aux serments religieux. Les lignes suivantes, page 20, reprochent à l'Angleterre d'imposer le rejet de la transsubstantiation et ajoutent: 'Votre Parlement est-il une assemblée de Théologiens? Non, c'en est une de Citoyens.' Un autre passage, qui précise la composition des Etats provinciaux (p.35-36), surprend par sa définition des 'hommes vraiment nationaux'. Il s'agit des 'propriétaires fonciers' mais 'on peut [...] y joindre encore ceux qui sont pensionnés par l'état, soit pour des services rendus, soit pour l'exercice de quelques fonctions publiques'. Cela contraste avec la doxa physiocratique telle, par exemple, qu'énoncée par Mirabeau.[15] La seconde *Lettre* donne ensuite des conditions précises (il faut avoir un revenu minimum) pour 'entrer dans les Etats provinciaux', ce qui est permis aux 'Entrepreneurs de culture [...] obligés de faire de grandes avances pour de telles entreprises'.[16] Nous sommes là très proches du futur mémoire sur les assemblées municipales évoqué dans l'introduction.

Le livre de de Lolme, Constitution de l'Angleterre

Ce livre fut un bestseller.[17] Editions et traductions se succédèrent, le livre intéressa d'illustres contemporains[18] et les commentaires ont continué jusqu'à nos jours.[19] L'auteur, s'inspirant de Montesquieu,

---

15. Voir Mirabeau (1776): 'Les propriétaires fonciers sont les seuls vrais [...] nationaux' (p.34).

16. Turgot (qui était en liaison constante avec Du Pont) venait de publier dans les *Ephémérides* les *Réflexions sur la formation et la distribution des richesses* et d'y théoriser le rôle du 'capitaliste, devenu entrepreneur de culture ou d'industrie'; voir *Ephémérides* 1 (1770), p.113-73 (160).

17. Jean-Louis de Lolme, *Constitution de l'Angleterre* (Amsterdam, E. Van Harrevelt, 1771). Sauf avis contraire, on renvoie à cette première édition dans tout le présent texte.

18. On trouve à Magdalen College (Oxford) un reçu montrant que Gibbon acheta à de Lolme deux exemplaires de son livre. Je dois cette information au regretté Robert Mankin.

19. Voir Edouard Tillet, *La Constitution anglaise: un modèle politique et institutionnel*

Le modèle politique anglais confronté avec une Amérique rêvée 297

mais avec des nuances importantes, décrivait un système politique anglais passablement idéalisé. La seule divergence entre Montesquieu et de Lolme explicitement reconnue par ce dernier, et la seule qui nous concerne ici car elle a probablement accentué le rejet du livre par Du Pont, porte sur la corruption du Parlement britannique, pour laquelle de Lolme est plus indulgent que son prédécesseur.[20] Une phrase de la dédicace, datée de décembre 1770, qui fut probablement écrite après le reste de l'ouvrage,[21] le résume parfaitement: on voit 'la liberté, non dans les prérogatives de telle ou telle partie du Gouvernement, mais dans l'équilibre de toutes'. La lecture du livre dissipe certains des mystères des *Lettres à Abraham Mansword* et notamment ce qui concerne le rejet de la transsubstantiation. C'est une réponse directe à la page 47 du livre de de Lolme qui défendait la proscription du catholicisme en Angleterre (en faisant allusion à la transsubstantiation).

Ce qui frappe aujourd'hui est le contraste entre le silence presque total avec lequel le livre fut reçu en 1771 en France et son retentissement à la fin des années 1780. Une historienne a ainsi résumé la situation: 'first published in 1770 [*sic*] but not appraised correctly in France until the 1780s'.[22] L'explication est fournie par l'interdiction stricte du livre en France: au début de sa *Lettre à Scheffer* (écrite en 1773 et imprimée en 1788, comme précédemment indiqué), Du Pont disait du livre de de Lolme: 'il est encore tout nouveau, & très-rare en France, grace aux précautions qu'on prend pour interdire l'entrée [...] des Livres étrangers qui ont quelque rapport à la politique.' Cela est confirmé par les *Mémoires* de Bachaumont:[23] à la date du 11 novembre 1771, moult éloges du livre précèdent une glose sur 'la sévérité avec laquelle le gouvernement en empêche l'introduction'.

---

    dans la France des Lumières (Aix-en-Provence, 2001). Cet ouvrage sera dorénavant désigné par Tillet (2001).

20. Après avoir cité p.266 la prédiction de Montesquieu selon laquelle l'Angleterre pourrait perdre sa liberté en raison de la corruption de la puissance législative – voir Montesquieu, *De l'esprit des lois*, t.1 (Genève, Barillot & fils, 1748), p.260 – de Lolme consacre de nombreuses pages à la réfuter, non sans avoir fait état de son approbation pour presque toutes les opinions de Montesquieu.

21. Le livre était sans doute achevé en 1770: l'auteur a affirmé l'avoir écrit en neuf mois, un an après son arrivée en 1768 en Angleterre; voir de Lolme, *Constitution de l'Angleterre*, 2 vol. (Londres, G. Robinson, J. Murray, 1785), t.1, p.vi.

22. Frances Acomb, *Anglophobia in France, 1763-1789: an essay in the history of constitutionalism and nationalism* (Durham, NC, 1950), p.104.

23. Voir Louis Petit de Bachaumont, *Mémoires secrets*, éd. Christophe Cave, t.4 (Paris, 2010), p.22.

On trouve alors un extrait des pages 50-51 du livre de de Lolme commentant la révolution de 1688 dont voici trois lignes: 'Il fut décidé que les nations n'appartiennent point aux rois. Tous ces principes d'obéissance passive, de droit divin [...] cet échafaudage de notions funestes [...] sur lesquelles l'autorité royale avait porté [...] fut détruit.'

La permission de vendre l'ouvrage en France fut refusée.[24] Le refus n'est pas daté mais on peut supposer, en examinant d'autres décisions (datées) de la même page du registre, qu'il eut lieu en septembre 1771. L'ouvrage fut soumis à la censure par le biais de la chambre syndicale, ce qui explique qu'un long délai a pu s'écouler entre l'arrivée du volume en France[25] et la décision. Il est certain que l'ouvrage avait été publié en Hollande au début de 1771.[26] Il reçut probablement à Amsterdam un accueil favorable.[27]

Il est difficile de trouver en France un écho du livre de de Lolme avant le milieu des années 1780.[28] En 1779 le comte d'Albon, disciple chéri de Quesnay, publia, mais en Suisse, le premier volet de ses *Discours politiques*, consacré à l'Angleterre, la Hollande et la Suisse. Le tiers des 160 pages dévolues à l'Angleterre[29] est une critique sans nuances du système politique anglais avec là encore une vive attaque

24. Voir Bibliothèque nationale de France, Paris, MS fr. 21993, p.380.
25. Il fut envoyé par l'auteur ou l'éditeur ou saisi par la douane.
26. L'obligeance de la Bibliothèque de l'université d'Amsterdam m'a permis d'examiner plusieurs années de la *Gazette littéraire de l'Europe* (Amsterdam) qui, au numéro d'avril 1771, inclut le livre dans sa liste de 'parutions récentes'. Comme le *Journal des savants* (Amsterdam), la *Gazette littéraire de l'Europe* copiait allègrement la presse périodique française en général et les *Ephémérides* en particulier. Il n'y a aucune raison de croire que ces réimpressions étaient autorisées. C'est pourquoi je néglige les variantes (peu significatives) de la réimpression dans le *Journal des savants* des *Lettres d'Abraham Mansword* relevées dans Paul-Pierre Le Mercier de La Rivière, *Pennsylvaniens et Féliciens: œuvres utopiques (1771 et 1792)*, éd. Bernard Herencia (Genève, 2014). Cet ouvrage sera désormais désigné par Le Mercier de La Rivière (2014).
27. La *Gazette littéraire d'Amsterdam* en donna de longs extraits dans ses numéros de mai et juin 1771.
28. Cependant la future Mme Roland, qui l'a probablement obtenu par un horloger suisse, Moré, l'a attentivement lu, et son enthousiasme éclate dans un résumé rédigé à la fin de l'année 1776 mais non publié alors; voir Jeanne-Marie Roland de La Platière, *Lettres*, éd. Claude Perroud, 2 vol. (Paris, 1913-1915), t.1, p.538, et t.2, p.4-13.
29. J'utilise l'édition originale de 1779, comportant trois parties séparément paginées, avec 160 pages pour l'Angleterre, 145 pour la Hollande et 126 pour la Suisse: *Discours politiques, historiques et critiques, sur quelques gouvernements de l'Europe* (Neufchâtel, De l'imprimerie de la Société typographique, 1779).

contre la vénalité du personnel politique et une défense des colonies américaines[30] (il est plus que probable que d'Albon lisait régulièrement les *Ephémérides* et avait pris connaissance des *Lettres d'Abraham Mansword*). Une mention du livre de de Lolme, 'un des Panégyristes les plus outrés de l'Angleterre', figure à la page 45. L'ouvrage fut l'objet d'un long compte rendu dans le *Mercure de France*, entièrement consacré à la Hollande et la Suisse, sauf pour quelques lignes dans lesquelles le commentateur faisait état précautionneusement du désaccord probable des 'Anglomanes' avec d'Albon.[31]

En 1785, dans le même journal,[32] Garat fut moins prudent[33] et encensa 'De Lolme […] Auteur d'un excellent ouvrage sur la constitution de l'Angleterre […] qu'on admire dans toute l'Europe'. La censure devenait moins stricte et le *Mercure* était bien informé: la permission de diffuser le livre fut accordée le 20 novembre 1785,[34] par Vergennes en personne.[35] Dès lors plusieurs éditions du livre circulèrent normalement en France.

La Lettre à Scheffer

Précisons d'abord ce qui fut dit à propos de l'*Examen du gouvernement d'Angleterre, comparé aux constitutions des Etats-Unis*. Les pages 73 et 158 de cet ouvrage sont reprises de la *Lettre à Scheffer*.[36] L'abondante littérature consacrée à cette traduction ne remarqua jamais que la

---

30. Le 25 décembre 1782 d'Albon envoya à Franklin une édition (incomplète) de son ouvrage (la dernière partie parut en 1785), mais comportant le volume sur l'Angleterre: la lettre d'envoi de d'Albon, publiée dans *The Papers of Benjamin Franklin* – voir franklinpapers.org –, mentionnait sa défense 'des intérêts d'un peuple opprimé dont vous êtes aujourd'hui le représentant'.

31. *Mercure de France* (15 juin 1779), p.151.

32. *Mercure de France* (27 août 1785), p.181.

33. Il éprouva cependant le besoin d'indiquer que son texte imprimé depuis trois semaines avait été retardé pour des 'raisons dont il est inutile que le public soit instruit'; *Mercure de France* (27 août 1785), p.155. On peut encore une fois songer à la censure.

34. Voir Bibliothèque nationale de France, Paris, MS fr. 21987, f.28r. L'extrait cité plus haut des p.50-51 de l'édition originale est présent dans les éditions publiées en France à la fin des années 1780.

35. Il est normal que le livre ait été soumis à Vergennes puisqu'il traitait d'une puissance étrangère. Il est intéressant de noter qu'un manuscrit fragmentaire des *Discours* de d'Albon avait été communiqué à Vergennes en 1781; voir Tillet (2001), p.360, n.1868.

36. Voir *Lettre à Scheffer*, n° 35, p.268 et 265.

Lettre à Scheffer y était reprise ni que cette lettre datait de 1773, bien avant la controverse provoquée par un livre d'Adams, à laquelle cette traduction répondit.[37] Cela montre que l'histoire admise de cette controverse, qui est au fond assez éloignée du sujet de cette étude car très postérieure, est inexacte.

Voici quelques passages de cette *Lettre*. Un extrait particulièrement remarquable et souligné par une note de l'éditeur insistant qu'il s'agit d'un texte écrit en 1773 est relatif aux colonies américaines et peut être comparé à la page 91 de la première *Lettre* sur le système mercantile et les colonies: 'les prohibitions [...] les douanes [...] les réglemens tyranniques [...] qui brouilleront sans retour (l'Angleterre) [...] avec ses Colonies'.[38]

D'autres passages sont encore plus semblables à certains de ceux cités des *Lettres*. Du Pont condamne la vénalité des élections (et des électeurs): 'les suffrages de la pluralité dans deux cents Electeurs ne coûtent pas cher [...] la Nation se vend [...] à des députés qui la revendent.'[39] Après avoir recommandé de 'lier [...] les intérêts de tous les Membres de l'Etat et que toutes les forces réunies élèvent avec rapidité l'édifice du bien public',[40] Du Pont propose des mesures permettant à 'chaque député de porter à l'Assemblée Nationale le vœu de ses commettans'[41] et à l'Angleterre d'avoir 'effectivement une constitution fondée sur un intérêt commun'.[42]

La comparaison de la *Lettre à Scheffer* et de la seconde *Lettre d'Abraham Mansword* est particulièrement frappante. Nous mettons en parallèle ci-dessous les pages 288-89 du numéro 36 de l'*Analyse des papiers anglois* et les pages 13-14 de la seconde *Lettre*:

---

37. Un excellent traitement récent 'traditionnel' de cette controverse se trouve dans Victor Riqueti de Mirabeau et P.-S. Du Pont de Nemours, *Dialogues physiocratiques sur l'Amérique, éd.* Manuela Albertone (Paris, 2015), p.45. Cet ouvrage sera dorénavant désigné par Albertone (2015). Le livre de John Adams, *A Defence of the constitutions of government of the United States of America* (Londres, C. Dilly, 1787-1788), ne put être traduit en français que bien plus tard.
38. *Lettre à Scheffer*, n° 36, p.288.
39. *Lettre à Scheffer*, n° 36, p.286-87.
40. *Lettre à Scheffer*, n° 36, p.291.
41. *Lettre à Scheffer*, n° 36, p.294.
42. *Lettre à Scheffer*, n° 36, p.296.

Analyse des papiers anglois	Seconde *Lettre d'Abraham Mansword*
Leur principe est, qu'une fois admis au nombre des Membres du Parlement, ils ne sont plus seulement représentans du lieu qui les a députés, mais de la Grande-Bretagne entière. Cette belle supposition fait qu'aucun d'eux ne se croit astreint à suivre exactement les instructions ni les intentions de ceux qui l'ont député.	Jamais les Districts ne s'assemblent pour ouir le rapport de ce qui s'est passé au Parlement, & de la conduite que leurs Députés y ont tenue [...] Des Députés qui n'y portent point le voeu commun de leur District, & qui [...] n'ont aucun compte à rendre à leurs commettants,[43] ne forment point la nation.

ii. Quelques autres articles de Du Pont

Les textes les plus importants relatifs aux colonies américaines publiés dans les *Ephémérides* sont les *Lettres d'Abraham Mansword* et deux publications antérieures: la *Lettre de Mr. H. à l'auteur des Ephémérides sur un pays très florissant où il n'y a point de villes*, datée du 12 mars 1769, et sa correction.[44] Ces deux textes ayant été attribués à Barbeu Du Bourg par Aldridge, à Beaurieu par Echeverria et à Du Pont par Schelle (1888) et Herencia (2014), il n'est pas superflu d'observer que *la seule lecture* des *Ephémérides* permet d'attribuer les deux textes de Mr. H. à Du Pont, qui avait ainsi dès 1769 un fort intérêt pour les colonies américaines.[45]

Les deux textes de 1769 ont le même auteur, qui, le 12 mars 1769, fait allusion à un compte rendu d'un livre de Justi, annoncé plus tard par Du Pont comme écrit par lui.[46] Ce compte rendu avait été publié dans le tome 2 des *Ephémérides* de 1769, approuvé par le censeur le 6 mars 1769. Le tome 2 de 1769 n'ayant pu circuler avant au moins le 15 ou 20 mars, il était impossible à Mr. H. le 12 mars

---

43. Ce terme, 'commettants', est utilisé dans la *Lettre à Scheffer*; voir la note 41. La similitude des deux textes confrontés est ici éclatante.
44. Voir *Ephémérides* 3 (1769), p.68-77, et *Ephémérides* 8 (1769), p.39-52. La lettre du 12 mars 1769 affirmait à tort que la province de New York n'avait point de ville.
45. Manuela Albertone, 'Décentralisation territoriale et unité de la nation: *Les Lettres d'Abraham Mansword* entre physiocratie et modèle américain', dans *Centralisation et fédéralisme: les modèles et leur circulation dans l'espace européen francophone, germanophone et italophone*, éd. Michel Biard et autres (Mont-Saint-Aignan, 2018), p.103-14, rappelle, p.106, les attributions à Barbeu Du Bourg et Du Pont et considère comme 'très probable' cette dernière. Voir aussi A. O. Aldridge, 'Jacques Barbeu-Dubourg, a French disciple of Benjamin Franklin', *Proceedings of the American Philosophical Society* 95:4 (1951), p.331-92. Ces textes d'Albertone et Aldridge seront désignés dans la suite par Albertone (2018) et Aldridge (1951).
46. Voir *Ephémérides* 1 (1770), p.39.

302 *Gabriel Sabbagh*

de connaître l'existence de ce compte rendu, sauf si Mr. H. était l'éditeur du journal ou l'auteur du compte rendu, dans les deux cas Du Pont. Cela démontre chez Du Pont, manifestement influencé par Franklin, un tropisme américain précoce. Du Pont exploite le mythe américain pour vanter la prospérité d'une contrée sans ville, lui qui célèbre constamment les campagnes et dénigre les 'citadins', ce que l'on retrouve sous la signature de Mr. H. dans une troisième *Lettre à l'auteur des Ephémérides*.[47]

Il est pour nous intéressant de considérer d'autres articles de Du Pont. En 1769 Du Pont publie dans les *Ephémérides* une longue série sur les finances et l'histoire de l'Angleterre qui ne sera jamais terminée mais qui donne une vision du régime féodal anglais à l'opposé exact de celle que de Lolme développera. Dans sa *Lettre à Scheffer* Du Pont explique très longuement[48] que de Lolme se trompe en prétendant trouver dans le régime féodal anglais l'origine de la liberté de l'Angleterre et renvoie pour réfuter de Lolme à un de ces articles.[49] Un autre article de Du Pont, assez troublant parce qu'il suit de peu la parution du livre de de Lolme[50] et précède les *Lettres à Abraham Mansword*, est un compte rendu des trois premiers volumes d'un livre de Gaillard sur la rivalité franco-anglaise.[51] Ses premières pages esquissent une histoire de la féodalité très proche de ce que Du Pont écrira au début de la lettre à Scheffer et sont suivies d'un extrait du livre de Gaillard: Du Pont a privilégié ce que Gaillard a écrit sur... la Pennsylvanie! On peut encore signaler un autre écrit de Du Pont, probablement de mars 1771,[52] sur la République de Genève, qui lui aussi permet de penser que Du Pont a lu le livre de de Lolme à sa parution: il contient une brève critique de la constitution anglaise et de Montesquieu qui annonce la *Lettre à Scheffer*.[53]

Les textes de Du Pont les plus intéressants pour ce travail et qui sont très proches de certains thèmes des *Lettres d'Abraham Mansword* sont philosophiques et religieux ou esthétiques. Dans la première

---

47. *Ephémérides* 2 (1770), p.5-15.
48. Le premier tiers du texte est dévolu à cette réfutation.
49. Voir *Ephémérides* 5 (1769), p.135-68.
50. Voir *Ephémérides* 2 (1771), p.108-56. Ce tome reçut l'approbation du censeur le 13 juin 1771.
51. Gabriel-Henri Gaillard, *Histoire de la rivalité de la France et de l'Angleterre*, 11 vol. (Paris, 1771-1777).
52. Voir *Ephémérides* 12 (1770), p.237 et 244.
53. Voir *Ephémérides* 12 (1770), p.187.

catégorie il y a trois brefs opuscules, importants et négligés, dans lesquels Du Pont expose ses croyances religieuses:

- *Des bases de la morale: observations lues le 22 thermidor An VI à [...] l'Institut*; Du Pont y sépare la morale de la religion.
- *Irénée bonfils, sur la religion de ses pères et de nos pères*, 1808. C'est un écrit extraordinaire,[54] qui est une autobiographie religieuse et le récit fictionnel des appartenances religieuses de tous ses ancêtres jusqu'à une époque très reculée. Du Pont affirme son déisme et s'interdit de se prononcer sur les dogmes qui ne lui semblent pas évidents, tels que la transsubstantiation (la situation de l'Angleterre avait été fortement critiquée à ce propos dans la seconde *Lettre d'Abraham Mansword*): le mot est en toutes lettres dans le texte et cela n'est point anodin. Du Pont a utilisé un pseudonyme assez transparent (un de ses fils était prénommé Eleuthère Irénée) qui lui permet d'affirmer qu'il était jeune à l'époque de la révolution.
- *Sur le déisme: lettre aux auteurs du publiciste*, An XIV. C'est un écrit téméraire, surtout à l'époque du Concordat. Du Pont se proclame déiste et énumère une série de grands hommes qui selon lui l'étaient, dont Quesnay et Turgot.

Il convient de citer ici quelques lignes écrites par Du Pont le 5 novembre 1771,[55] donc contemporaines des *Lettres d'Abraham Mansword*, dans lesquelles Du Pont verse dans le prosélytisme et tente de faire du très luthérien margrave de Bade un déiste 'pennsylvanien': 'Votre Altesse [...] pourra faire [...] en Europe, ce qui est commencé en Pennsylvanie; où comme le disait le célèbre Benjamin Franklin, toutes les sectes se fondent insensiblement [...] dans une religion pure, simple, naturelle, morale, civile, débarrassée de toute fable [...], digne de l'homme et du Dieu qu'il doit adorer.' Il s'agit là d'un rapport très étroit reliant le déisme de Du Pont à la Pennsylvanie par le truchement de Benjamin Franklin qui fait immédiatement songer au préambule déiste de la première *Lettre d'Abraham Mansword*.

Pour les textes esthétiques de Du Pont, je signale celui qui est le plus proche des *Lettres*, intitulé *Des spectacles nationaux*,[56] envoyé au fils du margrave de Bade le 31 décembre 1772. Du Pont vante 'la cérémonie de l'ouverture des terres' en Chine, proclame que 'les

---

54. La traduction en anglais de 1947 reproduit la page de titre de l'exemplaire de la Library of Congress de l'édition originale sur laquelle Jefferson a inscrit le nom de l'auteur.
55. Il s'agit d'une lettre écrite au margrave de Bade; voir Knies (1892), t.1, p.132-33.
56. Voir Knies (1892), t.2, p.15-25.

spectacles du peuple sont des fêtes [...] civiles, politiques, religieuses, relatives à de grands objets d'une utilité générale' et propose quatre fêtes annuelles célébrant les saisons. Il décrira un peu plus tard la fête du printemps.[57] La conception moralisatrice de l'utilité des beaux-arts et de la littérature est fréquente chez Du Pont, et je renvoie pour d'autres textes semblables à une analyse de Liana Vardi.[58] Ces pages de Vardi, consacrées à ce qu'elle nomme 'Physiocratic Aesthetics', sont d'autant plus intéressantes que son étude de la conception 'utilitaire' des beaux-arts chez les physiocrates est consacrée presque exclusivement à Du Pont mais conclut avec quelques lignes extraites de *L'Heureuse Nation, ou Relations du gouvernement des Féliciens* de Le Mercier de La Rivière, utopie plus ou moins physiocratique publiée en 1792, soit plus de vingt ans après les *Lettres d'Abraham Mansword*. Je reviendrai bientôt sur ce livre.

Il reste à évoquer des textes envoyés par Du Pont au margrave de Bade qui ne sont pas de lui mais qui semblent confirmer le retentissement du livre de de Lolme chez des proches de Du Pont. Dans sa *Lettre à Scheffer*, envoyée également comme indiqué au margrave de Bade, Du Pont reconnaissait de 'Bonnes Loix' en Angleterre et incluait 'celles relatives à la procédure criminelle' en ajoutant qu'il les discuterait dans une prochaine lettre.[59] Du Pont se contenta d'envoyer au margrave de Bade une correspondance entre Condorcet et Turgot[60] qui portait sur cette question. La correspondance débuta apparemment par une lettre de Turgot à Condorcet du 12 février 1771. Elle ne mentionne pas le livre de de Lolme et il est possible que, quand Turgot envoya cette première lettre, il ignorait l'existence du livre (je rappelle qu'il fut annoncé en Hollande en avril 1771). La 'jurisprudence anglaise' intervint dans la première lettre de Condorcet du 25 avril 1771. La réponse de Turgot du 17 mai 1771 est fort troublante: Turgot regrette de ne pouvoir 'traiter [la matière] comme elle le devrait' et ajoute 'Vous êtes accoutumé à entendre à demi mot.' Cela semble un appel à la prudence: il était dangereux de faire allusion à ce livre interdit dans une correspondance dont

---

57. Voir Knies (1892), t.2, p.149-57.
58. Voir Liana Vardi, *The Physiocrats and the world of the Enlightenment* (Cambridge et New York, 2012), p.192-202.
59. Voir *Lettre à Scheffer*, n° 35, p.269.
60. Elle fut publiée dans Knies (1892) à la suite du texte de la lettre à Scheffer, à partir de la p.232 du t.2.

rien ne garantissait le secret.[61] Je conjecture que l'apparition du livre de de Lolme explique en bonne partie cet échange et sa date. On peut ajouter une coïncidence remarquable qui renforce cette conjecture et établit l'importance accordée par les physiocrates au livre de de Lolme: le 13 mai 1774, en clôturant la huitième année des 'assemblées Economiques' tenues chez le marquis de Mirabeau,[62] Du Pont fit référence aux travaux qu'il y avait présentés en nommant dans le même paragraphe 'quelques morceaux [...] sur la Constitution d'Angleterre', allusion à sa *Lettre à Scheffer* qui circula donc à Paris dans l'année 1773-1774 sous forme orale ou écrite, et 'les *Lettres sur la procédure criminelle* que j'ai eu l'honneur de vous lire il y a quelques jours'.

iii. A qui faut-il attribuer les *Lettres d'Abraham Mansword*?

Tillet (2001, p.424), avait consacré quelques lignes aux *Lettres* mais avait pris pour argent comptant la fiction de la traduction d'un article du *Pennsylvany's chronicle*. Aldridge (1951), suivi par Albertone (2015), privilégia l'interprétation 'américaine' des *Lettres* et les attribua à Barbeu Du Bourg, alors que la correspondance de Franklin exclut à elle seule cette hypothèse.[63] En 2014, Herencia attribuait les *Lettres* à Le Mercier de La Rivière. Cette attribution est rendue très improbable par l'examen de la seule lettre connue de Le Mercier à Franklin. Dans cette lettre du 21 septembre 1774, donc bien postérieure aux *Lettres d'Abraham Mansword*, Le Mercier se présente à Franklin en excipant de leurs amis communs parisiens, ce qui implique que les deux hommes n'avaient aucun contact jusqu'alors.[64] On peut penser que, si Le Mercier avait été l'auteur des *Lettres*, il s'en serait prévalu auprès de

---

61. La procédure criminelle anglaise occupe les p.104-41 du livre de de Lolme dans l'édition de 1771.

62. Voir Knies (1892), t.2, p.196 et 201.

63. Cependant Manuela Albertone, informée de mon enquête, corrigea son attribution et reconnut l'importance du livre de de Lolme; voir Albertone (2018), p.105. Cette correction rend inutile la réfutation de l'attribution à Barbeu Du Bourg.

64. Cette lettre, datant d'une époque cruciale du ministère Turgot, dans laquelle l'austère magistrat propose une 'spéculation' consistant à importer en France '100 mille quintaux [...] de farine [des colonies américaines]' et à exporter en Amérique le vin de Le Mercier de La Rivière produit en Anjou, fut signalée, mais non publiée, par Herencia dans sa thèse (non publiée), 'Physiocratie et gouvernementalité: l'œuvre de Lemercier de La Rivière', 2 vol., Paris Ouest Nanterre La Défense, 2011.

306 *Gabriel Sabbagh*

Franklin, et on se demande comment un Le Mercier non proche de Franklin aurait pu inventer la fiction du *Pennsylvany's chronicle.*

Le principal argument pour cette attribution est l'existence d'un exemplaire fragmentaire des *Ephémérides* à la bibliothèque municipale de Lyon dans lequel Du Pont a inscrit les noms des auteurs des articles. Ces annotations de Du Pont semblent largement fiables, mais comportent une anomalie évidente: Du Pont attribue l'ouvrage d'Abeille, *Principes sur la liberté du commerce des grains* (1768), à Le Mercier de La Rivière. L'écriture des annotations étant tardive, on peut les dater de la période 1800-1815.

Il existe une explication raisonnable à l'annotation de Du Pont attribuant les *Lettres* à Le Mercier, suggérée en fait par sa lettre à Jefferson du 31 mars 1816 relative à son projet constitutionnel pour les 'Républiques Equinoxiales' précédemment évoqué.[65] Du Pont indique qu'il n'est pas question pour lui d'imprimer cet ouvrage en français, car il redoute les persécutions que pourrait entraîner la publication d'un chapitre, celui sur 'la représentation nationale, et du gouvernement en général',[66] qui exposeraient une centaine de cartons, 'le travail de ma vie', à la destruction.

Dans les *Lettres d'Abraham Mansword* les passages qui pouvaient déclencher l'ire des autorités du Consulat ou de l'Empire abondaient: ceux politiques, relatifs à 'la représentation nationale', et d'autres que Du Pont pouvait difficilement avouer, alors qu'il souhaitait être nommé sénateur ou obtenir la Légion d'honneur: le texte était alors certainement sulfureux, en particulier mais pas seulement par son déisme; le passage, précédemment cité, sur 'les prohibitions [...] les douanes [...] les réglemens tyranniques' pouvait être interprété comme une critique de la politique économique du Consulat et de l'Empire. A cette époque Du Pont était attaché à la bibliothèque de l'Arsenal et dans une situation précaire. Le plus commode pour Du Pont était d'attribuer les *Lettres* à un physiocrate mort.[67]

L'Heureuse Nation, évoquée à la fin de la section précédente, a été présentée par Bernard Herencia comme une œuvre 'duale' des *Lettres* et les Féliciens comme d'autres Pennsylvaniens. Le titre de son édition

---

65. Voir https://founders.archives.gov/documents/Jefferson/03-09-02-0426-0001 (date de dernière consultation le 11 décembre 2024).
66. Du Pont indique qu'il s'agit du treizième chapitre, qui porte sur 'la représentation nationale, et du gouvernement en général', si l'on se fie au catalogue Freeman's mentionné à la note 8.
67. Le Mercier est décédé en 1801.

des *Œuvres utopiques* de Le Mercier de La Rivière, dans laquelle il a inclus les *Lettres d'Abraham Mansword*, est éloquent. Dans ce livre le seul rôle de Du Pont est d'être l'auteur des annotations de Lyon, et de Lolme n'y est jamais mentionné. L'interprétation des *Lettres* par Herencia peut être résumée par cette citation: 'le physiocrate [Le Mercier], sous couvert d'une identité supposée pennsylvanienne, s'adresse aux Français.'[68] Herencia a-t-il raison de rassembler deux ouvrages écrits à vingt ans de distance dans des circonstances totalement différentes? Il y a un point dans *L'Heureuse Nation* qui fait songer aux *Lettres*, l'évolution doctrinale de Le Mercier sur les 'hommes nationaux': Le Mercier revient sur la primauté accordée aux propriétaires fonciers et s'inspire des 'cahiers des états'.[69] De manière plus générale, Le Mercier modifie de manière si fondamentale sa doctrine dans ce livre, en préconisant dans certains cas 'l'interdiction de l'exportation', en corrigeant sur ce point les 'économistes', et en s'en prenant aux 'spéculations des particuliers, et à la concurrence des vendeurs', que l'on se demande ce que l'auteur de ce livre a gardé de ses convictions physiocratiques.[70]

Manuela Albertone a émis dans sa correspondance avec moi et dans Albertone (2018) l'hypothèse intéressante d'une collaboration entre Le Mercier de La Rivière et Du Pont. Si l'on ne peut l'exclure, l'examen des divers arguments pousse à privilégier la part de Du Pont.

Il est utile de revenir à l'exemplaire de la Fondation Heertje qui apporte des renseignements précieux. Cet exemplaire est dans sa condition d'origine, broché mais avec des couvertures renforcées

---

68. P.-P. Le Mercier de La Rivière, *Pennsylvaniens*, p.12.
69. Voir Paul-Pierre Le Mercier de La Rivière, *L'Heureuse Nation, ou Relations du gouvernement des Féliciens, peuple souverainement libre sous l'empire absolu de ses loix*, 2 vol. (Paris, Chez Buisson, 1792), t.1, p.108-14. Les 'cahiers des états' sont nommément cités p.110.
70. Voir P.-P. Le Mercier de La Rivière, *L'Heureuse Nation*, t.2, p.436: 'la nécessité de conserver à l'Industrie Nationale les matieres premieres de sa main-d'œuvre, paroît n'avoir point été apperçue par les Ecrivains auxquels on a donné le nom d'économistes.' On est très loin de la condamnation des 'prohibitions' des *Lettres d'Abraham Mansword*. On trouve plus loin au même ouvrage, p.438, une attaque surprenante contre la 'liberté indéfinie dans le Commerce d'une denrée de *premier besoin* [qui] conduit naturellement à son Monopole' (c'est Le Mercier qui souligne). Mathilde Lemée, 'Le citoyen dans *L'Heureuse Nation ou Gouvernement des Féliciens* de Le Mercier de La Rivière (1792)', *Revue juridique de l'Ouest* 3 (2013), þ.271-303, a signalé et longuement analysé le changement des idées *politiques* de Le Mercier (sans cependant examiner ses nouvelles convictions en économie).

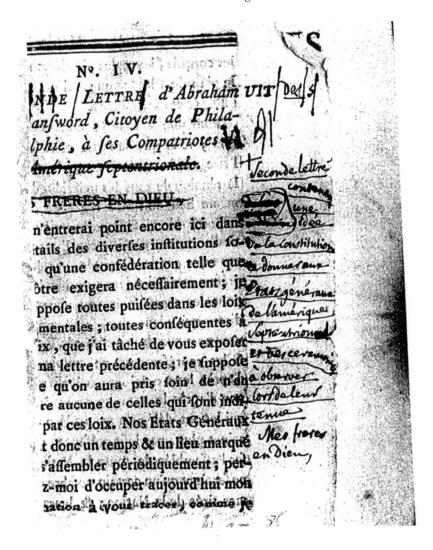

Figure 1: feuillet récupéré sous le papier de garde du premier plat de la couverture du numéro 12 des *Ephémérides* de 1771, broché, de la collection Arnold Heertje, par M. Herre de Vries, de l'atelier de photographie Restauratie Nijhoff Asser.

avec des feuillets rejetés par la censure ou des épreuves corrigées par Du Pont, le tout dissimulé sous les gardes des couvertures. Tous les feuillets qui ont pu être déchiffrés grâce à des techniques photographiques complexes (rayons ultra-violets, etc.) correspondent à des textes qui sont certainement de Du Pont, sauf éventuellement un feuillet correspondant au début de la seconde des *Lettres d'Abraham Mansword*, qui est une épreuve corrigée de la main de Du Pont (voir Figure 1): le titre de la *Lettre* a été modifié et d'autres changements ont été opérés. Il est difficile de croire que Du Pont aurait pris en 1772 ces libertés avec un texte de Le Mercier de La Rivière, auguste aîné hautement considéré par Quesnay et auteur d'un livre qualifié de 'sublime' par Du Pont et ses amis, *L'Ordre naturel et essentiel des sociétés politiques*. Cette découverte matérielle fortuite renforce tous les éléments qui plaident pour une implication étroite de Du Pont dans les *Lettres d'Abraham Mansword*: son déisme, son intérêt constant pour l'Angleterre, l'importance qu'il attachait au rôle des beaux-arts, sa paternité des *Lettres* 'américaines' signées H.

***

Je crois avoir élucidé la raison d'être des *Lettres d'Abraham Mansword*: elles sont au moins autant une réaction au livre de de Lolme et une critique du modèle anglais qu'une préfiguration du modèle américain. Les interprétations précédentes des *Lettres d'Abraham Mansword*, Tillet (2001), Herencia dans son édition des *Œuvres utopiques* de Le Mercier de La Rivière (2014), Albertone (2015),[71] supposaient que l'auteur de ces *Lettres* ait eu le don de prophétie et ait anticipé dès 1771-1772 que les colonies américaines seraient indépendantes, formeraient une confédération et tenteraient d'avoir une constitution républicaine. Certes Franklin était un grand esprit et Du Pont l'a certainement compris, mais rien n'était décidé en 1771-1772. L'étincelle qui a donné naissance aux *Lettres* est le livre de de Lolme, dont le retentissement fut probablement accentué par son interdiction en France: Du Pont a dit vrai dans la *Lettre à Scheffer* en soulignant que l'interdiction d'un livre accroissait son attractivité.[72]

Je crois aussi avoir montré que Du Pont est au moins le coauteur des *Lettres*, premier écrit de la série de ses textes constitutionnels inspirés par l'Angleterre et l'Amérique, qui s'achève avec le projet de 1815, et j'ai fourni une preuve intrinsèque claire de sa paternité des *Lettres* signées H., qui sont le premier volet des *Lettres* 'américaines'

---

71. Voir p.15: '[les *Lettres d'Abraham Mansword* constituent] la première lecture de la réalité américaine [...] Cinq ans avant la parution du *Common Sense* de Thomas Paine, Dubourg devinait déjà la révolution et la création d'une république fédérale.' Le mot 'réalité' ne semble pas justifié.
72. Voir *Lettre à Scheffer*, n° 34, p.242.

310 *Gabriel Sabbagh*

des *Ephémérides*. Il est cependant impossible d'exclure une collaboration avec Le Mercier de La Rivière, au moins pour la première *Lettre d'Abraham Mansword*, pour laquelle aucun élément matériel, comparable à celui fourni par l'exemplaire de la Fondation Heertje, n'est connu, alors que la seconde *Lettre* rassemble la plupart des éléments que l'on retrouve dans d'autres écrits de Du Pont, notamment sa critique de la vénalité des institutions anglaises, sa défense de la liberté religieuse, le refus de l'obligation de rejeter la transsubstantiation, l'importance accordée aux beaux-arts et aux cérémonies. La comparaison avec un texte presque contemporain de Du Pont, la *Lettre à Scheffer*, fut, je l'espère, suffisamment convaincante.

De nombreuses questions demeurent, notamment celle de l'influence des *Lettres*. Qui les a lues? Quelle place ont-elles dans le 'mythe américain'? Le cas de Beaurieu, auquel il fut rapidement fait allusion, qui s'est manifestement inspiré de ces *Lettres* dans un ouvrage qu'il convient de lui restituer, montre que l'influence en France de ces *Lettres* fut plus grande qu'on ne le suppose en général, et cela bien avant l'indépendance des colonies américaines.[73]

On n'en a pas fini avec les *Lettres d'Abraham Mansword*.

---

73. Gaspard Guillard de Beaurieu, *La Ferme de Pennsylvanie* (Philadelphie, PA, et Paris, Chez Ribou, 1775). La p.24 établit que Beaurieu est l'auteur de cet ouvrage anonyme. L'auteur nous assure que 'la Pennsylvanie se gouverne aujourd'hui par les Loix éternelles de l'ordre' et associe les *Ephémérides* et la Pennsylvanie. Il avait auparavant incorporé au t.2 d'une édition tardive de *L'Elève de la nature*, 3 vol. (Lille, J.-B. Henry, 1771) les *Lettres* signées H.

Pontiana: Du Pont de Nemours's physiocratic dream in America

AYA TANAKA

NYU Stern School of Business

This two-part article examines the business plan devised by Pierre-Samuel Du Pont de Nemours in the late 1790s to raise funds for his family's immigration to the United States and the establishment of his American enterprise. First, I discuss the relationship between the business plan and economic theory (physiocracy), showing that Du Pont's aim was principally a land-speculation scheme, and that this scheme would in turn allow Du Pont to eventually buy enough land to establish his own physiocratic colony in the United States. In the second part I explore what this physiocratic colony would have looked like by examining mythical, utopian and pastoral allusions in contemporary works, both fiction and non-fiction.

i. Business imperatives and physiocratic dreams

Following the Directoire coup of 4 September 1797, and what he perceived as his public-service career dead-end, Du Pont abruptly decided to leave France and move to the United States with his family to start a business.[1] His connection to the United States, however, had been established many years earlier. Du Pont had not only studied and published on American trading as well as economic and political issues, he had also developed friendships with Benjamin Franklin and especially Thomas Jefferson. His eldest son, Victor Du Pont, had been a French diplomat in the United States for twelve years. Notably, Du Pont seems to have collected extensive information about the business environment in the United States in the run up to his move.[2]

1. Mack Thompson, 'Causes and circumstances of the Du Pont family's emigration', *French historical studies* 6:1 (1969), p.67-77.
2. Martin Giraudeau, 'The predestination of capital: projecting E. I. Du Pont

312   *Aya Tanaka*

Du Pont needed a substantial initial investment to finance his move to America and establish a business. Between 1797 and 1799, he turned his assets into cash, and did what any modern entrepreneur would: he devised a business plan explaining the reasons why investors should back him and showing how he planned to generate profits for them; then he printed a prospectus and set off to raise the needed funds among the members of his network. Du Pont's prospectus is a forty-page document, named *Compagnie d'Amérique*, detailing the operations of his new company.[3] The prospectus is divided into two parts, the *plan* and the *actes de la société* (incorporation deed). The first is a detailed description of how the Du Ponts planned to establish two *maisons de commerce de commission* and an *opération territoriale d'acqui-sitions et revente de terres*. The careful implementation and subsequent interaction between the three were at the core of the money-making scheme. The commercial houses would provide more immediate revenues, while the territorial operation would require more upfront funds and time to appreciate. The deed summarises the venture as such:

> Ayant résolu de se réunir en Société pour multiplier les rapports utiles de Commerce entre la France et les Etats-Unis de l'Amérique, et faire la commission pour les Citoyens qui voudraient envoyer, soit des fonds, soit des marchandises, d'Europe en Amérique, ou d'Amérique en Europe, comme aussi pour acheter des terres dans les Etats-Unis,

---

de Nemours and Company into the New World', *Critical historical studies* 6:1 (2019), p.33-62. Giraudeau argues that P.-S. Du Pont de Nemours did extensive research on the business environment in America before leaving France.

3.   Pierre-Samuel Du Pont de Nemours, *Compagnie d'Amérique: mémoire qui contient le plan des opérations de la Société* (Paris, n.n., 1799). There are four additional summaries describing Du Pont's business project. The first, *Esquisse d'un projet d'établissement dans l'Amérique septentrionale* (Hagley Museum and Library, Wilmington, DE, hereafter HML, W3-1337), dated from 1797, is in the hand of Mme Bureaux de Pusy, Du Pont's stepdaughter. Mme Bureaux de Pusy included it in a letter to Victor Du Pont, who was still in the United States, asking him for advice and approval. A more detailed one is the *Extrait d'un plan d'une opération rurale et commerciale à exécuter dans les Etats-Unis de l'Amérique* (HML, L1-469). The last two are the *Notes et observations sur le plan d'un établissement rural et commercial dans les Etats Unis de l'Amérique* (HML, L1-471) and the *Aperçu sur l'établissement commercial & rural que va former en Amérique la maison Dupont de Nemours père & fils & Cie* (HML, L1-472). The paper I presented at the 'Colloque Du Pont de Nemours' in December 2017 was based on the *Extrait*, but since then I have found the original business prospectus upon which all these summaries are based.

Pontiana: Du Pont de Nemours's physiocratic dream in America 313

les améliorer, tant par la culture, que par d'autres travaux, et qu'en ouvrant des débouchés à leurs productions, et les revendre lorsqu'elles seront augmentées de valeur, ont arrêté les conditions fondamentales de leur association, ainsi qu'il suit.[4]

Du Pont also proposed a generous return in the form of increasing yearly dividends, title to land, and the prospect of substantial returns on capital at the end of twelve years – up to twenty times the initial investment.

Du Pont aimed at raising up to 4, and no less than 2, million francs.[5] However, the family set sail in late 1799 with just over 200,000 francs,[6] or 10 per cent of the minimum amount. While, in the business plan, commercial and territorial activities are described as both separate and mutually reinforcing, a hierarchy of interest developed as early as 1798. Due to the low amount of capital available, Du Pont had already determined before his departure to the US to delay the purchase of land and raise the lacking funds for their territorial purchases via their trading company business.[7]

Du Pont's American territorial enterprise has often been characterised as a physiocratic colony.[8] The plan to improve land to increase

4. Du Pont, *Compagnie d'Amérique*, p.33.
5. On paper, Du Pont claimed to have raised 2.14 million francs, with 214 of the 400 shares, at 10,000 francs each, subscribed, but this number reflects the interest, more than the funds actually received. Four months before the family's departure, Du Pont hoped for 1 million francs in funds, but acknowledged the possibility that it would be closer to 600,000. HML, Longwood Manuscripts, L1-209, letter from P.-S. Du Pont to Bureaux de Pusy, April 1799.
6. Ambrose Saricks cites funds of 214,347 francs, but he does not cite sources; see Ambrose Saricks, *Pierre Samuel Du Pont de Nemours* (Lawrence, KS, 1965), p.273. The suspiciously precise number may be a calculation using numbers from the 'Etat au vrai de notre affaire', a confidential document in the hand of Victor Du Pont (HML, Longwood Manuscripts, L1-483). In 1801, Victor Du Pont explains that, 'Au lieu d'avoir placé 400 actions, nous n'en avons pas eu plus de 80 souscrites et 60 payées jusqu'à ce jour'; letter from Victor Du Pont to Necker de Germany, 21 March 1801, in *De Staël-Du Pont letters: correspondence of Madame de Staël and Pierre Samuel Du Pont de Nemours and other members of the Necker and Du Pont families*, ed. and translated by James F. Marshall (Madison, WI, 1968), p.53. This translates into 120,000 francs in cash, although it is not clear whether this includes the personal investments of Du Pont himself and Bureaux de Pusy.
7. From Du Pont de Nemours to Bureaux de Pusy, April 1799.
8. 'The scheme around which Du Pont's mind revolved was most agreeable to his physiocratic predilections. Somewhere in the vast and fertile reaches of America might one not establish a model agricultural community operated on the best scientific principles and on a scale large enough to return substantial

314   *Aya Tanaka*

its value may be based on the physiocratic idea that agriculture forms the base of an economy, but Du Pont was not set on agriculture. 'Cultivating the land', in the plan he proposed, meant to raise cattle:

> On fera d'abord peu de culture, parce que la main-d'œuvre est trop chère, et que les hommes sont trop rares dans ce pays neuf. On se bornera prudemment pendant quelques années, et comme les habitants actuels, à l'éducation des bestiaux *qui vont eux-mêmes au marché*. Il n'y a point de pays où ils réussissent mieux. Ayant des capitaux libres, on montera sur ces bestiaux une branche de commerce.[9]

The focus on cattle-raising, in turn, underscores the idea that Du Pont simply wanted to make his land investment more attractive to future buyers. In physiocratic doctrine, cattle are not an output, but an input, essentially sources of fertiliser and machines to be used in agriculture.[10] Besides cattle-raising, the commercial operations Du Pont proposed for the colony were explicitly logging, cured meats and cheesemaking, along with the establishment of commercial outposts to trade them.[11] Together, these activities were simply meant to make the land more liveable and increase its asset value.

The fact that Du Pont veers away from proposing a stricter physiocratic plan is indicative of a dissociation between the idea of physiocracy as economic policy and the reality of business practice.

---

profits?' (Saricks, *Pierre Samuel Du Pont de Nemours*, p.269); 'The community would be composed of Frenchmen and other Europeans and would, of course, practice physiocracy' (James McLain, *The Economic writings of Du Pont de Nemours*, Wilmington, DE, 1977, p.47); 'As one can see, Du Pont's physiocratic doctrine guided his business action in its overall structure: wealth was meant to come exclusively from the agricultural production of a "rural house"' (Martin Giraudeau, 'Performing physiocracy: Pierre Samuel Du Pont de Nemours and the limits of political engineering', *Journal of cultural economy* 3:2, 2010, p.225-42, 234); 'In Du Pont's eyes, the business prospects appeared bright; and he, physiocrat and student of Turgot, seemed about to prove that theory can lead to good practice' (Raymond Betts, 'Du Pont de Nemours in Napoleonic France, 1802-1815', *French historical studies* 5:2, 1967, p.188-203, 189).

9. Du Pont, *Compagnie d'Amérique*, p.18 (original emphasis).

10. 'Qu'on favorise la multiplication des bestiaux; car ce sont eux qui fournissent aux terres les engrais qui procurent les riches moissons'; François Quesnay, *Maximes générales du gouvernement économique d'un royaume agricole*, in *Physiocratie, ou Constitution naturelle du gouvernement le plus avantageux au genre humain*, 2 vols (Leiden and Paris, Merlin, 1768), vol.1, p.114.

11. Du Pont, *Compagnie d'Amérique*, p.18-21.

Du Pont's plan aimed at making his investors, his family and himself rich, but the path to riches was not physiocracy; rather, Du Pont's plan detailed how his firm would take advantage of a particular situation in the United States: first, the infrastructural needs of the region surrounding the nation's new capital, Washington, DC, and labour scarcity. Du Pont was quite precise about the location of his land purchase: the region he targeted for development was not only very fertile, but also conveniently located not far from Washington, DC, and easily accessible via river boat (see Figure 1). One of the trading houses, in turn, would be established in Alexandria, VA, across the Potomac River from the capital. Du Pont's plan was smart and ambitious – to place himself in the vicinity of a new town, in the state led by his friend Jefferson, to be ready to capitalise on the influx of people and money in the region. However, Du Pont underestimated the extent of land speculation already under way in the United States. The territorial enterprise, already jeopardised by the lack of investment funds, was further dealt a blow only three weeks after Du Pont's arrival in the United States when Thomas Jefferson advised him in no uncertain terms to avoid land purchases at all costs.[12]

I have argued so far that the core of Du Pont's business plan was land speculation: he wanted to buy land, improve it and sell it at a considerable profit after twelve years. In fact, the shareholders' deed requires the sale and dissolution of the partnership at the end of the period. Yet some inconsistencies and references in the business prospectus itself point to a different and vastly more ambitious project. The first one is the very location for his twenty-by-sixty league land plot itself, as shown in Figure 2. Du Pont's plan placed his colony in Northern Virginia, one of the original thirteen colonies, a state since 1776, and headed by his friend Thomas Jefferson. On the business

---

12. 'The present agonizing state of commerce, and the swarms of speculators in money and in land, would induce me to beseech you to trust no-body, in whatever form they may approach you till you are fully informed' (letter from Thomas Jefferson to Pierre-Samuel Du Pont de Nemours, 17 January 1800). Du Pont takes the advice to heart: 'Les idées que j'ai conçues en Europe tendent à me rapprocher de vous en plaçant le centre de mon travail dans la haute Virginie. Mais je ne puis m'arrêter à aucun Plan avant d'être plus éclairé. Je savais déjà qu'il faut être ici extrêmement réservé, surtout lorsqu'on y veut gérer en honnête homme les intérêts d'autrui' (letter from Pierre-Samuel Du Pont de Nemours to Thomas Jefferson, 20 January 1800); *The Papers of Thomas Jefferson*, vol.31: *1 February 1799-31 May 1800*, ed. Barbara B. Oberg (Princeton, NJ, 2004), p.326-29.

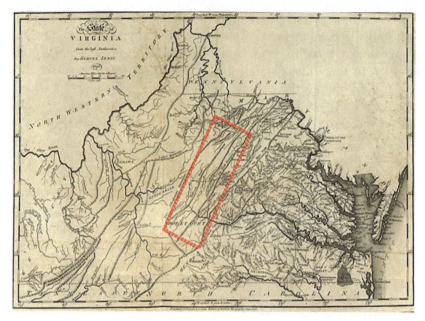

Figure 2: Samuel Lewis, *The State of Virginia from the best authorities* (1794), engraved by James Smithers, printed for Mathew Carey, with the enterprise's projected territory calculated and demarcated by Hernando Cortina (2017), based on Du Pont's coordinates in *Compagnie d'Amérique*, p.10-11.

plan, Du Pont predicted that his company's main establishment would become the capital of the county, and perhaps one day of the state:

> Ce dépôt d'actes amènera naturellement où il se trouvera placé, les archives, la *court-house*, le séjour du tribunal, les assemblées politiques, judiciaires et d'élection. Il en résultera que le principal établissement de la Compagnie deviendra, sans que l'on ait paru y prétendre, par le consentement commun, pour la plus grande commodité de tous, la capitale du *comté*, et par la suite, de l'ÉTAT dont il fera partie.[13]

Du Pont's projections for a capital, with government offices and official record-keeping, also point to his ultimate desire to establish a legitimate government – although positioning a new capital city with a new government in the middle of the already established state of Virginia did not make much sense. Du Pont's ambition to found a

---

13. Du Pont, *Compagnie d'Amérique*, p.28.

Pontiana: Du Pont de Nemours's physiocratic dream in America 317

state is further underscored by another business-plan provision that a university (*collège*) should be erected in the fifth or sixth year of their twelve-year plan.[14] This suggests that Du Pont was trying to adapt his plans to the newly created 1787 Northwest Ordinance, which laid out rules for territorial expansion west of the Ohio River and for the formation of new states. An important feature of the Ordinance is the mandatory creation of a university as communities made their way to legal statehood. Furthermore, his characterisation of Kentucky as a *république indépendante* shows us the more ambitious nature of Du Pont's plan. Kentucky and Tennessee had achieved statehood in 1792 and 1796 respectively, and exemplify the potential for his own colony to achieve the same prodigious status. The establishment of an 'independent republic' clearly goes much beyond the idea of settling a rectangular plot of land in Northern Virginia to resell it in twelve years.

Such slippages in Du Pont's business prospectus imply that he had more ambitious plans than the land-speculation scheme let on. These plans are further developed in his private correspondence with his new son-in-law Jean-Xavier Bureaux de Pusy.[15] Pusy was married to Ile de France, daughter of the second Mme Du Pont, formerly Mme Pierre Poivre. Pusy was closely associated with the marquis de Lafayette, whom he followed to exile in 1792 for five years. He was the fourth managing partner in Du Pont's enterprise, in addition to Du Pont and his sons Victor and Eleuthère Irénée. Pusy was sent to America in advance of the official family move to look for lodgings and establish contacts, bearing a detailed letter from Du Pont with instructions. This letter serves as metacommentary on the business plan: among other things, it further delineates Du Pont's private ambition underlying the official purposes of the enterprise, as he characterises the territorial project as his 'véritable affaire',[16] or his true business.

---

14. Du Pont, *Compagnie d'Amérique*, p.28.
15. HML, Longwood Manuscripts, L1-209.
16. 'Mais je reviens à ma thèse de prudence, c'est que durant notre première année, il faut nous tenir en très grande réserve sur nos projets territoriaux, qui sont notre véritable affaire, et n'en parler que comme de vues que nous pourrions proposer à nos amis.' Also, 'Quant à notre véritable affaire, c'est celle dont il faut le moins parler. On n'a que trop dit que nous voulions spéculer en terres, et de là, nous verrons résulter une concurrence de propositions insidieuses de la part de gens extrêmement habiles, *clever-men*, qui ont l'air loyal, ingénu, et dans ce cas affectueux même. Il faut vous défier des américains, dès qu'ils

Du Pont's letter to Pusy corroborates the idea that there is more than a land-speculation scheme at play. While the term 'véritable affaire' could certainly indicate that Du Pont thought land ownership should take precedence over commercial establishment, further details in the letter keep pointing to something else, of a much greater magnitude: 'Il faut fonder un Empire, c'est-à-dire, une République, si nous pouvons, mais il faut surtout faire les affaires de notre compagnie.'[17] The distinction between empire/republic and the company's business, coupled with the allusion that they had a 'true business' beyond their company business, indicates that Du Pont's republic is his mysterious 'true business', which goes much beyond his Northern Virginia plans. This republic, financed by the returns of his business scheme, can in turn be further understood by further details he provides in his letter to Pusy.

While the founding of a republic may be Du Pont's ultimate secret project, the republic was clearly dependent on the financial success of the more immediate business plan. Funding was not forthcoming for either, as he plainly puts to Pusy. Du Pont knows well that they are leaving France with inadequate funds.[18] Du Pont cautions his son-in-law about the likelihood of hardship: 'Nous aurions donc la patience de compléter nos fonds par notre travail, et d'attendre qu'ils fussent suffisants pour reprendre nos projets de Numa: nous aurions même l'avantage d'être, lorsqu'il nous deviendrait enfin possible de nous y livrer, parfaitement éclairés sur tous les moyens de succès. Nous ne commencerions à peindre qu'après avoir longtemps dessiné.'[19]

Du Pont warns Pusy that to go ahead with their grand territorial project, named Numa, they will need to put in a lot of work to raise the faltering funds. Du Pont expects a five- to six-year delay but hopes

---

sont caressants, leur nature est froide et indifférente.' See HML, Longwood Manuscripts, L1-209.

17. HML, Longwood Manuscripts, L1-209.

18. 'Nous ne pouvons avoir aujourd'hui une idée juste de nos moyens. Je ne les connaitrai avec certitude que dans trois mois; il se peut que les héros et les législateurs ne soient que de médiocres propriétaires et de petits négociants. / Et sur cette possibilité notre courage doit être préparé, nos arrangements subsidiaires pris au moins dans notre prévoyance. / Je ne crois pas que dans la supposition la plus malheureuse nous puissions avoir moins d'un million; mais un million serait absolument insuffisant pour nos grands projets. / Que faire alors? que faire s'il arrivait même que nous n'eussions que six cent mille francs?' HML, Longwood Manuscripts, L1-209.

19. HML, Longwood Manuscripts, L1-209.

to use these years for gathering local intelligence to firmly launch his territorial project. Here, the painting metaphor is telling: he proposes that the delay would afford the opportunity for them to draw before painting the picture. The business prospectus, in this light, could be the sketch to the great republican plan. With Numa as the ultimate goal, Du Pont sends Pusy across the Atlantic with the mission of establishing the family's first roots on the American continent. Although Du Pont did not know where Numa would be placed, he had a clear vision of what it should look like.

> Mais quand on embrasse des millions d'acres, l'étendue d'un ou de plusieurs départements, il faut bien s'attendre qu'il y aura de tout, des rocs, des sables, des *pire barrens*, et des vallées très fertiles. On exploite celles-ci, on ouvre les communications par les autres, on y laisse les bois, on y trouve des cours d'eau importants pour les usines. On y rencontre des mines exploitables en talus, et sans qu'on soit obligé de creuser des puits. Tout est bon pourvu que la masse soit considérable et le pays salubre, qu'il y ait une assez grande quantité en bonnes terres et une autre variée dont l'intelligence et le génie tirent parti.[20]

Numa required vast amounts of land: millions of acres where the landscape and economic activity were as varied as a country could be expected to be. This all-encompassing landscape somewhere in the middle of the United States was to be an independent nation, self-sufficient, no longer tied to the development of the United States' capital. More importantly, this description gives us a glimpse of what a physiocratic nation should look like: a place for nature, but one where human intelligence takes advantage of land for wealth.

ii. Envisioning physiocracy

While this letter to Bureaux de Pusy further substantiates the idea that there is a much larger plan than that proposed in the business prospectus, this is still only a limited sketch of Numa. Other contemporary texts allow us to colour in this drawing, painting a fuller picture of Du Pont's inspiration and vision. I have chosen but a few related texts of fiction and non-fiction that help us understand the context of Du Pont's Numa in the eighteenth century – and how Numa, as it rests in imaginative territory, is exemplary of the intersection of history, political economy and literature.

20. HML, Longwood Manuscripts, L1-209.

Du Pont's territorial project is sometimes referred to as Pontiana, following a common practice in early American history: Georgia, the Carolinas, Virginia, Louisiana, to name a few, were all feminised nouns derived from kings' and queens' names. The name Pontiana betrays the centrality of Du Pont and his ideals in the inception of a new state, and that his ambition went well beyond a twenty- by sixty-league plot of land in the middle of Virginia. It also places the project more firmly in the context of American territorial expansion. However, Du Pont named his project Numa in his letter to Bureaux de Pusy. The name Numa builds on the greater mythical, nation-building vision alluded to before.

Numa seems to refer to Numa Pompilius, the second king of Rome, the one who, after the city's establishment by Romulus and Remus, codified the rules of government. Numa Pompilius is the subject of many a study about the role of religion in politics. Jean-Jacques Rousseau, in his *Considérations sur le gouvernement de Pologne*, praises him as one of the few great leaders of Antiquity precisely because he codified the spiritual relationships between people and their land. In Rousseau's view, the establishment of early nations goes hand-in-hand with the establishment of religious rites; these, in turn, are tied not to God or gods, but to the land itself:

> Ceux qui n'ont vu dans Numa qu'un instituteur de rites et de cérémonies religieuses ont bien mal jugé ce grand homme. Numa fut le vrai fondateur de Rome. Si Romulus n'eût fait qu'assembler des brigands qu'un revers pouvait disperser, son ouvrage imparfait n'eût pu résister au temps. Ce fut Numa qui le rendit solide et durable en unissant ces brigands en un corps indissoluble, en les transformant en Citoyens, moins par des lois, dont leur rustique pauvreté n'avait guère encore besoin, que par des institutions douces qui les attachaient les uns aux autres et tous à leur sol en rendant enfin leur ville sacrée par ces rites frivoles et superstitieux en apparence, dont si peu de gens sentent la force et l'effet, et dont cependant Romulus, le farouche Romulus lui-même, avait jeté les premiers fondements.[21]

Numa also appears in Jean-Pierre Claris de Florian's oeuvre, and this time as the ultimate physiocratic king. The author is principally known for edifying genres such as fables and pastorals, but, in

---

21. Jean-Jacques Rousseau, *Considérations sur le gouvernement de Pologne, et sur sa réformation projetée* (1782), https://fr.wikisource.org/wiki/Considérations_sur_le_gouvernement_de_Pologne (last accessed 11 December 2024), p.424-25.

Numa Pompilius, Florian launches into the education of kings – an influence of François Fénelon's *Télémaque*. Numa is counseled by the nymph Egeria as he reluctantly begins his reign of Rome. Egeria tells Numa Pompilius that men assemble together freely in society to defend themselves and to procure their basic needs and wants. The fundamental truth upon which Numa Pompilius' laws should be based is thus the idea of freedom and individual self-interest – in other words, liberalism: 'Tu te souviendras que les hommes se sont rassemblés librement en société, pour se procurer les secours nécessaires à leur sécurité, aux besoins et aux consolations de la vie. Du développement de cette vérité, tu verras naître tous les principes de législation.'[22]

Notably, Egeria firmly establishes agriculture as the primary economic activity of Rome. Agriculture, private property and marriage all work together and should be dignified by Numa Pompilius as the basis of this society: 'Une subsistance facile et assurée doit être le premier effet de tes loix: c'est à l'agriculture à la donner. Tu regarderas donc la classe des agriculteurs comme la plus utile; tu l'honoreras: tu assureras leurs propriétés, tu encourageras leurs mariages, tu rendras à l'art qui nourrit les hommes la dignité qu'il doit avoir.'[23] All other activities – commerce and the arts in particular – derive from the solid establishment of agriculture.[24] Still, it is only once agriculture starts producing a surplus that anything else can flourish.[25] Finally, Egeria reminds Numa Pompilius that, underlying it all, natural law is the ultimate rule, and at the base of natural law there is a love of humanity. Florian's Numa Pompilius is thus clearly charged by the nymph Egeria with establishing a physiocratic nation, where the

---

22. Jean-Pierre Claris de Florian, *Numa Pompilius: second roi de Rome* (Hamburg, Pierre François Fauche, 1788), p.308.
23. Florian, *Numa Pompilius*, p.308.
24. 'L'agriculture ne peut fleurir sans les autres arts; elle les fait naître, et les récompense. Tu les protégeras, tu les appelleras dans ton empire; et tu verras que ces arts faciliteront les travaux champêtres, en occupant, en nourrissant un grand nombre de citoyens.' Florian, *Numa Pompilius*, p.308.
25. 'Lorsque les champs et les coteaux auront donné ce qu'ils peuvent produire, il se trouvera des cultivateurs riches d'un superflu de productions qui manqueront à une autre terre. De la naîtra le commerce, que tu favoriseras, que tu laisseras toujours libre: mais tu n'oublieras jamais que le commerce, qui fait fleurir les arts, ne peut augmenter qu'en proportion des progrès de l'agriculture.' Florian, *Numa Pompilius*, p.309.

322   *Aya Tanaka*

government stays mostly out of the way, where agriculture is honoured as the most important activity, and where natural law is the rule.[26]

Florian's *Numa Pompilius* draws a clear connection between Numa the monarch and physiocracy: in Florian's account, the Roman king is called on by higher powers to establish a kingdom based on the primacy of agriculture. Yet Florian's *Essai sur la pastorale* further theorises the relationship between literature (pastoral genre) and its uses for government. According to Florian, pastorals should not exclusively feature shepherds: characters of higher social status should be brought in, as they stand to learn from the pastoral life's simplicity and their shared love of nature and virtue.[27]

Florian's prescriptions of self-governance, nature and virtue form a theoretical basis for the literary representation of physiocracy. These themes are more fully developed and integrated in a faraway colonial context by Bernardin de Saint-Pierre's 'espèce de pastorale', *Paul et Virginie*.[28] The relationship between Bernardin's *Paul et Virginie* and Du Pont's Numa is not random. First, Du Pont and Bernardin were colleagues at the Institut de France. More importantly, Du Pont's second wife, Marie Françoise Robin, was the widow of Pierre Poivre, superintendent of the Ile de France (Mauritius) when Bernardin passed by the island. Virginie's character, in turn, is said to have been inspired by Mme Poivre, who became Mme Du Pont in 1795. Du Pont had certainly read and admired *Paul et Virginie*.[29]

---

26. 'Quand tu auras établi ces trois bases fondamentales de la prospérité des états, l'agriculture, les arts et le commerce, tu t'occuperas des autres loix, auxquelles seront également soumis tous les ordres des citoyens. Elles seront en petit nombre, pour que chacun de tes sujets puisse les étudier: elles seront fondées sur l'amour de l'humanité, qui est la première, la plus sacrée de toutes les loix, la seule que la nature ait rédigée.' Florian, *Numa Pompilius*, p.309.

27. Jean-Pierre Claris de Florian, *Essai sur la pastorale*, in *Œuvres de M. de Florian* (Paris, 1805), p.146.

28. Jacques-Henri Bernardin de Saint-Pierre, 'Avant-propos', in *Paul et Virginie*, ed. Pierre Trahard (Paris, 1958), p.cxlvi.

29. 'Mon cher collègue, Je vous dois des remerciements pour les plaisirs que vous me procurez à l'autre bout du monde. Je viens de fondre en larmes en relisant *Paul et Virginie*. C'est ce que je connais de plus parfait pour la simplicité du plan, l'excellence des sentiments, et la beauté pure de l'exécution. Je ne sais qui a dit qu'on ne va pas à la posterité avec un gros bagage. Avec un diamant comme celui-là, on y est riche. C'est bien la cinquième ou sixième fois que ce modèle des petits romans me charme. Il m'a semblé que c'était la première.' HML, Longwood Manuscripts, L1-211, letter from Pierre-Samuel Du Pont de Nemours to Bernardin de Saint-Pierre, 21 July 1800.

Paul et Virginie may well be the ultimate fictional representation of physiocracy. The fundamental rule for a well-functioning relationship is a clear delineation of property rights, and, even before Virginie is born, land is divided evenly between the two families. They are counselled by the old man who narrates the story to a traveler in Mauritius: 'Je dis à ces deux dames qu'il convenait, pour l'intérêt de leurs enfants, et surtout pour empêcher l'établissement de quelque autre habitant, de partager entre elles le fond de ce bassin, qui contient environ vingt arpents.'[30] Although they treat the entire property as communal, Mme de La Tour owns the upper half of the property, and Marguerite the lower half.

While the children are briefly described as goatherds – an allusion to the pastoral theme – the mothers weave. Most of the hard work is carried out by their slaves, Domingue and Marie, but Domingue in particular cultivates the land:

> Domingue, était un noir yolof, encore robuste, quoique déjà sur l'âge. Il avait de l'expérience et un bon sens naturel. Il cultivait indifféremment sur les deux habitations les terrains qui lui semblaient les plus fertiles, et il y mettait les semences qui leur convenaient le mieux. Il semait du petit mil et du maïs dans les endroits médiocres, un peu de froment dans les bonnes terres, du riz dans les fonds marécageux; et au pied des roches, des giraumons, des courges et des concombres, qui se plaisent à y grimper. Il plantait dans les lieux secs des patates qui y viennent très sucrées, des cotonniers sur les hauteurs, des cannes à sucre dans les terres fortes, des pieds de café sur les collines, où le grain est petit, mais excellent; le long de la rivière et autour des cases, des bananiers qui donnent toute l'année de longs régimes de fruits avec un bel ombrage, et enfin quelques plantes de tabac pour charmer ses soucis et ceux de ses bonnes maîtresses. Il allait couper du bois à brûler dans la montagne, et casser des roches çà et là dans les habitations pour en aplanir les chemins. Il faisait tous ces ouvrages avec intelligence et activité, parce qu'il les faisait avec zèle.[31]

The terrain he cultivates is as varied as a small country, much like Numa. The seamless connection between the landscape and the slave's activities emphasises an attachment to the land and the incipient desire for self-sufficiency and self-determination – the beginning of nation-building. Yet, while Domingue is a 'natural

---

30. Jacques-Henri Bernardin de Saint-Pierre, *Paul et Virginie* (Paris, 1806), p.9.
31. Bernardin de Saint-Pierre, *Paul et Virginie*, p.12.

324   *Aya Tanaka*

farmer', he eventually passes his skill to Paul; in Paul, we get a second stage of land management:

> Paul, à l'âge de douze ans, plus robuste et plus intelligent que les Européens à quinze, avait embelli ce que le noir Domingue ne faisait que cultiver. [...] Sa main laborieuse avait répandu la fécondité jusque dans les lieux les plus stériles de cet enclos. [...] Mais en assujettissant ces végétaux à son plan, il ne s'était pas écarté de celui de la nature.[32]

Like Florian's Numa, he further organises the relationship between people and their soil. He subjects the landscape to the family's needs, his hard work increases soil fertility and he goes further: he transforms their small paradise into a work of art, much like Egeria had predicted to Numa: agriculture both creates and supports other arts and is nurtured by it. *Paul et Virginie*, as such, could be seen as Bernardin's application of Florian's physiocratic rules in *Numa Pompilius* to a colonial pastoral setting. Du Pont's Numa, in turn, invokes the same characteristics of mythical Rome and pastoral Mauritius: it aims to be a self-contained, self-sufficient, virtuous nation, where private property is protected, agriculture is privileged and every other activity follows this natural law.

Pursuing Numa's literary connections to the fiction of Florian and Bernardin de Saint-Pierre allows us to gain insight into Du Pont's vision for his American republic. This vision may be further substantiated by travel accounts – especially those of experienced administrators such as Pierre Poivre and Le Mercier de La Rivière, who experimented with physiocracy on the Ile de France and in Martinique respectively. Louis-Antoine de Bougainville, the first Frenchman to lead an expedition around the globe, is perhaps less known as a governor of the Malouines – now the Falkland Islands – than he is for his sojourn in Tahiti. Bougainville's description of the Malouines points to his true utopian vision, one similar to Du Pont's, and even Bernardin's own:

Cependant le temps et l'expérience nous apprirent que le travail et la constance n'y seraient pas sans fruits. Des baies immenses à l'abri des vents par ces mêmes montagnes qui répandent de leur sein les cascades et les ruisseaux; des prairies couvertes de gras pâturages, faits pour alimenter des troupeaux nombreux, des lacs et des étangs pour les abreuver; point de contestations pour la propriété du lieu;

---

32. Bernardin de Saint-Pierre, *Paul et Virginie*, p.42.

point d'animaux à craindre par leur férocité, leur venin ou leur importunité; une quantité innombrable d'amphibies des plus utiles, d'oiseaux et de poissons du meilleur goût; une matière combustible pour suppléer au défaut du bois; des plantes reconnues spécifiques aux maladies des navigateurs; un climat salubre par sa température également éloignée du chaud et du froid, et bien plus propre à former des hommes robustes et sains, que ces contrées enchanteresses où l'abondance même devient un poison, et la chaleur une obligation de ne rien faire.[33]

Bougainville had been in charge of the colonisation of the Malouines between 1764 and 1767. Like Du Pont's Numa, the Malouines presented a variety of landscape features that would allow a society to emerge and thrive. We see here again the idea that such a great landscape is a canvas for the ruler's imagination, and hard work and industriousness are all that is needed to find agricultural bounty and happiness. However, this description of the Malouines also points to a problem with these utopian views and plans: people. At the very end of this paragraph, Bougainville alludes to Tahiti as an enchanting corner of the world. He saw Tahiti as hopelessly populated. His stay in that island was marked by the threat of attack by the Tahitians, whom he regarded as unruly. The Malouines, in turn, were uninhabited until he brought twenty-seven fellow Frenchmen to colonise the islands. Likewise, Numa would flourish in an area Du Pont imagined as 'empty lands'.[34] This is indeed one of the few guarantees for the proper regulation of private property, which, as we have seen, is the basis of all other physiocratic principles. Regardless of geographic location, what all these literary – fictional or non-fictional – representations of physiocracy assert is that land can be subjected to and modified by human genius, for the benefit and ultimate happiness of humankind. However, they also regard humankind ambivalently, in an us-versus-them dichotomy that promotes isolation and highlights the dangers of cultural contamination.

Du Pont had a similar plan for Numa: 'Mais si je parviens à

33. Louis Antoine de Bougainville, *Voyage autour du monde*, ed. Michel Bideaux and Sonia Faesel (Paris, 2001), p.96.
34. 'The indifferent state [regarding agriculture] of that among us does not proceed from a want of knowledge merely; it is from our having such quantities of land to waste as we please. In Europe the object is to make the most of their land, labor being abundant: here it is to make the most of our labor, land being abundant.' Thomas Jefferson, 'Notes on the state of Virginia', in *Thomas Jefferson: writings*, ed. Merrill Peterson (New York, 1984), p.212.

rassembler seulement trois cents familles sous un climat salubre, sur un terroir fertile, et à faire deux autres bons petits livres à l'usage de leurs enfants, mes petits-enfants verront encore un très bel ordre des choses, qui pourra être durable et se propager, parce qu'il aura commencé par le commencement.'[35] And, if we follow the money that did come in from his investors (to Irénée's gunpowder mill starting in 1802), we can finally discern a third and successful version of a colony, on a much smaller scale: the Eleutherian Mills and Hagley in Wilmington, Delaware. In her anthropological study of the Du Ponts' myths and family traditions, Kaori O'Connor argues that, while the company's official narratives tend to obfuscate the family's communism and physiocratic ideals in its early years, supplementary documents show precisely that. O'Connor suggests that, 'bound by ties of blood, marriage and employment intensified by physical and social isolation, living and dying within sound of the powder works, the Duponts developed a strong attachment to and identification with the land on the Brandywine.'[36]

In O'Connor's account, the Du Ponts essentially formed a physio-cratic colony near Wilmington, Delaware in consecutive stages. In the nineteenth century, the family and their workers lived in physical and social isolation, remaining a closed group. Life was characterised by hard, dusty work, communal property, and a steady improvement in production and workers' conditions. Only in the twentieth century did Eleutherian Mills become a place of myth, where the dirty industrial past was beautified, the Arcadian landscape dominated and human genius was celebrated. It is at Hagley that Pontiana finally rests.

35. Cambridge, Houghton Library, Harvard University, MS Fr80 4, letter from P.-S. Du Pont to Marie-Anne Lavoisier, 23 October 1798.
36. Kaori O'Connor, *Lycra: how a fiber shaped America* (New York, 2011), p.26-53.

Des finances et des banques américaines: autour des rapports entre Du Pont de Nemours et Thomas Jefferson

MANUELA ALBERTONE

Université de Turin

'Je veux mourir dans un pays où la liberté ne soit pas seulement dans les loix', écrivait Du Pont de Nemours à Thomas Jefferson en 1798, en lui annonçant son souhait d'émigrer en Virginie.[1] Du Pont débarqua aux Etats-Unis en janvier 1800, l'année de la victoire de Jefferson à la présidence. Pendant ses premières années américaines, le vieux physiocrate collabora à la création de l'université de Virginie, en envoyant à Jefferson en juillet 1800 un plan complet d'éducation nationale, et en 1803 il favorisa l'acquisition de la Louisiane.[2] Ses premiers pas américains furent donc marqués par une attitude dynamique, qui laisse deviner sa volonté de s'ancrer dans la réalité politique des Etats-Unis. Une parenthèse longue et inattendue força toutefois Du Pont à rester en France entre 1802 et 1815. Elle fut l'occasion pour les deux hommes politiques de nouer une intense correspondance et pour Du Pont de réfléchir sur l'Amérique aussi par des travaux restés inédits.

Notre essai vise à analyser, à travers les contacts entre Jefferson et Du Pont tout au long de ces années cruciales pour leurs pays et

1. Lettre de Du Pont de Nemours à Jefferson, 27 août 1798, dans T. Jefferson, *The Papers of Thomas Jefferson*, t.30, éd. Julian P. Boyd (Princeton, NJ, 1950), p.501. Voir aussi *The Correspondence of Jefferson and Du Pont de Nemours, with an introduction on Jefferson and the physiocrats*, éd. Gilbert Chinard (Baltimore, MD, 1931).
2. Pierre-Samuel Du Pont de Nemours, *Sur l'éducation nationale dans les Etats-Unis d'Amérique*, 2ᵉ éd. (Paris, 1812). Voir aussi Manuela Albertone, 'Du Pont de Nemours et l'instruction publique pendant la Révolution: de la science économique à la formation du citoyen', *Revue française d'histoire des idées politiques* 20:2 (2004), p.353-71.

328   *Manuela Albertone*

leurs vies, un moment fort de cette relation d'échange intellectuel qui s'instaura entre la France et l'Amérique autour de la double expérience de leurs révolutions. Ce dialogue permet aussi de saisir le rôle joué par Du Pont dans les transformations de la physiocratie face à de nouveaux contextes et son apport à la pensée post-physiocratique, dont Jefferson apprécia la dimension sociale.

i. Jefferson et Du Pont de Nemours: un échange mutuel

Les rapports entre Jefferson et Du Pont remontent aux années du séjour du représentant américain en France entre 1784 et 1789: 'vous m'avez vu pendant votre Ambassade lutter en faveur de votre Patrie, et pour les principes de libéralité, d'amitié sincère entre les deux nations, contre tous les préjugés fiscaux et mercantiles qu'avait alors notre gouvernement.'[3] Après le retour de Jefferson aux Etats-Unis, Du Pont représenta pour lui le lien vivant avec la physiocratie et joua le rôle d'intermédiaire avec les milieux français. De la correspondance des deux premières années américaines de Du Pont ressort toute l'entente intellectuelle entre le président américain et le vieil Economiste: Du Pont partageait l'aversion pour Hamilton et sa politique économique, Jefferson était méfiant à l'égard de Bonaparte, tous les deux étaient partisans d'un développement économique pour les Etats-Unis bâti sur l'agriculture et alternatif au modèle anglais.[4]

Les années de leur intense échange intellectuel, lors du retour de Du Pont en France, coïncident avec des moments qui ont marqué la vie politique des deux pays: entre 1807 et 1813 les intellectuels français connurent des années difficiles sous l'Empire; la période qui va de 1802 à 1820 marqua une phase de vives discussions autour de la *Richesse des nations* d'Adam Smith, reléguant enfin la physiocratie au rang de moment de l'histoire de la pensée économique; en 1811 le privilège accordé à la Banque des Etats-Unis ne fut plus renouvelé; en 1812 les Etats-Unis entrèrent en guerre contre la Grande-Bretagne. Dans ce contexte international, où les questions politiques et économiques se croisent, Jefferson et Du Pont profitèrent mutuellement de leurs

---

3. Lettre de Du Pont de Nemours à Jefferson, Paris, 27 août 1798, dans T. Jefferson, *The Papers*, t.30, p.501.
4. Lettre de Du Pont de Nemours à Jefferson, New York, 17 décembre 1801, Washington, 18 janvier 1802, dans T. Jefferson, *The Papers of Thomas Jefferson*, t.36, éd. Julian P. Boyd (Princeton, NJ, 2010), p.128-29, 391-92.

échanges intellectuels, qui se révèlent également précieux pour comprendre les persistances et les métamorphoses de la physiocratie.

Par le biais d'une réflexion économique affermie à côté des milieux proches de la physiocratie, lors de son séjour en France,[5] Jefferson élabora son projet économique, bâti sur le modèle d'une agriculture commercialisée, qu'il partagea avec les Républicains contre le programme des Fédéralistes d'Alexander Hamilton, qui privilégiaient les manufactures, le commerce et les intérêts financiers. Nourrie de l'idée physiocratique de la productivité exclusive de l'agriculture à laquelle Jefferson resta toujours fidèle, et conçue comme expression de la spécificité et de l'identité américaine en opposition au modèle britannique, l'idéologie de la démocratie agraire américaine trouva dans la physiocratie sa légitimation scientifique. La lutte acharnée entre les Républicains et les Fédéralistes tout au long des années 1790 s'alimenta de la culture économique française. Jefferson devenu président, son pragmatisme politique et sa vocation à la pacification le poussèrent à nuancer ses positions. Tout en demeurant partisan de la primauté de l'agriculture, face aux circonstances de la guerre de 1812, Jefferson fut enfin amené à se rallier à l'opinion favorable à l'essor des manufactures, bien que subordonnée aux intérêts agraires.[6]

A une époque où Du Pont incarnait par sa réputation la tradition physiocratique et avait placé l'Amérique au cœur de son projet de vie, le dialogue avec Jefferson joua pour le vieux physiocrate un rôle humain, politique et intellectuel à la fois. Du Pont mit par conséquent sa science économique au service des Etats-Unis, ayant en vue la spécificité de la nouvelle nation. Il en ressortit un échange mutuel, qui permit à l'homme politique de profiter de la science de l'économie et qui fut l'occasion pour l'Economiste de donner sa contribution sur deux questions, qui durant ces années touchèrent au cœur de la politique des Etats-Unis: le rôle d'une banque nationale et le lien entre système financier et développement économique. Du Pont avait déjà

---

5.   Sur les rapports entre Jefferson et les milieux physiocratiques lors de son séjour français, voir mon ouvrage, M. Albertone, *National identity and the agrarian republic: the transatlantic commerce of ideas between America and France (1750-1830)* (Farnham, 2014).

6.   Sur les mutations des positions de Jefferson, une référence encore utile est l'article de W. D. Grampp, 'A re-examination of Jeffersonian economics', *The Southern economic journal* 12 (1945-1946), p.263-82; sur la complexité de la figure de Jefferson, voir Bernard Bailyn, 'Jefferson and the ambiguities of freedom', dans *To begin the world anew: the genius and ambiguities of the American Founders* (New York, 2003), p.37-59.

330   *Manuela Albertone*

assoupli la rigueur de ses principes pendant son activité au sein des comités révolutionnaires.[7] Sollicité par la réalité américaine et dans le cadre de l'économie politique post-physiocratique, il retoucha ses positions, tout en gardant sa vocation physiocratique.

L'engagement pour l'édition des œuvres de Turgot fut une des raisons du long séjour de Du Pont en France.[8] En juin 1809 il envoya à Jefferson les premiers volumes publiés, en intensifiant le dialogue avec le désormais ex-président, qui était enfin en état de reprendre avec plus de liberté d'action les contacts avec ses interlocuteurs français.[9] En 1809, un mois après avoir quitté la présidence, Jefferson était désormais persuadé de la nécessité de parvenir à l'équilibre entre les activités économiques, même s'il concevait l'essor des manufactures comme borné à la consommation intérieure et alimenté par le surplus de l'agriculture, afin de garder l'indépendance.[10]

Dans ce cadre politique et intellectuel Du Pont rédigea deux travaux, restés inédits, conçus comme contributions aux discussions américaines: un mémoire sur les finances, écrit en 1810,[11] et *Des banques*

---

7.   Voir Pierre-Henri Goutte, 'Economie et transition: l'œuvre de Du Pont de Nemours sous la Révolution française', dans *Idées économiques sous la Révolution 1789-1794*, éd. Jean-Michel Servet (Lyon, 1989), p.145-233.

8.   Anne-Robert-Jacques Turgot, *Œuvres de M. Turgot, ministre d'Etat, précédées et accompagnées de mémoires et de notes sur sa vie, son administration et ses ouvrages*, éd. Pierre-Samuel Du Pont de Nemours, 9 vol. (Paris, 1808-1811).

9.   Lettre de Du Pont de Nemours à Jefferson, Paris, 12 juin 1809, dans Thomas Jefferson, *The Papers of Thomas Jefferson: retirement series*, t.1, éd. J. Jefferson Looney (Princeton, NJ, 2004), p.263.

10.   Lettre de Jefferson à John Jay, Monticello, 7 avril 1809, dans T. Jefferson, *The Papers: retirement*, t.1, p.110; voir aussi Jefferson à Thomas Leiper, Washington, 21 janvier 1809, dans T. Jefferson, *The Writings of Thomas Jefferson*, éd. Andrew A. Lipscomb et Albert Ellery Bergh, 20 vol. (Washington, DC, 1903), t.12, p.238.

11.   Le mémoire sur les finances, dont le manuscrit est conservé au Hagley Museum and Library, Wilmington, DE (dorénavant HML), Papers of Pierre-Samuel Du Pont de Nemours, Winterthur Manuscripts, series B, n° 44, *Memoir of Du Pont de Nemours on the finances of the United States*, est reproduit dans T. Jefferson, *The Papers of Thomas Jefferson: retirement series*, t.2, éd. J. Jefferson Looney (Princeton, NJ, 2006), p.569-656. Dans la lettre du [28] juillet 1810, attachée au manuscrit, Du Pont écrit: 'Permettez-moi d'examiner successivement ces trois systèmes, et de soumettre cet examen à votre prompte sagacité.' Dans la lettre du 14 septembre 1810, il annonce: 'Vous trouverez ci-joint mon petit Traité Sur les Finances des Etats-Unis' (T. Jefferson, *The Papers of Thomas Jefferson: retirement series*, t.3, éd. J. Jefferson Looney, Princeton, NJ, 2007, p.80). Jefferson envoya l'écrit de Du Pont à James Madison (lettre de Jefferson à James Madison, 8 décembre 1810, dans T. Jefferson, *The Papers: retirement*, t.3, p.248-49). Du Pont

en général et des banques américaines en particulier, composé en 1812.[12] Tous les deux furent élaborés sous l'impulsion des circonstances.

La rédaction des deux textes correspond à une phase de la réflexion de Du Pont à côté de la pensée économique post-physiocratique, que la correspondance et la familiarité intellectuelle avec Jefferson permettent de capturer. La publication du *Commentary and review of Montesquieu's Spirit of laws*, que Du Pont attribua faussement à Jefferson, fut pour le vieux physiocrate l'occasion de préciser ses positions. Elle est aussi révélatrice de la triangulation entre Du Pont, Jefferson et Destutt de Tracy et des suggestions qui venaient du milieu des Idéologues. Tel fut le contexte intellectuel et politique où ces deux textes manuscrits se placent.

ii. Autour du *Commentaire sur l'Esprit des lois* de Destutt de Tracy

A travers la médiation de Lafayette, duquel il fut proche par des liens de famille, Destutt de Tracy envoya à Jefferson le 12 juin 1809 le manuscrit de son *Commentaire sur Montesquieu*, en lui demandant de le faire paraître anonymement en anglais, en raison du climat politique français.[13] En juillet 1811 le *Commentary and review of Montesquieu's Spirit of laws* fut enfin publié par l'éditeur William Duane.[14]

---

avait déjà annoncé son écrit dans ses lettres à Jefferson du 20 janvier et 10 avril, dans T. Jefferson, *The Papers: retirement*, t.2, p.162-63, 330-31. Le 4 juillet 1811, Du Pont annonçait à Jefferson qu'il allait envoyer à Madison une copie corrigée de la minute qu'il avait reçue l'année précédente (lettre de Du Pont de Nemours à Jefferson, 4 juillet 1811, dans T. Jefferson, *The Papers of Thomas Jefferson: retirement series*, éd. J. Jefferson Looney, t.4, Princeton, NJ, 2008, p.22).

12. Pierre-Samuel Du Pont de Nemours, *Des banques en général et des banques américaines en particulier* [1812], HML, Box 3, II, Special Papers and Writings, 1793-1816, Papers of Pierre-Samuel Du Pont de Nemours (Accession LMSS:I), DE 19807. Il s'agit de trente et une feuilles, de la main d'un copiste, avec des corrections et en partie de la main de Du Pont. La référence à la guerre et au système de John Law (f.23), comme remontant à quatre-vingt-seize ans auparavant, permet de dater le manuscrit de 1812.

13. Lettre de Destutt de Tracy à Jefferson, Auteuil, 12 juin 1809, dans *Jefferson et les Idéologues d'après sa correspondance inédite*, éd. Gilbert Chinard (Baltimore, MD, et Paris, 1925), p.43-44.

14. Antoine Destutt de Tracy, *A Commentary and review of Montesquieu's Spirit of laws, prepared for press from the original manuscript, in the hands of the publishers, to which are annexed, observations on the thirty-first book, by the late M. Condorcet, and two letters of Helvétius, on the merits of the same work* (Philadelphia, PA, 1811).

332 *Manuela Albertone*

Jefferson révisa la traduction et traduit de sa main le chapitre 11 sur la liberté publique et la constitution, en suggérant aussi le titre anglais et en rédigeant l'introduction, sous forme de lettre d'un Français émigré aux Etats-Unis pour échapper à Robespierre. Il partageait les critiques de Tracy à l'encontre de Montesquieu et du modèle politique britannique,[15] qui découlaient du rationalisme politique physiocratique, métamorphosé par les Idéologues, après l'expérience de la Révolution.[16] En dépit des écarts entre leurs positions, Jefferson faisait siens plusieurs arguments économiques et politiques de Tracy: la critique d'un pouvoir exécutif fort, l'exaltation de la souveraineté populaire et du gouvernement représentatif, les attaques contre le colonialisme, la justification de la seule guerre défensive, la séparation entre l'Etat et l'Eglise, la nécessité de l'instruction publique.[17]

L'œuvre parut en français en 1817 sans l'autorisation de Tracy, qui en fit une réédition en 1819, où on lit: 'Un savant français distingué avait commencé à le traduire en 1812: cette traduction n'a pas été achevée.'[18] Le savant mentionné était Du Pont, qui avait entrepris la traduction du *Commentaire*, persuadé que Jefferson en était l'auteur:

> C'est l'ouvrage d'un grand Homme d'Etat; et c'est vous qui l'avez fait. Vous y avez mis une petite dédicace comme s'il était offert par un Français aux Etats-Unis [...] Mais il n'y a pas en Amérique un Français et il n'y en a pas même en France un seul, qui eût pu suivre tant de discussions du premier ordre avec une si sévère logique et une si étonnante profondeur.[19]

L'ouvrage reflétait à tel point un patrimoine intellectuel et politique commun entre la France et les Etats-Unis que, dans les milieux américains, on arriva à imaginer qu'il était sorti de l'entourage de Du Pont et qu'un de ses enfants en était l'auteur. La correspondance entre Du Pont et Jefferson est le témoignage de ce climat.

L'analyse de Du Pont se concentra surtout sur le chapitre 13, 'Des

---

15. Lettre de Jefferson à William Duane, Monticello, 12 août 1810, dans G. Chinard, *Jefferson*, p.57.
16. Gilbert Chinard, *Pensées choisies de Montesquieu tirées du 'Common-place book' de Thomas Jefferson* (Paris, 1925).
17. Lettre de Jefferson à William Duane, Monticello, 12 août 1810, dans G. Chinard, *Jefferson*, p.55.
18. Antoine Destutt de Tracy, *Commentaire sur L'Esprit des lois de Montesquieu: édition entièrement conforme à celle publiée à Liège en 1817* (Paris, 1819), p.5.
19. Lettre de Du Pont à Jefferson, 25 janvier 1812, dans T. Jefferson, *The Papers: retirement*, t.4, p.436.

Des finances et des banques américaines: Du Pont et Thomas Jefferson 333

rapports que la levée des tributs et la grandeur des revenus publics ont avec la liberté', en rejetant l'idée que l'impôt foncier pût être un poids pour les propriétaires.[20] A la différence de Jefferson et Tracy, Du Pont considérait le rôle de l'Etat compatible avec les intérêts des individus: 'l'existence d'un Gouvernement est un des premiers besoins de la Société.'[21] Le cadre théorique de ses arguments demeurait la physiocratie, mais l'on devinait la lecture réfléchie des auteurs de son époque, car, sans avoir une notion claire du concept de capital, Du Pont parlait de 'travail utile', de 'salaire des ouvriers', de 'profit', de 'services' offerts 'aux Entrepreneurs de culture'. Il rattachait Malthus à la physiocratie par les mêmes arguments, auxquels il aurait recours dans l'*Examen de Malthus*.[22] Du Pont discutait aussi en détail le chapitre 11, traduit par Jefferson. En réservant l'exercice des droits de vote et d'éligibilité aux seuls propriétaires fonciers, il dévoilait toute la distance qui séparait son libéralisme de la démocratie de Jefferson.[23]

Tout en demeurant fidèle à ses principes, Du Pont apprécia l'œuvre, en jugeant que les principes de la science économique qu'elle contenait concouraient à consolider la république américaine:

> Votre livre est une belle consolidation de ce Gouvernement qui n'existe qu'imparfaitement en Angleterre et dans sa pureté que chez vous [...] Jefferson n'est pas fait pour s'arrêter sur les traces de Smith et de Mr Say au point où ils ont stationné! Quoique tous deux, et surtout le premier, soient des hommes d'un éminent mérite, il a la tête encore plus profonde et les reins plus forts qu'eux.[24]

Du Pont parvint à traduire jusqu'au chapitre 11 de l'ouvrage, quand Jefferson lui dévoila enfin qu'il n'en était pas l'auteur. Il partageait les appréciations du vieux physiocrate pour 'the most profound and logical work which has been presented to the present generation on

---

20. A. Destutt de Tracy, *A Commentary and review of Montesquieu*, p.160-61.
21. Lettre de Du Pont à Jefferson, 25 janvier 1812, dans T. Jefferson, *The Papers: retirement*, t.4, p.438.
22. Pierre-Samuel Du Pont de Nemours, *Examen du livre de M. Malthus sur le principe de population, auquel on a joint la traduction de quatre chapitres de ce livre supprimés dans l'édition française, et une lettre à M. Say sur son Traité d'économie politique* (Philadelphie, PA, 1817).
23. Lettre de Du Pont à Jefferson, 14 avril 1812, dans T. Jefferson, *The Papers: retirement*, t.4, p.607. Voir aussi dans le présent ouvrage la contribution d'Annie Léchenet.
24. Lettre de Du Pont à Jefferson, 25 janvier 1812, dans T. Jefferson, *The Papers: retirement*, t.4, p.446 et 448.

the subject on government',[25] à une époque difficile pour le commerce international, troublé en 1812 par la guerre entre l'Angleterre et les Etats-Unis. C'était l'époque où Jefferson, à côté des Idéologues, en premier lieu Say et Destutt de Tracy, et de Du Pont même, raffermit ses convictions sur l'équilibre nécessaire entre les activités économiques.

En dépit des critiques adressées par l'idéologue aux physiocrates, Du Pont apprécia constamment Tracy, dont l'approche déductive était plus proche de l'esprit systématique physiocratique que l'économie politique pratique de Say:[26]

> Si vous eussiez écrit ce livre trente ans plutôt, vous seriez à la tête de notre Philosophie, de notre Littérature et de notre Economie Politique, bien au-dessus de Say qui pourtant a beaucoup de mérite, et qui s'efforce de nous couper l'herbe sous le pied avec la faucille de Smith, un peu raiguisée [*sic*] mais trop courte des trois quarts. Au lieu de cela il faudra encore trente ans et deux ou trois révolutions pour que ce livre si important ait toute son utilité, toute sa gloire.[27]

La place que Tracy accordait à l'économie dans le cadre de la science sociale déployait les liens entre économie et politique. Ceux-ci s'accordaient avec les convictions de Du Pont, qui faisait de l'économie politique 'la *science des constitutions*'.[28] Après son retour aux Etats-Unis, Du Pont joua le rôle d'intermédiaire entre Jefferson et Tracy, anxieux de voir publié en anglais son *Traité de la volonté*, envoyé le 15 novembre

---

25. Lettre de Jefferson à Du Pont, 29 novembre 1813, dans T. Jefferson, *The Papers: retirement*, t.4, p.6.

26. Philippe Steiner, 'L'économie politique pratique contre les systèmes: quelques remarques sur la méthode de J.-B. Say', *Revue d'économie politique* 100:5 (1990), p.664-87.

27. Lettre manuscrite de Du Pont à Tracy, Paris, 14 août 1816, HML, Papers of Pierre-Samuel Du Pont de Nemours, Winterthur Manuscripts, series A, Correspondence.

28. Lettre de Du Pont à Jean-Baptiste Say, 22 avril 1814, dans *Physiocrates: Quesnay, Dupont de Nemours, Mercier de La Rivière, l'abbé Baudeau, Le Trosne, avec une introduction sur la doctrine des physiocrates, des commentaires et des notices historiques*, éd. Eugène Daire, 2 vol. (Paris, 1846), t.1, p.397 (c'est Du Pont qui souligne). Du Pont reproduit la lettre en appendice, dans l'*Examen du livre de M. Malthus*, p.117-59.

Des finances et des banques américaines: Du Pont et Thomas Jefferson 335

1811,[29] et qui parut enfin en 1817, comme *Treatise on political economy* avec un *Prospectus* anonyme de Jefferson.[30]

Dans un contexte compliqué, fait de relations personnelles, d'un cadre international troublé, des fermentations de la politique américaine et de l'effacement du legs de la physiocratie, Du Pont rédigea les deux mémoires restés manuscrits. Tous les deux concernent le rapport entre manufactures, finances et politiques dans un contexte républicain.

iii. Un physiocrate au service des Etats-Unis: Du Pont de Nemours et les finances américaines

Le premier texte, une sorte d'histoire des systèmes fiscaux depuis l'Antiquité, est plus strictement fidèle aux principes physiocratiques et reflète les idées, exprimées parfois même textuellement, que Du Pont avance à la même époque dans sa correspondance avec Jefferson.

Il souligne l'importance de la réception de la pensée économique française aux Etats-Unis et il en saisit tout l'apport qui revenait à la France, enrichi de la spécificité américaine:

> Vous rendrez ainsi service à la France elle-même dont l'ancienne amitié ne peut pas être oubliée des Américains fiers et reconnaissans de leur indépendance à laquelle les Français ont eu le bonheur de puissamment contribuer. Il vous sera honorable, il est très désirable pour les deux Nations que vous renvoyez à la France ses propres lumières confirmées par une expérience dont le succès n'est pas douteux et peut d'avance être démontré par des calculs dont l'évidence est palpable.[31]

Du Pont avait été sollicité pour rédiger son mémoire par la décision du gouvernement américain d'encourager l'essor des manufactures, face au bloc continental, ce qui aurait eu pour effet une réduction des douanes, vitales pour les finances américaines. Il jugeait qu'un

---

29. Lettre de Tracy à Jefferson, 15 novembre 1811, dans G. Chinard, *Jefferson*, p.99-101.
30. Antoine Destutt de Tracy, *A Treatise on political economy, to which is prefixed a supplement to a preceding work on the understanding, or elements of ideology, with an analytical table, and an introduction on the faculty of the will, translated from the unpublished French original* (Georgetown, DC, 1817).
31. P.-S. Du Pont de Nemours, *Memoir on the finances*, f.39.

tel tournant de la politique économique imposait une réorganisation fiscale.

Le mémoire débute par l'analyse des différents systèmes fiscaux, selon une approche synchronique par types d'impôts, mais présentés de façon diachronique. Du Pont distingue trois systèmes, qu'il catalogue comme: 'système anglais', bâti originairement sur un prélèvement sur le revenu des terres, suppléé ensuite par les impôts indirects, face aux résistances de l'aristocratie; 'systèmes domaniaux de finances', caractérisés par l'impôt sur la terre, pratiqué par les Egyptiens, les Hébreux, les Chinois et durant un an en France par l'Assemblée constituante; 'système domanial de finances à partage de revenu', qui correspondait à l'impôt unique territorial physiocratique.

L'écrit est caractérisé par sa forte empreinte politique et le rôle central joué par le principe de liberté, au-delà de sa dimension économique. Les coordonnées théoriques demeurent solidement physiocratiques. Du Pont visait à persuader les Américains de conjurer une hausse des impôts indirects, face à la réduction des douanes, et d'opérer une réorganisation générale de la fiscalité, bâtie sur l'impôt unique territorial, le seul où 'tous les Revenus nets contribuent, mais nul d'eux dans une proportion plus forte qu'aucune autre.' Les arguments de Du Pont n'étaient pas toutefois centrés uniquement sur l'agriculture, car la recette de l'impôt était censée assurer les capitaux nécessaires à l'essor des manufactures et à la préservation de 'la classe moyenne, la classe vertueuse, honnête, laborieuse, libérale'.[32] On devine un Du Pont qui a lu Jean-Baptiste Say sans renier la physiocratie.[33] La validité de l'impôt territorial s'inscrivait dans l'ordre naturel, du fait que 'la loi physique' demandait de taxer uniquement les propriétaires fonciers, qui payaient les salaires et étaient le centre d'où tout partait et où tout revenait, 'tels sont dans les animaux vertébrés le cœur et le cerveau'.[34]

L'abondance de terres et le gouvernement républicain, qui plaçait les *farmers* au cœur de la société, faisaient de l'Amérique un laboratoire pour la mise en œuvre du projet fiscal physiocratique. Du Pont mettait au service de la nouvelle nation américaine l'expérience ministérielle acquise sous l'Ancien Régime et la Révolution. En discutant

32. P.-S. Du Pont de Nemours, *Memoir on the finances*, f.16.
33. P.-S. Du Pont de Nemours, *Memoir on the finances*, f.39.
34. P.-S. Du Pont de Nemours, *Memoir on the finances*, f.21. Voir aussi Julien Vincent, '"Un dogue de forte race": Dupont de Nemours, ou la physiocratie réincarnée (1793-1807)', *La Révolution française* 14 (2018), p.1-34.

Des finances et des banques américaines: Du Pont et Thomas Jefferson 337

de la dîme, adoptée par les Hébreux et améliorée par les Chinois, qui proportionnaient le taux de la contribution au rendement de différentes classes de terres, Du Pont renouvelait ses appréciations pour l'impôt de quotité et les critiques adressées à la subvention territoriale en nature, proposée à l'Assemblée des notables en 1787 par Calonne, dont il avait été le collaborateur:

> Le principe de la dîme a quelque apparence d'équité, il présente une perception chère en voitures, granges, greniers, celliers et manutention, mais peu litigieuse et peu embarrassante. Cependant, il est très inique en ce qu'il prend la même part sur les terres fertiles dont la culture n'est pas très coûteuse et sur celles qui sont peu fécondes pour l'exploitation desquelles les frais absorbent presque toute la récolte [...] Le système de la dîme a donc une tendance perpétuelle à enrichir toujours plus l'opulence, à toujours aggraver la pauvreté, à augmenter toujours l'inégalité des fortunes.[35]

Du Pont développe à maintes reprises dans son manuscrit les arguments en faveur des avantages de l'impôt de quotité sur l'impôt de répartition, fidèle au noyau de la théorie physiocratique, même s'il célébrait notamment la portée politique d'un prélèvement qu'il considérait non pas proprement comme un impôt, mais plutôt comme une 'concession sociale', par le biais d''une portion régulière et uniforme du revenu net de toutes les terres'.[36] Du Pont exaltait la valeur patriotique de l'impôt, en ligne avec la tradition physiocratique, dont *De l'administration provinciale et de la réforme de l'impôt* de Le Trosne avait été la formulation la plus complète. Au milieu de la réalité républicaine, l'impôt de quotité s'affirmait comme une garantie pour la liberté des personnes et du travail, à travers l'assignation d'une portion constante du revenu des terres aux besoins publics, et comme le moyen de consolider les liens entre les citoyens et l'Etat:[37]

> Les produits annuels n'offrent rien de disponible et d'applicable aux besoins publics, que ce qui reste des récoltes après que les frais de culture aient été payés, ainsi que l'intérêt des capitaux nécessaires à l'exploitation [...] Ce reste qui est la propriété des possesseurs du

35. P.-S. Du Pont de Nemours, *Memoir on the finances*, f.28.
36. P.-S. Du Pont de Nemours, *Memoir on the finances*, f.35. Voir aussi la lettre de Du Pont à Carl Friedrich von Baden, 11 juillet 1787 dans P.-S. Du Pont de Nemours, *Carl Friedrichs von Baden brieflicher Verkehr mit Mirabeau und Du Pont*, éd. Carl Knies, 2 vol. (Heidelberg, 1892), t.1, p.273-74.
37. P.-S. Du Pont de Nemours, *Memoir on the finances*, f.79.

338 *Manuela Albertone*

sol, est [...] la seule que le propriétaire ou la société politique aient la faculté d'employer comme il leur convient le mieux; la seule aussi qui acquitte toutes les dépenses publiques.[38]

La reprise de la notion physiocratique d'impôt de quotité était donc adaptée au contexte américain. Du Pont considérait que les Américains pouvaient même devenir un modèle pour les Français. Face à l'abondance de terres, les différences territoriales rendaient la mise en œuvre de l'impôt de quotité plus difficile en Amérique qu'en Europe. Du Pont détaillait ces différences, qui découlaient des pratiques diffusées en France et en Angleterre d'affermer les terres à des entrepreneurs qui fournissaient les avances. La fixation des valeurs des terres devenait par conséquent plus facile, le prix du fermage donnant l'estimation du revenu net. En Amérique en revanche le revenu des terres n'était pas si évident, car on louait rarement les terres, en raison de leur abondance, ce qui encourageait la propriété.[39] Dans les *Ephémérides du citoyen* et avant la révolution des colonies contre la Grande-Bretagne, Du Pont avait concouru à diffuser les connaissances sur l'Amérique et ses potentialités.[40] Il célébrait ici l'aisance américaine:

> Vos cultivateurs sont si bien logés, si bien nourris, si bien vêtus, se lèvent si tard, travaillent si peu, ménagent toute leur peine, donnent tant à leur plaisir, passent si longtemps à déjeuner, à dîner, à prendre le thé, à souper, que la récolte toute entière est consommée et parait n'avoir produit que ses frais. La seule chose à laquelle on puisse reconnaître un bénéfice est l'augmentation des bâtiments, et l'embellissement des meubles.[41]

Le rôle central assigné à la grande propriété dans la théorie physiocratique n'empêchait pas Du Pont d'apprécier la spécificité du *farmer*, 'le cultivateur propriétaire d'une terre qu'il n'afferme pas', mot

---

38. P.-S. Du Pont de Nemours, *Memoir on the finances*, f.70.
39. P.-S. Du Pont de Nemours, *Memoir on the finances*, f.42.
40. Voir Manuela Albertone, 'Décentralisation territoriale et unité de la nation: *Les Lettres d'Abraham Mansword* entre physiocratie et modèle américain', dans *Centralisation et fédéralisme: les modèles et leur circulation dans l'espace européen francophone, germanophone et italophone*, éd. Michel Biard et autres (Mont-Saint-Aignan, 2018), p.103-14.
41. P.-S. Du Pont de Nemours, *Memoir on the finances*, f.46.

intraduisible, ajoutait-il, qui 'n'a pas le même sens qu'en Angleterre quoique les deux nations parlent la même langue'.[42]

Dans son mémoire Du Pont non seulement énonçait les principes, mais esquissait aussi les détails pour la mise en œuvre de l'impôt territorial. Une partie de son mémoire était consacrée à fixer le taux de l'impôt de quotité. En dépit des difficultés à estimer la valeur des terres, il jugeait possible d'y parvenir à partir des contrats de vente. La création de *land offices* visait à en rendre l'enregistrement obligatoire.[43] Si le recours à un cinquième du revenu national était censé être indispensable pour les pays européens qui entretenaient des armées permanentes, un septième suffisait pour la république américaine, où il y avait un moindre risque de guerre.

Une forte dimension politique aux fondements économiques marque le mémoire. Du Pont conçut son écrit pour une république, où la liberté était un pilier à la fois économique et politique, où la propriété définissait l'adhésion sociale et où l'appartenance territoriale forgeait l'esprit du citoyen *farmer*. Fidèle à son approche centrée sur le lien entre économie et politique, Du Pont répondit aux sollicitations qui lui venaient de la réalité américaine et qui l'amenèrent à avancer des propositions concrètes et à nuancer ses positions au niveau de la théorie. Tout en demeurant fidèle au principe de la productivité exclusive de l'agriculture – partagé aussi par Jefferson – Du Pont se ralliait aux décisions du gouvernement américain de favoriser l'essor des manufactures pour garder l'indépendance face à l'Europe. Tout en souhaitant un système fiscal bâti sur l'impôt foncier et alternatif au modèle anglais, il jugeait nécessaire le maintien provisoire des douanes pour protéger les manufactures naissantes. Il estimait quand même que les tarifs ne devaient pas encourager la contrebande, en accord avec les arguments qu'il avait déjà exposés dans les *Ephémérides du citoyen*, dans le cadre d'une polémique avec Cesare Beccaria.[44] Les Etats-Unis ne pouvaient pas se passer des douanes, car la main-d'œuvre y était plus chère par rapport à l'Angleterre surtout, qui possédait plus de compétences et de capitaux. Un impôt sur les produits américains au profit des manufacturiers américains s'imposait. Il reste que, pour répondre aux coûts de l'administration, au paiement de la dette et

---

42. P.-S. Du Pont de Nemours, *Memoir on the finances*, f.47.
43. P.-S. Du Pont de Nemours, *Memoir on the finances*, f.50.
44. [Pierre-Samuel Du Pont de Nemours], 'De la fondation d'une chaire d'économie politique, et de l'utilité de cette institution', *Ephémérides du citoyen* 3 (1769), p.160-81.

340 *Manuela Albertone*

à l'affaiblissement d'une partie des douanes, Du Pont appelait à la création d'un nouvel impôt sur le revenu des terres, confiant qu'il était dans la force et l'unité politique de l'Amérique pour faire appel à la raison et au patriotisme.

On décèle donc dans ce texte un mouvement dans les idées de Du Pont par rapport aux positions exprimées juste deux années auparavant, quand en 1808 il redoutait qu'une guerre entre les Etats-Unis et l'Europe pût entraîner la création de manufactures et d'impôts sur les consommations: 'Il ne faut rien prohiber, mais rien exciter. Les fabriques viendront en leur tems à mesure que la Population et les capitaux manqueront d'emploi. Mais les mêmes causes ameneront la concurrence dans la culture, distingueront l'Etat de Fermier de celui de Propriétaire, feront jaillir et discerner le Produit net.'[45]

Jefferson apprécia la logique physiocratique du mémoire de Du Pont et sa capacité à l'adapter à la situation américaine. 'He is, as you know – écrivait-il à Madison en décembre 1810 – a rigorous economist, and although the system be not new, yet he always gives something new, and places his subject in strong lights. The application of the system to our situation also is new.'[46] En 1815, il n'avait toujours pas perdu l'espoir d'arriver à faire publier le mémoire:[47] 'your observations [...] bear the stamps of logic and eloquence which mark everything coming from you, and place the doctrines of the Economists in their strongest point of view.'[48] Il ne partageait pas néanmoins l'empressement de Du Pont à modifier le système des finances face à l'essor des manufactures, et il défendait la politique économique américaine, expression des différences locales, les Etats du Sud privilégiant l'impôt foncier et les Etats du Nord-Est les douanes. Tandis que Du Pont en acceptait la nécessité momentanée, Jefferson reconnaissait la validité des douanes: 'We are all the more

---

45. Lettre de Du Pont de Nemours à Jefferson, Paris, 23 juillet 1808, dans Chinard, *The Correspondence*, p.131.

46. Lettre de Jefferson à Madison, 8 décembre 1810, dans T. Jefferson, *The Papers: retirement*, t.3, p.248.

47. Lettre de Jefferson à Du Pont, Monticello, 28 février 1815, dans T. Jefferson, *The Writings*, t.14, p.257. Dans sa lettre à Jefferson du 12 décembre 1811 (T. Jefferson, *The Papers: retirement*, t.4, p.327-36), Du Pont mentionnait comme traducteur Paterson, recommandé par Jefferson pour la traduction aussi de l'*Essai sur l'éducation nationale* et de la *Table raisonnée des principes de l'économie politique*.

48. Lettre de Jefferson à Du Pont, Monticello, 15 avril 1811, dans T. Jefferson, *The Writings*, t.13, p.37-38.

reconciled to the tax on importations, because it falls exclusively on the rich, and with the equal partition of intestate's estates, constitutes the best agrarian law.[49]

En dépit de l'adaptation au contexte américain, les principes de Du Pont demeurèrent fidèlement physiocratiques. En décembre 1811, ayant été informé que la situation financière était moins urgente que ce qu'il semblait, le remboursement de la dette étant en cours et les consommations des produits de luxe étant en mesure d'alimenter la recette des douanes, Du Pont réaffirma la nécessité de continuer à propager les principes physiocratiques: 'La Science de l'Economie politique ne doit pas être ignorée, ni négligée aux Etats-Unis. Où traiterait-on Ses questions les plus importantes, Si ce n'était pas dans une République qui respecte la liberté de la presse?'[50]

iv. Un physiocrate au service des Etats-Unis: Du Pont de Nemours et les banques américaines

Une nouvelle circonstance poussa bientôt Du Pont à s'occuper de nouveau de la finance américaine. En 1812, pendant qu'il discutait avec Jefferson du *Commentaire sur Montesquieu* et au moment de l'essor de la guerre avec l'Angleterre, qui déclencha la *banking mania* et accéléra la crise de l'économie financière et la spéculation, Du Pont rédigea un autre texte demeuré inédit, *Des banques en général et des banques américaines en particulier*. Ses connaissances du système des banques françaises et sa longue expérience renforçaient les arguments politiques qu'il adressait aux Etats-Unis. Il s'agit d'un écrit précieux pour saisir la rencontre entre la culture économique de Du Pont et le contexte politique, économique et social américain.

Du point de vue de la réflexion économique, le texte ne contient pas d'éléments originaux. Du Pont revient à l'idée que la valeur de la monnaie métallique est toujours supérieure à celle en papier, qu'il avait déjà exprimée en 1790 dans *Effet des assignats sur le prix du pain*.[51] Il réaffirmait ses appréciations pour les banques d'émission, en tant qu'établissements qui permettaient de se passer d'une très

---

49. Lettre de Jefferson à Du Pont, Monticello, 15 avril 1811, dans T. Jefferson, *The Writings*, t.13, p.39.
50. Lettre de Du Pont à Jefferson, 12 décembre 1811, dans T. Jefferson, *The Writings*, t.4, p.327.
51. Pierre-Samuel Du Pont de Nemours, *Effet des assignats sur le prix du pain, par un ami du peuple* (s.l.n.d. [1790]).

grande quantité de monnaie métallique, contribuaient à la stabilité, encourageaient le commerce et favorisaient la réduction de l'intérêt de l'argent. Il avait traité ces mêmes questions en 1806 dans *Sur la Banque de France*,[52] en reprenant les arguments sur l'utilité de l'escompte commercial, énoncés en 1789 dans sa défense de la Caisse d'escompte.[53] Les liens entre Banque et Nation, indépendance de l'une et crédit de l'autre, sont développés dans ces pages dans lesquelles transparaissent les discussions américaines et la réalité d'une république aux fondements économiques. Les arguments politiques du texte manuscrit dépassaient le récit technique et la prudence de l'écrit de 1806.

Du Pont avait acquis une connaissance approfondie du contexte américain à travers les contacts avec un interlocuteur privilégié comme Jefferson, qui lui fournit le cadre intellectuel et politique au moyen duquel il élabore ses réflexions.

La batterie d'arguments contre la spéculation financière, les banques et le crédit public, avancés par la physiocratie, avait donné à Jefferson et aux Républicains de puissants instruments de lutte contre les Fédéralistes d'Alexandre Hamilton. Dès les débuts de 1793, les attaques de George Logan – le seul véritable physiocrate américain[54] – contre la Banque des Etats-Unis opposèrent l'idéologie de la démocratie agraire, raffermie par la théorie économique physiocratique, au modèle fédéraliste, bâti sur un projet de développement économique qui privilégiait le commerce et la richesse financière. Les Fédéralistes firent de la création d'une banque nationale, à côté de la dette publique et de la richesse financière, l'instrument pour raffermir le pouvoir central. Par son métallisme convaincu, Jefferson redoutait l'excès de papier monnaie. Au nom du

---

52. Pierre-Samuel Du Pont de Nemours, *Sur la Banque de France, les causes de la crise qu'elle a éprouvée, les tristes effets qui en sont résultés, et les moyens d'en prévenir le retour, avec une théorie des banques, rapport fait à la Chambre de commerce par une commission spéciale* (Paris, 1806).

53. Pierre-Samuel Du Pont de Nemours, *Discours prononcé à l'Assemblée nationale, par M. Du Pont, sur les banques en général, sur la caisse d'escompte en particulier, et sur le projet du premier ministre des finances relativement à cette dernière* (Paris, Chez Baudouin, 1789).

54. J'ai approfondi l'étude des idées économiques de George Logan dans mes contributions: M. Albertone, 'George Logan: un physiocrate américain', dans *La Diffusion internationale de la physiocratie (XVIIIe-XIXe)*, éd. Bernard Delmas et autres (Grenoble, 1995), p.421-39; M. Albertone, *National identity and the agrarian republic*, p.139-50.

rejet de toute forme de monopole et d'instrument financier au service du gouvernement, il mena une résistance acharnée contre la création de la Banque des Etats-Unis, jugée inconstitutionnelle, d'après une interprétation restrictive du domaine d'action de l'Etat.[55] Devenu président et face à la situation internationale, Jefferson nuança ses positions. A côté de l'utilité du développement des manufactures, il plaça aussi les bénéfices des banques d'escompte: 'To the existence of banks of discount for cash, as on the continent of Europe, there can be no objection, because there can be no danger of abuse, and they are a convenience both to merchants and individuals.'[56]

En 1811, on n'avait plus renouvelé le privilège d'action fédérale de la Banque des Etats-Unis, considérée par ses adversaires comme un instrument qui favorisait la centralisation au profit des intérêts commerciaux. L'essor de la guerre en 1812 ressuscitait les arguments en sa faveur.[57] Dans ce contexte et par une lecture de la situation à travers le filtre de Jefferson, Du Pont élabora ses réflexions sur le rôle des banques en Amérique en s'appuyant sur une perspective fortement politique, qui donne un aperçu efficace du mouvement de ses idées.

Les exemples de banques qui pratiquaient l'escompte des effets commerciaux, pris en considération par Du Pont, étaient la Banque d'Angleterre et, pour France, la Caisse d'escompte, fondée en 1797 et fusionnée avec la Banque de France en 1803, la Caisse des comptes courants du commerce, fondée en juin 1796 sur les reliquats de la Caisse d'escompte liquidée en 1793, et le Comptoir commercial, une banque privée, qui opéra entre 1800 et 1813. La Banque d'Angleterre demeurait le modèle du lien entre intérêt privé et intérêt public, tandis que les références françaises renvoyaient aux banques qui, sous le Directoire, avaient concouru à la reconstruction financière de la France, laquelle aboutit sous Napoléon à la création de la Banque de

55. Thomas Jefferson, *Opinion on the constitutionality of the bill for establishing a national bank*, dans *The Writings*, t.19, p.276.
56. Lettre de Jefferson à J. W. Eppes, Monticello, 6 novembre 1813, dans *The Writings*, t.13, p.431.
57. La seconde Banque des Etats-Unis fut créée en 1816 sur le modèle de la première. Face à la bulle foncière qui provoqua la crise financière de 1819, Jefferson écrit à John Taylor: 'I sincerely believe, with you that banking establishments are more dangerous than standing armies; and that the principle of spending money to be paid by posterity, under the name of funding, is but swindling futurity on a large scale' (lettre de Jefferson à John Taylor, Monticello, 28 mai 1816, dans *The Writings*, t.15, p.23).

France.[58] Les points de référence de Du Pont étaient donc les banques publiques, créées pour soutenir la circulation des effets commerciaux et pratiquer l'escompte, face à la diminution de la monnaie métallique, et pour accélérer la circulation de l'argent. Il s'agissait d'instituts de crédit, dont la naissance était liée à une conjoncture particulière.

Au-delà des aspects financiers, le manuscrit traitait aussi du rapport entre dimension économique et politique, dans le contexte du patriotisme républicain américain et d'une situation extraordinaire occasionnée par la guerre.

Modelées d'après les établissements de crédit européens, les banques américaines avaient modifié leur rôle, à la suite des transformations survenues dans la société. La diffusion des produits de luxe avait entraîné la hausse des importations de l'Angleterre, déterminant le déséquilibre de la balance commerciale, responsable de la pénurie de monnaie métallique, qui laissait les banques américaines à court d'argent pour rembourser les billets des négociants.[59]

Face à l'embargo et à la guerre, s'était formée une classe d'entrepreneurs que Du Pont jugeait mus par l'intérêt aussi bien que par le patriotisme, destinée à consolider l'indépendance des Etats-Unis. Bien qu'ils ne pussent se passer des banques, les entrepreneurs et les négociants n'étaient pas en état de respecter la brièveté de termes imposés. Du Pont soulignait la valeur républicaine des crédits accordés aux entrepreneurs par les banques. Il appréciait aussi les soutiens aux fermiers venant des banques des petites villes, qui encourageaient l'élargissement des cultures dans les campagnes.[60] L'évolution de la pensée de Du Pont s'accompagnait de celle de Jefferson. Le contexte américain avait imposé à tous les deux une reconsidération du rapport entre agriculture, manufactures et finances.

Par rapport au mémoire sur les finances, rédigé deux ans avant, Du Pont délaissa tout dogmatisme dans le manuscrit sur les banques. S'il imputait la nouvelle situation au luxe et à la guerre, il renonça à imposer un modèle économique rigide: 'Quand une chose a été faite et a produit de certaines circonstances, aucun pouvoir humain ne saurait empêcher qu'elle n'ait été faite et que ces circonstances

---

58. Louis Bergeron, *Banquiers, négociants et manufacturiers parisiens du Directoire à l'Empire*, 2 vol. (1978; Paris, 1999); Arnaud Manas, 'Le premier business model de la Banque de France en 1800', *Revue d'économie financière* 122 (2016), p.249-54.
59. P.-S. Du Pont de Nemours, *Des banques en général*, f.5, 8.
60. P.-S. Du Pont de Nemours, *Des banques en général*, f.9-10.

Des finances et des banques américaines: Du Pont et Thomas Jefferson   345

n'existent. Dieu lui-même ne s'est pas réservé ce pouvoir. Ce qui est. Ce qui fait la raison suprême est de se conduire avec sagesse et bonté d'après ce qui est.'[61]

Alors que le renouvellement de la Banque des Etats-Unis se profilait, Du Pont niait l'utilité de la création d'une banque nationale. L'on devine la présence dans la réflexion de Du Pont de l'exemple de la Banque de France et de l'opposition entre les intérêts de Paris et du reste du pays, et qu'il transplantait dans le contexte d'un Etat fédéral tel que les Etats-Unis. La Banque des Etats-Unis avait été créée pour profiter d'un papier monnaie uniforme. Face à la difficulté d'assurer une quantité suffisante de monnaie métallique, on avait imposé de verser tous les revenus de l'Etat dans les caisses de la banque.[62] Liant le crédit d'une banque nationale au crédit de l'Etat, d'après l'exemple de la Banque d'Angleterre, Du Pont célébrait la confiance qu'inspirait désormais la stabilité de la république américaine, exprimée par le crédit de sa trésorerie. Il proposait par conséquent de créer à la place d'une banque nationale des notes de trésorerie, qui étaient censées atteindre une valeur supérieure aux billets de banque:

> Cela n'empêcherait pas que l'on créât une banque nationale si on le jugeait convenable, ou que l'on ne donnât l'existence à celle qui vient d'être établie; qu'on lui laissât se procurer des fonds comme elle le pourrait, à quoi son titre honorable l'aiderait vraisemblablement; établir des branches banques où elle le voudrait en concurrence avec les autres banques qui existent: ce qui donnerait à tous billets un sens général dans tous les Etats-Unis. J'entre au marché: est une phrase portant sur une chose qui doit être permise à tout le monde. Je te chasse du marché est une chose et une phrase qui ne doivent être permises à personne, pas même au gouvernement. Tu suivras la police du marché est un droit de règlement qui appartient à tous les gouvernements du monde.[63]

La république donnait plus de garanties que les monarchies, la Constitution empêchant le Congrès américain d'exercer son influence sur les revenus publics comme en Angleterre. Du Pont rejetait la présence d'une autorité intermédiaire entre la nation et le gouvernement, qu'une banque nationale aurait illustrée. Si, malgré ses

---

61. P.-S. Du Pont de Nemours, *Des banques en général*, f.17 (c'est Du Pont qui souligne).
62. P.-S. Du Pont de Nemours, *Des banques en général*, f.23.
63. P.-S. Du Pont de Nemours, *Des banques en général*, f.24-25.

arguments, on arrivait à rétablir une banque nationale, Du Pont souhaitait donc qu'elle rivalisât avec les autres banques et il revenait à l'Etat de fixer les règles de la concurrence. Il prenait en exemple la France, qui imposait aux administrateurs de la Banque de France et des autres banques françaises un compte rendu public annuel.[64]

Les Etats-Unis représentaient un modèle de république aux fondements économiques, centrée sur le binôme liberté économique et liberté politique, qui s'accordait aux convictions physiocratiques de Du Pont, passées à travers l'expérience des révolutions américaine et française et opposées au modèle anglais. La spécificité du contexte américain fut pour lui l'occasion de reformuler ses arguments sur le rôle des banques d'émission, fortifiés et adaptés au système américain: l'impossibilité de rembourser en argent la totalité des billets, l'inutilité de la circulation d'une trop grande quantité de monnaie métallique,[65] l'utilité des banques d'escompte pour soutenir les entreprises, la supériorité de la monnaie métallique sur le papier monnaie.

La reformulation des principes physiocratiques de Du Pont s'exprima dans le respect de la spécificité américaine. Il souhaitait l'inclusion des Etats-Unis dans le commerce international pour rivaliser avec l'Angleterre, au nom des principes de la liberté économique et politique. Ses contacts avec Jefferson et la réflexion économique post-physiocratique l'amenèrent à nuancer la rigidité de ses positions dans le but prioritaire de préserver la stabilité politique de la république américaine et d'encourager le développement de son économie. Au fond, ses propositions fiscales et sa défense de la politique américaine de soutien aux entrepreneurs et aux négociants pour favoriser les ouvriers domestiques, qui par leurs subsistances favorisaient l'agriculture et assuraient l'indépendance du pays, s'inscrivaient dans sa cohérence physiocratique.

---

64. P.-S. Du Pont de Nemours, *Des banques en général*, f.25.

65. Il avait déjà exprimé en 1789 dans le *Discours sur les banques* l'idée de l'inutilité d'une abondance de monnaie métallique (P.-S. Du Pont de Nemours, *Discours sur les banques*, p.18).

Du Pont de Nemours, between physiocratic loyalty and political versatility

ANTHONY MERGEY

Paris-Panthéon-Assas University

ARNAULT SKORNICKI

University Paris Nanterre

As this volume draws to a close, it is clear that Du Pont de Nemours was not only remarkable for the astonishing variety of his intellectual and professional interests and activities, between the *Ancien Régime* and the Restoration, between France and America: he also never ceased to reclassify himself politically according to the upheavals imposed on him by his 'century'. This 'versatility' should not be taken in the wrong way; it has less to do with inconstancy of character than with the instability of the situation. All in all, Du Pont appears remarkably constant on one point, among all the changes he was forced to make: the maintenance, against all odds, of his intellectual and public identity as a physiocrat or 'Economist', even though the school founded by Dr Quesnay and the marquis de Mirabeau had disintegrated and demonetised over time.

From then on, Du Pont de Nemours poses a thorny question for the history of political ideas: how can we understand the tension between his versatility and political mobility on the one hand and a form of intellectual constancy on the other? How was he able to move from 'legal despotism' (which, admittedly, he did not defend as such for very long) to a form of republicanism, and what reasons did he give for this? He was trained and spent most of his career under the *Ancien Régime*, and was approaching his fifties when the Revolution broke out. This kaleidoscopic impression of his character is certainly linked to the institutions and hierarchies of the *Ancien Régime*, which did not offer much stability to a commoner who was certainly educated and had good introductions into society but who was without fortune, a Huguenot, the son of a watchmaker, despite having noble ancestry through his mother. Half-educated, he had a lasting complex about this, seeing his virtual absence from higher education as an irremediable handicap to his recognition, manifested in a disordered style.[1] As a man of letters, Du Pont was a propagandist of physiocracy, a journalist and a leader of the economic press until the end of the *Ancien Régime*. As an administrator, he held various positions: adviser to the Controller-General of Finances L'Averdy, but above all personal secretary to Turgot; inspector general of manufactures; collaborator of the minister of Foreign Affairs Vergennes and then of the minister Calonne; and, finally, secretary to the Assembly of Notables on the eve of the Revolution. By 1785, Du Pont had become one of the most influential figures in the administration of commerce. Now a public figure recognised for his talents, skills and professionalism, he nevertheless remained a regular in the supporting role of 'secretary' to ministers. As Nicolas Schapira explains regarding secretaries under the *Ancien Régime*, this position was fundamentally ambivalent, situated between the domestic and the political, 'between statutory dependence and potential power linked to proximity to the master': it constantly surrounded his 'real situation with a halo of uncertainty'.[2] The revolutionary upheavals changed the situation, but without offering Du Pont a stable and lasting solution. Moreover, Du Pont's versatility was due not only to the chronic instability of the period from the end of the *Ancien Régime* to the fall of the Empire, which profoundly transformed the relationship between the Republic of Letters and political power, but also to the ambiguities that this same period 'between two waters' entailed.

---

1. Of himself, he says: '*Dupont* n'était qu'un artiste, quittant à peine la lime et le tour. Il ne manquait pas d'une sorte de verve dans le cœur, et de quelque justesse dans la tête; mais n'ayant fait que de très mauvaises études [...] il n'atteignait jamais cette correction, sans laquelle aucun écrit ne demeure' (Pierre-Samuel Du Pont de Nemours, 'Lettre aux auteurs de la *Décade*, sur les Economistes, 30 frimaire An III', *La Décade philosophique, littéraire et politique, par une société de républicains* 4 (1794), 30 décembre 1794, p.70-84 (78)). A well-known obituary writer seems to confirm this: 'Il ne rédigeait point sa pensée, il la donnait, la confiait telle qu'il l'avait conçue'; Joseph-Marie de Gérando, *Notice sur M. Du Pont de Nemours, lue à la séance générale de la Société d'encouragement pour l'industrie nationale, le 23 septembre 1818*, *Moniteur* (16 October 1818), p.3.
2. Nicolas Schapira, *Maîtres et secrétaires (XVIᵉ-XVIIIᵉ siècles): l'exercice du pouvoir dans la France d'Ancien Régime* (Paris, 2020), p.15. All translations are our own unless otherwise indicated.

i. A second-Enlightenment figure?

The century of Du Pont is a difficult in-between period to name: a *pivotal moment* in political modernity according to Reinhart Koselleck, it has also been called the 'second Enlightenment', *Spätaufklärung* or 'late Enlightenment', to designate the period from the end of the *Ancien Régime* to the end of the Empire – and even to the beginnings of the Restoration – during which the last generations of the Enlightenment were able to live and act. These historiographical categories, which are hardly satisfactory, at least have the advantage of making the problems visible, if not solving them. Nor can they be reduced to simple artificial chronological divisions, of which the French Revolution and Napoleon would be the main scansions. A period that is difficult to describe culturally, a 'period without a name',[3] includes movements that are apparently far apart. Some, like the Ideologues and the Institut de France founded in 1795, were consciously part of the French philosophical heritage of the mid-eighteenth century, that of the encyclopedists, who were inclined to value the sciences and arts and criticise the 'infamous'.[4] Other tendencies, which in the past might have been improperly described as 'pre-Romantic', drew the Enlightenment towards a rediscovery of sensibility and even spirituality. The complexity of the matter lies in the fact that these two directions do not separate two opposing camps but lie at the heart of the 'second Enlightenment' and its ambiguities, during this period of troubled waters, marked by a series of sociopolitical upheavals as well as the beginnings of the Romantic movement and conservatism.[5] To speak of the 'second Enlightenment' is to draw attention to two major developments that affected the generations of this period.

The first concerns the relationship between political power and the Republic of Letters and Science. Du Pont belonged to the generation of Condorcet and Lavoisier, whom he worked closely with, born around half a century after Voltaire and Montesquieu and twenty-five years after Diderot and Rousseau. This generation entered the service

---

3. *Une 'Période sans nom': les années 1780-1820 et la fabrique de l'histoire littéraire*, ed. Fabienne Bercegol *et al.* (Paris, 2016).
4. Bertrand Binoche, *Ecrasez l'infâme! Philosopher à l'âge des Lumières* (Paris, 2018).
5. See the historiographical synthesis by Anouchka Vasak, 'Introduction', in *Entre deux eaux: les secondes Lumières et leurs ambiguïtés (1789-1815)*, ed. Anouchka Vasak (Paris, 2012), p.9-18. See also the analyses of Michel Delon, 'Questions de périodisation', *SVEC* 2005:10, p.322-34; 'Quarante ans de recherche sur un objet protéiforme', in *Une 'Période sans nom'*, ed. F. Bercegol *et al.*, p.37-49.

of the monarchy under the active reign of Louis XV, amid the Seven Years War. After many trials and tribulations, the *philosophes* and their allies eventually conquered the great academies, reduced censorship and established themselves in the public arena, even including some of their close allies in the government under Louis XVI, such as Turgot and, to a certain extent, Jacques Necker.[6] Du Pont's career is a good illustration of this rapprochement between the state and the Enlightenment elite, some of whom also took part in the Revolution. However, unlike Condorcet or Lavoisier, his much more modest origins were a permanent obstacle to his social success.

The second type of transformation highlighted by the notion of the 'second Enlightenment' refers to the spiritual dimension of the Enlightenment, as mentioned above. These late-Enlightenment movements were no longer satisfied with cautious deism and the joys of experimental research alone; they appeared to be searching for new cosmologies capable of marrying reason and sentiment, empiricism and metaphysics, in such a way as to blur the boundary between belief and science.[7] Mesmerism and the theories of animal magnetism were the most famous and popular manifestations of this at the end of the *Ancien Régime*.[8] Du Pont was certainly not an eminently religious man. Trained as a young man in the Protestant faith, he did at one time envisage a career as a pastor. Later, he affirmed his classically deist convictions, and, in a pamphlet, he made an ecumenical plea for a natural religion in line with the main teachings of Christian revelation. If he did grant Protestantism superiority over Catholicism, it was not in the field of theology but in that of practical morality: he considered it more accessible and less dogmatic, more attached to the spirit than to the letter, more concerned with freedom of conscience. Protestantism made people more reasonable and virtuous.[9] However, during the Revolution, Du Pont was no longer content to put forward this civic religion; he gave its metaphysical underpinnings in a work

6. See for example the remarks by Michel Delon in *L'Idée d'énergie au tournant des Lumières (1770-1820)* (Paris, 1988), p.22-33.
7. Jessica Riskin, *Science in the age of sensibility: the sentimental empiricists of the French Enlightenment* (Chicago, IL, 2002).
8. Robert Darnton, *Mesmerism and the end of the Enlightenment in France* (Cambridge, MA, 1968). French translation: *La Fin des Lumières: le mesmérisme et la Révolution*, translated by Marie-Alyx Revellat (Paris, 1984).
9. Pierre-Samuel Du Pont de Nemours, *Sur les institutions religieuses dans l'intérieur des familles, avec un essai de traduction nouvelle de l'Oraison dominicale* (Paris, October 1806; read before the Institut national 31 October 1806), p.5-6.

detailing his theories on metempsychosis, which he said he had been developing for thirty-five years.[10] He then became a member of the first Theophilanthropy Committee under the Directoire.[11] Against the backdrop of the Enlightenment's quest for spirituality and pantheism,[12] Du Pont forged a personal 'doctrine' on the transmigration of souls and cosmology: 'Partout où l'*Intelligence* se manifeste, il y a un DIEU. Il y en a dans le polype [...]. Il y en a dans l'huître à l'écaille. Il y en a un très-respectable dans l'éléphant. Il y en avait un sublime dans Confucius, dans Socrate.'[13] This conception is faithful to a scheme widespread in European thought, of which there are many variants, and which was renewed under the influence of modern science: the 'Great Chain of Being', according to which each being is placed according to a continuous and hierarchical gradation, achieving perfection in the history of the world and of mankind.[14] 'Telle est ma *Religion*', says Du Pont.[15] It remains to be seen what precise links there are between his spiritual development and the physiocratic doctrine in general, the theological character of which has often been pointed out,[16] as well as with the development of the physiocratic collective itself. The marquis de Mirabeau never ceased to assert his Christian identity loud and clear, and in some of his later works indulged in quasi-mystical developments on the divine breath of universal beneficence that freedom of trade and high culture were to raise over

10. Pierre-Samuel Du Pont de Nemours, *Philosophie de l'univers* (Paris, De l'imprimerie de Du Pont, [1793]).
11. Albert Mathiez, *La Théophilanthropie et le culte décadaire: essai sur l'histoire de la Révolution 1796-1801* (Paris, 1903), p.109-14.
12. See *The Super-Enlightenment: daring to know too much*, ed. Dan Edelstein, *SVEC* 2010:01; *Let there be enlightenment: the religious and mystical sources of rationality*, ed. Dan Edelstein and Anton M. Matytsin (Baltimore, MD, 2018).
13. 'Sur Haller, sur Bonnet, sur leur très louable-philosophie', read at the class of moral and political sciences of the Institut, on 27 messidor Year VI (15 July 1798), in Pierre-Samuel Du Pont de Nemours, *Quelques mémoires sur différens sujets, la plupart d'histoire naturelle, ou de physique générale et particulière*, 2nd edn (Paris, 1813), p.372-73 (original emphasis).
14. Arthur Oncken Lovejoy, *The Great Chain of Being: a study of the history of an idea* (Cambridge and London, 1964).
15. Du Pont de Nemours, *Philosophie de l'univers*, p.236. See also Julien Vincent, '"Un dogue de forte race": Dupont de Nemours, ou la physiocratie réincarnée (1793-1807)', *La Révolution française* 14 (2018), p.1-34.
16. Michael Sonenscher, 'Physiocracy as a theodicy', *History of political thought* 23:2 (2002), p.326-39.

the entire planet.[17] Du Pont shared this idea of beneficence conceived as solidarity between human beings, to the point of drawing from it plans to reform public charity and hospitals to care for the sick and the poor, as Jean-Baptiste Masméjan shows in his contribution.

ii. A thinker of the bourgeois revolution?

A singular and revealing figure of the 'second Enlightenment', did Du Pont also represent 'the bourgeoisie of talent that wished for Eighty-Nine, endured Year II, then re-emerged after Thermidor', as one of his most well-known biographers claims?[18] Marc Bouloiseau takes as his starting point the long-unquestioned Marxist thesis that the 'bourgeoisie', a dominated but rising social class under the *Ancien Régime*, played a leading role in the initiation and unfolding of the French Revolution. This thesis has been widely discussed and even overturned over the last three decades by so-called 'revisionist' historians, the most radically sceptical position being brilliantly defended by Sarah Maza, who sees the very existence of this bourgeoisie as a myth pure and simple.[19] If it did not exist, how could it have been active in 1789? From this perspective, the bourgeoisie simply disappears from the landscape, to become nothing more than a 'social imaginary' that revolutionary discourse has shaped as a repellent.

Relaunched by Sarah Maza, the debate has since been further enriched and nuanced, and even turned on its head again: talk of bourgeoisie(s) in the eighteenth century has once again become legitimate, but at the cost of a series of definitional shifts and nuances. On the one hand, the causal links between emerging capitalism and revolutionary dynamics often appear indirect and polycentric. With little representation in the revolutionary assemblies, the major capitalist merchants were able to consciously act as a distinct social

17. See for example Victor Riqueti de Mirabeau, *Entretiens d'un jeune prince avec son gouverneur* (London, Moutard, 1785).
18. Marc Bouloiseau, *Bourgeoisie et révolution: les Du Pont de Nemours (1788-1799)* (Paris, 1972), p.14.
19. Sarah C. Maza, *The Myth of the French bourgeoisie: an essay on the social imaginary, 1750-1850* (Cambridge, MA, 2003); see also the illuminating synthesis of the debate by Lauren R. Clay, 'The bourgeoisie, capitalism, and the origins of the French Revolution', in *The Oxford handbook of the French Revolution*, ed. David Andress (Oxford, 2015), p.21-39; as well as chapter 2 of Laurent Coste, *Les Bourgeoisies en France: du XVIe au milieu du XIXe siècle* (Paris, 2013).

Du Pont, between physiocratic loyalty and political versatility 353

group within the nation, lobbying behind the scenes. Above all, however, the link between the expansion of commercial society in the eighteenth century and the revolutionary dynamic is more indirect than the determined action of a social group mobilised to assert its interests. The 'consumer revolution'[20] and the development of educated middle classes led to cultural transformations that undermined the hierarchical vision of the social world in favour of a more horizontal and egalitarian 'Great Chain' of the market, based on criteria of wealth and taste rather than privilege and birth,[21] favouring a culture of civic equality opposed to the traditional monarchical culture.[22] For many contemporaries, the advent of 'trading nations' was a tangible reality, as was the 'progress of commerce' marked by the expansion of the world market and colonial trade.[23] Du Pont and the Economists were among the major contributors to this debate on the value and consequences of these upheavals. Although they did not directly *cause* the Revolution, they were part of its *origins*, in the sense given to the term by Roger Chartier: they made it *possible* by making it *thinkable*.[24]

On the other hand, even if we admit that the bourgeoisie is not just a myth, which bourgeoisie are we talking about? A rising social class of entrepreneurs and capitalists relatively united by a core of common sociopolitical interests and aspirations (ousting the nobility from political power and using the state for its own ends)? Or a plurality of social groups with heterogeneous socioprofessional occupations, and whose community of interests and values is anything but obvious?[25] Within this spectrum of bourgeoisies, merchants and manufacturers weighed heavily without dominating, and were in the minority in the various revolutionary assemblies. By contrast, the 'talented bourgeoisie' – to use Marc Bouloiseau's expression – was pre-eminent,

---

20. Daniel Roche, *Histoire des choses banales: naissance de la consommation dans les sociétés traditionnelles (XVIIᵉ-XIXᵉ siècle)* (Paris, 1997).
21. Colin Jones, 'The great chain of buying: medical advertisement, the bourgeois public sphere, and the origins of the French Revolution', *American historical review* 101:1 (1996), p.13-40.
22. William H. Sewell, *Capitalism and the emergence of civic equality in eighteenth-century France* (Chicago, IL, 2021).
23. Paul Cheney, *Revolutionary commerce: globalization and the French monarchy* (Cambridge, MA, 2010).
24. Roger Chartier, *Les Origines culturelles de la Révolution française* (Paris, 1990), p.10.
25. We borrow some of the critical arguments of Sarah Maza's thesis from Colin Jones, 'La (les) bourgeoisie(s) de la France d'Ancien Régime', in *Vers un ordre bourgeois?*, ed. Jean-Pierre Jessenne (Rennes, 2007), p.161-70.

354 *Anthony Mergey and Arnault Skornicki*

whether it was the lawyers who made up the 'bourgeoisie de robe'[26] or other commoners who – like Du Pont – made a career in the various echelons of the royal administration (officers, clerks, commissioners, etc.) or, to a lesser extent, the medical professions.[27]

What brought all these groups together was perhaps above all a position between the working classes and the nobility. This negative definition does not yet give rise to a class identity: it refers only to a plurality of notables and officers from Paris and the provinces, and the economic elites of trade, manufacturing and agriculture. These well-to-do commoners were not generally income-earners: they had to work for a living, in the hope of joining the elite of the nobility through the purchase of offices, which were both economically advantageous and symbolically rewarding, to the point of diverting certain merchant vocations to the service of the state.[28] In this sense, it is doubtful that these bourgeoisies, in all their plurality, *wanted* 1789: they simply put up with it once it came. In this respect, there is a long way to go from the 'class on paper'[29] to the class mobilised and experienced by those concerned as a sociopolitical identity.

In the eighteenth century, there was certainly no shortage of attempts to describe the 'middle classes'[30] (in the plural) in a *positive light*, particularly in the network of the *intendant du commerce* Vincent de Gournay. Instead, they were associated with the economic bourgeoisie, the heads of farming, trading or manufacturing businesses. In contrast to the nobility, they were valued for their merits, skills and key role in economic development, but also for their moral qualities of honesty and moderation.[31] This type of classification contributed to the

26. Hervé Leuwers, 'La robe révolutionnée', in *Vers un ordre bourgeois?*, ed. J.-P. Jessenne, p.105-18.
27. Edna Hindie Lemay, 'La composition de l'Assemblée nationale constituante: les hommes de la continuité?', *Revue d'histoire moderne et contemporaine* 3 (1977), p.341-63.
28. Guy Chaussinand-Nogaret, 'Capital et structure sociale sous l'Ancien Régime', *Annales. Histoire, sciences sociales* 25:2 (1970), p.463-76; Eric Brian, *La Mesure de l'Etat: administrateurs et géomètres au XVIIIe siècle* (Paris, 1994), p.149-50; Jean-Pierre Hirsch, 'Les milieux du commerce, l'esprit de système et le pouvoir à la veille de la Révolution', *Annales* 30:6 (1975), p.1337-70.
29. Pierre Bourdieu, 'Espace social et genèse des "classes"', *Actes de la recherche en sciences sociales* 52:1 (1984), p.3-14.
30. François Véron Duverger de Forbonnais, *Elémens du commerce*, 2 vols (Leiden and Paris, Chez Briasson, 1754), vol.1, p.268.
31. Frédéric Lefebvre, 'L'honnêteté du négociant: une enquête sociologique française au milieu du XVIIIe siècle', in *Le Cercle de Vincent de Gournay: savoirs*

existence of these groups in the public arena, and perhaps to the creation of a social identity. Du Pont de Nemours and the physiocrats defended an original position in this debate. On the one hand, they systematised the use of the vocabulary of 'classes' to designate the main types of position in the economic circuit.[32] On the other hand, it would be hard to find any bourgeoisie or middle class in their tripartition:[33] the 'landlords' are more like an aristocracy of rentiers whose vocation is to run the state; the farmers or 'agricultural entrepreneurs' are perhaps the closest thing to it, but in the circumscribed form of a large capitalist bourgeoisie in the agricultural sector.

Du Pont's social profile appears to be 'bourgeois', but not without ambiguity. From a wealthy background, but with no assets of his own, he began studying medicine, but abandoned his studies in favour of a career in the administration. His upward trajectory led him, in 1785, to a comfortable income of around 20,000 pounds a year,[34] but not without uncertainty. Perfectly integrated into the kingdom's ruling and intellectual elites, he belonged to that social stratum of the state bourgeoisie that constantly rubbed shoulders with the nobility. As Christophe Le Digol shows in this volume, this 'double man' was torn between aspiring to join the aristocracy – to which he was related through his mother's line – and asserting his social dignity as a deserving commoner. It may be said that Du Pont also had a taste for *business*. But this vocation only came to him later, under duress. First, following the dissolution of the Constituent Assembly, he had no choice but to embark on an entrepreneurial adventure by setting up a printing works in Paris with the financial support of his friend Lavoisier and opening a printing company. However, the business proved to be unprofitable. Then, after surviving the Terror and taking

---

économiques et pratiques administratives en France au milieu du XVIIIe siècle, ed. Loïc Charles *et al.* (Paris, 2011), p.201-34; Michel Morineau, 'Entre usurier et "philistin": le "bon marchand" et le "négociant éclairé"', in *Cultures et formations négociantes dans l'Europe moderne*, ed. Franco Angiolini and Daniel Roche (Paris, 1995), p.421-38.

32. Marie-France Piguet, *Classe: histoire du mot et genèse du concept des physiocrates aux historiens de la Restauration* (Lyon, 1996).

33. Quesnay's *Tableau économique* lists three classes: the landowning class, the productive class (farm workers and managers) and the sterile class (craftsmen and shopkeepers).

34. This enabled him to invest in colonial trade; see Loïc Charles and Christine Théré, 'The physiocratic movement: a revision', in *The Economic turn: recasting political economy in Enlightenment Europe*, ed. Steven L. Kaplan and Sophus A. Reinert (New York, 2019), p.35-70 (50).

on new political and academic responsibilities at the beginning of the Directoire, he lost his positions after the coup d'état of 18 fructidor Year V (4 September 1797), which prompted him to raise funds over a two-year period to set up a joint-stock company in the United States. This attempt to retrain a bourgeois from the state bureaucracy proved costly and tricky: unable to pay his rent arrears in Paris on the eve of his departure for America, he begged the Directoire finance minister to grant him a reprieve in the name of his 'patriotic zeal' and services rendered to the Republic and the Institute.[35] The disappointments that followed did not put him on the road to fortune either, even though the firm founded in 1802 by his son Eleuthère Irénée went on to achieve the astonishing success that we know today.

Is Du Pont's thinking bourgeois? The question is as dubious as the answer is delicate. It is at this point that the debate on the bourgeois character of the Revolution – or even of the Enlightenment – telescopes with another, more situated one, on the general socio-historical interpretation that should be given to the physiocratic doctrine. It was also Marx who set the terms. According to Marx, François Quesnay's *Tableau économique* was the 'most ingenious' discovery in the history of political economy, representing in remarkably simple macroeconomic terms the consubstantial link between the circulation of wealth and the reproduction of capital, based on the *net product* of agricultural labour.[36] This scientific discovery definitively relegated mercantilism to the rank of obsolete old age, accused of limiting itself to the sphere of circulation without ever opening the secret laboratory of production. However, the physiocratic thesis of the *exclusive* productivity of agriculture, which many of his contemporaries already considered unusual, appeared to him to be indefensible three quarters of a century after the start of the Industrial Revolution. To explain this snag in the theory, Marx ascribed a precise ideological function to it: to justify the contradictions of a *transitional period between feudalism and capitalism* in a nation dominated by the agricultural sector, by formulating a compromise solution, namely, to transform the nobility into the bourgeoisie by turning them into agricultural capitalists,

---

35. Letter to 'citoyen Ramel ministre des Finances', n.p., undated, BnF, NAF 1303, f.240.

36. Karl Marx, *Théories sur la plus-value: livre IV du 'Capital'*, ed. Gilbert Badia (Paris, 1974), p.399. See also the study by Bernard Delmas and Thierry Demals, 'Karl Marx et la physiocratie', in *La Diffusion internationale de la physiocratie (XVIIIe-XIXe)*, ed. Bernard Delmas *et al.* (Grenoble, 1995), p.149-73.

to maintain their social pre-eminence. Thus, the physiocrats would propose 'a bourgeois replica of the feudal system, of the domination of landed property [...]. While feudalism acquires in this way a bourgeois aspect, bourgeois society takes on a feudal appearance.'[37]

This thesis has been criticised many times. Du Pont, like his other companions, was not the theoretician of nobles in the process of capitalist conversion, nor of a 'rural bourgeoisie' in search of ennoblement. Nor could the Economists have anticipated the advent of industrial society. Far from fully espousing the interests of the large landowners, they recommended placing the entire tax burden on their shoulders, while making the *farmers* the true capitalist entrepreneurs and their main partners in business, as equals. Their project of development centred on 'great cultivation', and agricultural capitalism implied the pure and simple abolition of feudalism, not the transformation of the old aristocracy into new capitalists of the countryside. Marx himself recognised the radical scope of the physiocratic ideas, which were far more likely to herald the French Revolution than to safeguard the *Ancien Régime*.

However, the men of the eighteenth century, including the revolutionaries, understood 'feudalism' to mean something quite different from what Marx understood it to mean: not so much a mode of production based on land ownership as a legal order in its own right.[38] Quesnay equated 'feudal government' with serfdom,[39] the principle of fiefdom constituting a major infringement of the natural right to freely dispose of one's body. On the strength of his legal expertise, another physiocrat, Guillaume-François Le Trosne, identified its historical legacy in the legal ramifications of the absolute monarchy, which had seriously degraded seigneurial power. While the latter abolished personal servitude, it maintained 'landed servitude' with the division between *useful domain* and *direct domain*, which preserved certain exorbitant rights of the seigneur over the rights of the farmer.[40] By advocating the elimination of the last vestiges of feudal tenure, as

37. Marx, *Théories sur la plus-value*, p.37-38.
38. Rafe Blaufarb, *The Great demarcation: the French Revolution and the invention of modern property* (Oxford and New York, 2016), p.8-11; French translation: *L'Invention de la propriété privée: une autre histoire de la Révolution*, translated by Christophe Jaquet (Ceyzérieu, 2019).
39. François Quesnay, 'Hommes' (1757-1758), in *Œuvres économiques complètes et autres textes*, ed. Christine Théré *et al.*, 2 vols (Paris, 2005), vol.1, p.313-14.
40. Guillaume-François Le Trosne, 'Dissertation sur la féodalité, dans laquelle on discute son origine, son état actuel, ses inconvéniens, & les moyens de la

358   *Anthony Mergey and Arnault Skornicki*

well as the venality of offices, the Economists were calling for the 'great demarcation' between private property and political power well before the Revolution, which effectively implemented it. In all its purity, this project of 'great demarcation' championed by Du Pont and his companions was designed less to serve the interests of the bourgeoisie – even the rural bourgeoisie – than to bring about a 'new civic order' stripped of privilege and feudalism.[41] However, as Jean-Pierre Jessenne points out, this civic order can legitimately be described as a *bourgeois order* if we consider it 'not as the result of the inevitable seizure of power by an inevitably conquering bourgeoisie, but as a multifactorial, cumulative process',[42] and if its result was to pave the way for capitalism. The physiocrats had neither wished for nor anticipated that this civic order based on land ownership would eventually be transformed into an *industrial society* far removed from their original 'rural philosophy'. And Du Pont, the only one of them to live long enough to witness the devastating effects of the Industrial Revolution, which became apparent in the early nineteenth century, deplored the fact that the United Kingdom had taken this path of capitalist development to the detriment of agriculture.[43]

iii. A weathervane of the extreme centre?

In 1793, Danton demanded that 'that old rascal' Du Pont be brought before the Revolutionary Tribunal.[44] In 1797, Jean-Lambert Tallien, whose versatility is itself well documented, denounced him in turn, describing him as 'l'homme qui a travaillé le plus opiniâtrement à rétablir l'Ancien Régime'.[45] In his defence, the accused described

---

supprimer', in Guillaume-François Le Trosne, *De l'administration provinciale, et de la réforme de l'impôt* (Basel, n.n., 1779), p.617-50 (625).

41. Isser Woloch, *The New regime: transformations of the French civic order, 1789-1820s* (New York, 1994).

42. Jean-Pierre Jessenne, 'Introduction', in *Vers un ordre bourgeois?*, ed. J.-P. Jessenne, p.9-15 (12).

43. Pierre-Samuel Du Pont de Nemours, *Examen du livre de M. Malthus sur le principe de population, auquel on a joint la traduction de quatre chapitres de ce livre supprimés dans l'édition française, et une lettre à M. Say sur son Traité d'économie politique* (Philadelphia, PA, 1817), p.19-20.

44. Session of 12 July 1793, in François-Alphonse Aulard, *La Société des Jacobins: recueil de documents pour l'histoire du club des Jacobins de Paris*, vol.5 (Paris, 1895), p.300.

45. Quoted in Bouloiseau, *Bourgeoisie et révolution*, p.130.

Du Pont, between physiocratic loyalty and political versatility 359

himself as a 'Dogue de forte race':[46] faithful to his convictions and loyal to his protectors, a tireless servant of the public good through all changes of regime and devoted to his friends and protectors. Others, including an adversary such as Jacques Necker,[47] spoke of his upright and trustworthy character. Honest man and champion of liberty? An unrepentant monarchist who treacherously hid behind republican declamations, opportunistic enough to survive the turbulence of history? This troubled public image was that of a man who lived through and survived the Terror, the Directoire, the Consulate and the Empire.

Without making Du Pont de Nemours a perfect model of political constancy, we can distinguish three scales of loyalty: to power, to friendship and to his principles. The first fluctuated. The second was undoubtedly solid, and inspired Du Pont to write this self-portrait for Mme de Staël: 'Pourquoi m'accordez-vous une bienveillance qui m'est très précieuse? C'est que vous m'avez vu très fidèle à mes patrons, à mes compagnons, à mes alliés et confédérés.'[48] The third is the most problematic, because his ideological evolution, which was real, was accompanied by the unshakeable maintenance of his public identity as an 'Economist'. What happened to all these loyalties when the Revolution was put to the test?

Let us first dispense with the facile hypothesis of opportunism, which is undoubtedly less common than we think because it presupposes a degree of utilitarian rationality rarely displayed by individuals. To understand the logic behind Du Pont's repositioning, we first need to look at the fluctuations in the political situation itself, which was extremely fluid even before the Revolution. Like the other deputies of the Third Estate, he had no subversive fervour at the beginning of 1789, but, once the Revolution had come, he put up with it very well and seemed to have thrown overboard the principles of absolute monarchy that had long been defended – in

---

46. P.-S. Du Pont de Nemours, *Philosophie de l'univers*, 3rd edn (Paris, Chez Goujon fils, 1798), p.167.
47. Letter from Necker to Du Pont de Nemours, 7 May 1800, in Germaine de Staël-Holstein and Pierre-Samuel Du Pont de Nemours, *De Staël-Du Pont letters: correspondence of Madame de Staël and Pierre Samuel Du Pont de Nemours and other members of the Necker and Du Pont families*, ed. and translated by James F. Marshall (Madison, WI, 1968), p.22.
48. Letter from Du Pont de Nemours to Mme de Staël, 8 February 1800 (19 pluviôse An VIII), in Staël-Holstein and Du Pont de Nemours, *De Staël-Du Pont letters*, p.15.

360   *Anthony Mergey and Arnault Skornicki*

their own way and to varying degrees – by the physiocrats. As the next day's republican after the fall of royalty, he also had to come to terms with a situation he had wanted even less. There is therefore little reason to be surprised by Du Pont's changes in position. In other words, his supposed political inconstancy cannot be understood without reference to the inconstancy of the regimes themselves, and to the shifting and uncertain identity of the political camps during the Revolution, in accordance with the famous formula of the former minister Edgar Faure – incidentally a qualified professor in Roman law and legal history – according to whom 'it's not the weather vane that turns, it's the wind.'[49]

But we don't want to paint a picture of Du Pont simply being tossed about by the gusts of history. Faced with the crisis of an institution, in this case an entire political regime, the economist and sociologist Albert O. Hirschman asserted that there are three main responses available to the players: *exit, voice* and *loyalty*.[50] These three responses are not mutually exclusive. It is striking to note that Du Pont, at the beginning of his revolutionary commitment, switched from one 'loyalty' to another without giving the impression of betraying the monarchy, but on the contrary taking advantage of the opportunity he was given to recast it from within. In other words, the unprecedented broadening of political participation inaugurated by the Constituent Assembly offered him the opportunity to *speak at the highest level*, to play an active and direct part in shaping the future institutions of a remodelled kingdom. His attachment to the old monarchy was all the weaker because he had been a harsh critic of its institutions and, despite his tireless efforts, he never felt entirely secure in his position. It was therefore understandable that he should move from critical loyalty to the *Ancien Régime* to active participation in the constituent process, which enabled him, briefly, to play a political role to which he had never aspired: aside from the presidency of the Constituent Assembly, which did not last two weeks, he was a member of eleven committees. Threatened under the Terror, rehabilitated under the Directoire (he was appointed to the Conseil des Anciens) and then sidelined again, he never ceased to enliven public debate.

---

49. See *Politix: revue des sciences sociales du politique* 14:56 (2001), special issue: *Inconstances politiques*, ed. Brigitte Gaïti and Pierre Serna.
50. Albert Hirschman, *Exit, voice, and loyalty: responses to decline in firms, organizations, and states* (Cambridge, MA, 2004); *Défection et prise de parole: théorie et applications*, translated by Claude Besseyrias (Paris, 1995).

Even when he went into exile – or, in Hirschman's terms, 'exited' – he directed his interventions towards the young American Republic and its leaders, particularly Thomas Jefferson.

All in all, Du Pont's political procrastinations were limited. They resembled successive compromises marked sometimes by support and sometimes by reluctance, guided by an ideological compass even more precious as it enabled him to maintain stable reference points in a world in perpetual upheaval. On a personal and professional level, he was able to expect the introduction of representative government to stabilise his political and administrative career, which until then had depended on the goodwill or good fortune of his aristocratic patrons. In political terms, he could also expect it to bring to fruition the great project of rebuilding the political order based on citizenship defined by property instead of birth and rank. In other words, his ability to adapt was neither a guilty passivity in the face of events and *faits accomplis*, nor a strict denial.

iv. The invention of a neo-physiocracy? From legal despotism to republicanism

'Quand on a cru devoir adopter une doctrine et des principes, il faut les suivre en tout et toute sa vie', declared Du Pont de Nemours.[51] At first sight, the gulf between the physiocratic doctrine of 'legal despotism' and his later republicanism is no less striking. Although he questioned the institutions of the *Ancien Régime* very early on, he hardly ever questioned the principle of monarchy. That is why we can be legitimately surprised when he states in 1798: 'Si l'on excepte les nations entièrement abusées on trouvera partout des sentiments républicains. Et même sous un certain aspect tous les Etats sont déjà des Républiques, ou très prêts à le devenir.'[52] Just after Thermidor, he was already trumpeting: 'la République triomphe et triomphera de toutes les tyrannies.'[53] These statements lead us to the following question: how are we to appreciate the apparent political versatility of

---

51. Pierre-Samuel Du Pont de Nemours, 'Notes sur le second chant', in *L'Arioste: essai de traduction en vers du Roland furieux de l'Arioste (par Dupont de Nemours)* (Paris, 1812), p.196-204 (198). The first edition, which we have not been able to consult, dates from 1781.
52. Letter dated 5 floréal An VI (24 April 1798), quoted in Bouloiseau, *Bourgeoisie et révolution*, p.135-36.
53. Du Pont de Nemours, 'Lettre aux auteurs de la *Décade*', p.71.

Du Pont, who moved from 'legal despotism' to the defence of constitutional monarchy, before defining himself as a republican? How can we understand that he never ceased to maintain his public identity as a physiocrat against all odds and constantly defended a doctrine that had fallen into disuse with the international success of the ideas of Adam Smith, Thomas Robert Malthus,[54] David Ricardo and Jean-Baptiste Say?[55] Du Pont himself theorised *ex post* the coherence of his political career: physiocracy, he explained, would have greatly contributed to planting 'l'arbre de la liberté française', and the Economists – including Turgot, rightly or wrongly – would have been the 'précurseurs de la République'.[56] Just as the anatomy of man is a key to the anatomy of the ape, the late Du Pont could help shed light on the political thinking of the physiocrats under the *Ancien Régime*.

To cut a long story short, Du Pont de Nemours's political views, from the *Ancien Régime* to the beginning of the nineteenth century, were characterised by an undeniable thread running through them: a perpetual search for moderation and a constant exercise of it, which were not always easy to grasp in the midst of the events that punctuated this tumultuous period. In political parlance, Du Pont is what is commonly known as a 'moderate', concerned about the authority of laws (natural and positive), attentive to the balance of power, vigilant about respect for rights and freedoms and worried about arbitrary excesses. And it is precisely this permanent attachment to moderation that largely explains his winding political path and his various ideological adjustments.[57] From a bold reformer under the *Ancien Régime*, he became a moderate revolutionary in 1789, then a moderate conservative after Thermidor.

His fleeting and not very energetic defence of legal despotism is striking proof of this. Theorised and developed by Le Mercier de La Rivière in his work *L'Ordre naturel et essentiel des sociétés politiques* published in 1767, legal despotism is defined by the abbé Baudeau, in

---

54. See Du Pont de Nemours, *Examen du livre de M. Malthus*.
55. To Say, who regretted the physiocratic confusion between political economy and the science of government, he replied in his letter of 22 April 1815; see Jean-Baptiste Say, *Mélanges et correspondance d'économie politique*, ed. Charles Comte (Paris, 1833), p.9.
56. Du Pont de Nemours, 'Lettre aux auteurs de la *Décade*', p.83.
57. On this cardinal idea of moderation, see Aurelian Craiutu, *A Virtue for courageous minds: moderation in French political thought (1748-1830)* (Princeton, NJ, 2012).

a review of the book by the former intendant of the Windward Islands, as follows:

> *Despotisme*, c'est-à-dire *force* supérieure à toute force privée, appartenant à un *maître* qui en est propriétaire à titre patrimonial; mais *légal*, c'est-à-dire qu'il n'est que pour garantir à chacun ses *propriétés*, et pour donner à tous les connaissances de l'ordre naturel et social, pour dissiper l'*ignorance* et réprimer les *usurpations, force* dont la base est l'association indissoluble et manifestement connue des intérêts du Souverain avec ceux de chaque propriétaire particulier.[58]

This legal despot, instructed in the rules of evidence and advised by competent persons and bodies[59] who must apply and respect the principles of the natural order to satisfy the general interest, *obviously* has nothing in common with an arbitrary despot who would be satisfied with an authoritarian drift of the regime to satisfy the needs linked to the satisfaction of his particular interest. Legal despotism is nothing less than a regenerated absolute monarchy, amended, corrected and framed by the principles of natural order, which is further distinguished by the obligation placed on the prince-legislator to strictly respect the hierarchy of norms under the expert eye of the magistrates. Out of loyalty to his school of thought, Du Pont obviously relayed the virtues and advantages of what the abbé Baudeau called the 'true monarchy'.[60] But often he did so by repeating verbatim or paraphrasing the words of his most convinced fellow students. Make no mistake about it: at the end of the 1760s, Du Pont fully embraced the physiocratic political doctrine in that he was convinced, at that moment, that the government of one, guided by the laws of natural order, with a renewed monarchy as its framework, was the only regime suitable for guaranteeing the happiness of all.[61]

---

58. Nicolas Baudeau, 'Critique raisonnée de *L'Ordre naturel et essentiel des sociétés politiques*', *Ephémérides du citoyen* 12 (1767), p.207-208 (original emphasis).

59. See Anthony Mergey, 'Conseiller le prince dans l'idéal physiocratique: le rôle de la magistrature', in *Education des citoyens, éducation des gouvernants* (Aix-en-Provence, 2020), p.171-81.

60. Nicolas Baudeau, *Première introduction à la philosophie économique, ou Analyse des Etats policés* (Paris, Didot l'aîné, 1771), p.366.

61. Pierre-Samuel Du Pont de Nemours, *De l'origine et des progrès d'une science nouvelle* (1768), ed. A. Dubois (Paris, 1910), p.35: 'Ce n'est que dans ce Gouvernement simple et naturel, que les Souverains sont véritablement *despotes*; qu'ils peuvent tout ce qu'ils veulent pour leur bien, lequel se trouve inséparablement et manifestement attaché à celui des Nations qu'ils gouvernent.'

364   *Anthony Mergey and Arnault Skornicki*

But then, how do you explain his reluctance to promote legal despotism? Like so many others, he felt uneasy about using the term 'legal despotism', which fuelled confusion and misunderstanding. One need only look at the explanatory note he wrote in 1768 in *De l'origine et des progrès d'une science nouvelle* to justify the choice of the term 'despot' to immediately grasp his discomfort in trying to convince the reader of the validity of using such an expression. Quite logically, opponents of the physiocrats were quick to criticise the physiocrats' political theory in general and their choice of term in particular. Grimm considered that 'the government of an enlightened, active, vigilant, wise and firm despot' was a utopia,[62] and criticised the Economists for using 'an abundance [of] empty words'[63] to conceal the establishment of the most arbitrary despotism imaginable. As for Mably, convinced that a despot can only be a man blinded by the excess of his power and his ignorance, he concluded that 'legal despotism only serves to increase the delirium and strength of passions.'[64] Beardé de L'Abbaye,[65] Galiani,[66] the baron d'Holbach,[67] Morellet[68] and Voltaire[69] were also outspoken in their condemnation of the phrase, describing it as a veritable linguistic monstrosity. Even

62. Friedrich Melchior, baron von Grimm, *Correspondance littéraire, philosophique et critique (1747-1793)*, ed. M. Tourneux, vol.7 (Paris, 1879), p.435: 'Ce sont les despotes endormis sur le trône qui font le malheur des nations. Or si la morale vous dit que le trône est l'endroit le moins propre au sommeil, l'histoire vous apprendra que c'est cependant le lieu où l'on sommeille le plus.'
63. Grimm, *Correspondance littéraire*, p.437.
64. Gabriel Bonnot de Mably, *Doutes proposés aux philosophes économistes sur l'ordre naturel et essentiel des sociétés politiques* (The Hague and Paris, Chez Nyon, 1768), p.274.
65. M. Beardé de L'Abbaye, *Recherches sur les moyens de supprimer les impôts, précédées de l'examen de la nouvelle science* (Amsterdam, Marc-Michel Rey, 1770).
66. Ferdinando Galiani, *Dialogues sur le commerce des blés* (London and Paris, Joseph Merlin, 1770).
67. Paul Heinrich Dietrich von Holbach, *Système social, ou Principes naturels de la morale et de la politique, avec un examen de l'influence du gouvernement sur les mœurs* (London, n.n., 1773).
68. André Morellet, *Sur le despotisme légal et contre M. de La Rivière*, ed. Eugenio Di Rienzo, in *Individualismo, assolutismo, democrazia*, ed. Centro studi di filosofia politica (Naples, 1992), p.329-44. See also Eugenio Di Rienzo, 'Pour une histoire du concept de despotisme du XVIIIe siècle français: le manuscrit inédit de l'abbé Morellet: *Sur le despotisme légal et contre M. de La Rivière*', *Proceedings of the 8th International Congress of the Enlightenment*, vol.1 (Oxford, 1992), p.292-96.
69. Voltaire, *L'Homme aux quarante écus*, ed. Brenda M. Bloesch, in *Œuvres complètes de Voltaire*, vol.66 (Oxford, 1999), p.211-409.

Du Pont, between physiocratic loyalty and political versatility 365

Rousseau, although he had never publicly entered a polemic with a supporter of physiocracy, could not help expressing his scepticism, seeing in the phrase 'nothing but two contradictory words, which together mean nothing'.[70] Supporters of the physiocratic movement were also cautious. Turgot was a typical example, and it was hardly surprising that he confided in his friend Du Pont, certain that he would find an attentive and probably understanding ear. Although a faithful and loyal supporter of strong royal power, the man who was still intendant of Limousin did not hesitate, in various letters, to openly state his rejection of such a political regime tending inexorably towards arbitrariness, to the point of considering that this doctrine of legal despotism 'never ceases to sully the works of Economists',[71] encouraging them to find another formulation such as, for example, 'public authority'.[72] The contentious expression adopted by Le Mercier de La Rivière was regularly defended and justified in the years that followed, notably by Baudeau and the marquis de Mirabeau, to demonstrate that the legal despot was in no way a 'despotic *despot*'.[73] In vain. The unfortunate use of a word that still had a strong pejorative connotation in the eighteenth century,[74] and whose

---

70. Jean-Jacques Rousseau, 'Lettre à M. le marquis de Mirabeau (26 juillet 1767)', in *Correspondance générale de J.-J. Rousseau, collationnée sur les originaux, annotés et commentés par T. Dufour*, vol.17 (Paris, 1932), p.158.

71. Anne-Robert-Jacques Turgot, 'Lettre XCVIII à Dupont (10 mai 1771)', in *Œuvres de Turgot et documents le concernant*, ed. Gustave Schelle, 5 vols (Paris, 1913-1923), vol.3, p.486-87; A.-R.-J. Turgot, 'Lettre LXXXV à Dupont (21 décembre 1770)', in *Œuvres de Turgot et documents le concernant*, p.398 : 'MM. les Economistes ne peuvent se défaire de leur tic sur l'autorité tutélaire, laquelle déshonore leur doctrine et est l'inconséquence la plus inconséquente à leur dogme de l'évidence'; A.-R.-J. Turgot, 'Lettre XCVII à Dupont (7 mai 1771)', in *Œuvres de Turgot et documents le concernant*, p.486: 'Ce diable de despotisme, quoique plus déguisé, nuira toujours à la propagation de votre doctrine.'

72. A.-R.-J. Turgot, 'Lettre CXXXIII à Dupont (14 mars 1774)', in *Œuvres de Turgot et documents le concernant*, p.662.

73. François Quesnay, 'Despotisme de la Chine', *Ephémérides du citoyen* 6 (1767), p.10.

74. On the meaning and history of the term 'despotism', see Richard Koebner, 'Despot and despotism: vicissitudes of a political term', *Journal of the Warburg and Courtauld Institutes* 14:3-4 (1951), p.275-302; Charles Porset, 'Despotisme: du mot à l'histoire', in *L'Etat moderne: regards sur la pensée politique de l'Europe occidentale entre 1715 et 1848*, ed. Simone Goyard-Fabre (Paris, 2000), p.53-61; Melvin Richter, 'Le concept de despotisme et l'abus des mots', *Dix-huitième siècle* 34 (2002), p.373-88; Franco Venturi, 'Despotisme oriental', in *Europe des Lumières: recherches sur le 18ᵉ siècle* (Paris, 1971), p.131-42; *Il dispotismo: genesi*

image Montesquieu's typology of governments did little to improve, contributed greatly to the disqualification of the political doctrine of the physiocrats, whose initial aim was simply to regenerate and perfect the old French monarchy. Given this context and the constant concern for moderation that governed Du Pont's political thinking, it is hardly surprising that he showed a kind of restraint in his defence of 'despotism', even if it was described as 'legal'. Indeed, he openly distanced himself from it after the Revolution, referring to 'an unfortunate expression' that 'gave a little too much credit to *absolute power*', reducing it to a 'particular branch' of physiocracy associated with Le Mercier de La Rivière, Baudeau and Quesnay himself, and blaming it for the bad reputation of the Economists.[75]

Although monarchy, under the aegis of the *moderate* power of one, remained for him, at that precise moment, the most appropriate regime for transposing the principles of natural order, it must be admitted that he was hardly expansive when it came to extolling its merits, although he was careful to mention as early as the 1760s his hostility to English-style temperate monarchy. However, he was more prolix on one of the necessary conditions for the regeneration of the monarchy, which he wanted as much as his fellow writers. For the monarchy to be in conformity with the higher rules of the natural order, a profound restructuring of its territorial administration was necessary to restore local administrative bodies to their natural places and thus ensure the proper functioning of the institutions. In short, it was a matter of reviving, in the words of the marquis de Mirabeau, 'cette république subordonnée qui [doit] entrer dans la composition de la monarchie, et qui peut seule en maintenir le jeu intérieur et la stabilité'.[76] Du Pont is well-known for having drafted, in conjunction with Turgot, the famous *Mémoire sur les municipalités*, which laid the foundations for a far-reaching reform of the monarchy, and influenced both the ministerial plans at the end of the *Ancien Régime* and the thinking of the Constituents at the start of the

---

    e sviluppo di un concetto filosofico-politico, ed. Domenico Felice, 2 vols (Naples, 2002); Mario Turchetti, 'Droit de résistance, à quoi? Unmasking despotism and tyranny today', *Revue historique* 4 (2006), p.831-78.

75. Pierre-Samuel Du Pont de Nemours, 'Notice sur les Economistes', in A.-R.-J. Turgot, *Œuvres de Turgot*, ed. Eugène Daire (Paris, 1844), p.258-61 (260); 'Lettre aux auteurs de la *Décade*', p.78 (original emphasis).

76. Victor Riqueti, marquis de Mirabeau, *Traité de la monarchie* (1757-1759), ed. G. Longhitano (Paris, 1999), p.108.

Revolution.[77] It was on this occasion that Du Pont developed his ideas on the economic foundations of the right to citizenship. This close association between land ownership and citizenship, which was typical of physiocracy and of the marquis de Mirabeau,[78] was a valuable intellectual resource during the Revolution. It enabled him to move his thinking towards a certain idea of representative government without giving the impression of betraying his principles. His appointment as a member of the Constitutional Committee, in the company of Bureaux de Pusy, Aubry-Dubochet and Gossuin, as deputy commissioner responsible for continuing the work of dividing up the territory (from the end of November 1789 until February 1790) and as president of the National Assembly (from 16 to 30 August 1790), is perhaps an acknowledgement of his consistency and moderation. More generally, Du Pont was far from being a strict defender of the monarchy before the Revolution: before his conversion to physiocracy, he carefully annotated Jean-Jacques Rousseau's *Du contrat social* from its publication in 1762, without following it entirely, as Thierry Demals and Alexandra Hyard show in this volume; as early as 1771, he envisaged a republican and confederal constitution for America, notes Gabriel Sabbagh in his contribution on Du Pont's participation in the *Letters of Abraham Mansword*,[79] and promptly showed a particular interest in the first steps of the young republic as his correspondence with Franklin and Jefferson attests. While it is inaccurate to assert that the question of the best regime was of secondary interest to the physiocrats, as has been argued,[80] this assertion does have some resonance when it comes to Du Pont de

---

77. The reference text of the *Mémoire sur les municipalités* can be found in Gustave Schelle's edition of the *Œuvres de Turgot et documents le concernant*, vol.4, p.568-621. Turgot was the instigator of the plan; Du Pont de Nemours was the one who gave it shape, even though the minister declared himself dissatisfied with the final result.

78. See Antonella Alimento, 'Tra fronda e fisiocrazia: il pensiero di Mirabeau sulle municipalità (1750-1767)', *Annali della Fondazione Luigi Einaudi* 22 (1988), p.97-141; Anthony Mergey, 'La question des "municipalités" dans l'*Introduction au Mémoire sur les Etats provinciaux* du marquis de Mirabeau (1758)', *Revue de la recherche juridique – droit prospectif* 4 (2006), p.2523-48.

79. Based on a critique of the English model famously developed by Jean-Louis de Lolme, *Constitution de l'Angleterre* (Amsterdam, E. Van Harrevelt, 1771).

80. Prosper Duvergier de Hauranne, *Histoire du gouvernement parlementaire en France*, vol.1 (Paris, 1857), p.40; Luigi Cossa, *Histoire des doctrines économiques* (Paris, 1899), p.281; Philippe Steiner, *La 'Science nouvelle' de l'économie politique* (Paris, 1998), p.105; Georges Weulersse, *Le Mouvement physiocratique en France (de 1756*

368   *Anthony Mergey and Arnault Skornicki*

Nemours who, without displaying total indifference to political forms, seemed to set as his main condition that natural laws be conscientiously applied and respected by the governing state. In fact, this was the thrust of his address to the king of Sweden, Gustav III, in 1772:

> Que votre administration soit monarchique, aristocratique, démocratique ou mixte, cela est indifférent au bonheur de vos peuples, si chacun de vos sujets sait, ainsi que le souverain, que l'autorité légitime est aussi sacrée, selon l'ordre naturel, que le droit de propriété qui comprend celle des biens et des personnes; si le souverain convient avec eux qu'il n'a aucun droit pour les juger que d'après les lois de l'ordre et de la justice.[81]

In the ordeal of the Revolution, it seems that Du Pont's physiocratic identity was a plumb line in the tumult of events. But there was more to it than that. The sociology of political crises uses the somewhat convoluted expression of *regression towards the habitus* to designate a mechanism that is both simple and counterintuitive. When a social order collapses, the actors in history, far from simply unleashing their imagination and creative power, fall back on their most secure, deep-rooted social and intellectual assets; these serve as a compass in rough weather, as landmarks when all other reference points dissipate and when they must carry out the 'reconstruction' of the social world.[82] Paradoxically, however, this inertia of social dispositions does not so much pull people back as generate new practices and representations, as the players are led to transpose them into new institutions and social spaces.[83] Thus, the invention of the National Assembly, the proliferation of clubs and the lifting of censorship offered Du Pont a new arena for his talents and skills. One might even wonder *whether the Revolution did not allow him to free his speech* by authorising him to

---

à 1770), vol.2 (Paris, 1910), p.43 and 654; Georges Weulersse, *La Physiocratie à la fin du règne de Louis XV (1770-1774)* (Paris, 1959), p.89.

81. Pierre-Samuel Du Pont de Nemours, 'Conseils demandés en Suède', *Ephémérides du citoyen* 1 (1772), p.193-94.

82. Michel Dobry, *Sociologie des crises politiques: la dynamique des mobilisations multisectorielles* (Paris, 1986), p.202.

83. Regression to habitus is understood as 'the transferability of patterns of action and perception from the social places or "contexts" where they have been internalised to other places, other "contexts" or other theatres of operation': Michel Dobry, *'Postface* / Eléments de réponse: principes et implications d'une perspective relationnelle', in *La Logique du désordre*, ed. Myriam Aït-Aoudia and Antoine Roger (Paris, 2015), p.261-332 (305).

Du Pont, between physiocratic loyalty and political versatility 369

free himself entirely from a certain monarchist physiocratic rhetoric with absolutist tendencies. This perspective may also give a slightly different view of physiocracy: a living, mobile and diverse way of thinking capable of redefining itself without betraying itself, in other words, of updating the meaning of its main principles (liberty, property, safety).

Du Pont's support for the idea of a constitutional monarchy in the early months of 1789 attests to this. A member of the influential Société des Trente since the end of the previous year and an active participant in drafting the grievances of the Third Estate of the bailiwick of Nemours, of which he would be one of the representatives at the Estates General, Du Pont fully supported the establishment of a new political system in which the prince would be subject to constitutional rules, sovereignty transferred to the nation, and legislative power exercised by the nation's representatives. Taking up the wish expressed by the majority of the *cahiers de doléances* that France should take the form of a 'monarchical government tempered by laws', Du Pont gave a definition that was far removed from that of the legal despotism proposed by the physiocrats: 'L'on entend par gouvernement monarchique, celui où un seul, qu'on nomme roi ou monarque, est chargé avec la plus grande étendue de puissance, de faire exécuter les lois faites par la nation et sanctionnées par lui, ou faites par lui et consenties par la nation'.[84] The separation and collaboration of powers,[85] while still insisting on the legitimate authority of the monarch, the representative system and national sovereignty,[86] now seemed to him to be the necessary ingredients for the exercise of moderate power. There was no longer any question of entrusting a single authority, namely the prince, with the exercise of executive and legislative functions; any confusion of powers had to be outlawed; otherwise, 'government would be arbitrary.'[87] This concept of the exercise of power is still far removed from that of legal despotism, which Du Pont never really endorsed, and which he implicitly rejected

---

84. Pierre-Samuel Du Pont de Nemours, *Tableau comparatif des demandes contenues dans les cahiers des trois ordres remis à MM. les députés aux Etats généraux* (n.p., n.n., 1789), p.9.
85. Du Pont de Nemours, *Tableau comparatif*, p.6-7.
86. Pierre-Samuel Du Pont de Nemours, *De la périodicité des assemblées nationales, de leur organisation, de la forme à suivre pour amener les propositions qui pourront y être faites, à devenir des lois et de la sanction nécessaire pour que ces lois soient obligatoires* (Paris, Chez Baudouin, 1789), p.4.
87. Du Pont de Nemours, *De la périodicité*, p.6.

at the time of the Revolution, and is also far removed from the concept he embraced in the last decades of the *Ancien Régime*, namely the *moderate* government of a single individual governed by natural laws and, increasingly, during the 1780s, by positive rules. But, in 1789, the criteria for establishing this moderate power changed: constitutional monarchy emerged as the appropriate regime for enshrining property and freedom.

The argument that Du Pont was politically fickle cannot be accepted. To be convinced of this, it is enough to appreciate the ideological path taken by some of his fellow travellers within the physiocratic school to grasp the sudden and unexpected effects of the pre-revolutionary context and of the Revolution itself on people's minds. As early as 1787, in his *Idées d'un citoyen presque sexagénaire*, without completely disregarding certain features of legal despotism, the abbé Baudeau adopted radical positions that reflected a clear return to an absolutist conception of monarchical government. More generally, in this text and in his few subsequent writings, he came to defend a vision of society with strong hints of the *Ancien Régime*, in which the 'patriarchal government of a hereditary monarch, who regards the entire state as his patrimony and all his subjects as his children', was to take its place.[88] In fact, this radicalisation observed in Baudeau was not without reason in retrospect for Du Pont, who never ceased to be suspicious of this porous boundary between absolute monarchy and legal despotism.

The career of Le Mercier de La Rivière is even more instructive. In *Les Vœux d'un Français*, published in 1788, there was no longer any question of instituting a legal despot. In this troubled period in France, the maintenance of an absolute monarchy by divine right was demanded, as this remained the 'principle of all justice and of all security'.[89] Although he was the main theorist of legal despotism, Le Mercier de La Rivière, like most of his fellow students, had long since stopped using the term for fear of being reviled by his critics. Nevertheless, although the monarch of 1788 was not the legal despot of 1767, the monarchical regime he defended remained imbued

---

88. Nicolas Baudeau, 'Avant-propos aux *Mémoires sur l'état des paysans polonais* de M. le comte Massalski', *Nouvelles éphémérides économiques* 2 (1788), part 2, p.73-74 (74).

89. Paul-Pierre Le Mercier de La Rivière, *Les Vœux d'un Français, ou Considérations sur les principaux objets dont le roi et la nation vont s'occuper* (Paris, Mme Vallat La Chapelle, 1788), p.9.

with the same physiocratic values and principles that he had greatly contributed to shaping in the preceding years: 'L'autorité tutélaire d'un monarque, quoiqu'absolue, n'est point cependant arbitraire et sans bornes, puisque ses sujets ont des droits et une liberté qu'elle est tenue de leur conserver.'[90] The words 'tutelary authority', 'absolute', 'arbitrary' and 'limits' express the delicate phase of transition in which the former intendant found himself, since they echo the features of both physiocratic and absolutist thinking. To see the influence of the traditional monarchical model on his thinking, we need only look at his efforts to distinguish between 'absolute' and 'arbitrary' authority,[91] echoing the difference he once made between 'legal despotism' and 'arbitrary despotism'. Basically, what was once 'legal' had become 'absolute' in 1788. A few months later, Le Mercier de La Rivière, an advocate of a monarchy with strong absolutist overtones, radically changed his point of view in his 1789 *Essais sur les maximes et loix fondamentales*: he validated the principle of the separation of legislative and executive powers, adopting a different conception of freedom, one that was more political and less natural. From then on, he recognised the power to legislate of the Estates General, which were assimilated to representatives of the nation who met periodically, and the executive function of the prince.[92] Clearly under pressure from the political and social context, the physiocrat also rallied, at the same time as Du Pont de Nemours, to this increasingly mainstream trend, which called for the sharing of government functions. Despite everything, his attachment to the monarchical principle seemed stronger than ever: the prince remained the sovereign, he alone had executive power, and representative government in the strict sense of the term was not yet a reality due to the regularity of the Estates General.[93] In his view, all these indicators were sufficient to conclude that kingship was likely to endure, as otherwise 'government would cease to be monarchical'.[94] In other words, it was a tempered

90. Le Mercier de La Rivière, *Les Vœux d'un Français*, p.12-13, 54. See also Catherine Larrère, 'L'apport de la physiocratie à la tradition française du libéralisme', in *Les Libéralismes, la théorie politique et l'histoire*, ed. S. Stuurman (Amsterdam, 1994), p.72-89 (76).

91. Le Mercier de La Rivière, *Les Vœux d'un Français*, p.13-14.

92. Paul-Pierre Le Mercier de La Rivière, *Essais sur les maximes et loix fondamentales de la monarchie française, ou Canevas d'un code constitutionnel* (Paris and Versailles, Mme Vallat La Chapelle, 1789), p.3, 41.

93. Le Mercier de La Rivière, *Essais*, p.25, 27.

94. Le Mercier de La Rivière, *Essais*, p.27, n.1.

monarchy, incorporating counterforces, that he was recommending, even though he had denounced it a few years earlier. The motivation that drove him was basically always the same: 'Dare to believe in the forthcoming regeneration of the state',[95] even if this means adapting the form of monarchical government. In 1792, in a work worthy of Thomas More entitled *L'Heureuse Nation, ou Relations du gouvernement des Féliciens*, he took full account of the country's new political and institutional reality. While he maintained the monarchical form of government and still recognised the nation's right to legislate, he now made the nation the sole holder of sovereignty and openly validated the principle of counterforces.[96] Now that we have looked at the ideological trajectory of Le Mercier de La Rivière, we can see that Du Pont's was a normal one, given his convictions and the events he witnessed.

Despite the approaching revolutionary whirlwind, only the marquis de Mirabeau remained faithful to his last breath to the most orthodox version of legal despotism, firmly believing in its establishment 'in its own time'.[97] This gave him the opportunity to denounce in general terms those who wished to 'demonarchise France'[98] and to deplore more specifically the increasing scarcity of spokesmen for the doctrine of the natural order, on the understanding that 'what sowers remain are no more than invalids, or heads warped by a series of pacts with impiety.'[99] There is no doubt that Du Pont was the target of this mocking remark, so characteristic of the marquis. Be that as it may, there was no longer any need for consensus in the ranks of physiocracy.

Du Pont adapted perfectly to the new political and social order that gradually came into being in the spring of 1789, seeing it as an

---

95. Le Mercier de La Rivière, *Essais*, p.xix.
96. P.-P. Le Mercier de La Rivière, *L'Heureuse Nation, ou Relations du gouvernement des Féliciens, peuple souverainement libre sous l'empire absolu de ses loix*, 2 vols (Paris, Chez Buisson, 1792), p.87, 4, 15-16, 269-70. On this utopia, see Mathilde Lemée, 'Le citoyen dans *L'Heureuse nation ou Gouvernement des Féliciens* de Le Mercier de La Rivière (1792)', *Revue juridique de l'Ouest* 3 (2013), p.271-303.
97. 'Lettre du marquis de Mirabeau à Charles de Butré du 9 janvier 1789', in Rodolphe Reuss, *Charles de Butré, un physiocrate tourangeau en Alsace et dans le margraviat de Bade d'après ses papiers inédits et sa correspondance* (Paris, 1887), p.98.
98. 'Lettre du marquis de Mirabeau au bailli de Mirabeau du 12 janvier 1789', in *Lettres inédites du marquis de Mirabeau (1787-1789)*, ed. Dauphin Meunier, *Le Correspondant* (25 April 1913), p.314.
99. 'Lettre du marquis de Mirabeau à Charles de Butré du 9 janvier 1789', p.98.

opportunity to put into practice a much-needed rational policy that would enshrine property, liberty, security, equality, obedience to the law and respect for the Constitution. From then on, after the adoption of the Constitution of 1791, true to his principles and convictions, he approved of representative government on condition that it was placed under the reign of enlightened public opinion informed by free discussion, with a restrictive definition of political participation. It is under this regime that political obligation and the duty of obedience of citizens are founded. At best, the law expresses the collective recognition of justice and reason by the enlightened majority. At worst, a defective law nevertheless protects citizens from arbitrariness.[100] However, aware of the existing balance of power within the Assembly and the fragility of the new institutions, he regularly took care to remind all true patriots to remain reasonable, not to resort to violence or excess, and to remain 'constitutional'.[101]

The period that began with the disappearance of royalty in August 1792 and ended with the murderous period of the Terror in July 1794 was a difficult one for Du Pont de Nemours. Forced into hiding because of his role in the defence of the Tuileries to protect Louis XVI from the mob, he was finally arrested by the Jacobins in 1794, imprisoned at La Force and then sentenced to the guillotine. Meanwhile, in September 1792, the Republic was proclaimed. When did Du Pont embrace the republican ideal? In one of his letters to his son Eleuthère Irénée dated 21 thermidor Year II, written from the depths of his prison, he answers this question as follows: 'Je n'ai jamais rien fait contre la République. Je l'ai demandée avant qu'elle existât, servie dès qu'elle a existé.'[102] While it is easy to understand Du Pont's immediate interest, in such circumstances, in expressing his attachment and loyalty to the Republic to save his own head, the fact remains that his statement takes on a completely different dimension if we put it into perspective with his ideological and political journey since the 1760s. If the Republic is now the political form best suited

---

100. Pierre-Samuel Du Pont de Nemours, 'De l'amour de la constitution et de celui de la liberté', in *Correspondance patriotique entre les citoyens qui ont été membres de l'Assemblée nationale constituante*, vol.2 (Paris, De l'imprimerie de Du Pont, 1791), p.70-79 (76).
101. Du Pont de Nemours, 'De l'amour de la constitution et de celui de la liberté', p.79.
102. Pierre-Samuel Du Pont de Nemours, *Lettres de Du Pont de Nemours écrites de la prison de la Force: 5 thermidor-8 fructidor An II*, ed. Gilbert Chinard (Paris, 1929), p.57.

374   *Anthony Mergey and Arnault Skornicki*

to the exercise of moderate government that preserves the rights and freedoms of everyone, separates the powers, ensures submission to the law and requires respect for the Constitution, Du Pont in fact 'asked for it before it existed'. An avowed 'Modérantiste', he has been pursuing the same objective for over thirty years: to put the *res publica*, the public thing, the state, in good hands. From then on, pragmatism helped, and the advent of the republic-state seemed inseparable from the establishment of the republic-government.[103]

His first publication of a political and legal nature after the Terror, *Du pouvoir législatif et du pouvoir exécutif convenables à la République française*, published in 1795, draws on a well-known lexical field already widely used under the *Ancien Régime* and in the early years of the Revolution:

> La Nation française veut être constituée en République, et en République démocratique, où l'égalité des droits, la liberté des actions honnêtes et utiles, la propriété des biens, la sûreté des personnes, soient efficacement garantis à tous et à chacun. C'est sur ces bases, et uniquement sur elles, qu'il faut asseoir un gouvernement sage et puissant; qui mette naturellement en place les lumières et la vertu; qui leur assure l'autorité nécessaire pour faire jouir le peuple de tous ses droits, et obliger chaque citoyen à remplir tous ses devoirs; qui prévienne les contre-révolutions; qui soit énergique au-dehors, paisible et protecteur au-dedans. Cette entreprise n'est peut-être pas aussi difficile qu'elle est belle. Les lois constitutives essentielles à un bon gouvernement ne sont pas nombreuses; il suffit qu'elles soient sages et bien combinées.[104]

It is not surprising, therefore, that he has continued to demand, without interruption since the 1770s, the abolition of physical restraint, a real attack on personal freedom, as Thérence Carvalho demonstrates in one of the essays in this volume. Behind the neo-republican, it is, in fact, the physiocrat who continues to express himself. The persistence of ideas, principles and hopes is palpable.

Once again, a player in the political game as a member of the Council of Elders, Du Pont stuck to a line he had adopted in the autumn of 1789, firmly adopting conservative, but not counter-revolutionary,

---

103. Eric Gojosso, *Le Concept de République en France (XVIe-XVIIIe siècle)* (Aix-en-Provence, 1998), p.472.

104. Pierre-Samuel Du Pont de Nemours, *Du pouvoir législatif et du pouvoir exécutif, convenables à la République française* (Paris, Chez Du Pont, 1795), p.5.

positions.[105] This stance appears close to that of the 'extreme centre' referred to by Pierre Serna, made up of political technicians adaptable to all regimes and who, to oust both the democratic 'left' and the royalist 'right', restored and justified the pre-eminence of executive power within representative government in the name of republican order, moderation and enlightened pragmatism.[106] Du Pont contributed to the right of the Directoire, to this paradoxical dream of a 'Republic without Revolution'.[107] But he did not derive much personal benefit from this middle ground: although he was no doubt more faithful to his earlier positions than many of the Thermidorians, his freedom of tone and his imprecations against the Jacobin weathervanes, which Liana Vardi discusses in her contribution, made him rather suspect in the eyes of the new power. However, this did not prevent him, in an approach like that of Condorcet, even if he did not follow him down the road of universal suffrage, from exploiting the republican potential of the association between citizenship and property by varying the degrees and extent of the right to citizenship with that to property, even granting a place to heads of family who were simply tenants.[108] This undeniable development is not, therefore, a contradiction.

A collateral victim of the coup d'état of 18 fructidor orchestrated by the Jacobins, suspected of royalism, Du Pont was arrested and again briefly imprisoned at La Force. Having narrowly escaped deportation to French Guiana thanks to his public reputation and private connections, Du Pont realised, helped by his growing financial difficulties, that his future lay not in France but on the other side of the Atlantic. For a long time already, his mind had been turned towards the young American republic, whose first steps he had followed, partly through his correspondence with Franklin and Jefferson, whose institutions corresponded to his political schemas and whose vast expanses constituted an ideal testing ground for his theories. He then turned away from politics proper to embark on an economic-political

---

105. Du Pont de Nemours, *Du pouvoir*, p.38-39: '*Nous ne voulons plus* [...] *de révolutions, pas plus que de contre-révolutions*' (original emphasis).
106. Pierre Serna, *La République des girouettes, 1789-1815 et au-delà: une anomalie politique, la France de l'extrême centre* (Seyssel, 2005).
107. *1795, pour une république sans révolution*, ed. Roger Dupuy (Rennes, 1996).
108. The latter were granted provisional citizenship 'by concession' from the landowner, limited to primary assemblies, and admitted to serve as national guards, since, if they did not have a 'place', they did have a 'fire'; see Du Pont de Nemours, *Du pouvoir*, p.16-18.

376   *Anthony Mergey and Arnault Skornicki*

project for a colony in Northern Virginia, behind which lay the dream of a small republic, discussed by Aya Tanaka in this volume, or to deal with diplomacy, as shown by his involvement in the sale of Louisiana by France to the United States, a subject dealt with here by Alfred Steinhauer. Although he was exiled to the United States, his late republicanism, which was formal, was still characterised by the continued defence of suffrage reserved for landowners, including for the young American republic, as Annie Léchenet shows in her contribution. This defence was also reaffirmed in the constitutional recommendations that Du Pont made to the three United Provinces of New Grenada, Cartagena and Caracas at their request.

On Du Pont's return to France in 1802, his intense activity focused mainly on managing his American business without him playing any political role, even though the fall of the Empire brought him back onto the political scene very briefly but always in the background. In any case, during the last twenty years of his life, he never failed to reiterate his support for the Republic when the opportunity arose, as in a paper read on 6 October 1815, the year of his return to the United States, at a meeting of the *American Philosophical Society*: 'Je suis un vieux Grammairien de l'Europe, retiré chez vous, parce que les rois et les empereurs m'ont donné pour jamais et irrévocablement attaché aux Républiques.'[109]

***

Du Pont de Nemours's successive political choices ranged from advocating an absolute monarchy regenerated by the laws of natural order under the *Ancien Régime* to defending a constitutional monarchy in the early years of the Revolution, to championing the virtues of

---

109. 'Patrie, république et "country" d'après Pierre Samuel Du Pont de Nemours et Peter Stephen Duponceau', *Bulletin de l'Institut français de Washington* 5-6 (1957), p.54-62 (56). Similarly, in a letter to Jefferson dated 26 May 1815, he declared: 'Nous rirons alors de ceux qui ont cru si longtemps qu'on ne pouvait organiser de République hors de l'enceinte d'une petite ville ou d'un petit canton. Nous en rirons, mais avec une indulgente modération. Ils n'avaient point encore l'idée de gouvernements représentatifs, et ils avaient l'expérience du danger des assemblées tumultueuses. Les gouvernements représentatifs commencés en Angleterre, et perfectionnés aux Etats-Unis par des Sénats qui ne sont point héréditaires, n'ont encore nulle part atteint la perfection dont ils sont susceptibles'; *The Correspondence of Jefferson and Du Pont de Nemours, with an introduction on Jefferson and the physiocrats*, ed. Gilbert Chinard (Baltimore, MD, 1931), p.218.

the republican regime in the mid-1790s. However, they all shared a common denominator that guided our author's career: the constant and renewed search for a government capable of exercising its power in a moderate way, with respect for the constitution, institutions, and the rights and freedoms of all. Finally, we must agree with Gustave Schelle that,

> as a politician, he must be regarded as one of the founders of the liberal school; the form of government quickly became indifferent to him; what he demanded was the abolition of all arbitrariness, whether it came from the great, the prince or the populace. He detested the oppression of majorities as much as Caesarism, and court intrigues as much as parliamentarianism.[110]

This 'moderation' remains that of a thinker and a man of action attached above all to a certain social order, summed up in the famous physiocratic motto, taken up in the first *Declaration of the rights of man*: 'liberty, property, safety'. Right up to the twilight of his life, this was probably the key to understanding the unity of the man behind the plurality of his commitments.

---

110. Gustave Schelle, *Du Pont de Nemours et l'école physiocratique* (Paris, 1888), p.2-3.

Bibliography

Archive and manuscripts

Cambridge, MA, Houghton Library, Harvard University, MS Fr80 4, letter from P.-S. Du Pont to Marie-Anne Lavoisier, 23 October 1798.

Chicago, IL, Newberry Library, 'Opinion de Du Pont de Nemours sur la résolution du premier messidor, relative à l'urgence des paiements et aux négociations à faire par la trésorerie' (Paris, Imprimerie nationale, messidor An v [1797]), case FRC 18066.

La Courneuve, Archives du ministère des Affaires étrangères

Correspondance politique Angleterre 539, 555, 557.

Du Pont 'de Nemours, Pierre-Samuel, *Mémoire sur les opérations qui sont à faire dans l'intérieur du royaume pour que la concurrence ouverte par le traité de commerce, entre les manufactures anglaises et les françaises, ne soit pas nuisible à ces dernières,* f.226-34v.

–, *Observations sur les avantages que trouvera la France dans la diminution des droits actuellement imposés à l'entrée des marchandises françaises en Angleterre,* f.199-223.

–, *Observations sur les motifs particuliers qui peuvent déterminer le traité de commerce,* f.9-21.

–, *Réflexions sur le bien que peuvent se faire réciproquement la France et l'Angleterre,* f.3-8.

–, *Remarques sur les observations faites au comité du 9 août 1786, relativement à la lettre confidentielle de M. Eden,* f.199-223.

–, *Sur le Traité de commerce entre la France et l'Angleterre: observations sur la note concernant la base du traité de commerce, communiquées par Monsieur le comte de Vergennes à Monseigneur le contrôleur général,* f.23-175v.

Mémoires et documents Angleterre 65, 74; France 587.

La Courneuve, Archives nationales, Fonds des hospices et secours, F^{15} 3590.

London, National Archives, Public Record Office, Privy Council, *Troisième mémoire sur le Traité de commerce entre la France et*

380 *Bibliography*

l'Angleterre: observations sur la note concernant la base du traité de commerce, communiquées par Monsieur le comte de Vergennes à Monseigneur le contrôleur général, I, box 123.

Paris, Archives nationales de France, AFIII/463, dossiers 2804-2806.

Paris, Bibliothèque nationale de France, MS fr. 21993, MS fr. 21987, NAF 1303.

Wilmington, DE, Hagley Library, no.B2019.D85, f.1-40.

Wilmington, DE, Hagley Museum and Library.

Brochure for the New York-based company Du Pont de Nemours, Père et Fils & Cie addressed to 'Perregaux, Banquier à Paris', dated New York, 27 ventôse An VIII (18 March 1800), W2-570.

Du Pont de Nemours, Pierre-Samuel, annotations on *Emile, ou De l'éducation*, 2 vols (Amsterdam and Paris, Jean Néaulme, 1765), vol.2, N LB 511a.

–, annotations on J.-J. Rousseau, *Du contrat social, ou Principes du droit politique* (Amsterdam, Chez Marc Michel Rey, 1762), N* JC179. R864c.

–, *Aperçu sur l'établissement commercial & rural que va former en Amérique la maison Dupont de Nemours père & fils & Cie*, L1-472.

–, *Compte rendu par Du Pont (de Nemours) aux actionnaires de la Compagnie* (18 April 1808), L1-526.

–, *De la vie pastorale: troisième état naturel de l'homme. Changement qu'elle introduit dans la forme de la Société. Elle n'en apporte aucun dans les droits de ses membres*, W2-4732.

–, *Des banques en général et des banques américaines en particulier* [1812], Box 3, II, Special Papers and Writings, 1793-1816, Papers of Pierre-Samuel Du Pont de Nemours (Accession LMSS:I), DE 19807.

–, *Elémens de philosophie économique*, W2-4579.

–, *Esquisse d'un projet d'établissement dans l'Amérique septentrionale*, W3-1337.

–, *Extrait d'un plan d'une opération rurale et commerciale à exécuter dans les Etats-Unis de l'Amérique*, L1-469.

–, letter from Du Pont to Bureaux de Pusy (April 1799), Longwood Manuscripts, L1-209.

–, letter from Du Pont to Destutt de Tracy, Paris (14 August 1816), Papers of Pierre-Samuel Du Pont de Nemours, Winterthur Manuscripts, series A, Correspondence.

–, letter from Du Pont to Le Mercier de La Rivière (November 1767), W2-11.

–, *Mémoires de Pierre Samuel Du Pont de Nemours adressés à ses enfans, le 4 septembre 1792*, Winterthur Manuscripts, W2-4796.

–, *Mémoire sur les finances*, Papers of Pierre-Samuel Du Pont de Nemours, Winterthur Manuscripts, series B, no.44.

–, *Memoir of Du Pont de Nemours*

Bibliography

on the finances of the United
States, Papers of Pierre-
Samuel Du Pont de Nemours,
Winterthur Manuscripts, series
B, no.44.
–, microfilm, Archives nationales
reel 7, accession 700 Du Pont
de Nemours.
–, Notes et observations sur le
plan d'un établissement rural et
commercial dans les Etats Unis de
l'Amérique, L1-471.
–, to Senn, Bidermann & Cie
dated 'Paris 9.bre [novembre]
1787', W2-326; to M. de La
Boullaye, Paris (November
1787), W2-327 and W2-328; and
the enclosure 'Etablissement
proposé par la maison Senn et
Bidermann', W2-329.
–, to the Assemblée nationale

constituante, 'Séance du 25
septembre 1790', in Archives
parlementaires de 1787 à 1860:
recueil complet des débats législatifs
& politiques des chambres
françaises. Première série (1789
à 1799), ed. Jérôme Mavidal
and Emile Laurent, 96 vols
(Paris, 1867-1990), vol.19 (1884),
p.224-37.
Du Pont de Nemours,
Victor-Marie, 'Etat au vrai
de notre affaire', Longwood
Manuscripts, L1-483.
Liste des ouvrages de M. Du Pont,
Longwood Manuscripts,
L1-467, and Liste des livres,
Winterthur Manuscripts,
W2-5131.
Packing list (1799), W2-5129.

Primary sources

Adams, John, A Defence of the
constitutions of government of the
United States of America (London,
C. Dilly, 1787-1788).
Albon, Claude-Camille-François,
comte d', Discours politiques,
historiques et critiques, sur
quelques gouvernements de l'Europe
(Neufchâtel, De l'imprimerie de
la Société typographique, 1779).
Aquinas, Thomas, Summa theologiae
(1266-1274), translated by Ceslas
Spicq (Paris, 1934).
L'Arioste, Roland furieux, poème
héroïque de l'Arioste, traduction
nouvelle par M*** (The Hague,
P. Gosse, 1741).
Aulard, François-Alphonse, La
Société des Jacobins: recueil de
documents pour l'histoire du club

des Jacobins de Paris, vol.5 (Paris,
1895).
Aulus Gellius, Les Nuits attiques,
vol.3 (Paris, 1846).

Bachaumont, Louis Petit de,
Mémoires secrets, ed. Christophe
Cave, vol.4 (Paris, 2010).
Barras, Paul, Mémoires de Barras
(Paris, 2010).
Barruel, Augustin, Mémoires pour
servir à l'histoire du jacobinisme,
vol.2 (Augsburg, Les librairies
associées, 1799).
Baudeau, Nicolas, 'Avant-propos
aux Mémoires sur l'état des
paysans polonais de M. le comte
Massalski', Nouvelles éphémérides
économiques 2 (1788), part 2,
p.73-74.

–, 'Critique raisonnée de *L'Ordre naturel et essentiel des sociétés politiques*', *Ephémérides du citoyen* 12 (1767), p.207-208.

–, 'Les doutes éclaircis ou réponse aux objections de M. l'abbé de Mably', *Ephémérides du citoyen* 7 (1768), p.208-10.

–, *Explication du Tableau économique à Madame de **** (1767; Paris, Delalain, 1776).

–, *Première introduction à la philosophie économique, ou Analyse des Etats policés* (Paris, Didot l'aîné, 1771).

–, and Pierre-Samuel Du Pont de Nemours, *Avis au peuple sur son premier besoin, ou Second traité économique sur le commerce des blés*, in *Discussions et développements sur quelques-unes des notions de l'économie politique*, vol.5 (Yverdon, Fortunato Bartolomeo de Felice, 1769), p.3-110.

Bayle, Pierre, *Œuvres*, vol.3 (The Hague, n.n., 1727).

Beardé de L'Abbaye, M., *Recherches sur les moyens de supprimer les impôts, précédées de l'examen de la nouvelle science* (Amsterdam, Marc-Michel Rey, 1770).

Beccaria, Cesare, *Des délits et des peines*, ed. Philippe Audegean (Paris, 2009).

Bernardin de Saint-Pierre, Jacques-Henri, *Paul et Virginie* (Paris, 1806).

–, *Paul et Virginie*, ed. Pierre Trahard (Paris, 1958).

La Bible: traduction œcuménique de la Bible, comprenant l'Ancien et le Nouveau Testament (Paris, 1993).

Bidermann, Jacques Antoine, 'Article VII. D'un commerce

national', *La Chronique du mois, ou les Cahiers patriotiques* (Paris, Imprimerie du Cercle social, An III [January 1792]), bound in vol.1, p.83-88.

Bloch, Camille, and Alexandre Tuetey (ed.), *Procès-verbaux et rapports du comité de mendicité de la Constituante 1790-1791* (Paris, 1911).

Boissy d'Anglas, François Antoine de, *Projet de constitution pour la République française, et discours préliminaire prononcé par Boissy d'Anglas, au nom de la Commission des Onze, dans la séance du 5 messidor An III* (Paris, Imprimerie de la République, messidor An III).

Bougainville, Louis Antoine de, *Voyage autour du monde*, ed. Michel Bideaux and Sonia Faesel (Paris, 2001).

Boug d'Orschwiller, François-Henri de, *Recueil des états, lettres patentes, arrêts du Conseil d'Etat et du Conseil souverain d'Alsace*, vol.2 (Colmar, Chez Jean-Henri Decker, 1775).

Burlamaqui, Jean-Jacques, *Principes du droit naturel* (Geneva, n.n., 1748).

Butré, Richard de, *Principes sur l'impôt, ou la Liberté et l'immunité des hommes et de leurs travaux* (London, Chez les libraires associés, 1775).

Chinard, Gilbert (ed.), *The Correspondence of Jefferson and Du Pont de Nemours, with an introduction on Jefferson and the physiocrats* (Baltimore, MD, 1931).

– (ed.), *The Correspondence of Jefferson and Du Pont de Nemours, with an*

introduction on Jefferson and the physiocrats (New York, 1971).
– (ed.), *Jefferson et les Idéologues d'après sa correspondance inédite* (Baltimore, MD, and Paris, 1925).
–, *Pensées choisies de Montesquieu tirées du 'Common-place book' de Thomas Jefferson* (Paris, 1925).
Condorcet, Jean-Antoine-Nicolas de Caritat, marquis de, *Eloge par Condorcet et pensées de Pascal* (Paris, 1832).
–, *Réflexions sur l'esclavage des nègres* (Paris, 2009).
–, 'Vie de M. Turgot' (1786), in *Œuvres de Condorcet, ed. Arthur O'Connor and François Arago*, vol.8.5 (Paris, 1847), p.5-233.
–, and Anne-Robert-Jacques Turgot, baron de L'Aulne, *Correspondance inédite de Condorcet et de Turgot 1770-1779*, ed. Charles Henry (Paris, 1883).
Constant, Benjamin, *Des réactions politiques* (n.p., n.n., 1796).
Coquéau, Claude-Philibert, *Essai sur l'établissement des hôpitaux dans les grandes villes* (Paris, De l'imprimerie de Ph.-D. Pierres, 1787).
Correspondance patriotique entre les citoyens qui ont été membres de l'Assemblée nationale constituante, vol.1 (Paris, De l'imprimerie de Du Pont, 1791).

Dain, Charles, 'De l'abolition de l'esclavage, suivi d'un article de M. Fourier' (1836), in *Abolition-nistes de l'esclavage et réformateurs des colonies, 1820-1851: analyse et documents*, ed. Nelly Schmidt (Paris, 2000), p.633-44.
Danton, Georges Jacques, *Discours*

civiques de Danton, ed. Hector Fleischmann (Paris, 1920).
Décret de la Convention nationale du 9 mars 1793, l'An second de la République française, qui donne l'élargissement des prisonniers détenus pour dettes, et qui abolit la contrainte par corps (Paris, Imprimerie de Praut, 1793).
Destutt de Tracy, Antoine, *Commentaire et revue de L'Esprit des lois de Montesquieu* (Caen, 1992).
–, *Commentaire sur L'Esprit des lois de Montesquieu: édition entièrement conforme à celle publiée à Liège en 1817* (Paris, 1819).
–, *A Commentary and review of Montesquieu's Spirit of laws, prepared for press from the original manuscript, in the hands of the publishers, to which are annexed, observations on the thirty-first book, by the late M. Condorcet, and two letters of Helvétius, on the merits of the same work* (Philadelphia, PA, 1811).
–, *A Treatise on political economy, to which is prefixed a supplement to a preceding work on the understanding, or elements of ideology, with an analytical table, and an introduction on the faculty of the will, translated from the unpublished French original* (Georgetown, DC, 1817).
Dictionnaire de l'Académie françoise dédié au roy (Paris, Coignard, 1718).
Diderot, Denis, 'Plan d'une université pour le gouvernement de Russie', in *Œuvres complètes*, vol.3 (Paris, 1875), p.409-551.
–, 'Supplément au *Voyage* de Bougainville', in *Opuscules philosophiques et littéraires* (Paris,

384 *Bibliography*

De l'imprimerie de Chevet, 1796), p.187-270.

[Dumas, Hilaire], *Histoire des cinq propositions de Jansenius* (Liège, n.n., 1700).

Du Pont, Bessie Gardner, *Life of Eleuthère Irénée Du Pont from contemporary correspondence*, 11 vols (Newark, DE, 1923-1926).

Du Pont de Nemours, Pierre-Samuel, *Abrégé des principes de l'économie politique* (1772), in *Physiocrates: Quesnay, Dupont de Nemours, Mercier de La Rivière, l'abbé Baudeau, Le Trosne, avec une introduction sur la doctrine des physiocrates, des commentaires et des notices historiques*, ed. Eugène Daire, 2 vols (Paris, 1846), vol.1, p.367-85.

–, *Avant-dernier chapitre de l'histoire des Jacobins: lettre de M. Du Pont aux citoyens constitutionnaires* (Paris, De l'imprimerie de l'auteur, 1796).

–, 'Bienfaisance en Russie', *Ephémérides du citoyen* 11 (1771), part 1, p.237.

–, *Carl Friedrichs von Baden brieflicher Verkehr mit Mirabeau und Du Pont*, ed. Carl Knies, 2 vols (Heidelberg, 1892).

–, 'Commentaire de l'article "Hôpital" de l'*Encyclopédie économique*', *Ephémérides du citoyen* 11 (1771), part 1, p.167.

–, *Compagnie d'Amérique: mémoire qui contient le plan des opérations de la Société* (Paris, n.n., 1799).

–, 'Conseils demandés en Suède', *Ephémérides du citoyen* 1 (1772), p.193-94.

–, 'Considération sur la position politique de la France, de

l'Angleterre et de l'Espagne', *Journal de la Société de 1789* 4 (26 June 1790), p.5-29.

–, 'De la fondation d'une chaire d'économie politique, et de l'utilité de cette institution', *Ephémérides du citoyen* 3 (1769), p.160-81.

–, *De la manière la plus favorable d'effectuer les emprunts qui seront nécessaires, tant afin de pourvoir aux besoins du moment, que pour opérer le remboursement des dettes de l'Etat dont les intérêts sont trop onéreux, par un député du bailliage de Nemours à l'Assemblée nationale* (Paris, Chez Baudouin, 1789).

–, 'De l'amour de la constitution et de celui de la liberté', in *Correspondance patriotique entre les citoyens qui ont été membres de l'Assemblée nationale constituante*, vol.2 (Paris, De l'imprimerie de Du Pont, 1791), p.70-79.

–, 'De l'amour de la constitution et de celui de la liberté', https://www.institutcoppet.org/de-lamour-de-la-constitution-et-celui-de-la-liberte/ (last accessed 7 December 2024).

–, *De la périodicité des assemblées nationales, de leur organisation, de la forme à suivre pour amener les propositions qui pourront y être faites, à devenir des lois et de la sanction nécessaire pour que ces lois soient obligatoires* (Paris, Chez Baudouin, 1789).

–, *De l'origine et des progrès d'une science nouvelle* (London and Paris, Desaint, 1768).

–, *De l'origine et des progrès d'une science nouvelle* (1768), in *Physiocrates: Quesnay, Dupont de*

Nemours, Mercier de La Rivière, l'abbé Baudeau, Le Trosne, avec une introduction sur la doctrine des physiocrates, des commentaires et des notices historiques, ed. Eugène Daire, 2 vols (Paris, 1846), vol.1, p.335-66.

–, De l'origine et des progrès d'une science nouvelle (1768), ed. A. Dubois (Paris, 1910).

–, De quelques améliorations dans la perception de l'impôt et de l'usage utile, qu'on peut faire des employés réformés, par M. Du Pont, député de Nemours (Paris, Imprimerie nationale, 1791).

–, 'Discours de l'éditeur', in François Quesnay, Physiocratie, ou Constitution naturelle du gouvernement le plus avantageux au genre humain, 2 vols (Leiden and Paris, Merlin, 1768), vol.1, p.i-cxx.

–, Discours prononcé à l'Assemblée nationale, par M. Du Pont, sur les banques en général, sur la caisse d'escompte en particulier, et sur le projet du premier ministre des finances relativement à cette dernière (Paris, Chez Baudouin, 1789).

–, Discours prononcé à l'Assemblée nationale par M. Du Pont sur l'état & les ressources des finances (Versailles, Chez Baudouin, 1789).

–, Du commerce et de la compagnie des Indes, 2nd edn (Paris, Delalain, 1769).

–, Du pouvoir législatif et du pouvoir exécutif, convenables à la République française (Paris, Chez Du Pont, 1795).

–, 'Economie rurale', La Décade philosophique, littéraire et politique 26 (20 nivôse An III), p.69-84.

–, Effet des assignats sur le prix du pain, par un ami du peuple (n.p., n.d. [1790]).

–, L'Enfance et la jeunesse de Du Pont de Nemours racontées par lui-même (Paris, 1906).

–, Examen du gouvernement d'Angleterre, comparé aux constitutions des Etats-Unis (London and Paris, Chez Froullé, 1789).

–, Examen du livre de M. Malthus sur le principe de population, auquel on a joint la traduction de quatre chapitres de ce livre supprimés dans l'édition française, et une lettre à M. Say sur son Traité d'économie politique (Philadelphia, PA, 1817).

–, Idées sur les secours à donner aux pauvres malades dans une grande ville (Philadelphia, PA, and Paris, Chez Moutard, 1786).

–, Irénée bonfils, sur la religion de ses pères et de nos pères (Paris, 1808; insert to the Journal des arts et des sciences).

–, Lettre à la Chambre du commerce de Normandie, sur le mémoire qu'elle a publié relativement au traité de commerce avec l'Angleterre (Rouen and Paris, chez Moutard, 1788).

–, 'Lettre aux auteurs de la Décade, sur les Economistes, 30 frimaire An III', La Décade philosophique, littéraire et politique, par une société de républicains 4 (1794), 30 December 1794, p.70-84.

–, 'Lettres africaines, ou histoire de Phédima et d'Abensar par Mr. Butini', Ephémérides du citoyen, ou Bibliothèque raisonnée des sciences morales et politiques 8 (1771), part 2, p.68-118.

–, Lettres d'Abraham Mansword, citoyen de Philadelphie, à ses compatriotes de l'Amérique

septentrionale, traduites du Pennsyl-
vany's chronicle, Ephémérides 11
(1771), p.74-112, and *Ephémérides*
12 (1771), p.6-45.
–, 'Lettres de Du Pont de Nemours
à Félix Faulcon', ed. Gilbert
Chinard, *French American review*
1:3 (1948), p.174-83.
–, *Lettres de Du Pont de Nemours*
écrites de la prison de la Force: 5
thermidor-8 fructidor An II, ed.
Gilbert Chinard (Paris, 1929).
–, *Lettres de M. Du Pont à M. Pétion*,
in *Histoire parlementaire de la*
Révolution française, ed. Philippe-
Joseph-Benjamin Buchez and
Pierre-Célestin Roux, vol.14
(Paris, 1835).
–, *Maximes du Docteur Quesnay*, in
Physiocrates: Quesnay, Dupont de
Nemours, Mercier de La Rivière,
l'abbé Baudeau, Le Trosne, avec
une introduction sur la doctrine des
physiocrates, des commentaires et
des notices historiques, ed. Eugène
Daire, 2 vols (Paris, 1846), vol.1,
p.389-93.
–, *Mémoire lu à la classe des sciences*
physiques et mathématiques de
l'Institut national, dans les séances
du 21 juillet, du 11 et du 18 août
1806 (Paris, 1806).
–, *Mémoires sur la vie et les ouvrages*
de M. Turgot, ministre d'Etat
(Philadelphia, PA, n.n., 1782).
–, *Mémoire sur l'agriculture et les*
manufactures aux Etats-Unis, in
The Correspondence of Jefferson
and Du Pont de Nemours, with an
introduction on Jefferson and the
physiocrats, ed. Gilbert Chinard
(New York, 1971).
–, 'Notes sur le second chant', in
L'Arioste: essai de traduction en vers

du Roland furieux de l'Arioste (par
Dupont de Nemours) (Paris, 1812),
p.196-204.
–, *Notice sur la vie de M. Poivre,*
chevalier de l'Ordre du roi, ancien
intendant des Iles de France et de
Bourbon (Philadelphia, PA, and
Paris, Chez Moutard, 1786).
–, 'Notice sur les Economistes', in
A.-R.-J. Turgot, *Œuvres de Turgot*,
ed. Eugène Daire (Paris, 1844),
p.258-61.
–, *Observations sur la constitution*
proposée par la commission des
Onze (Paris, Chez Du Pont
imprimeur-libraire, 1795).
–, *Observations sur les principes qui*
doivent déterminer le nombre des
districts et celui des tribunaux dans
les départemens, par M. Du Pont
(Paris, Imprimerie nationale, 1790).
–, *Les Œuvres posthumes de M. Turgot,*
ou Mémoire sur les administrations
provinciales (Lausanne, n.n., 1787).
–, 'Opinion de Du Pont (de
Nemours) sur la résolution
relative à la loi du 3 brumaire',
session of 27 brumaire An V
(Paris, Imprimerie nationale,
frimaire An V).
–, *Opinion de M. Du Pont, député*
de Nemours, sur le projet de créer
pour dix-neuf cent millions d'assig-
nats-monnaie, sans intérêt, exposée à
l'Assemblée nationale, le 25 septembre
1790 (Paris, Chez Baudouin,
1790).
–, *Opinion de M. Dupont sur l'exercice*
du droit de la guerre et de la paix,
exposée à l'Assemblée nationale
(Paris, Imprimerie nationale,
19 May 1790).
–, *Opinion sur la contrainte par corps:*
séance du 24 ventôse An V [14 March

1797] (Paris, Imprimerie nationale, germinal An v).

–, *Le Pacte de famille, Journal de la Société de 1789* (July 1790), p.15-36.

–, *Le Pacte de famille et les conventions subséquentes, entre la France et l'Espagne* (Paris, Imprimerie nationale, 1790).

–, *Philosophie de l'univers* (Paris, De l'imprimerie de Du Pont, [1793]).

–, *Philosophie de l'univers* (1793), 2nd edn (Paris, De l'imprimerie de Du Pont, fructidor An IV [1796]).

–, *Philosophie de l'univers* (1793), 3rd edn (Paris, Chez Goujon fils, 1798).

–, *Principes constitutionnels relativement au renvoi et à la nomination des ministres: discours prononcé à la Société des amis de la liberté et de la constitution de 1789, dans leur séance du 20 octobre 1790, par M. Du Pont, député de Nemours à l'Assemblée nationale* (Paris, Imprimerie nationale, 1790).

–, *Quelques mémoires sur différens sujets, la plupart d'histoire naturelle, ou de physique générale et particulière*, 2nd edn (Paris, 1813).

–, *Rapport fait, au nom du Comité de l'imposition, par M. Du Pont, député de Nemours, sur les impositions indirectes en général et sur les droits à raison de la consommation des vins, et des boissons en particulier* (Paris, Imprimerie nationale, 1790).

–, *Réflexions sur l'écrit intitulé: Richesse de l'Etat* (London, n.n., 1763).

–, *Réponse demandée par Monsieur le marquis de M*** à celle qu'il a faite aux Réflexions sur l'écrit intitulé: Richesse de l'Etat* (London, n.n.,1763).

–, review of *Essais sur les principes des finances, Ephémérides du citoyen* 3 (1770), p.158-95.

–, *Seconde lettre de Monsieur Du Pont à Pétion* (Paris, n.n., 1792).

–, *Sur la Banque de France, les causes de la crise qu'elle a éprouvée, les tristes effets qui en sont résultés, et les moyens d'en prévenir le retour, avec une théorie des banques, rapport fait à la Chambre de commerce par une commission spéciale* (Paris, 1806).

–, *Sur l'éducation nationale dans les Etats-Unis d'Amérique*, 2nd edn (Paris, 1812).

–, *Sur les institutions religieuses dans l'intérieur des familles, avec un essai de traduction nouvelle de l'Oraison dominicale* (Paris, October 1806; read before the Institut national 31 October 1806).

–, *Tableau comparatif des demandes contenues dans les cahiers des trois ordres remis à MM. les députés aux Etats généraux* (n.p., n.n., 1789).

–, 'Ziméo, ou de l'esclavage des nègres par Jean-François de Saint-Lambert', in *Ephémérides du citoyen, ou Bibliothèque raisonnée des sciences morales et politiques* 6 (1771), part 2, p.178-246.

Duvergier de Hauranne, Prosper, *Histoire du gouvernement parlementaire en France*, vol.1 (Paris, 1857).

Edit du roi, portant création de dix officiers-gardes du commerce, et règlement pour les contraintes par corps pour dettes civiles dans la ville, faubourgs et banlieue de Paris, donné à Fontainebleau au mois de novembre

1772, registré en Parlement le 2 janvier 1773 (Paris, P.-G. Simon, 1773).

Encyclopédie, ou Dictionnaire raisonné des sciences, des arts et des métiers, ed. Denis Diderot and Jean D'Alembert, 17 vols (Paris, Briasson, 1751-1772).

Florian, Jean-Pierre Claris de, *Numa Pompilius: second roi de Rome* (Hamburg, Pierre François Fauche, 1788).

–, *Œuvres de M. de Florian* (Paris, 1805).

Forbonnais, François Véron Duverger de, *Elémens du commerce*, 2 vols (Leiden and Paris, Chez Briasson, 1754).

Franklin, Benjamin, *The Papers of Benjamin Franklin*, https://franklinpapers.org/ (last accessed 25 November 2024).

–, *The Writings of Benjamin Franklin*, vol.9 (New York, 1906).

Gaillard, Gabriel-Henri, *Histoire de la rivalité de la France et de l'Angleterre*, 11 vols (Paris, 1771-1777).

Galiani, Ferdinando, *Dialogues sur le commerce des blés* (London and Paris, Joseph Merlin, 1770).

Gérando, Joseph-Marie de, *Histoire comparée des systèmes de philosophie relativement aux principes des connaissances humaines* (Paris, 1804).

Godechot, Jacques, and Hervé Faupin, *Les Constitutions de la France depuis 1789* (Paris, 2006).

Grimm, Friedrich Melchior, baron von, *Correspondance littéraire, philosophique et critique (1747-1793)*, ed. M. Tourneux, vol.7 (Paris, 1879).

Grotius, Hugo, *Le Droit de la guerre et de la paix*, translated by Jean Barbeyrac, 2 vols (Basel, Chez E. Thourneisen, 1746).

Guibert, Jacques de, *De la force publique* (1790), ed. Jean-Pierre Bois (Paris, 2005).

Guillard de Beaurieu, Gaspard, *L'Elève de la nature*, 3 vols (Lille, J.-B. Henry, 1771).

–, *La Ferme de Pennsylvanie* (Philadelphia, PA, and Paris, Chez Ribou, 1775).

Hamilton, Alexander, *et al.*, *Le Fédéraliste*, ed. and translated by Anne Amiel (Paris, 2012).

L'Historien (Paris, Chez Du Pont, 1795-1797).

Holbach, Paul Heinrich Dietrich von, *Système social, ou Principes naturels de la morale et de la politique, avec un examen de l'influence du gouvernement sur les mœurs* (London, n.n., 1773).

Jefferson, Thomas, *Autobiography of Thomas Jefferson 1743-1970* (New York and London, 1914).

–, *The Papers of Thomas Jefferson*, vol.8, ed. Julian P. Boyd (Princeton, NJ, 1953).

–, *The Papers of Thomas Jefferson*, vol.15, ed. Julian P. Boyd (Princeton, NJ, 1950).

–, *The Papers of Thomas Jefferson*, vol.30, ed. Julian P. Boyd (Princeton, NJ, 1950).

–, *The Papers of Thomas Jefferson*, vol.31: *1 February 1799-31 May 1800*, ed. Barbara B. Oberg (Princeton, NJ, 2004).

–, *The Papers of Thomas Jefferson*, vol.36, ed. Julian P. Boyd (Princeton, NJ, 2010).

–, *The Papers of Thomas Jefferson: retirement series*, vol.1, ed. J. Jefferson Looney (Princeton, NJ, 2004).

–, *The Papers of Thomas Jefferson: retirement series*, vol.2, ed. J. Jefferson Looney (Princeton, NJ, 2006).

–, *The Papers of Thomas Jefferson: retirement series*, vol.3, ed. J. Jefferson Looney (Princeton, NJ, 2007).

–, *The Papers of Thomas Jefferson: retirement series*, vol.4, ed. J. Jefferson Looney (Princeton, NJ, 2008).

–, *The Writings of Thomas Jefferson*, ed. Andrew A. Lipscomb and Albert Ellery Bergh, 20 vols (Washington, DC, 1903).

Jourdan, Anasthase-Jean-Léger, et al. (ed.), *Recueil général des anciennes lois françaises, depuis l'an 420 jusqu'à la Révolution de 1789*, 29 vols (Paris, 1821-1833).

Journal des sçavans (Paris, n.n., 1665-1790).

Jurieu, Pierre, *Histoire critique des dogmes et des cultes* (Amsterdam, n.n., 1704).

La Législation civile, commerciale et criminelle de la France, par M. le baron Locré, vol.15 (Paris, 1828).

La Révellière-Lépeaux, Louis-Marie de, *Mémoires de La Révellière-Lépeaux, publiés par son fils*, 3 vols (Paris, 1895).

Le Maistre de Sacy, Isaac-Louis (ed. and trans.), *La Sainte Bible, en latin et en français, avec des notes littérales pour l'intelligence des endroits les plus difficiles et la concorde des quatre évangélistes, par Le Maistre de Saci*, 4 vols (Paris, chez Guillaume Desprez, 1717).

Le Mercier de La Rivière, Paul-Pierre, *De l'instruction publique, ou Considérations morales et politiques sur la nécessité, la nature et la source de cette intruction* (Stockholm and Paris, Didot l'aîné, 1775).

–, *Essais sur les maximes et loix fondamentales de la monarchie française, ou Canevas d'un code constitutionnel* (Paris and Versailles, Mme Vallat La Chapelle, 1789).

–, *L'Heureuse Nation, ou Relations du gouvernement des Féliciens, peuple souverainement libre sous l'empire absolu de ses loix*, 2 vols (Paris, Chez Buisson, 1792).

–, *L'Intérêt général de l'Etat, ou la Liberté du commerce des blés* (Amsterdam and Paris, Desaint, 1770).

[–], *L'Ordre naturel et essentiel des sociétés politiques*, 2 vols (London and Paris, Nourse, Desaint, 1767).

–, *L'Ordre naturel et essentiel des sociétés politiques* (1767), in *Physiocrates: Quesnay, Dupont de Nemours, Mercier de La Rivière, l'abbé Baudeau, Le Trosne, avec une introduction sur la doctrine des physiocrates, des commentaires et des notices historiques*, ed. Eugène Daire, 2 vols (Paris, 1846), vol.2, p.445-638.

–, *L'Ordre naturel et essentiel des sociétés politiques* (Geneva, 2017).

–, *Pennsylvaniens et Féliciens: œuvres utopiques (1771 et 1792)*, ed. Bernard Herencia (Geneva, 2014).

–, *Pour la Pologne, la Suède, l'Espagne et autres textes: œuvres d'expertise (1772-1790)*, ed. Bernard Herencia (Geneva, 2016).

–, *Les Vœux d'un Français, ou Considérations sur les principaux objets dont le roi et la nation vont s'occuper* (Paris, Mme Vallat La Chapelle, 1788).

Le Trosne, Guillaume-François, *De l'administration provinciale, et de la réforme de l'impôt* (Basel, n.n., 1779).

–, *De l'ordre social, ouvrage suivi d'un traité élémentaire sur la valeur, l'argent, la circulation, l'industrie & le commerce intérieur & extérieur* (Paris, Chez les freres Debure, 1777).

–, *Les Lois naturelles de l'ordre social*, ed. T. Carvalho (Geneva, 2019).

–, *Recueil de plusieurs morceaux économiques* (Amsterdam and Paris, Desaint, 1768).

Lettre à M. le comte Charles de Scheffer, Analyse des papiers anglois 34-36 (1788), p.241-48, 265-72, 283-96.

Locke, John, *Essai philosophique concernant l'entendement humain*, translated by P. Coste (Amsterdam, n.n., 1742).

–, *Traité du gouvernement civil* (Paris, 1991).

–, *Two treatises of government* (1690), ed. P. Laslett (Cambridge, 1960).

Loi portant que la contrainte par corps ne pourra être exercée pour dettes de mois de nourrice, donnée à Paris, le 25 août 1792, l'An 4ᵉ de la liberté (Paris, Imprimerie nationale, 1792).

Lolme, Jean-Louis de, *Constitution de l'Angleterre* (Amsterdam, E. Van Harrevelt, 1771).

–, *Constitution de l'Angleterre*, 2 vols (London, G. Robinson, J. Murray, 1785).

Louis XIV, *Ordonnance de Louis XIV, roy de France et de Navarre, donnée à Saint-Germain-en-Laye au mois d'avril 1667* (Paris, chez les associés choisis par ordre de Sa Majesté pour l'impression de ses nouvelles ordonnances, 1667).

Mably, Gabriel Bonnot de, *Doutes proposés aux philosophes économistes sur l'ordre naturel et essentiel des sociétés politiques* (The Hague and Paris, Chez Nyon, 1768).

Madison, James, *Writings*, ed. Jack N. Rakove (New York, 1999).

Malone, Dumas (ed.), *Correspondence between Thomas Jefferson and Pierre Samuel Du Pont de Nemours, 1798-1817* (New York, 1930).

Marmontel, Jean-François, *La Voix des pauvres, épître au roi sur l'incendie de l'Hôtel-Dieu* (Paris, Valade, 1773).

Mavidal, Jérôme, and Emile Laurent (ed.), *Archives parlementaires de 1787 à 1860: recueil complet des débats législatifs & politiques des chambres françaises. Première série (1789 à 1799)*, 96 vols (Paris, 1867-1990).

Mélanges législatifs, historiques et politiques pendant la durée de la Constitution de l'An III (Paris, 1801).

Mercure de France (Paris, 1724-1823).

Mirabeau, Honoré-Gabriel de, *Analyse des papiers anglois* (Paris, 1788).

Bibliography

Mirabeau, Victor Riqueti de, *Entretiens d'un jeune prince avec son gouverneur* (London, Moutard, 1785).

–, *Lettres inédites du marquis de Mirabeau (1787-1789)*, ed. Dauphin Meunier, *Le Correspondant* (25 April 1913).

–, *Philosophie rurale, ou Economie générale et politique de l'agriculture* (Amsterdam and Paris, Les libraires associés, 1763).

–, *Supplément à la théorie de l'impôt* (The Hague, P.-F. Gosse, 1776).

–, *Traité de la monarchie (1757-1759)*, ed. G. Longhitano (Paris, 1999).

–, and Pierre-Samuel Du Pont de Nemours, *Dialogues physiocratiques sur l'Amérique*, ed. Manuela Albertone (Paris, 2015).

Montaigne, Michel de, *Les Essais* (1580), ed. Claude Pinganaud (Paris, 2002).

Montesquieu, Charles-Louis de Secondat, baron de, *De l'esprit des lois*, vol.1 (Geneva, Barillot & fils, 1748).

–, *De l'esprit des lois* (Paris, 1979).

–, *Pensées et fragments inédits de Montesquieu*, ed. G. Gounouilhou, vol.1 (Bordeaux, 1899).

Morellet, André, *Sur le despotisme légal et contre M. de La Rivière*, ed. Eugenio Di Rienzo, in *Individualismo, assolutismo, democrazia*, ed. Centro studi di filosofia politica (Naples, 1992), p.329-44.

Moreri, Louis, *Le Grand Dictionnaire historique*, vol.8 (Paris, Les libraires associés, 1759).

Necker, Jacques, *Cours de morale religieuse* (Geneva, An IX [1800]).

–, *De l'importance des opinions religieuses* (London and Paris, Panckoucke and Thou, 1788).

–, *Eloge de Jean-Baptiste Colbert, discours qui a remporté le prix de l'Académie française en 1773* ([Paris], J. B. Brunet, 1773).

–, *Sur la législation et le commerce des grains*, 2 vols in 1 (Paris, Pissot, 1775).

Peterson, Merrill (ed.), *Thomas Jefferson: writings* (New York, 1984).

Peuchet, Jacques, *Mémoires tirés des archives de la police de Paris pour servir à l'histoire de la morale et de la police, depuis Louis XIV jusqu'à nos jours*, 6 vols (Paris, 1838).

Piarron de Chamousset, Claude Humbert, *Plan d'une maison d'association, dans laquelle au moyen d'une somme très-modique chaque associé s'assurera dans l'état de maladie toutes les sortes de secours qu'on peut désirer* (n.p., n.n., 1754).

Poivre, Pierre, 'Discours aux habitants de l'Isle de France' (1767), in *Œuvres complettes de P. Poivre, intendant des isles de France et de Bourbon, correspondant de l'Académie des sciences, etc., précédées de sa vie, et accompagnées de notes* (Paris, Fuchs, 1797), p.199-232.

Portalis, Jean-Etienne-Marie, *Opinion sur la contrainte par corps: séance du 24 ventôse An v [14 March 1797]* (Paris, Imprimerie nationale, germinal An v).

Quesnay, François, 'Despotisme de la Chine', *Ephémérides du citoyen* 6 (1767), p.10.

–, 'Le droit naturel', in *Œuvres*

économiques complètes et autres textes, ed. Christine Théré et al., 2 vols (Paris, 2005), vol.1, p.111-23.

–, 'Hommes' (1757-1758), in Œuvres économiques complètes et autres textes, ed. Christine Théré et al., 2 vols (Paris, 2005), vol.1, p.313-14.

–, Physiocratie, ou Constitution naturelle du gouvernement le plus avantageux au genre humain, 2 vols (Leiden and Paris, Merlin, 1768).

Rabaut Saint-Etienne, Jean-Paul, Rapport de M. Rabaud sur l'organisation de la force publique, in Archives parlementaires de 1787 à 1860: recueil complet des débats législatifs & politiques des chambres françaises. Première série (1789 à 1799), ed. Jérôme Mavidal and Emile Laurent, 96 vols (Paris, 1867-1990), vol.20 (1885), p.592-97.

Recueil général des lois, décrets, ordonnances, etc., depuis le mois de juin 1789 jusqu'au mois d'août 1830, 16 vols (Paris, 1834-1837).

Réimpression de l'ancien Moniteur, vol.5 (Paris, 1860).

Roland de La Platière, Jeanne-Marie, Lettres, ed. Claude Perroud, 2 vols (Paris, 1913-1915).

Rousseau, Jean-Jacques, Considérations sur le gouvernement de Pologne, et sur sa réformation projetée (1782), https://fr.wikisource. org/wiki/Considérations_sur_le_ gouvernement_de_Pologne (last accessed 11 December 2024).

–, Correspondance générale de J.-J. Rousseau, collationnée sur les originaux, annotés et commentés par T. Dufour, vol.16 (Paris, 1931).

–, Correspondance générale de J.-J. Rousseau, collationnée sur les originaux, annotés et commentés par T. Dufour, vol.17 (Paris, 1932).

–, Discours sur l'économie politique (1755), in Œuvres politiques (Paris, 1989), p.119-52.

–, Discours sur l'origine & les fondements de l'inégalité parmi les hommes (Amsterdam, Chez Marc Michel Rey, 1755).

–, Du contrat social, ou Principes du droit politique (Amsterdam, Chez Marc Michel Rey, 1762).

–, Emile, ou De l'éducation, vol.1 (Amsterdam and Paris, Jean Néaulme, 1762).

–, Œuvres complètes de Jean-Jacques Rousseau, ed. Bernard Gagnebin and Marcel Raymond, vol.4: Emile. Education. Morale. Botanique (Paris, 1969).

Rousselot de Surgy, Jacques-Philibert, 'De la Sibérie', in Mélanges intéressans & curieux, vol.3 (Paris, Lacombe, 1766), p.15-204.

Say, Jean-Baptiste, Mélanges et correspondance d'économie politique, ed. Charles Comte (Paris, 1833).

Sieyès, Joseph-Emmanuel, Projet de loi contre les délits qui peuvent se commettre par la voie de l'impression, in Histoire parlementaire de la Révolution française, ed. Philippe-Joseph-Benjamin Buchez and Pierre-Célestin Roux, vol.4 (Paris, 1834), p.280-88.

–, What is the Third Estate?, https://pages.uoregon.edu/ dluebke/301ModernEurope/ Sieyes3dEstate.pdf (last accessed 4 December 2024).

Smith, Adam, An Inquiry into the nature and causes of the wealth of nations, ed. R. H. Campbell and A. S. Skinner, 2 vols (Oxford, 1979), vol.2, p.545-1080.

Staël-Holstein, Germaine de, and Pierre-Samuel Du Pont de Nemours, *De Staël-Du Pont letters: correspondence of Madame de Staël and Pierre Samuel Du Pont de Nemours and other members of the Necker and Du Pont families*, ed. and translated by James F. Marshall (Madison, WI, 1968).

Thibaudeau, A. C., *Mémoires sur la Convention et sur le Directoire*, vol.2: *Directoire* (Paris, 1824).

Turgot, Anne-Robert-Jacques, *Circulaire aux officiers de police des villes (1727-1781)* (Paris, 1914).

–, *Œuvres de M. Turgot, ministre d'Etat, précédées et accompagnées de mémoires et de notes sur sa vie, son administration et ses ouvrages*, ed. Pierre-Samuel Du Pont de Nemours, 9 vols (Paris, 1808-1811).

–, *Œuvres de Turgot et documents le concernant*, ed. Gustave Schelle, 5 vols (Paris, 1913-1923).

–, *Réflexions sur la formation et la distribution des richesses*, *Ephémérides* 1 (1770), p.113-73.

–, *Turgot: textes choisis*, ed. Pierre Vigreux (Paris, 1947).

Voltaire, *L'A, B, C: dix-sept dialogues traduits de l'anglais de Monsieur Huet*, ed. Roland Mortier and Christophe Paillard, in *Œuvres complètes de Voltaire*, vol.65A (Oxford, 2011), p.169-348.

–, *L'Homme aux quarante écus*, ed. Brenda M. Bloesch, in *Œuvres complètes de Voltaire*, vol.66 (Oxford, 1999), p.211-409.

Wateville, Adolphe de, *Législation charitable* (Paris, 1843).

Biographies of Pierre-Samuel Du Pont de Nemours and his family

Aimé-Azam, Denise, *Du Pont de Nemours, honnête homme* (Paris, 1933).

Boullée, A., 'Dupont de Nemours', in *Annuaire de la Société Montyon et Franklin pour l'an 1835*, no.3: *Bulletin des hommes utiles* (Paris, 1835), p.147-50.

Bouloiseau, Marc, *Bourgeoisie et révolution: les Du Pont de Nemours (1788-1799)* (Paris, 1972).

Du Pont, Bessie Gardner, *Du Pont de Nemours, 1739-1817*, vol.2 (Newark, DE, 1933).

Gérando, Joseph-Marie de, *Notice sur M. Du Pont de Nemours, lue à la séance générale de la Société d'encouragement pour l'industrie nationale, le 23 septembre 1818, Moniteur* (16 October 1818).

Giraudeau, Martin, 'Performing physiocracy: Pierre Samuel Du Pont de Nemours and the limits of political engineering', *Journal of cultural economy* 3:2 (2010), p.225-42.

–, 'The predestination of capital: projecting E. I. Du Pont de Nemours and Company into the New World', *Critical historical studies* 6:1 (2019), p.33-62.

Jolly, Pierre, *Du Pont de Nemours, soldat de la liberté* (Paris, 1956).

Monchanin, Jules, *Notice sur la vie de Du Pont de Nemours* (Paris, 1818).

Pérouse, Maurice, 'Françoise Robin, la citoyenne Du Pont de Nemours', *La Revue des deux mondes* (1985), p.578-86.

Rink, Evald, 'A family heritage: the library of the immigrant Du Ponts' (n.d., unpublished, courtesy of the Hagley Library).

Saricks, Ambrose, *Pierre Samuel Du Pont de Nemours* (Lawrence, KS, 1965).

Schelle, Gustave, *Du Pont de Nemours et l'école physiocratique* (Paris, 1888).

Starobinski, Jean, *Action et réaction: vie et aventures d'un couple* (Paris, 1999).

Thompson, Mack, 'Causes and circumstances of the Du Pont family's emigration', *French historical studies* 6:1 (1969), p.67-77.

Tonet, Aureliano, 'Du Pont de Nemours, une saga franco-américaine', *Le Monde* (18-24 August 2020).

Works on Pierre-Samuel Du Pont de Nemours and the physiocratic school

Albertone, Manuela, 'Décentralisation territoriale et unité de la nation: *Les Lettres d'Abraham Mansword* entre physiocratie et modèle américain', in *Centralisation et fédéralisme*, ed. Michel Biard *et al.* (Mont-Saint-Aignan, 2018), p.103-14.

–, 'Du Pont de Nemours et l'instruction publique pendant la Révolution: de la science économique à la formation du citoyen', *Revue française d'histoire des idées politiques* 20:2 (2004), p.353-71.

–, 'George Logan: un physiocrate américain', in *La Diffusion internationale de la physiocratie (XVIIIe-XIXe)*, ed. Bernard Delmas *et al.* (Grenoble, 1995), p.421-39.

–, 'Instruction et ordre naturel: le point de vue physiocratique', *Revue d'histoire moderne et contemporaine* 33:4 (1986), p.589-607.

Alimento, Antonella, 'Tra fronda e fisiocrazia: il pensiero di Mirabeau sulle municipalità (1750-1767)', *Annali della*

Fondazione Luigi Einaudi 22
(1988), p.97-141.

Bach, Reinhard, 'Rousseau et les
physiocrates: une cohabitation
contradictoire', *Etudes Jean-Jacques
Rousseau* 11 (2000), p.9-82.

Bergamasco, Lucia, 'Thomas
Jefferson et Du Pont de Nemours:
un dialogue décalé', in *Entre
deux eaux: les secondes Lumières et
leurs ambiguïtés (1789-1815)*, ed.
Anouchka Vasak (Paris, 2012),
p.203-36.

Betts, C. J., *Early deism in France:
from the so-called 'déistes' of
Lyon (1564) to Voltaire's 'Lettres
philosophiques' (1734)* (The Hague,
1984).

Betts, Raymond, 'Du Pont de
Nemours in Napoleonic France,
1802-1815', *French historical studies*
5:2 (1967), p.188-203.

Carvalho, Thérence, 'La
correspondance littéraire et
politique de Du Pont de Nemours:
vecteur de diffusion du modèle
physiocratique en Europe', in
*Entente culturelle: l'Europe des
correspondances littéraires*, ed. Ulla
Kölving (Ferney-Voltaire, 2021),
p.165-84.

–, *La Physiocratie dans l'Europe des
Lumières: circulation et réception d'un
modèle de réforme de l'ordre juridique
et social* (Paris, 2020).

Charles, Loïc, and Paul Cheney,
'The colonial machine
dismantled: knowledge and
empire in the French Atlantic',
Past & present 219:1 (2013),
p.127-63.

–, and Guillaume Daudin, 'La
collecte du chiffre au XVIIIe

siècle: le Bureau de la balance
du commerce et la production
des données sur le commerce
extérieur de la France', *Revue
d'histoire moderne & contemporaine*
58:1 (2011), p.128-55.

–, and Christine Théré, 'The
physiocratic movement: a
revision', in *The Economic turn:
recasting political economy in
Enlightenment Europe*, Steven
L. Kaplan and Sophus A. Reinert
(New York, 2019), p.35-70.

Clément, Alain, 'Du bon et du
mauvais usage des colonies:
politique coloniale et pensée
économique française au XVIIIe
siècle', *Cahiers d'économie politique
/ Papers in political economy* 56:1
(2009), p.101-27.

Daire, Eugène (ed.), *Physiocrates:
Quesnay, Dupont de Nemours, Mercier
de La Rivière, l'abbé Baudeau, Le
Trosne, avec une introduction sur la
doctrine des physiocrates, des commentaires et des notices historiques*, 2 vols
(Paris, 1846).

Delmas, Bernard, *et al.* (ed.),
*La Diffusion internationale de
la physiocratie (XVIIIe-XIXe)*
(Grenoble, 1995).

Demals, Thierry, and Alexandra
Hyard, 'Forbonnais, the two
balances and the Economistes',
*The European journal of the history
of economic thought* 22:3 (2015),
p.445-72.

DuPont, Henry Algernon, *The Early
generations of the Du Pont and allied
families*, 2 vols (New York, 1923).

Dupuy, Romuald, 'Liberté et
rationalité chez Quesnay', *Revue
de philosophie économique* 12
(2011-2012), p.117-42.

Gauthier, Florence, 'Le Mercier de La Rivière et les colonies d'Amérique', *Revue française d'histoire des idées politiques* 20:2 (2004), p.37-59.

Goutte, Pierre-Henri, 'Economie et transition: l'œuvre de Du Pont de Nemours sous la Révolution française', dans *Idées économiques sous la Révolution 1789-1794*, ed. Jean-Michel Servet (Lyon, 1989), p.145-233.

Haggard, Robert F., 'The politics of friendship: DuPont, Jefferson, Madison and the physiocratic dream for the New World', *Proceedings of the American Philosophical Society* 153:4 (2009), p.419-40.

Hall, John C., *Abraham DuPont: a Huguenot flees to Carolina, 1695: the DuPont-Buyck lineages* (Baltimore, MD, 2016).

Harvey, David Allen, 'Slavery on the balance sheet: Pierre-Samuel Dupont de Nemours and the physiocratic case for free labor', *Journal of the Western Society for French History* 42 (2014), http://hdl.handle.net/2027/spo.0642292.0042.008 (last accessed 10 December 2024).

Herencia, Bernard, *Les 'Ephémérides du citoyen' et les 'Nouvelles Ephémérides économiques', 1765-1788* (Ferney-Voltaire, 2014).

–, 'Physiocratie et gouvernementalité: l'œuvre de Lemercier de La Rivière', doctoral dissertation, 2 vols, Paris Ouest Nanterre La Défense, 2011.

–, 'Présentation', in Paul Pierre Lemercier de La Rivière, *L'Ordre naturel et essentiel des sociétés politiques* (Geneva, 2017), p.9-38.

Jacoud, Gilles, 'Jean-Baptiste Say et la critique de la physiocratie: l'opposition à Pierre Samuel Dupont de Nemours', in *Les Voies de la richesse? La physiocratie en question (1760-1850)*, ed. Gérard Klotz *et al.* (Rennes, 2017), p.245-62.

Kaplan, Steven L., 'The grain question as the social question: Necker's antiphysiocracy', in *The Economic turn: recasting political economy in Enlightenment Europe*, Steven L. Kaplan and Sophus A. Reinert (New York, 2019), p.505-84.

–, and Sophus A. Reinert (ed.), *The Economic turn: recasting political economy in Enlightenment Europe* (New York, 2019).

Klotz, Gérard, *et al.* (ed.), *Les Voies de la richesse? La Physiocratie en question (1760-1850)* (Rennes, 2017).

Labrouquère, André, *Les Idées coloniales des physiocrates (documents inédits)* (Paris, 1927).

Larrère, Catherine, 'L'apport de la physiocratie à la tradition française du libéralisme', in *Les Libéralismes, la théorie politique et l'histoire*, ed. S. Stuurman (Amsterdam, 1994), p.72-89.

–, *L'Invention de l'économie au XVIIIe siècle: du droit naturel à la physiocratie* (Paris, 1992).

Laval-Reviglio, Marie-Claire, 'Les conceptions politiques des physiocrates', *Revue française de science politique* 37:2 (1987), p.181-213.

Lavergne, Léonce de, *Les Economistes français du dix-huitième siècle* (Paris, 1870).

Le Masne, Pierre, 'La colonisation et l'esclavage vus par les physiocrates', *L'Economie politique* 71:3 (2016), p.101-12.

Lemée, Mathilde, 'Le citoyen dans *L'Heureuse Nation ou Gouvernement des Féliciens* de Le Mercier de La Rivière (1792)', *Revue juridique de l'Ouest* 3 (2013), p.271-303.

Lilti, Antoine, 'Sociabilité mondaine et réseaux intellectuels: les salons au XVIIIᵉ siècle', in *Réseaux de l'esprit en Europe des Lumières au XIXᵉ siècle*, ed. Wladimir Berelowitch and Michel Porret (Geneva, 2009), p.89-104.

McLain, James, *The Economic writings of Du Pont de Nemours* (Wilmington, DE, 1977).

May, Louis-Philippe, *Le Mercier de La Rivière (1719-1801): aux origines de la science économique* (Paris, 1975).

Mergey, Anthony, 'Conseiller le prince dans l'idéal physiocratique: le rôle de la magistrature', in *Education des citoyens, éducation des gouvernants* (Aix-en-Provence, 2020), p.171-81.

–, 'Le contrôle de l'activité législative de la nation en 1789: l'opinion de Dupont de Nemours', *Journal of interdisciplinary history of ideas* 3:5 (2014), p.1-33.

–, *L'Etat des physiocrates: autorité et décentralisation* (Aix-en-Provence, 2010).

–, 'La question des "municipalités"

dans l'*Introduction* au *Mémoire sur les Etats provinciaux* du marquis de Mirabeau (1758)', *Revue de la recherche juridique – droit prospectif* 4 (2006), p.2523-48.

–, et al. (ed.), *Guillaume-François Le Trosne: itinéraire d'une figure intellectuelle orléanaise au siècle des Lumières* (Le Kremlin-Bicêtre, 2023).

Mille, Jérôme, *Un Physiocrate oublié: G.-F. Le Trosne – étude économique, fiscale et politique* (Paris, 1905).

Murphy, Orville T., *Charles Gravier, comte de Vergennes: French diplomacy in the age of revolution, 1719-1787* (Albany, NY, 1982).

–, 'DuPont de Nemours and the Anglo-French commercial treaty of 1786', *The Economic history review* 19:3 (1966), p.569-80.

Perkins, Jean A., 'Rousseau jugé par Du Pont de Nemours', *Annales de la Société Jean-Jacques Rousseau* 39 (1972-1977), p.171-96.

Pisanelli, Simona, 'Political power vs "natural laws": physiocracy and slavery', *History of economic thought and policy* 6:1 (2017), p.67-85.

Reuss, Rodolphe, *Charles de Butré, un physiocrate tourangeau en Alsace et dans le margraviat de Bade d'après ses papiers inédits et sa correspondance* (Paris, 1887).

Røge, Pernille, *Economists and the reinvention of empire: France in the Americas and Africa, c.1750-1802* (Cambridge, 2019).

Sabbagh, Gabriel, 'An unrecorded physiocratic précis by Charles

Richard de Butré and the experiment of Karl Friedrich of Baden-Durlach in Dietlingen', *The European journal of the history of economic thought* 24:1 (2017), p.1-24.

Schlobach, Jochen, 'Une correspondance littéraire de Du Pont de Nemours adressée à Stockholm et à Karlsruhe', in *Nouvelles, gazettes, mémoires secrets*, ed. Birgitta Berglund-Nilsson (Karlstad, 1998), p.101-11.

–, 'Physiocratie, critique sociale et éducation princière: à propos d'un texte inconnu de Du Pont de Nemours', in *Chemins ouverts: mélanges offerts à Claude Sicard* (Toulouse, 1998), p.77-84.

Skornicki, Arnault, *L'Economiste, la cour et la patrie: l'économie politique dans la France des Lumières* (Paris, 2011).

–, 'Liberté, propriété, sûreté: retour sur une devise physiocratique', *Corpus* 66 (2014), p.16-36.

Sonenscher, Michael, 'Physiocracy as a theodicy', *History of political thought* 23:2 (2002), p.326-39.

Steiner, Philippe, 'L'économie politique du royaume agricole: François Quesnay', in *Nouvelle histoire de la pensée économique: des scolastiques aux classiques*, ed. Alain Béraud and Gilbert Faccarello, vol.1 (Paris, 1993), p.230-36.

–, *La 'Science nouvelle' de l'économie politique* (Paris, 1998).

Vardi, Liana, *The Physiocrats and the world of the Enlightenment* (Cambridge and New York, 2012).

Vincent, Julien, '"Un dogue de forte race": Dupont de Nemours, ou la physiocratie réincarnée (1793-1807)', *La Révolution française* 14 (2018), p.1-34.

Weulersse, Georges, *Le Mouvement physiocratique en France (de 1756 à 1770)*, vol.2 (Paris, 1910).

–, *La Physiocratie à la fin du règne de Louis XV (1770-1774)* (Paris, 1959).

–, *La Physiocratie à l'aube de la Révolution (1781-1792)* (Paris, 1985).

Whatmore, Richard, 'Dupont de Nemours et la politique révolutionnaire', *Revue française d'histoire des idées politiques* 20 (2004), p.335-51.

General works

Abramson, Julia L., 'Narrating "finances" after John Law: complicity, critique, and the bonds of obligation in Duclos and Mouhy', *Finance and society* 2:1 (2016), p.25-44.

–, 'Put your money where your friends are: finance and loyalty in a nineteenth-century Du Pont shareholder report', https://www.hagley.org/librarynews/put-your-money-where-your-friends-are-finance-and-loyalty-nineteenth-century-du-pont (last accessed 25 November 2024).

Acomb, Frances, *Anglophobia in France, 1763-1789: an essay in the history of constitutionalism and nationalism* (Durham, NC, 1950).

Bibliography

Agamben, Giorgio, *Qu'est-ce qu'un dispositif?* (Paris, 2007).

Aïnouddine Sidi, Nazlie, 'L'évolution de la contrainte par corps du XVIe au XXe siècle', doctoral dissertation, Université de Poitiers, 2020.

Albertone, Manuela, 'Deux générations autour de l'Amérique', in Victor Riqueti de Mirabeau and Pierre-Samuel Du Pont de Nemours, *Dialogues physiocratiques sur l'Amérique*, ed. M. Albertone (Paris, 2015), p.7-51.

–, *National identity and the agrarian republic: the transatlantic commerce of ideas between America and France (1750-1830)* (Farnham, 2014).

–, 'Thomas Jefferson and French economic thought: a mutual exchange of ideas', in *Rethinking the Atlantic world: Europe and America in the age of democratic revolutions*, ed. Manuela Albertone and Antonino De Francesco (New York, 2009), p.123-46.

–, and Antonino De Francesco (ed.), *Rethinking the Atlantic world: Europe and America in the age of democratic revolutions* (New York, 2009).

Aldridge, A. O., 'Jacques Barbeu-Dubourg, a French disciple of Benjamin Franklin', *Proceedings of the American Philosophical Society* 95:4 (1951), p.331-92.

Alimento, Antonella, 'Commercial treaties and the harmonisation of national interests: the Anglo-French case (1667-1713)', in *War, trade and neutrality: Europe and the Mediterranean in the seventeenth and eighteenth centuries*, ed. Antonella Alimento (Milan, 2011), p.107-28.

–, 'Il controverso cammino verso la reciprocità: pratica diplomatica e riflessione economica nella Francia d'Ancien Régime', *Società e storia* 165 (2019), p.549-65.

–, and Koen Stapelbroek (ed.), *The Politics of commercial treaties in the eighteenth century: balance of power, balance of trade* (Cham, 2017).

Ancelet-Netter, Dominique, '*Dettes* et *débiteurs* dans les versions françaises de la cinquième demande du *Notre Père* du XIIe au XXIe siècle: une mise en perspective par l'analyse sémantique', *Transversalités* 109 (2009), p.103-23.

Appleby, Joyce, 'What is still American in the political philosophy of Thomas Jefferson?', in *The Enlightenment: critical concepts in historical studies*, vol.5: *Revolutions*, ed. Ryan Patrick Hanley and Darrin McMahon (London and New York, 2010), p.287-309.

Arendt, Hannah, *Essai sur la révolution* (Paris, 1967).

Aron, Raymond, *Le tappe del pensiero sociologico* (Milan, 1972).

Artigas-Menant, Geneviève, *et al.* (ed.), *Protestants, protestantisme et pensée clandestine en France* (Paris, 2004).

Bachofen, Blaise, *La Condition de la liberté: Rousseau, critique des raisons politiques* (Paris, 2002).

Baczko, Bronislaw, *Comment sortir de la Terreur* (Paris, 1989).

–, *Politiques de la Révolution française* (Paris, 2008).

Badinter, Elisabeth, and Robert Badinter, *Condorcet (1743-1794):*

un intellectuel en politique (Paris, 1988).

Bailyn, Bernard, 'Jefferson and the ambiguities of freedom', in *To begin the world anew: the genius and ambiguities of the American Founders* (New York, 2003), p.37-59.

Banks, Bryan A., 'The Huguenot diaspora and the politics of religion in revolutionary France', in *The French Revolution and religion in global perspective: freedom and faith*, ed. Bryan A. Banks and Erica Johnson (Cham, 2017), p.3-24.

Bart, Jean, *Histoire du droit privé* (Paris, 2009).

Baudens, Stéphane, 'Linguet, critique du droit romain: un jurisconsulte iconoclaste au Palais', in *Les Représentations du droit romain en Europe du Moyen Age aux Lumières* (Aix-en-Provence, 2007), p.233-51.

Beiner, Ronald, *Civil religion: a dialogue in the history of political philosophy* (Cambridge, 2011).

Belissa, Marc, *Fraternité universelle et intérêt national (1713-1795): les cosmopolitiques du droit des gens* (Paris, 1998).

–, and Yannick Bosc, *Le Directoire: la République sans la démocratie* (Paris, 2018).

Benoît, Daniel, *Les Frères Gibert: pasteurs du 'Désert' puis du 'Refuge'* (Paris, 2005).

Bercegol, Fabienne, *et al.* (ed.), *Une 'Période sans nom': les années 1780-1820 et la fabrique de l'histoire littéraire* (Paris, 2016).

Berelowitch, Wladimir, and Michel Porret, 'Introduction', in *Réseaux de l'esprit en Europe des Lumières au XIXe siècle*, ed. Wladimir Berelowitch and Michel Porret (Geneva, 2009), p.11-28.

Berg, Maxine, and Pat Hudson, *Slavery, capitalism and the industrial revolution* (Cambridge, 2023).

Bergeron, Louis, *Banquiers, négociants et manufacturiers parisiens du Directoire à l'Empire* (Paris, 1978).

–, *Banquiers, négociants et manufacturiers parisiens du Directoire à l'Empire*, 2 vols (1978; Paris, 1999).

Berman, Harold J., *Law and revolution: the formation of the western legal tradition* (Cambridge, MA, and London, 1983).

Bertaud, Jean-Paul, 'La crise sociale (septembre 1792-juillet 1796)', in *La Protection sociale sous la Révolution française*, ed. J. Imbert (Paris, 1990), p.205-84.

Biard, Michel, and Marisa Linton, *Terreur! La Révolution française face à ses démons* (Malakoff, 2020).

Binoche, Bertrand, *Ecrasez l'infâme! Philosopher à l'âge des Lumières* (Paris, 2018).

Birnstiel, Eckart, and Chrystel Bernat (ed.), *La Diaspora des Huguenots: les réfugiés protestants de France et leur dispersion dans le monde (XVIe-XVIIIe siècles)* (Paris, 2001).

Blacher, Philippe, 'L'étendue du suffrage universel sous la IIe République', *Revue française d'histoire des idées politiques* 38:2 (2013), p.257-68.

Blanning, Timothy C. W., *The Culture of power and the power of culture: Old Regime Europe, 1660-1789* (Oxford, 2002).

Blaufarb, Rafe, *The Great demarcation: the French Revolution and the invention of modern property* (Oxford and New York, 2016).

–, *L'Invention de la propriété privée: une autre histoire de la Révolution*, translated by Christophe Jaquet (Ceyzérieu, 2019).

Bloch, Camille, *L'Assistance et l'Etat à la veille de la Révolution* (Paris, 1907).

Boismorand, Pierre, *et al.* (ed.), *Protestants d'Aunis, Saintonge et Angoumois* (Paris, 1998).

Bosher, John F., *The Single duty project* (London, 1964).

Bouchary, Jean, 'Les manieurs d'argent sous la Révolution française: le banquier Edouard de Walckiers', *Annales historiques de la Révolution française* 86 (1938), p.133-55.

Bourdieu, Pierre, 'Espace social et genèse des "classes"', *Actes de la recherche en sciences sociales* 52:1 (1984), p.3-14.

Bourdin, Philippe (ed.), *Les Noblesses françaises dans l'Europe de la Révolution* (Rennes, 2010).

Brace, Richard Munthe, 'General Dumouriez and the Girondins 1792-1793', *The American historical review* 56:3 (1951), p.493-509.

Brétéché, Marion, and Héloïse Hermant (ed.), *Parole d'experts: une histoire sociale du politique (Europe, XVIe-XVIIIe siècle)* (Rennes, 2021).

Brian, Eric, *La Mesure de l'Etat: administrateurs et géomètres au XVIIIe siècle* (Paris, 1994).

Brown, Howard, *Ending the French Revolution* (Charlottesville, VA, 2006).

–, *War, Revolution, and the bureaucratic state* (Oxford, 1995).

–, and Judith Miller (ed.), *Taking liberties: problems of a new order from the French Revolution to Napoleon* (Manchester, 2002).

Cabanel, Patrick, *Histoire des protestants en France (XVIe-XXIe siècle)* (Paris, 2012).

–, *Juifs et protestants en France: les affinités électives (XVIe-XXIe siècle)* (Paris, 2004).

Caillé, Alain, *et al.* (ed.), *Histoire raisonnée de la philosophie morale et politique: le bonheur et l'utile* (Paris, 2001).

Carré, Jacques, *Ville et santé en Grande-Bretagne, XVIIIe-XXe siècles* (Clermont-Ferrand, 1989).

Carrot, Georges, *Révolution et maintien de l'ordre* (Paris, 1995).

Castel, Robert, *Les Métamorphoses de la question sociale* (Paris, 1995).

Célimène, Fred, and André Legris (ed.), *L'Economie de l'esclavage colonial* (Paris, 2012).

Cerami, Charles A., *Jefferson's great gamble: the remarkable story of Jefferson, Napoleon and the men behind the Louisiana purchase* (Naperville, IL, 2003).

Chabalier, Stanislas de, 'Réparer l'injustice d'un châtiment par l'oubli: l'amnistie de soldats du régiment suisse de Châteauvieux (31 décembre 1791)', *Criminocorpus* 16 (2020), https://journals. openedition.org/criminocorpus/7842 (last accessed 29 November 2024).

Challamel, Augustin, *Les Clubs contre-révolutionnaires* (Paris, 1895).

Chappey, Jean-Luc, 'The new

elites: questions about political, social, and cultural reconstruction after the Terror', in *The Oxford handbook of the French Revolution*, ed. David Andress (Oxford, 2015), p.556-72.

Charara, Youmna (ed.), *Fictions coloniales du XVIIIᵉ siècle: Ziméo, Lettres africaines, Adonis, ou le Bon Nègre, anecdote coloniale* (Paris, 2005).

Charle, Christophe, 'Le temps des hommes doubles', *Revue d'histoire moderne et contemporaine* 39:1 (1992), p.73-85.

Chartier, Jean-Luc A., *Portalis, père du Code civil* (Paris, 2004).

Chartier, Roger, *Les Origines culturelles de la Révolution française* (Paris, 1990).

Chauduri, Joyautpaul, 'Possession, ownership and access: a Jeffersonian view of property', *Political inquiry* 1 (1973), p.78-95.

Chaussinand-Nogaret, Guy, 'Capital et structure sociale sous l'Ancien Régime', *Annales. Histoire, sciences sociales* 25:2 (1970), p.463-76.

Chavanette, Loris (ed.), *Le Directoire: forger la République 1795-1799* (Paris, 2020).

–, *Quatre-vingt-quinze: la Terreur en procès* (Paris, 2017).

Cheney, Paul, *Revolutionary commerce: globalization and the French monarchy* (Cambridge, MA, 2010).

Chernillo, Daniel, *The Natural law foundations of modern social theory: a quest for universality* (Cambridge, 2013).

Cheymol, Jean, and René-Jean César, 'Hôtel-Dieu: treize

siècles d'histoire… panégyrique ou réquisitoire', presented on 26 November 1977 at the Société française d'histoire de la médecine, https://numera-bilis.u-paris.fr/ressources/pdf/sfhm/hsm/HSMx1977x011x004/HSMx1977x011x004x0263.pdf (last accessed 28 November 2024).

Choudhury, Mita, and Daniel J. Watkins (ed.), *Belief and politics in Enlightenment France: essays in honour of Dale K. Van Kley*, Oxford University Studies in the Enlightenment (Liverpool, Liverpool University Press / Voltaire Foundation, 2019).

Clark, Henry C., *Compass of society: commerce and absolutism in Old-Regime France* (Lanham, MD, 2007).

Clay, Lauren R., 'The bourgeoisie, capitalism, and the origins of the French Revolution', in *The Oxford handbook of the French Revolution*, ed. David Andress (Oxford, 2015), p.21-39.

Cossa, Luigi, *Histoire des doctrines économiques* (Paris, 1899).

Coste, Laurent, *Les Bourgeoisies en France: du XVIᵉ au milieu du XIXᵉ siècle* (Paris, 2013).

Cotta, Sergio, 'Introduzione', in Montesquieu, *Lo spirito delle leggi*, vol.1 (Turin, 2005), p.7-30.

Craiutu, Aurelian, *A Virtue for courageous minds: moderation in French political thought (1748-1830)* (Princeton, NJ, 2012).

Crépel, Pierre, 'Arithmétique politique et population dans les métamorphoses de l'*Encyclopédie*', in *Arithmétique politique dans la*

France du XVIIIe siècle, ed. Thierry Martin (Paris, 2003), p.47-70.

Crook, Malcolm, *Elections in the French Revolution* (Cambridge, 1996).

Cubéro, José, *Histoire du vagabondage* (Paris, 1998).

Curtin, Philip D., *The Rise and fall of the plantation complex: essays in Atlantic history* (Cambridge, 1999).

Darnton, Robert, *La Fin des Lumières: le mesmérisme et la Révolution*, translated by Marie-Alyx Revellat (Paris, 1984).

–, *Mesmerism and the end of the Enlightenment in France* (Cambridge, MA, 1968).

Davis, David Brion, *Il problema della schiavitù nella cultura occidentale* (Turin, 1971).

Davis, Natalie Zemon, 'Ghosts, kin, and progeny: some features of family life in early modern France', *Daedalus* 106 (spring 1997), p.87-114.

Delmas, Bernard, and Thierry Demals, 'Karl Marx et la physiocratie', in *La Diffusion internationale de la physiocratie (XVIIIe-XIXe)*, ed. Bernard Delmas et al. (Grenoble, 1995), p.149-73.

Delon, Michel (ed)., *Dictionnaire européen des Lumières* (Paris, 1997).

–, *L'Idée d'énergie au tournant des Lumières (1770-1820)* (Paris, 1988).

–, 'Quarante ans de recherche sur un objet protéiforme', in *Une 'Période sans nom': les années 1780-1820 et la fabrique de l'histoire littéraire*, ed. Fabienne Bercegol et al. (Paris, 2016), p.37-49.

–, 'Questions de périodisation', *SVEC* 2005:10, p.322-34.

Delpiano, Patrizia, *La schiavitù in età moderna* (Bari, 2009).

Denis, Vincent, and Bernard Gainot, 'De l'art du maintien de l'ordre chez Sieyès, 1791', in *Les Mémoires policiers, 1750-1850: écritures et pratiques policières du siècle des Lumières au Second Empire*, ed. Vincent Milliot (Rennes, 2006), p.219-33.

Derathé, Robert, *Jean-Jacques Rousseau et la science politique de son temps* (Paris, 1950).

Di Rienzo, Eugenio, 'Pour une histoire du concept de despotisme du XVIIIe siècle français: le manuscrit inédit de l'abbé Morellet: *Sur le despotisme légal et contre M. de La Rivière*', *Proceedings of the 8th International Congress of the Enlightenment*, vol.1 (Oxford, 1992), p.292-96.

Dobry, Michel, '*Postface* / Eléments de réponse: principes et implications d'une perspective relationnelle', in *La Logique du désordre*, ed. Myriam Aït-Aoudia and Antoine Roger (Paris, 2015), p.261-332.

–, *Sociologie des crises politiques: la dynamique des mobilisations multisectorielles* (Paris, 1986).

Donaghay, Marie, 'Calonne and the Anglo-French commercial treaty of 1786', *Journal of modern history* 50:3 (1978), p.1157-84.

–, 'The exchange of products of the soil and industrial goods in the Anglo-French commercial treaty of 1786', *The Journal of European economic history* 19:2 (1990), p.377-401.

Duby, Georges, *Histoire de la France: dynasties et révolutions, de 1348 à 1852* (Paris, 1987).

Dupuy, Pascal, 'French representations of the 1786 Franco-British commercial treaty', in *The Politics of commercial treaties in the eighteenth century: balance of power, balance of trade*, ed. Antonella Alimento and Koen Stapelbroek (Cham, 2017), p.371-99.

Dupuy, Roger (ed.), *1795, pour une république sans révolution* (Rennes, 1996).

Durelle-Marc, Yann-Arzel, 'Jean-Denis Lanjuinais, juriste et parlementaire (1753-1827): une biographie politique', *Parlement[s]: revue d'histoire politique* 11:1 (2009), p.8-24.

Edelstein, Dan (ed.), *The Super-Enlightenment: daring to know too much*, *SVEC* 2010:01.

–, and Anton M. Matytsin (ed.), *Let there be enlightenment: the religious and mystical sources of rationality* (Baltimore, MD, 2018).

Edelstein, Melvin, *The French Revolution and the birth of electoral democracy* (Farnham, 2014).

Egret, Jean, *Necker, ministre de Louis XVI, 1776-1790* (Paris, 1975).

–, *La Pré-Révolution française (1787-1788)* (Paris, 1962).

Ehrard, Jean, *Lumières et esclavage: l'esclavage colonial et l'opinion publique en France au XVIIIᵉ siècle* (Brussels, 2008).

Ehrman, John, *The British government and commercial negotiations with Europe 1783-1793* (Cambridge, 1962).

Elbow, Matthew H., *French corporative theory, 1789-1948: a chapter in the history of ideas* (New York, 1953).

Elias, Norbert, *La Société de cour* (Paris, 1985).

Fabre, Jean, 'Mirabeau, interlocuteur et protecteur de Rousseau', in *Les Mirabeau et leur temps* (Paris, 1968), p.71-90.

Faccarello, Gilbert, 'Galiani, Necker and Turgot: a debate on economic reform and policy in eighteenth-century France', in *Studies in the history of French political economy from Bodin to Walras*, ed. Gilbert Faccarello (London, 1998), p.120-95.

Fauchois, Yann, 'La difficulté d'être libre: les droits de l'homme, l'Eglise catholique et l'Assemblée constituante, 1789-1791', *Revue d'histoire moderne et contemporaine* 48:1 (2001), p.71-101.

–, *Religion et France révolutionnaire* (Paris, 1989).

Faure, Olivier, and Dominique Dessertine, *Les Cliniques privées: deux siècles de succès* (Paris, 2012).

Felice, Domenico (ed.), *Il dispotismo: genesi e sviluppo di un concetto filosofico-politico*, 2 vols (Naples, 2002).

Félix, Joël, 'The problem with Necker's *Compte rendu au roi* (1781)', in *The Crisis of the absolute monarchy: France from Old Regime to Revolution*, ed. Julian Swann and Joël Félix (Oxford, 2013), p.107-26.

Fiori, Stefano, *Ordine, mano invisibile, mercato: una rilettura di Adam Smith* (Turin, 2001).

Foucault, Michel, *Histoire de la folie à l'âge classique* (Paris, 1975).

Freeman's, *Catalogue de vente* (22 October 2015).

Frey, Linda, and Marsha Frey, *The Culture of French revolutionary diplomacy: in the face of Europe* (London, 2018).

Fryer, W. R., *Republic or Restoration in France? 1794-7, the politics of French royalism, with particular reference to the activities of A. B. J. d'André* (Manchester, 1965).

Furet, François, and Mona Ozouf (ed.), *Dictionnaire critique de la Révolution française: événements* (Paris, 1992).

– (ed.), *Dictionnaire critique de la Révolution française: institutions et créations* (Paris, 1992).

Gainot, Bernard, 'Le contentieux électoral sous le Directoire: monisme et pluralisme dans la culture politique de la France révolutionnaire', *Revue historique* 642:2 (2007), p.325-53.

Gaïti, Brigitte, and Pierre Serna (ed.), *Politix: revue des sciences sociales du politique* 14:56 (2001), special issue: *Inconstances politiques*.

Garrioch, David, *Neighborhood and community in Paris, 1740-1790* (Cambridge, 1986).

Gauchet, Marcel, *Robespierre: l'homme qui nous divise le plus* (Paris, 2018).

Gauthier, Florence, *Triomphe et mort du droit naturel en Révolution, 1789-1795-1802* (Paris, 1992), reprinted in 2014.

Gaven, Jean-Christophe, *Le Crime de lèse-nation: histoire d'une invention juridique et politique (1789-1791)* (Paris, 2016).

Gervais, Pierre, 'Why profit and loss didn't matter: the historicized rationality of early modern merchant accounting', in *Merchants and profits in the age of commerce, 1680-1830*, ed. Pierre Gervais *et al.* (London, 2014), p.33-52.

Godechot, Jacques, 'The business classes and the Revolution outside France', *The American historical review* 64:1 (1958), p.1-13.

–, *Institutions de la France sous la Révolution* (Paris, 1985).

Goetzmann, William N., *et al.* (ed.), *The Great mirror of folly: finance, culture, and the crash of 1720* (New Haven, CT, 2013).

Goggi, Gianluigi, 'Diderot–Raynal, l'esclavage et les Lumières écossaises', *Lumières* 3 (2004), p.52-94.

Gojosso, Eric, *Le Concept de République en France (XVIe-XVIIIe siècle)* (Aix-en-Provence, 1998).

–, 'Le *Mémoire sur les municipalités* (1775) et la réforme administrative à la fin de l'Ancien Régime', *Cahiers poitevins d'histoire du droit* 1 (2007), p.127-38.

Gough, Hugh, *The Newspaper press in the French Revolution* (London, 1988).

Goyard-Fabre, Simone, *Les Embarras philosophiques du droit naturel* (Paris, 2002).

Graafland, Johan J., 'Weber revisited: critical perspectives from Calvinism on capitalism in economic crisis', in *Calvinism and the making of the European mind*, ed. Gijsbert van den Brink and Harro M. Höpfls (Boston, MA, 2014), p.177-98.

Grampp, W. D., 'A re-examination of Jeffersonian economics', *The Southern economic journal* 12 (1945-1946), p.263-82.

Grange, Henri, *Les Idées de Necker* (Paris, 1974).

Granshaw, Lindsay, and Roy Porter (ed.), *The Hospital in history* (London, 1989).

Greengrass, Mark, 'Thinking with Calvinist networks: from the "Calvinist international" to the "Venice affair" (1608-1610)', in *Huguenot networks, 1560-1780*, ed. Vivienne M. Larminie (New York, 2018), p.9-27.

Groffier, Ethel, *Un Encyclopédiste réformateur: Jacques Peuchet (1758-1830)* (Quebec, 2009).

Grosclaude, Pierre, *Malesherbes témoin et interprète de son temps* (Paris, 1961).

Gueniffey, Patrice, *Le Nombre et la raison: la Révolution française et les élections* (Paris, 1993).

–, *La Politique de la Terreur* (Paris, 2000).

Haara, Heiki, *Pufendorf's theory of sociability: passions, habits and social order* (Cham, 2018).

Harris, Robert D., *Necker and the Revolution of 1789* (Lanham, MD, 1986).

–, *Necker: reform statesman of the Ancien Régime* (Berkeley, CA, 1979).

Harris, Seymour Edwin, *The Assignats* (Cambridge, 1930).

Haussonville, Vicomte Othénien d' [Gabriel Paul Othénien de

Cléron, comte d'Haussonville], *Le Salon de Mme Necker: d'après les documents tirés des archives de Coppet*, vol.2 (Paris, 1882).

Heater, Derek, *A Brief history of citizenship* (Edinburgh, 2004).

Herland, Michel, 'Penser l'esclavage: de la morale à l'économie', in *L'Economie de l'esclavage colonial*, ed. Fred Célimène and André Legris (Paris, 2012), p.53-76.

Hermann, Johannes, *Zur Geschichte der Familie Necker* (Berlin, 1886).

Herriot, Edouard, 'Préface', in Denise Aimé-Azam, *Du Pont de Nemours, honnête homme* (Paris, 1933), p.i-ii.

Hildesheimer, Françoise, and Christian Gut, *L'Assistance hospitalière* (Paris, 1992).

Hirsch, Jean-Pierre, 'Les milieux du commerce, l'esprit de système et le pouvoir à la veille de la Révolution', *Annales* 30:6 (1975), p.1337-70.

Hirschman, Albert, *Défection et prise de parole: théorie et applications*, translated by Claude Besseyrias (Paris, 1995).

–, *Exit, voice, and loyalty: responses to decline in firms, organizations, and states* (Cambridge, MA, 2004).

–, *The Passions and the interests: political arguments for capitalism before its triumph* (Cambridge, MA, 2013).

Holt, Mack P., *The French wars of religion, 1562-1629* (Cambridge, 1995).

Horn, Jeff, *The Path not taken: French industrialization in the age of revolution, 1750-1830* (Cambridge, MA, 2006).

Imbert, Jean, *Le Droit hospitalier de l'Ancien Régime* (Paris, 1993).
–, 'Vers le redressement: le Directoire', in *La Protection sociale sous la Révolution française*, ed. J. Imbert (Paris, 1990), p.419-22.

Jacoud, Gilles, 'L'esclavage colonial: une comparaison des approches de Say, Sismondi et des saint-si-moniens', Œconomia: *history, methodology, philosophy* 6:3 (2016), p.363-402.
Jameson, Russell Parsons, *Montesquieu et l'esclavage: étude sur les origines de l'opinion antiesclav-agiste en France au XVIIIᵉ siècle* (Paris, 1911).
Jessenne, Jean-Pierre, 'Introduction', in *Vers un ordre bourgeois?*, ed. Jean-Pierre Jessenne (Rennes, 2007), p.9-15.
Jones, Colin, 'La (les) bourgeoisie(s) de la France d'Ancien Régime', in *Vers un ordre bourgeois?*, ed. Jean-Pierre Jessenne (Rennes, 2007), p.161-70.
–, 'The great chain of buying: medical advertisement, the bourgeois public sphere, and the origins of the French Revolution', *American historical review* 101:1 (1996), p.13-40.

Kammen, Michael, 'The rights of property, and the property in rights: the problematic nature of "property" in the political thought of the founders and the early republic', in *Liberty, property, and the foundations of the American Constitution*, ed. Ellen Frankel Paul and Howard Dickman (Albany, NY, 1989), p.1-22.

Kaplan, Steven L., *The Bakers of Paris and the bread question, 1700-1775* (Durham, NC, 1996).
Kastor, Peter J., *The Nation's crucible: the Louisiana purchase and the creation of America* (New Haven, CT, and London, 2004).
Katz, Stanley N., 'Thomas Jefferson and the right to property in revolutionary America', *Journal of law and economics* 19 (1976), p.467-88.
Kessler, Amalia D., 'Limited liability in context: lessons from the French origins of the American limited partnership', *The Journal of legal studies* 32:2 (2003), p.511-48.
Kettering, Sharon, *Patrons, brokers, and clients in seventeenth-century France* (New York, 1986).
Koebner, Richard, 'Despot and despotism: vicissitudes of a political term', *Journal of the Warburg and Courtauld Institutes* 14:3-4 (1951), p.275-302.
Koselleck, Reinhart, *L'Expérience de l'histoire*, ed. Michael Werner, translated by Alexandre Escudier (Paris, 2011).
Kuciski, Auguste, *Les Députés au corps législatif, Conseil des Cinq-Cents, Conseil des Anciens, de l'An IV à l'An VII* (1905; Delhi, 2019).

Lafrance, Geneviève, *Qui perd gagne: imaginaire du don et Révolution française* (Montreal, 2008).
Lameth, Alexandre, *Histoire de l'Assemblée constituante*, vol.2 (Paris, 1829).
Larrère, Catherine, 'Montesquieu et les pauvres', *Cahiers d'économie politique* 59:2 (2010), p.24-43.

Lauget, Pierre-Louis, and Françoise Salaün, 'Aux origines de l'hôpital moderne, une évolution européenne', *Les Tribunes de la santé* 3 (2004), p.19-28.

Léchenet, Annie, 'Indépendance et citoyenneté dans la république selon Jefferson', doctoral dissertation, Université de Nancy, 1990.

–, *Jefferson-Madison, un débat sur la République* (Paris, 2002).

–, 'Le républicanisme américain: Jefferson (1743-1826) et la poursuite du bonheur', in *Histoire raisonnée de la philosophie morale et politique*, vol.2: *Des Lumières à nos jours*, ed. Alain Caillé *et al.* (Paris, 2007), p.133-38.

–, 'Le républicanisme américain: Jefferson et la poursuite du bonheur', in *Histoire raisonnée de la philosophie morale et politique: le bonheur et l'utile*, ed. Alain Caillé *et al.* (Paris, 2001), p.500-504.

Lefebvre, Frédéric, 'L'honnêteté du négociant: une enquête sociologique française au milieu du XVIIIe siècle', in *Le Cercle de Vincent de Gournay: savoirs économiques et pratiques administratives en France au milieu du XVIIIe siècle*, ed. Loïc Charles *et al.* (Paris, 2011), p.201-34.

Lefebvre, Georges, *La France sous le Directoire (1795-1799)*, ed. Jean-René Suratteau (Paris, 1984).

Lefebvre-Teillard, Anne, 'Le nom et la loi', *Mots: les langages du politique* 63 (2000), p.9-18.

Le Gal, Sébastien, 'Origines de l'état de siège en France (Ancien Régime – Révolution)', doctoral dissertation, University Lyon 3, 2011.

–, 'La réforme de la constitution militaire durant la pré-révolution (Guibert et le Conseil de la Guerre)', *Cahiers poitevins d'histoire du droit* 8-9 (2017), p.109-27.

Lemay, Edna Hindie, 'La composition de l'Assemblée nationale constituante: les hommes de la continuité?', *Revue d'histoire moderne et contemporaine* 3 (1977), p.341-63.

–, *Dictionnaire des constituants, 1789-1791*, 2 vols (Paris, 1991).

Le Mentheour, Rudy, 'Au berceau de l'appropriation: Rousseau, Locke et l'enfance du propriétaire', *Annales Jean-Jacques Rousseau* 50 (2012), p.161-82.

Leuwers, Hervé, 'La robe révolutionnée', in *Vers un ordre bourgeois?*, ed. Jean-Pierre Jessenne (Rennes, 2007), p.105-18.

–, *Robespierre* (Paris, 2014).

Lever, Evelyne, *Paris sous la Terreur* (Paris, 2019).

Levieil de La Marsonnière, Jules, *Histoire de la contrainte par corps* (Paris, 1843).

Levratto, Nadine, 'Abolition de la contrainte par corps et évolution du capitalisme au XIXe siècle', *Economie et institutions* 10-11 (2007), p.221-49.

Lévy, Jean-Philippe, and André Castaldo, *Histoire du droit civil* (Paris, 2010).

Ligou, Daniel, *Le Protestantisme en France de 1598 à 1715* (Paris, 1968).

Ljublinski, Vladimir S., *La Guerre des farines: contribution à l'histoire de la lutte des classes en France, à la veille de la Révolution* (Grenoble, 1979).

Bibliography

Long, Marceau, and Jean-Claude Monier, *Portalis: l'esprit de justice* (Paris, 1997).

Lougee, Carolyn Chappell, *Facing the Revocation: Huguenot families, faith, and the king's will* (New York, 2016).

–, 'Family bonds across the Refuge', in *Memory and identity: the Huguenots in France and the Atlantic diaspora*, ed. Bertrand Van Ruymbeke and Randy J. Sparks (Columbia, SC, 2003), p.172-93.

Lovejoy, Arthur Oncken, *The Great Chain of Being: a study of the history of an idea* (Cambridge and London, 1964).

Lüthy, Herbert, *La Banque protestante en France de la Révocation de l'Edit de Nantes à la Révolution*, vol.1: *Dispersion et regroupement (1685-1730)* (Paris, 1959).

–, *La Banque protestante en France de la Révocation de l'Edit de Nantes à la Révolution*, vol.2: *De la banque aux finances (1730-1794)* (Paris, 1961).

Luzzatto, Sergio, *L'Automne de la Révolution: luttes et cultures politiques dans la France thermidorienne* (Paris, 2001).

Lyons, Martin, *France under the Directory* (Cambridge, 1975).

McKay, Derek, and Hamish M. Scott, *The Rise of the great powers, 1648-1815* (London, 1983).

McLean, Ian, 'The Paris years of Thomas Jefferson', in *A Companion to Thomas Jefferson*, ed. Francis D. Cogliano (Malden, MA, 2012), p.110-27.

Magdelain, André, 'La loi *Poetelia papiria* et la loi *Iulia de pecuniis mutuis*', in *Jus imperium auctoritas: études de droit romain* (Rome, 1990), p.707-11.

Manas, Arnaud, 'Le premier business model de la Banque de France en 1800', *Revue d'économie financière* 122 (2016), p.249-54.

Margairaz, Dominique, *François de Neufchâteau: biographie intellectuelle* (Paris, 2005).

Margolf, Diane C., 'Identity, law, and the Huguenots of early modern France', in *Memory and identity: the Huguenots in France and the Atlantic diaspora*, ed. Bertrand Van Ruymbeke and Randy J. Sparks (Columbia, SC, 2003), p.26-44.

Martin, Jean-Clément, *Les Echos de la Terreur: vérités d'un mensonge d'Etat 1794-2001* (Paris, 2018).

–, *Nouvelle histoire de la Révolution française* (Paris, 2012).

–, *La Terreur: vérités et légendes* (Paris, 2017).

–, *Violence et Révolution: essai sur la naissance d'un mythe national* (Paris, 2006).

Martin, Thierry (ed.), *Arithmétique politique dans la France du XVIIIe siècle* (Paris, 2003).

Martin, Xavier, 'Images négatives de la Rome antique et du droit romain (1789-1814)', in *Droit romain, jus civile, et droit français*, ed. Jacques Krynen (Toulouse, 1999), p.49-66.

Martin-Ginouvier, F., *Un Philanthrope méconnu du XVIIIe siècle: Piarron de Chamousset* (Paris, 1905).

Marx, Karl, *Capital: a critique of political economy*, translated by

David Fernbach, vol.3 (London, 1991).

–, *Théories sur la plus-value: livre IV du 'Capital'*, ed. Gilbert Badia (Paris, 1974).

Masméjan, Jean-Baptiste, 'Le comité de mendicité mandaté par la nation: vers une harmonisation de la politique d'assistance des valides (1790-1791)', *Cahiers Jean-Moulin* 2 (2016), https://revues.univ-lyon3.fr/cjm/index.php?id=280#bodyftn33 (last accessed 28 November 2024).

Mathiez, Albert, 'Les élections de l'An v', *Annales historiques de la Révolution française* 6:35 (1929), p.425-46.

–, *Rome et le clergé français sous la Constituante* (Paris, 1911).

–, *La Théophilanthropie et le culte décadaire: essai sur l'histoire de la Révolution 1796-1801* (Paris, 1903).

Matsumoto, Akihito, 'Priestley and Smith against slavery', *The Kyoto economic review* 80:1 (2011), p.119-31.

Mayer, Arno J., *The Furies: violence and terror in the French and Russian revolutions* (Princeton, NJ, 2000).

Maza, Sarah C., *The Myth of the French bourgeoisie: an essay on the social imaginary, 1750-1850* (Cambridge, MA, 2003).

Menard, Russell R., *Sweet negotiations: sugar, slavery, and plantation agriculture in early Barbados* (Charlottesville, VA, 2006).

Menichetti, Johan, 'Pierre-Louis Roederer (1754-1835): science sociale et législation', doctoral dissertation, University Paris-Est, 2020.

Mentzer, Raymond A., and Bertrand Van Ruymbeke (ed.), *A Companion to the Huguenots* (Boston, MA, 2016).

Michelet, Jules, *Histoire de la Révolution française*, vol.1 (Paris, 1952).

Milliot, Vincent (ed.), *Histoire des polices en France: des guerres de religion à nos jours* (Paris, 2020).

Mindock, David, 'The role of the Clichy Club in the French Revolution from October 26, 1795 to September 4, 1795', MA dissertation, University of Wisconsin, 1969.

Les Mirabeau et leur temps (Paris, 1968).

Mollat, Michel, *Les Pauvres au Moyen Age* (Brussels, 2006).

Moravia, Sergio, *Il tramonto dell'illuminismo: filosofia e politica nella società francese (1770-1810)* (1968; Rome and Bari, 1986).

Morineau, Michel, 'Entre usurier et "philistin": le "bon marchand" et le "négociant éclairé"', in *Cultures et formations négociantes dans l'Europe moderne*, ed. Franco Angiolini and Daniel Roche (Paris, 1995), p.421-38.

Mousnier, Roland, *L'Assassinat d'Henri IV, 14 mai 1610* (Paris, 1964).

Murphy, Antoin E., *John Law: economic theorist and policy maker* (Oxford, 1997).

Namer, Gérard, 'Mirabeau et Rousseau: réflexions sur un texte inédit', in *Les Mirabeau et leur temps* (Paris, 1968), p.67-70.

Napoli, Paolo, 'Mesure de police: une approche

historico-conceptuelle à l'âge moderne', *Tracés* 11 (2011), p.151-73.

–, *Naissance de la police moderne: pouvoir, normes, société* (Paris, 2003).

Negroni, Barbara de, *Intolérances: catholiques et protestants en France, 1560-1787* (Paris, 1996).

O'Connor, Kaori, *Lycra: how a fiber shaped America* (New York, 2011).

Onorio, Joël-Benoît d', *Portalis: l'esprit des siècles* (Paris, 2005).

Orain, Arnaud, *La Politique du merveilleux: une autre histoire du système de Law (1695-1795)* (Paris, 2018).

Oslington, Paul (ed.), *The Oxford handbook of Christianity and economics* (New York, 2014).

–, *et al.* (ed.), *Recent developments in economics and religion* (Northampton, 2018).

Oudin-Bastide, Caroline, and Philippe Steiner, *Calculation and morality: the costs of slavery and the value of emancipation in the French Antilles* (Oxford, 2019).

–, *Calcul et morale: coûts de l'esclavage et valeur de l'émancipation (XVIII⁰-XIX⁰ siècle)* (Paris, 2015).

Pålss, Ale, *Our side of the water: political culture in the Swedish colony of St Barthélemy, 1800-1825* (Stockholm, 2016).

'Patrie, république et "country" d'après Pierre Samuel Du Pont de Nemours et Peter Stephen Duponceau', *Bulletin de l'Institut français de Washington* 5-6 (1957), p.54-62.

Perelman, Chaïm, *L'Empire rhétorique, rhétorique et argumentation* (Paris, 2002).

–, and Lucie Olbrechts-Tyteca, *Traité de l'argumentation* (Brussels, 2008).

Pertué, Michel, 'La loi martiale', in *Mélanges Henri Jacquot* (Orléans, 2006), p.459-70.

Petitimbert, Jean-Paul, 'Les traductions liturgiques du "Notre Père": un point de vue sémiotique sur les théologies qui les sous-tendent', *Actes sémiotiques* 119 (2016), https://www.unilim. fr/actes-semiotiques/5594 (last accessed 28 November 2024).

Picavet, François, *Les Idéologues: essai sur l'histoire des idées et des théories scientifiques, philosophiques, religieuses, etc. en France depuis 1789* (Paris, 1891).

Pigman, Geoffrey Allen, *Trade diplomacy transformed: why trade matters for global prosperity* (London, 2016).

Piguet, Marie-France, *Classe: histoire du mot et genèse du concept des physiocrates aux historiens de la Restauration* (Lyon, 1996).

Pocock, John G. A., *The Machiavellian moment: Florentine political thought and the Atlantic republican tradition* (Princeton, NJ, 1975).

Poisson, Charles, *Les Fournisseurs aux armées sous la Révolution française: le Directoire des achats (1792-1793) – J. Bidermann, Cousin, Marx-Berr* (Paris, 1932).

Polanyi, Karl, *La Grande Transformation* (Paris, 1983).

Poovey, Mary, *Genres of the credit economy: mediating value in eighteenth- and nineteenth-century Britain* (Chicago, IL, 2008).

Popkin, Jeremy D., *La Presse de la Révolution: journaux et journalistes (1789-1799)* (Paris, 2011).

–, *The Right-wing press in France, 1792-1800* (Chapel Hill, NC, 1980).

Porset, Charles, 'Despotisme: du mot à l'histoire', in *L'Etat moderne: regards sur la pensée politique de l'Europe occidentale entre 1715 et 1848*, ed. Simone Goyard-Fabre (Paris, 2000), p.53-61.

Poton, Didier, and Patrick Cabanel, *Les Protestants français du XVIe au XXe siècle* (Paris, 1994).

Quastana, François, 'Du bon usage du droit romain: Voltaire et la réforme des législations civile et pénale', in *Les Représentations du droit romain en Europe du Moyen Age aux Lumières* (Aix-en-Provence, 2007), p.203-31.

–, *La Pensée politique de Mirabeau (1771-1789), 'républicanisme classique' et régénération de la monarchie* (Paris, 2007).

Rabier, Christelle (ed.), *Fields of expertise: a comparative history of expert procedures in Paris and London, 1600 to present* (Newcastle, 2007).

Rahe, Paul A., 'Cicero and the classical republican legacy in America', in *Thomas Jefferson, the classical world and early America*, ed. Peter S. Onuf and Nicholas B. Cole (Charlottesville, VA, and London, 2011), p.248-64.

Raynaud, Philippe, *Trois révolutions de la liberté: Angleterre, Amérique, France* (Paris, 2009).

Renaut, Marie-Hélène, 'La contrainte par corps: une voie d'exécution civile à coloris pénal', *Revue de science criminelle et de droit pénal comparé* 4 (2002), p.791-808.

Riccobono, Salvatore, *et al.* (ed.), *Fontes iuris Romani anteiustiniani*, vol.1 (Florence, 1941).

Richter, Melvin, 'Le concept de despotisme et l'abus des mots', *Dix-huitième siècle* 34 (2002), p.373-88.

Riskin, Jessica, *Science in the age of sensibility: the sentimental empiricists of the French Enlightenment* (Chicago, IL, 2002).

Roche, Daniel, *Histoire des choses banales: naissance de la consommation dans les sociétés traditionnelles (XVIIe-XIXe siècle)* (Paris, 1997).

Rosanvallon, Pierre, *Le Sacre du citoyen* (Paris, 1992).

–, *La Société des égaux* (Paris, 2011).

Rose, John Holland, 'The Franco-British commercial treaty of 1786', *The English historical review* 23:92 (1908), p.709-24.

Sadosky, Leonard J., 'Jefferson and international relations', in *A Companion to Thomas Jefferson*, ed. Francis D. Cogliano (Malden, MA, 2012), p.99-217.

Sagnac, Philippe, *La Révolution du 10 août 1792: la chute de la royauté* (Paris, 1909).

Sahlins, Peter, *Unnaturally French: foreign citizens in the Old Regime and after* (Ithaca, NY, and London, 2004).

Savage, Gary, 'Favier's heirs: the French Revolution and the *secret du roi*', *Historical journal* 41:1 (1998), p.225-58.

Scattola, Mario, 'Before and after natural law: models of natural law in ancient and modern times', in *Early modern natural law theories: contexts and strategies in the early Enlightenment*, ed. Timothy J. Hochstrasser and Peter Schröder (Dordrecht, 2003), p.1-30.

–, '*Scientia iuris* and *ius naturae*: the jurisprudence of the Holy Roman Empire in the seventeenth and eighteenth centuries', in *A History of the philosophy of law in the civil law world, 1600-1900*, ed. Damiano Canale *et al.* (Dodrecht, 2009), p.1-41.

Schapira, Nicolas, *Maîtres et secrétaires (XVIe-XVIIIe siècles): l'exercice du pouvoir dans la France d'Ancien Régime* (Paris, 2020).

Schocket, Andrew M., *Founding corporate power in early national Philadelphia* (DeKalb, IL, 2007).

Serna, Pierre, *La République des girouettes, 1789-1815 et au-delà: une anomalie politique, la France de l'extrême centre* (Seyssel, 2005).

– (ed.), *Républiques sœurs: le Directoire et la Révolution atlantique* (Rennes, 2009).

Sewell, William H., *Capitalism and the emergence of civic equality in eighteenth-century France* (Chicago, IL, 2021).

Shankman, Andrew, *Crucible of American democracy: the struggle to fuse egalitarianism & capitalism in Jeffersonian Pennsylvania* (Lawrence, KS, 2004).

Shovlin, John, *The Political economy of virtue: luxury, patriotism, and the origins of the French Revolution* (Ithaca, NY, 2006).

–, *Trading with the enemy: Britain, France, and the 18th-century quest for a peaceful world order* (New Haven, CT, and London, 2021).

Soboul, Albert, 'Hospices/ Hôpitaux', in *Dictionnaire historique de la Révolution française* (Paris, 2005).

Söderhjelm, Alma, 'Le régime de la presse française pendant la Révolution française', doctoral dissertation, University of Helsingfors, 1900.

Spang, Rebecca L., 'The ghost of Law: speculating on money, memory and Mississippi in the French Constituent Assembly', *Historical reflections / Réflexions historiques* 31:1 (2005), p.3-25.

Spector, Céline, 'L'inaliénabilité de la liberté', in *Rousseau et Locke: dialogues critiques*, ed. Céline Spector and Johanna Lenne-Cormuez, Oxford University Studies in the Enlightenment (Liverpool, Liverpool University Press / Voltaire Foundation, 2022), p.181-207.

–, *Rousseau et la critique de l'économie politique* (Bordeaux, 2017).

Stapelbroek, Koen, 'Reinventing the Dutch Republic: Franco-Dutch commercial treaties from Ryswick to Vienna', in *The Politics of commercial treaties in the eighteenth century: balance of power, balance of trade*, ed. Antonella Alimento and Koen Stapelbroek (Cham, 2017), p.195-215.

Steiner, Philippe, 'L'économie politique pratique contre les systèmes: quelques remarques sur la méthode de J.-B. Say', *Revue d'économie politique* 100:5 (1990), p.664-87.

Stone, Bailey, *Rethinking revolutionary change in Europe* (Lanham, MD, 2020).

414   *Bibliography*

Suratteau, Jean-René, 'Les élections de l'An V aux Conseils du Directoire', *Annales historiques de la Révolution française* 301:154 (1958), p.21-63.

Tackett, Timothy, *Becoming a revolutionary: the deputies of the French National Assembly and the emergence of a revolutionary culture (1789-1790)* (Princeton, NJ, 1996).

–, *Par la volonté du peuple: comment les députés de 1789 sont devenus révolutionnaires* (Paris, 1997).

–, *Religion, revolution, and regional culture in eighteenth-century France: the Ecclesiastical Oath of 1791* (Princeton, NJ, 1986).

Tagliapietra, Andrea, *Che cos'è l'illuminismo? I testi e la genealogia del concetto* (Milan, 2000).

Terjanian, Anoush Fraser, *Commerce and its discontents in eighteenth-century French political thought* (Cambridge, 2013).

Tessier, Philippe, *François Denis Tronchet, ou la Révolution par le droit* (Paris, 2016).

Tillet, Edouard, *La Constitution anglaise: un modèle politique et institutionnel dans la France des Lumières* (Aix-en-Provence, 2001).

Tilly, Louise A., 'The food riot as a form of political conflict in France', *The Journal of interdisciplinary history* 2:1 (summer 1971), p.23-57.

Todd, David, *L'Identité économique de la France: libre-échange et protectionnisme, 1814-1851* (Paris, 2008).

Trénard, Louis, 'L'idéologie révolutionnaire et ses incidences', in *La Protection sociale sous la Révolution française*, ed. J. Imbert (Paris, 1990), p.95-204.

Trim, David J. B. (ed.), *The Huguenots: history and memory in transnational context: essays in honour and memory of Walter C. Utt* (Leiden and Boston, MA, 2011).

Troper, Michel, *Terminer la Révolution: la Constitution de 1795* (Paris, 2006).

Tully, James, *A Discourse on property: John Locke and his adversaries* (Cambridge, 1978).

Turchetti, Mario, 'Droit de résistance, à quoi? Unmasking despotism and tyranny today', *Revue historique* 4 (2006), p.831-78.

Vachet, André, *L'Idéologie libérale: l'individu et sa propriété* (Paris, 1970).

Valsania, Maurizio, 'Thomas Jefferson and private property: myths and reality', *Ricognizioni: rivista di lingue, letterature e culture moderne* 7 (2020), p.123-36.

Van Kley, Dale K., *The Religious origins of the French Revolution: from Calvin to the Civil Constitution 1560-1791* (New Haven, CT, 1996).

Van Ruymbeke, Bertrand, and Randy J. Sparks (ed.), *Memory and identity: the Huguenots in France and the Atlantic diaspora* (Columbia, SC, 2003).

Vasak, Anouchka, 'Introduction', in *Entre deux eaux: les secondes Lumières et leurs ambiguïtés (1789-1815)*, ed. Anouchka Vasak (Paris, 2012), p.9-18.

Venturi, Franco, 'Despotisme oriental', in *Europe des Lumières: recherches sur le 18ᵉ siècle* (Paris, 1971), p.131-42.

Villey, Michel, *La Formation de la pensée juridique moderne: cours d'histoire de la philosophie du droit* (Paris, 1975).

Vovelle, Michel, *Religion et Révolution: la déchristianisation de l'An II* (Paris, 1976).

Walton, Charles, 'Capitalism's alter ego: the birth of reciprocity in eighteenth-century France', *Critical historical studies* (2018), p.1-43.

–, 'The fall from Eden: the free-trade origins of the French Revolution', in *The French Revolution in global perspective*, ed. Suzanne Desan *et al.* (Ithaca, NY, 2013), p.44-56 and 193-97.

–, *La Liberté d'expression en Révolution* (Rennes, 2014).

Weber, Max, *The Protestant ethic and the 'spirit' of capitalism and other writings* (1905), ed. and translated by Peter Baehr and Gordon C. Wells (New York, 2002).

Whiteman, Jeremy J., *Reform, Revolution, and French global policy, 1787-1791* (Aldershot, 2003).

Williamson, Chilton, *American suffrage from property to democracy, 1760-1860* (Princeton, NJ, 1968).

Woloch, Isser, *The New regime: transformations of the French civic order, 1789-1820s* (New York, 1994).

Wolodkiewicz, Witold, *Le Droit romain et l'Encyclopédie* (Naples, 1986).

Woronoff, Denis, *La République bourgeoise: de thermidor à brumaire 1794-1799* (Paris, 1972).

Xifaras, Mikhaïl, 'La destination politique de la propriété chez Jean-Jacques Rousseau', *Les Etudes philosophiques* 66 (2003), p.331-70.

Yarbrough, Jean M., *American virtues: Thomas Jefferson on the character of a free people* (Lawrence, KS, 1998).

–, 'Jefferson and property rights', in *Liberty, property, and the foundations of the American Constitution*, ed. Ellen Frankel Paul and Howard Dickman (Albany, NY, 1989), p.65-84.

Ziesche, Philipp, *Cosmopolitan patriots: Americans in Paris in the age of Revolution* (Charlottesville, VA, 2010).

Indices

Index nominum

Adams, John, 266n, 300

Albertone, Manuela, 5, 17, 68n, 83n, 85, 206n, 211-12, 220n, 259n, 269n, 270, 288n, 291n, 300n, 301n, 305, 307, 309, 327n, 329n, 338n, 342n

Albon, Claude-Camille-François, comte d', 298-99

Alembert, Jean Le Rond d', 135, 166, 170

Alimento, Antonella, 16, 230n, 232n, 253, 270, 367n

Arendt, Hannah, 255, 265-66

Argenson, René-Louis de Voyer de Paulmy, marquis d', 168, 170

Arioste, Ludovico, dit L'Arioste (Ludovico Ariosto), 125, 361n

Bachaumont, Louis Petit de, 297

Bade, Charles-Frédéric, Margrave de, 102, 337n

Bade, Charles-Louis, Margrave de, 63n, 68, 103n, 104n, 105n, 106n, 107n, 108n, 132, 133n, 268, 293n, 303-304

Barbeu-Dubourg, Jacques, 301n45, 309n

Barras, Paul, 201-202

Barruel, Augustin (abbé), 81

Baudeau, Nicolas (abbé), 83n, 129n, 156n, 158n, 275n, 362, 363, 365, 366, 370

Bayle, Pierre, 39, 150n

Beaurieu, Gaspard Guillard de, 301, 310

Beccaria, Cesare, 107, 110, 187n, 339

Bernardin de Saint-Pierre, Jacques-Henri, 322-24

Bidermann, Jacques-Antoine, 10, 31-33, 35-36, 57

Boissy d'Anglas, François Antoine de, 44n, 112, 198

Bonaparte, Napoléon, 30, 36, 57n, 183n, 256, 260-61, 328, 343, 349

Bougainville, Louis Antoine de, 324-25

Bouloiseau, Marc, 3-4, 9n, 11n, 13n, 17n, 164, 172n, 173n, 176n, 186n, 202, 352-53, 358n

Bourdieu, Pierre, 354n

Brissot, Jacques Pierre, 96n

Bureaux de Pusy, Jean-Xavier, 80, 311, 313n, 317, 319, 320, 367

Burlamaqui, Jean-Jacques, 150n

Butini, Jean-François, 275, 280

Butré, Charles de, 292n, 372n

Calonne, Charles Alexandre de, 130n, 172, 241n, 258n, 337, 348

Carvalho, Thérence, 11, 41n, 63n, 100n, 106n, 268n, 374

Charles, Loïc, 14n, 233n, 355n

Chartier, Roger, 353

Cheney, Paul, 14n, 48n, 353n

Condillac, Étienne Bonnot de, 68

Condorcet, Nicolas de, 16, 41-42, 258, 278-81, 283, 287, 294, 304, 349-50, 375

Constant, Benjamin, 13, 182n

418   *Indices*

Coquéau, Claude-Philibert, 62n
Crauford, George, 230

Danton, Georges Jacques, 107, 113,
  358
Darnton, Robert, 350n
Demals, Thierry, 235n, 356n, 367
Destutt de Tracy, Antoine, 216n,
  331-35
Diderot, Denis, 62n, 105, 129, 271,
  349
Dobry, Michel, 368
Du Pont de Nemours,
  Eleuthère Irénée, ix, 1-2, 4n, 8-11,
  23, 31, 36, 57, 80, 303, 317, 356,
  373
Du Pont de Nemours, Victor-Marie,
  2, 9, 23, 31, 33
Duvergier de Hauranne, Prosper,
  367n

Eden, William, 15, 229, 230-32, 234,
  235
Elias, Norbert, 404n

Fénelon, François, 321
Florian, Jean-Pierre Claris de,
  320-24
Forbonnais, François Véron Duverger
  de, 183, 235n, 354
Foucault, Michel, 75n, 255n
Fourqueux, Michel Bouvard de,
  172
Franklin, Benjamin, 15n, 134n,
  258-59, 286, 291-94, 229n,
  302-306, 309-11, 367, 375

Gaillard, Gabriel-Henri, 302
Galiani, Ferdinando, 16, 364
Gérando, Joseph-Marie de, 14, 67n,
  163, 348n
Grimm, Friedrich Melchior, baron
  von, 364
Grotius, Hugo, 139, 140, 157, 255n,
  266n
Goutte, Pierre-Henri, 5, 330n
Guibert, Jacques, comte de, 89-91, 93
Guillard de Beaurieu, Gaspard, 301,
  310
Gustav III (king of Sweden), 102,
  241n, 293, 368

Harrington, James, 219
Helvétius, Anne-Catherine de
  Ligniville, Madame, 258
Helvétius, Claude Adrien, 68, 182n
Herencia, Bernard, 99n, 127n, 291n,
  301, 305-307, 309
Hirschman, Albert O., 263n,
  360-61
Hobbes, Thomas, 129, 136, 152, 153,
  255n, 266n
Holbach, Paul Heinrich Dietrich,
  baron d', 364
Horn, Jeff, 241
Hyard, Alexandra, 235n

Jay, John, 330n
Jefferson, Thomas, 8, 168n, 204-25,
  253-70, 293n, 303n, 306, 311,
  315, 325n, 327-46, 361, 367, 375,
  376n
Jurieu, Pierre, 150n

Kaplan, Steven L., 15n, 25n, 40n,
  41n, 56n
Klotz, Gérard, 5, 68n
Koselleck, Reinhart, 16, 349

La Révellière-Lépeaux, Louis-Marie
  de, 185n, 201
Lanjuinais, Jean-Denis, 113, 116, 183,
  198
Larrère, Catherine, 5, 64n, 210, 213,
  265n, 371n
Lavoisier, Antoine, 9, 176, 349, 350,
  355
Lavoisier, Marie-Anne, 9, 326n
Le Maistre de Sacy, Isaac-Louis, 21n,
  53n, 54n
Le Mercier de La Rivière, Pierre-
  Paul, 14n, 15, 16n, 79, 82, 99, 122,
  123-24, 127, 129, 132, 150, 152,
  158, 210n, 213, 214n, 224, 274,
  295, 298n, 304-307, 309-10, 324,
  365-66, 370-72
  *L'Ordre naturel et essentiel des sociétés
  politiques* (1767), 79, 82, 122-23,
  127, 132n, 150n, 152n, 158n,
  214n, 224n, 309, 362
Le Trosne, Guillaume- François,
  99, 106n, 156n, 235-37, 337,
  357-58

Indices

Lettre à la Chambre du commerce de
Normandie, sur le mémoire qu'elle
a publié relativement au traité de
commerce avec l'Angleterre (1788), 17,
231-32, 244n, 245-46
Lilti, Antoine, 269n
Locke, John, 68, 72n, 128n, 153-56,
213n, 217, 255n, 266n
Lolme, Jean-Louis de, 291-99, 302,
304-305, 307-309, 367n
Loménie de Brienne, Etienne-Charles
de, 11n, 172-73
Louis XIV, 28, 39, 101
Louis XV, 102-103, 169, 350
Louis XVI, ix, 28, 85, 350, 373
Louis XVIII, 196
Louisiane, 151n, 253-54, 256-57, 261,
262-64, 267, 327

Mably, Gabriel Bonnot de (abbé),
158n, 364
Machiavel, Nicolas, 261
Madison, James, 204n, 205, 209, 213,
215n, 217n, 219n, 221n, 224, 258n,
259n, 330n, 332n, 340
Malouet, Pierre-Victor, 96-97
Malthus, Thomas Robert, 17, 333-34,
362
Marmontel, Jean-François, 63n
Marx, Karl, 37, 38, 356-57
Maupeou, René Nicolas Charles
Augustin de, 100, 103
Maza, Sarah, 352-53
Mergey, Anthony, 5, 21n, 66n, 67n,
83n, 85n, 100n, 121n, 157n, 185n,
203n, 292n, 363n, 367n
Michelet, Jules, 80n, 87
Mirabeau, Honoré-Gabriel de, 294n
Mirabeau, Jean-Antoine, 14n
Mirabeau, Victor Riqueti (marquis
de), v, 5, 123, 125-26, 133, 156n,
248, 270, 274n, 292n, 296, 305,
347, 351, 352n, 365-67, 372
Monroe, James, 204
Montaigne, Michel de, 25-26
Montesquieu, Charles-Louis de
Secondat, baron de la Brède, 17,
64, 84, 114n, 135, 271-73, 276-78,
281n, 287, 296-97, 302, 331-32,
341, 349, 366

De l'Esprit des lois (Of Spirit of Laws),
64n, 84, 331
More, Thomas, 372
Morellet, André, 182n, 183, 186n,
198, 364
Moreri, Louis, 151n

Napoléon, see Bonaparte
Necker, Jacques, 10, 16, 27, 32-36,
38-43, 50, 55-57, 62, 73-74, 76,
173, 182n, 233n, 350, 359
Necker de Germany, Louis, 10,
32-33, 36, 50, 313n
Numa Pompilius (second king of
Rome), 9, 318-25

Orain, Arnaud, 38n

Paine, Thomas, 309n
Peuchet, Jacques, 80-81, 183
Philosophie de l'univers (1792), 22,
27-28, 136-38, 149n, 151n, 153n,
351n, 359n
Piarron de Chamousset, Claude
Humbert, 76
Platon (Plato), 266n
Pocock, John, 261, 269
Poivre, Pierre, 2, 274, 281n, 282, 317,
322, 324
Polanyi, Karl, 70
Polybe, 261
Portalis, Jean-Étienne-Marie, 113,
114, 116
Pufendorf, Samuel von, 255n, 264,
266n

Quastana, François, 105n, 294n
Quesnay, François, v, ix, 5, 6, 14,
17, 39, 65, 66n, 68-70, 107, 125,
127, 133-36, 151-53, 156n, 160,
169, 170n, 171, 234, 252, 255n,
268, 274, 298, 303, 309, 314n, 347,
355n, 356-57, 365n, 366

Rabaut Saint-Etienne, Jean-Paul, 42,
89
Rayneval, Joseph Matthias Gérard
de, 15, 230, 241n
Robespierre, Maximilien, 27, 81, 87,
94, 190, 332

420 *Indices*

Roche, Daniel, 353n
Roederer, Pierre-Louis, 96n, 182n
Roland, Jeanne-Marie de La Platière, 298n
Rosanvallon, Pierre, 48n, 207n
Rousseau, Jean-Jacques, 16, 26, 128-60, 271, 320, 349, 365, 367
  Du Contrat Social (1762), 121, 122, 124, 128n, 131, 134-36, 138, 148, 155-59, 271n, 367

Saint-Lambert, Jean-François de, 275-77
Say, Jean-Baptiste, 17, 100, 183, 333, 334, 336, 362
Scheffer, Charles de (Comte), 292n, 293, 294, 297, 299-302, 304-305, 309-10
Serna, Pierre, 178n, 194n, 375
Shovlin, John, 16n, 38n, 48n
Sieyès, Joseph-Emmanuel, 89, 96-98, 162n, 209
Skornicki, Arnault, 11n, 21n, 107n, 121n, 122n, 171n, 203n, 210n, 213n, 218n, 220n, 221n, 253n, 267n, 269n
Smith, Adam, 17, 76, 281, 282n, 283n, 287, 328, 333, 334, 362
Spector, Céline, 124n, 154n
Staël, Germaine de, 6, 9n, 10, 36, 50, 182n, 259n, 359

Steiner, Philippe, 5, 38n, 69n, 276n, 277n, 279n, 287n, 334n, 367n

Terray, Joseph Marie (abbé), 110
Théré, Christine, 274n, 291n, 355n
Thibaudeau, Antoine-Claire, 194, 199, 202
Thomas d'Aquin (Thomas Aquinas), 155n
Trudaine, Daniel-Charles (intendant des finances), 245
Turgot, Anne Robert Jacques, 10, 17, 31, 33, 39-42, 47, 57, 61, 64-65, 75, 86, 131n, 134, 135n, 159, 170, 172, 184, 207n, 230, 233, 238, 240, 245, 258, 266n, 271-72, 282-87, 292, 294, 296n, 303, 304, 305n, 314n, 330, 348, 350, 362, 365-66, 367n

Vergennes, Charles Gravier, comte de, 16, 172, 230-34, 238-39, 241, 244-46, 249-50, 252, 253, 269, 299, 348
Villey, Michel, 266, 267n
Voltaire, François-Marie Arouet, dit, 8, 105, 271, 349, 364

Wateville, Adolphe de, 77n
Weulersse, Georges, 5, 258, 367n, 368n
Whatmore, Richard, 5, 17, 81n, 175n, 291n

Index rerum

agriculture, ix, 98, 125-27, 130, 132-33, 135-36, 138, 151, 175, 181, 182, 223-25, 243, 273-74, 280, 284, 287, 314, 321-22, 324, 325n, 328-30, 336, 339, 344, 346, 354, 356, 358
  Comité d'administration de l'agri-culture, 233
Amérique, Etats-Unis d' (America, United States of), 1, 2, 4, 5, 8-9, 10, 23-24, 29, 30, 38, 45, 89n, 98, 116, 205-206, 208, 220, 239, 241, 253-54, 256-59, 261-65, 267, 268, 279, 311-12, 315, 317, 319, 346-47, 356, 361, 367, 375-76

Américains (Americans), 204, 213, 269, 317n, 335-36, 338-39
Angleterre (England), 5, 45, 73n, 74, 77, 146, 208, 229, 238, 243, 248, 253, 262, 282n, 284, 294, 296-300, 302-305, 309, 333-34, 338, 339, 341, 343-46, 376n
  Grande-Bretagne (Great Britain), 301, 328, 338
  United Kingdom, 16, 358
argent, *see* monnaie (money)
aristocracy (aristocratie), 85, 93, 167, 168, 336, 355, 357
  aristocrates (aristocrats), 175, 187, 189

Indices

armée (army), 89, 90, 93, 94, 179,
135, 200, 201, 330, 339
Assemblée nationale (National
Assembly), 8, 80-81, 85, 87, 92, 93,
108, 109n, 180, 247, 251, 300, 367,
368
assistance (to the poor), 10, 46, 63n,
66, 69, 71-72, 74, 76-78
see also bienfasiance
Athens, 9
Austria, 242, 243

balance
de puissance (of power), 242, 251,
362, 373
of trade (du commerce), 10, 233n,
235-36, 344
see also équilibre
banque(s) (bank(s)), 10, 17, 49
des États-Unis, 327-31, 341-46
bienfaisance, 52, 56, 77, 106, 127, 295
bourgeoisie, 165, 169, 173, 210n,
352-58
business, 2-4, 8-10, 21-26, 30-39, 41, 48,
50-57, 233, 311-19, 354-55, 357, 376

capitalisme (capitalism), 9, 25-26, 55,
117, 352, 356-58
catholicisme, catholique (Catholicism,
Catholic), 25-29, 40-44, 48-49, 51,
183n, 297, 350
citoyen (citizen), 14, 28, 56, 84-86,
90, 95, 97, 107, 108n, 114, 135,
138, 142-43, 145, 147, 159, 177, 179,
181, 185, 187, 196-97, 204n, 207,
211, 216, 220, 222, 224, 225, 241,
245, 254, 261, 296, 312, 320, 321n,
322n, 337-39, 367, 373, 374
citoyenneté (citizenship), 179, 361,
367, 375
Clichy, club de, 12, 193-95, 198-200
colonialisme (colonialism), 271, 332
colonies, 15, 205, 238, 248, 249, 256,
272n, 273-75, 277-80, 293, 295,
299-301, 305n, 309-10, 315, 338
commerce, 17, 23, 30, 34, 38, 57n,
64, 98, 100, 101n, 103, 109, 112-14,
126, 135-38, 181-82, 188, 190,
219-20, 223, 230, 233-50, 258, 286,
312, 314, 315n, 321-22, 329, 334,
342-43, 346, 348, 353-54

Chamber of Commerce of Paris,
9, 31, 36
Bureau de, 9, 24, 32
transatlantic commerce, 9, 23
see also liberté; libre-échange
(free-trade; trade)
concurrence, 75, 221, 232, 236, 244,
307, 317n, 340, 345, 346
Constitution, 12, 13, 27, 85, 89-90,
93, 95-98, 100, 105, 115-16,
135-36, 175, 177, 178, 180-87,
192-216, 220, 292, 299-300, 302,
305, 309, 332, 334, 345, 367,
373-74, 377
Consulat (Consulate), 117, 306, 359
Contrat social, 135, 136
Du Contrat social, see Rousseau
pacte social, 124, 141-43, 157
Convention Nationale, 11, 13, 63, 77,
98, 102, 107, 109, 110, 178, 180,
185-86, 188n, 231
Council of the Elders (Conseil des
Anciens), 115-16, 177, 180-81, 186-87,
192, 194, 198, 200-202, 360, 374
crédit (credit), 17, 23, 35, 37-38, 48,
52, 57, 117, 161, 172n, 173, 200,
342, 344, 345

démocratie (democracy), 204n, 211,
225, 329, 333, 342
despotisme (despotism), 74, 84, 127,
130, 133, 192
légal (legal), 124, 136, 160, 203n,
347, 361-66, 369-71
dette (debt), 21, 31, 35-38, 53-55, 57,
73, 101, 103-12, 113, 172n, 175,
201, 267, 330, 339, 341, 342
diplomacy (diplomatie), 16, 99,
231-32, 238, 247, 252, 376
Directoire (Directory), 2, 8, 12, 32,
77, 78, 98, 102, 109, 116, 177, 178n,
183-84, 187, 189, 190n, 193, 200,
201-202, 311, 343, 351, 356, 359,
360, 375
droit (law)
civil, 103n, 106n, 117, 149
naturel (natural), 65-67, 72, 78,
100, 106, 122-24, 127, 140,
149, 151-53, 155, 159-60, 161n,
213-20, 223, 254-55, 264-67, 269,
274, 321-22, 324, 368, 370

422 *Indices*

pénal (criminal), 7, 101, 110
privé, 99
public, 99, 269
romain, 104-106, 112, 158n

économie politique (political
economy), 5, 7, 10n, 15n, 17, 25n,
40-41, 48, 56, 99, 100, 136, 142,
187, 188, 191, 223, 229, 261, 276,
283, 319, 330, 335, 356, 362n
égalité (equality), 40, 53, 85, 95, 163,
180, 186n, 203n, 250n, 254, 255,
270, 353, 373-74
see also inégalité(s)
élection (election), 98, 175, 177-80,
182-83, 197-99, 208-209, 300, 316
see also suffrage; vote
empire, 2, 17, 133, 242, 246, 318
colonial français (French colonial),
249
napoléonien (napoleonian), 121,
254, 306, 348-49, 359, 376
England, *see* Angleterre
enterprise (entreprise), 23, 117, 296,
311, 313, 315, 316-17, 346
entrepreneur, 2, 9, 67n, 75, 275, 296,
312, 333, 338, 344, 346, 353, 355,
357
équilibre, 235-36, 297, 330, 334
see also balance de puissance (of
power)
esclavage (slavery), 15, 37n, 75, 101,
104-106, 110-11, 139, 140, 210,
271-88
Espagne (Spain), 112, 128n, 146, 229,
234n, 241, 242, 246-51, 256, 267,
284
Amérique espagnole, 210
Colonies espagnoles, 256, 293
Commerce espagnol (Spanish
commerce), 248, 250
état de guerre, *see* guerre (war)
état de nature (state of nature), 66,
82, 122, 140, 141, 148, 150, 152-55,
266n, 267
États généraux (Estates General), ix,
11, 85, 86, 175, 179, 295, 369, 371
*Examen du gouvernement d'Angleterre,
comparé aux constitutions des
Etats-Unis* (1789), 40, 88n, 294, 299

family compact, *see* Pacte de famille
féodalité (feudalism), 218n, 302,
356-58
gouvernement féodal, régime
féodal (feudal system), 130, 140,
302, 357
fermier (farmer), 188, 283, 324, 336,
338, 339, 340, 344, 355, 357
finance, 10, 35, 40-43, 123n, 182,
188n, 192, 220-21, 224, 302, 330,
335-36, 340-41, 344
financier, 23, 39, 45, 191
fiscalité, 336
fraternité (fraternity), 147, 180,
250-51
free trade, *see*
libre-échange (free-trade)
freedom, *see* liberté (liberty, freedom)

Girondin, 10
Grande-Bretagne (Great Britain), *see*
Angleterre (England)
guerre (war), 12, 17, 90-91, 95,
129-30, 132-33, 135n, 137, 139-41,
143, 145, 146, 151-55, 157-58, 184,
189, 235, 242, 243, 246, 247, 249,
254, 256-57, 260-64, 267, 281,
281, 284, 328-29, 331n, 332, 334,
339-41, 343-44
état de guerre (state of war), 12, 85,
85, 129, 139, 153, 155, 158,
281
des Farines, 40

Hollande (Holland), 39, 45, 112,
241-42, 246, 298-99, 304
hôpital (hospital), 10, 62n, 70-75, 78,
137, 352
Huguenot(s), *see* Protestantism

Idéologues, 331-32, 334
impôt(s), 125-26, 159, 191, 207n,
222-23, 236, 238n, 243, 333,
336-40
tax, taxation, 17, 30, 76, 85, 91,
188, 191-92, 235, 238, 244, 269,
341, 357
industrie (industry), ix, 9, 31, 152,
163, 217, 217n, 219n, 225, 236, 243,
244, 248, 273, 280, 296n, 307n

Indices

inégalité(s), 56, 129, 135, 141, 148,
153, 169, 218, 219n, 337
intérêt (interest)
  financier (financial) 73, 101n, 175,
  221, 337, 342
  privé, personnel (private), 70n, 150,
  158n, 162, 180, 215, 222, 225,
  251, 255, 265n, 267, 276, 281,
  300, 321, 333, 343, 344, 363
  public, national, commun, 77, 126,
  138, 209, 211-14, 223, 230n, 235,
  237, 240, 247, 242, 245, 255, 263,
  295, 299n, 300, 343
intolerance, *see* tolerance

Jacobins, Jacobinism, 2, 12, 93, 176,
177, 180, 185, 187, 193, 195, 196,
198, 202, 373, 375
justice, 3, 85, 94, 100, 106, 110, 127,
138-39, 144-45, 147, 152, 153,
182, 186n, 194, 199, 213-14, 222,
237-38, 245, 295, 368, 370, 373
jusnaturalisme, jusnaturaliste (natural
law theory), 64, 65, 67, 106, 254,
265, 266, 270

landowner(s), *see* propriétaire(s)
Lettres africaines (1771), 275n, 280
liberté (freedom, liberty), ix, 11-13, 16,
26, 28, 38, 65, 69, 75, 79, 82-85, 88,
90-91, 93, 95-97, 98, 106-10, 112-17,
124, 127, 130, 135-37, 139-40,
142-44, 148-50, 152-53, 155, 157,
160, 163, 170, 180, 188-89, 191-92,
197, 203n, 204-205, 208, 213n, 215,
217, 219, 221-23, 229, 236-38, 240,
245, 247, 250-51, 262-63, 269-70,
279-80, 295, 297, 302, 307, 321,
327, 332-33, 336-37, 339, 341, 346,
350-51, 359, 362, 369, 370, 371,
373-75, 377
  liberté du commerce (commercial
  freedom), 126, 135, 210, 231, 234,
  231, 238, 245, 307n
    see also libre-échange (free-trade,
    freedom of trade)
  liberté religieuse (religious freedom,
  freedom of conscience), 28, 310,
  350
    see also tolérance (tolerance)

libre-échange (free-trade, freedom
of trade), 16, 229, 231-32, 235,
237, 242, 245, 256, 269, 351
loi(s) (law(s)), 28, 30, 53n, 56, 77, 88,
95, 101, 103, 104-106, 108, 111-17,
129, 131-32, 135, 138-40, 143-44,
146-47, 156-58, 160, 170, 181, 187,
189, 196, 199, 208-11, 213, 217,
219n, 220, 222, 233, 236-38, 245,
258, 278n, 281, 295, 304, 321, 322n,
327, 369, 371, 374
  naturelle(s), de la nature, de l'ordre
  naturel (natural law), 65, 75, 83,
  100, 129, 144, 147, 153, 195n,
  235, 255, 265, 266n, 274, 278n,
  310n, 321-22, 324, 336, 368, 370
  martiale (martial), 89-90, 92, 94

manufacture(s), 98, 172, 181-82,
191-92, 231, 246, 249, 329-30,
335-36, 339-40, 343-44, 348
  manufacturing activities (or
  production, or sector), 32, 240,
  243, 244, 246, 354
Mexique, 261-62
monarchie (monarchy), 7, 27, 84, 174,
201, 205, 212n, 247, 346, 360-63,
366-67, 369-72
  absolue (absolute), 357, 359, 363,
  367-71, 376
  constitutionnelle (constitutional), ix,
  198, 203n, 369, 376
monnaie (money), 26, 33, 46, 52, 93,
97, 173, 192, 267n, 312, 315, 326,
341-42, 344-46
  Argent, 40-41, 46, 93, 126, 172n,
  200, 263, 267, 342, 343, 346

noblesse (nobility), 11, 93, 94, 163,
165-67, 169, 172n, 189, 212n, 221n,
353-56

ordre (order)
  naturel (natural), 69, 83, 85, 100,
  106, 123, 129, 151, 160, 211,
  214n, 222, 363, 366, 368, 372
  public, 11, 28, 79, 81-82, 87-90,
  92-98
  social, 75, 82, 86, 158n, 165, 167,
  271, 278n, 363, 372, 377

424 *Indices*

Pacte de famille (family compact), 229, 242, 248-52

Pacte social, *see* Contrat social

paix (peace), 12, 17, 80, 81, 89, 95, 134, 140, 158, 181n, 182, 184, 189-90, 197, 200, 229, 232-35, 237-38, 242-45, 247, 250-52, 261, 267-68, 279, 281n

patriotisme, 80, 89, 212, 340, 344

pauvreté, pauvres (poverty, poor), 10, 63-64, 66, 69-76, 78, 134, 138, 159, 166, 168, 188, 263, 267n, 273, 277, 320, 337, 352

poor laws, 73, 76

paysans, 210n

personne, 85, 88, 102, 105, 107, 108n, 115, 127-30, 134, 136-37, 139-42, 144-47, 153, 155-56, 187, 191, 195, 196, 215, 222, 247, 270, 337, 368, 374

physiocrate(s), physiocratie, physiocratique (physiocrat(s), physiocracy, physiocratic), v, ix, 5, 6, 14-17, 39, 43, 62, 64-65, 73, 75, 76, 79-88, 91-93, 97-100, 102-103, 105-106, 114, 116, 122-27, 130, 135n, 136, 159, 160, 174, 177-79, 188, 191, 202, 205, 206, 210, 211, 213-15, 218, 220, 221, 224, 230, 234-35, 246, 253, 258-59, 265-67, 270, 273-74, 291, 292, 295-96, 304-307, 311, 313-15, 319-20, 322-26, 327-42, 346, 347, 351, 355-58, 360-72, 374, 377

police, 83, 88, 89-91, 96, 98, 104, 345

des pauvres, 66, 72, 159

Pologne (Poland), 14, 210n, 242, 244

Portugal, 112, 113n, 229, 234n, 241

produit net (net product), 44, 55, 57, 83, 125, 127, 159, 274, 340, 356

propriétaire(s), 128, 145, 146, 255

terrien(s) (landowner(s)), viii, 72, 127, 130, 137, 159-60, 177, 179, 188, 190, 193, 196, 203, 205, 207-208, 212-15, 218-19, 221-25, 283, 292n, 296, 307, 318n, 333, 336, 338, 340, 357, 363, 375n, 376

propriété (property), 11-12, 15, 56, 65, 79n, 81-88, 95, 98, 106-107, 115, 127-30, 132, 134, 136-37, 140, 143-46, 148, 150, 152-53, 170, 177, 179, 185-87, 189, 195, 197, 203n, 205, 213-20, 222-25, 245, 266n, 295, 321, 324-26, 337-39, 357-59, 361, 363, 368-70, 374, 375

mobilière, 128, 134

terrienne, foncière (landed), 129, 145, 213, 215, 220, 225, 266n, 357

Protestant(s), 2, 24-26, 28-32, 37-51, 55, 57, 165, 183n, 350

Huguenot(s), 2, 24, 29, 37, 39, 40, 43, 45, 48, 49, 169, 347

Protestantism, 22-26, 29, 43-49, 55, 350

Prussia (Prusse), 45, 235, 242, 243, 246

Refuge (Huguenot), 24, 45

religion, 22, 24-29, 37, 39, 41-46, 49-53, 56, 183n, 294, 303, 320, 350-51

représentation [politique] ([political] representation), 204, 208, 306, 352, 368

Republicanism, 12, 347, 361, 376

république (republic), 17, 28, 84, 98, 105, 112, 131, 134-36, 142, 149, 186, 190, 195-96, 199, 201, 202, 203-208, 210, 212, 215, 219-25, 237n, 253-54, 273, 292-93, 302, 306, 309n, 317-18, 324, 333, 339, 341-42, 345-46, 348, 356, 361-62, 367, 373-76

République des Lettres (Republic of Letters), 7, 254, 349

révolution (revolution), 12-13, 56, 148, 155, 185, 193, 197, 222, 261, 268, 295, 303, 309n, 328, 332, 334, 346

américaine (American), 255, 262, 266, 338

anglaise (English or Glorious), 205, 298

française (French), ix, 76, 108, 109, 121, 162, 165, 176, 187, 205, 255, 259, 303, 332, 336, 346, 352

Rome, 9, 111, 320-21, 324

Russie (Russia), 74, 105, 235, 241-43

Indices 425

santé, 63, 71, 147, 273
 Maisons de santé, 67n, 69-70
slavery, *see* esclavage
souveraineté (sovereignty), 76, 124,
 131, 146, 215, 223, 224, 256, 332,
 369, 372
Suède (Sweden), 102, 172, 241, 242,
 293, 368
suffrage, 12, 135-36, 140, 146, 157-59,
 205, 208-209, 215, 216, 219-20,
 300, 320, 375-76
 see also élection (election); vote
Suisse (Switzerland), 31, 45, 189, 198,
 298, 299

tax(es), *see* impôt(s)
tolerance, toleration, 28-29, 39-40,
 42, 44, 49
 intolerance, 28
trade
 balance of trade (balance du
  commerce), 10, 233n, 235-36
 colonial trade, 353-55

Eden-Rayneval trade treaty, 15,
 229-35, 238-41, 243-46, 249-50
free trade, freedom of trade, 16,
 229, 231-32, 235, 237, 242, 245,
 351
international trade, 232, 252, 273,
 279
 see also commerce

United Kingdom, *see* Angleterre
 (England)
Utopia, utopian, utopianism (utopie),
 8, 16, 311, 324, 325, 364, 372n

vertu (virtue), 9n, 25, 68, 70, 84, 95,
 143, 147, 161, 189, 194, 198, 212,
 219, 322, 374
vote, 159, 177, 179, 197n, 205,
 207-209, 212-16, 218, 220, 223,
 225, 333
 see also élection (election); suffrage

war, *see* Guerre